Vauxhall/Opel Zafira
Owners Workshop Manual

Martynn Randall

Models covered

(6366 - 384)

Petrol: 1.6 litre (1598cc) normally-aspirated & 1.8 litre (1796cc)
Turbo-diesel: 1.7 litre (1686cc) & 1.9 litre (1910cc)

Does NOT cover 1.6 litre turbo, 2.0 litre or 2.2 litre petrol models,1.3 litre diesel models, or dual fuel versions
Does NOT cover Zafira Tourer range ('C' Series) introduced 2012

© Haynes Publishing 2017

ABCDE
FGHIJ
KLMNO
PQRST

A book in the **Haynes Owners Workshop Manual Series**

Printed in Malaysia

ISBN **978 1 78521 366 3**

Haynes Publishing
Sparkford, Yeovil, Somerset BA22 7JJ, England

British Library Cataloguing in Publication Data
A catalogue record for this book is available from the British Library.

Haynes North America, Inc
859 Lawrence Drive, Newbury Park, California 91320, USA

Printed using NORBRITE BOOK 48.8gsm (CODE: 40N6533) from NORPAC; procurement system certified under Sustainable Forestry Initiative standard. Paper produced is certified to the SFI Certified Fiber Sourcing Standard (CERT - 0094271)

Contents

LIVING WITH YOUR VAUXHALL/OPEL ZAFIRA

Introduction   Page   **0•4**

Safety first!   Page   **0•5**

Roadside repairs

If your car won't start   Page   **0•6**

Jump starting   Page   **0•7**

Wheel changing   Page   **0•8**

Identifying leaks   Page   **0•10**

Towing   Page   **0•10**

Weekly checks

Introduction   Page   **0•11**

Underbonnet check points   Page   **0•11**

Engine oil level   Page   **0•13**

Coolant level   Page   **0•14**

Brake/clutch fluid level   Page   **0•14**

Battery   Page   **0•15**

Washer fluid level   Page   **0•15**

Tyre condition and pressure   Page   **0•16**

Electrical systems   Page   **0•17**

Wiper blades   Page   **0•17**

Lubricants and fluids   Page   **0•18**

Tyre pressures   Page   **0•18**

MAINTENANCE

Routine maintenance and servicing – petrol models

Servicing specifications   Page   **1A•2**

Maintenance schedule   Page   **1A•3**

Maintenance procedures   Page   **1A•5**

Routine maintenance and servicing – diesel models

Servicing specifications   Page   **1B•2**

Maintenance schedule   Page   **1B•3**

Maintenance procedures   Page   **1B•6**

Contents

REPAIRS AND OVERHAUL

Engine and Associated Systems

Petrol engine in-car repair procedures   Page   2A•1

1.7 litre diesel engine in-car repair procedures   Page   2B•1

1.9 litre SOHC diesel engine in-car repair procedures   Page   2C•1

1.9 litre DOHC diesel engine in-car repair procedures   Page   2D•1

Engine removal and overhaul procedures   Page   2E•1

Cooling, heating and air conditioning systems   Page   3•1

Fuel and exhaust systems – petrol engine   Page   4A•1

Fuel and exhaust systems – diesel engines   Page   4B•1

Emissions control systems   Page   4C•1

Starting and charging systems   Page   5A•1

Ignition system – petrol engine   Page   5B•1

Transmission

Clutch   Page   6•1

Manual transmission   Page   7A•1

Automatic transmission   Page   7B•1

Easytronic transmission   Page   7C•1

Driveshafts   Page   8•1

Brakes and suspension

Braking system   Page   9•1

Suspension and steering systems   Page   10•1

Body equipment

Bodywork and fittings   Page   11•1

Body electrical system   Page   12•1

Wiring diagrams   Page   12•17

REFERENCE

Dimensions and weights   Page   REF•1

Fuel economy   Page   REF•2

Conversion factors   Page   REF•6

Buying spare parts   Page   REF•7

Vehicle identification   Page   REF•7

General repair procedures   Page   REF•8

Jacking and vehicle support   Page   REF•9

Disconnecting the battery   Page   REF•9

Tools and working facilities   Page   REF•10

MOT test checks   Page   REF•12

Fault finding   Page   REF•16

Glossary of technical terms   Page   REF•26

Index   Page   REF•30

The Vauxhall/Opel Zafira-B model was introduced in the UK in the Spring of 2005 as a replacement for the previous Zafira, the 'A' model. This manual covers the Zafira-B model, from 2009 when it was facelifted, and several new engines introduced. The Zafira is available with only one body style, that of a 5-door Multi Personnel Vehicle (MPV), and with 1.6 and 1.8 petrol engines, along with 1.7 and 1.9 litre diesel engines. 2.0 litre turbo, and 2.2 litre petrol engines are also available, but are not covered in this manual. All the petrol engines are DOHC 16-valve units, whereas the diesel engines are available in either SOHC 8-valve, or DOHC 16-valve form.

According to engine type, the manual gearbox is of the 5- or 6-speed all synchromesh type, with a 4- or 6-speed electronically-controlled automatic transmission optionally available on certain models.

All models have front-wheel-drive with fully-independent front suspension, and semi-independent rear suspension with a torsion beam and trailing arms.

A wide range of standard and optional equipment is available within the Zafira range to suit most tastes, including electro/hydraulic power steering, air conditioning, remote central locking, electric windows, electric sunroof, anti-lock braking system, electronic alarm system and supplemental restraint systems.

For the home mechanic, the Zafira is a relatively straightforward vehicle to maintain, and most of the items requiring frequent attention are easily accessible.

Your Vauxhall/Opel Zafira manual

The aim of this manual is to help you get the best value from your vehicle. It can do so in several ways. It can help you decide what work must be done (even should you choose to get it done by a garage), provide information on routine maintenance and servicing, and give a logical course of action and diagnosis when random faults occur. However, it is hoped that you will use the manual by tackling the work yourself. On simpler jobs, it may even be quicker than booking the car into a garage and going there twice, to leave and collect it. Perhaps most important, a lot of money can be saved by avoiding the costs a garage must charge to cover its labour and overheads.

The manual has drawings and descriptions to show the function of the various components, so that their layout can be understood. Then the tasks are described and photographed in a clear step-by-step sequence.

References to the 'left' or 'right' are in the sense of a person in the driver's seat, facing forward.

Project vehicles

The main vehicle used in the preparation of this manual, and which appears in many of the photographic sequences, was a Vauxhall Zafira with a 1.7 litre diesel engine. Additional work was carried out on a Zafira with a 1.6 litre petrol engine.

Acknowledgements

Thanks are also due to Draper Tools Limited, who provided some of the workshop tools, and to all those people at Sparkford who helped in the production of this manual.

We take great pride in the accuracy of information given in this manual, but vehicle manufacturers make alterations and design changes during the production run of a particular vehicle of which they do not inform us. No liability can be accepted by the authors or publishers for loss, damage or injury caused by any errors in, or omissions from, the information given.

Vauxhall Zafira

Working on your car can be dangerous. This page shows just some of the potential risks and hazards, with the aim of creating a safety-conscious attitude.

General hazards

Scalding

• Don't remove the radiator or expansion tank cap while the engine is hot.
• Engine oil, transmission fluid or power steering fluid may also be dangerously hot if the engine has recently been running.

Burning

• Beware of burns from the exhaust system and from any part of the engine. Brake discs and drums can also be extremely hot immediately after use.

Crushing

• When working under or near a raised vehicle, always supplement the jack with axle stands, or use drive-on ramps.
Never venture under a car which is only supported by a jack.
• Take care if loosening or tightening high-torque nuts when the vehicle is on stands. Initial loosening and final tightening should be done with the wheels on the ground.

Fire

• Fuel is highly flammable; fuel vapour is explosive.
• Don't let fuel spill onto a hot engine.
• Do not smoke or allow naked lights (including pilot lights) anywhere near a vehicle being worked on. Also beware of creating sparks (electrically or by use of tools).
• Fuel vapour is heavier than air, so don't work on the fuel system with the vehicle over an inspection pit.
• Another cause of fire is an electrical overload or short-circuit. Take care when repairing or modifying the vehicle wiring.
• Keep a fire extinguisher handy, of a type suitable for use on fuel and electrical fires.

Electric shock

• Ignition HT and Xenon headlight voltages can be dangerous, especially to people with heart problems or a pacemaker. Don't work on or near these systems with the engine running or the ignition switched on.

• Mains voltage is also dangerous. Make sure that any mains-operated equipment is correctly earthed. Mains power points should be protected by a residual current device (RCD) circuit breaker.

Fume or gas intoxication

• Exhaust fumes are poisonous; they can contain carbon monoxide, which is rapidly fatal if inhaled. Never run the engine in a confined space such as a garage with the doors shut.
• Fuel vapour is also poisonous, as are the vapours from some cleaning solvents and paint thinners.

Poisonous or irritant substances

• Avoid skin contact with battery acid and with any fuel, fluid or lubricant, especially antifreeze, brake hydraulic fluid and Diesel fuel. Don't syphon them by mouth. If such a substance is swallowed or gets into the eyes, seek medical advice.
• Prolonged contact with used engine oil can cause skin cancer. Wear gloves or use a barrier cream if necessary. Change out of oil-soaked clothes and do not keep oily rags in your pocket.
• Air conditioning refrigerant forms a poisonous gas if exposed to a naked flame (including a cigarette). It can also cause skin burns on contact.

Asbestos

• Asbestos dust can cause cancer if inhaled or swallowed. Asbestos may be found in gaskets and in brake and clutch linings. When dealing with such components it is safest to assume that they contain asbestos.

Special hazards

Hydrofluoric acid

• This extremely corrosive acid is formed when certain types of synthetic rubber, found in some O-rings, oil seals, fuel hoses etc, are exposed to temperatures above 4000C. The rubber changes into a charred or sticky substance containing the acid. *Once formed, the acid remains dangerous for years. If it gets onto the skin, it may be necessary to amputate the limb concerned.*
• When dealing with a vehicle which has suffered a fire, or with components salvaged from such a vehicle, wear protective gloves and discard them after use.

The battery

• Batteries contain sulphuric acid, which attacks clothing, eyes and skin. Take care when topping-up or carrying the battery.
• The hydrogen gas given off by the battery is highly explosive. Never cause a spark or allow a naked light nearby. Be careful when connecting and disconnecting battery chargers or jump leads.

Air bags

• Air bags can cause injury if they go off accidentally. Take care when removing the steering wheel and trim panels. Special storage instructions may apply.

Diesel injection equipment

• Diesel injection pumps supply fuel at very high pressure. Take care when working on the fuel injectors and fuel pipes.

Warning: Never expose the hands, face or any other part of the body to injector spray; the fuel can penetrate the skin with potentially fatal results.

Remember...

DO

• Do use eye protection when using power tools, and when working under the vehicle.

• Do wear gloves or use barrier cream to protect your hands when necessary.

• Do get someone to check periodically that all is well when working alone on the vehicle.

• Do keep loose clothing and long hair well out of the way of moving mechanical parts.

• Do remove rings, wristwatch etc, before working on the vehicle – especially the electrical system.

• Do ensure that any lifting or jacking equipment has a safe working load rating adequate for the job.

DON'T

• Don't attempt to lift a heavy component which may be beyond your capability – get assistance.

• Don't rush to finish a job, or take unverified short cuts.

• Don't use ill-fitting tools which may slip and cause injury.

• Don't leave tools or parts lying around where someone can trip over them. Mop up oil and fuel spills at once.

• Don't allow children or pets to play in or near a vehicle being worked on.

The following pages are intended to help in dealing with common roadside emergencies and breakdowns. You will find more detailed fault finding information at the back of the manual, and repair information in the main chapters.

If your car won't start and the starter motor doesn't turn

- ☐ If it's a model with automatic transmission, make sure the selector is in P or N.
- ☐ Open the bonnet and make sure that the battery terminals are clean and tight.
- ☐ Switch on the headlights and try to start the engine. If the headlights go very dim when you're trying to start, the battery is probably flat. Get out of trouble by jump starting using a friend's car.

If your car won't start even though the starter motor turns as normal

- ☐ Is there fuel in the tank?
- ☐ Is there moisture on electrical components under the bonnet? Switch off the ignition, then wipe off any obvious dampness with a dry cloth. Spray a water-repellent aerosol product (WD-40 or equivalent) on ignition and fuel system electrical connectors like those shown in the photos.

1 Check that the airflow meter wiring is connected securely.

2 Check the security and condition of the battery connections.

Check that electrical connections are secure (with the ignition switched off) and spray them with a water-dispersant spray like WD-40 if you suspect a problem due to damp.

3 Check all multiplugs and wiring connectors for security.

4 Check that all fuses are still in good condition and none have blown.

Jump starting

 HAYNES HINT *Jump starting will get you out of trouble, but you must correct whatever made the battery go flat in the first place. There are three possibilities:*

1 *The battery has been drained by repeated attempts to start, or by leaving the lights on.*

2 *The charging system is not working properly (alternator drivebelt slack or broken, alternator wiring fault or alternator itself faulty).*

3 *The battery itself is at fault (electrolyte low, or battery worn out).*

When jump-starting a car using a booster battery, observe the following precautions:

✓ Before connecting the booster battery, make sure that the ignition is switched off. Caution: Remove the key in case the central locking engages when the jump leads are connected.

✓ Ensure that all electrical equipment (lights, heater, wipers, etc) is switched off.

✓ Take note of any special precautions printed on the battery case.

✓ Make sure that the booster battery is the same voltage as the discharged one in the vehicle.

✓ If the battery is being jump-started from the battery in another vehicle, the two vehicles MUST NOT TOUCH each other.

✓ Make sure that the transmission is in neutral (or PARK, in the case of automatic transmission).

 HAYNES HINT *Budget jump leads can be a false economy, as they often do not pass enough current to start large capacity or diesel engines. They can also get hot.*

1 Connect one end of the red jump lead to the positive (+) terminal of the flat battery

Connect the other end of the red lead to

2 the positive (+) terminal of the booster battery.

3 Connect one end of the black jump lead to the negative (-) terminal of the booster battery

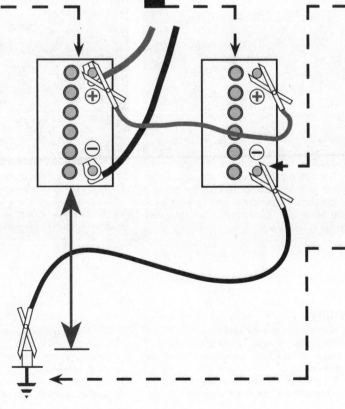

4 Connect the other end of the black jump lead to a bolt or bracket on the engine block, well away from the battery, on the vehicle to be started.

5 Make sure that the jump leads will not come into contact with the fan, drive-belts or other moving parts of the engine.

6 Start the engine using the booster battery and run it at idle speed. Switch on the lights, rear window demister and heater blower motor, then disconnect the jump leads in the reverse order of connection. Turn off the lights etc.

Wheel changing

Note: *Most Zafira models are equipped with a puncture repair kit and do not have a spare wheel and jack. If your car has a puncture repair kit, refer to the information below.*

Warning: Do not change a wheel in a situation where you risk being hit by other traffic. On busy roads, try to stop in a lay-by or a gateway. Be wary of passing traffic while changing the wheel – it is easy to become distracted by the job in hand.

Preparation

☐ When a puncture occurs, stop as soon as it is safe to do so.

☐ Park on firm level ground, if possible, and well out of the way of other traffic.

☐ Use hazard warning lights if necessary.

☐ If you have one, use a warning triangle to alert other drivers of your presence.

☐ Apply the handbrake and engage first or reverse gear gear (or Park on models with automatic transmission).

☐ Chock the wheel diagonally opposite the one being removed – a couple of large stones will do for this.

☐ If the ground is soft, use a flat piece of wood to spread the load under the jack.

Changing the wheel

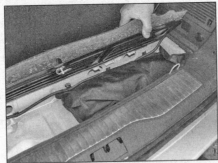

1 Lift the floor covering and open the storage compartment by lifting and turning the retaining ring. Release the strap and lift out the tool bag.

3 From under the car, unhook the catch and lower the spare wheel cradle. Detach the safety cable and lower the cradle to the ground. Lift out the spare wheel.

2 The spare wheel is located under the rear of the car. Unscrew the spare wheel cradle retaining bolt in the luggage compartment floor using the wheel brace.

4 On models with steel wheels, use the special tool to pull the wheel trim from the wheel. On models with alloy wheels, use the screwdriver provided inserted at the wheel bolt holes to prise off the trim. Slacken each wheel bolt by half a turn.

5 Locate the jack head below the jacking point nearest the wheel to be changed; the jacking point is indicated by an arrow in the sill. Turn the handle until the base of the jack touches the ground ensuring that the jack is vertical. Raise the vehicle until the wheel is clear of the ground. If the tyre is flat make sure that the vehicle is raised sufficiently to allow the spare wheel to be fitted.

6 Remove the bolts and lift the wheel from the vehicle. Place it beneath the sill as a precaution against the jack failing. Fit the spare wheel and tighten the bolts moderately with the wheel brace.

7 Lower the vehicle to the ground, then finally tighten the wheel bolts in a diagonal sequence. Refit the wheel trim. Note that the wheel bolts should be tightened to the specified torque at the earliest opportunity.

Finally . . .

☐ Remove the wheel chocks.

☐ Place the damaged wheel or tyre in the spare wheel cradle, then raise and secure the cradle.

☐ Stow the jack and tools in the storage compartment and refit the cover.

☐ Check the tyre pressure on the wheel just fitted. If it is low, drive slowly to the nearest garage and inflate the tyre to the right pressure.

☐ Have the punctured wheel repaired at the earliest opportunity.

Using the puncture repair kit

 Warning: Do not attempt to repair a punctured tyre in a situation where you risk being hit by other traffic. On busy roads, try to stop in a lay-by or a gateway. Be wary of passing traffic while using the kit – it is easy to become distracted by the job in hand.

 Warning: Repair of a tyre using the puncture repair kit must be regarded as a 'get you home' emergency repair only. A new tyre must be fitted as soon as possible.

Preparation

☐ When a puncture occurs, stop as soon as it is safe to do so.
☐ Park on firm level ground, if possible, and well out of the way of other traffic.
☐ Use hazard warning lights if necessary.
☐ If you have one, use a warning triangle to alert other drivers of your presence.
☐ Apply the handbrake and engage first or reverse gear gear (or Park on models with automatic transmission).

1 Open the storage compartment cover located at the right-hand side of the luggage compartment. Take out the sealant bottle and bracket together with the air hose.

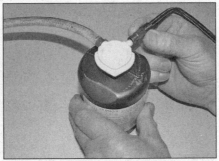

2 Detach the air hose from the bracket and screw it onto the sealant bottle connection. Slide the sealant bottle onto the bracket making sure it is fully located and will not fall over.

3 Unscrew the dust cap from the punctured tyre, and screw the sealant bottle short air hose onto the tyre valve.

4 Take the long air hose into the car and screw it onto the connection on the electric pump.

5 Open the cover on the front of the electric pump, pull out the wiring plug and insert it into the adjacent accessory socket. To avoid discharging the battery when the electric pump is running, it is advisable to start the engine.

6 Press the '+' button on the electric pump to start the pump. The pump will initially pump the sealant into the tyre which will take approximately 30 seconds, and then start to inflate the tyre. During the initial 30 second period the pressure gauge on the pump will indicate up to 6 bar (87 psi) and then drop. The correct tyre pressure (see end of Weekly checks) should be obtained within 10 minutes. The electric pump can then be switched off by pressing the '+' button again.

Important notes

☐ If the correct tyre pressure is not obtained within 10 minutes, it is likely that the tyre is too badly damaged to be repaired with the kit.
☐ If it is necessary to release the pressure in the tyre, press the '–' button on the electric pump.
☐ The maximum speed sticker attached to the sealant bottle should be placed in the driver's field of view. Do not exceed the permitted maximum speed until an undamaged wheel and tyre have been fitted.
☐ On completion, disconnect the sealant bottle, tyre repair kit and long air hose, and connect the end of the short air hose to the free connection on the sealant bottle. This will prevent any remaining sealant from leaking out.
☐ Continue driving immediately so that the sealant is evenly distributed around the inside of the tyre.
☐ After driving approximately 6 miles (but no more than 10 minutes) stop and check the tyre pressure by connecting the long air hose directly to the tyre valve. As long as the pressure indicated on the gauge is more than 1.3 bar (19 psi) it may be adjusted using the electric pump. If the pressure has fallen below 1.3 bar (19 psi) the repair has not been successful and the car should not be driven. It will therefore be necessary to seek roadside assistance.

Finally . . .

☐ Stow the puncture repair kit in the storage compartment and refit the storage compartment cover.
☐ Do not exceed 50 mph until a new tyre has been fitted.
☐ Obtain a new sealant bottle as soon as possible, or another puncture will leave you stranded.

Identifying leaks

Puddles on the garage floor or drive, or obvious wetness under the bonnet or underneath the car, suggest a leak that needs investigating. It can sometimes be difficult to decide where the leak is coming from, especially if an engine undershield is fitted. Leaking oil or fluid can also be blown rearwards by the passage of air under the car, giving a false impression of where the problem lies.

⚠ *Warning: Most automotive oils and fluids are poisonous. Wash them off skin, and change out of contaminated clothing, without delay.*

 The smell of a fluid leaking from the car may provide a clue to what's leaking. Some fluids are distinctively coloured. It may help to remove the engine undershield, clean the car carefully and to park it over some clean paper overnight as an aid to locating the source of the leak. Remember that some leaks may only occur while the engine is running.

Sump oil

Engine oil may leak from the drain plug...

Oil from filter

...or from the base of the oil filter.

Gearbox oil

Gearbox oil can leak from the seals at the inboard ends of the driveshafts.

Antifreeze

Leaking antifreeze often leaves a crystalline deposit like this.

Brake fluid

A leak occurring at a wheel is almost certainly brake fluid.

Power steering fluid

Power steering fluid may leak from the pipe connectors on the steering rack.

Towing

When all else fails, you may find yourself having to get a tow home – or of course you may be helping somebody else. Long-distance recovery should only be done by a garage or breakdown service. For shorter distances, DIY towing using another car is easy enough, but observe the following points:

☐ Use a proper tow-rope – they are not expensive. The vehicle being towed must display an ON TOW sign in its rear window.

☐ Always turn the ignition key to the 'on' position when the vehicle is being towed, so that the steering lock is released, and the direction indicator and brake lights work.

☐ Only attach the tow-rope to the towing eyes provided.

☐ To fit the towing eye, remove the circular cover from the front or rear bumper, as required, then screw in the towing eye anti-clockwise as far as it will go using the handle of the wheel brace to turn the eye. Note that the towing eye has a left-hand thread.

☐ A towing eye is provided with the tool kit in the luggage compartment.

☐ Before being towed, release the handbrake and select neutral on the transmission. On models with automatic transmission, special precautions apply. If in doubt, do not tow, or transmission damage may result.

☐ Note that greater-than-usual pedal pressure will be required to operate the brakes, since the vacuum servo unit is only operational with the engine running.

☐ Greater-than-usual steering effort will also be required.

☐ The driver of the car being towed must keep the tow-rope taut at all times to avoid snatching.

☐ Make sure that both drivers know the route before setting off.

☐ Only drive at moderate speeds and keep the distance towed to a minimum. Drive smoothly and allow plenty of time for slowing down at junctions.

Introduction

There are some very simple checks which need only take a few minutes to carry out, but which could save you a lot of inconvenience and expense.

These Weekly checks require no great skill or special tools, and the small amount of time they take to perform could prove to be very well spent, for example:

☐ Keeping an eye on tyre condition and pressures, will not only help to stop them wearing out prematurely, but could also save your life.

☐ Many breakdowns are caused by electrical problems. Battery-related faults are particularly common, and a quick check on a regular basis will often prevent the majority of these.

☐ If your car develops a brake fluid leak, the first time you might know about it is when your brakes don't work properly. Checking the level regularly will give advance warning of this kind of problem.

☐ If the oil or coolant levels run low, the cost of repairing any engine damage will be far greater than fixing the leak, for example.

Underbonnet check points

▶ 1.6 litre petrol engine

1 *Engine oil level dipstick*
2 *Engine oil filler cap*
3 *Coolant reservoir (expansion) tank*
4 *Washer fluid reservoir*
5 *Battery*

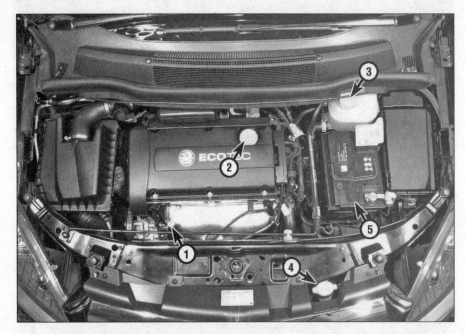

▶ 1.8 litre petrol engine

1 *Engine oil level dipstick*
2 *Engine oil filler cap*
3 *Coolant reservoir (expansion) tank*
4 *Washer fluid reservoir*
5 *Battery*

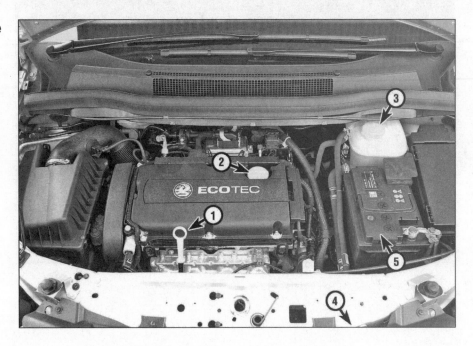

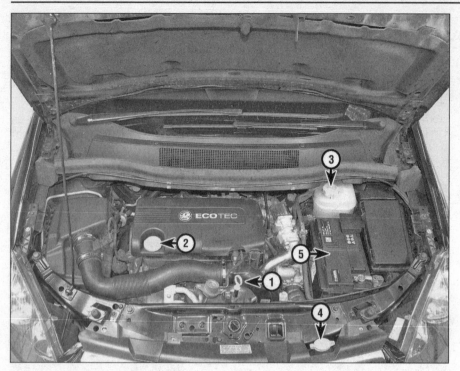

◄ 1.7 litre diesel engine

1 *Engine oil level dipstick*
2 *Engine oil filler cap*
3 *Coolant reservoir (expansion) tank*
4 *Washer fluid reservoir*
5 *Battery*

◄ 1.9 litre diesel engine

1 *Engine oil level dipstick*
2 *Engine oil filler cap*
3 *Coolant reservoir (expansion) tank*
4 *Washer fluid reservoir*
5 *Battery*

Engine oil level

Before you start

✔ Make sure that the car is on level ground.
✔ The oil level must be checked with the engine at normal operating temperature, however, wait at least 5 minutes after the engine has been switched off.

 HAYNES HINT *If the oil is checked immediately after driving the vehicle, some of the oil will remain in the upper engine components, resulting in an inaccurate reading on the dipstick.*

The correct oil

Modern engines place great demands on their oil. It is very important that the correct oil for your car is used (see *Lubricants and fluids*).

Car care

● If you have to add oil frequently, you should check whether you have any oil leaks. Remove the engine undershield and place some clean paper under the car overnight, and check for stains in the morning. If there are no leaks, then the engine may be burning oil, or the oil may only be leaking when the engine is running.
● Always maintain the level between the upper and lower dipstick marks (see photo 3). If the level is too low, severe engine damage may occur. Oil seal failure may result if the engine is overfilled by adding too much oil.

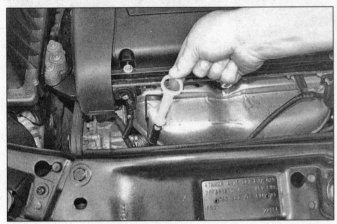

1 The dipstick is brightly coloured for easy identification (see Underbonnet check points for exact location). Withdraw the dipstick.

2 Using a clean rag or paper towel remove all oil from the dipstick. Insert the clean dipstick into the tube as far as it will go, then withdraw it again.

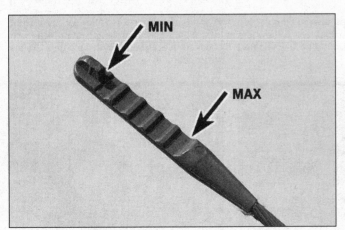

MIN

MAX

3 Note the level on the end of the dipstick, which should be between the upper (MAX) mark and lower (MIN) mark. Approximately 1.0 litre of oil will raise the level from the lower mark to the upper mark.

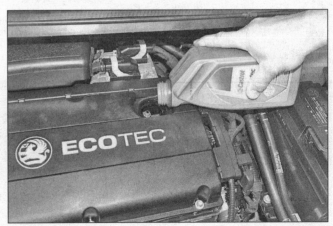

4 Oil is added through the filler cap. Unscrew the cap and top-up the level. A funnel may help to reduce spillage. Add the oil slowly, checking the level on the dipstick frequently. Avoid overfilling (see *Car care*).

Coolant level

> *Warning: Do not attempt to remove the expansion tank pressure cap when the engine is hot, as there is a very great risk of scalding. Do not leave open containers of coolant about, as it is poisonous.*

Car care

● Adding coolant should not be necessary on a regular basis. If frequent topping-up is required, it is likely there is a leak. Check the radiator, all hoses and joint faces for signs of staining or wetness, and rectify as necessary.

● It is important that antifreeze is used in the cooling system all year round, not just during the winter months. Don't top-up with water alone, as the antifreeze will become diluted.

1 The coolant level varies with the temperature of the engine. When the engine is cold, the coolant level should be slightly above the KALT/COLD mark on the side of the tank. When the engine is hot, the level will rise.

2 If topping-up is necessary, wait until the engine is cold. Slowly unscrew the expansion tank cap, to release any pressure present in the cooling system, and remove it.

3 Add a mixture of water and antifreeze to the expansion tank until the coolant is up to the KALT/COLD level mark. Refit the cap and tighten it securely.

Brake (and clutch) fluid level

Note: *Models with the Easytronic transmission have a clutch fluid reservoir mounted on the transmission (see Chapter 1A).*

> *Warning: Brake fluid can harm your eyes and damage painted surfaces, so use extreme caution when handling and pouring it.*
> *Warning: Do not use fluid that has been standing open for some time, as it absorbs moisture from the air, which can cause a dangerous loss of braking effectiveness.*

Safety first!

● If the reservoir requires repeated topping-up this is an indication of a fluid leak somewhere in the system, which should be investigated immediately.

 The fluid level in the reservoir will drop slightly as the brake pads wear down, but the fluid level must never be allowed to drop below the MIN mark.

● If a leak is suspected, the car should not be driven until the braking system has been checked. Never take any risks where brakes are concerned.

1 The MAX and MIN marks are indicated on the side of the reservoir. The fluid level must be kept between the marks at all times.

2 If topping-up is necessary, first wipe clean the area around the filler cap to prevent dirt entering the hydraulic system. Unscrew the reservoir cap.

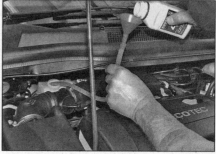

3 Using a funnel and clear plastic tube, carefully add fluid, taking care not to spill it onto the surrounding components. Use only the specified fluid; mixing different types can cause damage to the system. After topping-up to the correct level, securely refit the cap and wipe off any spilt fluid.

Battery

Caution: Before carrying out any work on the vehicle battery, read the precautions given in 'Safety first!' at the start of this manual. If the battery is to be disconnected, refer to Chapter 5A Section 4, before proceeding.

✔ Make sure that the battery tray is in good condition, and that the clamp is tight. Corrosion on the tray, retaining clamp and the battery itself can be removed with a solution of water and baking soda. Thoroughly rinse all cleaned areas with water. Any metal parts damaged by corrosion should be covered with a zinc-based primer, then painted.

✔ Periodically (approximately every three months), check the charge condition of the battery as described in Chapter 5A Section 3.

✔ If the battery is flat, and you need to jump start your vehicle, see *Jump starting*.

Battery corrosion can be kept to a minimum by applying a layer of petroleum jelly to the clamps and terminals after they are reconnected.

1 The battery is located at the front, left-hand side of the engine compartment. Where fitted, open the insulation jacket around the battery, then check the tightness of battery clamps to ensure good electrical connections. You should not be able to move them. Also check each cable for cracks and frayed conductors.

2 If corrosion (white, fluffy deposits) is evident, remove the cables from the battery terminals, clean them with a small wire brush, then refit them. Automotive stores sell a tool for cleaning the battery post …

3 … as well as the battery cable clamps.

Washer fluid level

● Screenwash additives not only keep the windscreen clean during bad weather, they also prevent the washer system freezing in cold weather – which is when you are likely to need it most. Don't top-up using plain water, as the screenwash will become diluted, and will freeze in cold weather.

 Warning: On no account use engine coolant antifreeze in the screen washer system – this may damage the paintwork.

1 The reservoir for the windscreen, rear window and headlight (where applicable) washer systems is located on the front left-hand side of the engine compartment. If topping-up is necessary, open the filler cap.

2 When topping-up the reservoir a screen wash additive should be added in the quantities recommended on the bottle.

Tyre condition and pressure

It is very important that tyres are in good condition, and at the correct pressure – having a tyre failure at any speed is highly dangerous.

Tyre wear is influenced by driving style – harsh braking and acceleration, or fast cornering, will all produce more rapid tyre wear. As a general rule, the front tyres wear out faster than the rears. Interchanging the tyres from front to rear ("rotating" the tyres) may result in more even wear. However, if this is completely effective, you may have the expense of replacing all four tyres at once!

21 Remove any nails or stones embedded in the tread before they penetrate the tyre to cause deflation. If removal of a nail does reveal that the tyre has been punctured, refit the nail so that its point of penetration is marked. Then immediately change the wheel, and have the tyre repaired by a tyre dealer.

Regularly check the tyres for damage in the form of cuts or bulges, especially in the sidewalls. Periodically remove the wheels, and clean any dirt or mud from the inside and outside surfaces. Examine the wheel rims for signs of rusting, corrosion or other damage. Light alloy wheels are easily damaged by "kerbing" whilst parking; steel wheels may also become dented or buckled. A new wheel is very often the only way to overcome severe damage.

New tyres should be balanced when they are fitted, but it may become necessary to re-balance them as they wear, or if the balance weights fitted to the wheel rim should fall off. Unbalanced tyres will wear more quickly, as will the steering and suspension components. Wheel imbalance is normally signified by vibration, particularly at a certain speed (typically around 50 mph). If this vibration is felt only through the steering, then it is likely that just the front wheels need balancing. If, however, the vibration is felt through the whole car, the rear wheels could be out of balance. Wheel balancing should be carried out by a tyre dealer or garage.

1 Tread Depth - visual check
The original tyres have tread wear safety bands (B), which will appear when the tread depth reaches approximately 1.6 mm. The band positions are indicated by a triangular mark on the tyre sidewall (A).

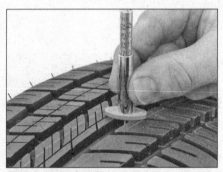

2 Tread Depth - manual check
Alternatively, tread wear can be monitored with a simple, inexpensive device known as a tread depth indicator gauge.

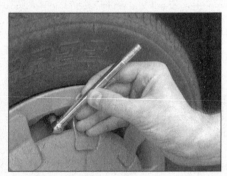

3 Tyre Pressure Check
Check the tyre pressures regularly with the tyres cold. Do not adjust the tyre pressures immediately after the vehicle has been used, or an inaccurate setting will result.

Tyre tread wear patterns

Shoulder Wear

Underinflation (wear on both sides)
Under-inflation will cause overheating of the tyre, because the tyre will flex too much, and the tread will not sit correctly on the road surface. This will cause a loss of grip and excessive wear, not to mention the danger of sudden tyre failure due to heat build-up.
Check and adjust pressures
Incorrect wheel camber (wear on one side)
Repair or renew suspension parts
Hard cornering
Reduce speed!

Centre Wear

Overinflation
Over-inflation will cause rapid wear of the centre part of the tyre tread, coupled with reduced grip, harsher ride, and the danger of shock damage occurring in the tyre casing.
Check and adjust pressures

If you sometimes have to inflate your car's tyres to the higher pressures specified for maximum load or sustained high speed, don't forget to reduce the pressures to normal afterwards.

Uneven Wear

Front tyres may wear unevenly as a result of wheel misalignment. Most tyre dealers and garages can check and adjust the wheel alignment (or "tracking") for a modest charge.
Incorrect camber or castor
Repair or renew suspension parts
Malfunctioning suspension
Repair or renew suspension parts
Unbalanced wheel
Balance tyres
Incorrect toe setting
Adjust front wheel alignment
Note: *The feathered edge of the tread which typifies toe wear is best checked by feel.*

Electrical systems

✔ Check all external lights and the horn. Refer to the appropriate Sections of Chapter 12 for details if any of the circuits are found to be inoperative.

✔ Visually check all accessible wiring connectors, harnesses and retaining clips for security, and for signs of chafing or damage.

 HAYNES HiNT *If you need to check your brake lights and indicators unaided, back up to a wall or garage door and operate the lights. The reflected light should show if they are working properly.*

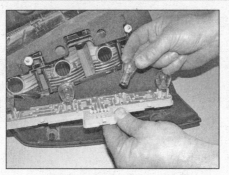

1 If a single indicator light, stop-light or headlight has failed, it is likely that a bulb has blown and will need to be renewed. Refer to Chapter 12 for details. If both stop-lights have failed, it is possible that the switch has failed (see Chapter 9).

2 If more than one indicator light or headlight has failed, it is likely that either a fuse has blown or that there is a fault in the circuit (see Chapter 12). The main fuses are located behind the trim panel on the left-hand side of the luggage compartment. Turn the catches and open the cover for access to the fuses.

3 Additional fuses and relays are located in the fuse/relay box on the left-hand side of the engine compartment. Refer to the wiring diagrams at the end of Chapter 12 for details of the fuse locations and circuits protected.

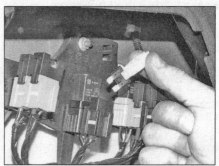

4 To renew a blown fuse, remove it, where applicable, using the plastic tool provided. Fit a new fuse of the same rating, available from car accessory shops. It is important that you find the reason that the fuse blew (see Electrical fault finding in Chapter 12).

Wiper blades

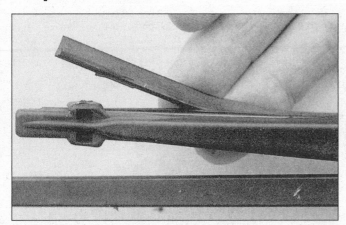

1 Check the condition of the wiper blades; if they are cracked or show any signs of deterioration, or if the glass swept area is smeared, renew them. Wiper blades should be renewed annually.

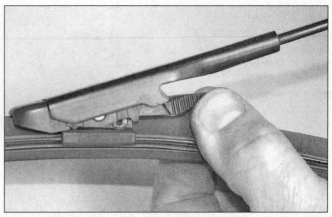

2 To remove a windscreen wiper blade, pull the arm fully away from the screen until it locks. Swivel the blade through 90°, then press the two catches on the wiper blade and remove the blade. Don't forget to check the tailgate wiper blade as well which is removed in a similar way.

Lubricants and fluids

Engine	Multigrade engine oil, viscosity SAE 0W/30, 0W/40 (below -25°C) or 5W/30 or 5W/40 (down to -25°C). DEXOS 2 for all petrol and diesel engines.
Petrol engines...	If DEXOS 2 is unavailable, use oil to specification GM-LL-A-025. If this is unavailable, use oil to specification ACEA-A3/B3 or A4/B4 (or higher)
Diesel engines	If DEXOS 2 is unavailable, use oil to specification GM-LL-B-025. If this is unavailable, use oil to specification ACEA-A3/B4 (engines without diesel particulate filter), or ACEA-C3 (engine with diesel particulate filter)
Manual and Easytronic transmissions	Vauxhall/Opel gear oil (09 120 541)
AF22 transmission	Vauxhall/Opel automatic transmission fluid (91 117 946)
AF40 transmission	Vauxhall/Opel automatic transmission fluid (93 165 147)
Power steering reservoir............................	Vauxhall/Opel steering fluid (90 544 116)
Cooling system	Vauxhall/Opel silicate-free coolant (09 194 431/19 40 650)
Brake/clutch fluid reservoir........................	Hydraulic fluid to DOT 4

Tyre pressures (cold)

Note: *Pressures apply to original-equipment tyres, and may vary if any other make or type of tyre is fitted; check with the tyre manufacturer or supplier for correct pressures if necessary.*

Normal load (up to 3 passengers)	Front	Rear
Petrol models		
195/65 R 15, 205/55 R 16 and 225/45 R 17 tyres	2.0 bar (29 psi)	2.0 bar (29 psi)
225/40 R 18 tyres.......................................	2.2 bar (32 psi)	2.2 bar (32 psi)
Diesel models		
195/60 R 16 tyres.......................................	2.6 bar (38 psi)	2.4 bar (35 psi)
205/55 R 16 and 225/45 R 17 tyres...........................	2.4 bar (35 psi)	2.2 bar (32 psi)
225/40 R 18 tyres.......................................	2.5 bar (36 psi)	2.3 bar (33 psi)
Fully laden		
Petrol models		
195/65 R 15, 205/55 R 16 and 225/45 R 17 tyres	2.1 bar (30 psi)	2.6 bar (38 psi)
225/40 R 18 tyres.......................................	2.3 bar (33 psi)	2.8 bar (41 psi)
Diesel models		
195/60 R 16 tyres.......................................	2.8 bar (41 psi)	3.2 bar (46 psi)
205/55 R 16 and 225/45 R 17 tyres...........................	2.6 bar (38 psi)	3.1 bar (45 psi)
225/40 R 18 tyres.......................................	2.7 bar (39 psi)	3.1 bar (45 psi)
Space-saver temporary spare tyre		
All models..	4.2 bar (61 psi)	4.2 bar (61 psi)

Chapter 1 Part A
Routine maintenance and servicing – petrol models

Contents

Section number

Air cleaner element renewal – petrol models 30
Automatic transmission fluid renewal. 33
Auxiliary drivebelt check and renewal 23
Bodywork and underbody condition check 16
Brake fluid pipe and hose check 11
Brake pad and disc check 10
Clutch hydraulic fluid level check – Easytronic models 9
Component location – petrol models 3
Coolant renewal 28
Driveshaft check. 13
Electrical systems check 19
Engine oil and filter renewal – petrol models 6
Exhaust emission check. 29
Exhaust system check 14
Front suspension and steering check 12
General Information 4
Handbrake operation and adjustment check. 24

Section number

Headlight beam alignment check. 25
Hinge and lock lubrication 18
Hose and fluid leak check 7
Hydraulic fluid renewal. 27
Maintenance schedule – petrol models 2
Pollen filter renewal 22
Power steering fluid level check. 8
Rear suspension check 15
Regular maintenance 5
Remote control battery renewal 26
Road test 20
Roadwheel bolt tightness check 17
Service interval indicator reset 21
Servicing specifications 1
Spark plug renewal. 31
Timing belt, tensioner and idler pulley renewal 32
Valve clearance check and adjustment 34

Degrees of difficulty

Easy, suitable for novice with little experience	**Fairly easy,** suitable for beginner with some experience	**Fairly difficult,** suitable for competent DIY mechanic	**Difficult,** suitable for experienced DIY mechanic	**Very difficult,** suitable for expert DIY or professional

1 Servicing specifications

Lubricants and fluids. . . . . Refer to *Weekly checks*

Capacities

Engine oil (including oil filter)

All engines . . . . 4.5 litres
Difference between MIN and MAX dipstick marks. . . . . 1.0 litre

Cooling system

All engines:
  Without air conditioning . . . . 6.1 litres
  With air conditioning. . . . . 6.3 litres

Transmission

Manual transmission:
  F17+ transmission . . . . 1.6 litres
  M32 transmission . . . . 2.4 litres
Automatic transmission (at fluid change):
  AF22 transmission . . . . 4.0 litres (approximately)
  AF40 transmission . . . . 3.0 litres (approximately)
Easytronic transmission . . . . 1.6 litres

Washer fluid reservoir

Without headlight washers. . . . . 2.3 litres
With headlight washers . . . . 4.2 litres

Fuel tank

All models. . . . . 58 litres

Cooling system

Antifreeze mixture:
  50% antifreeze . . . . Protection down to -40°C

Ignition system

Spark plugs: *

	Type	Electrode gap
1.6 litre engines:		
Z16XE1, Z16XEP and Z16XER engine codes.	NGK ZFR5F	0.9 mm
A16XER engine code	NGK ZFR6V-G	0.9 mm
1.8 litre engines:		
Z18XER engine code	NGK ZFR5F	0.9 mm
A18XER engine code	ZFR6V-G	0.9 mm

* Seek manufacturer's latest recomendations

Brakes

Brake pad friction material minimum thickness. . . . . 2.0 mm

Torque wrench settings

	Nm	lbf ft
Oil filter housing cap-to-filter housing (paper element filter):		
1.6 litre engines:		
Z16XE1, Z16XEP and Z16 XER engine codes	12	9
A16XER engine code	25	18
1.8 litre engines	25	18
Roadwheel bolts.	110	81
Spark plugs	25	18
Sump drain plug:		
1.6 and 1.8 litre engines	15	11

2 Maintenance schedule – petrol models

The maintenance intervals in this manual are provided with the assumption that you, not the dealer, will be carrying out the work. These are the minimum maintenance intervals based on the standard service schedule recommended by the manufacturer for vehicles driven daily. If you wish to keep your vehicle in peak condition at all times, you may wish to perform some of these procedures more often. We encourage frequent maintenance, because it enhances the efficiency, performance and resale value of your vehicle.

If the vehicle is driven in dusty areas, used to tow a trailer, or driven frequently at slow speeds (idling in traffic) or on short journeys, more frequent maintenance intervals are recommended.

When the vehicle is new, it should be serviced by a dealer service department (or other workshop recognised by the vehicle manufacturer as providing the same standard of service) in order to preserve the warranty. The vehicle manufacturer may reject warranty claims if you are unable to prove that servicing has been carried out as and when specified, using only original equipment parts or parts certified to be of equivalent quality.

Every 250 miles or weekly

☐ Refer to Weekly checks

Every 10 000 miles or 6 months – whichever comes first

☐ Renew the engine oil and filter (Section 6)

Note: *Vauxhall/Opel recommend that the engine oil and filter are changed every 20 000 miles or 12 months. However, oil and filter changes are good for the engine and we recommend that the oil and filter are renewed more frequently, especially if the vehicle is used on a lot of short journeys.*

Every 20 000 miles or 12 months – whichever comes first

☐ Check all underbonnet and underbody components, pipes and hoses for leaks (Section 7)
☐ Check the power steering fluid level (Section 8)
☐ Check the Easytronic clutch hydraulic fluid level (Section 9)
☐ Check the condition of the brake pads, calipers and discs (Section 10)
☐ Check the condition of all brake fluid pipes and hoses (Section 11)
☐ Check the condition of the front suspension and steering components, particularly the rubber gaiters and seals (Section 12)
☐ Check the condition of the driveshaft joint gaiters, and the driveshaft joints (Section 13)
☐ Check the condition of the exhaust system components (Section 14)
☐ Check the condition of the rear suspension components (Section 15)
☐ Check the bodywork and underbody for damage and corrosion, and check the condition of the underbody corrosion protection (Section 16)
☐ Check the tightness of the roadwheel bolts (Section 17)
☐ Lubricate all door, bonnet and tailgate hinges and locks (Section 18)
☐ Check the operation of the horn, all lights, and the wipers and washers (Section 19)
☐ Carry out a road test (Section 20)
☐ Reset the service interval indicator (Section 21)

Every 40 000 miles or 2 years – whichever comes first

☐ Renew the pollen filter (Section 22)
☐ Check the auxiliary drivebelt and tensioner (Section 23)
☐ Check the operation of the handbrake and adjust if necessary (Section 24)
☐ Check the headlight beam alignment (Section 25)

Every 2 years, regardless of mileage

☐ Renew the battery for the remote control handset (Section 26)
☐ Renew the brake and clutch fluid (Section 27)
☐ Renew the coolant (Section 28)*
☐ Exhaust emission test (Section 29)

*Note: *Vehicles using Vauxhall/Opel silicate-free coolant do not need the coolant renewed on a regular basis.*

Every 40 000 miles or 4 years – whichever comes first

☐ Renew the air cleaner filter element (Section 30)
☐ Renew the spark plugs (Section 31)
☐ Renew the timing belt, tensioner and idler pulleys – 1.6 and 1.8 litre engines (Section 32)*
☐ Renew the automatic transmission fluid (Section 33)

*Note: *The normal interval for timing belt renewal is 90 000 miles or 6 years. However, it is strongly recommended that the interval used is 40 000 miles on vehicles which are subjected to intensive use, ie, mainly short journeys or a lot of stop-start driving. The actual belt renewal interval is therefore very much up to the individual owner, but bear in mind that severe engine damage will result if the belt breaks.*

Every 100 000 miles or 10 years – whichever comes first

☐ Check, and if necessary adjust, the valve clearances – 1.6 litre and 1.8 litre engines (Section 34)

3 Component location – petrol models

Underbonnet view of a 1.6 litre model (other models similar)

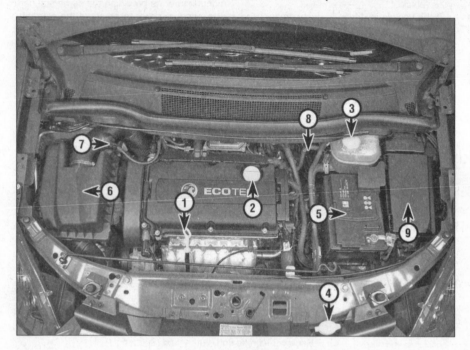

1 Engine oil level dipstick
2 Engine oil filler cap
3 Coolant expansion tank
4 Screen washer fluid reservoir
5 Battery
6 Air cleaner assembly
7 Inlet air temperature sensor
8 Power steering fluid reservoir
9 Fuse/relay box

Front underbody view

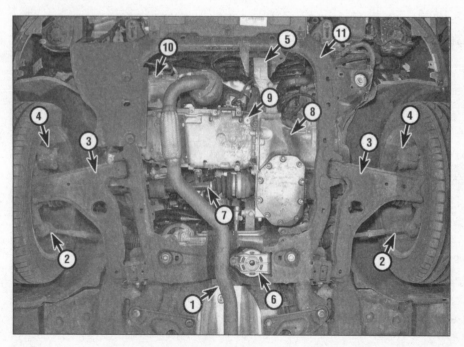

1 Exhaust front pipe
2 Steering track rods
3 Front suspension lower arms
4 Front brake calipers
5 Engine mounting front torque link
6 Engine mounting rear torque link
7 Right-hand driveshaft
8 Manual transmission
9 Engine oil drain plug
10 Air conditioning compressor
11 Front subframe

Rear underbody view

1 Exhaust tailpipe and silencer
2 Rear suspension torsion beam and trailing arms
3 Fuel tank
4 Handbrake cables
5 Rear coil springs
6 Rear shock absorber lower mountings

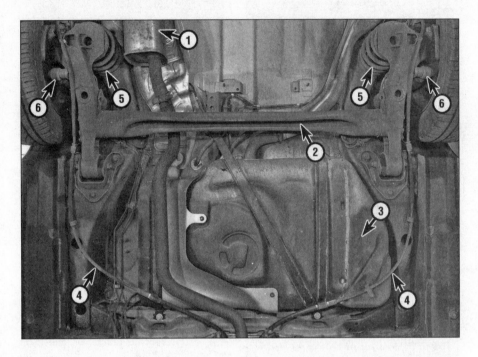

4 General Information

1 This Chapter is designed to help the home mechanic maintain his/her vehicle for safety, economy, long life and peak performance.

2 The Chapter contains a master maintenance schedule, followed by Sections dealing specifically with each task in the schedule. Visual checks, adjustments, component renewal and other helpful items are included. Refer to the accompanying illustrations of the engine compartment and the underside of the vehicle for the locations of the various components.

3 Servicing your vehicle in accordance with the mileage/time maintenance schedule and the following Sections will provide a planned maintenance programme, which should result in a long and reliable service life. This is a comprehensive plan, so maintaining some items but not others at the specified service intervals, will not produce the same results.

4 As you service your vehicle, you will discover that many of the procedures can – and should – be grouped together, because of the particular procedure being performed, or because of the proximity of two otherwise-unrelated components to one another. For example, if the vehicle is raised for any reason, the exhaust can be inspected at the same time as the suspension and steering components.

5 The first step in this maintenance programme is to prepare yourself before the actual work begins. Read through all the Sections relevant to the work to be carried out, then make a list and gather all the parts and tools required. If a problem is encountered, seek advice from a parts specialist, or a dealer service department.

5 Regular maintenance

1 If, from the time the vehicle is new, the routine maintenance schedule is followed closely, and frequent checks are made of fluid levels and high-wear items, as suggested throughout this manual, the engine will be kept in relatively good running condition, and the need for additional work will be minimised.

2 It is possible that there will be times when the engine is running poorly due to the lack of regular maintenance. This is even more likely if a used vehicle, which has not received regular and frequent maintenance checks, is purchased. In such cases, additional work may need to be carried out, outside of the regular maintenance intervals.

3 If engine wear is suspected, a compression test (refer to the appropriate part of Chapter 2) will provide valuable information regarding the overall performance of the main internal components. Such a test can be used as a basis to decide on the extent of the work to be carried out. If, for example, a compression test indicates serious internal engine wear, conventional maintenance as described in this Chapter will not greatly improve the performance of the engine, and may prove a waste of time and money, unless extensive overhaul work is carried out first.

4 The following series of operations are those most often required to improve the performance of a generally poor-running engine:

Primary operations

a) Clean, inspect and test the battery (refer to Weekly checks).
b) Check all the engine-related fluids (refer to Weekly checks).
c) Check the condition and tension of the auxiliary drivebelt (Section 23).
d) Renew the spark plugs (Section 31).
e) Check the condition of the air cleaner element, and renew if necessary (Section 30).
f) Check the condition of all hoses, and check for fluid leaks (Section 7).

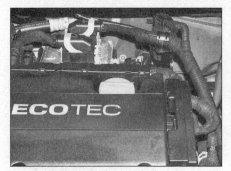

6.3 Removing the oil filler cap

As the drain plug threads release, move it sharply away so the stream of oil issuing from the sump runs into the container, not up your sleeve.

6.7 Using an oil filter removal tool to slacken the canister-type filter

5 If the above operations do not prove fully effective, carry out the following secondary operations:

Secondary operations

6 All items listed under Primary operations, plus the following:
a) *Check the ignition system (Chapter 5B).*
b) *Check the charging system (Chapter 5A).*
c) *Check the fuel, exhaust and emission control systems (refer to the appropriate Parts of Chapter 4A).*

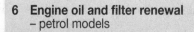

6 Engine oil and filter renewal – petrol models

Frequent oil and filter changes are the most important preventative maintenance procedures which can be undertaken by the DIY owner. As engine oil ages, it becomes diluted and contaminated, which leads to premature engine wear.

1 Before starting this procedure, gather together all the necessary tools and materials.

Also make sure that you have plenty of clean rags and newspapers handy, to mop-up any spills. Ideally, the engine oil should be warm, as it will drain more easily, and more built-up sludge will be removed with it. Take care not to touch the exhaust or any other hot parts of the engine when working under the vehicle. To avoid any possibility of scalding, and to protect yourself from possible skin irritants and other harmful contaminants in used engine oils, it is advisable to wear gloves when carrying out this work.

2 Access to the underside of the vehicle will be greatly improved if it can be raised on a lift, driven onto ramps, or jacked up and supported on axle stands (see *Jacking and vehicle support*). Whichever method is chosen, make sure that the vehicle remains level, or if it is at an angle, that the drain plug is at the lowest point.

3 Remove the oil filler cap from the camshaft cover (twist it through a quarter-turn anti-clockwise and withdraw it) **(see illustration)**.

4 Using a spanner, or preferably a suitable socket and bar, slacken the drain plug about

half a turn. Position the draining container under the drain plug, then remove the plug completely (see **Haynes Hint**).

5 Allow some time for the oil to drain, noting that it may be necessary to reposition the container as the oil flow slows to a trickle.

6 Position another container under the oil filter, located on the front left-hand side of the cylinder block. Two different types of filter may be encountered. The oil filter may be either a paper element type or a metal canister type.

7 Where a canister-type oil filter is fitted, use an oil filter removal tool to slacken the filter initially, then unscrew it by hand the rest of the way **(see illustration)**. Empty the oil from the old filter into the container. In order to ensure that all the old oil is removed, puncture the 'dome' of the filter in two places and allow the oil to drain from the filter completely.

8 Where a paper element-type oil filter is fitted, unscrew the filter cap and withdraw it, together with the element, then separate the element, and remove the O-ring seal from the cap **(see illustrations)**.

9 Use a clean rag to remove all oil, dirt and sludge from the filter sealing area on the block or from the inside of the filter housing.

10 On the canister-type filter, apply a light

6.8a Separate the paper-element type filter from the cap ...

6.8b ... then remove the O-ring seal

6.11a Locate the new seal into the groove in the cap

6.11b Insert the new filter, then lubricate the seal

6.12 If necessary, renew the sump plug O-ring

coating of clean engine oil to the sealing ring on the new filter, then screw the filter into position on the engine. Tighten the filter firmly by hand only – do not use any tools.

11 On the paper element-type filter, locate a new O-ring seal in the groove on the retaining cap, then locate the new element in the cap. Lubricate the seal with a little clean engine oil, then insert the cap and filter into filter housing **(see illustrations)**. Screw on the cap and tighten to the specified torque.

12 After all the oil has drained, wipe the drain plug and the sealing washer/O-ring with a clean rag. Examine the condition of the sealing washer/O-ring, and renew it if it shows signs of damage which may prevent an oil-tight seal **(see illustration)**. Clean the area around the drain plug opening, and refit the plug complete with the washer/O-ring. Tighten the plug to the specified torque, using a torque wrench.

13 Remove the old oil and all tools from under the vehicle then lower the vehicle to the ground.

14 Fill the engine through the filler hole in the camshaft cover, using the correct grade and type of oil (refer to *Weekly checks* for details of topping-up). Pour in half the specified quantity of oil first, then wait a few minutes for the oil to drain into the sump. Continue to add oil, a small quantity at a time, until the level is up to the lower mark on the dipstick. Adding approximately a further 1.0 litre will bring the level up to the upper mark on the dipstick.

15 Start the engine and run it until it reaches normal operating temperature. While the engine is warming-up, check for leaks around the oil filter and the sump drain plug.

16 Stop the engine, and wait at least five minutes for the oil to settle in the sump once more. With the new oil circulated and the filter now completely full, recheck the level on the dipstick, and add more oil as necessary.

17 Dispose of the used engine oil and filter safely, with reference to *General repair procedures* in the Reference chapter of this manual. Do not discard the old filter with domestic household waste. The facility for waste oil disposal provided by many local council refuse tips and/or recycling centres generally has a filter receptacle alongside.

7 Hose and fluid leak check

Note: *Also refer to Section 11.*

1 Visually inspect the engine joint faces, gaskets and seals for any signs of water or oil leaks. Pay particular attention to the areas around the camshaft cover, cylinder head, oil filter and sump joint faces. Similarly, check the transmission and (where applicable) the air conditioning compressor for oil leakage. Bear in mind that, over a period of time, some very slight seepage from these areas is to be expected; what you are really looking for is any indication of a serious leak. Should a leak be found, renew the offending gasket or oil seal by referring to the appropriate Chapters in this manual.

2 Also check the security and condition of all the engine-related pipes and hoses. Ensure that all cable ties or securing clips are in place, and in good condition. Clips which are broken or missing can lead to chafing of the hoses pipes or wiring, which could cause more serious problems in the future.

3 Carefully check the radiator hoses and heater hoses along their entire length. Renew any hose which is cracked, swollen or deteriorated. Cracks will show up better if the hose is squeezed. Pay close attention to the hose clips that secure the hoses to the

HAYNES HiNT

A leak in the cooling system will usually show up as white- or antifreeze coloured deposits on the area adjoining the leak.

cooling system components. Hose clips can pinch and puncture hoses, resulting in cooling system leaks. If wire-type hose clips are used, it may be a good idea to update them with Jubilee clips.

4 Inspect all the cooling system components (hoses, joint faces, etc) for leaks. Where any problems of this nature are found on system components, renew the component or gasket with reference to Chapter 3 (see **Haynes Hint**).

5 Where applicable, inspect the automatic transmission fluid cooler hoses for leaks or deterioration.

6 With the vehicle raised, inspect the fuel tank and filler neck for punctures, cracks and other damage. The connection between the filler neck and tank is especially critical. Sometimes, a rubber filler neck or connecting hose will leak due to loose retaining clamps or deteriorated rubber.

7 Carefully check all rubber hoses and metal or plastic fuel lines leading away from the fuel tank. Check for loose connections, deteriorated hoses, crimped lines and other damage. Pay particular attention to the vent pipes and hoses, which often loop up around the filler neck and can become blocked or crimped. Follow the lines to the front of the vehicle, carefully inspecting them all the way. Renew damaged sections as necessary. Similarly, whilst the vehicle is raised, take the opportunity to inspect all underbody brake fluid pipes and hoses.

8 From within the engine compartment, check the security of all fuel hose attachments and pipe unions, and inspect the fuel hoses and vacuum hoses for kinks, chafing and deterioration.

8 Power steering fluid level check

1 The power steering fluid reservoir is located on RHD vehicles on the left-hand side of the engine compartment between the transmission and the bulkhead. On LHD vehicles, the reservoir is located between the engine and bulkhead on the right-hand side of the engine compartment. The fluid level should be checked with the engine cold.

8.2 Power steering fluid reservoir filler cap (arrowed)

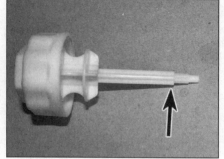

8.3 The fluid level should be up to the MAX mark (arrowed) on the dipstick

8.4 Use a clean funnel and a long length of flexible pipe to top-up the reservoir

EHPS Generation II

2 Wipe clean the reservoir and filler cap, then unscrew the filler cap from the top of the reservoir **(see illustration)**. The filler cap has a bayonet fitting and has a dipstick incorporated into it.

3 Wipe all fluid from the dipstick with a clean rag. Refit the dipstick, then remove it again. Note the fluid level on the dipstick which should be up to the MAX mark **(see illustration)**.

4 If topping-up is necessary, obtain a clean funnel and a long length of flexible pipe to fit the end of the funnel. Insert the pipe down behind the engine and into the top of the reservoir **(see illustration)**. Using power steering fluid of the specified type (see *Lubricants and fluids*), top-up the reservoir by means of the funnel and tube until the level is up to the MAX mark on the dipstick. Do this slowly and carefully, checking the level with the dipstick frequently. Take care not to overfill the reservoir.

EHPS-ZF

5 The fluid level is visible through the side of the reservoir **(see illustration)**.

6 If topping-up is necessary, obtain a clean funnel and a long length of flexible pipe to fit the end of the funnel. Unscrew the cap and insert the pipe down behind the engine and into the top of the reservoir. Using power steering fluid of the specified type (see *Lubricants and fluids*), top-up the reservoir by means of the funnel and tube until the level is up to the MAX mark on the reservoir. Do this

slowly and carefully. Take care not to overfill the reservoir.

Both systems

7 When the level is correct, remove the funnel and tube and refit the reservoir filler cap.

9 Clutch hydraulic fluid level check – Easytronic models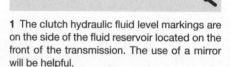

1 The clutch hydraulic fluid level markings are on the side of the fluid reservoir located on the front of the transmission. The use of a mirror will be helpful.

2 Check that the level of the fluid is at or near the MAX marking on the side of the reservoir **(see illustration)**.

3 If topping-up is required, unscrew the filler cap and pour in fresh fluid until the level is at the MAX marking. Retighten the cap on completion.

10 Brake pad and disc check

1 Firmly apply the handbrake, then jack up the front and rear of the vehicle and support it securely on axle stands (see *Jacking and vehicle support*). Remove the roadwheels.

2 For a quick check, the pad thickness can be carried out via the inspection hole on the caliper **(see Haynes Hint)**. Using a steel rule, measure the thickness of the pad friction

linings. This must not be less than that indicated in the Specifications.

3 The view through the caliper inspection hole gives a rough indication of the state of the brake pads. For a comprehensive check, the brake pads should be removed and cleaned. The operation of the caliper can then also be checked, and the condition of the brake disc itself can be fully examined on both sides. Chapter 9 contains a detailed description of how the brake disc should be checked for wear and/or damage.

4 If any pad's friction material is worn to the specified thickness or less, all four pads must be renewed as a set. Refer to Chapter 9 for details.

5 On completion, refit the roadwheels and lower the vehicle to the ground.

11 Brake fluid pipe and hose check

1 The brake hydraulic system includes a number of metal pipes, which run from the master cylinder to the hydraulic modulator of the anti-lock braking system (ABS) and then to the front and rear brake assemblies. Flexible hoses are fitted between the pipes and the front and rear brake assemblies, to allow for steering and suspension movement.

2 When checking the system, first look for

8.5 The maximum and minimum marks are indicated on the side of the reservoir

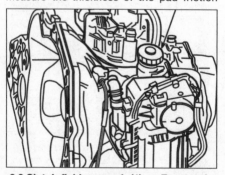

9.2 Clutch fluid reservoir (1) on Easytronic models

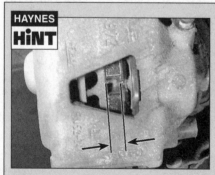

HAYNES HiNT

For a quick check, the thickness of friction material remaining on the inner brake pad can be measured through the aperture in the caliper body.

signs of leakage at the pipe or hose unions, then examine the flexible hoses for signs of cracking, chafing or deterioration of the rubber. Bend the hoses sharply between the fingers (but do not actually bend them double, or the casing may be damaged) and check that this does not reveal previously-hidden cracks, cuts or splits. Check that the pipes and hoses are securely fastened in their clips.

3 Carefully working along the length of the metal pipes, look for dents, kinks, damage of any sort, or corrosion. Light corrosion can be polished off, but if the depth of pitting is significant, the pipe must be renewed.

12 Front suspension and steering check

1 Apply the handbrake, then raise the front of the vehicle and securely support it on axle stands (see *Jacking and vehicle support*).

2 Inspect the balljoint dust covers and the steering gear gaiters for splits, chafing or deterioration.

3 Any wear of these components will cause loss of lubricant, and may allow water to enter the components, resulting in rapid deterioration of the balljoints or steering gear.

4 Grasp each roadwheel at the 12 o'clock and 6 o'clock positions, and try to rock it **(see illustration)**. Very slight free play may be felt, but if the movement is appreciable, further investigation is necessary to determine the source. Continue rocking the wheel while an assistant depresses the footbrake. If the movement is now eliminated or significantly reduced, it is likely that the hub bearings are at fault. If the free play is still evident with the footbrake depressed, then there is wear in the suspension joints or mountings.

5 Now grasp each wheel at the 9 o'clock and 3 o'clock positions, and try to rock it as before. Any movement felt now may again be caused by wear in the hub bearings or the steering track rod end balljoints. If the track rod end balljoint is worn, the visual movement will be obvious.

6 Using a large screwdriver or flat bar, check for wear in the suspension mounting bushes by levering between the relevant suspension component and its attachment point. Some movement is to be expected, as the mountings are made of rubber, but excessive wear should be obvious. Also check the condition of any visible rubber bushes, looking for splits, cracks or contamination of the rubber.

7 Check for any signs of fluid leakage around the suspension struts, or from the rubber gaiters around the piston rods. Should any fluid be noticed, the suspension strut is defective internally, and should be renewed. **Note:** *Suspension struts should always be renewed in pairs on the same axle.*

8 With the vehicle standing on its wheels, have an assistant turn the steering wheel back-and-forth about an eighth of a turn each way. There should be very little, if any, lost movement between the steering wheel and roadwheels. If this is not the case, closely observe the joints and mountings previously described. In addition, check the steering column universal joints for wear, and also check the rack-and-pinion steering gear itself.

9 The efficiency of each suspension strut may be checked by bouncing the vehicle at each front corner. Generally speaking, the body will return to its normal position and stop after being depressed. If it rises and returns on a rebound, the suspension strut is probably suspect. Also examine the suspension strut upper mountings for any signs of wear.

13 Driveshaft check

1 Firmly apply the handbrake, then jack up the front of the car and support it securely on axle stands (see *Jacking and vehicle support*).

2 Turn the steering onto full lock then slowly rotate the roadwheel. Inspect the condition of the outer constant velocity (CV) joint rubber gaiters while squeezing the gaiters to open out the folds **(see illustration)**. Check for signs of cracking, splits or deterioration of the rubber which may allow the grease to escape and lead to water and grit entry into the joint. Also check the security and condition of the retaining clips. Repeat these checks on the inner CV joints. If any damage or deterioration is found, the gaiters should be renewed as described in Chapter 8 Section 5.

3 At the same time, check the general condition of the CV joints themselves by first holding the driveshaft and attempting to rotate the wheel. Repeat this check by holding the inner joint and attempting to rotate the driveshaft. Any appreciable movement indicates wear in the joints, wear in the driveshaft splines or loose driveshaft retaining nut.

14 Exhaust system check

1 With the engine cold (at least an hour after the vehicle has been driven), check the complete exhaust system from the engine to the end of the tailpipe. The exhaust system is most easily checked with the vehicle raised on a hoist, or suitably-supported on axle stands, so that the exhaust components are readily visible and accessible (see *Jacking and vehicle support*).

2 Check the exhaust pipes and connections for evidence of leaks, severe corrosion and damage. Make sure that all brackets and mountings are in good condition, and that all relevant nuts and bolts are tight. Leakage at any of the joints or in other parts of the system will usually show up as a black sooty stain in the vicinity of the leak.

3 Rattles and other noises can often be traced to the exhaust system, especially the brackets and mountings **(see illustration)**. Try to move the pipes and silencers. If the components are able to come into contact with the body or suspension parts, secure the system with new mountings. Otherwise separate the joints (if possible) and twist the pipes as necessary to provide additional clearance.

15 Rear suspension check

1 Chock the front wheels, then jack up the rear of the vehicle and support securely on axle stands (see *Jacking and vehicle support*).

12.4 Check for wear in the hub hearings by grasping the wheel and trying to rock it

13.2 Check the condition of the driveshaft gaiters (1) and retaining clips (2)

14.3 Exhaust mountings

2 Inspect the rear suspension components for any signs of obvious wear or damage. Pay particular attention to the rubber mounting bushes, and renew if necessary (see Chapter 10).

3 Grasp each roadwheel at the 12 o'clock and 6 o'clock positions **(see illustration 12.4)**, and try to rock it. Any excess movement indicates wear in the wheel bearings. Wear may also be accompanied by a rumbling sound when the wheel is spun, or a noticeable roughness if the wheel is turned slowly. The wheel bearing can be renewed as described in Chapter 10 Section 9.

4 Check for any signs of fluid leakage around the shock absorber bodies. Should any fluid be noticed, the shock absorber is defective internally, and should be renewed. **Note:** *Shock absorbers should always be renewed in pairs on the same axle.*

5 With the vehicle standing on its wheels, the efficiency of each shock absorber may be checked by bouncing the vehicle at each rear corner. Generally speaking, the body will return to its normal position and stop after being depressed. If it rises and returns on a rebound, the shock absorber is probably suspect.

16 Bodywork and underbody condition check

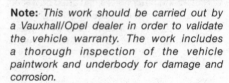

Note: *This work should be carried out by a Vauxhall/Opel dealer in order to validate the vehicle warranty. The work includes a thorough inspection of the vehicle paintwork and underbody for damage and corrosion.*

Bodywork damage/ corrosion check

1 Once the car has been washed, and all tar spots and other surface blemishes have been cleaned off, carefully check all paintwork, looking closely for chips or scratches. Pay particular attention to vulnerable areas such as the front panels (bonnet and spoiler), and around the wheel arches. Any damage to the paintwork must be rectified as soon as possible, to comply with the terms of the manufacturer's anti-corrosion warranties; check with a Vauxhall/Opel dealer for details.

2 If a chip or light scratch is found which is recent and still free from rust, it can be touched-up using the appropriate touch-up stick which can be obtained from Vauxhall/Opel dealers. Any more serious damage, or rusted stone chips, can be repaired as described in Chapter 11, but if damage or corrosion is so severe that a panel must be renewed, seek professional advice as soon as possible.

3 Always check that the door and ventilation opening drain holes and pipes are completely clear, so that water can drain out.

Corrosion protection check

4 The wax-based underbody protective coating should be inspected annually, preferably just prior to Winter, when the underbody should be washed down as thoroughly as possible without disturbing the protective coating. Any damage to the coating should be repaired using a suitable wax-based sealer. If any of the body panels are disturbed for repair or renewal, do not forget to re-apply the coating. Wax should be injected into door cavities, sills and box sections, to maintain the level of protection provided by the vehicle manufacturer – seek the advice of a Vauxhall/Opel dealer.

17 Roadwheel bolt tightness check

1 Where applicable, remove the wheel trims from the wheels.

2 Using a torque wrench on each wheel bolt in turn, ensure that the bolts are tightened to the specified torque.

3 Where applicable, refit the wheel trims on completion, making sure they are fitted correctly.

18 Hinge and lock lubrication

1 Work around the vehicle and lubricate the hinges of the bonnet, doors and tailgate with a light machine oil.

2 Lightly lubricate the bonnet release mechanism and exposed section of inner cable with a smear of grease.

3 Check the security and operation of all hinges, latches and locks, adjusting them where required. Check the operation of the central locking system.

4 Check the condition and operation of the tailgate support struts, renewing them both if either is leaking or no longer able to support the tailgate securely when raised.

19 Electrical systems check

1 Check the operation of all the electrical equipment, ie, lights, direction indicators, horn, etc. Refer to the appropriate sections of Chapter 12 for details if any of the circuits are found to be inoperative.

2 Note that the stop-light switch is described in Chapter 9 Section 15.

3 Check all accessible wiring connectors, harnesses and retaining clips for security, and for signs of chafing or damage. Rectify any faults found.

20 Road test

Instruments and electrical equipment

1 Check the operation of all instruments, warning lights and electrical equipment.

2 Make sure that all instruments read correctly, and switch on all electrical equipment in turn, to check that it functions properly.

Steering and suspension

3 Check for any abnormalities in the steering, suspension, handling or road 'feel'.

4 Drive the vehicle, and check that there are no unusual vibrations or noises.

5 Check that the steering feels positive, with no excessive 'sloppiness', or roughness, and check for any suspension noises when cornering and driving over bumps.

Drivetrain

6 Check the performance of the engine, clutch, transmission and driveshafts.

7 Listen for any unusual noises from the engine, clutch and transmission.

8 Make sure that the engine runs smoothly when idling, and that there is no hesitation when accelerating.

9 Check that, where applicable, the clutch action is smooth and progressive, that the drive is taken up smoothly, and that the pedal travel is not excessive. Also listen for any noises when the clutch pedal is depressed.

10 Check that all gears can be engaged smoothly without noise, and that the gear lever action is smooth and not abnormally vague or 'notchy'.

11 On automatic transmission models, make sure that all gearchanges occur smoothly, without snatching, and without an increase in engine speed between changes. Check that all of the gear positions can be selected with the vehicle at rest. If any problems are found, they should be referred to a Vauxhall/Opel dealer.

12 Listen for a metallic clicking sound from the front of the vehicle, as the vehicle is driven slowly in a circle with the steering on full-lock. Carry out this check in both directions. If a clicking noise is heard, this indicates wear in a driveshaft joint (see Chapter 8).

Braking system

13 Make sure that the vehicle does not pull to one side when braking.

14 Check that there is no vibration through the steering when braking. **Note:** *Under heavy braking on models equipped with ABS, vibration may be felt through the brake pedal. This is a normal feature of ABS operation, and does not constitute a fault.*

15 Check that the handbrake operates correctly, without excessive movement of the lever, and that it holds the vehicle stationary on a slope.

16 Test the operation of the brake servo unit as follows. Depress the footbrake four or five times to exhaust the vacuum, then start the engine. As the engine starts, there should be a noticeable 'give' in the brake pedal as vacuum builds-up. Allow the engine to run for at least two minutes, and then switch it off. If the brake pedal is now depressed again, it should be possible to detect a hiss from the servo as the pedal is depressed. After about four or five applications, no further hissing should be heard, and the pedal should feel considerably harder.

22.2a Extract the plastic rivet ...

22.2b ... and remove the footwell air duct

21 Service interval indicator reset

1 With the ignition switched off, the display on the instrument panel must show the trip odometer.
2 With the ignition still switched off, depress and hold the trip odometer reset button located on the instrument panel.
3 With the reset button depressed, switch on the ignition, wait until the service interval display changes (approximately 10 seconds).
4 After approximately 10 seconds the display will show the service symbol and the maximum mileage before the next required service, followed by 'InSP'. When '-– -' appears in the display, release the reset button and switch off the ignition. When the button is released, the odometer reading will appear again.

22 Pollen filter renewal

1 Remove the glovebox as described in Chapter 11 Section 26.
2 Extract the plastic rivet and remove the footwell air duct on the passenger's side **(see illustrations)**.
3 Prise-off the 6 metal clips and open the pollen filter access cover from the side of the

heater/ventilation air distribution housing **(see illustration)**. Take care as the clips are easily lost.
4 Withdraw the pollen filter from the housing **(see illustration)**.
5 Fit the new filter using a reversal of the removal procedure; make sure that the filter is fitted the correct way up as indicated on the edge of the filter.

23 Auxiliary drivebelt check and renewal

Note: *The manufacturers recommend that the tensioner roller is checked and if necessary renewed at the same time as the drivebelt.*

Checking

1 Due to their function and material make-up, drivebelts are prone to failure after a long period of time and should therefore be inspected regularly.
2 Apply the handbrake, then jack up the front of the vehicle and support it on axle stands (see *Jacking and vehicle support*). Remove the right-hand front roadwheel and the wheel arch liner cover for access to the right-hand side of the engine.
3 With the engine stopped, inspect the full length of the drivebelt for cracks and separation of the belt plies. It will be necessary to turn the engine (using a spanner or socket

and bar on the crankshaft pulley bolt) so that the belt can be inspected thoroughly. Twist the belt between the pulleys so that both sides can be viewed. Also check for fraying, and glazing which gives the belt a shiny appearance. Check the pulleys for nicks, cracks, distortion and corrosion. If the belt shows signs of wear or damage, it should be renewed as a precaution against breakage in service.

Renewal

4 If not already done, apply the handbrake, then jack up the front of the vehicle and support it on axle stands (see *Jacking and vehicle support*). Remove the right-hand front roadwheel and the wheel arch liner cover for access to the right-hand side of the engine.
5 Remove the air cleaner housing as described in Chapter 4A Section 2.
6 If the drivebelt is to be re-used, mark it to indicate its normal running direction.
7 Note the routing of the drivebelt, then, using a socket or spanner on the raised projection on the tensioner arm, turn the tensioner anti-clockwise against the spring tension. Hold the tensioner in this position by inserting a suitable locking pin/bolt through the special hole provided **(see illustration)**.
8 Slip the auxiliary drivebelt off of the pulleys.
9 Locate the auxiliary drivebelt onto the pulleys in the correct routing. If the drivebelt is being re-used, make sure it is fitted the correct way around.
10 Turn back the tensioner and remove the

22.3 Prise-off the 6 metal clips and open the pollen filter access cover

22.4 Withdraw the pollen filter from the housing

23.7 Auxiliary drivebelt tensioner

1 Raised projection on tensioner arm
2 Locking pin/bolt hole

locking pin/bolt, then release it, making sure that the drivebelt ribs locate correctly on each of the pulley grooves.

11 Refit the air cleaner housing, then refit the wheel arch liner and roadwheel, and lower the vehicle to the ground.

24 Handbrake operation and adjustment check

1 With the vehicle on a slight slope, apply the handbrake lever by up to 4 clicks of the ratchet, and check that it holds the vehicle stationary, then release the lever and check that there is no resistance to movement of the vehicle.

2 If necessary, adjust the handbrake as follows.

3 Chock the front wheels then jack up the rear of the vehicle and securely support it on axle stands (see *Jacking and vehicle support*).

4 From inside the vehicle, lift out the rubber mat from the base of the centre console. The handbrake cable adjuster nut is accessible through the access opening in the console base **(see illustration)**.

5 Move the handbrake lever to the fully released position then, using a deep socket, turn the cable adjuster nut anti-clockwise to remove all tension from the cables.

6 Depress the footbrake five times, then fully apply and release the handbrake lever five times.

7 With the handbrake lever set on the second notch of the ratchet mechanism, rotate the adjuster nut clockwise until a reasonable amount of force is required to turn each wheel. **Note:** *The force required should be equal for each wheel.*

8 Now pull the handbrake lever up to the third notch of the ratchet mechanism and check that both rear wheels are locked. Once this is so, fully release the handbrake lever and check that the wheels rotate freely. Check the adjustment by applying the handbrake fully whilst counting the clicks emitted from the handbrake ratchet and, if necessary, re-adjust.

9 On completion of adjustment, refit the rubber mat to the centre console, then lower the vehicle to the ground.

25 Headlight beam alignment check

1 Accurate adjustment of the headlight beam is only possible using optical beam-setting equipment, and this work should therefore be carried out by a Vauxhall/Opel dealer or service station with the necessary facilities. Refer to Chapter 12 Section 8 for further information.

26 Remote control battery renewal

Vehicles without keyless entry

1 Using a screwdriver, prise the battery cover from the ignition key fob **(see illustration)**.

2 Note how the circular battery is fitted, then carefully remove it from the contacts **(see illustration)**.

3 Fit the new battery (type CR 2032) and refit the cover making sure that it clips fully onto the base.

4 After changing the battery, lock and unlock the driver's door with the key in the lock to synchronise the remote control unit.

Vehicles with keyless entry

5 No information was available at the time of writing. Consult a Vauxhall dealer.

27 Hydraulic fluid renewal

Note: *It is not possible for the home mechanic to bleed the clutch hydraulic system on Easytronic models. Refer to Chapter 7C for additional information.*

⚠️ **Warning: Hydraulic fluid can harm your eyes and damage painted surfaces, so use extreme caution when handling and pouring it. Do not use fluid that has been standing open for some time, as it absorbs moisture**

from the air. Excess moisture can cause a dangerous loss of braking effectiveness.

1 The procedure is similar to that for the bleeding of the hydraulic system as described in Chapter 9 Section 2 (brake) and Chapter 6 Section 2 (clutch).

> **HAYNES HiNT** *Old hydraulic fluid is invariably much darker in colour than the new, making it easy to distinguish the two.*

2 Working as described in Chapter 9 Section 2, open the first bleed screw in the sequence, and pump the brake pedal gently until nearly all the old fluid has been emptied from the master cylinder reservoir. Top-up to the MAX level with new fluid, and continue pumping until only the new fluid remains in the reservoir, and new fluid can be seen emerging from the bleed screw. Tighten the screw, and top the reservoir level up to the MAX level line.

3 Work through all the remaining bleed screws in the sequence until new fluid can be seen at all of them. Be careful to keep the master cylinder reservoir topped-up to above the MIN level at all times, or air may enter the system and greatly increase the length of the task.

4 Bleed the fluid from the clutch hydraulic system as described in Chapter 6 Section 2.

5 When the operation is complete, check that all bleed screws are securely tightened, and that their dust caps are refitted. Wash off all traces of spilt fluid, and recheck the master cylinder reservoir fluid level.

6 Check the operation of the brakes and clutch before taking the car on the road.

28 Coolant renewal

Note: *Vauxhall/Opel do not specify renewal intervals for the antifreeze mixture, as the mixture used to fill the system when the vehicle is new is designed to last the lifetime of the vehicle. However, it is strongly recommended that the coolant is renewed at the intervals specified in the Maintenance schedule, as a precaution against possible*

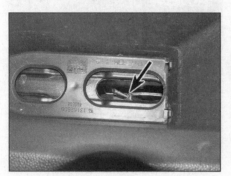

24.4 Handbrake cable adjuster nut (arrowed)

26.1 Prise the battery cover from the ignition key fob

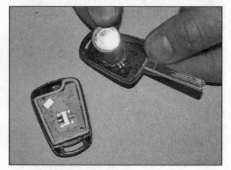

26.2 Carefully remove the battery from the contacts

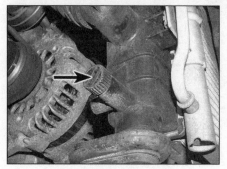

28.3 Radiator drain plug

engine corrosion problems. This is particularly advisable if the coolant has been renewed using an antifreeze other than that specified by Vauxhall/Opel. With many antifreeze types, the corrosion inhibitors become progressively less effective with age. It is up to the individual owner whether or not to follow this advice.

⚠️ **Warning: Wait until the engine is cold before starting this procedure. Do not allow antifreeze to come in contact with your skin, or with the painted surfaces of the vehicle. Rinse off spills immediately with plenty of water. Never leave antifreeze lying around in an open container, or in a puddle in the driveway or on the garage floor. Children and pets are attracted by its sweet smell, but antifreeze can be fatal if ingested.**

Cooling system draining

1 To drain the cooling system, first cover the expansion tank cap with a wad of rag, and slowly turn the cap anti-clockwise to relieve the pressure in the cooling system (a hissing sound will normally be heard). Wait until any pressure remaining in the system is released, then continue to turn the cap until it can be removed.
2 Position a suitable container beneath the right-hand side of the radiator.
3 The coolant drain plug is located at the bottom of the radiator right-hand end tank. Unscrew the drain plug and allow the coolant to drain **(see illustration)**.
4 When the flow of coolant stops, refit and tighten the drain plug.
5 As no cylinder block drain plug is fitted, it is not possible to drain all of the coolant. Due consideration must be made for this when refilling the system, in order to maintain the correct concentration of antifreeze.
6 If the coolant has been drained for a reason other than renewal, then provided it is clean and less than two years old, it can be re-used.

Cooling system flushing

7 If coolant renewal has been neglected, or if the antifreeze mixture has become diluted, then in time, the cooling system may gradually lose efficiency, as the coolant passages become restricted due to rust, scale deposits, and other sediment. The cooling system efficiency can be restored by flushing the system clean.

8 The radiator should be flushed independently of the engine, to avoid unnecessary contamination.

Radiator flushing

9 Disconnect the top and bottom hoses and any other relevant hoses from the radiator, with reference to Chapter 3 Section 3.
10 Insert a garden hose into the radiator top inlet. Direct a flow of clean water through the radiator, and continue flushing until clean water emerges from the radiator bottom outlet.
11 If after a reasonable period, the water still does not run clear, the radiator can be flushed with a good proprietary cleaning agent. It is important that the manufacturer's instructions are followed carefully. If the contamination is particularly bad, remove the radiator, insert the hose in the radiator bottom outlet, and reverse-flush the radiator.

Engine flushing

12 To flush the engine, the thermostat must be removed, because it will be shut, and would otherwise prevent the flow of water around the engine. The thermostat can be removed as described in Chapter 3 Section 4. Take care not to introduce dirt or debris into the system if this approach is used.
13 With the bottom hose disconnected from the radiator, insert a garden hose into the thermostat opening. Direct a clean flow of water through the engine, and continue flushing until clean water emerges from the radiator bottom hose.
14 On completion of flushing, refit the thermostat with reference to Chapter 3 Section 4, and reconnect the hoses.

Cooling system filling

15 Before attempting to fill the cooling system, make sure that all hoses and clips are in good condition, and that the clips are tight. Note that an antifreeze mixture must be used all year round, to prevent corrosion of the engine components.
16 Remove the expansion tank filler cap.
17 Fill the system by slowly pouring the coolant into the expansion tank until it is up to the filler neck.
18 Top-up the expansion tank until the coolant level is up to the KALT/COLD mark on the side of the tank.
19 Refit and tighten the expansion tank filler cap.
20 Start the engine and run it at 2000 to 2500 rpm until the cooling fan switches on. Continue running the engine at between 2000 and 2500 rpm for a further 2 minutes.
21 Stop the engine, and allow it to cool, then recheck the coolant level with reference to *Weekly checks*. Top-up the level if necessary and refit the expansion tank filler cap.

Antifreeze mixture

22 Always use an ethylene-glycol based antifreeze which is suitable for use in mixed-metal cooling systems (see *Lubricants*

and *fluids*). The quantity of antifreeze and levels of protection are given in the Specifications.
23 Before adding antifreeze, the cooling system should be completely drained, preferably flushed, and all hoses checked for condition and security.
24 After filling with antifreeze, a label should be attached to the expansion tank, stating the type and concentration of antifreeze used, and the date installed. Any subsequent topping-up should be made with the same type and concentration of antifreeze.
Caution: Do not use engine antifreeze in the windscreen/tailgate washer system, as it will cause damage to the vehicle paintwork. A screenwash additive should be added to the washer system in the quantities stated on the bottle.

29 Exhaust emission check

1 The exhaust emission check is carried out initially after 3 years, then every 2 years, however, on vehicles which are subject to intensive use (eg, taxis/hire cars/ambulances) it must be carried out annually. The check involves checking the engine management system operation by plugging an electronic tester into the system diagnostic socket to check the electronic control unit (ECU) memory for faults (see Chapter 4A).
2 In reality, if the vehicle is running correctly and the engine management warning light in the instrument panel is functioning normally, then this check need not be carried out.

30 Air cleaner element renewal – petrol models

1 The air cleaner is located in the front right-hand corner of the engine compartment.
2 Disconnect the wiring connector from the side of the inlet air temperature sensor or airflow meter **(see illustration)**.
3 Slacken the retaining clip securing the air duct to the air cleaner cover.

30.2 Disconnect the wiring connector from the inlet air temperature sensor or airflow meter

30.4a Undo the retaining screws …

30.4b … then lift off the air cleaner cover, and detach it from the air duct

30.5 Lift out the filter element

4 Undo the screws, lift off the air cleaner cover, and detach it from the air duct **(see illustrations)**.

5 Lift out the filter element **(see illustration)**.

6 Wipe out the casing and the cover.

7 Fit the new filter, noting that the rubber locating flange should be uppermost, and secure the cover with the screws.

8 Reconnect the inlet air temperature sensor or airflow meter wiring connector and the air duct.

31 Spark plug renewal

1 The correct functioning of the spark plugs is vital for the correct running and efficiency of the engine. It is essential that the plugs fitted are appropriate for the engine; suitable types are specified at the beginning of this Chapter, or in the vehicle's Owner's Handbook. If the correct type is used and the engine is in good condition, the spark plugs should not need attention between scheduled renewal intervals. Spark plug cleaning is rarely necessary, and should not be attempted unless specialised equipment is available, as damage can easily be caused to the firing ends.

2 Where applicable, remove the engine top cover after removing the oil filler cap. Refit the cap.

3 Remove the ignition module from the spark plugs with reference to Chapter 5B Section 3.

4 It is advisable to remove the dirt from the spark plug recesses using a clean brush, vacuum cleaner or compressed air before removing the plugs, to prevent dirt dropping into the cylinders.

5 Unscrew the spark plugs from the cylinder head using a spark plug spanner, suitable box spanner or a deep socket and extension bar **(see illustrations)**. Keep the socket aligned with the spark plug – if it is forcibly moved to one side, the ceramic insulator may be broken off.

6 Examination of the spark plugs will give a good indication of the condition of the engine. As each plug is removed, examine it as follows. If the insulator nose of the spark plug is clean and white, with no deposits, this is indicative of a weak mixture or too hot a plug (a hot plug transfers heat away from the electrode slowly, a cold plug transfers heat away quickly).

7 If the tip and insulator nose are covered with hard black-looking deposits, then this is indicative that the mixture is too rich. Should the plug be black and oily, then it is likely that the engine is fairly worn, as well as the mixture being too rich.

8 If the insulator nose is covered with light tan to greyish-brown deposits, then the mixture is correct and it is likely that the engine is in good condition.

9 The spark plug electrode gap is of considerable importance. If the gap is too large or too small, the size of the spark and its efficiency will be seriously impaired and it will not perform correctly under all engine speed and load conditions. For the best results, the spark plug gap should be set in accordance with the Specifications at the beginning of this Chapter.

10 To set the gap, measure it with a feeler blade or spark plug gap gauge and then carefully bend the outer plug electrode until the correct gap is achieved. The centre electrode should never be bent, as this may crack the insulator and cause plug failure,

31.5a Unscrew the spark plugs …

31.5b … and remove them

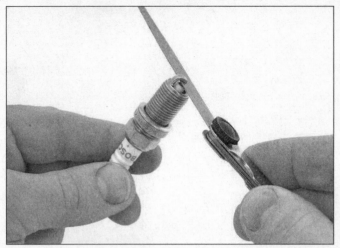

31.10a Measuring a spark plug electrode gap using a feeler blade

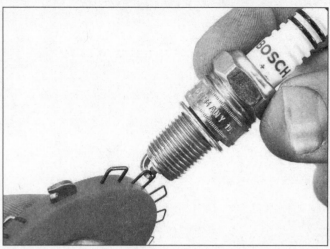

31.10b Measuring a spark plug electrode gap using a wire gauge

HAYNES HiNT

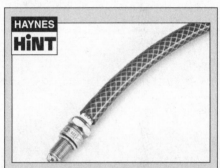

It's often difficult to insert spark plugs into their holes without cross-threading them. To avoid this possibility, fit a short piece of rubber hose over the end of the spark plug. The flexible hose acts as a universal joint, to help align the plug with the plug hole. Should the plug begin to cross-thread, the hose will slip on the spark plug, preventing thread damage.

if nothing worse. If using feeler blades, the gap is correct when the appropriate-size blade is a firm sliding fit **(see illustrations)**.

11 Special spark plug electrode gap adjusting tools are available from most motor accessory shops, or from some spark plug manufacturers.

12 Before fitting the spark plugs, check that the threaded connector sleeves on the top of the plug are tight, and that the plug exterior surfaces and threads are clean.

13 Screw in the spark plugs by hand where possible, then tighten them to the specified torque. Take extra care to enter the plug threads correctly, as the cylinder head is of light alloy construction (see **Haynes Hint**).

14 On completion, refit the ignition module as described in Chapter 5B Section 3 then, where applicable, refit the engine top cover.

32 Timing belt, tensioner and idler pulley renewal

1 Refer to the procedures contained in Chapter 2A.

33 Automatic transmission fluid renewal

1 Refer to the procedures contained in Chapter 7B Section 2.

34 Valve clearance check and adjustment

1 Refer to the procedures contained in Chapter 2A Section 11.

Chapter 1 Part B
Routine maintenance and servicing – diesel models

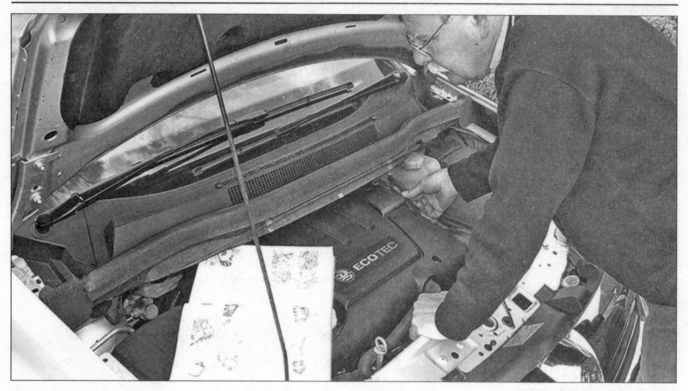

Contents

Section number

Air cleaner element renewal – diesel models 32
Automatic transmission fluid renewal. 34
Auxiliary drivebelt condition check and renewal – diesel models . . . 24
Bodywork and underbody condition check 16
Brake fluid pipe and hose check 11
Brake pad and disc check 10
Component localion – diesel models 3
Coolant renewal 30
Driveshaft check. 13
Electrical systems check 19
Engine oil and filter renewal – diesel models 6
Exhaust emission check. 31
Exhaust system check 14
Front suspension and steering check 12
Fuel filter renewal – diesel models 23
Fuel filter water draining. 8
General Information 4
Handbrake operation and adjustment check. 26

Section number

Headlight beam alignment check. 27
Hinge and lock lubrication 18
Hose and fluid leak check 7
Hydraulic fluid renewal. 29
Maintenance schedule – diesel models 2
Pollen filter renewal 22
Power steering fluid level check. 9
Rear suspension check 15
Regular maintenance 5
Remote control battery renewal 28
Road test 20
Roadwheel bolt tightness check 17
Service interval indicator reset 21
Servicing specifications 1
Timing belt, tensioner and idler pulley renewal 33
Valve clearance check and adjustment – 1.7 litre engines. 35
Valve clearance check and adjustment – SOHC (Z19DT and Z19DTL)
   engines. 25

Degrees of difficulty

| Easy, suitable for novice with little experience | | Fairly easy, suitable for beginner with some experience | | Fairly difficult, suitable for competent DIY mechanic | | Difficult, suitable for experienced DIY mechanic | 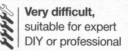 | Very difficult, suitable for expert DIY or professional | |

1 Servicing specifications

Lubricants and fluids. . . . .   Refer to *Weekly checks*

Capacities

Engine oil

Oil change including filter
1.7 litre engines . . . .   5.4 litres
1.9 litre engines . . . .   4.3 litres
Difference between MIN and MAX dipstick marks. . . . .   1.0 litre

Cooling system . . . .   7.1 litres

Transmission

Manual transmission . . . .   2.4 litres
Automatic transmission (at fluid change).   3.0 (approximately)

Washer fluid reservoir

Without headlight washers. . . . .   2.3 litres
With headlight washers . . . .   4.2 litres

Fuel tank

All models. . . . .   56 litres

Cooling system

Antifreeze mixture:
50% antifreeze . . . .   Protection down to -40°C

Brakes

Brake pad friction material minimum thickness. . . . .   2.0 mm

Torque wrench settings

	Nm	lbf ft
Engine oil filter:		
1.7 litre engines	25	18
1.9 litre SOHC (Z19DT and Z19DTH) engines	25	18
1.9 litre DOHC (Z19DTL) engines.	15	11
Fuel filter central bolt (1.7 litre engines)	6	4
Fuel filter housing cover retaining ring (1.9 litre engines).	30	22
Roadwheel bolts.	110	81
Sump drain plug.	20	15

2 Maintenance schedule – diesel models

1 The maintenance intervals in this manual are provided with the assumption that you, not the dealer, will be carrying out the work. These are the minimum maintenance intervals based on the standard service schedule recommended by the manufacturer for vehicles driven daily. If you wish to keep your vehicle in peak condition at all times, you may wish to perform some of these procedures more often. We encourage frequent maintenance, because it enhances the efficiency, performance and resale value of your vehicle.

2 If the vehicle is driven in dusty areas, used to tow a trailer, or driven frequently at slow speeds (idling in traffic) or on short journeys, more frequent maintenance intervals are recommended.

3 When the vehicle is new, it should be serviced by a dealer service department (or other workshop recognised by the vehicle manufacturer as providing the same standard of service) in order to preserve the warranty. The vehicle manufacturer may reject warranty claims if you are unable to prove that servicing has been carried out as and when specified, using only original equipment parts or parts certified to be of equivalent quality.

Every 250 miles or weekly

☐ Refer to Weekly checks

Every 10 000 miles or 6 months – whichever comes first

☐ Renew the engine oil and filter (Section 6)

Note: *Vauxhall/Opel recommend that the engine oil and filter are changed every 20 000 miles or 12 months if the vehicle is being operated under the standard service schedule. However, oil and filter changes are good for the engine and we recommend that the oil and filter are renewed more frequently, especially if the vehicle is used on a lot of short journeys.*

Every 20 000 miles or 12 months – whichever comes first

☐ Check all underbonnet and underbody components, pipes and hoses for leaks (Section 7)
☐ Drain the water from the fuel filter (Section 8)
☐ Check the power steering fluid level (Section 9)
☐ Check the condition of the brake pads, calipers and discs (Section 10)
☐ Check the condition of all brake fluid pipes and hoses (Section 11)
☐ Check the condition of the front suspension and steering components, particularly the rubber gaiters and seals (Section 12)
☐ Check the condition of the driveshaft joint gaiters, and the driveshaft joints (Section 13)
☐ Check the condition of the exhaust system components (Section 14)
☐ Check the condition of rear suspension components (Section 15)
☐ Check the bodywork and underbody for damage and corrosion, and check the condition of the underbody corrosion protection (Section 16)
☐ Check the tightness of the roadwheel bolts (Section 17)
☐ Lubricate all door, bonnet and tailgate hinges and locks (Section 18)
☐ Check the operation of the horn, all lights, and the wipers and washers (Section 19)
☐ Carry out a road test (Section 20)
☐ Reset the service interval indicator (Section 21)

Every 40 000 miles or 2 years – whichever comes first

☐ Renew the pollen filter (Section 22)
☐ Renew the fuel filter (Section 23)
☐ Check the auxiliary drivebelt and tensioner (Section 24)
☐ Check, and if necessary adjust, the valve clearances – SOHC (Z19DT and Z19DTL) engines (Section 25)
☐ Check the operation of the handbrake and adjust if necessary (Section 26)
☐ Check the headlight beam alignment (Section 27)

Every 2 years, regardless of mileage

☐ Renew the battery for the remote control handset (Section 28)
☐ Renew the brake and clutch fluid (Section 29)
☐ Renew the coolant (Section 30)*
☐ Exhaust emission test (Section 31)

*Note: *Vehicles using Vauxhall/Opel silicate-free coolant do not need the coolant renewed on a regular basis.*

Every 40 000 miles or 4 years – whichever comes first

☐ Renew the air cleaner filter element (Section 32)
☐ Renew the timing belt, tensioner and idler pulleys (Section 33)*

Note: **The normal interval for timing belt renewal is 90 000 miles or 6 years. However, it is strongly recommended that the interval used is 40 000 miles on vehicles which are subjected to intensive use, ie, mainly short journeys or a lot of stop-start driving. The actual belt renewal interval is therefore very much up to the individual owner, but bear in mind that severe engine damage will result if the belt breaks.*

Every 50 000 miles or 6 years – whichever comes first

☐ Renew the automatic transmission fluid (Section 34)

Every 80 000 miles or 10 years – whichever comes first

☐ Renew the auxiliary drivebelt (Section 24)

Every 100 000 miles or 10 years – whichever comes first

☐ Check, and if necessary, adjust the valve clearances – 1.7 litre engines (Section 35)

3 Component location – diesel models

Underbonnet view of an SOHC engine model

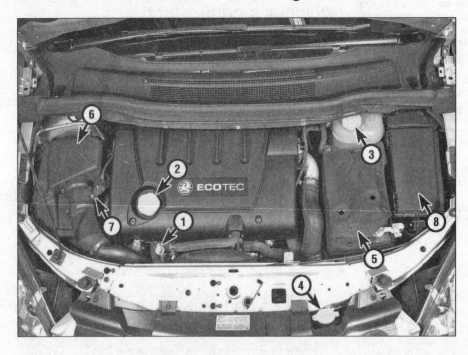

1 Engine oil level dipstick
2 Engine oil filler cap
3 Coolant expansion tank
4 Screen washer fluid reservoir
5 Battery
6 Air cleaner assembly
7 Airflow meter
8 Fuse/relay box

Underbonnet view of a 1.7 litre model

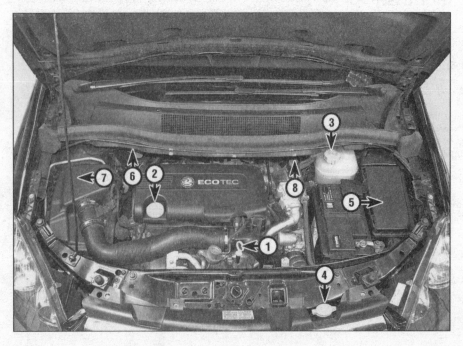

1 Engine oil level dipstick
2 Engine oil filler cap
3 Coolant expansion tank
4 Screen washer fluid reservoir
5 Fuse/relay box
6 Brake/clutch fluid reservoir
7 Air cleaner assembly
8 Power steering reservoir

Front underbody view

1 Exhaust front pipe
2 Steering track rods
3 Front suspension lower arms
4 Front brake calipers
5 Engine mounting front torque link
6 Engine mounting rear torque link
7 Right-hand driveshaft/intermediate shaft
8 Manual transmission
9 Engine oil drain plug
10 Air conditioning compressor
11 Front subframe

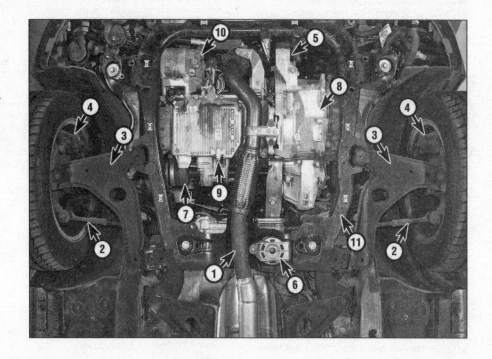

Rear underbody view

1 Exhaust tailpipe and silencer
2 Rear suspension torsion beam and trailing
   arms
3 Fuel tank
4 Handbrake cables
5 Rear coil springs
6 Rear shock absorber lower mountings

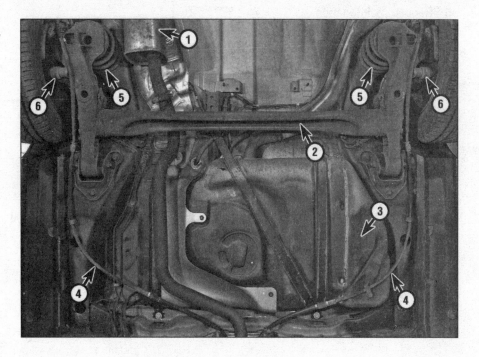

4   General Information

1 This Chapter is designed to help the home mechanic maintain his/her vehicle for safety, economy, long life and peak performance.

2 The Chapter contains a master maintenance schedule, followed by Sections dealing specifically with each task in the schedule. Visual checks, adjustments, component renewal and other helpful items are included. Refer to the accompanying illustrations of the engine compartment and the underside of the vehicle for the locations of the various components.

3 Servicing your vehicle in accordance with the mileage/time maintenance schedule and the following Sections will provide a planned maintenance programme, which should result in a long and reliable service life. This is a comprehensive plan, so maintaining some items but not others at the specified service intervals, will not produce the same results.

4 As you service your vehicle, you will discover that many of the procedures can – and should – be grouped together, because of the particular procedure being performed, or because of the proximity of two otherwise-unrelated components to one another. For example, if the vehicle is raised for any reason, the exhaust can be inspected at the same time as the suspension and steering components.

5 The first step in this maintenance programme is to prepare yourself before the actual work begins. Read through all the Sections relevant to the work to be carried out, then make a list and gather all the parts and tools required. If a problem is encountered, seek advice from a parts specialist, or a dealer service department.

5   Regular maintenance

1 If, from the time the vehicle is new, the routine maintenance schedule is followed closely, and frequent checks are made of fluid levels and high-wear items, as suggested throughout this manual, the engine will be kept in relatively good running condition, and the need for additional work will be minimised.

2 It is possible that there will be times when the engine is running poorly due to the lack of regular maintenance. This is even more likely if a used vehicle, which has not received regular and frequent maintenance checks, is purchased. In such cases, additional work may need to be carried out, outside of the regular maintenance intervals.

3 If engine wear is suspected, a compression test (refer to the appropriate part of Chapter 2) will provide valuable information regarding the overall performance of the main internal components. Such a test can be used as a basis to decide on the extent of the work to be carried out. If, for example, a compression test indicates serious internal engine wear, conventional maintenance as described in this Chapter will not greatly improve the performance of the engine, and may prove a waste of time and money, unless extensive overhaul work is carried out first.

4 The following series of operations are those most often required to improve the performance of a generally poor-running engine:

Primary operations

a) *Clean, inspect and test the battery (refer to Weekly checks).*
b) *Check all the engine-related fluids (refer to Weekly checks).*
c) *Check the condition and tension of the auxiliary drivebelt (Section 24).*
d) *Check the condition of the air cleaner element, and renew if necessary (Section 32).*
e) *Renew the fuel filter (Section 23).*
f) *Check the condition of all hoses, and check for fluid leaks (Section 7).*

5 If the above operations do not prove fully effective, carry out the following secondary operations:

Secondary operations

6 All items listed under Primary operations, plus the following:
a) *Check the charging system (refer to Chapter 5A).*
b) *Check the pre/post-heating system (refer to Chapter 5A).*
c) *Check the fuel, exhaust and emission control systems (refer to the appropriate Parts of Chapter 4).*

6   Engine oil and filter renewal – diesel models

> **HAYNES HiNT**
> *Frequent oil and filter changes are the most important preventative maintenance procedures which can be undertaken by the DIY owner. As engine oil ages, it becomes diluted and contaminated, which leads to premature engine wear.*

1 Before starting this procedure, gather together all the necessary tools and materials. Also make sure that you have plenty of clean rags and newspapers handy, to mop-up any spills. Ideally, the engine oil should be warm, as it will drain more easily, and more built-up sludge will be removed with it. Take care not to touch the exhaust or any other hot parts of the engine when working under the vehicle. To avoid any possibility of scalding, and to protect yourself from possible skin irritants and other harmful contaminants in used engine oils, it is advisable to wear gloves when carrying out this work.

2 Access to the underside of the vehicle will be greatly improved if it can be raised on a lift, driven onto ramps, or jacked up and supported on axle stands (see *Jacking and vehicle support*). Whichever method is chosen, make sure that the vehicle remains level, or if it is at an angle, that the drain plug is at the lowest point. Where fitted, remove the screws and clips and remove the engine undertray for access.

3 Remove the oil filler cap from the camshaft cover (twist it through a quarter-turn anti-clockwise and withdraw it) **(see illustration)**.

4 Using a spanner, or preferably a suitable socket and bar, slacken the drain plug about half a turn **(see illustration)**. Position the draining container under the drain plug, then remove the plug completely (see **Haynes Hint**).

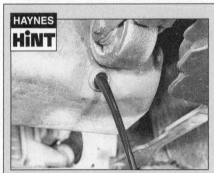

> **HAYNES HiNT**
>
> *As the drain plug releases from the threads, move it away quickly so that the stream of oil running out of the sump goes into the drain pan.*

6.3 Removing the oil filler cap

6.4 Engine oil drain plug location (arrowed)

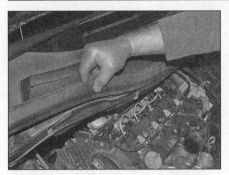

6.7 Pull up the rubber weatherstrip

6.8 Release the clips and remove the water deflector

6.9a Unclip the cable at the front edge...

5 Allow some time for the oil to drain, noting that it may be necessary to reposition the container as the oil flow slows to a trickle.
6 Position another container under the oil filter. The oil filter is located at the rear of the engine and is accessible from under the car.

1.7 litre engines

7 On these engines, the oil filter is accessed from above. Begin by pulling up the rubber weatherstrip at the engine compartment bulkhead **(see illustration)**.
8 Unclip the water deflector, and disconnect the washer jet tube **(see illustration)**. Where applicable, disconnect the air quality sensor wiring plug.
9 Undo the 2 bolts at each end, unclip the wiring harness and cables, then remove the bulkhead cover plate insulation **(see illustrations)**.

All engines

10 Unscrew the filter housing cap and withdraw it, together with the element, then separate the element, and remove the O-ring seals from the cover **(see illustrations)**.
11 Use a clean rag to remove all oil, dirt and sludge from the oil filter housing and cover.
12 Locate the new O-ring seals in their grooves on the housing cover, lubricate them with a little clean engine oil, then locate the new element in the cover and insert them both in the filter housing **(see illustration)**. Screw on the cover and tighten to the specified torque.

6.9b ...and undo the two bolts at each end

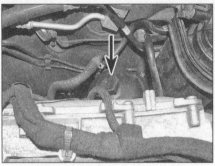

6.10a The oil filter cap is at the rear of the engine and accessed from above (1.7 litre engines)

6.10b Unscrew the filter cap and withdraw it together with the element (1.9 litre engine)

6.10c ... then separate the element from the cap ...

6.10d ... and remove the two O-ring seals (1.9 litre engines)...

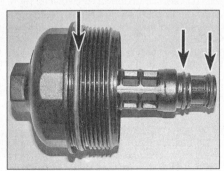

6.10e ...or three O-ring seals (1.7 litre engines). Note that the smaller seal are different sizes

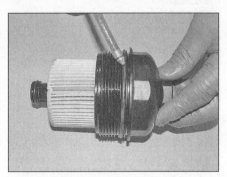

6.12 Lubricate the new seal with clean engine oil

6.13 Renew the O-ring seal if necessary

13 After all the oil has drained, wipe the drain plug and the sealing washer/O-ring with a clean rag. Examine the condition of the sealing washer/O-ring, and renew it if it shows signs of damage which may prevent an oil-tight seal **(see illustration)**. Clean the area around the drain plug opening, and refit the plug complete with the washer/O-ring. Tighten the plug to the specified torque, using a torque wrench.

14 Remove the old oil and all tools from under the vehicle then refit the undertray (where applicable) and lower the vehicle to the ground.

15 On 1.7 litre engines, refit the bulkhead cover plate insulation.

16 Fill the engine through the filler hole in the camshaft cover, using the correct grade and type of oil (refer to *Weekly checks* for details of topping-up). Pour in half the specified quantity of oil first, then wait a few minutes for the oil to drain into the sump. Continue to add oil, a small quantity at a time, until the level is up to the lower mark on the dipstick. Adding approximately a further 1.0 litre will bring the level up to the upper mark on the dipstick.

17 Start the engine and run it until it reaches normal operating temperature. While the engine is warming-up, check for leaks around the oil filter and the sump drain plug.

18 Stop the engine, and wait at least five minutes for the oil to settle in the sump once more. With the new oil circulated and the filter

A leak in the cooling system will usually show up as white- or antifreeze-coloured deposits on the area adjoining the leak.

now completely full, recheck the level on the dipstick, and add more oil as necessary.

19 Dispose of the used engine oil and filter safely, with reference to *General repair procedures*. Do not discard the old filter with domestic household waste. The facility for waste oil disposal provided by many local council refuse tips and/or recycling centres generally has a filter receptacle alongside.

7 Hose and fluid leak check

Note: *Also refer to Section 11.*

1 Visually inspect the engine joint faces, gaskets and seals for any signs of water or oil leaks. Pay particular attention to the areas around the camshaft cover, cylinder head, oil filter and sump joint faces. Similarly, check the transmission and (where applicable) the air conditioning compressor for oil leakage. Bear in mind that, over a period of time, some very slight seepage from these areas is to be expected; what you are really looking for is any indication of a serious leak. Should a leak be found, renew the offending gasket or oil seal by referring to the appropriate Chapters in this manual.

2 Also check the security and condition of all the engine-related pipes and hoses. Ensure that all cable ties or securing clips are in place, and in good condition. Clips which are broken or missing can lead to chafing of the hoses pipes or wiring, which could cause more serious problems in the future.

3 Carefully check the radiator hoses and heater hoses along their entire length. Renew any hose which is cracked, swollen or deteriorated. Cracks will show up better if the hose is squeezed. Pay close attention to the hose clips that secure the hoses to the cooling system components. Hose clips can pinch and puncture hoses, resulting in cooling system leaks. If wire-type hose clips are used, it may be a good idea to update them with Jubilee clips.

4 Inspect all the cooling system components (hoses, joint faces, etc) for leaks. Where any problems of this nature are found on system components, renew the component or gasket with reference to Chapter 3 **(see Haynes Hint)**.

5 Where applicable, inspect the automatic transmission fluid cooler hoses for leaks or deterioration.

6 With the vehicle raised, inspect the fuel tank and filler neck for punctures, cracks and other damage. The connection between the filler neck and tank is especially critical. Sometimes, a rubber filler neck or connecting hose will leak due to loose retaining clamps or deteriorated rubber.

7 Carefully check all rubber hoses and metal or plastic fuel lines leading away from the fuel tank. Check for loose connections, deteriorated hoses, crimped lines and other damage. Pay particular attention to the vent pipes and hoses, which often loop up around

the filler neck and can become blocked or crimped. Follow the lines to the front of the vehicle, carefully inspecting them all the way. Renew damaged sections as necessary. Similarly, whilst the vehicle is raised, take the opportunity to inspect all underbody brake fluid pipes and hoses.

8 From within the engine compartment, check the security of all fuel hose attachments and pipe unions, and inspect the fuel hoses and vacuum hoses for kinks, chafing and deterioration.

8 Fuel filter water draining

Caution: Before starting any work on the fuel filter, wipe clean the filter assembly and the area around it; it is essential that no dirt or other foreign matter is allowed into the system. Obtain a suitable container into which the filter can be drained and place rags or similar material under the filter assembly to catch any spillages. Do not allow diesel fuel to contaminate components such as the alternator and starter motor, the coolant hoses and engine mountings, and any wiring.

1 The fuel filter is located at the rear of the engine compartment, in the centre of the bulkhead. Access to the drain screw is from under the car.

2 Firmly apply the handbrake, then jack up the front of the vehicle and support it securely on axle stands (see *Jacking and vehicle support*). Remove the engine undertray.

3 With a suitable container in place to collect escaping water and fuel, reach up from below and loosen the drain screw approximately one complete turn. Allow the filter to drain until clean fuel, free of dirt or water, emerges from the drain screw (approximately 100 cc is usually sufficient).

4 Tighten the drain screw securely, then refit the undertray and lower the car to the ground.

5 On completion, dispose of the drained fuel safely. Check all disturbed components to ensure that there are no leaks (of air or fuel) when the engine is restarted.

9 Power steering fluid level check

1 The power steering fluid reservoir is located on RHD vehicles on the left-hand side of the engine compartment between the transmission and the bulkhead. On LHD vehicles, the reservoir is located between the engine and bulkhead on the right-hand side of the engine compartment. The fluid level should be checked with the engine cold.

EHPS Generation II

2 Wipe clean the reservoir and filler cap, then unscrew the filler cap from the top of

9.2 Power steering fluid reservoir filler cap (arrowed)

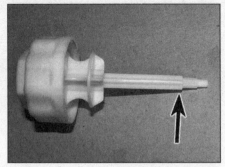

9.3 The fluid level should be up to the MAX mark (arrowed) on the dipstick

9.4 Use a clean funnel and a long length of flexible pipe to top-up the reservoir

the reservoir **(see illustration)**. The filler cap has a bayonet fitting and has a dipstick incorporated into it.

3 Wipe all fluid from the dipstick with a clean rag. Refit the dipstick, then remove it again. Note the fluid level on the dipstick which should be up to the MAX mark **(see illustration)**.

4 If topping-up is necessary, obtain a clean funnel and a long length of flexible pipe to fit the end of the funnel. Insert the pipe down behind the engine and into the top of the reservoir **(see illustration)**. Using power steering fluid of the specified type (see *Lubricants and fluids*), top-up the reservoir by means of the funnel and tube until the level is up to the MAX mark on the dipstick. Do this slowly and carefully, checking the level with the dipstick frequently. Take care not to overfill the reservoir.

EHPS-ZF

5 The fluid level is visible through the side of the reservoir **(see illustration)**.

6 If topping-up is necessary, obtain a clean funnel and a long length of flexible pipe to fit the end of the funnel. Unscrew the cap and insert the pipe down behind the engine and into the top of the reservoir. Using power steering fluid of the specified type (see *Lubricants and fluids*), top-up the reservoir by means of the funnel and tube until the level is up to the MAX mark on the reservoir. Do this slowly and carefully.Take care not to overfill the reservoir.

9.5 The maximum and minimum marks are indicated on the side of the reservoir

Both systems

7 When the level is correct, remove the funnel and tube and refit the reservoir filler cap.

10 Brake pad and disc check

1 Firmly apply the handbrake, then jack up the front and rear of the vehicle and support it securely on axle stands (see *Jacking and vehicle support*). Remove the roadwheels.

2 For a quick check, the pad thickness can be carried out via the inspection hole on the caliper (see **Haynes Hint**). Using a steel rule, measure the thickness of the pad friction linings. This must not be less than that indicated in the Specifications.

3 The view through the caliper inspection hole gives a rough indication of the state of the brake pads. For a comprehensive check, the brake pads should be removed and cleaned. The operation of the caliper can then also be checked, and the condition of the brake disc itself can be fully examined on both sides. Chapter 9 contains a detailed description of how the brake disc should be checked for wear and/or damage.

4 If any pad's friction material is worn to the specified thickness or less, all four pads must

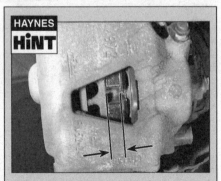

HAYNES HINT

For a quick check, the thickness of friction material remaining on the inner brake pad can be measured through the aperture in the caliper body.

be renewed as a set. Refer to Chapter 9 for details.

5 On completion, refit the roadwheels and lower the vehicle to the ground.

11 Brake fluid pipe and hose check

1 The brake hydraulic system includes a number of metal pipes, which run from the master cylinder to the hydraulic modulator of the anti-lock braking system (ABS) and then to the front and rear brake assemblies. Flexible hoses are fitted between the pipes and the front and rear brake assemblies, to allow for steering and suspension movement.

2 When checking the system, first look for signs of leakage at the pipe or hose unions, then examine the flexible hoses for signs of cracking, chafing or deterioration of the rubber. Bend the hoses sharply between the fingers (but do not actually bend them double, or the casing may be damaged) and check that this does not reveal previously-hidden cracks, cuts or splits. Check that the pipes and hoses are securely fastened in their clips.

3 Carefully working along the length of the metal pipes, look for dents, kinks, damage of any sort, or corrosion. Light corrosion can be polished off, but if the depth of pitting is significant, the pipe must be renewed.

12 Front suspension and steering check

1 Apply the handbrake, then raise the front of the vehicle and securely support it on axle stands (see *Jacking and vehicle support*).

2 Inspect the balljoint dust covers and the steering gear gaiters for splits, chafing or deterioration.

3 Any wear of these components will cause loss of lubricant, and may allow water to enter the components, resulting in rapid deterioration of the balljoints or steering gear.

4 Grasp each roadwheel at the 12 o'clock and 6 o'clock positions, and try to rock it

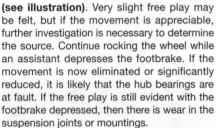

12.4 Check for wear in the hub bearings by grasping the wheel and trying to rock it

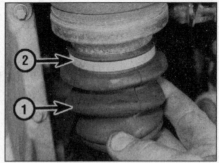

13.2 Check the condition of the driveshaft gaiters (1) and the retaining clips (2)

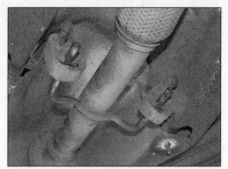

14.3 Exhaust mountings

(see illustration). Very slight free play may be felt, but if the movement is appreciable, further investigation is necessary to determine the source. Continue rocking the wheel while an assistant depresses the footbrake. If the movement is now eliminated or significantly reduced, it is likely that the hub bearings are at fault. If the free play is still evident with the footbrake depressed, then there is wear in the suspension joints or mountings.

5 Now grasp each wheel at the 9 o'clock and 3 o'clock positions, and try to rock it as before. Any movement felt now may again be caused by wear in the hub bearings or the steering track rod end balljoints. If the track rod end balljoint is worn, the visual movement will be obvious.

6 Using a large screwdriver or flat bar, check for wear in the suspension mounting bushes by levering between the relevant suspension component and its attachment point. Some movement is to be expected, as the mountings are made of rubber, but excessive wear should be obvious. Also check the condition of any visible rubber bushes, looking for splits, cracks or contamination of the rubber.

7 Check for any signs of fluid leakage around the suspension struts, or from the rubber gaiters around the piston rods. Should any fluid be noticed, the suspension strut is defective internally, and should be renewed. **Note:** *Suspension struts should always be renewed in pairs on the same axle.*

8 With the vehicle standing on its wheels, have an assistant turn the steering wheel back-and-forth about an eighth of a turn each way. There should be very little, if any, lost movement between the steering wheel and roadwheels. If this is not the case, closely observe the joints and mountings previously described. In addition, check the steering column universal joints for wear, and also check the rack-and-pinion steering gear itself.

9 The efficiency of each suspension strut may be checked by bouncing the vehicle at each front corner. Generally speaking, the body will return to its normal position and stop after being depressed. If it rises and returns on a rebound, the suspension strut is probably suspect. Also examine the suspension strut upper mountings for any signs of wear.

13 Driveshaft check

1 Firmly apply the handbrake, then jack up the front of the car and support it securely on axle stands (see *Jacking and vehicle support*).
2 Turn the steering onto full lock then slowly rotate the roadwheel. Inspect the condition of the outer constant velocity (CV) joint rubber gaiters while squeezing the gaiters to open out the folds **(see illustration)**. Check for signs of cracking, splits or deterioration of the rubber which may allow the grease to escape and lead to water and grit entry into the joint. Also check the security and condition of the retaining clips. Repeat these checks on the inner CV joints. If any damage or deterioration is found, the gaiters should be renewed as described in Chapter 8 Section 5.
3 At the same time, check the general condition of the CV joints themselves by first holding the driveshaft and attempting to rotate the wheel. Repeat this check by holding the inner joint and attempting to rotate the driveshaft. Any appreciable movement indicates wear in the joints, wear in the driveshaft splines or loose driveshaft retaining nut.

14 Exhaust system check

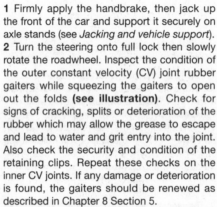

1 With the engine cold (at least an hour after the vehicle has been driven), check the complete exhaust system from the engine to the end of the tailpipe. The exhaust system is most easily checked with the vehicle raised on a hoist, or suitably-supported on axle stands, so that the exhaust components are readily visible and accessible (see *Jacking and vehicle support*).
2 Check the exhaust pipes and connections for evidence of leaks, severe corrosion and damage. Make sure that all brackets and mountings are in good condition, and that all relevant nuts and bolts are tight. Leakage at any of the joints or in other parts of the system will usually show up as a black sooty stain in the vicinity of the leak.
3 Rattles and other noises can often be traced

to the exhaust system, especially the brackets and mountings **(see illustration)**. Try to move the pipes and silencers. If the components are able to come into contact with the body or suspension parts, secure the system with new mountings. Otherwise separate the joints (if possible) and twist the pipes as necessary to provide additional clearance.

15 Rear suspension check

1 Chock the front wheels, then jack up the rear of the vehicle and support securely on axle stands (see *Jacking and vehicle support*).
2 Inspect the rear suspension components for any signs of obvious wear or damage. Pay particular attention to the rubber mounting bushes, and renew if necessary (see Chapter 10).
3 Grasp each roadwheel at the 12 o'clock and 6 o'clock positions **(see illustration 12.4)**, and try to rock it. Any excess movement indicates wear in the wheel bearings. Wear may also be accompanied by a rumbling sound when the wheel is spun, or a noticeable roughness if the wheel is turned slowly. The wheel bearing can be renewed as described in Chapter 10 Section 9.
4 Check for any signs of fluid leakage around the shock absorber bodies. Should any fluid be noticed, the shock absorber is defective internally, and should be renewed. **Note:** *Shock absorbers should always be renewed in pairs on the same axle.*
5 With the vehicle standing on its wheels, the efficiency of each shock absorber may be checked by bouncing the vehicle at each rear corner. Generally speaking, the body will return to its normal position and stop after being depressed. If it rises and returns on a rebound, the shock absorber is probably suspect.

16 Bodywork and underbody condition check

Note: *This work should be carried out by a Vauxhall/Opel dealer in order to validate*

the vehicle warranty. The work includes a thorough inspection of the vehicle paintwork and underbody for damage and corrosion.

Bodywork damage/ corrosion check

1 Once the car has been washed, and all tar spots and other surface blemishes have been cleaned off, carefully check all paintwork, looking closely for chips or scratches. Pay particular attention to vulnerable areas such as the front panels (bonnet and spoiler), and around the wheel arches. Any damage to the paintwork must be rectified as soon as possible, to comply with the terms of the manufacturer's anti-corrosion warranties; check with a Vauxhall/Opel dealer for details.

2 If a chip or light scratch is found which is recent and still free from rust, it can be touched-up using the appropriate touch-up stick which can be obtained from Vauxhall/ Opel dealers. Any more serious damage, or rusted stone chips, can be repaired as described in Chapter 11, but if damage or corrosion is so severe that a panel must be renewed, seek professional advice as soon as possible.

3 Always check that the door and ventilation opening drain holes and pipes are completely clear, so that water can drain out.

Corrosion protection check

4 The wax-based underbody protective coating should be inspected annually, preferably just prior to Winter, when the underbody should be washed down as thoroughly as possible without disturbing the protective coating. Any damage to the coating should be repaired using a suitable wax-based sealer. If any of the body panels are disturbed for repair or renewal, do not forget to re-apply the coating. Wax should be injected into door cavities, sills and box sections, to maintain the level of protection provided by the vehicle manufacturer – seek the advice of a Vauxhall/ Opel dealer.

17 Roadwheel bolt tightness check

1 Where applicable, remove the wheel trims from the wheels.

2 Using a torque wrench on each wheel bolt in turn, ensure that the bolts are tightened to the specified torque.

3 Where applicable, refit the wheel trims on completion, making sure they are fitted correctly.

18 Hinge and lock lubrication

1 Work around the vehicle and lubricate the hinges of the bonnet, doors and tailgate with a light machine oil.

2 Lightly lubricate the bonnet release mechanism and exposed section of inner cable with a smear of grease.

3 Check the security and operation of all hinges, latches and locks, adjusting them where required. Check the operation of the central locking system.

4 Check the condition and operation of the bonnet and tailgate support struts, renewing them both if either is leaking or no longer able to support the bonnet/tailgate securely when raised.

19 Electrical systems check

1 Check the operation of all the electrical equipment, ie, lights, direction indicators, horn, etc. Refer to the appropriate sections of Chapter 12 for details if any of the circuits are found to be inoperative.

2 Note that the stop-light switch is described in Chapter 9 Section 15.

3 Check all accessible wiring connectors, harnesses and retaining clips for security, and for signs of chafing or damage. Rectify any faults found.

20 Road test

Instruments and electrical equipment

1 Check the operation of all instruments, warning lights and electrical equipment.

2 Make sure that all instruments read correctly, and switch on all electrical equipment in turn, to check that it functions properly.

Steering and suspension

3 Check for any abnormalities in the steering, suspension, handling or road 'feel'.

4 Drive the vehicle, and check that there are no unusual vibrations or noises.

5 Check that the steering feels positive, with no excessive 'sloppiness', or roughness, and check for any suspension noises when cornering and driving over bumps.

Drivetrain

6 Check the performance of the engine, clutch, transmission and driveshafts.

7 Listen for any unusual noises from the engine, clutch and transmission.

8 Make sure that the engine runs smoothly when idling, and that there is no hesitation when accelerating.

9 Check that, where applicable, the clutch action is smooth and progressive, that the drive is taken up smoothly, and that the pedal travel is not excessive. Also listen for any noises when the clutch pedal is depressed.

10 Check that all gears can be engaged smoothly without noise, and that the gear lever action is smooth and not abnormally vague or 'notchy'.

11 On automatic transmission models, make sure that all gearchanges occur smoothly, without snatching, and without an increase in engine speed between changes. Check that all of the gear positions can be selected with the vehicle at rest. If any problems are found, they should be referred to a Vauxhall/Opel dealer.

12 Listen for a metallic clicking sound from the front of the vehicle, as the vehicle is driven slowly in a circle with the steering on full-lock. Carry out this check in both directions. If a clicking noise is heard, this indicates wear in a driveshaft joint (see Chapter 8).

Braking system

13 Make sure that the vehicle does not pull to one side when braking.

14 Check that there is no vibration through the steering when braking. **Note:** *Under heavy braking on models equipped with ABS, vibration may be felt through the brake pedal. This is a normal feature of ABS operation, and does not constitute a fault.*

15 Check that the handbrake operates correctly, without excessive movement of the lever, and that it holds the vehicle stationary on a slope.

16 Test the operation of the brake servo unit as follows. Depress the footbrake four or five times to exhaust the vacuum, then start the engine. As the engine starts, there should be a noticeable 'give' in the brake pedal as vacuum builds-up. Allow the engine to run for at least two minutes, and then switch it off. If the brake pedal is now depressed again, it should be possible to detect a hiss from the servo as the pedal is depressed. After about four or five applications, no further hissing should be heard, and the pedal should feel considerably harder.

21 Service interval indicator reset

1 With the ignition switched off, the display on the instrument panel must show the trip odometer.

2 With the ignition still switched off, depress and hold the trip odometer reset button located on the instrument panel. The service interval indicator will appear after approximately 2 seconds.

3 With the reset button still depressed, also depress the brake pedal, then switch on the ignition. 'InSP – – -' will appear in the display.

4 After approximately 10 seconds the display will show 'InSP' and the maximum mileage before the next required service. Release the reset button and switch off the ignition. When the button is released, the odometer reading will appear again.

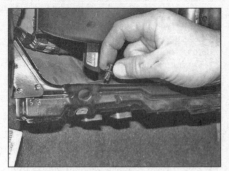

22.2a Extract the plastic rivet …

22.2b … and remove the footwell air duct

22.3 Prise off the 6 clips and open the pollen filter access cover

22.4 Withdraw the pollen filter from the housing

23.4a Depress the clip above and below each connector…

23.4b …and pull them from the housing

22 Pollen filter renewal

1 Remove the glovebox (see Chapter 11 Section 26).

2 Extract the plastic rivet and remove the footwell air duct on the passenger's side **(see illustrations)**.

3 Prise-off the 6 metal clips, and open the pollen filter access cover from the side of the heater/ventilation air distribution housing **(see illustration)**. Take care as the clips are easily lost.

4 Withdraw the pollen filter from the housing **(see illustration)**.

5 Fit the new filter using a reversal of the removal procedure; make sure that the filter is fitted the correct way up as indicated on the edge of the filter.

23 Fuel filter renewal – diesel models

Caution: Before starting any work on the fuel filter, wipe clean the filter assembly and the area around it; it is essential that no dirt or other foreign matter is allowed into the system. Obtain a suitable container into which the filter can be drained and place rags or similar material under the filter assembly to catch any spillages. Do not allow diesel fuel to contaminate components such as the starter motor, the coolant hoses and engine mountings, and any wiring.

1 The fuel filter and crash box are located at the rear of the engine compartment, in the centre of the bulkhead.

2 Remove the bulkhead insulation panel as described in paragraphs 7 to 9 of Section 6.

1.7 litre engines

3 Disconnect the wiring plug from the pre-heater on the top of the filter housing.

4 Detach the two fuel hose quick-release connectors and remove the hoses from the fuel filter housing. A Vauxhall/Opel special tool (KM-796-A) is available to disconnect the hose connectors, but provided care is taken, the connections can be released using two screwdrivers, a pair of long-nosed pliers, or similar, to depress the retaining tangs **(see illustrations)**. Suitably cover or plug the open hose connections to prevent dirt entry.

5 Pull the filter housing upwards from the crash box **(see illustration)**.

6 Unscrew the central bolt, and pull the cover upwards from the housing with the filter element **(see illustrations)**. Be prepared for fuel spillage.

23.5 Pull the filter housing upwards – it may be stiff

23.6a Use a Torx key to unscrew the central bolt

23.6b Lift up the cover with the element

23.8a Renew the large O-ring seal in the housing...

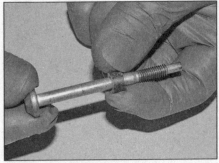

23.8b ...and the small O-ring on the central bolt

23.9 Insert the element into the housing

23.10 Align the slot in the cover with the tab on the housing

23.11 Slide the filter housing firmly into the crash box

23.20 Using a home-made tool to slacken the filter housing cover retaining ring

7 Pull the element from the cover, then drain and clean the filter housing.

8 Renew the O-ring seal on the filter housing, and the seal on the central bolt (see illustrations).

9 Insert the new element into the housing, the fill the housing with clean fuel (see illustration).

10 Refit the filter housing cover, aligning the slot in the cover with the tab on the housing, and tighten the central bolt to the specified torque (see illustration).

11 Insert the filter housing into the crash box (see illustration).

12 Reconnect the fuel hoses and the wiring connectors.

1.9 litre engines

Note: Vauxhall/Opel special tool EN-46784-010 or a suitable alternative will be

required to unscrew the filter housing cover retaining ring.

13 Release the fuel supply and return hoses from the clips on the crash box cover.

14 Undo the three bolts and detach the cover from the crash box.

15 Detach the two fuel hose quick-release connectors and remove the hoses from the fuel filter housing. A Vauxhall/Opel special tool (KM-796-A) is available to disconnect the hose connectors, but provided care is taken, the connections can be released using two screwdrivers, a pair of long-nosed pliers, or similar, to depress the retaining tangs. Suitably cover or plug the open hose connections to prevent dirt entry.

16 Disconnect the heater element wiring connector from the fuel filter cover and, where fitted, the water level sensor wiring connector from the base of the filter housing.

17 Pull the fuel filter upwards and remove it from the crash box.

18 Loosen the drain screw on the base of the filter housing one complete turn and drain the fuel into a suitable container. Tighten the drain screw securely once the filter has drained.

19 Lay the filter on its side and clamp the two filter housing mounting lugs in a soft-jawed vice. Take great care not to damage the lugs and only tighten the vice sufficiently to hold the housing while the cover retaining ring is slackened.

20 Slacken the filter housing cover retaining ring using the Vauxhall/Opel special tool or a suitable alternative (see illustration).

21 Reposition the filter housing vertically in the vice and tighten the vice lightly.

22 Fully unscrew the cover retaining ring, then lift the cover together with the filter element from the housing. Recover the O-ring seal (see illustrations).

23.22a Unscrew and remove the cover retaining ring ...

23.22b ... then lift the cover together with the filter element ...

23.22c ... and recover the O-ring seal

23.23 Turn the filter element approximately 50° anti-clockwise to release it from the cover

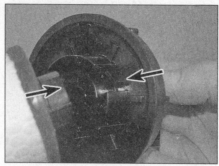

23.25a Align the arrow on the new filter element with the corresponding arrow on the cover ...

23.25b ... then push the filter onto the cover until it locks in position

23 Turn the filter element approximately 50° anti-clockwise to release it from the cover **(see illustration)**.

24 Empty the fuel from the filter housing, then thoroughly clean the housing and cover with a lint-free cloth.

25 Align the arrow on the new filter element with the corresponding arrow on the cover then push the filter onto the cover until it locks in position **(see illustrations)**.

26 Locate a new O-ring seal on the filter housing, then fit the element and cover to the housing **(see illustrations)**.

27 Lubricate the threads of the retaining ring with a little diesel fuel then screw the ring onto the housing. Reposition the housing horizontally in the vice as before, and tighten the retaining ring to the specified torque using the special tool or alternative.

28 Insert the filter assembly into the crash box, making sure that the retaining clip engages. Reconnect the fuel hoses and the wiring connectors.

29 Refit the crash box cover and tighten the retaining bolts securely. Clip the fuel hoses into the cover.

All engines

30 Bleed the fuel system as described

in Chapter 4B Section 5 and check all disturbed components to ensure that there are no leaks (of air or fuel) when the engine is restarted.

31 Refit the bulkhead cover plate insulation.

32 On completion, safely dispose of the drained fuel.

24 Auxiliary drivebelt condition check and renewal – diesel models

Note: *The manufacturers recommend that the tensioner roller is checked and if necessary renewed at the same time as the drivebelt.*

Checking

1 Due to their function and material make-up, drivebelts are prone to failure after a long period of time and should therefore be inspected regularly.

2 Apply the handbrake, then jack up the front of the vehicle and support it on axle stands (see *Jacking and vehicle support*). Remove the right-hand front roadwheel and the wheel arch liner cover for access to the right-hand side of the engine.

3 With the engine stopped, inspect the

full length of the drivebelt for cracks and separation of the belt plies. It will be necessary to turn the engine (using a spanner or socket and bar on the crankshaft pulley bolt) so that the belt can be inspected thoroughly. Twist the belt between the pulleys so that both sides can be viewed. Also check for fraying, and glazing which gives the belt a shiny appearance. Check the pulleys for nicks, cracks, distortion and corrosion. If the belt shows signs of wear or damage, it should be renewed as a precaution against breakage in service.

Renewal

4 If not already done, apply the handbrake, then jack up the front of the vehicle and support it on axle stands (see *Jacking and vehicle support*). Remove the right-hand front roadwheel and the wheel arch liner cover for access to the right-hand side of the engine.

5 For additional working clearance, remove the air cleaner housing as described in Chapter 4B Section 3.

6 If the drivebelt is to be re-used, mark it to indicate its normal running direction.

7 Using a spanner on the pulley centre bolt, turn the tensioner against the spring tension. Hold the tensioner in this position by inserting

23.26a Locate a new O-ring seal on the filter housing ...

23.26b ... then fit the element and cover to the housing

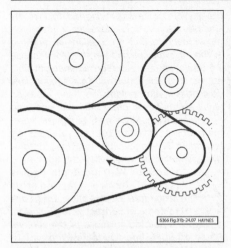

24.7a Rotate the tensioner bolt clockwise, and lock it by inserting a drill bit (arrowed) through the hole above the tensioner (1.7 litre engines)

24.7b Turn the drivebelt tensioner using a spanner on the pulley centre bolt (arrowed) …

24.7c … then lock the tensioner by inserting a drill bit (arrowed) through the hole on the underside of the tensioner (1.9 litre engines)

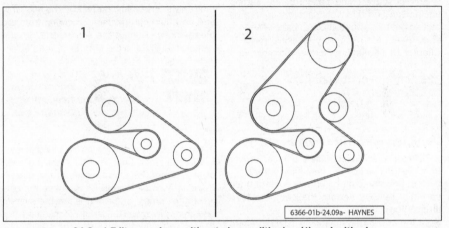

24.9a 1.7 litre engines without air conditioning (1) and with air conditioning (2)

a suitable locking pin or drill bit through the special hole provided **(see illustrations)**.

8 Slip the drivebelt from the pulleys.

9 Locate the new drivebelt on the pulleys in the correct routing **(see illustrations)**. If the drivebelt is being re-used, make sure it is fitted the correct way around.

10 Turn back the tensioner and remove the locking pin/drill bit, then release it, making sure that the drivebelt ribs locate correctly on each of the pulley grooves.

11 Refit the air cleaner housing (if removed), then refit the wheel arch liner and roadwheel, and lower the vehicle to the ground.

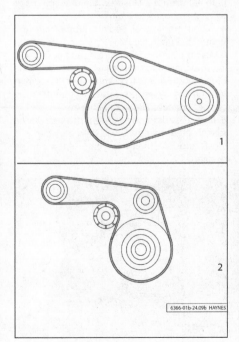

24.9b 1.9 litre engines with air conditioning (1) and without air conditioning (2)

25 Valve clearance check and adjustment – SOHC (Z19DT and Z19DTL) engines

1 Refer to the procedures contained in Chapter 2C Section 10.

26 Handbrake operation and adjustment check

1 With the vehicle on a slight slope, apply

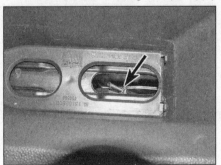

26.4 Handbrake cable adjuster nut (arrowed)

the handbrake lever by up to 4 clicks of the ratchet, and check that it holds the vehicle stationary, then release the lever and check that there is no resistance to movement of the vehicle.

2 If necessary, adjust the handbrake as follows.

3 Chock the front wheels then jack up the rear of the vehicle and securely support it on axle stands (see *Jacking and vehicle support*).

4 From inside the vehicle, lift out the rubber mat from the base of the centre console. The handbrake cable adjuster nut is accessible through the access opening in the console base **(see illustration)**.

5 Move the handbrake lever to the fully released position then, using a deep socket, turn the cable adjuster nut anti-clockwise to remove all tension from the cables.

6 Depress the footbrake five times, then fully apply and release the handbrake lever five times.

7 With the handbrake lever set on the second notch of the ratchet mechanism, rotate the adjuster nut clockwise until a reasonable amount of force is required to turn each wheel. **Note:** *The force required should be equal for each wheel.*

8 Now pull the handbrake lever up to the third

notch of the ratchet mechanism and check that both rear wheels are locked. Once this is so, fully release the handbrake lever and check that the wheels rotate freely. Check the adjustment by applying the handbrake fully whilst counting the clicks emitted from the handbrake ratchet and, if necessary, re-adjust.
9 On completion of adjustment, refit the rubber mat to the centre console, then lower the vehicle to the ground.

27 Headlight beam alignment check

1 Accurate adjustment of the headlight beam is only possible using optical beam- setting equipment, and this work should therefore be carried out by a Vauxhall/Opel dealer or service station with the necessary facilities. Refer to Chapter 12 Section 8 for further information.

28 Remote control battery renewal

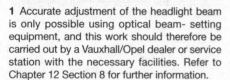

Vehicles without keyless entry

1 Using a screwdriver, prise the battery cover from the ignition key fob **(see illustration)**.
2 Note how the circular battery is fitted, then carefully remove it from the contacts **(see illustration)**.
3 Fit the new battery (type CR 2032) and refit the cover making sure that it clips fully onto the base.
4 After changing the battery, lock and unlock the driver's door with the key in the lock to synchronise the remote control unit.

Vehicles with keyless entry

5 No information was available at the time of writing. Consult a Vauxhall dealer.

29 Hydraulic fluid renewal

⚠ **Warning: Hydraulic fluid can harm your eyes and damage painted surfaces, so use extreme caution**

when handling and pouring it. **Do not use fluid that has been standing open for some time, as it absorbs moisture from the air. Excess moisture can cause a dangerous loss of braking effectiveness.**
Note: *The brake and clutch hydraulic systems share a common reservoir.*

1 The procedure is similar to that for the bleeding of the hydraulic system as described in Chapter 9 Section 2 (brake) and Chapter 6 Section 2 (clutch).
2 Working as described in Chapter 9 Section 2, open the first bleed screw in the sequence, and pump the brake pedal gently until nearly all the old fluid has been emptied from the master cylinder reservoir. Top-up to the MAX level with new fluid, and continue pumping until only the new fluid remains in the reservoir, and new fluid can be seen emerging from the bleed screw. Tighten the screw, and top the reservoir level up to the MAX level line.

> **HAYNES HINT** *Old hydraulic fluid is invariably much darker in colour than the new, making it easy to distinguish the two.*

3 Work through all the remaining bleed screws in the sequence until new fluid can be seen at all of them. Be careful to keep the master cylinder reservoir topped-up to above the MIN level at all times, or air may enter the system and greatly increase the length of the task.
4 Bleed the fluid from the clutch hydraulic system as described in Chapter 6 Section 2.
5 When the operation is complete, check that all bleed screws are securely tightened, and that their dust caps are refitted. Wash off all traces of spilt fluid, and recheck the master cylinder reservoir fluid level.
6 Check the operation of the brakes and clutch before taking the car on the road.

30 Coolant renewal

Note: *Vauxhall/Opel do not specify renewal intervals for the antifreeze mixture, as the mixture used to fill the system when*

the vehicle is new is designed to last the lifetime of the vehicle. However, it is strongly recommended that the coolant is renewed at the intervals specified in the Maintenance schedule, as a precaution against possible engine corrosion problems. This is particularly advisable if the coolant has been renewed using an antifreeze other than that specified by Vauxhall/Opel. With many antifreeze types, the corrosion inhibitors become progressively less effective with age. It is up to the individual owner whether or not to follow this advice.

⚠ **Warning: Wait until the engine is cold before starting this procedure. Do not allow antifreeze to come in contact with your skin, or with the painted surfaces of the vehicle. Rinse off spills immediately with plenty of water. Never leave antifreeze lying around in an open container, or in a puddle in the driveway or on the garage floor. Children and pets are attracted by its sweet smell, but antifreeze can be fatal if ingested.**

Cooling system draining

1 To drain the cooling system, first cover the expansion tank cap with a wad of rag, and slowly turn the cap anti-clockwise to relieve the pressure in the cooling system (a hissing sound will normally be heard). Wait until any pressure remaining in the system is released, then continue to turn the cap until it can be removed.
2 Remove the engine undertray (where fitted), then position a suitable container beneath the right-hand side of the radiator.
3 The coolant drain plug is located at the bottom of the radiator right-hand end tank **(see illustration)**. Unscrew the drain plug and allow the coolant to drain..
4 When the flow of coolant stops, refit and tighten the drain plugs.
5 As no cylinder block drain plug is fitted, it is not possible to drain all of the coolant. Due consideration must be made for this when refilling the system, in order to maintain the correct concentration of antifreeze.
6 If the coolant has been drained for a reason other than renewal, then provided it is clean and less than two years old, it can be re-used.

28.1 Prise the battery cover from the ignition key fob

28.2 Carefully remove the battery from the contacts

30.3 Radiator drain plug

Cooling system flushing

7 If coolant renewal has been neglected, or if the antifreeze mixture has become diluted, then in time, the cooling system may gradually lose efficiency, as the coolant passages become restricted due to rust, scale deposits, and other sediment. The cooling system efficiency can be restored by flushing the system clean.

8 The radiator should be flushed independently of the engine, to avoid unnecessary contami-nation.

Radiator flushing

9 Disconnect the top and bottom hoses and any other relevant hoses from the radiator, with reference to Chapter 3.

10 Insert a garden hose into the radiator top inlet. Direct a flow of clean water through the radiator, and continue flushing until clean water emerges from the radiator bottom outlet.

11 If after a reasonable period, the water still does not run clear, the radiator can be flushed with a good proprietary cleaning agent. It is important that the manufacturer's instructions are followed carefully. If the contamination is particularly bad, remove the radiator, insert the hose in the radiator bottom outlet, and reverse-flush the radiator.

Engine flushing

12 To flush the engine, the thermostat must be removed, because it will be shut, and would otherwise prevent the flow of water around the engine. The thermostat can be removed as described in Chapter 3 Section 4. Take care not to introduce dirt or debris into the system if this approach is used.

13 With the bottom hose disconnected from the radiator, insert a garden hose into the thermostat opening. Direct a clean flow of water through the engine, and continue flushing until clean water emerges from the radiator bottom hose.

14 On completion of flushing, refit the thermostat with reference to Chapter 3 Section 4, and reconnect the hoses.

Cooling system filling

15 Before attempting to fill the cooling system, make sure that all hoses and clips are in good condition, and that the clips are tight. Note that an antifreeze mixture must be used all year round, to prevent corrosion of the engine components.

16 Remove the expansion tank filler cap.

17 Fill the system by slowly pouring the coolant into the expansion tank until it is up to the filler neck.

18 On 1.9 litre engines, open the bleed screw in the coolant pipe above the exhaust manifold **(see illustration)**. Close the coolant pipe bleed screw as soon as coolant emerges.

19 Top-up the expansion tank until the coolant level is up to the KALT/COLD mark on the side of the tank.

20 Refit and tighten the expansion tank filler cap.

21 Start the engine and run it at 2000 to 2500 rpm until the cooling fan switches on. Continue running the engine at between 2000 and 2500 rpm for a further 2 minutes.

22 Stop the engine, and allow it to cool, then recheck the coolant level with reference to *Weekly checks*. Top-up the level if necessary and refit the expansion tank filler cap. Refit the engine undertray (where applicable).

Antifreeze mixture

23 Always use an ethylene-glycol based antifreeze which is suitable for use in mixed-metal cooling systems (see *Lubricants and fluids*). The quantity of antifreeze and levels of protection are given in the Specifications.

24 Before adding antifreeze, the cooling system should be completely drained, preferably flushed, and all hoses checked for condition and security.

25 After filling with antifreeze, a label should be attached to the expansion tank, stating the type and concentration of antifreeze used, and the date installed. Any subsequent topping-up should be made with the same type and concentration of antifreeze.

Caution: Do not use engine antifreeze in the windscreen/tailgate washer system, as it will cause damage to the vehicle paintwork. A screenwash additive should be added to the washer system in the quantities stated on the bottle.

31 Exhaust emission check

1 The exhaust emission check is carried out initially after 3 years, then every 2 years, however, on vehicles which are subject to intensive use (eg, taxis/hire cars/ambulances) it must be carried out annually. The check involves checking the engine management system operation by plugging an electronic tester into the system diagnostic socket to check the electronic control unit (ECU) memory for faults (see Chapter 4B Section 10).

2 In reality, if the vehicle is running correctly and the engine management warning light in the instrument panel is functioning normally, then this check need not be carried out.

32 Air cleaner element renewal – diesel models

1 The air cleaner is located in the front right-hand corner of the engine compartment.

2 Slacken the retaining clip and disconnect the air duct from the air cleaner cover **(see illustration)**.

3 Slide out the locking clip and disconnect

30.18 Open the bleed screw (arrowed) in the coolant pipe above the exhaust manifold

32.2 Slacken the clip and disconnect the air intake duct from the airflow meter

32.3 Disconnect the wiring connector from the airflow meter

32.4a Undo the retaining screws ...

32.4b ... lift off the air cleaner cover ...

32.4c ... then lift out the filter element

the wiring connector from the side of the airflow meter (see illustration).

4 Undo the screws and lift off the air cleaner cover, then lift out the filter element (see illustrations).

5 Wipe out the casing and the cover.

6 Fit the new filter, noting that the rubber locating flange should be uppermost, and secure the cover with the screws.

7 Reconnect the airflow meter wiring connector.

33 Timing belt, tensioner and idler pulley renewal

1 Refer to the procedures contained in the relevant Part of Chapter 2.

34 Automatic transmission fluid renewal

1 Refer to the procedures contained in Chapter 7B Section 2.

35 Valve clearance check and adjustment – 1.7 litre engines

1 Refer to the procedures in Chapter 2B Section 10.

Chapter 2 Part A
Petrol engine in-car repair procedures

Contents

Section number

Camshaft cover – removal and refitting 4
Camshaft oil seals – renewal 10
Camshafts and followers – removal, inspection and refitting 12
Compression test – general information 2
Crankshaft oil seals – renewal 17
Crankshaft pulley – removal and refitting 5
Cylinder head – removal and refitting. 13
Engine/transmission mountings – inspection and renewal 19
Flywheel/driveplate – removal, inspection and refitting 18
General Information 1
Oil filter housing (VVT engines) – removal and refitting 16

Oil pump – removal, overhaul and refitting. 15
Sump – removal and refitting 14
Timing belt – removal and refitting. 7
Timing belt covers – removal and refitting 6
Timing belt sprockets, tensioner and idler pulley –
  removal and refitting. 8
Top Dead Centre (TDC) for No 1 piston – locating 3
Valve clearances – checking and adjustment 11
VVT oil control valves (A16XER and 1.8 litre engines) –
  removal and refitting. 9

Degrees of difficulty

| **Easy,** suitable for novice with little experience | **Fairly easy,** suitable for beginner with some experience | **Fairly difficult,** suitable for competent DIY mechanic | **Difficult,** suitable for experienced DIY mechanic | **Very difficult,** suitable for expert DIY or professional |

Specifications

General

Engine type.	Four-cylinder, in-line, water-cooled. Double overhead camshafts, belt-driven
Manufacturer's engine code: *	
1.6 litre engines	Z16XEP, Z16XE1, Z16XER and A16XER
1.8 litre engines	Z18XER and A18XER
Bore:	
1.6 litre engines	79.0 mm
1.8 litre engines	80.5 mm
Stroke:	
1.6 litre engines	81.5 mm
1.8 litre engines	88.2 mm
Capacity:	
1.6 litre engines	1598 cc
1.8 litre engines	1796 cc
Compression ratio	10.5: 1
Firing order.	1-3-4-2 (No 1 cylinder at timing belt end)
Direction of crankshaft rotation	Clockwise (viewed from timing belt end of engine)

*For details of engine code location, see 'Vehicle identification'.

Compression pressures
Maximum difference between any two cylinders . . . . 1 bar

Valve clearances
Engine cold:
    Intake . . . . 0.21 to 0.29 mm
    Exhaust . . . . 0.26 to 0.35 mm

Lubrication system
Minimum oil pressure at 80ºC . . . . 1.3 bar at idle speed
Oil pump type . . . . Rotor-type, driven directly from crankshaft
Rotor-to-housing clearance (endfloat) . . . . 0.020 to 0.058 mm

Torque wrench settings

	Nm	lbf ft
Auxiliary drivebelt tensioner retaining bolt	50	37
Camshaft bearing cap bolts	8	6
Camshaft bearing support bolts (A16XER and 1.8 litre engines)	8	6
Camshaft cover bolts	8	6
Camshaft sprocket bolt: *		
1.6 litre engines (non-VVT engines): *		
Stage 1	50	37
Stage 2	Angle-tighten a further 60°	
Stage 3	Angle-tighten a further 15°	
1.6 litre engines (VVT-engines):		
Stage 1	50	37
Stage 2	Angle-tighten a further 150°	
Stage 3	Angle-tighten a further 15°	
1.8 litre engines:		
Stage 1	50	37
Stage 2	Angle-tighten a further 150°	
Stage 3	Angle-tighten a further 15°	
Connecting rod big-end bearing cap bolt: *		
Stage 1	35	26
Stage 2	Angle-tighten a further 45°	
Stage 3	Angle-tighten a further 15°	
Coolant pipe flange to coolant pump (1.6 litre engines)	10	7
Crankshaft pulley bolt: *		
Stage 1	95	70
Stage 2	Angle-tighten a further 45°	
Stage 3	Angle-tighten a further 15°	
Cylinder head bolts: *		
Stage 1	25	18
Stage 2	Angle-tighten a further 90°	
Stage 3	Angle-tighten a further 90°	
Stage 4	Angle-tighten a further 90°	
Stage 5	Angle-tighten a further 45°	
Engine/transmission mountings:		
Front mounting/torque link:		
Mounting-to-transmission bolts	80	59
Mounting to subframe	55	41
Left-hand mounting:		
Mounting-to-body bolts	25	18
Mounting bracket to transmission bracket	55	41
Rubber mounting through-bolt	55	41
Transmission bracket to transmission	35	26
Rear mounting/torque link:		
Mounting-to-bracket bolts	55	41
Mounting-to-subframe bolts	55	41
Bracket-to-transmission bolts	80	59
Right-hand mounting:		
Engine bracket-to-engine bolts	50	37
Mounting-to-body bolts	35	26
Mounting-to-engine bracket bolts	55	41
Rubber mounting through-bolt	55	41
Engine-to-transmission bolts	60	44
Flywheel bolts: *		
Stage 1	35	26
Stage 2	Angle-tighten a further 30°	
Stage 3	Angle-tighten a further 15°	

Torque wrench settings (continued)

	Nm	lbf ft
Main bearing cap bolts: *		
Stage 1	50	37
Stage 2 . . . . .ˑ.	Angle-tighten a further 45°	
Stage 3	Angle-tighten a further 15°	
Oil filter housing to cylinder block (A16 XER and 1.8 litre engines)	25	18
Oil pump:		
Retaining bolts	20	15
Pump cover screws	8	6
Oil pressure relief valve cap	15	11
Roadwheel bolts.	110	81
Sump bolts:		
Sump-to-cylinder block/oil pump bolts	10	7
Sump flange-to-transmission bolts	40	30
Timing belt cover bolts.	6	4
Timing belt idler pulley bolt*:		
Stage 1	20	15
Stage 2	Angle-tighten a further 120°	
Timing belt tensioner bolt*:		
Stage 1	20	15
Stage 2	Angle-tighten a further 120°	
VVT oil control valve bolts (A16XER and 1.8 litre engines only)	6	4

*Do not re-use

1 General Information

How to use this Chapter

1 This Part of Chapter 2 describes the repair procedures which can reasonably be carried out on the engine while it remains in the vehicle. If the engine has been removed from the vehicle and is being dismantled as described in Chapter 2E, any preliminary dismantling procedures can be ignored.

2 Note that, while it may be possible physically to overhaul items such as the piston/connecting rod assemblies while the engine is in the vehicle, such tasks are not usually carried out as separate operations, and usually require the execution of several additional procedures (not to mention the cleaning of components and of oilways); for this reason, all such tasks are classed as major overhaul procedures, and are described in Chapter 2E.

3 Chapter 2E describes the removal of the engine/transmission unit from the vehicle, and the full overhaul procedures which can then be carried out.

Engine description

4 The engine is a double overhead camshaft (DOHC), four-cylinder, in-line unit, mounted transversely at the front of the car, with the transmission attached to its left-hand end.

5 The 1.6 litre Z16XE1 and Z16XER power units are known as 'Twinport' engines due to the design of the intake manifold and cylinder head combustion chambers. Vacuum operated flap valves located in the intake manifold are opened or closed according to engine operating conditions, to create a variable venturi manifold arrangement. This system has significant advantages in terms of engine power, fuel economy and reduced exhaust emissions.

6 The crankshaft is supported within the cylinder block on five shell-type main bearings. Thrustwashers are fitted to number 3 main bearing, to control crankshaft endfloat.

7 The connecting rods are attached to the crankshaft by horizontally-split shell-type big-end bearings, and to the pistons by interference-fit gudgeon pins. The aluminium alloy pistons are of the slipper type, and are fitted with three piston rings, comprising two compression rings and a scraper-type oil control ring.

8 The camshafts run directly in the cylinder head, and are driven by the crankshaft via a toothed composite rubber timing belt. The camshafts operate each valve via a camshaft follower. One camshaft operates the intake valves, and the other operates the exhaust valves. The camshaft followers are available in various thicknesses to facilitate valve clearance adjustment.

9 On the 1.6 litre A16XER and 1.8 litre engines, a variable valve timing (VVT) system is employed. The VVT system allows the intake and exhaust camshaft timing to be varied under the control of the engine management system, to boost both low-speed torque and top-end power, as well as reducing exhaust emissions. The VVT camshaft adjuster is integral with each camshaft timing belt sprocket, and is supplied with two pressurised oil feeds through passages in the camshaft itself. Two electro-magnetic oil control valves, one for each camshaft and operated by the engine management system, are fitted to the cylinder head, and are used to supply the pressurised oil to each camshaft adjuster through the two oil feeds. Each adjuster contains two chambers – depending on which of the two oil feeds is enabled by the control valve, the oil pressure will turn the camshaft clockwise (advance) or anti-clockwise (retard) to adjust the valve timing as required. If pressure is removed from both feeds, this induces a timing 'hold' condition. Thus the valve timing is infinitely variable within a given range.

10 Lubrication is by pressure-feed from a rotor-type oil pump, which is mounted on the right-hand end of the crankshaft. The pump draws oil through a strainer located in the sump, and then forces it through an externally mounted full-flow oil filter. The oil flows into galleries in the cylinder block/crankcase, from where it is distributed to the crankshaft (main bearings) and camshafts. The big-end bearings are supplied with oil via internal drillings in the crankshaft, while the camshaft bearings also receive a pressurised supply. The camshaft lobes and valves are lubricated by splash, as are all other engine components.

11 A semi-closed crankcase ventilation system is employed; crankcase fumes are drawn from cylinder head cover, and passed via a hose to the intake manifold.

12 The coolant pump is located externally on the engine, and is driven by the auxiliary drivebelt.

Operations with engine in car

13 The following operations can be carried out without having to remove the engine from the car.

a) Removal and refitting of the camshaft cover.
b) Adjustment of the valve clearances.
c) Removal and refitting of the VVT oil control valves.
d) Removal and refitting of the cylinder head.
e) Removal and refitting of the timing belt, tensioner and sprockets.
f) Renewal of the camshaft oil seals.

g) Removal and refitting of the camshafts and followers.

h) Removal and refitting of the sump.

i) Removal and refitting of the connecting rods and pistons.*

j) Removal and refitting of the oil pump.

k) Removal and refitting of the oil filter housing (A16 XER and 1.8 litre engines).

l) Renewal of the crankshaft oil seals.

m) Renewal of the engine mountings.

n) Removal and refitting of the flywheel.

* Although the operation marked with an asterisk can be carried out with the engine in the car (after removal of the sump), it is preferable for the engine to be removed, in the interests of cleanliness and improved access. For this reason, the procedure is described in Chapter 2E.

2 Compression test – general information

1 When engine performance is down, or if misfiring occurs which cannot be attributed to the ignition or fuel systems, a compression test can provide diagnostic clues as to the engine's condition. If the test is performed regularly, it can give warning of trouble before any other symptoms become apparent.

2 Due to the electronic throttle control system used on these engines, a compression test can only be carried out with the engine management electronic control unit connected to Vauxhall/Opel diagnostic test

equipment, or a compatible alternative unit. Without the test equipment, the throttle valve cannot be opened (as there is no accelerator cable) and the test will be inconclusive. Note that even with the accelerator pedal fully depressed, the engine management ECU will only control the throttle valve position when the engine is actually running. The test equipment independently actuates the throttle valve (irrespective of ECU commands) and opens the throttle valve fully.

3 As the equipment needed for the compression test is unlikely to be available to the home mechanic, it is recommended that the test is performed by a Vauxhall/Opel dealer, or suitably-equipped garage.

3 Top Dead Centre (TDC) for No 1 piston – locating

1 Top dead centre (TDC) is the highest point in the cylinder that a piston reaches as the crankshaft turns. Each piston reaches TDC at the end of the compression stroke, and again at the end of the exhaust stroke. For the purpose of timing the engine, TDC refers to the position of No 1 piston at the end of its compression stroke. No 1 piston and cylinder are at the timing belt end of the engine.

2 Disconnect the battery negative terminal (refer to Chapter 5A Section 4). If necessary, remove all the spark plugs as described in Chapter 1A Section 31 to enable the engine to be easily turned over.

3 Remove the timing belt upper cover as described in Section 6.

4 Apply the handbrake, then jack up the front of the vehicle and support it on axle stands (see *Jacking and vehicle support*). Remove the right-hand front roadwheel, then remove the wheel arch liner inner cover for access to the crankshaft pulley.

5 Using a socket and extension bar on the crankshaft pulley bolt, rotate the crankshaft until the timing marks on the camshaft sprockets are facing towards each other, and an imaginary straight line can be drawn through the camshaft sprocket bolts and the timing marks. With the camshaft sprocket marks correctly positioned, align the notch on the crankshaft pulley rim with the mark at the base of the timing belt lower cover **(see illustrations)**. The engine is now positioned with No 1 piston at TDC on its compression stroke.

6 If the crankshaft pulley and lower timing belt cover have been removed, the timing mark on the crankshaft sprocket can be used instead of the mark on the pulley. The mark on the crankshaft sprocket must align with the corresponding mark on the oil pump housing **(see illustration)**.

4 Camshaft cover – removal and refitting

Non-VVT engines
Removal

1 Remove the air cleaner assembly and intake ducts as described in Chapter 4A Section 2.

2 Remove the ignition module from the spark plugs as described in Chapter 5B Section 3.

3 Remove the timing belt upper cover as described in Section 6.

4 Release the fitting and disconnect the breather hose from the camshaft cover.

5 Unclip the wiring harness trough from the vicinity of the camshaft cover and move it to one side.

6 Unscrew the three camshaft cover retaining bolts at the timing belt end of the cover. Pull the captive bolts upward from the cover as far as possible and retain them in this position with adhesive tape.

7 Unscrew the remaining six bolts securing the camshaft cover to the cylinder head.

8 Lift the camshaft cover away from the cylinder head and recover the rubber seal. Examine the seal for signs of wear or damage and renew if necessary.

Refitting

9 Ensure that the camshaft cover grove and rubber seal are clean and dry with all traces of oil removed. If necessary, degrease the seal and cover groove with brake cleaner or a similar product.

10 Clean the mating surface of the cylinder head and the area around the camshaft bearing caps at the timing belt end, ensuring that all traces of oil are removed.

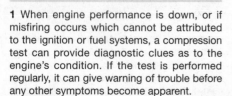

3.5a Align the camshaft sprocket timing marks (arrowed) on non-VVT engines ...

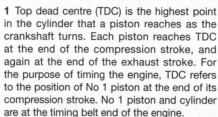

3.5b ... and VVT engines

3.5c The notch on the crankshaft pulley rim with the mark at the base of the timing belt lower cover (arrowed)

3.6 Crankshaft sprocket and rear timing belt cover alignment marks (crankshaft pulley removed)

4.11 Locate the rubber seal into the grooves of the camshaft cover, ensuring that it is fully seated

11 Locate the rubber seal into the grooves of the camshaft cover, ensuring that it is fully seated, with no chance of it falling out as the cover is fitted **(see illustration)**.
12 Carefully manoeuvre the camshaft cover into position, taking great care to ensure the seal remains correctly seated. Locate the flywheel end of the camshaft cover on the cylinder head, then carefully bring the timing belt end of the cover down onto the head.
13 Remove the adhesive tape from the three timing belt end retaining bolts. Screw in all the cover retaining bolts and tighten them to the specified torque, working in a spiral pattern from the centre outwards.
14 Clip the wiring harness trough back into position, then reconnect the engine breather hose.
15 Refit the timing belt upper cover as described in Section 6.
16 Refit the ignition module to the spark plugs as described in Chapter 5B Section 3.
17 Refit the air cleaner assembly and intake ducts as described in Chapter 4A Section 2.

VVT engines

Removal

18 Remove the ignition module from the spark plugs as described in Chapter 5B Section 3.
19 Lift the wiring harness up and out of the support on the right-hand end of the camshaft cover **(see illustration)**.
20 Unclip the wiring harness trough from the rear of the camshaft cover **(see illustration)**.
21 Pull out the retaining wire clip and

4.21 Pull out the retaining wire clip and disconnect the breather hose from the camshaft cover

disconnect the breather hose from the camshaft cover **(see illustration)**.
22 Unscrew the eleven bolts securing the camshaft cover to the cylinder head.
23 Lift the camshaft cover away from the cylinder head and recover the rubber seal. Examine the seal for signs of wear or damage and renew if necessary.

Refitting

24 Ensure that the camshaft cover grove and rubber seal are clean and dry with all traces of oil removed. If necessary, degrease the seal and cover groove with brake cleaner or a similar product.
25 Clean the mating surface of the cylinder head and the area around the camshaft bearing caps at the timing belt end, ensuring that all traces of oil are removed.
26 Locate the rubber seal into the grooves of the camshaft cover, ensuring that it is fully seated, with no chance of it falling out as the cover is fitted **(see illustration 4.11)**.
27 Carefully manoeuvre the camshaft cover into position, taking great care to ensure the seal remains correctly seated. Screw in all the cover retaining bolts and tighten them to the specified torque, working in a spiral pattern from the centre outwards.
28 Reconnect the engine breather hose, then clip the wiring harness trough back into position. Engage the wiring harness with the support on cover.
29 Refit the ignition module to the spark plugs as described in Chapter 5B Section 3.

4.19 Lift the wiring harness out of the support on the camshaft cover

5.3 Engage a strip of metal with the flywheel ring gear teeth through the access slot (arrowed) to lock the flywheel

4.20 Unclip the wiring harness trough from the rear of the camshaft cover

5 Crankshaft pulley – removal and refitting

Note: *A new pulley retaining bolt will be required on refitting.*

Removal

1 Firmly apply the handbrake, then jack up the front of the car and support it securely on axle stands (see *Jacking and vehicle support*). Remove the right-hand roadwheel, then remove the wheel arch liner inner cover for access to the crankshaft pulley.
2 Remove the auxiliary drivebelt as described in Chapter 1A Section 23. Prior to removal, mark the direction of rotation on the belt to ensure the belt is refitted the same way around.
3 Slacken the crankshaft pulley retaining bolt. To prevent crankshaft rotation, have an assistant select top gear and apply the brakes firmly. Alternatively engage a strip of metal with the flywheel ring gear teeth through the access slot located just above the front engine mounting/torque link **(see illustration)**.
4 Unscrew the retaining bolt and washer and remove the crankshaft pulley from the end of the crankshaft.

Refitting

5 Refit the crankshaft pulley, aligning the pulley cut-out with the raised notch on the timing belt sprocket, then fit the washer and new retaining bolt **(see illustration)**.

5.5 Align the pulley cut-out with the raised notch

6 Lock the crankshaft by the method used on removal, and tighten the pulley retaining bolt to the specified Stage 1 torque setting, then angle-tighten the bolt through the specified Stage 2 angle, using a socket and extension bar, and finally through the specified Stage 3 angle. It is recommended that an angle-measuring gauge is used during the final stages of the tightening, to ensure accuracy. If a gauge is not available, use white paint to make alignment marks between the bolt head and pulley prior to tightening; the marks can then be used to check that the bolt has been rotated through the correct angle.

7 Refit the auxiliary drivebelt as described in Chapter 1A Section 23 using the mark made prior to removal to ensure the belt is fitted the correct way around.

8 Refit the wheel arch liner inner cover and the roadwheel. Lower the car to the ground and tighten the wheel bolts to the specified torque.

6 Timing belt covers –
removal and refitting

Upper cover

1 Remove the air cleaner assembly and intake ducts as described in Chapter 4A Section 2.

2 Undo the two retaining bolts then unclip the upper cover from the rear cover and remove it from the engine compartment **(see illustration)**.

3 Refitting is the reverse of removal, tightening the cover retaining bolts to the specified torque.

Lower cover

4 On non-VVT engines, remove the upper cover as described in paragraphs 1 and 2.

5 Remove the crankshaft pulley as described in Section 5.

6 Undo the retaining bolt and remove the auxiliary drivebelt tensioner **(see illustration)**.

7 Undo the four retaining bolts then manoeuvre the lower cover off the engine **(see illustrations)**.

8 Refitting is the reverse of removal, tightening the cover retaining bolts and auxiliary drivebelt tensioner bolt to the specified torque.

Centre cover (VVT engines)

9 Remove the upper and lower covers as described previously.

10 Remove the right-hand engine mounting as described in Section 19, then undo the three retaining bolts and remove the mounting bracket bolted to the cylinder block.

11 Release the two clips securing the centre cover to the rear cover and manoeuvre the centre cover off the engine.

12 Refitting is the reverse of removal, tightening the engine mounting bracket retaining bolts to the specified torque.

Rear cover

13 Remove the timing belt as described in Section 7.

6.2 Timing belt upper cover retaining bolts (arrowed)

6.7a Timing belt lower cover upper retaining bolts (arrowed) …

14 Remove the camshaft sprockets, timing belt tensioner and idler pulley as described in Section 8.

15 Unclip the wiring harness from the cover, then undo the four bolts securing the cover to the cylinder head. On non-VVT engines, remove the camshaft sensor from the cover by turning it slightly, then remove the cover from the cylinder head.

16 Refitting is the reverse of removal, tightening the cover retaining bolts to the specified torque.

7 Timing belt –
removal and refitting

Note: *The timing belt must be removed and refitted with the engine cold.*

Removal

1 Position No 1 cylinder at TDC on its compression stroke as described in Section 3.

2 On non-VVT engines, remove the timing belt lower cover as described in Section 6. On VVT engines, remove the timing belt lower cover and centre cover as described in Section 6.

3 Check that the timing marks on the camshaft sprockets are still correctly aligned and facing towards each other, and the timing mark on the crankshaft sprocket is aligned with the corresponding mark on the oil pump housing.

4 On non-VVT engines, remove the right-hand

6.6 Auxiliary drivebelt tensioner retaining bolt (arrowed)

6.7b … and lower retaining bolts (arrowed)

engine mounting as described in Section 19, then undo the three retaining bolts and remove the mounting bracket bolted to the cylinder block.

5 Using an Allen key inserted in the slot on the face of the timing belt tensioner, rotate the tensioner clockwise to relieve the tension in the timing belt **(see illustration)**. Insert Vauxhall/Opel special tool KM-6333 or similar into the slot on the inner edge of the tensioner body to lock the tensioner in the released position. If the special tool is not available, a length of welding rod or drill bit is a suitable alternative.

6 Slide the timing belt from its sprockets and remove it from the engine. If the belt is to be re-used, use white paint or similar to mark the

7.5 Insert an Allen key in the timing belt tensioner slot (arrowed) and rotate the tensioner clockwise to relieve the tension in the belt

direction of rotation on the belt. Do not rotate the crankshaft or camshafts until the timing belt has been refitted.

7 Check the timing belt carefully for any signs of uneven wear, splitting or oil contamination, and renew it if there is the slightest doubt about its condition. If the engine is undergoing an overhaul and is approaching the manufacturer's specified interval for belt renewal (see Chapter 1A) renew the belt as a matter of course, regardless of its apparent condition. If signs of oil contamination are found, trace the source of the oil leak and rectify it, then wash down the engine timing belt area and all related components to remove all traces of oil.

Refitting

8 On reassembly, thoroughly clean the timing belt sprockets and tensioner/idler pulleys.

9 Check that the camshaft and crankshaft sprocket timing marks are still correctly aligned as described in paragraph 3.

10 Fit the timing belt over the crankshaft and camshaft sprockets and around the idler pulley, ensuring that the belt front run is taut (ie, all slack is on the tensioner side of the belt), then fit the belt over the tensioner pulley. Do not twist the belt sharply while refitting it. Ensure that the belt teeth are correctly seated centrally in the sprockets, and that the timing marks remain in alignment. If a used belt is being refitted, ensure that the arrow mark made on removal points in the normal direction of rotation, as before.

11 Using the Allen key, turn the tensioner clockwise slightly and remove the tool used to lock the tensioner. Slowly release the tensioner and allow it to turn anti-clockwise and automatically tension the timing belt.

12 Check the sprocket timing marks are still correctly aligned. If adjustment is necessary, release the tensioner again then disengage the belt from the sprockets and make any necessary adjustments.

13 Using a socket on the temporarily refitted crankshaft pulley bolt, rotate the crankshaft smoothly through two complete turns (720º) in the normal direction of rotation to settle the timing belt in position.

14 Set the crankshaft back in the timing position and check that all the sprocket timing marks are still correctly aligned. If this is not the case, repeat the timing belt refitting procedure.

15 If everything is satisfactory, refit the timing belt covers as described in Section 6.

16 On non-VVT engines, refit the engine mounting bracket, tightening the three retaining bolts to the specified torque, then refit the right-hand engine mounting as described in Section 19

17 Refit the crankshaft pulley as described in Section 5.

8 Timing belt sprockets, tensioner and idler pulley – removal and refitting

Camshaft sprockets – non-VVT engines

Note: New sprocket retaining bolt(s) will be required for refitting.

Removal

1 Remove the timing belt as described in Section 7.

2 Turn the crankshaft 60° anti-clockwise away from TDC, to move the pistons away from the valves in the cylinder head. This is purely a precaution to prevent valve-to-piston contact if the camshafts are inadvertently rotated during the sprocket bolt removal/refitting procedure.

3 The camshaft sprocket must be prevented from turning as the sprocket bolt is unscrewed. Vauxhall/Opel special tools KM-6347 and KM-956-1 are available for this purpose, however a home-made tool can easily be fabricated (see **Tool Tip 1**).

4 Hold the sprocket with the tool, then unscrew the retaining bolt and washer and remove the sprocket from the end of the camshaft. If the sprocket locating pin is a loose fit in the camshaft end, remove it and store it with the sprocket for safe-keeping.

5 If necessary, remove the remaining sprocket using the same method. The intake and exhaust sprockets are different; the exhaust camshaft sprocket can be easily identified by the lugs which activate the camshaft position sensor.

Refitting

6 Prior to refitting check the oil seal(s) for signs of damage or leakage. If necessary, renew as described in Section 10.

7 Ensure the locating pin is in position in the camshaft end.

8 Refit the sprocket to the camshaft end, aligning its cut-out with the locating pin, and fit the washer and new retaining bolt. If both sprockets have been removed, ensure each sprocket is fitted to the correct shaft; the exhaust camshaft sprocket can be identified by the lugs on the sprocket outer face which trigger the camshaft position sensor.

9 Retain the sprocket by the method used on removal, and tighten the pulley retaining bolt to the specified Stage 1 torque setting then angle-tighten the bolt through the specified Stage 2 angle, using a socket and extension bar, and finally through the specified Stage 3 angle. It is recommended that an angle-measuring gauge is used during the final stages of the tightening, to ensure accuracy. If a gauge is not available, use white paint to make alignment marks between the bolt head and pulley prior to tightening; the marks can then be used to check that the bolt has been rotated through the correct angle.

10 Carefully rotate the crankshaft 60° clockwise until the mark on the crankshaft sprocket aligns with the mark at the base of the oil pump housing, then refit the timing belt as described in Section 7.

Camshaft sprockets – VVT engines

Note: Vauxhall/Opel special tools KM-6340 and KM-6628 or suitable alternatives will be required for this procedure.

Note: New sprocket retaining bolt(s) and a new sprocket closure bolt seal will be required for refitting.

Removal

11 Remove the camshaft cover as described in Section 4.

12 Remove the timing belt as described in Section 7.

13 Insert Vauxhall/Opel special tool KM-6628 into the slots on the end of the camshafts to lock the camshafts in the TDC position. In the absence of the special tool, a suitable alternative can be fabricated from a steel strip

Make up a sprocket-holding tool using two lengths of steel strip (one long, the other short), and three nuts and bolts; one nut and bolt forms the pivot of a forked tool, with the remaining two nuts and bolts at the tips of the 'forks' to engage with the sprocket spokes.

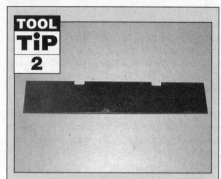

TOOL TiP 2

A camshaft locking tool can be made from a steel strip approximately 4.5 mm thick, with two grooves filed in the strip to clear the camshaft sensor trigger lugs.

8.13 Insert the special tool into the slots on the end of the camshafts to lock the camshafts in the TDC position – VVT engines

8.14 Camshaft sprocket closure bolts (arrowed) – VVT engines

(see **Tool Tip 2 and illustration**). It may be necessary to turn the camshafts slightly using an open-ended spanner on the flats provided, to allow the tool to fully engage with the slots.

14 Unscrew the closure bolt from the relevant camshaft sprocket **(see illustration)**. Note that a new closure bolt seal will be required for refitting.

15 Hold the camshaft using an open-ended spanner on the flats provided, and unscrew the camshaft sprocket retaining bolt. Withdraw the sprocket from the end of the camshaft.

16 If necessary, remove the remaining sprocket using the same method.

Refitting

17 Prior to refitting check the oil seal(s) for signs of damage or leakage. If necessary, renew as described in Section 10.

18 Refit the sprocket to the camshaft end and fit the new retaining bolt. Tighten the bolt finger tight only at this stage. If both sprockets have been removed, ensure each sprocket is fitted to the correct shaft; the exhaust camshaft sprocket has the timing belt guide flange on its inner face and the intake sprocket has the guide flange on its outer face.

19 Turn the camshaft sprocket(s) until the timing marks are facing towards each other and aligned. It will now be necessary to retain the sprockets in the timing position while the sprocket retaining bolt is tightened. Engage Vauxhall/Opel special tool KM-6340 or a suitable alternative with the teeth on both sprockets, to lock the sprockets together.

20 With the camshafts and sprockets locked in the timing position with the special tools, hold the camshaft using an open-ended spanner on the flats provided and tighten the sprocket retaining bolt to the specified Stage 1 torque setting. Now angle-tighten the bolt through the specified Stage 2 angle, using a socket and extension bar, and finally through the specified Stage 3 angle. It is recommended that an angle-measuring gauge is used during

the final stages of the tightening, to ensure accuracy. If a gauge is not available, use white paint to make alignment marks between the bolt head and sprocket prior to tightening; the marks can then be used to check that the bolt has been rotated through the correct angle.

21 Fit a new seal to the camshaft sprocket closure bolt, then refit the closure bolt and tighten securely.

22 Remove the special tools, then refit the timing belt as described in Section 7, and the camshaft cover as described in Section 4.

Crankshaft sprocket

Removal

23 Remove the timing belt as described in Section 7.

24 Slide the sprocket off from the end of the crankshaft, noting which way around it is fitted.

Refitting

25 Align the sprocket locating key with the crankshaft groove then slide the sprocket into position

26 Refit the timing belt as described in Section 7.

Tensioner assembly

27 A new tensioner retaining bolt will be required for refitting.

Removal

28 Remove the timing belt as described in Section 7.

29 Slacken and remove the central retaining bolt and remove the tensioner assembly from the engine.

Refitting

30 Clean the tensioner retaining bolt threads in the oil pump housing, ensuring that all traces of sealant, oil or grease are removed.

31 Fit the tensioner to the engine, making sure that the projecting end of the tensioner spring engages with the slot on the oil pump housing. Ensure the tensioner is correctly seated then fit the new retaining bolt and tighten it to the specified torque.

32 Refit the timing belt as described in Section 7.

Idler pulley

Note: *A new idler pulley retaining bolt will be required for refitting.*

Removal

33 Remove the timing belt as described in Section 7.

34 Slacken and remove the retaining bolt and remove the idler pulley from the engine.

Refitting

35 Clean the idler pulley retaining bolt threads in the oil pump housing, ensuring that all traces of sealant, oil or grease are removed.

36 Refit the idler pulley and tighten the new retaining bolt to the specified torque.

37 Refit the timing belt as described in Section 7.

9 VVT oil control valves (A16XER and 1.8 litre engines) – removal and refitting

Removal

1 The VVT oil control valves are fitted to the camshaft bearing support, adjacent to the camshaft sprockets. Two oil control valves are used, one for each camshaft.

2 Disconnect the wiring connector from the relevant oil control valve **(see illustration)**.

3 Undo the retaining bolt located below the valve, and withdraw the valve from the

9.2 Disconnect the wiring connector (arrowed) from the VVT oil control valve

camshaft bearing support. Be prepared for oil spillage.

Refitting

4 Lubricate the valve sealing rings with clean engine oil and insert the valve into the camshaft bearing support.
5 Refit and tighten the retaining bolt to the specified torque, then reconnect the wiring connector.
6 On completion, check and if necessary top-up the engine oil as described in *Weekly checks*.

10 Camshaft oil seals – renewal

1 Remove the relevant camshaft sprocket as described in Section 8.
2 Carefully punch or drill two small holes opposite each other in the oil seal. Screw a self-tapping screw into each, and pull on the screws with pliers to extract the seal **(see illustration)**.
3 Clean the seal housing, and polish off any burrs or raised edges which may have caused the seal to fail in the first place.
4 Press the new seal into position using a suitable tubular drift (such as a socket) which bears only on the hard outer edge of the seal **(see illustration)**. Take care not to damage the seal lips during fitting; note that the seal lips should face inwards.
5 Refit the camshaft sprocket as described in Section 8.

11 Valve clearances – checking and adjustment

Checking

1 The importance of having the valve

10.2 Camshaft oil seal removal method

clearances correctly adjusted cannot be overstressed, as they vitally affect the performance of the engine. The engine must be cold for the check to be accurate. The clearances are checked as follows.
2 Firmly apply the handbrake, then jack up the front of the vehicle and support it securely on axle stands (see *Jacking and vehicle support*). Remove the right-hand front roadwheel then remove the wheel arch liner inner cover for access to the crankshaft pulley.
3 Remove the camshaft cover as described in Section 4.
4 Position No 1 cylinder at TDC on its compression stroke as described in Section 3.
5 With the engine at TDC on compression for No 1 cylinder, the intake camshaft lobes for No 2 cylinder and the exhaust camshaft lobes for No 3 cylinder are pointing upwards and slightly towards the centre. This indicates that these valves are completely closed, and the clearances can be checked.
6 On a piece of paper, draw the outline of the engine with the cylinders numbered from the timing belt end. Show the position of each valve, together with the specified valve clearance.
7 With the cam lobes positioned as described in paragraph 5, using feeler blades, measure the clearance between the base of both No 2

10.4 Refit the camshaft oil seal with a tool that bears only on the hard outer edge of the seal

cylinder intake cam lobes and No 3 cylinder exhaust cam lobes and their followers. Record the clearances on the paper **(see illustrations)**.
8 Rotate the crankshaft pulley in the normal direction of rotation through a half a turn (180°) to position No 1 cylinder intake camshaft lobes and No 4 cylinder exhaust camshaft lobes pointing upwards and slightly towards the centre. Measure the clearance between the base of the camshaft lobes and their followers and record the clearances on the paper.
9 Rotate the crankshaft pulley through a half a turn (180°) to position No 3 cylinder intake camshaft lobes and No 2 cylinder exhaust camshaft lobes pointing upwards and slightly towards the centre. Measure the clearance between the base of the camshaft lobes and their followers and record the clearances on the paper.
10 Rotate the crankshaft pulley through a half a turn (180°) to position No 4 cylinder intake camshaft lobes and No 1 cylinder exhaust camshaft lobes pointing upwards and slightly towards the centre. Measure the clearance between the base of the camshaft lobes and their followers and record the clearances on the paper.

11.7a Using feeler blades, measure the intake valve clearances …

11.7b … and the exhaust valve clearances

11 If all the clearances are correct, refit the camshaft cover (see Section 4), then refit the wheel arch liner inner cover and the roadwheel. Lower the vehicle to the ground and tighten the wheel bolts to the specified torque. If any clearance measured is not correct, adjustment must be carried out as described in the following paragraphs.

Adjustment

12 If adjustment is necessary, remove the relevant camshaft(s) and camshaft followers as described in Section 12.
13 Clean the followers of the valves that require clearance adjustment and note the thickness marking on the follower. The thickness marking is stamped on the underside of each follower. For example, a 3.20 mm thick follower will have a 20 thickness marking, a 3.21 mm thick follower will have a 21 thickness marking, etc.
14 Add the measured clearance of the valve to the thickness of the original follower then subtract the specified valve clearance from this figure. This will give you the thickness of the follower required. For example:

Clearance measured of valve	0.31 mm
Plus thickness of the follower	3.20 mm
Equals	3.51 mm
Minus clearance required	0.25 mm
Thickness of follower required	3.26 mm

15 Repeat this procedure on the remaining valves which require adjustment, then obtain the correct thickness of follower(s) required.
16 Refit the camshaft followers and the relevant camshaft(s) as described in Section 12. Rotate the crankshaft a few times to settle all the components, then recheck the valve clearances before refitting the camshaft cover (Section 4).
17 Refit the wheel arch liner inner cover and roadwheel then lower the vehicle to the ground and tighten the wheel bolts to the specified torque.

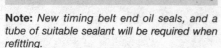

12 Camshafts and followers
– removal, inspection and refitting

Note: *New timing belt end oil seals, and a tube of suitable sealant will be required when refitting.*

Non-VVT engines

Removal

1 Remove the camshaft cover as described in Section 4.
2 Remove the timing belt as described in Section 7.
3 Remove the camshaft sprockets as described in Section 8.
4 Starting on the intake camshaft, working in a spiral pattern from the outside inwards, slacken the camshaft bearing cap retaining

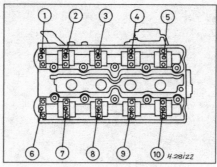

12.4a Camshaft bearing cap numbering sequence (No 1 at timing belt end) – non-VVT engines

bolts by half a turn at a time, to relieve the pressure of the valve springs on the bearing caps gradually and evenly (the reverse of illustration 12.15). Once the valve spring pressure has been relieved, the bolts can be fully unscrewed and removed along with the caps; the bearing caps are numbered intake camshaft 1 to 5, exhaust camshaft 6 to 10 (or 6 to 0) to ensure the caps are correctly positioned on refitting **(see illustrations)**. Take care not to loose the locating dowels (where fitted).
Caution: If the bearing cap bolts are carelessly slackened, the bearing caps might break. If any bearing cap breaks then the complete cylinder head assembly must be renewed; the bearing caps are matched to the head and are not available separately.
5 Lift the camshaft out of the cylinder head and slide off the oil seal.
6 Repeat the operations described in paragraphs 4 and 5 and remove the exhaust camshaft.
7 Obtain sixteen small, clean plastic containers, and label them for identification. Alternatively, divide a larger container into compartments. Using a rubber sucker tool, lift the followers out from the top of the cylinder head and store each one in its respective fitted position **(see illustration)**.

Inspection

8 Examine the camshaft bearing surfaces and cam lobes for signs of wear ridges

12.7 Use a valve lapping tool to remove the cam followers

and scoring. Renew the camshaft if any of these conditions are apparent. Examine the condition of the bearing surfaces both on the camshaft journals and in the cylinder head. If the head bearing surfaces are worn excessively, the cylinder head will need to be renewed.
9 Examine the follower bearing surfaces which contact the camshaft lobes for wear ridges and scoring. Check the followers and their bores in the cylinder head for signs of wear or damage. If any follower is thought to be faulty or is visibly worn it should be renewed.

Refitting

10 Where removed, lubricate the followers with clean engine oil and carefully insert each one into its original location in the cylinder head.
11 Lubricate the camshaft followers with molybdenum disulphide paste (or clean engine oil) then lay the camshafts in position.
12 Ensure the mating surfaces of the bearing caps and cylinder head are clean and dry and lubricate the camshaft journals and lobes with clean engine oil.
13 Apply a smear of sealant to the mating surfaces of both the intake (No 1) and exhaust (No 6) camshaft right-hand bearing caps **(see illustration)**.
14 Ensure the locating dowels (where fitted) are in position then refit the camshaft bearing caps and the retaining bolts in their original locations on the cylinder head.

12.4b Camshaft bearing cap numbers (arrowed – intake camshaft shown)

12.13 Apply a smear of sealant to the right-hand bearing caps

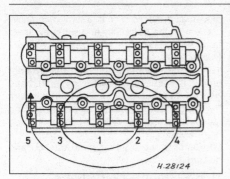

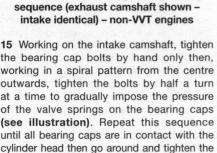

12.15 Camshaft bearing cap tightening sequence (exhaust camshaft shown – intake identical) – non-VVT engines

12.28 Camshaft bearing support retaining bolts (arrowed) – VVT engines

12.40 Camshaft bearing cap tightening sequence (intake camshaft shown – exhaust identical) – VVT engines

15 Working on the intake camshaft, tighten the bearing cap bolts by hand only then, working in a spiral pattern from the centre outwards, tighten the bolts by half a turn at a time to gradually impose the pressure of the valve springs on the bearing caps **(see illustration)**. Repeat this sequence until all bearing caps are in contact with the cylinder head then go around and tighten the camshaft bearing cap bolts to the specified torque.

16 Caution: If the bearing cap bolts are carelessly tightened, the bearing caps might break. If any bearing cap breaks then the complete cylinder head assembly must be renewed; the bearing caps are matched to the head and are not available separately.

17 Tighten the exhaust camshaft bearing cap bolts as described in paragraph 15.

18 Fit new camshaft oil seals as described in Section 10.

19 Refit the camshaft sprockets as described in Section 8.

20 Align all the sprocket timing marks to bring the camshafts and crankshaft back to TDC then refit the timing belt as described in Section 7.

21 Refit the camshaft cover as described in Section 4.

VVT engines

Removal

22 Remove the camshaft cover as described in Section 4.

23 Remove the timing belt as described in Section 7.

24 Remove the camshaft sprockets as described in Section 8.

25 Remove the timing belt rear cover as described in Section 6.

26 Remove the special tool used to lock the camshafts in the TDC position.

27 Disconnect the wiring connector at the intake camshaft and exhaust camshaft VVT oil control valves **(see illustration 9.2)**.

28 Undo the four bolts securing the camshaft bearing support at the timing belt end of the engine **(see illustration)**. Undo the two outer bolts first, followed by the two inner bolts. Using a plastic mallet, gently tap the bearing

support free and remove it from the cylinder head.

29 Starting on the intake camshaft, working in a spiral pattern from the outside inwards, slacken the camshaft bearing cap retaining bolts by half a turn at a time, to relieve the pressure of the valve springs on the bearing caps gradually and evenly (the reverse of illustration 12.39). Once the valve spring pressure has been relieved, the bolts can be fully unscrewed and removed along with the caps; the bearing caps are numbered intake camshaft 2 to 5, exhaust camshaft 6 to 9 to ensure the caps are correctly positioned on refitting **(see illustration 12.4b)**. Take care not to loose the locating dowels (where fitted).

Caution: If the bearing cap bolts are carelessly slackened, the bearing caps might break. If any bearing cap breaks then the complete cylinder head assembly must be renewed; the bearing caps are matched to the head and are not available separately.

30 Lift the camshaft out of the cylinder head and slide off the oil seal.

31 Repeat the operations described in paragraphs 28 and 29 and remove the exhaust camshaft.

32 Obtain sixteen small, clean plastic containers, and label them for identification. Alternatively, divide a larger container into compartments. Using a rubber sucker tool, lift the followers out from the top of the cylinder head and store each one in its respective fitted position **(see illustration 12.7)**.

Inspection

33 Refer to the information contained in paragraphs 8 and 9.

Refitting

34 Commence refitting by turning the crankshaft anti-clockwise by 60°. This will position Nos 1 and 4 pistons a third of the way down the bore, and prevent any chance of the valves touching the piston crowns as the camshafts are being fitted.

35 Thoroughly clean the mating surfaces of the camshaft bearing support and cylinder head, ensuring all traces of old sealant are removed.

36 Where removed, lubricate the followers

with clean engine oil and carefully insert each one into its original location in the cylinder head.

37 Lubricate the camshaft followers with molybdenum disulphide paste (or clean engine oil) then lay the camshafts in position.

38 Ensure the mating surfaces of the bearing caps and cylinder head are clean and dry and lubricate the camshaft journals and lobes with clean engine oil.

39 Ensure the locating dowels (where fitted) are in position then refit camshaft bearing caps 2 to 9 and the retaining bolts in their original locations on the cylinder head.

40 Working on the intake camshaft, tighten the bearing cap bolts by hand only then, working in a spiral pattern from the centre outwards, tighten the bolts by half a turn at a time to gradually impose the pressure of the valve springs on the bearing caps **(see illustration)**. Repeat this sequence until all bearing caps are in contact with the cylinder head then go around and tighten the camshaft bearing cap bolts to the specified torque.

Caution: If the bearing cap bolts are carelessly tightened, the bearing caps might break. If any bearing cap breaks then the complete cylinder head assembly must be renewed; the bearing caps are matched to the head and are not available separately.

41 Tighten the exhaust camshaft bearing cap bolts as described in paragraph 39.

42 Apply a smear of sealant to the mating surface of the camshaft bearing support, ensuring that the oil grooves remain free of sealant. Do not apply sealant to the area immediately adjacent to the bearing surface on the inside of the oil groove.

43 Place the camshaft bearing support in position and refit the four retaining bolts. Tighten the bolts to the specified torque, starting with the two inner bolts, then the two outer bolts.

44 If new components have been fitted, the valve clearances should now be checked and, if necessary adjusted, before proceeding with the refitting procedure. Temporarily refit the camshaft sprockets and secure with their retaining bolts, to allow the camshafts to be turned for the check. Refer to the procedure contained in Section 11, but as the timing belt is not fitted, check the clearances of each camshaft individually. Use the sprocket retaining bolt to turn the camshafts as necessary until the cam lobes for each pair of valves are pointing upward, away from the valves.

45 Once the valve clearances have been checked and if necessary adjusted, position the camshafts so that their timing slots are parallel with the cylinder head surface and refit the locking tool to the slots. Undo the retaining bolts and remove the camshaft sprockets.

46 Reconnect the wiring connector at the intake camshaft and exhaust camshaft VVT oil control valves.

47 Refit the timing belt rear cover as described in Section 6.

48 Fit new camshaft oil seals as described in Section 10.

49 Refit the camshaft sprockets as described in Section 8.

50 Align all the sprocket timing marks to bring the camshafts and crankshaft back to TDC then refit the timing belt as described in Section 7.

51 Refit the camshaft cover as described in Section 4.

---

13 Cylinder head – removal and refitting

Note: *The engine must be cold when removing the cylinder head. A new cylinder head gasket and new cylinder head bolts must be used on refitting.*

Removal

1 Depressurise the fuel system as described in Chapter 4A Section 5.

2 Disconnect the battery negative terminal (refer to Chapter 5A Section 4).

3 Apply the handbrake, then jack up the front of the vehicle and support it on axle stands (see *Jacking and vehicle support*). Remove the right-hand front roadwheel and the wheel arch liner inner cover for access to the right-hand side of the engine.

4 Drain the cooling system as described in Chapter 1A Section 28.

5 Remove the camshaft cover as described in Section 4.

6 Remove the spark plugs as described in Chapter 1A Section 31.

7 Remove the timing belt as described in Section 7.

8 Remove the camshaft sprockets, timing belt tensioner, and the timing belt idler roller, as described in Section 8.

9 Remove the rear timing belt cover with reference to Section 6.

10 Refer to Chapter 4A Section 18 and unbolt the exhaust front pipe from the catalytic converter, taking care to support the flexible section. **Note:** *Angular movement in excess*

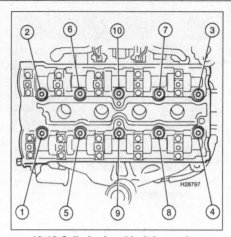

13.18 Cylinder head bolt loosening sequence

of 10° can cause permanent damage to the flexible section. Release the mounting rubbers and support the front of the exhaust pipe to one side.

11 Disconnect the wiring connectors from the following components:

a) *Crankshaft speed/position sensor.*
b) *Camshaft sensor(s).*
c) *Oil pressure switch.*
d) *Thermostat.*
e) *Coolant temperature sensor.*
f) *EGR valve.*

12 Release the cable ties and place the wiring loom to one side.

13 Remove the intake and exhaust manifolds as described in Chapter 4A.

14 Undo the five bolts and remove the metal coolant pipe from the coolant pump and thermostat housing.

15 Referring to Chapter 3 Section 9, disconnect the coolant hoses from the heater matrix unions on the engine compartment bulkhead.

16 Loosen the clips and remove the coolant hose from the radiator and thermostat housing.

17 Make a final check to ensure that all relevant hoses, pipes and wires have been disconnected.

18 Working in sequence, progressively loosen the cylinder head bolts **(see illustration)**. First loosen all the bolts by quarter of a turn, then

13.27 Ensure the head gasket is fitted with its OBEN/TOP marking uppermost

loosen all the bolts by half a turn, then finally slacken all the bolts fully and withdraw them from the cylinder head. Recover the washers (where fitted).

19 Lift the cylinder head from the cylinder block. If necessary, tap the cylinder head gently with a soft-faced mallet to free it from the block, but do not lever at the mating faces. Note that the cylinder head is located on dowels.

20 Recover the cylinder head gasket, and discard it.

Preparation for refitting

21 The mating faces of the cylinder head and block must be perfectly clean before refitting the head. Use a scraper to remove all traces of gasket and carbon, and also clean the tops of the pistons. Take particular care with the aluminium surfaces, as the soft metal is damaged easily. Also, make sure that debris is not allowed to enter the oil and water channels – this is particularly important for the oil circuit, as carbon could block the oil supply to the camshaft or crankshaft bearings. Using adhesive tape and paper, seal the water, oil and bolt holes in the cylinder block. To prevent carbon entering the gap between the pistons and bores, smear a little grease in the gap. After cleaning the piston, rotate the crankshaft so that the piston moves down the bore, then wipe out the grease and carbon with a cloth rag. Clean the other piston crowns in the same way.

22 Check the block and head for nicks, deep scratches and other damage. If slight, they may be removed carefully with a file. More serious damage may be repaired by machining, but this is a specialist job.

23 If warpage of the cylinder head is suspected, use a straight-edge to check it for distortion. Refer to Chapter 2E Section 7 if necessary.

24 Ensure that the cylinder head bolt holes in the crankcase are clean and free of oil. Syringe or soak up any oil left in the bolt holes. This is most important in order that the correct bolt tightening torque can be applied and to prevent the possibility of the block being cracked by hydraulic pressure when the bolts are tightened.

25 Renew the cylinder head bolts regardless of their apparent condition.

Refitting

26 Ensure that the two locating dowels are in position at each end of the cylinder block/crankcase surface.

27 Fit the new cylinder head gasket to the block, making sure it is fitted with the correct way up with its OBEN/TOP mark uppermost **(see illustration)**.

28 Carefully refit the cylinder head, locating it on the dowels.

29 Fit the washers (where applicable) to the new cylinder head bolts then carefully insert them into position (do not drop), tightening them finger-tight only at this stage.

30 Working progressively and in sequence, first tighten all the cylinder head bolts to the Stage 1 torque setting **(see illustrations)**.
31 Once all bolts have been tightened to the Stage 1 torque, again working in sequence, tighten each bolt through its specified Stage 2 angle, using a socket and extension bar. It is recommended that an angle-measuring gauge is used during this stage of the tightening, to ensure accuracy **(see illustration)**.
32 Working in the specified sequence, go around again and tighten all bolts through the specified Stage 3 angle.
33 Working again in the specified sequence, go around and tighten all bolts through the specified Stage 4 angle.
34 Finally go around in the specified sequence again and tighten all bolts through the specified Stage 5 angle.
35 Using new gaskets, refit the metal coolant pipe to the coolant pump and thermostat housing, tightening the bolts securely.
36 Reconnect the coolant hose to the radiator and thermostat housing.
37 Reconnect the coolant hoses to the heater matrix unions on the engine compartment bulkhead.
38 Refit the intake and exhaust manifolds as described in Chapter 4A.
39 Reconnect the wiring to the components listed in paragraph 11, then secure the wiring with cable ties.
40 Refer to Chapter 4A Section 18 and refit the exhaust front pipe to the exhaust manifold. Refit the mounting rubbers.
41 Refit the rear timing belt cover with reference to Section 6.
42 Refit the camshaft sprockets, timing belt tensioner, and the timing belt idler roller, with reference to Section 8.
43 Refit the timing belt as described in Section 7.
44 Refit the spark plugs as described in Chapter 1A Section 31.
45 Refit the camshaft cover as described in Section 4.
46 Refit the wheel arch liner inner cover and front roadwheel, then lower the vehicle to the ground.

47 Reconnect the battery negative terminal (Chapter 5A Section 4)
48 Check that all relevant hoses, pipes and wires, etc, have been reconnected. Check the security of the fuel hose connections.
49 Refill and bleed the cooling system with reference to Chapter 1A Section 28.
50 When the engine is started, check for signs of oil or coolant leakage.

14 Sump – removal and refitting

Removal

1 Disconnect the battery negative terminal (refer to Chapter 5A Section 4).
2 Apply the handbrake, then jack up the front of the vehicle and support it on axle stands (see *Jacking and vehicle support*). Remove the right-hand front roadwheel and the wheel arch liner inner cover for access to the right-hand side of the engine.
3 Drain the engine oil as, then fit a new sealing washer and refit the drain plug, tightening it to the specified torque (Chapter 1A Section 6).
4 Remove the exhaust system as described in Chapter 4A Section 18.
5 Disconnect the wiring connector from the oil level sensor.
6 Undo the retaining bolt and remove the oil dipstick guide tube.
7 Slacken and remove the bolts securing the sump flange to the transmission housing.
8 On early models, remove the rubber plugs from the transmission end of the sump flange to gain access to the sump end retaining bolts.
9 Progressively slacken and remove the bolts securing the sump to the base of the cylinder block/oil pump. Using a wide-bladed scraper or similar tool inserted between the sump and cylinder block, carefully break the joint, then remove the sump from under the car.

Refitting

10 Thoroughly clean the sump and baffle plate, then remove all traces of sealer and oil from the mating surfaces of the sump and cylinder block.

11 Apply a smear of suitable sealant (available form Vauxhall/Opel dealers) to the areas of the cylinder block mating surface around the areas of the of the oil pump housing and rear main bearing cap joints.
12 Apply a bead of suitable sealant (available from Vauxhall/Opel dealers) approximately 2.5 mm thick to the sealing surface of the sump. Around the No 5 main bearing cap area, increase the thickness of the bead to 3.5 mm.
13 Offer up the sump, and loosely refit all the retaining bolts. Working out from the centre in a diagonal sequence, progressively tighten the bolts securing the sump to the cylinder block/oil pump to their specified torque setting.
14 Tighten the bolts securing the sump flange to the transmission housing to their specified torque settings. Refit the rubber plugs to the sump flange cut-outs (where fitted).
15 Refit the oil dipstick guide tube.
16 Refit the exhaust system (see Chapter 4A Section 18) and reconnect the oil level sender wiring connector.
17 Refit the wheel arch liner inner cover and front roadwheel, then lower the vehicle to the ground. Fill the engine with fresh oil, with reference to Chapter 1A Section 6.

15 Oil pump – removal, overhaul and refitting

Non-VVT engines
Removal

1 Remove the alternator as described in Chapter 5A Section 8.
2 Remove the timing belt as described in Section 7.
3 Remove the timing belt tensioner and Idler pulley as described in Section 8.
4 Remove the sump as described in Section 14.
5 Undo the two bolts securing the metal coolant pipe to the rear of the coolant pump.
6 Slacken and remove the eight retaining bolts (noting their different lengths) then slide the oil pump housing assembly off of the end of the crankshaft, taking great care not to lose the locating dowels. Remove the housing gasket and discard it.

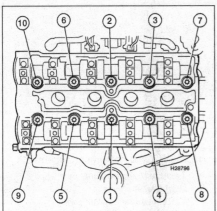
13.30a Cylinder head bolt tightening sequence

13.30b Tighten the cylinder head bolts to the specified Stage 1 torque setting ...

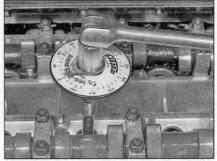
13.31 ... and then through the various specified angles as described in the text

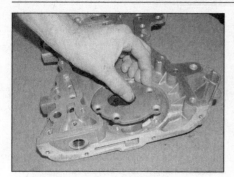

15.7 Remove the securing screws and withdraw the oil pump cover from the rear of the housing

15.9a Unscrew the oil pressure relief valve cap ...

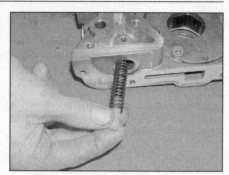

15.9b ... then withdraw the spring ...

15.9c ... and the plunger

15.11 Check the oil pump rotor endfloat using a straight-edge and feeler gauge

Overhaul

7 Remove the securing screws/bolts and withdraw the oil pump cover from the rear of the oil pump housing **(see illustration)**.

8 Remove the inner and outer rotor from the pump housing, noting which way round they are fitted, and wipe them clean. Also clean the rotor location in the oil pump housing.

9 The oil pressure relief valve components can also be removed from the oil pump housing by unscrewing the cap. Withdraw the cap, spring and plunger **(see illustrations)**.

10 Locate the inner and outer rotor back in the oil pump housing, ensuring they are fitted the right way round as noted during removal.

11 Check the clearance between the end faces of the rotors and the housing (endfloat) using a straight-edge and a feeler gauge **(see illustration)**.

12 If the clearance is outside the specified limits, renew the components as necessary.

13 Examine the pressure relief valve spring and plunger, and renew if any sign of damage or wear is evident.

14 Ensure that the rotor location in the interior of the oil pump housing is scrupulously clean before commencing reassembly.

15 Thoroughly clean the pressure relief valve components, and lubricate them with clean engine oil before refitting. Insert the plunger and spring, then refit the cap and tighten to the specified torque.

16 Ensure that the rotors are clean, then lubricate them with clean engine oil, and refit them to the pump body ensuring they are fitted the right way round as noted during removal.

17 Wipe clean the mating faces of the rear cover and the pump housing, then refit the rear cover. Refit and tighten the securing screws securely. Prime the oil pump by filling it with clean engine oil whilst rotating the inner rotor.

Refitting

18 Prior to refitting, carefully lever out the crankshaft oil seal using a flat-bladed screwdriver. Fit the new oil seal, ensuring its sealing lip is facing inwards, and press it squarely into the housing using a tubular drift

which bears only on the hard outer edge of the seal. Press the seal into position so that it is flush with the housing.

19 Ensure the mating surfaces of the oil pump housing and cylinder block are clean and dry and the locating dowels are in position.

20 Fit a new gasket to the cylinder block.

21 Carefully manoeuvre the oil pump into position and engage the inner rotor with the crankshaft end. Locate the pump on the dowels, taking great care not damage the oil seal lip.

22 Refit the pump housing retaining bolts in their original locations and tighten them to the specified torque.

23 Using a new gasket, refit the metal coolant pipe flange to the coolant pump and tighten the retaining bolts to the specified torque.

24 Refit the sump as described in Section 14.

25 Refit the timing belt tensioner and idler pulley, then refit the timing belt as described in Sections 8 and 7.

26 Refit the alternator as described in Chapter 5A Section 8.

27 On completion, fit a new oil filter and fill the engine with clean oil as described in Chapter 1A Section 6.

VVT engines

Removal

28 Drain the cooling system as described in Chapter 1A Section 28.

29 Remove the alternator as described in Chapter 5A Section 8.

30 Remove the exhaust manifold as described in Chapter 4A Section 17.

31 Remove the timing belt as described in Section 7.

32 Remove the timing belt tensioner and idler pulley, and the crankshaft sprocket as described in Section 8.

33 Remove the sump as described in Section 14.

34 Release the clamp and disconnect the coolant hose from the coolant pump.

35 Undo the two bolts securing the upper metal coolant pipe to the rear of the coolant pump **(see illustration)**.

36 Undo the support bracket bolt securing the lower metal coolant pipe to the oil filter housing.

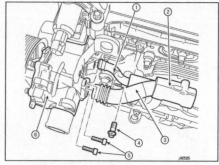

15.35 Oil pump housing attachements

1 Lower metal coolant pipe
2 Oil filter housing
3 Upper metal coolant pipe
4 Support bracket bolt
5 Upper metal coolant pipe bolts
6 Coolant pump housing

37 Slacken and remove the eight retaining bolts (noting their different lengths) then slide the oil pump housing assembly off of the end of the crankshaft, taking great care not to lose the locating dowels. Remove the housing gasket and discard it.

38 Remove the metal coolant pipes and renew the four seals.

Overhaul

39 Refer to the information contained in paragraphs 7 to 17.

Refitting

40 Prior to refitting, carefully lever out the crankshaft oil seal using a flat-bladed screwdriver. Fit the new oil seal, ensuring its sealing lip is facing inwards, and press it squarely into the housing using a tubular drift which bears only on the hard outer edge of the seal. Press the seal into position so that it is flush with the housing.

41 Refit the two previously removed metal coolant pipes.

42 Ensure the mating surfaces of the oil pump housing and cylinder block are clean and dry and the locating dowels are in position.

43 Fit a new gasket to the cylinder block.

44 Carefully manoeuvre the oil pump into position and engage the inner rotor with the crankshaft end. Engage the coolant pipes, then locate the pump on the dowels, taking great care not to damage the oil seal lip.

45 Refit the pump housing retaining bolts in their original locations and tighten them to the specified torque.

46 Refit the metal coolant pipe retaining bolts and tighten securely.

47 Reconnect the coolant hose to the pump and secure with the retaining clip.

48 Refit the sump as described in Section 14.

49 Refit the timing belt tensioner and idler pulley and the crankshaft sprocket, then refit the timing belt as described in Sections 8 and 7.

50 Refit the exhaust manifold as described in Chapter 4A Section 17.

51 Refit the alternator as described in Chapter 5A Section 8.

52 On completion, refer to Chapter 1A Section 6 and fit a new oil filter and fill the engine with clean oil, then refill the cooling system.

16 Oil filter housing (VVT engines) – removal and refitting

Removal

1 The oil filter housing with integral oil cooler is located at the front, left-hand side of the cylinder block.

2 Disconnect the battery negative terminal (refer to Chapter 5A Section 4).

3 Apply the handbrake, then jack up the front of the vehicle and support it on axle stands (see *Jacking and vehicle support*).

4 Drain the cooling system as described in Chapter 1A Section 28.

5 Remove the engine oil filter element as described in Chapter 1A Section 6.

6 Remove the exhaust manifold as described in Chapter 4A Section 17.

7 Undo the two bolts and release the coolant pipe flange from the thermostat housing. Push the coolant pipe into the oil filter housing.

8 Undo the two bolts securing the wiring harness bracket and coolant pipe flange to the rear of the coolant pump. Move the wiring harness bracket to one side and release the pipe flange from the coolant pump. Push the coolant pipe into the oil filter housing.

9 Undo the bolt securing the remaining coolant pipe to the oil filter housing and push the pipe into the housing.

10 Undo the four bolts securing the oil filter housing to the cylinder block. Remove the housing and recover the two gaskets. Note that new gaskets will be required for refitting.

Refitting

11 Thoroughly clean the oil filter housing and cylinder block mating faces, then fit the two new gaskets to the filter housing.

12 Position the oil filter housing on the cylinder block and refit the retaining bolts. Tighten the bolts to the specified torque.

13 Refit the coolant pipe to the oil filter housing and tighten the retaining bolt securely.

14 Using new gaskets/seals where necessary, refit the coolant pipe and wiring harness bracket to the coolant pump and securely tighten the two retaining bolts.

15 Using new gaskets/seals where necessary, refit the coolant pipe to the thermostat housing and securely tighten the retaining bolts.

16 Refit the exhaust manifold as described in Chapter 4A Section 17.

17 Lower the car to the ground then fit a new oil filter element as described in Chapter 1A Section 6.

18 Check, and if necessary, top-up the engine oil as described in *Weekly checks*.

19 Refill the cooling system as described in Chapter 1A Section 28, then reconnect the battery negative terminal.

17 Crankshaft oil seals – renewal

Right-hand (timing belt end)

1 Remove the crankshaft sprocket as described in Section 8.

2 Carefully punch or drill two small holes opposite each other in the oil seal. Screw a self-tapping screw into each and pull on the screws with pliers to extract the seal **(see illustration)**.

Caution: Great care must be taken to avoid damage to the oil pump.

3 Clean the seal housing and polish off any burrs or raised edges which may have caused the seal to fail in the first place.

4 Carefully ease the new seal into position on the end of the crankshaft. Press the seal squarely into position until it is flush with the housing. If necessary, a suitable tubular drift, such as a socket, which bears only on the hard outer edge of the seal can be used to tap the seal into position **(see illustration)**. Take great care not to damage the seal lips during fitting and ensure that the seal lips face inwards.

5 Wash off any traces of oil, then refit the crankshaft sprocket as described in Section 8.

Left-hand (flywheel end)

6 Remove the flywheel as described in Section 18.

7 Renew the seal as described in paragraphs 2 to 4 **(see illustration)**.

8 Refit the flywheel as described in Section 18.

17.2 Removing the crankshaft oil seal

17.4 Fitting a new crankshaft oil seal

17.7 Left-hand crankshaft oil seal – transmission and flywheel removed

18 Flywheel/driveplate – removal, inspection and refitting

Removal

Note: *New flywheel/driveplate retaining bolts will be required on refitting.*

Manual transmission models

1 Remove remove the clutch assembly as described in Chapter 6 Section 6.
2 Prevent the flywheel from turning by locking the ring gear teeth with a similar arrangement to that shown **(see illustration)**.
3 Slacken and remove the retaining bolts and remove the flywheel **(see illustrations)**.
Caution: Take care, as the flywheel is heavy.

Automatic transmission models

4 Remove the transmission as described in Chapter 7B Section 13, then remove the driveplate as described in paragraphs 2 and 3.

Inspection

Single-mass (solid) flywheel

5 Examine the flywheel for wear or chipping of the ring gear teeth. Renewal of the ring gear is not possible and if the wear or chipping is significant, a new flywheel will be required.
6 Examine the flywheel for scoring of the clutch face. If the clutch face is scored significantly, a new flywheel will be required.
7 If there is any doubt about the condition of the flywheel, seek the advice of a Vauxhall/Opel dealer or engine reconditioning specialist.

Dual-mass flywheel

8 A dual-mass flywheel has the effect of reducing engine and transmission vibrations and harshness. The flywheel consists of a primary mass and a secondary mass constructed in such a way that the secondary mass is allowed to rotate slightly in relation to the primary mass. Springs within the assembly restrict this movement to set limits.
9 Dual-mass flywheels have earned an unenviable reputation for unreliability and have been known to fail at quite low mileages (sometimes as low as 20 000 miles). As well as the checks described above in paragraphs 7 and 8, some additional checks should be performed as follows.
10 Look through the bolt hole and inspection openings in the secondary mass and check for any visible damage in the area of the centre bearing.
11 Place your thumbs on the clutch face of the secondary mass at the 3 o'clock and 9 o'clock positions and try to rock it. The maximum movement should not exceed 3 mm. Repeat this check with your thumbs at the 12 o'clock and 6 o'clock positions.
12 Rotate the secondary mass clockwise and anti-clockwise. It should move freely in both directions until spring resistance is felt, with no abnormal grating or rattling noises. The maximum rotational movement should not exceed a distance of eight teeth of the ring gear.
13 If there is any doubt about the condition of the flywheel, seek the advice of a Vauxhall/Opel dealer or engine reconditioning specialist. They will be able to advise if the flywheel is an acceptable condition, or whether renewal is necessary.

Driveplate

14 Closely examine the driveplate and ring gear teeth for signs of wear or damage and check the driveplate surface for any signs of cracks.
15 If there is any doubt about the condition of the driveplate, seek the advice of a Vauxhall/Opel dealer or engine reconditioning specialist.

Refitting

Manual transmission models

16 Clean the mating surfaces of the flywheel and crankshaft.
17 Offer up the flywheel and engage it on the crankshaft. Apply a drop of locking compound to the threads of each new flywheel retaining bolt (unless they are already precoated) and install the new bolts.
18 Lock the flywheel by the method used on removal then, working in a diagonal sequence, evenly and progressively tighten the retaining bolts to the specified torque and through the specified angles.
19 Refit the clutch as described in Chapter 6 Section 6, then remove the locking tool and refit the transmission as described in Chapter 7A Section 7 or Chapter 7C Section 7.

Automatic transmission models

20 Clean the mating surfaces of the driveplate and crankshaft.
21 Offer up the driveplate and engage it on the crankshaft. Apply a drop of locking compound to the threads of each new driveplate retaining bolt (unless they are already precoated) and install the new bolts.
22 Lock the driveplate by the method used on removal then, working in a diagonal sequence, evenly and progressively tighten the retaining bolts to the specified torque.
23 Remove the locking tool, and refit the transmission as described in Chapter 7B Section 13.

19 Engine/transmission mountings – inspection and renewal

Inspection

1 To improve access, firmly apply the handbrake, then jack up the front of the vehicle and support it on axle stands (see *Jacking and vehicle support*).
2 Check the mounting blocks (rubbers) to see if they are cracked, hardened or separated from the metal at any point. Renew the mounting block if any such damage or deterioration is evident.
3 Check that all the mounting securing nuts and bolts are securely tightened, using a torque wrench to check if possible.
4 Using a large screwdriver, or a similar tool, check for wear in the mounting blocks by carefully levering against them to check for free play. Where this is not possible, enlist the aid of an assistant to move the engine/ transmission unit back-and-forth, and from side-to-side, while you observe the mountings. While some free play is to be expected, even from new components,

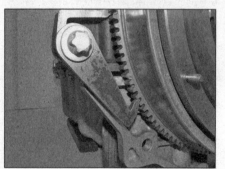

18.2 Prevent the flywheel from turning by locking the ring gear teeth with a suitable tool

18.3a Unscrew the retaining bolts...

18.3b ...and remove the flywheel

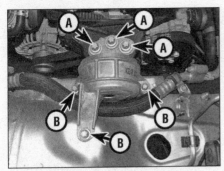

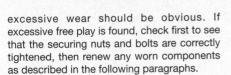

19.7 Right-hand engine mounting-to-engine bracket bolts (A) and mounting-to-body bolts (B)

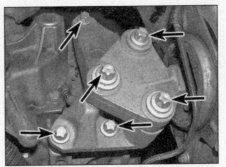

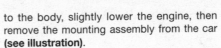

19.13 Left-hand engine mounting bracket and transmission bracket bolts (arrowed)

19.14 Undo the four bolts and remove the left-hand mounting from the body

excessive wear should be obvious. If excessive free play is found, check first to see that the securing nuts and bolts are correctly tightened, then renew any worn components as described in the following paragraphs.

Renewal

Note: *Before slackening any of the engine mounting bolts/nuts, the relative positions of the mountings to their various brackets should be marked to ensure correct alignment upon refitting.*

Right-hand mounting

5 With reference to Chapter 4A Section 2, remove the air cleaner housing.
6 Support the weight of the engine using a trolley jack with a block of wood placed on its head.
7 Remove the three bolts securing the right-hand engine mounting to the engine mounting support bracket **(see illustration)**.
8 Undo the bolts securing the mounting to the body, and withdraw the bracket with the mounting. If necessary, the engine mounting bracket may be unbolted from the cylinder block.
9 If required, the mounting can be separated by undoing the single bolt in the centre of the rubber element.
10 Refitting is a reversal of removal. Tighten the bolts to the specified torque.

Left-hand mounting

11 Remove the battery and battery tray as described in Chapter 5A Section 4.
12 Support the weight of the transmission using a trolley jack with a block of wood placed on its head.
13 Unscrew the bolts securing the mounting bracket to the transmission bracket, and the bolts securing the transmission bracket to the transmission **(see illustration)**.
14 Undo the four bolts securing the mounting

to the body, slightly lower the engine, then remove the mounting assembly from the car **(see illustration)**.
15 If necessary, undo the through-bolt and separate the rubber mounting from the mounting bracket.
16 Refitting is a reversal of removal. Ensure all bolts are tightened to their specified torques.

Front mounting/torque link

17 Firmly apply the handbrake, then jack up the front of the car and support it securely on axle stands (see *Jacking and vehicle support*).
18 Support the weight of the engine/transmission using a trolley jack with a block of wood placed on its head.
19 Slacken and remove the nut and washer securing the mounting to the subframe, then withdraw the bolt **(see illustration)**.
20 Undo the two bolts securing the mounting bracket to the transmission, then manoeuvre the mounting and bracket out of position.
21 Refitting is a reversal of removal. Ensure all bolts/nuts are tightened to their specified torques.

Rear mounting/torque link

22 Firmly apply the handbrake, then jack up the front of the car and support it securely on axle stands (see *Jacking and vehicle support*).
23 Support the weight of the engine/transmission using a trolley jack with a block of wood placed on its head. Position the jack underneath the transmission and raise the transmission slightly to remove all load from the rear mounting.
24 Slacken and remove the two bolts securing the rear mounting to the subframe, and the nut securing the mounting to the transmission bracket, then manoeuvre the assembly out from underneath the vehicle **(see illustration)**.
25 On refitting, manoeuvre the mounting into position and refit the bolts/nuts securing it to the subframe. Ensure that the mounting is correctly engaged with the transmission bracket and fit the mounting-to-bracket retaining nut. Tighten the mounting bolts/nuts to their specified torque settings. Remove the jack from underneath the engine/transmission.
26 Lower the vehicle to the ground.

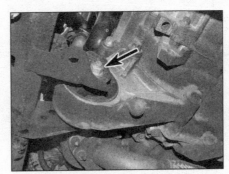

19.19 Front engine mounting/torque link-to-subframe nut/bolt (arrowed)

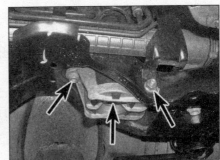

19.24 Rear engine mounting/torque link retaining bolts and nut (arrowed)

Notes

Chapter 2 Part B
1.7 litre diesel engine in-car repair procedures

Contents

Section number

Camshaft cover – removal and refitting 4
Camshaft housing – removal and refitting 12
Camshaft oil seal – renewal 9
Camshafts and followers – removal, inspection and refitting 11
Compression and leakdown tests – description and interpretation. . 2
Crankshaft oil seals – renewal 19
Crankshaft pulley – removal and refitting. 5
Cylinder head – removal and refitting. 13
Engine/transmission mountings – inspection and renewal 20
Flywheel – removal, inspection and refitting 18

Section number

General Information 1
Oil filter housing – removal and refitting. 17
Oil pump – removal, inspection and refitting 15
Oil pump seal – renewal. 16
Sump – removal and refitting 14
Timing belt – removal and refitting. 7
Timing belt covers – removal and refitting. 6
Timing belt tensioner and sprockets – removal and refitting 8
Top Dead Centre (TDC) for No 1 piston – locating. 3
Valve clearances – checking and adjustment 10

Degrees of difficulty

Easy, suitable for novice with little experience 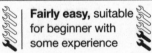 | **Fairly easy,** suitable for beginner with some experience | **Fairly difficult,** suitable for competent DIY mechanic | **Difficult,** suitable for experienced DIY mechanic | **Very difficult,** suitable for expert DIY or professional

Specifications

General

Engine type. . . . . Four-cylinder, in-line, water-cooled. Belt-driven double overhead camshafts, 16 valves
Manufacturer's engine codes* A17DTJ, A17DTR
Bore . . . . 79.0 mm
Stroke . . . . 86.0 mm
Capacity . . . . 1686 cc
Firing order. . . . . 1-3-4-2 (No 1 cylinder at timing belt end)
Direction of crankshaft rotation . . . . Clockwise (viewed from timing belt end of engine)
Compression ratio 18.2: 1
Output:
  A17DTR . . . . 92 kW @ 4000 rpm, 280 Nm @ 2300 rpm
  A17DTJ. . . . . 81 kW @ 3800 rpm, 260 Nm @ 2300 rpm
*For details of engine code location, see 'Vehicle identification'

Compression pressures
Maximum difference between any two cylinders. . . . . 1.5 bar

Valve clearances
Engine cold:
  Inlet and exhaust . . . . 0.40 ± 0.05 mm

Lubrication system
Oil pump type. . . . . Rotor-type, driven by timing belt
Oil pressure at 80ºC (approximate) . . . . 1.5 bar @ idle speed, 3.5 bar @ 4000 rpm

Oil pump clearances:	Standard	Service limit
Outer rotor-to-body clearance	0.24 to 0.36 mm	0.40 mm
Inner-to-outer rotor clearance	0.13 to 0.15 mm	0.20 mm
Rotor endfloat.	0.035 to 0.100 mm	0.150 mm

Torque wrench settings

	Nm	lbf ft
Auxiliary drive belt tensioner bolt	90	66
Auxiliary drivebelt guide roller bolt	50	37
Baffle plate-to-cylinder block bolts	19	14
Camshaft bearing cap bolts/nuts	27	20
Camshaft cover bolts	10	7
Camshaft housing-to-cylinder head:		
M8 bolts	22	16
M10 bolts	27	20
Camshaft sprocket bolt	111	82
Coolant pump pulley bolts	15	11
Connecting rod big-end bearing cap nuts*:		
Stage 1	25	18
Stage 2	Angle-tighten a further 100°	
Stage 3	Angle-tighten a further 15°	
Crankshaft pulley bolts	20	15
Crankshaft oil seal housing bolts	10	7
Crankshaft sprocket bolt	196	145
Cylinder head bolts*:		
Stage 1	50	37
Stage 2	Angle-tighten a further 90°	
Stage 3	Angle-tighten a further 90°	
Driveshaft support bearing housing bolts	58	43
Engine mountings:		
Front mounting/torque link:		
Mounting-to-transmission bolts	80	60
Mounting to subframe	55	41
Left-hand mounting:		
Mounting-to-body bolts	20	15
Mounting bracket-to-transmission bracket	55	41
Rear mounting/torque link:		
Mounting-to-transmission bracket	55	41
Mounting-to-subframe	55	41
Right-hand mounting:		
Mounting bracket-to-engine	55	41
Mounting-to-body	55	41
Mounting-to-mounting bracket	55	41
Engine-to-transmission bolts:		
M10 bolts	40	32
M12 bolts	60	44
Flywheel bolts*:		
Stage 1	85	63
Stage 2	Angle-tighten a further 30°	
Stage 3	Angle-tighten a further 15°	
High-pressure fuel pipe union nuts	25	18
High-pressure fuel pump sprocket nut	69	51
Main bearing cap bolts*:		
Stage 1	39	29
Stage 2	Angle-tighten a further 60°	
Oil dipstick guide tube bolts	10	7
Oil filter housing to cylinder block:		
Exhaust pressure sensor bracket bolt	20	15
Filter housing flange bolt	46	34
Filter housing hollow bolt	110	81
Oil pump cover retaining bolts	10	7
Oil pump sprocket nut	60	44
Oil pump pick-up/strainer bolts	26	19
Sump bolts:		
Drain plug	20	15
Temperature sensor bracket bolt	46	34
Main casting-to-block bolts	10	7
Main casting-to-transmission bolts	40	32
Sump pan-to-main casting bolts	10	7
Roadwheel nuts	110	81
Timing belt cover bolts	10	7
Timing belt idler pulley bolt	80	59
Timing belt tensioner pulley bolt	49	36

*Use new fasteners

1 General Information

How to use this Chapter

1 This Part of Chapter 2 describes the repair procedures which can reasonably be carried out on the engine while it remains in the vehicle. If the engine has been removed from the vehicle and is being dismantled as described in Chapter 2E, any preliminary dismantling procedures can be ignored.

2 Note that, while it may be possible physically to overhaul items such as the piston/connecting rod assemblies while the engine is in the vehicle, such tasks are not usually carried out as separate operations, and usually require the execution of several additional procedures (not to mention the cleaning of components and of oil ways); for this reason, all such tasks are classed as major overhaul procedures, and are described in Chapter 2E.

3 Chapter 2E describes the removal of the engine/transmission unit from the vehicle, and the full overhaul procedures which can then be carried out.

Engine description

4 The 1.7 litre common-rail diesel engine is of the sixteen-valve, in-line four-cylinder, double overhead camshaft (DOHC) type, mounted transversely at the front of the car with the transmission attached to its left-hand end.

5 The crankshaft runs in five main bearings. Thrustwashers are fitted to No 2 main bearing shell (upper half) to control crankshaft endfloat.

6 The connecting rods rotate on horizontally-split bearing shells at their big-ends. The pistons are attached to the connecting rods by gudgeon pins, which are a sliding fit in the connecting rod small-end eyes and retained by circlips. The aluminium-alloy pistons are fitted with three piston rings – two compression rings and an oil control ring.

7 The cylinder block is made of cast iron and the cylinder bores are an integral part of the block. On this type of engine the cylinder bores are sometimes referred to as having dry liners.

8 The inlet and exhaust valves are each closed by coil springs, and operate in guides pressed into the cylinder head.

9 The inlet camshaft is driven by the crankshaft by a timing belt and rotates directly in the camshaft housing. The exhaust camshaft is driven by the inlet camshaft via a spur gear. The camshafts operate the valves via followers, which are situated directly below the camshafts. Valve clearances are adjusted using camshaft followers of different thickness.

10 Lubrication is by means of an oil pump, which is driven by the timing belt. It draws oil through a strainer located in the sump, and then forces it through an externally-mounted filter into galleries in the cylinder block/ crankcase. From there, the oil is distributed to the crankshaft (main bearings) and camshaft. The big-end bearings are supplied with oil via internal drillings in the crankshaft, while the camshaft bearings also receive a pressurised supply. The camshaft lobes and valves are lubricated by splash, as are all other engine components. An oil cooler is fitted to keep the oil temperature stable under arduous operating conditions.

Operations with engine in place

11 The following operations can be carried out without having to remove the engine from the vehicle.

a) *Compression pressure testing.*
b) *Camshaft cover – removal and refitting.*
c) *Timing belt cover – removal and refitting.*
d) *Timing belt – removal and refitting.*
e) *Timing belt tensioner and sprockets – removal and refitting.*
f) *Valve clearances – checking and adjustment.*
g) *Camshaft and followers – removal, inspection and refitting.*
h) *Cylinder head – removal and refitting.*
i) *Connecting rods and pistons – removal and refitting*.*
j) *Sump – removal and refitting.*
k) *Oil pump – removal, overhaul and refitting.*
l) *Oil cooler – removal and refitting.*
m) *Crankshaft oil seals – renewal.*
n) *Engine/transmission mountings – inspection and renewal.*
o) *Flywheel – removal, inspection and refitting.*
p) *Camshaft housing – removal and refitting.*

Note: **Although the operation marked with an asterisk can be carried out with the engine in the car after removal of the sump, it is better for the engine to be removed, in the interests of cleanliness and improved access. For this reason, the procedure is described in Chapter 2E Section 9.*

2 Compression and leakdown tests – description and interpretation

Compression test

Note: *A compression tester specifically designed for diesel engines must be used for this test.*

Note: *The battery must be in a good state of charge, the air filter must be clean, and the engine should be at normal operating temperature.*

1 When engine performance is down, or if misfiring occurs which cannot be attributed to the fuel system, a compression test can provide diagnostic clues as to the engine's condition. If the test is performed regularly, it can give warning of trouble before any other symptoms become apparent.

2 The tester is connected to an adapter which screws into the glow plug holes. It is unlikely to be worthwhile buying such a tester for occasional use, but it may be possible to borrow or hire one – if not, have the test performed by a Vauxhall/Opel dealer, or suitably-equipped garage. If the necessary equipment is available, proceed as follows.

3 Remove the glow plugs as described in Chapter 5A, then open the cover on the engine compartment fuse/relay box and remove the fuel pump relay **(see illustrations)**.

4 Screw the compression tester adapter in to the glow plug hole of No 1 cylinder.

5 With the help of an assistant, crank the engine on the starter motor; after one or two revolutions, the compression pressure should build-up to a maximum figure, and then stabilise. Record the highest reading obtained.

6 Repeat the test on the remaining cylinders, recording the pressure in each.

7 All cylinders should produce very similar pressures; any difference greater than the maximum figure given in the Specifications indicates the existence of a fault. Note that the compression should build-up quickly in a healthy engine; low compression on the first stroke, followed by gradually-increasing pressure on successive strokes, indicates worn piston rings. A low compression reading on the first stroke, which does not build-up during successive strokes, indicates leaking valves or a blown head gasket (a cracked head could also be the cause). **Note:** *The cause of poor compression is less easy to establish on a diesel engine than on a petrol one. The effect of introducing oil into the cylinders ('wet' testing) is not conclusive, because there is a risk that the oil will sit in the recess on the piston crown instead of passing to the rings.*

2.3a Open the cover on the fuse/relay box ...

2.3b ... and remove the fuel pump relay (arrowed)

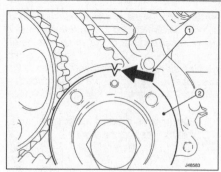

3.6 Rotate the crankshaft until the notch (1) on the sprocket (2) is aligned with the mark on the oil pump housing

3.8a The camshaft sprocket can be locked using a 6 mm bolt (arrowed)...

3.8b ...and the high-pressure fuel pump sprocket by an 8 mm bolt (arrowed)

8 On completion of the test, refit the fuel pump relay, then refit the glow plugs as described in Chapter 5A.

Leakdown test

9 A leakdown test measures the rate at which compressed air fed into the cylinder is lost. It is an alternative to a compression test, and in many ways it is better, since the escaping air provides easy identification of where pressure loss is occurring (piston rings, valves or head gasket).

10 The equipment needed for leakdown testing is unlikely to be available to the home mechanic. If poor compression is suspected, have the test performed by a Vauxhall/Opel dealer, or suitably-equipped garage.

3 Top Dead Centre (TDC) for No 1 piston – locating

Note: If the engine is to be locked in position with No 1 piston at TDC on its compression stroke then two M6 bolts will be required.

1 In its travel up and down its cylinder bore, Top Dead Centre (TDC) is the highest point that each piston reaches as the crankshaft rotates. While each piston reaches TDC both at the top of the compression stroke and again at the top of the exhaust stroke, for the

purpose of timing the engine, TDC refers to the piston position (usually number 1) at the top of its compression stroke.

2 Number 1 piston (and cylinder) is at the right-hand (timing belt) end of the engine, and its TDC position is located as follows. Note that the crankshaft rotates clockwise when viewed from the right-hand side of the car.

3 Disconnect the battery negative terminal (refer to Chapter 5A Section 4).

4 Firmly apply the handbrake, then jack up the front of the car and support it securely on axle stands (see *Jacking and vehicle support*). Remove the right-hand front roadwheel.

5 Remove the timing belt upper and lower covers as described in Section 6.

6 Using a socket and extension bar on the crankshaft sprocket bolt, rotate the crankshaft until the notch on the sprocket is aligned with the mark on the oil pump housing **(see illustration)**. Once the notch is correctly aligned, No 1 and 4 pistons are at TDC.

7 To determine which piston is at TDC on its compression stroke, check the position of the timing holes in the camshaft and high-pressure fuel pump sprockets. When No 1 piston is at TDC on its compression stroke, both sprocket holes will be aligned with the threaded holes in the cylinder head/block, and both exhaust camshaft lobes for cylinder No 1 are pointing upwards if viewed through the oil filler hole. If the timing holes are out of alignment, continue rotating the crankshaft until they align. Note

that because the sprockets are of different diameters, it may take up to six revolutions of the crankshaft to achieve alignment.

8 With No 1 piston at TDC on its compression stroke, if necessary, the camshaft and high-pressure fuel pump sprockets can be locked in position. Secure the camshaft sprocket in position by screwing an M6 bolt into the hole in the cylinder head and lock the high-pressure fuel pump sprocket in position by screwing an M8 bolt into the cylinder block **(see illustrations)**.

4 Camshaft cover – removal and refitting

Removal

 Warning: Refer to the information contained in Chapter 4B Section 2 before proceeding.

1 Disconnect the battery negative terminal (refer to Chapter 5A Section 4).

2 Remove the air cleaner housing as described in Chapter 4B Section 3.

3 Remove the engine oil filler cap, then lift off the plastic cover over the top of the engine **(see illustrations)**. Refit the oil filler cap.

4 Pull up the rubber seal from the engine compartment bulkhead **(see illustration)**.

4.3a Remove the engine oil filler cap...

4.3b ...then lift off the plastic cover over the top of the engine

4.4 Pull up the rubber seal

4.5 Unclip the water deflector and disconnect the washer jet tube

4.6a Unclip the cable at the front edge

4.6b Undo the two bolts at each end of the plate

5 Unclip the water deflector, and disconnect the washer jet tube **(see illustration)**. Where applicable, disconnect the air quality sensor wiring plug.
6 Undo the 2 bolts at each end, unclip the wiring harness and cables, then remove the bulkhead cover plate insulation **(see illustrations)**.
7 Squeeze together the legs of the retaining clip and disconnect the crankcase ventilation hose from the air cleaner outlet air duct **(see illustration)**.
8 Unclip the vacuum hose then undo the bolt securing the outlet air duct to the camshaft cover **(see illustration)**.

9 Undo the three bolts securing the wiring harness trough to the top of the camshaft cover **(see illustration)**.
10 Disconnect the wiring connectors from the following components:
a) Coolant temperature sensor.
b) EGR valve.
c) Throttle housing.
d) Fuel injectors.
e) Glow plugs.
f) Camshaft sensor.
g) Airflow meter.
h) Inlet manifold vacuum solenoid valves.
i) Charge (boost) pressure sensor.
j) Engine management electronic control unit.

k) Pre/post heating system control unit.
l) Wiring harness connection plug.
11 Release the wiring harness from the cable ties and retaining clips and move the harness to one side, clear of the camshaft cover.
12 Using a small screwdriver, carefully prise off the retaining clips securing the fuel leak-off hose connection to the top of each fuel injector. Lift the leak-off hose off the injectors and suitably plug or cover the open injector unions to prevent dirt entry **(see illustrations)**.
13 Open the retaining clip securing the fuel leak-off hose to the banjo union on the fuel

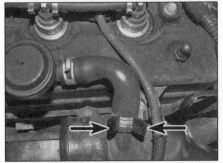

4.7 Squeeze together the retaining clip legs and disconnect the crankcase ventilation hose from the outlet air duct

4.8 Undo the bolt securing the outlet air duct to the camshaft cover

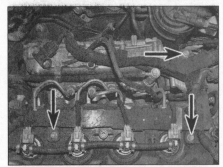

4.9 Undo the three bolts (arrowed) securing the wiring harness trough to the top of the camshaft cover

4.12a Carefully prise off the retaining clips securing the fuel leak-off hose connection to the top of each fuel injector...

4.12b ...lift the leak-off hose off the injectors...

4.12c ...and suitably plug or cover the open injector unions

4.13a Open the retaining clip securing the fuel leak-off hose to the banjo union on the fuel rail...

4.13b ...then disconnect the hose from the banjo union

4.14 Undo the bolt (arrowed) securing the fuel leak-off hose support clip to the inlet manifold

rail, then disconnect the hose from the banjo union **(see illustrations)**.

14 Undo the bolt securing the fuel leak-off hose support clip to the inlet manifold.

4.15a Unscrew the union nuts (arrowed)...

Release the leak-off hose from the guides on the timing belt cover and move the hose assembly to one side **(see illustration)**. Slip a plastic bag over the disconnected leak off hose to prevent dirt entry.

15 Thoroughly clean the fuel pipe unions on the fuel injectors and fuel rail. Using an open-ended spanner, unscrew the union nuts securing the high-pressure fuel pipes to the injectors and fuel rail. Withdraw the high-pressure fuel pipes and plug or cover the open unions to prevent dirt entry **(see illustrations)**.

16 Using a suitable screwdriver, prise free the four fuel injector seal rings and remove them from the camshaft cover **(see illustrations)**.

17 Undo the two bolts securing the timing belt upper cover to the camshaft cover **(see illustration)**.

18 Unscrew the ten retaining bolts and lift away the camshaft cover, complete with rubber seal **(see illustration)**.

19 Prior to refitting, obtain four new high-pressure fuel pipes, four new fuel injector seal rings, fuel leak-off hose retaining clips, a tube of Vauxhall/Opel sealant and a new camshaft cover rubber seal.

Refitting

20 Thoroughly clean the camshaft cover and the mating surfaces of the cover and camshaft housing ensuring that all traces of oil and old sealant are removed from the mating surfaces.

21 Fit the new rubber seal to the camshaft cover ensuring it is fully seated in the cover groove **(see illustration)**.

22 Apply Vauxhall/Opel sealant to the camshaft housing mating surfaces at the end

4.15b ...and remove the high-pressure fuel pipes

4.16a Prise free the four fuel injector seal rings...

4.16b ...and remove them from the camshaft cover

4.17 Undo the two bolts (arrowed) securing the timing belt upper cover to the camshaft cover

4.18 Unscrew the retaining bolts and lift away the camshaft cover

4.21 Fit the new rubber seal to the camshaft cover ensuring it is fully seated in the cover groove

4.22a Apply sealant to the camshaft housing mating surfaces at the left-hand end (arrowed)...

4.22b ...and right-hand end (arrowed) of each camshaft...

4.22c ...ensuring that the oil borehole (arrowed) at the right-hand end of the exhaust camshaft is not covered in sealant

of each camshaft. Ensure that the oil borehole at the right-hand end of the exhaust camshaft is not covered in sealant (see illustrations).

23 Carefully lower the cover into position, ensuring the seal remains correctly seated. Refit the timing belt upper cover and camshaft cover retaining bolts and tighten them finger tight only at this stage. With all the bolts installed, tighten the camshaft cover retaining bolts to the specified torque in the sequence shown (see illustration). When all the camshaft cover bolts have been tightened, tighten the two timing belt cover bolts to the specified torque.

24 Fit the four new fuel injector seal rings, ensuring they are pushed fully home in the camshaft cover (see illustration).

25 Working on one fuel injector at a time, remove the blanking plugs from the fuel pipe unions on the fuel rail and the relevant injector. Locate the new high-pressure fuel pipe over the unions and screw on the union nuts finger tight. Tighten the union nuts to the specified torque using a torque wrench and crow-foot adaptor (see illustrations). Repeat this operation for the remaining three injectors.

26 Place the fuel leak-off hose in position, locating it in the guides in the timing belt cover. Refit the bolt securing the leak-off hose support clip to the inlet manifold and tighten it securely.

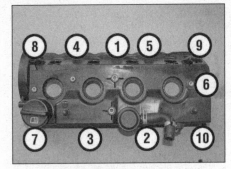

4.23 Camshaft cover retaining bolt tightening sequence

4.24 Fit the four new fuel injector seal rings, ensuring they are pushed fully home in the camshaft cover

27 Reconnect the leak-off hose to the banjo union on the fuel rail and secure the hose with a new retaining clip.

28 Engage the fuel-leak-off hose connectors with the four injectors and secure using new retaining clips.

29 Place the wiring harness trough in position over the camshaft cover and reconnect the wiring connectors to the components listed in paragraph 12. Secure the wiring harness with the three retaining bolts, cable clips and cable ties.

30 Place the air cleaner outlet air duct in position, attach the lower end to the turbocharger and secure with the retaining clip.

31 Reconnect the intercooler outlet duct to the throttle housing, ensuring that the wire retaining clip is correctly seated in its slots.

32 Refit the EGR vacuum valve to the studs on the EGR cooler. Refit the retaining nuts and tighten securely. Reconnect the vacuum hose to the valve and secure the hose with the retaining clips.

33 Refit and tighten the bolt securing the outlet air duct to the camshaft housing.

34 Engage the outlet air duct with the airflow meter and tighten the retaining clip. Refit and tighten the bolt securing the outlet air duct to the support bracket.

35 Reconnect the crankcase ventilation hose to the outlet air duct.

36 Refit the bulkhead cover plate insulation using a reversal of the removal procedures.

37 Reconnect the battery negative terminal.

38 Observing the precautions listed in Chapter 4B Section 2, prime the fuel system as described in Chapter 4B Section 5, then start the engine and allow it to idle. Check for leaks at the high-pressure fuel pipe unions with the engine idling. If satisfactory, increase the engine speed to 4000 rpm and check again for leaks. Take the car for a short road test and check for leaks once again on return. If any leaks are detected, obtain and fit a new high-pressure fuel pipe(s).

39 Refit the engine cover on completion.

4.25a Locate the new high-pressure fuel pipes over the unions and screw on the union nuts finger tight...

4.25b ...then tighten the union nuts using a torque wrench and crow-foot adaptor

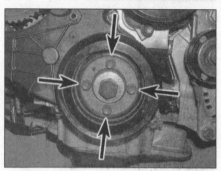

5.3 Remove the bolts (arrowed) securing the crankshaft pulley to the sprocket

5.4a Refit the pulley to the crankshaft sprocket, aligning the pulley hole (arrowed)…

5.4b …with the sprocket locating pin (arrowed)

5 Crankshaft pulley – removal and refitting

Removal

1 Firmly apply the handbrake, then jack up the front of the car and support it securely on axle stands (see *Jacking and vehicle support*). Remove the right-hand roadwheel.
2 Remove the auxiliary drivebelt as described in Chapter 1B Section 24. Prior to removal, mark the direction of rotation on the belt to ensure the belt is refitted the same way around.
3 Slacken and remove the four small retaining bolts securing the pulley to the crankshaft sprocket and remove the pulley from the engine (see illustration). If necessary, prevent crankshaft rotation by holding the sprocket retaining bolt with a suitable socket.

Refitting

4 Refit the pulley to the crankshaft sprocket, aligning the pulley hole with the sprocket locating pin (see illustrations). Refit the pulley retaining bolts, tightening them to the specified torque.
5 Refit the auxiliary drivebelt as described in Chapter 1B Section 24, using the mark made prior to removal to ensure the belt is fitted the correct way around.
6 Refit the roadwheel, then lower the car to the ground and tighten the roadwheel nuts to the specified torque.

6 Timing belt covers – removal and refitting

Removal

Upper cover

1 Disconnect the battery negative terminal (refer to Chapter 5A Section 4).
2 Remove the engine oil filler cap, then lift off the plastic cover over the top of the engine (see illustrations 4.2a and 4.2b). Refit the oil filler cap.
3 Remove the air cleaner assembly and outlet duct as described in Chapter 4B Section 3.
4 Undo the nut and bolt, then remove the shield at the front edge of the upper cover (see illustration).
5 Disconnect the wiring connector from the camshaft position sensor, then undo the retaining bolt and remove the sensor (see illustration).
6 Support the weight of the engine using a trolley jack with a block of wood placed on its head.
7 Undo the three bolts securing the right-hand mounting to the body (see illustration).
8 Undo the three bolts securing the right-hand engine mounting support bracket to the engine (see illustrations). Access is

6.4 Undo the nut and bolt, then move the shield to one side

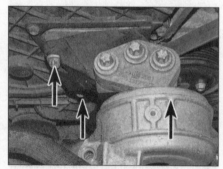

6.5 Disconnect the wiring connector from the camshaft position sensor

6.7 Mounting-to-body bolts

6.8a Undo the bracket-to-engine bolts (3rd bolt hidden beneath)…

6.8b …and remove the mounting with the bracket

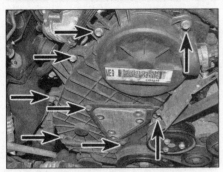

6.9 Undo the eight retaining bolts and withdraw the cover

6.15a Undo the three retaining bolts, and remove the lower cover from the oil pump housing

6.15b Recover the adapter plate

limited, but it is just possible to withdraw the bolts, then manoeuvre the mounting from place.

9 Undo the eight upper cover retaining bolts and withdraw the cover **(see illustration)**. Note the cover bolts are of different lengths.

Lower cover

10 Firmly apply the handbrake, then jack up the front of the car and support it securely on axle stands (see *Jacking and vehicle support*). Remove the right-hand roadwheel.

11 Remove the auxiliary drivebelt as described in Chapter 1B Section 24. Prior to removal, mark the direction of rotation on the belt to ensure the belt is refitted the same way around.

12 Remove the timing belt upper cover as described previously.

13 Slacken and remove the four small retaining bolts securing the crankshaft pulley to the crankshaft sprocket and remove the pulley from the engine **(see illustration 5.3)**. If necessary, prevent crankshaft rotation by holding the sprocket retaining bolt with a suitable socket.

14 Undo the three retaining bolts and remove the coolant pump pulley.

15 Undo the three retaining bolts, and remove the lower cover from the oil pump housing, and recover the mounting adapter plate **(see illustrations)**.

Rear cover

16 Remove timing belt as described in Section 7.

17 Remove the timing belt idler pulley, camshaft sprocket and high-pressure fuel pump sprocket as described in Section 8.

18 Undo the six retaining bolts, and remove the rear timing belt cover.

Refitting

19 Refitting is the reverse of removal, ensuring all retaining bolts are tightened to the specified torque, where given.

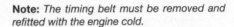

7 Timing belt – removal and refitting

Note: *The timing belt must be removed and refitted with the engine cold.*

Removal

1 Position No 1 cylinder at TDC on its compression stroke as described in Section 3. Lock the camshaft and high-pressure fuel pump sprockets in position by screwing the bolts into the threaded holes in the cylinder head/block.

2 Slacken the timing belt tensioner retaining bolt, then turn the tensioner anti-clockwise to relieve the belt tension, using a suitable hexagon bit or Allen key engaged with the hole provided in the tensioner front plate **(see illustration)**. Hold the tensioner in this position and tighten the retaining bolt.

3 Slide the timing belt off its sprockets and remove it from the engine. If the belt is to be re-used, use white paint or similar to mark the direction of rotation on the belt. Do not rotate the crankshaft until the timing belt has been refitted.

4 Check the timing belt carefully for any signs of uneven wear, splitting or oil contamination, and renew it if there is the slightest doubt about its condition. If the engine is undergoing

7.2 Slacken the timing belt tensioner retaining bolt (arrowed) and turn the tensioner anti-clockwise to relieve the belt tension

an overhaul and is approaching the specified interval for belt renewal (see Chapter 1B Section 2) renew the belt as a matter of course, regardless of its apparent condition. If signs of oil contamination are found, trace the source of the oil leak and rectify it, then wash down the engine timing belt area and all related components to remove all traces of oil.

Refitting

5 On reassembly, thoroughly clean the timing belt sprockets and ensure that No 1 cylinder is still positioned at TDC on its compression stroke, with the camshaft and high-pressure fuel pump sprockets locked correctly in position (see Section 3).

6 Fit the timing belt over the crankshaft, oil pump, high-pressure fuel pump and camshaft sprockets, then guide it over the tensioner pulley. Ensure that the belt rear run is taut (ie, all slack is on the tensioner pulley side of the belt). Do not twist the belt sharply while refitting it. Ensure that the belt teeth are correctly seated centrally in the sprockets, and that the timing mark remains in alignment. If a used belt is being refitted, ensure that the arrow mark made on removal points in the normal direction of rotation, as before.

7 Tension the belt by slackening the tensioner retaining bolt and allowing the tensioner to automatically take up the slack in the belt. Once the slack is taken up, tighten the tensioner retaining bolt to the specified torque.

8 Check that the crankshaft sprocket timing mark is still correctly positioned then unscrew the locking bolts from the high-pressure fuel pump and camshaft sprockets.

9 Rotate the crankshaft through two complete turns in the normal direction of rotation to settle the timing belt in position. Realign the crankshaft sprocket timing mark and check that the camshaft and high-pressure fuel pump sprocket locking bolts can be refitted. If it is not possible to fit the locking bolts with the crankshaft sprocket timing mark aligned, repeat the belt refitting procedure.

10 Refit the timing belt covers as described in Section 6.

To make a sprocket holding tool, obtain two lengths of steel strip about 6 mm thick by about 30 mm wide or similar, one 600 mm long, the other 200 mm long (all dimensions are approximate). Bolt the two strips together to form a forked end, leaving the bolt slack so that the shorter strip can pivot freely. At the other end of each 'prong' of the fork, drill a suitable hole and fit a nut and bolt to allow the tool to engage with the spokes in the sprocket.

8 Timing belt tensioner and sprockets – removal and refitting

Camshaft sprocket

Removal

1 Remove the timing belt as described in Section 7.
2 Remove the locking bolt securing the camshaft sprocket in the TDC position.
3 It will now be necessary to hold the camshaft sprocket to enable the retaining bolt to be removed. Vauxhall/Opel special tools EN-956-1 and EN-6347 are available for this purpose, however, a home-made tool can easily be fabricated (see **Tool-Tip**).
4 Using the holding tool to prevent rotation of the camshaft, slacken the sprocket retaining bolt. Remove the holding tool, unscrew the retaining bolt and remove the sprocket, noting which way round it is fitted **(see illustration)**.

8.4 Using the holding tool to prevent rotation of the camshaft, slacken the sprocket retaining bolt

If the sprocket locating pin is a loose fit, remove it from the camshaft end and store it with the sprocket for safe-keeping.

Refitting

5 Ensure the locating pin is in position then refit the sprocket to the camshaft end aligning its locating hole with the pin.
6 Refit the sprocket retaining bolt, then tighten the bolt to the specified torque using the holding tool to prevent rotation.
7 Turn the camshaft sprocket slightly, as necessary, then refit the locking bolt to secure the sprocket in the TDC position.
8 Refit the timing belt as described in Section 7.

High-pressure fuel pump sprocket

Removal

9 Remove the timing belt as described in Section 7.
10 Remove the locking bolt securing the high-pressure fuel pump sprocket in the TDC position.
11 Refer to the information contained in paragraph 3 and suitably hold the sprocket, then slacken and remove the sprocket retaining nut **(see illustration)**.
12 Remove the sprocket from the fuel pump shaft, noting which way around it is fitted. If the Woodruff key is a loose fit in the pump shaft, remove it and store it with the sprocket for safe-keeping. **Note:** *The sprocket is a tapered-fit on the fuel pump shaft and in some*

8.11 Using a sprocket holding tool to prevent rotation as the high-pressure fuel pump sprocket nut is slackened

cases a suitable puller may be needed to free it from the shaft **(see illustration)**.

Refitting

13 Ensure the Woodruff key is correctly fitted to the pump shaft then refit the sprocket, aligning the sprocket groove with the key **(see illustration)**.
14 Refit the retaining nut and tighten it to the specified torque whilst using the holding tool to prevent rotation.
15 If not already done, align the sprocket timing hole with the threaded hole in the cylinder block and screw in the locking bolt.
16 Refit the timing belt as described in Section 7.

Crankshaft sprocket

Removal

17 Remove the timing belt as described in Section 7.
18 Slacken the crankshaft sprocket retaining bolt. To prevent crankshaft rotation, have an assistant select top gear and apply the brakes firmly. If the engine is removed from the vehicle it will be necessary to lock the flywheel (see Section 18).
19 Unscrew the retaining bolt and washer and remove the crankshaft sprocket from the end of the crankshaft **(see illustration)**. If the sprocket is a tight fit, draw it off of the crankshaft using a suitable puller. If the Woodruff key is a loose fit in the crankshaft, remove it and store it with the sprocket for safe-keeping.

8.12 Using a puller to remove the high-pressure fuel pump sprocket

8.13 Align the keyway in the sprocket with the Woodruff key in the shaft

8.19 Slide the sprocket from the shaft

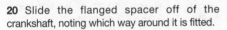

8.21 Fit the flanged spacer with the convex side away from the oil pump cover

8.23 Refit the sprocket retaining bolt and washer

8.26 Use a socket and extension bar on one of the oil pump cover bolts to prevent the sprocket from turning

20 Slide the flanged spacer off of the crankshaft, noting which way around it is fitted.

Refitting

21 Refit the flanged spacer to the crankshaft with its convex surface facing away from the oil pump housing **(see illustration)**.

22 Ensure the Woodruff key is correctly fitted then slide on the crankshaft sprocket aligning its groove with the key.

23 Refit the retaining bolt and washer then lock the crankshaft by the method used on removal, and tighten the sprocket retaining bolt to the specified torque setting **(see illustration)**.

24 Refit the timing belt as described in Section 7.

Oil pump sprocket

Removal

25 Remove the timing belt as described in Section 7.

26 Prevent the oil pump sprocket from rotating using a socket and extension bar fitted to one of the oil pump cover bolts then slacken and remove the sprocket retaining nut **(see illustration)**.

27 Remove the sprocket from the oil pump shaft, noting which way around it is fitted.

Refitting

28 Refit the sprocket, aligning it with the flat on the pump shaft, and fit the retaining nut. Tighten the sprocket retaining nut to the specified torque, using the socket and extension bar to prevent rotation.

29 Refit the timing belt as described in Section 7.

Tensioner assembly

Removal

30 Remove the timing belt as described in Section 7.

31 Unscrew the retaining bolt and remove the tensioner assembly from the engine. Disengage the tension spring from its locating stud as the tensioner is removed.

Refitting

32 Fit the tensioner assembly to the engine, engaging the tension spring over the stud. Screw in the tensioner retaining bolt, then turn the tensioner anti-clockwise using a suitable hexagon bit or Allen key engaged with the hole provided in the tensioner front plate. Hold the tensioner in this position and tighten the retaining bolt.

33 Refit the timing belt as described in Section 7.

Idler pulley

Removal

34 Remove the timing belt as described in Section 7.

35 Slacken and remove the retaining bolt and remove the idler pulley from the engine **(see illustration)**.

Refitting

36 Refit the idler pulley and tighten the retaining bolt to the specified torque.

37 Refit the timing belt as described in Section 7.

9 Camshaft oil seal – renewal

1 Remove the camshaft sprocket as described in Section 8.

2 Carefully punch or drill a small hole in the oil seal. Screw in a self-tapping screw, and pull on the screw with pliers to extract the seal **(see illustration)**.

3 Clean the seal housing, and polish off any burrs or raised edges which may have caused the seal to fail in the first place.

4 Press the new seal into position using a suitable tubular drift (such as a socket) which bears only on the hard outer edge of the seal. Take care not to damage the seal lips during fitting; note that the seal lips should face inwards **(see illustration)**.

5 Refit the camshaft sprocket as described in Section 8.

10 Valve clearances – checking and adjustment

Checking

1 The importance of having the valve clearances correctly adjusted cannot be overstressed, as they vitally affect the

8.35 Timing belt idler pulley retaining bolt

9.2 Pull the screw to extract the seal

9.4 Press the oil seal into position using a tubular drift such as a socket

performance of the engine. The engine must be cold for the check to be accurate. The clearances are checked as follows.

2 Firmly apply the handbrake, then jack up the front of the car and support it securely on axle stands (see *Jacking and vehicle support*). Remove the right-hand roadwheel.

3 Remove the camshaft cover as described in Section 4, then remove the fuel injectors as described in Chapter 4B Section 14.

4 Using a socket and extension on the crankshaft sprocket bolt, rotate the crankshaft in the normal direction (clockwise) until the inlet camshaft lobes for No 1 cylinder (nearest the timing belt end of the engine) and the exhaust camshaft lobes for No 3 cylinder are pointing away from the followers. This indicates that these valves are completely closed, and the clearances can be checked.

5 On a piece of paper, draw the outline of the engine with the cylinders numbered from the timing belt end. Show the position of each valve, together with the specified valve clearance. Note that the clearance for both the inlet and exhaust valves is the same.

6 With the cam lobes positioned as described in paragraph 4, using feeler blades, measure the clearance between the base of both No 1 cylinder inlet cam lobes and No 3 cylinder exhaust cam lobes and their followers. Record the clearances on the paper **(see illustration)**.

7 Rotate the crankshaft pulley through a half a turn (180º) to position No 3 cylinder inlet camshaft lobes and No 4 cylinder exhaust camshaft lobes pointing away from their followers. Measure the clearance between the base of the camshaft lobes and their followers and record the clearances on the paper.

8 Rotate the crankshaft pulley through a half a turn (180º) to position No 2 cylinder exhaust camshaft lobes and No 4 cylinder inlet camshaft lobes pointing away from their followers. Measure the clearance between the base of the camshaft lobes and their followers and record the clearances on the paper.

9 Rotate the crankshaft pulley through a half a turn (180º) to position No 1 cylinder exhaust camshaft lobes and No 2 cylinder inlet camshaft lobes pointing away from their followers. Measure the clearance between the

base of the camshaft lobes and their followers and record the clearances on the paper.

10 If all the clearances are correct, refit the fuel injectors as described in Chapter 4B Section 14, and the camshaft cover as described in Section 4. Refit the roadwheel, lower the vehicle to the ground and tighten the roadwheel nuts to the specified torque. If any clearance measured is not correct, adjustment must be carried out as described in the following paragraphs.

Adjustment

11 If adjustment is necessary, remove the relevant camshaft(s) and camshaft followers as described in Section 11.

12 Clean the followers of the valves that require clearance adjustment and note the thickness marking on the follower. The thickness marking is stamped on the underside of each follower. For example, a 3.46 mm thick follower will have a 46 thickness marking, a 3.48 mm thick follower will have a 48 thickness marking etc. New followers are available in thicknesses ranging from 3.46 mm to 4.14 mm in increments of 0.02 mm.

13 Add the measured clearance of the valve to the thickness of the original follower then subtract the specified valve clearance from this figure. This will give you the thickness of the follower required. For example:

Clearance measured of valve	0.48 mm
Plus thickness of the original follower	3.46 mm
Equals	3.94 mm
Minus clearance required	0.40 mm
Thickness of follower required	3.54 mm

14 Repeat this procedure on the remaining valves which require adjustment, then obtain the correct thickness of follower(s) required.

15 Refit the camshaft followers and the relevant camshaft(s) as described in Section 11. Rotate the crankshaft a few times to settle all the components, then recheck the valve clearances.

16 If all the clearances are correct, refit the fuel injectors as described in Chapter 4B Section 14, and the camshaft cover as described in Section 4. Refit the roadwheel, lower the vehicle to the ground and tighten the roadwheel nuts to the specified torque.

11 Camshafts and followers – removal, inspection and refitting

Removal

1 Remove the camshaft cover as described in Section 4.

2 Remove the fuel injectors as described in Chapter 4B Section 14.

3 Remove the vacuum pump as described in Chapter 9 Section 19.

4 Remove the camshaft sprocket as described in Section 8.

5 Undo the bolt and two nuts and remove the No 5 bearing cap from the left-hand (transmission) end of the camshafts.

6 The exhaust camshaft gear incorporates a backlash compensating gear. This must now be locked to the fixed exhaust camshaft gear by inserting a suitably-sized bolt/rod into the hole on the inboard face of the fixed gear, and through into the backlash compensating gear. This prevents the spring preload of the compensating gear being lost when either camshaft is removed **(see illustration)**.

7 Working in a spiral pattern from the outside in, slacken the remaining camshaft bearing cap retaining bolts and nuts by one turn at a time, to relieve the pressure of the valve springs on the bearing caps gradually and evenly. Once the valve spring pressure has been relieved, the bolts and nuts can be fully unscrewed and removed.

8 Caution: If the bearing cap nuts/bolts are carelessly slackened, the bearing caps might break. If any bearing cap breaks then the complete camshaft housing assembly must be renewed; the bearing caps are matched to the housing and are not available separately.

9 Remove the bearing caps, noting each caps correct fitted location. The bearing caps are numbered 1 to 5 and the arrow on each cap points towards the timing belt end of the engine **(see illustration)**.

10 Lift the camshafts out of the cylinder head.

11 Obtain sixteen small, clean plastic containers, and label them for identification.

10.6 With the camshaft lobe pointing away from the follower measure the clearance

11.6 Insert a screw through the fixed gear and into the backlash compensating gear (arrowed)

11.9 The camshaft bearing caps are numbered 1 to 5 and the arrow on each cap points towards the timing belt end of the engine

11.11 Lift the cam followers from the cylinder head

11.16 Align the camshaft gear marks (arrowed)

12.6 Remove the two bolts securing the rear timing belt cover to the camshaft housing

Alternatively, divide a larger container into compartments. Using a rubber sucker tool, lift the followers out from the top of the cylinder head and store each one in its respective fitted position. Make sure the followers are not mixed to ensure the valve clearances remain correctly adjusted on refitting **(see illustration)**.

Inspection

12 Examine the camshaft bearing surfaces and camshaft lobes for signs of wear ridges and scoring. Renew the camshaft if any of these conditions are apparent.

13 Examine the condition of the bearing surfaces both on the camshaft journals and in the cylinder head. If the head bearing surfaces are worn excessively, the cylinder head will need to be renewed.

14 Examine the followers and their bores in the cylinder head for signs of wear or damage. If any follower is visibly worn it should be renewed.

Refitting

15 Lubricate the followers with clean engine oil and carefully insert each one into its original location in the cylinder head.

16 Rotate the crankshaft approximately 60° backwards (anti-clockwise) as a precaution against accidental piston-to-valve contact. Lubricate the camshaft followers with clean engine oil then lay the camshafts in position. Check that the exhaust camshaft backlash compensating gear is still locked to the fixed gear. Ensure that the mark on the outer face exhaust camshaft gear lies between the two marks on the outer face of the inlet camshaft gear, and that the marks are approximately level with the upper edge of the camshaft housing **(see illustration)**. **Note:** *If the exhaust camshaft is being renewed, it will be necessary to obtain Vauxhall/Opel tool No KM 6092, and pre-tension the backlash compensating gear prior to installation.*

17 Ensure the mating surfaces of the bearing caps and camshaft housing are clean and dry and lubricate the camshaft journals and lobes with clean engine oil.

18 Refit the No 1 to 4 camshaft bearing caps in their original locations on the cylinder head. The caps are numbered 1 to 5 (No 1 cap being at the timing belt end of the engine) and the

arrow cast onto the top of each cap should point towards the timing belt end of the engine **(see illustration 11.8)**.

19 Refit the No 1 to 4 bearing cap bolts and nuts, tightening them by hand only.

20 Remove the bolt/rod locking the backlash compensating gear to the exhaust camshaft fixed gear, and refit the No 5 camshaft bearing cap.

21 Working in a spiral pattern from the inside out, tighten the bolts and nuts by one turn at a time to gradually impose the pressure of the valve springs evenly on the bearing caps. Repeat this sequence until all bearing caps are in contact with the cylinder head then go around again, in a spiral pattern from the inside out, and tighten them to the specified torque.

22 **Caution:** If the bearing cap nuts/bolts are carelessly tightened, the bearing caps might break. If any bearing cap breaks then the complete camshaft housing assembly must be renewed; the bearing caps are matched to the housing and are not available separately.

23 Fit a new camshaft oil seal as described in Section 9.

24 Refit the camshaft sprocket as described in Section 8 and the timing belt as described in Section 7.

25 Check the valve clearances as described in Section 10.

26 Refit the vacuum pump as described in Chapter 9 Section 19.

27 Refit the fuel injectors as described in Chapter 4B Section 14.

28 Refit the camshaft cover as described in Section 4.

12 Camshaft housing – removal and refitting

Removal

1 Remove the camshaft cover as described in Section 4.

2 Remove the fuel injectors as described in Chapter 4B Section 14.

3 Remove the vacuum pump as described in Chapter 9 Section 19.

4 Remove the camshaft sprocket as described in Section 8.

5 Remove the EGR valve cooler as described in Chapter 4C Section 3.

6 Undo the two bolts securing the rear timing belt cover to the camshaft housing **(see illustration)**.

7 Slacken the camshaft housing retaining bolts 1/2 turn at a time working in a spiral pattern from inside to outside.

8 Undo the bolts completely and remove the camshaft housing. Remove and discard the gasket.

Refitting

9 Ensure all mating surfaces are clean and free from any gasket or sealant residue.

10 Prior to refitting the housing, check that the camshaft gears are correctly aligned, with the mark on the outer face of the exhaust gear between the marks on the outer face of the inlet gear **(see illustration 11.15)**.

11 With a new gasket in place, position the camshaft housing on to the cylinder head, and tighten the housing bolts evenly and gradually to the specified torque, in a spiral pattern from outside to inside.

12 Refit the two bolts securing the rear timing belt cover to the camshaft housing and tighten the bolts to the specified torque.

13 Refit the EGR valve cooler as described in Chapter 4C Section 3.

14 Refit the camshaft sprocket as described in Section 8 and the timing belt as described in Section 7.

15 Check the valve clearances as described in Section 10.

16 Refit the vacuum pump as described in Chapter 9 Section 19.

17 Refit the fuel injectors as described in Chapter 4B Section 14.

18 Refit the camshaft cover as described in Section 4.

13 Cylinder head – removal and refitting

Caution: Be careful not to allow dirt into the fuel injection pump or injector pipes during this procedure.

Note: *New cylinder head bolts and a new high-pressure fuel pipe will be required for refitting.*

13.5 Store the followers the correct way up

13.11 Lift the cylinder head off the block

Removal

1 Drain the engine oil as described in Chapter 1B Section 6.

2 Drain the cooling system as described in Chapter 1B Section 30.

3 Remove the exhaust manifold as described in Chapter 4B Section 19.

4 Remove the camshaft housing as described in Section 12.

5 As a precaution, obtain sixteen small, clean plastic containers, and label them for identification. Alternatively, divide a larger container into compartments. Lift the followers out from the top of the cylinder head and store each one in its respective fitted position **(see illustration)**.

6 Thoroughly clean the fuel pipe unions on the fuel pump and fuel rail. Using an open-ended spanner, unscrew the union nuts securing the high-pressure fuel pipe to the fuel pump and fuel rail. Counterhold the union on the pump with a second spanner, while unscrewing the union nut. Undo the bolt securing the high-pressure fuel pipe to the support bracket and withdraw the pipe. Plug or cover the open unions to prevent dirt entry.

7 Release the retaining clips and disconnect the remaining coolant hoses from the thermostat housing and cylinder head.

8 Disconnect the two vacuum hoses from the solenoid valves at the rear of the inlet manifold. Release the hoses from their retaining clips.

9 Undo the bolt securing the rear timing belt cover to the cylinder head.

10 Working in the reverse of the tightening sequence **(see illustration 13.28)**, progressively slacken the cylinder head bolts by half a turn at a time, until all bolts can be unscrewed by hand. Lift out the cylinder head bolts.

11 Lift the cylinder head away; seek assistance if possible, as it is a heavy assembly **(see illustration)**. Remove the gasket, noting the two locating dowels fitted to the top of the cylinder block. If they are a loose fit, remove the locating dowels and store them with the head for safe-keeping. Keep the

head gasket for identification purposes (see paragraph 18).

12 If the cylinder head is to be dismantled for overhaul, then refer to Part E of this Chapter.

Preparation for refitting

13 The mating faces of the cylinder head and cylinder block/crankcase must be perfectly clean before refitting the head. Use a hard plastic or wood scraper to remove all traces of gasket and carbon; also clean the piston crowns. Take particular care, as the surfaces are damaged easily. Also, make sure that the carbon is not allowed to enter the oil and water passages – this is particularly important for the lubrication system, as carbon could block the oil supply to any of the engine's components. Using adhesive tape and paper, seal the water, oil and bolt holes in the cylinder block/crankcase. To prevent carbon entering the gap between the pistons and bores, smear a little grease in the gap. After cleaning each piston, use a small brush to remove all traces of grease and carbon from the gap, then wipe away the remainder with a clean rag. Clean all the pistons in the same way.

14 Check the mating surfaces of the cylinder block/crankcase and the cylinder head for nicks, deep scratches and other damage. If slight, they may be removed carefully with a file, but if excessive, machining may be the only alternative to renewal.

15 Ensure that the cylinder head bolt holes in the crankcase are clean and free of oil. Syringe or soak up any oil left in the bolt holes. This is most important in order that the correct bolt tightening torque can be applied and to prevent the possibility of the block being cracked by hydraulic pressure when the bolts are tightened.

16 The cylinder head bolts must be discarded and renewed, regardless of their apparent condition.

17 If warpage of the cylinder head gasket surface is suspected, use a straight-edge to check it for distortion. Refer to Part E of this Chapter if necessary.

18 On this engine, the cylinder head-to-piston clearance is controlled by fitting different thickness head gaskets. The gasket thickness can be determined by looking at the front centre of the gasket and checking on the number of holes.

Holes in gasket	Gasket thickness
One hole	0.95 mm
Two holes	1.00 mm
Three holes	1.05 mm

19 The correct thickness of gasket required is selected by measuring the piston protrusions as follows.

20 Mount a dial test indicator securely on the block so that its pointer can be easily pivoted between the piston crown and block mating surface. Turn the crankshaft to bring No 1 piston roughly to the TDC position. Move the dial test indicator probe over and in contact with No 1 piston. Turn the crankshaft back and forth slightly until the highest reading is shown on the gauge, indicating that the piston is at TDC.

21 Zero the dial test indicator on the gasket surface of the cylinder block then carefully move the indicator over No 1 piston. Measure its protrusion at the highest point between the valve cut-outs, and then again at its highest point between the valve cut-outs at 90° to the first measurement **(see illustration)**. Repeat this procedure with No 4 piston.

13.21 Measure the piston projection at the highest points between the valve cut-outs

13.25 Check the locating dowels are in place then fit the new gasket

22 Rotate the crankshaft half a turn (180°) to bring No 2 and 3 pistons to TDC. Ensure the crankshaft is accurately positioned then measure the protrusions of No 2 and 3 pistons at the specified points. Once both pistons have been measured, rotate the crankshaft through a further one and a half turns (540°) to bring No 1 and 4 pistons back to TDC.

23 Select the correct thickness of head gasket required by determining the largest amount of piston protrusion, and using the following table.

Piston protrusion measurement	Gasket thickness required
0.230 to 0.296 mm	0.95 mm
0.297 to 0.362 mm	1.00 mm
0.363 to 0.429 mm	1.05 mm

Refitting

24 Wipe clean the mating surfaces of the cylinder head and cylinder block/crankcase.

25 Check that the two locating dowels are in position then fit a new gasket to the cylinder block **(see illustration)**.

26 If not already positioned at TDC, rotate the crankshaft so that No 1 piston is at its highest point in the cylinder. Now turn the crankshaft 60° backwards (anti-clockwise). This is to ensure that whist the cylinder head and camshafts are being refitted, there is little chance of accidental piston-to-valve contact.

27 With the aid of an assistant, carefully refit the cylinder head assembly to the block, aligning it with the locating dowels.

28 Carefully enter each new cylinder head bolt into its relevant hole (do not drop them in). Screw all bolts in, by hand only, until finger-tight.

29 Working progressively in the sequence shown, tighten the cylinder head bolts to their Stage 1 torque setting, using a torque wrench and suitable socket **(see illustration)**.

30 Once all bolts have been tightened to the Stage 1 torque, working again in the same sequence, go around and tighten all bolts through the specified Stage 2 angle, then through the specified Stage 3 angle using an angle-measuring gauge.

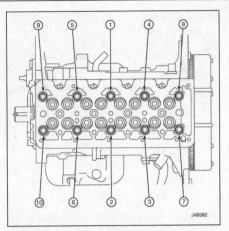

13.29 Cylinder head bolt tightening sequence

31 Refit the bolt securing the rear timing belt cover to the cylinder head and tighten the bolt to the specified torque.

32 Reconnect the two vacuum hoses to the solenoid valves at the rear of the inlet manifold. Refit the hoses to their retaining clips.

33 Reconnect the coolant hoses to the thermostat housing and cylinder head.

34 Remove the blanking plugs from the fuel pipe unions on the fuel rail and fuel pump. Locate the new high-pressure fuel pipe over the unions and screw on the union nuts finger tight. Tighten the union nuts to the specified torque using a torque wrench and crow-foot adaptor. Counterhold the union on the pump with an open-ended spanner, while tightening the union nut. Refit and tighten the bolt securing the high-pressure fuel pipe to the support bracket.

35 Lubricate the camshaft followers with clean engine oil and carefully insert each one into its original location in the cylinder head.

36 Refit the camshaft housing as described in Section 12.

37 Refit the exhaust manifold as described in Chapter 4B Section 19.

38 Refit the plastic cover over the top of the engine.

39 Refit the wheel arch liner and roadwheel, then lower the car to the ground and tighten the roadwheel nuts to the specified torque.

40 Refill the engine with fresh oil as described in Chapter 1B Section 6, then reconnect the battery negative terminal.

41 Refill the cooling system as described in Chapter 1B Section 30.

14 Sump – removal and refitting

Removal

1 Disconnect the battery negative terminal (refer to Chapter 5A Section 4).

14.4 If the lower pan is stuck to the main casting, carefully ease it away using a wide-bladed scraper

2 Firmly apply the handbrake, then jack up the front of the car and support it securely on axle stands (see *Jacking and vehicle support*).

3 Drain the engine oil as described in Chapter 1B Section 6, then fit a new sealing washer and refit the drain plug, tightening it to the specified torque.

4 Slacken and remove the bolts securing the sump lower pan to the main casting. Using a wide bladed scraper or similar tool inserted between the sump and main casting, carefully break the joint, then remove the sump from under the car **(see illustration)**.

5 To remove the main casting from the engine, remove the exhaust system front pipe as described in Chapter 4B Section 20.

6 Undo the two bolts securing the oil dipstick guide tube to the main sump casting and the bolt securing the guide tube to the exhaust manifold. Remove the guide tube and collect the O-ring seal. Note that a new seal will be required for refitting.

7 Undo the two bolts securing the driveshaft support bearing housing to the sump main casting.

8 Disconnect the wiring connector from the engine oil level sensor.

9 Release the exhaust temperature sensor wiring connector from the support bracket, then undo the retaining bolt securing the support bracket to the main casting.

10 Undo the two retaining nuts and remove the wiring harness trough from the studs at the front of the main casting.

11 Progressively slacken and remove the nuts and bolts securing the main casting to the base of the cylinder block/oil pump cover and transmission. Break the joint using a wide scraper or similar tool carefully inserted in the joint between the main casting and cylinder block. Lower the casting away from the engine and withdraw it from underneath the vehicle.

12 While the sump main casting is removed, take the opportunity to check the oil pump pick-up/strainer for signs of clogging or splitting. If necessary, unbolt the pick-up/strainer and remove it from the engine along with its sealing rings **(see illustration)**. The strainer can then be cleaned easily in solvent or renewed.

Refitting

13 Remove all traces of dirt, oil and sealant from the mating surfaces of the sump main casting and pan, the cylinder block and (where removed) the pick-up/strainer.

14 Where necessary, fit new sealing rings to the oil pump pick-up/strainer and fit the strainer to the base of the cylinder block. Refit the strainer retaining bolt and tighten it to the specified torque.

15 Ensure the main casting and cylinder block mating surfaces are clean and dry, and apply a coat of suitable sealant (available from Vauxhall/Opel dealers) to the upper mating surface of the casting.

16 Offer up the main casting and loosely refit all the retaining nuts and bolts **(see illustration)**. Note that the four long bolts correspond with the bolts holes at the rear of the casting. If the sump is being fitted with the engine removed from the vehicle and separated from the transmission, ensure that the rear face of the casting is flush with the transmission mounting face of the cylinder block. Working out from the centre in a diagonal sequence, progressively tighten the main casting retaining nuts/bolts to the specified torque setting.

17 Refit the bolts securing the main casting to the transmission housing and tighten them to the specified torque.

18 Place the wiring harness trough back in position over the two studs and secure with the two nuts tightened securely.

19 Refit the exhaust temperature sensor wiring connector support bracket and secure with the retaining bolt tightened securely. Refit the wiring connector to the support bracket.

20 Reconnect the wiring connector to the oil level sensor.

21 Fit new seals to the oil dipstick guide tube and insert the tube into the sump main casting. Refit the retaining bolts, and tighten to the specified torque.

22 Refit the two bolts securing the driveshaft support bearing housing to the sump main casting and tighten the bolts to the specified torque.

23 Refit the exhaust front pipe as described in Chapter 4B Section 20.

14.12 Remove the oil pick-up pipe and strainer

24 Ensure the main casting and sump pan mating surfaces are clean and dry and apply a coat of suitable sealant (available from Vauxhall/Opel dealers) to the upper mating surface of the pan. Refit the pan to the base of the main casting and tighten its retaining bolts to the specified torque.

25 Lower the vehicle to the ground and reconnect the battery negative terminal.

26 Fill the engine with fresh oil as described in Chapter 1B Section 6.

15 Oil pump – removal, inspection and refitting

Removal

1 Remove the timing belt as described in Section 7.

2 Remove the oil pump and crankshaft timing belt sprockets as described in Section 8.

3 Remove the sump main casting as described in Section 14. If the engine was supported on a trolley jack for removal of the timing belt, temporarily refit the right-hand engine mounting components, then remove the trolley jack from under the sump.

4 Slacken and remove the retaining bolts then slide the oil pump cover off of the end of the crankshaft, taking great care not to lose the locating dowels. Remove the sealing ring, which is fitted around the oil pump housing section of the cover, and discard it.

14.16 Refit the sump main casting

5 Using a suitable marker pen, mark the surface of the pump outer rotor; the mark can then be used to ensure the rotor is refitted the correct way around.

6 Remove the oil pump inner and outer rotors from the cylinder block **(see illustrations)**.

Inspection

7 Clean the components, and carefully examine the rotors, pump housing and cover for any signs of scoring or wear. Renew any component which shows signs of wear or damage. If the pump housing in the cylinder block is marked then seek the advice of a Vauxhall/Opel dealer on the best course of action.

8 If the components appear serviceable, fit the rotors into the housing and measure the clearance between the outer rotor and pump housing, and the inner rotor tip-to-outer rotor clearance using feeler blades **(see illustration)**. Also measure the rotor endfloat, and check the flatness of the end cover. If the clearances exceed the specified tolerances, renew the worn components.

Refitting

9 Lubricate the pump rotors with clean engine oil and refit them to the pump housing, using the mark made prior to removal to ensure the outer rotor is fitted the correct way around.

10 Prior to refitting, carefully lever out the crankshaft and oil pump oil seals using a flat-bladed screwdriver. Fit the new oil seals, ensuring that each seals sealing lip is facing

15.6a Remove the oil pump inner rotor...

15.6b ...and outer rotor

15.8 Measure the inner rotor tip-to-outer rotor clearance

15.10 The seal fits flush with the housing

15.12 Fit a new seal to the oil pump cover

16.2 Pull the screw to extract the seal

inwards, and press them squarely into the housing using a tubular drift which bears only on the hard outer edge of the seal. Press each seal into position so that it is flush with the housing **(see illustration)**.

11 Ensure the mating surfaces of the oil pump and cylinder block are clean and dry and the locating dowels are in position. Remove all traces of sealant from the threads of the pump cover bolts.

12 Fit a new seal into the groove around the oil pump housing section of the cover, and apply a bead of suitable sealant (available from Vauxhall/Opel dealers) to the pump cover mating surface **(see illustration)**.

13 Carefully manoeuvre the oil pump cover into position, taking great care not to damage the oil seal lips on the crankshaft and inner rotor shaft. Locate the cover on the dowels making sure the pump sealing ring remains correctly positioned.

14 Apply a smear of sealant to the threads of each cover retaining bolt then refit all bolts and tighten them to the specified torque. Note that the longer bolt corresponds to the lower left-hand bolt hole in the cover.

15 Refit the sump as described in Section 14.

16 Refit the timing belt sprockets as described in Section 8, then refit the timing belt as described in Section 7.

17 On completion refill the engine with fresh oil as described in Chapter 1B Section 6.

16 Oil pump seal – renewal

1 Remove the oil pump sprocket as described in Section 8.

2 Carefully punch or drill a small hole in the oil seal. Screw a self-tapping screw into the seal, and pull on the screw with pliers to extract the seal **(see illustration)**.

Caution: Great care must be taken to avoid damage to the oil pump.

3 Clean the seal housing, and polish off any burrs or raised edges which may have caused the seal to fail in the first place.

4 Press the new seal into position using a suitable tubular drift (such as a socket) which

bears only on the hard outer edge of the seal. Take care not to damage the seal lips during fitting; note that the seal lips should face inwards.

5 Refit the oil pump sprocket as described in Section 8.

17 Oil filter housing – removal and refitting

Removal

1 The oil filter housing and integral oil cooler is situated on the rear left-hand side of the cylinder block. Firmly apply the handbrake, then jack up the front of the car and support it securely on axle stands (see *Jacking and vehicle support*).

2 Drain the cooling system as described in Chapter 1B Section 30.

3 Position a suitable container beneath the oil filter. Release the retaining clip and disconnect the coolant return hose from the oil cooler.

4 Release the retaining clip and disconnect the oil return hose from the filter housing.

5 Undo the retaining bolt and remove the exhaust pressure sensor bracket from the side of the filter housing.

6 Disconnect the wiring connector from the oil pressure warning light switch on the side of the filter housing.

7 Undo the small retaining bolt securing the

oil filter housing flange to the cylinder block.

8 Undo the large hollow bolt securing the oil filter housing to the cylinder block and remove the assembly from the engine.

9 Remove and discard the filter housing sealing ring and the two O-ring seals on the hollow bolt. Obtain new seals for refitting.

Refitting

10 Refitting is a reversal of removal, bearing in mind the following points:

a) Fit new O-ring seals to the hollow bolt and a new sealing ring to the filter housing **(see illustrations)**.

b) Tighten all retaining bolts to the specified torque, where given.

c) Check and if necessary top-up the engine oil as described in Weekly checks.

d) Refill the cooling system as described in Chapter 1B Section 30.

18 Flywheel – removal, inspection and refitting

Note: *New flywheel retaining bolts will be required for refitting.*

Removal

1 Remove the clutch assembly as described in Chapter 6 Section 6.

2 Prevent the flywheel from turning by

17.10a Fit new O-ring seals (arrowed) to the hollow bolt...

17.10b ...and a new sealing ring to the filter housing

18.2 Prevent the flywheel from turning by locking the ring gear teeth with a suitable tool

jamming the ring gear teeth using a suitable tool **(see illustration)**.

3 Slacken and remove the retaining bolts and remove the flywheel.

Caution: Take care, as the flywheel is heavy.

Inspection

4 Examine the flywheel for wear or chipping of the ring gear teeth. Renewal of the ring gear is not possible and if the wear or chipping is significant, a new flywheel will be required.

5 Examine the flywheel for scoring of the clutch face. If the clutch face is scored significantly, a new flywheel will be required.

6 The dual-mass flywheel used on these engines has the effect of reducing engine and transmission vibrations and harshness. The flywheel consists of a primary mass and a secondary mass constructed in such a way that the secondary mass is allowed to rotate slightly in relation to the primary mass. Springs within the assembly restrict this movement to set limits.

7 Dual-mass flywheels have earned an unenviable reputation for unreliability and have been known to fail at quite low mileages

(sometimes as low as 20 000 miles). As well as the checks described above in paragraphs 5 and 6, some additional checks should be performed as follows.

8 Look through the bolt hole and inspection openings in the secondary mass and check for any visible damage in the area of the centre bearing.

9 Place your thumbs on the clutch face of the secondary mass at the 3 o'clock and 9 o'clock positions and try to rock it. The maximum movement should not exceed 3 mm. Repeat this check with your thumbs at the 12 o'clock and 6 o'clock positions.

10 Rotate the secondary mass clockwise and anti-clockwise. It should move freely in both directions until spring resistance is felt, with no abnormal grating or rattling noises. The maximum rotational movement should not exceed a distance of eight teeth of the ring gear.

11 If there is any doubt about the condition of the flywheel, seek the advice of a Vauxhall/Opel dealer or engine reconditioning specialist. They will be able to advise if the flywheel is an acceptable condition, or whether renewal is necessary.

Refitting

12 Clean the mating surfaces of the flywheel and crankshaft.

13 Apply a drop of locking compound to the threads of each of the new flywheel retaining bolts (unless they are already pre-coated) then refit the flywheel and install the new bolts.

14 Lock the flywheel using the method employed on removal then, working in a diagonal sequence, evenly and progressively tighten the retaining bolts to the specified torque setting, then through the specified angles.

15 Refit the clutch as described in Chapter 6 Section 6.

19 Crankshaft oil seals – renewal

Right-hand (timing belt end) oil seal

1 Remove the crankshaft sprocket as described in Section 8.

2 Carefully punch or drill two small holes opposite each other in the oil seal. Screw a self-tapping screw into each and pull on the screws with pliers to extract the seal.

3 Clean the seal housing and polish off any burrs or raised edges which may have caused the seal to fail in the first place.

4 Ease the new seal into position on the end of the crankshaft. Press the seal squarely into position until it is flush with the housing. If necessary, a suitable tubular drift which bears only on the hard outer edge of the seal can be used to tap the seal into position. Take great care not to damage the seal lips during fitting and ensure that the seal lips face inwards.

5 Wash off any traces of oil, then refit the crankshaft sprocket as described in Section 8.

Left-hand (flywheel end) oil seal

6 Remove the flywheel as described in Section 18.

7 Renew the seal as described in paragraphs 2 to 4.

8 Refit the flywheel as described in Section 18.

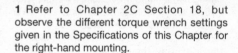

20 Engine/transmission mountings – inspection and renewal

1 Refer to Chapter 2C Section 18, but observe the different torque wrench settings given in the Specifications of this Chapter for the right-hand mounting.

Chapter 2 Part C
1.9 litre SOHC diesel engine in-car repair procedures

Contents

Section number

Camshaft and followers – removal, inspection and refitting 11
Camshaft cover – removal and refitting 5
Camshaft oil seal – renewal 09
Compression and leakdown tests – description and interpretation . . . 2
Crankshaft oil seals – renewal 16
Crankshaft pulley/vibration damper – removal and refitting 6
Cylinder head – removal and refitting 12
Engine/transmission mountings – inspection and renewal 18
Flywheel/driveplate – removal, inspection and refitting 17
General Information 1

Section number

Oil filter housing – removal and refitting 15
Oil pump – removal, overhaul and refitting 14
Sump – removal and refitting 13
Timing belt – removal and refitting 7
Timing belt sprockets, tensioner and idler pulley – removal and
    refitting 8
Top Dead Centre (TDC) for No 1 piston – locating 3
Valve clearances – checking and adjustment 10
Valve timing – checking and adjustment 4

Degrees of difficulty

Easy, suitable for novice with little experience 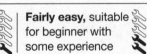 | **Fairly easy,** suitable for beginner with some experience | **Fairly difficult,** suitable for competent DIY mechanic | **Difficult,** suitable for experienced DIY mechanic | **Very difficult,** suitable for expert DIY or professional

Specifications

General

Engine type	Four-cylinder, in-line, water-cooled. Single overhead camshaft, belt-driven
Manufacturer's engine code	Z19DT and Z19DTL
Bore	82.0 mm
Stroke	90.4 mm
Capacity	1910 cc
Compression ratio	18.0: 1
Firing order	1-3-4-2 (No 1 cylinder at timing belt end of engine)
Direction of crankshaft rotation	Clockwise (viewed from timing belt end of engine)

Compression pressures

Maximum difference between any two cylinders	1.5 bar

Valve clearances

Engine cold (intake and exhaust)	0.30 to 0.40 mm

Lubrication system

Minimum oil pressure at 100°C	1.0 bar at idle speed
Oil pump type	Rotor-type, driven by crankshaft pulley/vibration damper from crankshaft

Torque wrench settings

	Nm	lbf ft
Air conditioning compressor mounting bracket to cylinder block/sump . .	50	37
Auxiliary drivebelt idler pulley bolt	50	37
Auxiliary drivebelt tensioner assembly bolts	50	37
Camshaft bearing cap bolts.	15	11
Camshaft cover bolts.	10	7
Camshaft sprocket bolt*.	120	89
Connecting rod big-end bearing cap bolt: *		
Stage 1	25	18
Stage 2	Angle-tighten a further 60°	
Crankshaft oil seal housing	9	7
Crankshaft pulley/vibration damper bolts	25	18
Crankshaft sprocket bolt*†.	340	251
Cylinder head bolts: *		
Stage 1	20	15
Stage 2	65	48
Stage 3	Angle-tighten a further 90°	
Stage 4	Angle-tighten a further 90°	
Stage 5	Angle-tighten a further 90°	
Driveplate bolts*.	160	118
Engine/transmission mountings:		
Front mounting/torque link:		
Mounting to subframe bracket.	55	41
Bracket to transmission	80	59
Left-hand mounting:		
Mounting-to-body bolts	25	18
Mounting bracket to transmission bracket.	80	59
Rubber mounting through-bolt.	55	41
Transmission bracket to transmission	55	41
Rear mounting/torque link:		
Mounting to subframe	55	41
Mounting-to-transmission bracket through-bolt	55	41
Transmission bracket to transmission	80	59
Right-hand mounting:		
Engine bracket-to-engine bolts:		
Lower bolts (M8)	25	18
Upper bolts (M10)	50	37
Mounting-to-body bolts	35	26
Mounting-to-engine bracket bolts	55	41
Engine-to-transmission unit bolts:		
M10 bolts	40	30
M12 bolts	60	44
Flywheel bolts*.	160	118
High-pressure fuel pump sprocket nut*.	50	37
Intermediate shaft bearing housing support bracket bolts	55	41
Main bearing cap bolts: *		
Stage 1	25	18
Stage 2	Angle-tighten a further 100°	
Oil filter housing to cylinder block	50	37
Oil pump housing to cylinder block	9	7
Oil pump pick-up/strainer bolts	9	7
Roadwheel bolts.	110	81
Sump bolts:		
M6 bolts	9	7
M8 bolts	25	18
M10 bolts	40	30
Timing belt idler pulley bolt	50	37
Timing belt tensioner bolt.	30	22
Timing belt upper cover bolts:		
M6 bolts	9	7
M8 bolts	25	18

*Use new fasteners

† Left-hand thread

1 General Information

How to use this Chapter

1 This Part of Chapter 2 describes the repair procedures which can reasonably be carried out on the engine while it remains in the vehicle. If the engine has been removed from the vehicle and is being dismantled as described in Chapter 2E, any preliminary dismantling procedures can be ignored.

2 Note that, while it may be possible physically to overhaul items such as the piston/connecting rod assemblies while the engine is in the vehicle, such tasks are not usually carried out as separate operations, and usually require the execution of several additional procedures (not to mention the cleaning of components and of oilways); for this reason, all such tasks are classed as major overhaul procedures, and are described in Chapter 2E.

3 Chapter 2E describes the removal of the engine/transmission unit from the vehicle, and the full overhaul procedures which can then be carried out.

Engine description

4 The 1.9 litre SOHC diesel engine is of the eight-valve, in-line four-cylinder, single overhead camshaft type, mounted transversely at the front of the car, with the transmission on its left-hand end.

5 The crankshaft is supported within the cylinder block on five shell-type main bearings. Thrustwashers are fitted to number 3 main bearing, to control crankshaft endfloat.

6 The connecting rods rotate on horizontally-split bearing shells at their big-ends. The pistons are attached to the connecting rods by gudgeon pins, which are retained by circlips. The aluminium-alloy pistons are fitted with three piston rings – two compression rings and scraper-type oil control ring.

7 The camshaft runs directly in the cylinder head, and is driven by the crankshaft via a toothed composite rubber timing belt (which also drives the high-pressure fuel pump and the coolant pump). The camshaft operates each valve via a camshaft follower with adjustment shim.

8 Lubrication is by pressure-feed from a rotor-type oil pump, which is mounted on the right-hand end of the crankshaft. The pump draws oil through a strainer located in the sump, and then forces it through an externally mounted full-flow cartridge-type filter. The oil flows into galleries in the cylinder block/crankcase, from where it is distributed to the crankshaft (main bearings) and camshaft. The big-end bearings are supplied with oil via internal drillings in the crankshaft, while the camshaft bearings also receive a pressurised supply. The camshaft lobes and valves are lubricated by splash, as are all other engine components.

9 A semi-closed crankcase ventilation system is employed; crankcase fumes are drawn from the oil separator (integral with the camshaft cover), and passed via a hose to the intake manifold.

Operations with engine in car

10 The following operations can be carried out without having to remove the engine from the vehicle.
a) Removal and refitting of the camshaft cover.
b) Adjustment of the valve clearances.
c) Removal and refitting of the cylinder head.
d) Removal and refitting of the timing belt, tensioner, idler pulleys and sprockets.
e) Renewal of the camshaft oil seal.
f) Removal and refitting of the camshaft and followers.
g) Removal and refitting of the sump.
h) Removal and refitting of the connecting rods and pistons.*
i) Removal and refitting of the oil pump.
j) Removal and refitting of the oil filter housing.
k) Renewal of the crankshaft oil seals.
l) Renewal of the engine mountings.
m) Removal and refitting of the flywheel.
* Although the operation marked with an asterisk can be carried out with the engine in the car (after removal of the sump), it is preferable for the engine to be removed, in the interests of cleanliness and improved access. For this reason, the procedure is described in Chapter 2E.

2 Compression and leakdown tests – description and interpretation

Compression test

Note: *A compression tester specifically designed for diesel engines must be used for this test.*

1 When engine performance is down, or if misfiring occurs which cannot be attributed to the fuel system, a compression test can provide diagnostic clues as to the engine's condition. If the test is performed regularly, it can give warning of trouble before any other symptoms become apparent.

2 The tester is connected to an adapter which screws into the injector holes. It is unlikely to be worthwhile buying such a tester for occasional use, but it may be possible to borrow or hire one – if not, have the test performed by a Vauxhall/Opel dealer, or suitably-equipped garage.

3 Unless specific instructions to the contrary are supplied with the tester, observe the following points:
a) *The battery must be in a good state of charge, the air filter must be clean, and the engine should be at normal operating temperature.*
b) *All the fuel injectors must be removed before starting the test (see Chapter 4B Section 14).*
c) *Open the cover on the engine compartment fuse/relay box and remove the fuel pump relay* **(see illustrations)**.

4 Screw the compression tester and adapter in to the fuel injector hole of No 1 cylinder.

5 With the help of an assistant, crank the engine on the starter motor; after one or two revolutions, the compression pressure should build-up to a maximum figure, and then stabilise. Record the highest reading obtained.

6 Repeat the test on the remaining cylinders, recording the pressure in each.

7 All cylinders should produce very similar pressures; any difference greater than the maximum figure given in the Specifications indicates the existence of a fault. Note that the compression should build-up quickly in a healthy engine; low compression on the first stroke, followed by gradually-increasing pressure on successive strokes, indicates worn piston rings. A low compression reading on the first stroke, which does not build-up during successive strokes, indicates leaking valves or a blown head gasket (a cracked head could also be the cause). **Note:** *The cause of poor compression is less easy to establish on a diesel engine than on a petrol one. The effect of introducing oil into the cylinders ('wet' testing) is not conclusive, because there is a risk that the oil will sit in the recess on the piston crown instead of passing to the rings.*

8 On completion of the test, refit the fuel pump relay, then refit the fuel injectors as described in Chapter 4B Section 14.

2.3a Open the cover on the fuse/relay box ...

2.3b ... and remove the fuel pump relay (arrowed)

3.0 Vauxhall/Opel special tool EN-46788 (or equivalent) is required to set the TDC position for No 1 piston

3.3a Remove the engine oil filler cap ...

3.3b ... undo the two retaining bolts (arrowed) ...

Leakdown test

9 A leakdown test measures the rate at which compressed air fed into the cylinder is lost. It is an alternative to a compression test, and in many ways it is better, since the escaping air provides easy identification of where pressure loss is occurring (piston rings, valves or head gasket).

10 The equipment needed for leakdown testing is unlikely to be available to the home mechanic. If poor compression is suspected, have the test performed by a Vauxhall/Opel dealer, or suitably-equipped garage.

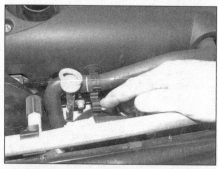

3.3c ... release the hose support clip ...

3.3d ... then lift off the plastic cover over the top of the engine

3	Top Dead Centre (TDC) for No 1 piston – locating

Note: *To accurately determine the TDC position for No 1 piston, it will be necessary to use Vauxhall/Opel special tool EN-46788 (or suitable equivalents) to set the crankshaft at the TDC position* **(see illustration).**

1 In its travel up and down its cylinder bore, Top Dead Centre (TDC) is the highest point that each piston reaches as the crankshaft rotates. While each piston reaches TDC both at the top of the compression stroke and again at the top of the exhaust stroke, for the purpose of timing the engine, TDC refers to the piston position of No 1 cylinder at the top of its compression stroke.

2 Number 1 piston (and cylinder) is at the right-hand (timing belt) end of the engine, and its TDC position is located as follows. Note that the crankshaft rotates clockwise when viewed from the right-hand side of the car.

3 Remove the engine oil filler cap, undo the two retaining bolts, release the hose support clip, then lift off the plastic cover over the top of the engine **(see illustrations)**. Refit the oil filler cap.

4 Remove the crankshaft pulley/vibration damper as described in Section 6.

5 Undo the central mounting bolt, and remove the auxiliary drivebelt tensioner assembly from the engine **(see illustration)**.

6 Remove the air cleaner assembly and air intake duct as described in Chapter 4B Section 3.

7 Place a trolley jack beneath the right-hand end of the engine with a block of wood on the jack head. Raise the jack until it is supporting the weight of the engine.

8 Mark the bolt positions for correct refitting, then undo the three bolts securing the right-hand engine mounting to the engine bracket, and the three bolts securing the mounting to the body. Remove the mounting **(see illustration)**.

9 Unclip the wiring harness from the top and side of the upper timing belt cover. Unscrew the six retaining bolts and lift off the upper timing belt cover **(see illustration)**.

10 Using a socket and extension bar on the crankshaft sprocket bolt, rotate the crankshaft in the normal direction of rotation until the mark on the camshaft sprocket is aligned

3.5 Undo the central mounting bolt (arrowed), and remove the auxiliary drivebelt tensioner assembly

3.8 Undo the retaining bolts and remove the right-hand engine mounting

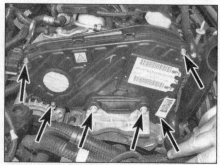

3.9 Upper timing belt cover retaining bolts (arrowed)

3.10 Rotate the crankshaft to align the mark on the camshaft sprocket (arrowed) with the pointer on the camshaft cover

3.11 Screw the fastening stud of special tool EN-46788 into the oil pump housing

3.12 Positioning ring of tool EN-46788 (arrowed) attached to the fastening stud and crankshaft sprocket

with the pointer on the camshaft cover **(see illustration)**.

11 Unscrew the bolt from the lower left-hand side of the oil pump housing and screw in the fastening stud of Vauxhall/Opel special tool EN-46788 **(see illustration)**.

12 Fit the positioning ring of tool EN-46788 over the fastening stud and engage it with the crankshaft sprocket. Ensure that the hole in the positioning ring engages with the lug on the sprocket. Secure the tool in position with the retaining bolt and nut **(see illustration)**.

13 With the crankshaft positioning ring in place and the mark on the camshaft sprocket aligned with the pointer on the camshaft cover, the engine is positioned with No 1 piston at TDC on compression.

4 Valve timing – checking and adjustment

1 Position No 1 cylinder at TDC on its compression stroke as described in Section 3.

2 With the crankshaft positioning ring in place, check that the mark on the camshaft sprocket is aligned with the pointer on the camshaft cover; if so, the valve timing is correct.

3 If the mark on the camshaft sprocket is not aligned with the pointer on the camshaft cover, readjust the timing belt position as described in Section 7.

5 Camshaft cover – removal and refitting

Removal

1 Remove the engine oil filler cap, undo the two retaining bolts, release the hose support clip, then undo the two bolts and lift off the plastic cover over the top of the engine **(see illustrations 3.3a to 3.3d)**. Refit the oil filler cap.

2 Undo the retaining bolt(s) to release the vacuum lines running over the top of the camshaft cover **(see illustration)**.

3 Release the retaining clips and disconnect

5.2 Undo the retaining bolt(s) to release the vacuum lines from the camshaft cover

the breather hoses from the front and rear of the camshaft cover **(see illustrations)**.

4 Disconnect the fuel leak-off hose connection at No 2 and No 3 injector by extracting the locking clip and lifting out the hose fitting. Refit the locking clips to the injectors after disconnecting the hose fitting.

5 Undo the seven retaining bolts securing the camshaft cover to the cylinder head **(see illustration)**.

6 Carefully move the disconnected leak-off hose assembly rearward, then lift the camshaft cover from the cylinder head **(see illustration)**.

Refitting

7 Ensure the cover and cylinder head

5.3a Release the retaining clips and disconnect the breather hoses from the front ...

5.3b ... and rear of the camshaft cover

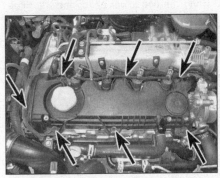

5.5 Undo the seven bolts (arrowed) securing the camshaft cover to the cylinder head

5.6 Move the leak-off hose assembly rearward, then lift the camshaft cover from the cylinder head

5.7 Fit the seal to the camshaft cover groove

6.3 Crankshaft pulley/vibration damper retaining bolts (arrowed)

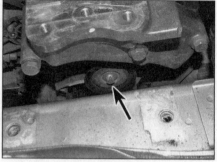

7.2 Undo the bolt (arrowed) and remove the auxiliary drivebelt idler pulley from the engine bracket

surfaces are clean and dry then fit the seal to the cover groove **(see illustration)**.

8 Move the leak-off hose assembly to the rear and carefully lower the cover into position. Screw in the retaining bolts and lightly tighten them. Once all bolts are hand-tight, go around and tighten them all to the specified torque setting.

9 Reconnect the leak-off hose fittings to the injectors by pushing in the locking clip, attaching the fitting, then releasing the locking clip. Ensure that each fitting is securely connected and retained by the clip.

10 Reconnect the breather hoses to the cover.

11 Refit and tighten the bolts securing the vacuum lines.

12 Refit the plastic cover to the top of the engine, tighten the two retaining bolts and resecure the hose.

6 Crankshaft pulley/vibration damper – removal and refitting

Removal

1 Apply the handbrake, then jack up the front of the vehicle and support it on axle stands (see *Jacking and vehicle support*). Remove the right-hand front roadwheel.

2 Remove the auxiliary drivebelt as described in Chapter 1B Section 24. Prior to removal, mark the direction of rotation on the belt

to ensure the belt is refitted the same way around.

3 Undo the four bolts securing the pulley to the crankshaft sprocket and remove the pulley from the sprocket **(see illustration)**.

Refitting

4 Locate the crankshaft pulley on the sprocket, ensuring that the hole on the rear face of the pulley engages with the lug on the sprocket.

5 Refit the four retaining bolts and tighten them progressively to the specified torque.

6 Refit the auxiliary drivebelt as described in Chapter 1B Section 24 using the mark made prior to removal to ensure the belt is fitted the correct way around.

7 Refit the roadwheel, then lower the car to the ground and tighten the wheel bolts to the specified torque.

7 Timing belt – removal and refitting

Note: *The timing belt must be removed and refitted with the engine cold.*

Removal

1 Position No 1 cylinder at TDC on its compression stroke as described in Section 3.

2 Undo the retaining bolt and remove the auxiliary drivebelt idler pulley from the engine bracket **(see illustration)**.

3 Undo the two lower bolts, and the three

upper bolts, and remove the engine bracket from the engine **(see illustrations)**.

4 Undo the nut and bolt and remove the crankshaft positioning tool (EN-46788) from the crankshaft sprocket.

5 Slacken the timing belt tensioner retaining bolt and allow the tensioner to retract, relieving the tension on the timing belt.

6 Slide the timing belt from its sprockets and remove it from the engine. If the belt is to be re-used, use white paint or similar to mark the direction of rotation on the belt. Do not rotate the crankshaft or camshafts until the timing belt has been refitted.

7 Check the timing belt carefully for any signs of uneven wear, splitting or oil contamination, and renew it if there is the slightest doubt about its condition. If the engine is undergoing an overhaul and is approaching the specified interval for belt renewal (see Chapter 1B Section 2) renew the belt as a matter of course, regardless of its apparent condition. If signs of oil contamination are found, trace the source of the oil leak and rectify it, then wash down the engine timing belt area and all related components to remove all traces of oil.

Refitting

8 On reassembly, thoroughly clean the timing belt sprockets and tensioner/idler pulleys.

9 Place the timing belt in position over the crankshaft sprocket. If the original belt is being refitted, ensure that the arrow mark made on removal points in the normal direction of rotation, as before.

7.3a Undo the two lower bolts (arrowed) …

7.3b … and the three upper bolts (arrowed) …

7.3c … and remove the engine bracket from the engine

7.12a Using a screwdriver resting on a pivot bolt (arrowed), move the adjusting lever on the tensioner …

7.12b … until the tensioner pointer (arrowed) is aligned with the mark on the backplate

10 Check that the camshaft and crankshaft are still correctly positioned with No 1 piston at TDC on compression as described in Section 3, and refit the crankshaft positioning tool.

11 Fit the timing belt over the crankshaft, camshaft and fuel pump sprockets and around the idler pulleys, ensuring that the belt front run is taut (ie, all slack is on the tensioner side of the belt), then fit the belt over the coolant pump sprocket and tensioner pulley. Do not twist the belt sharply while refitting it. Ensure that the belt teeth are correctly seated centrally in the sprockets, and that the timing mark on the camshaft sprocket remain in alignment.

12 Screw a suitable bolt, approximately 50 mm in length, into the threaded hole directly below the timing belt tensioner. Using a screwdriver resting on the bolt as a pivot, move the adjusting lever on the tensioner until the tensioner pointer is aligned with the mark on the backplate. Hold the tensioner in this position and tighten the tensioner retaining bolt **(see illustrations)**.

13 Remove the crankshaft positioning tool.

14 Using a socket on the crankshaft sprocket bolt, rotate the crankshaft smoothly through two complete turns (720°) in the normal direction of rotation to settle the timing belt in position. At the end of the second turn, align the mark on the camshaft sprocket with the pointer on the camshaft cover.

15 Refit the positioning ring of tool EN-46788 over the fastening stud and engage it with the crankshaft sprocket. Ensure that the hole in the positioning ring engages with the lug on the sprocket. Secure the tool in position with the retaining bolt and nut.

16 Slacken the timing belt tensioner retaining bolt and, using a screwdriver resting on the pivot bolt as before, move the adjusting lever on the tensioner until the tensioner pointer is once again aligned with the mark on the backplate. Hold the tensioner in this position and tighten the tensioner retaining bolt to the specified torque.

17 Remove all the positioning tools and again rotate the crankshaft smoothly through two complete turns (720°) in the normal direction of rotation. Check that the timing belt tensioner pointer is still aligned with the mark on the backplate. If not, repeat the procedure described in paragraph 16.

18 When all is correct, remove the tensioner position pivot bolt. Refit the bolt removed from the oil pump housing and tighten it to the specified torque.

19 Place the engine bracket in position and refit the two lower bolts, and the three upper bolts. Tighten the bolts to the specified torque. Refit the auxiliary drivebelt idler pulley to the engine bracket and tighten the retaining bolt to the specified torque.

20 Refit the upper timing belt cover and tighten the retaining bolts to the specified torque. Clip the wiring harness back into position.

21 Place the right-hand engine mounting assembly in position and refit the three bolts securing the mounting to the body. Tighten the bolts to the specified torque. Align the mounting in its original position, then fit and tighten the three mounting bracket bolts to the specified torque. Remove the jack from under the engine.

22 Refit the air cleaner assembly and air intake duct as described in Chapter 4B Section 3.

23 Place the auxiliary drivebelt tensioner assembly in position ensuring that the locating peg on the tensioner mounting surface engages correctly with the corresponding hole in the mounting bracket. Tighten the tensioner central mounting bolt to the specified torque.

24 Refit the crankshaft pulley/vibration damper as described in Section 6, then refit the auxiliary drivebelt as described in Chapter 1B Section 24.

25 Refit the plastic cover to the top of the engine and tighten the retaining bolts.

26 Refit the roadwheel, then lower the car to the ground and tighten the wheel bolts to the specified torque.

8 Timing belt sprockets, tensioner and idler pulley – removal and refitting

Note: *Certain special tools will be required for the removal and refitting of the sprockets. Read through the entire procedure to familiarise yourself with the work involved, then either obtain the manufacturer's special tools, or use the alternatives described.*

Camshaft sprocket

Note: *A new sprocket retaining bolt will be required for refitting.*

Removal

1 Remove the timing belt as described in Section 7.

2 It will now be necessary to hold the camshaft sprocket to enable the retaining bolt to be removed. Vauxhall/Opel special tools EN-46787 and KM-956-1 are available for this purpose, however, a home-made tool can easily be fabricated (see **Tool Tip**).

HAYNES HiNT

To make a sprocket holding tool, obtain two lengths of steel strip about 6 mm thick by about 30 mm wide or similar, one 600 mm long, the other 200 mm long (all dimensions are approximate). Bolt the two strips together to form a forked end, leaving the bolt slack so that the shorter strip can pivot freely. At the other end of each 'prong' of the fork, drill a suitable hole and fit a nut and bolt to allow the tool to engage with the spokes in the sprocket.

8.12a Remove the bolt and washer ...

8.12b ... and slide the sprocket off the end of the crankshaft

8.18 Engage the holding tool with the holes in the fuel pump sprocket and undo the retaining nut

3 Engage the tool with the holes in the camshaft sprocket, taking care not to damage the camshaft sensor located behind the sprocket

4 Unscrew the retaining bolt and remove the sprocket from the end of the camshaft.

Refitting

5 Prior to refitting check the oil seal for signs of damage or leakage. If necessary, renew as described in Section 9.

6 Refit the sprocket to the camshaft end, aligning its cut-out with the locating peg, and fit the new retaining bolt.

7 Retain the sprocket using the holding tool, and tighten the retaining bolt to the specified torque.

8 Refit the timing belt as described in Section 7.

Crankshaft sprocket

Note: The crankshaft sprocket retaining bolt is extremely tight. Ensure that the holding tool used to prevent rotation as the bolt is slackened is of sturdy construction and securely attached.

Note: A new sprocket retaining bolt will be required for refitting.

Removal

9 Remove the timing belt as described in Section 7.

10 It will now be necessary to hold the crankshaft sprocket to enable the retaining bolt to be removed. Vauxhall/Opel special tools EN-47630 and KM-956-1 are available for this purpose, however, a home-made tool

similar to that described in paragraph 2, can easily be fabricated.

11 Using the crankshaft pulley retaining bolts, securely attach the tool to the crankshaft sprocket. With the help of an assistant, hold the sprocket stationary and unscrew the retaining bolt. Note: The sprocket retaining bolt has a left-hand thread and is unscrewed by turning it clockwise.

12 Remove the bolt and washer and slide the sprocket off the end of the crankshaft (see illustrations). Note that a new bolt will be required for refitting.

Refitting

13 Align the sprocket location key with the crankshaft groove and slide the sprocket into position. Fit the new retaining bolt and washer.

14 Hold the sprocket stationary using the holding tool and tighten the retaining bolt to the specified torque. Remove the holding tool.

15 Refit the timing belt as described in Section 7.

High-pressure fuel pump sprocket

Note: A new sprocket retaining nut will be required for refitting.

Removal

16 Remove the timing belt as described in Section 7.

17 It will now be necessary to hold the fuel pump sprocket to enable the retaining nut to be removed. Vauxhall/Opel special tools KM-6347 and KM-956-1 are available for this

purpose, however, a home-made tool similar to that described in paragraph 2, can easily be fabricated.

18 Engage the tool with the holes in the fuel pump sprocket and undo the sprocket retaining nut (see illustration). Note that a new nut will be required for refitting.

19 Attach a suitable puller to the threaded holes in the fuel pump sprocket using bolts and washers similar to the arrangement shown (see illustration).

20 Tighten the puller centre bolt to release the sprocket from the taper on the pump shaft. Once the taper releases, remove the puller and withdraw the sprocket. Collect the Woodruff key from the pump shaft (see illustrations).

Refitting

21 Clean the fuel pump shaft and the sprocket hub ensuring that all traces of oil or grease are removed.

22 Refit the Woodruff key to the pump shaft, then locate the sprocket in position. Fit the new retaining nut.

23 Hold the sprocket stationary using the holding tool and tighten the retaining nut to the specified torque. Remove the holding tool.

24 Refit the timing belt as described in Section 7.

Tensioner assembly

Removal

25 Remove the timing belt as described in Section 7.

26 Slacken and remove the retaining bolt

8.19 Use a suitable puller to release the fuel pump sprocket taper

8.20a Once the taper releases, withdraw the sprocket ...

8.20b ... and collect the Woodruff key from the pump shaft

8.26 Slacken and remove the retaining bolt and remove the timing belt tensioner assembly

and remove the tensioner assembly from the engine **(see illustration)**.

Refitting

27 Fit the tensioner to the engine, making sure that the slot on the tensioner backplate is correctly located over the peg on the engine bracket **(see illustration)**.

28 Clean the threads of the retaining bolt and apply thread-locking compound to the bolt threads. Screw in the retaining bolt, set the tensioner in the retracted position and tighten the retaining bolt.

29 Refit the timing belt as described in Section 7.

Idler pulley

Removal

30 Remove the timing belt as described in Section 7.

31 Slacken and remove the retaining bolt and remove the idler pulley from the engine.

Refitting

32 Refit the idler pulley and tighten the retaining bolt to the specified torque.

33 Refit the timing belt as described in Section 7.

9 Camshaft oil seal – renewal

1 Remove the camshaft sprocket as described in Section 8.

10.4 Camshaft positioned with No 1 and No 6 cam lobes (arrowed) pointing upward

8.27 The slot on the tensioner backplate must locate over the peg (arrowed) on the engine bracket

2 Carefully punch or drill a small hole in the oil seal. Screw in a self-tapping screw, and pull on the screw with pliers to extract the seal.

3 Clean the seal housing, and polish off any burrs or raised edges which may have caused the seal to fail in the first place.

4 Press the new seal into position using a suitable tubular drift (such as a socket) which bears only on the hard outer edge of the seal. Take care not to damage the seal lips during fitting; note that the seal lips should face inwards.

5 Refit the camshaft sprocket as described in Section 8.

10 Valve clearances – checking and adjustment

Note: *Vauxhall/Opel special tools EN-46797 and EN-46799 (or suitable equivalents) will be required if adjustment is necessary.*

Checking

1 The importance of having the valve clearances correctly adjusted cannot be overstressed, as they vitally affect the performance of the engine. The engine must be cold for the check to be accurate. The clearances are checked as follows.

2 Apply the handbrake, then jack up the front of the vehicle and support it on axle stands (see *Jacking and vehicle support*). Remove the right-hand front roadwheel.

3 Remove the camshaft cover as described in Section 5.

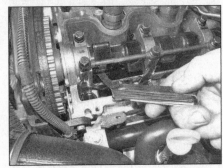

10.6 Valve clearance measurement

4 Using a socket and extension on the crankshaft pulley bolt, rotate the crankshaft in the normal direction of rotation (clockwise when viewed from the right-hand end of the engine) until camshaft lobes 1 and 6 are pointing upward **(see illustration)**.

5 On a piece of paper, draw the outline of the engine with the cylinders numbered from the timing belt end. Show the position of each valve, together with the specified valve clearance. Note that the clearance for both the intake and exhaust valves is the same.

6 With the cam lobes positioned as described in paragraph 4, using feeler blades, measure the clearance between the base of camshaft lobes 1 and 6 and the adjustment shim located on the top of the camshaft follower **(see illustration)**. Record the clearances on the paper.

7 Rotate the crankshaft until camshaft lobes 5 and 8 are pointing upward. Measure the clearance between the base of the camshaft lobes and the shims on their followers and record the clearances on the paper.

8 Rotate the crankshaft until camshaft lobes 4 and 7 are pointing upward. Measure the clearance between the base of the camshaft lobes and the shims on their followers and record the clearances on the paper.

9 Rotate the crankshaft until camshaft lobes 2 and 3 are pointing upward. Measure the clearance between the base of the camshaft lobes and the shims on their followers and record the clearances on the paper.

10 If all the clearances are correct, refit the camshaft cover as described in Section 5. Refit the roadwheel, then lower the car to the ground and tighten the wheel bolts to the specified torque.

11 If any clearance measured is not correct, adjustment must be carried out as described in the following paragraphs.

Adjustment

12 Rotate the crankshaft clockwise until camshaft lobes 1 and 6 are once again pointing upward. With the camshaft in this position, valve No 1 and valve No 6 can be adjusted as follows.

13 Rotate the follower until the groove on its upper edge is facing towards the front of the engine **(see illustration)**.

10.13 Rotate the follower until the groove (arrowed) is facing towards the front of the engine

10.16 The thickness of each shim should be stamped on one of its surfaces

11.6 Camshaft bearing cap retaining bolts (arrowed)

11.7 Carefully release the oil pipe (arrowed) from its location in the cylinder head

14 Insert Vauxhall/Opel special tool EN-46797 between the base of the camshaft lobe and the shim and lever downward to open the valve. Now insert Vauxhall/Opel special tool EN-46799 between the edge of the follower and the base of the camshaft to hold the valve open. Take care when doing this as it is possible for the valve to contact the piston. If any resistance is felt as the valve is opened, remove the tool and rotate the crankshaft slightly to move the piston down its bore.

15 Using a small screwdriver inserted in the groove on the edge of the follower, lift up the shim, then slide it out from between the follower and camshaft.

16 Clean the shim, and measure its thickness with a micrometer. The shims carry thickness markings, but wear may have reduced the original thickness, so be sure to double-check **(see illustration)**.

17 Add the measured clearance of the valve to the thickness of the original shim then subtract the specified valve clearance from this figure. This will give you the thickness of the shim required. For example:

Measured valve clearance	0.45 mm
Plus thickness of the original shim	2.70 mm
Equals	3.15 mm
Minus clearance required	0.40 mm
Thickness of shim required	2.75 mm

18 Obtain the correct thickness of shim required and lubricate it with clean engine oil. With the valve still held open with the special tool, slide the shim into position, with the thickness number downwards, ensuring it is correctly located.

19 Using the first special tool, lever down on the shim and remove the second special tool. Allow the valve to close and remove the first special tool. Check that the valve clearance is within limits.

20 Rotate the crankshaft clockwise until camshaft lobes 5 and 8 are once again pointing upward. Adjust No 5 and No 8 valve clearances as described in paragraphs 13 to 19.

21 Rotate the crankshaft clockwise until camshaft lobes 4 and 7 are once again

pointing upward. Adjust No 4 and No 7 valve clearances as described in paragraphs 13 to 19.

22 Rotate the crankshaft clockwise until camshaft lobes 2 and 3 are once again pointing upward. Adjust No 2 and No 3 valve clearances as described in paragraphs 13 to 19.

23 On completion, refit the camshaft cover as described in Section 5. Refit the roadwheel, then lower the car to the ground and tighten the wheel bolts to the specified torque.

11 Camshaft and followers
– removal, inspection and refitting

Removal

1 Remove the timing belt as described in Section 7.

2 Remove the camshaft sprocket as described in Section 8.

3 Remove the camshaft cover as described in Section 5.

4 Remove the braking system vacuum pump as described in Chapter 9.

5 Check for identification markings on the camshaft bearing caps. If no markings can be seen, make suitable identification marks on the caps, to indicate their number and which way round they are fitted.

6 Working in a spiral pattern from the outside inwards, slacken the twelve camshaft bearing cap retaining bolts by half a turn at a time, to relieve the pressure of the valve springs on the bearing caps gradually and evenly **(see illustration)**. Once the valve spring pressure has been relieved, the bolts can be fully unscrewed and removed.

Caution: If the bearing cap bolts are carelessly slackened, the bearing caps might break. If any bearing cap breaks then the complete cylinder head assembly must be renewed; the bearing caps are matched to the head and are not available separately.

7 Carefully release the oil supply pipe from its location in the cylinder head, then lift the pipe off the bearing caps **(see illustration)**.

8 Remove the bearing caps, then lift the

camshaft out of the cylinder head and slide off the oil seal.

9 Obtain eight small, clean plastic containers, and label them for identification. Alternatively, divide a larger container into compartments. Lift the followers and shims out from the top of the cylinder head and store each one in its respective fitted position. Make sure the followers and shims are not mixed up, to ensure the valve clearances remain correct on refitting.

Inspection

10 Examine the camshaft bearing surfaces and cam lobes for signs of wear ridges and scoring. Renew the camshaft if any of these conditions are apparent. Examine the condition of the bearing surfaces both on the camshaft journals and in the cylinder head. If the head bearing surfaces are worn excessively, the cylinder head will need to be renewed.

11 Check the camshaft followers and their bores in the cylinder head for signs of wear or damage. If any follower is thought to be faulty or is visibly worn it should be renewed.

Refitting

12 Commence refitting by turning the crankshaft anti-clockwise by 90°. This will position all the pistons half-way down their bores, and prevent any chance of the valves touching the piston crowns as the camshaft is being fitted.

13 Lubricate the camshaft followers with clean engine oil and carefully insert each one (together with its adjusting shim) into its original location in the cylinder head.

14 Lubricate the camshaft follower shims, and the bearing journals with clean engine oil, then lay the camshaft in position.

15 Apply a smear of sealant to the mating surfaces of both the No 1 and No 5 camshaft bearing caps. Using the marks made on removal as a guide, refit the camshaft bearing caps in their original locations on the cylinder head.

16 Carefully engage the oil supply pipe into its location in the cylinder head, then place the pipe in position on the bearing caps.

17 Refit the bearing cap retaining bolts and tighten them by hand until they just contact the bearing caps.

18 Working in a spiral pattern from the centre outwards, tighten the bolts by half a turn at a time to gradually impose the pressure of the valve springs on the bearing caps. Repeat this sequence until all bearing caps are in contact with the cylinder head then go around and tighten the camshaft bearing cap bolts to the specified torque.

Caution: If the bearing cap bolts are carelessly tightened, the bearing caps might break. If any bearing cap breaks then the complete cylinder head assembly must be renewed; the bearing caps are matched to the head and are not available separately.

19 Fit a new camshaft oil seal as described in Section 9.

20 Refit the braking system vacuum pump as described in Chapter 9 Section 19.

21 Refit the camshaft cover as described in Section 5.

22 Refit the camshaft sprocket as described in Section 8. Rotate the camshaft until the mark on the camshaft sprocket is aligned with the pointer on the camshaft cover (see Section 3).

23 Turn the crankshaft clockwise by 90° to bring No 1 and 4 pistons to approximately the TDC position.

24 Refit the timing belt as described in Section 7.

25 If any new components have been fitted, check, and if necessary adjust, the valve clearances as described in Section 10.

12 Cylinder head – removal and refitting

Note: *New cylinder head bolts will be required on refitting.*

Removal

1 Disconnect the battery negative terminal (refer to Chapter 5A Section 4).

2 Drain the cooling system as described in Chapter 1B Section 30.

3 Remove the timing belt as described in Section 7.

4 Disconnect the wiring harness connectors from the following components with reference to the Chapters indicated:
a) *Coolant temperature sensor (Chapter 3 Section 6).*
b) *Fuel pressure sensor (Chapter 4B Section 11).*
c) *Fuel pressure regulating valve (Chapter 4B Section 10).*
d) *Throttle housing (Chapter 4B Section 11).*
e) *Fuel injectors (Chapter 4B Section 14).*
f) *Air conditioning compressor (Chapter 3 Section 11).*
g) *EGR valve (Chapter 4C Section 3).*
h) *Charge (boost) pressure sensor (Chapter 4B Section 11).*
i) *High-pressure fuel pump (Chapter 4B Section 12).*
j) *Camshaft sensor (Chapter 4B Section 11).*

5 Undo the wiring harness support bracket bolts, release the retaining clips and move the harness to one side **(see illustration)**.

6 Remove the intake and exhaust manifolds as described in Chapter 4B.

7 Remove the camshaft cover as described in Section 5.

8 Remove the braking system vacuum pump as described in Chapter 9 Section 19.

9 Make a final check to ensure that all relevant hoses, pipes and wires have been disconnected.

10 Working in the reverse of the tightening sequence **(see illustration 12.28)**, progressively slacken the cylinder head bolts by half a turn at a time, until all bolts can be unscrewed by hand. Note that an M14 RIBE socket bit will be required to unscrew the bolts. Remove the cylinder head bolts and recover the washers.

11 Engage the help of an assistant and lift the cylinder head from the cylinder block. Take care as it is a bulky and heavy assembly.

Caution: Do not lay the head on its lower mating surface; support the head on wooden blocks, ensuring each block only contacts the head mating surface.

12 Remove the gasket and keep it for identification purposes (see paragraph 19).

13 If the cylinder head is to be dismantled for overhaul, then refer to Part E of this Chapter.

Preparation for refitting

14 The mating faces of the cylinder head and cylinder block/crankcase must be perfectly clean before refitting the head. Use a hard plastic or wood scraper to remove all traces of gasket and carbon; also clean the piston crowns. Take particular care, as the surfaces are damaged easily. Also, make sure that the carbon is not allowed to enter the oil and water passages – this is particularly important for the lubrication system, as carbon could block the oil supply to any of the engine's components. Using adhesive tape and paper, seal the water, oil and bolt holes in the cylinder block/crankcase. To prevent carbon entering the gap between the pistons and bores, smear a little grease in the gap. After cleaning each piston, use a small brush to remove all traces of grease and carbon from the gap, then wipe away the remainder with a clean rag. Clean all the pistons in the same way.

15 Check the mating surfaces of the cylinder block/crankcase and the cylinder head for nicks, deep scratches and other damage. If slight, they may be removed carefully with a file, but if excessive, machining may be the only alternative to renewal.

16 Ensure that the cylinder head bolt holes in the crankcase are clean and free of oil. Syringe or soak up any oil left in the bolt holes. This is most important in order that the correct bolt tightening torque can be applied and to prevent the possibility of the block being cracked by hydraulic pressure when the bolts are tightened.

17 The cylinder head bolts must be discarded and renewed, regardless of their apparent condition.

18 If warpage of the cylinder head gasket surface is suspected, use a straight-edge to check it for distortion. Refer to Part E of this Chapter if necessary.

19 On this engine, the cylinder head-to-piston clearance is controlled by fitting different thickness head gaskets. The gasket thickness can be determined by looking at the holes stamped on the edge of the gasket **(see illustration)**.

Number of holes	Gasket thickness
No holes	0.77 to 0.87 mm
One hole	0.87 to 0.97 mm
Two holes	0.97 to 1.07 mm

20 The correct thickness of gasket required is selected by measuring the piston protrusions as follows.

21 Mount a dial test indicator securely on the block so that its pointer can be easily pivoted between the piston crown and block mating surface. Turn the crankshaft to bring No 1 piston roughly to the TDC position. Move the dial test indicator probe over and in contact with No 1 piston. Turn the crankshaft back-and-forth slightly until the highest reading is shown on the gauge, indicating that the piston is at TDC.

22 Zero the dial test indicator on the gasket surface of the cylinder block then carefully

12.5 Undo the support bracket bolts (arrowed), release the retaining clips and move the wiring harness to one side

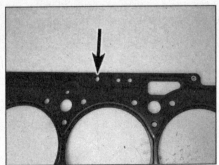

12.19 Cylinder head gasket thickness identification hole (arrowed)

12.22 Using a dial test indicator to measure piston protrusion

12.25 Place the new gasket in position with the words ALTO/TOP uppermost

12.29 Cylinder head bolt tightening sequence

move the indicator over No 1 piston. Measure its protrusion at the highest point between the valve cut-outs, and then again at its highest point between the valve cut-outs at 90° to the first measurement **(see illustration)**. Repeat this procedure with No 4 piston.

23 Rotate the crankshaft half a turn (180°) to bring No 2 and 3 pistons to TDC. Ensure the crankshaft is accurately positioned then measure the protrusions of No 2 and 3 pistons at the specified points. Once all pistons have been measured, rotate the crankshaft to position all the pistons at their mid-stroke.

24 Select the correct thickness of head gasket required by determining the largest amount of piston protrusion, and using the following table.

Piston protrusion measurement (mm)	Gasket thickness required
0.020 to 0.100	0.77 to 0.87 (no holes)
0.101 to 0.200	0.87 to 0.97 (one hole)
0.201 to 0.295	0.97 to 1.07 (two holes)

Refitting

25 Wipe clean the mating surfaces of the cylinder head and cylinder block/crankcase. Place the new gasket in position with the words ALTO/TOP uppermost **(see illustration)**.

26 If not already done, rotate the crankshaft to position all the pistons at their mid-stroke.

27 With the aid of an assistant, carefully refit the cylinder head assembly to the block, aligning it with the locating dowels.

28 Apply a thin film of engine oil to the bolt

13.4 Intermediate shaft bearing housing support bracket retaining bolts (arrowed)

threads and the underside of the bolt heads. Carefully enter each new cylinder head bolt into its relevant hole (do not drop them in). Screw all bolts in, by hand only, until finger-tight.

29 Working progressively in sequence, tighten the cylinder head bolts to their Stage 1 torque setting, using a torque wrench and suitable socket **(see illustration)**. Working again in the same sequence, go around and tighten all bolts through the specified Stage 2 torque setting.

30 Once all bolts have been tightened to the Stage 2 torque, working again in the same sequence, go around and tighten all bolts through the specified Stage 3 angle, then through the specified Stage 4 angle, and finally through the specified Stage 5 angle using an angle-measuring gauge.

31 Refit the braking system vacuum pump as described in Chapter 9 Section 19.

32 Refit the camshaft cover as described in Section 5.

33 Refit the intake and exhaust manifolds as described in Chapter 4B.

34 Reconnect the wiring harness connectors to the components listed in paragraph 4, then refit the wiring harness support bracket bolts, and secure the harness with the retaining clips.

35 Refit the timing belt as described in Section 7.

36 On completion, reconnect the battery negative terminal, then refill the cooling system as described in Chapter 1B Section 30.

13.9 Air conditioning compressor mounting bracket retaining bolts (arrowed)

13 Sump – removal and refitting

Removal

1 Disconnect the battery negative terminal (refer to Chapter 5A Section 4).

2 Apply the handbrake, then jack up the front of the vehicle and support it on axle stands (see *Jacking and vehicle support*). Remove the right-hand front roadwheel.

3 Remove the right-hand driveshaft and the intermediate shaft as described in Chapter 8.

4 Undo the three bolts securing the intermediate shaft bearing housing support bracket to the cylinder block and remove the support bracket **(see illustration)**.

5 Remove the exhaust system as described in Chapter 4B Section 20.

6 Undo the three bolts and remove the support bracket from the catalytic converter and sump.

7 Remove the crankshaft pulley/vibration damper as described in Section 6.

8 Disconnect the wiring connector from the air conditioning compressor. Undo the three bolts securing the air conditioning compressor to the mounting bracket and suitably support the compressor on the front subframe.

9 Undo the four bolts securing the compressor mounting bracket to the cylinder block and sump **(see illustration)**. Unclip the wiring harness and remove the mounting bracket.

10 Drain the engine oil as described in Chapter 1B Section 6. When the oil has completely drained, refit the drain plug with new sealing washer, and tighten to the specified torque.

11 Undo the upper bolt securing the oil dipstick guide tube to the coolant pipe. Undo the lower bolt securing the guide tube to the sump flange, then unclip the wiring harness and withdraw the tube from the sump flange sealing grommet.

12 Disconnect the wiring connector from the oil level sensor, then release the retaining clip and disconnect the oil return hose.

13 Undo the two bolts securing the sump flange to the transmission bellhousing.

14 Using a socket and extension on the

13.17 Removing the oil baffle plate from inside the sump

13.18 Renew the pick-up/strainer sealing ring prior to refitting

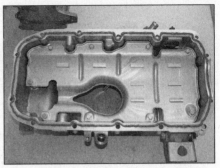

13.21 Apply a continuous bead of silicone sealing compound to the sump flange

crankshaft pulley bolt, rotate the crankshaft in the normal direction of rotation (clockwise when viewed from the right-hand end of the engine) until the opening in the flywheel is positioned to allow access to one of the rear sump retaining bolts. Undo and remove the bolt, then rotate the crankshaft again until the flywheel allows access to the second rear retaining bolt. Undo and remove the bolt.

15 Progressively slacken and remove the remaining twelve bolts securing the sump to the base of the cylinder block and oil pump housing. Using a wide-bladed scraper or similar tool inserted between the sump and cylinder block, carefully break the joint to release the sump.

16 Manoeuvre the sump out from under the car. Clearance is extremely limited between the sump and subframe, and it may be necessary to release the oil pump pick-up/strainer, by undoing its two retaining bolts, to enable the sump to be removed.

17 If required, undo the retaining bolts and remove the oil baffle plate from inside the sump **(see illustration)**.

18 While the sump is removed, take the opportunity to check the oil pump pick-up/strainer for signs of clogging or splitting. If not already done, unbolt the oil pump pick-up/strainer and remove it from the engine along with its sealing ring. The strainer can then be cleaned easily in solvent or renewed. Renew the pick-up/strainer sealing ring prior to refitting **(see illustration)**.

Refitting

19 Thoroughly clean the sump and remove all traces of silicone sealer and oil from the mating surfaces of the sump and cylinder block. If removed, refit the oil baffle plate and tighten its retaining bolts securely.

20 If clearance allows, refit the oil pump pick-up/strainer using a new sealing ring, and tighten its two retaining bolts securely. If it was necessary to unbolt the pick-up/strainer to allow the sump to be removed, place the unit in position and loosely screw in the bolt securing it to the main bearing cap. It must still be possible for the forward end of the pipe to be moved to the rear as the sump is refitted.

21 Apply a continuous bead of silicone sealing compound (available from your Vauxhall/Opel dealer) at approximately 1.0

mm from the inner edge of the sump **(see illustration)**. The bead of sealant should be between 2.0 and 2.5 mm in diameter.

22 Locate the sump over the pick-up/strainer then, where applicable, fit the forward end of the pick-up/strainer to the oil pump housing and fit the retaining bolt. Tighten both retaining bolts securely.

23 Engage the sump with the cylinder block and loosely refit all the retaining bolts.

24 Working out from the centre in a diagonal sequence, progressively tighten the bolts securing the sump to the cylinder block and oil pump housing. Tighten all the bolts to their specified torque setting.

25 Tighten the two bolts securing the sump flange to the transmission bellhousing to their specified torque settings.

26 Reconnect the wiring connector to the oil level sensor, then refit the oil return hose and secure with the retaining clip.

27 Refit the oil dipstick guide tube and secure with the two bolts tightened securely.

28 Locate the air conditioning compressor mounting bracket in position and refit the four retaining bolts. Tighten the bolts to the specified torque. Clip the wiring harness back into position on the bracket.

29 Position the air conditioning compressor on the mounting bracket. Fit and tighten the three retaining bolts to the specified torque (see Chapter 3 Section 11), then reconnect the compressor wiring connector.

30 Refit the crankshaft pulley/vibration damper as described in Section 6.

31 Refit the catalytic converter support bracket and securely tighten the three bolts.

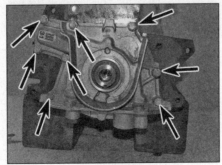

14.4 Oil pump housing retaining bolts (arrowed)

32 Refit the exhaust system as described in Chapter 4B Section 20.

33 Position the intermediate shaft bearing housing support bracket on the cylinder block and secure with the three retaining bolts tightened to the specified torque.

34 Refit the intermediate shaft and right-hand driveshaft as described in Chapter 8.

35 Refit the roadwheel, then lower the car to the ground and tighten the wheel bolts to the specified torque.

36 Fill the engine with fresh engine oil as described in Chapter 1B Section 6.

37 On completion, reconnect the battery negative terminal.

14 Oil pump – removal, overhaul and refitting

Removal

1 Remove the timing belt as described in Section 7.

2 Remove the crankshaft sprocket as described In Section 8.

3 Remove the sump and oil pump pick-up/strainer as described in Section 13.

4 Slacken and remove the seven retaining bolts then slide the oil pump housing assembly off of the end of the crankshaft **(see illustration)**. Remove the housing gasket and discard it.

Overhaul

5 Undo the retaining screws and lift off the pump cover from the rear of the housing **(see illustration)**.

14.5 Undo the retaining screws and lift off the oil pump cover

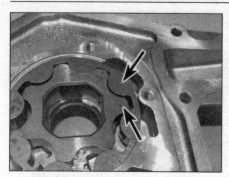

14.6 Oil pump inner and outer rotor identification dots (arrowed)

14.8a Unscrew the oil pressure relief valve bolt ...

14.8b ... and withdraw the spring ...

14.8c ... and plunger

14.10 Prime the oil pump by filling it with clean engine oil whilst rotating the inner rotor

14.13 Bend down the tabs on the edge of the gasket to retain it on the oil pump housing

6 Check the inner and outer rotors for identification dots indicating which way round they are fitted **(see illustration)**. If no marks are visible, use a suitable marker pen to mark the surface of both the pump inner and outer rotors.

7 Lift out the inner and outer rotors from the pump housing.

8 Unscrew the oil pressure relief valve bolt from the base of the housing and withdraw the spring and plunger, noting which way around the plunger is fitted **(see illustrations)**. Remove the sealing washer from the valve bolt.

9 Clean the components, and carefully examine the rotors, pump body and relief valve plunger for any signs of scoring or wear. If any damage or wear is noticed, it will be necessary to renew the complete pump assembly.

10 If the pump is satisfactory, reassemble the components in the reverse order of removal, noting the following.

a) Ensure both rotors are fitted the correct way around.

b) Fit a new sealing ring to the pressure relief valve bolt and securely tighten the bolt.

c) Apply a little locking compound to the threads, and securely tighten the pump cover screws.

d) On completion prime the oil pump by filling it with clean engine oil whilst rotating the inner rotor **(see illustration)**.

Refitting

11 Prior to refitting, carefully lever out the crankshaft oil seal using a flat-bladed screwdriver. Fit the new oil seal, ensuring its sealing lip is facing inwards, and press it squarely into the housing using a tubular drift which bears only on the hard outer edge of the seal. Press the seal into position so that it is flush with the housing and lubricate the oil seal lip with clean engine oil.

12 Ensure the mating surfaces of the oil pump and cylinder block are clean and dry.

13 Fit a new gasket to the oil pump housing and bend down the tabs on the edge of the gasket to retain it on the pump housing **(see illustration)**.

14 Locate the pump housing over the end of the crankshaft and into position on the cylinder block.

15 Refit the pump housing retaining bolts and tighten them to the specified torque.

16 Refit the oil pump pick-up/strainer and sump as described in Section 13.

17 Refit the crankshaft sprocket as described in Section 8.

18 Refit the timing belt as described in Section 7.

19 On completion, fit a new oil filter and fill the engine with clean oil as described in Chapter 1B Section 6.

15 Oil filter housing – removal and refitting

Removal

1 The oil filter housing with integral oil cooler is located at the rear of the cylinder block, above the right-hand driveshaft.

2 Disconnect the battery negative terminal (refer to Chapter 5A Section 4).

3 Apply the handbrake, then jack up the front of the vehicle and support it on axle stands (see Jacking and vehicle support). Remove the right-hand front roadwheel.

4 Drain the cooling system and remove the engine oil filter element as described in Chapter 1B.

5 Remove the exhaust system as described in Chapter 4B Section 20.

6 Remove the right-hand driveshaft and the intermediate shaft as described in Chapter 8.

7 Undo the three bolts securing the intermediate shaft bearing housing support bracket to the cylinder block and remove the support bracket **(see illustration 13.4)**.

8 Disconnect the wiring connector from the oil pressure switch.

9 Release the retaining clips and disconnect the two coolant hoses from the oil cooler on the oil filter housing.

15.10 Oil filter housing retaining bolts (arrowed)

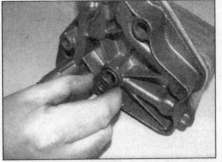

15.11a Fit a new sealing ring to the oil filter housing supply channel ...

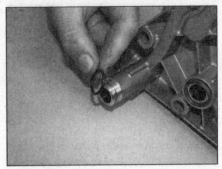

15.11b ... and to the return channel

10 Undo the three retaining bolts and remove the oil filter housing from the cylinder block **(see illustration)**. Recover the two rubber seals from the rear of the housing. Note that new seals will be required for refitting.

Refitting

11 Thoroughly clean the oil filter housing, then fit the two new sealing rings **(see illustrations)**.
12 Position the oil filter housing on the cylinder block and refit the retaining bolts. Tighten the bolts to the specified torque.
13 Refit the two coolant hoses and secure with their retaining clips. Reconnect the oil pressure switch wiring connector.
14 Position the intermediate shaft bearing housing support bracket on the cylinder block and secure with the three retaining bolts tightened to the specified torque.
15 Refit the intermediate shaft and right-hand driveshaft as described in Chapter 8.
16 Add new engine oil and fit a new oil filter element as described in Chapter 1B Section 6.
17 Refit the exhaust system as described in Chapter 4B Section 20.
18 Refit the roadwheel, then lower the car to the ground and tighten the wheel bolts to the specified torque.
19 Refill the cooling system as described in Chapter 1B Section 30.
20 On completion, reconnect the battery negative terminal.

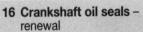

16 Crankshaft oil seals – renewal

Right-hand (timing belt end)

1 Remove the crankshaft sprocket as described in Section 8.
2 Carefully punch or drill a small hole in the oil seal. Screw in a self-tapping screw and pull on the screw with pliers to extract the seal **(see illustration)**.
3 Clean the seal housing and polish off any burrs or raised edges which may have caused the seal to fail in the first place.
4 Ease the new seal into position on the end

of the crankshaft. Press the seal squarely into position until it is flush with the housing. If necessary, a suitable tubular drift which bears only on the hard outer edge of the seal can be used to tap the seal into position **(see illustration)**. Take great care not to damage the seal lips during fitting and ensure that the seal lips face inwards.
5 Wash off any traces of oil, then refit the crankshaft sprocket as described in Section 8.

Left-hand (flywheel/driveplate end)

6 Remove the flywheel/driveplate as described in Section 17.
7 Remove the sump as described in Section 13.
8 Undo the five bolts and remove the oil seal

16.2 Screw in a self-tapping screw and pull on the screw with pliers to extract the oil seal

16.10 Fitting the new oil seal housing, with integral oil seal, over the crankshaft

housing. Note that the oil seal and the housing are a single assembly.
9 Clean the crankshaft and polish off any burrs or raised edges which may have caused the seal to fail in the first place.
10 Position the new oil seal housing, complete with seal over the crankshaft and into position on the cylinder block **(see illustration)**. Note that the new oil seal housing is supplied with a protector sleeve over the oil seal. Leave the sleeve in position as the housing is fitted.
11 Refit the five retaining bolts and tighten to the specified torque.
12 Remove the protector sleeve from the housing **(see illustration)**.
13 Refit the sump as described in Section 13.
14 Refit the flywheel/driveplate as described in Section 17.

16.4 Using a socket as a tubular drift to fit the new oil seal

16.12 After fitting, remove the protector sleeve from the housing

17 Flywheel/driveplate – removal, inspection and refitting

Note: *New flywheel/driveplate retaining bolts will be required on refitting.*

Removal

Manual transmission models

1 Remove the clutch assembly as described in Chapter 6 Section 6.

2 Prevent the flywheel from turning by locking the ring gear teeth with a similar arrangement to that shown **(see illustration)**.

3 Slacken and remove the retaining bolts and remove the flywheel **(see illustration)**. Do not drop it, as it is very heavy.

Automatic transmission models

4 Remove the transmission as described in Chapter 7B Section 13 then remove the driveplate as described in paragraphs 2 and 3.

Inspection

5 Examine the flywheel for wear or chipping of the ring gear teeth. Renewal of the ring gear is not possible and if the wear or chipping is significant, a new flywheel will be required.

6 Examine the flywheel for scoring of the clutch face. If the clutch face is scored significantly, a new flywheel will be required.

7 The dual-mass flywheel used on these engines has the effect of reducing engine and transmission vibrations and harshness. The flywheel consists of a primary mass and a secondary mass constructed in such a way that the secondary mass is allowed to rotate slightly in relation to the primary mass. Springs within the assembly restrict this movement to set limits.

8 Dual-mass flywheels have earned an unenviable reputation for unreliability and have been known to fail at quite low mileages (sometimes as low as 20 000 miles). As well as the checks described above in paragraphs 5 and 6, some additional checks should be performed as follows.

9 Look through the bolt hole and inspection openings in the secondary mass and check for any visible damage in the area of the centre bearing.

10 Place your thumbs on the clutch face of the secondary mass at the 3 o'clock and 9 o'clock positions and try to rock it. The maximum movement should not exceed 3 mm. Repeat this check with your thumbs at the 12 o'clock and 6 o'clock positions.

11 Rotate the secondary mass clockwise and anti-clockwise. It should move freely in both directions until spring resistance is felt, with no abnormal grating or rattling noises. The maximum rotational movement should not exceed a distance of eight teeth of the ring gear.

12 If there is any doubt about the condition of the flywheel, seek the advice of a Vauxhall/Opel dealer or engine reconditioning specialist. They will be able to advise if the flywheel is an acceptable condition, or whether renewal is necessary.

Refitting

Manual transmission models

13 Clean the mating surfaces of the flywheel and crankshaft.

14 Offer up the flywheel and engage it over the positioning dowel on the crankshaft. Apply a drop of locking compound to the threads of each new flywheel retaining bolt (unless they are precoated) and install the new bolts.

15 Lock the flywheel by the method used on removal then, working in a diagonal sequence, evenly and progressively tighten the retaining bolts to the specified torque.

16 Refit the clutch as described in Chapter 6 Section 6.

Automatic transmission models

17 Refit the driveplate as described in paragraphs 6 to 8.

18 Remove the locking tool, and refit the transmission as described in Chapter 7B Section 13.

18 Engine/transmission mountings – inspection and renewal

Inspection

1 If improved access is required, firmly apply the handbrake, then jack up the front of the car and support it securely on axle stands (see *Jacking and vehicle support*).

2 Check the mounting rubber to see if it is cracked, hardened or separated from the metal at any point; renew the mounting if any such damage or deterioration is evident.

3 Check that all the mounting's fasteners are securely tightened; use a torque wrench to check if possible.

4 Using a large screwdriver or a pry bar, check for wear in the mounting by carefully levering against it to check for free play; where this is not possible, enlist the aid of an assistant to move the engine/transmission unit back-and-forth, or from side-to-side, while you watch the mounting. While some free play is to be expected even from new components, excessive wear should be obvious. If excessive free play is found, check first that the fasteners are correctly secured, then renew any worn components as described below.

Renewal

Note: *Before slackening any of the engine mounting bolts/nuts, the relative positions of the mountings to their various brackets should be marked to ensure correct alignment upon refitting.*

Front mounting/torque link

5 Apply the handbrake, then jack up the front of the vehicle and support it on axle stands (see *Jacking and vehicle support*).

6 Slacken and remove the nut securing the mounting to the subframe bracket. Withdraw the through-bolt **(see illustration)**.

7 Undo the bolts securing the mounting bracket to the transmission, then manoeuvre the mounting and bracket out of position.

17.2 Prevent the flywheel from turning by locking the ring gear teeth

17.3 Flywheel retaining bolts (arrowed)

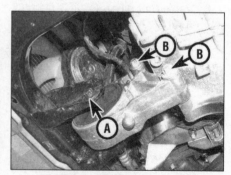

18.6 Front mounting/torque link through-bolt (A) and mounting bracket-to-transmission bolts (B)

8 Check all components for signs of wear or damage, and renew as necessary.

9 Locate the mounting in the subframe, refit the through-bolt and nut, then tighten the nut finger-tight at this stage.

10 Refit the mounting bracket to the transmission and tighten its bolts to the specified torque.

11 Tighten the through-bolt nut to the specified torque.

12 On completion, lower the vehicle to the ground.

Rear mounting/torque link

13 Apply the handbrake, then jack up the front of the vehicle and support it on axle stands (see *Jacking and vehicle support*).

14 Working under the vehicle, remove the centre nut and bolt securing the mounting to the transmission bracket.

15 Remove the two bolts securing the mounting to the subframe, and withdraw the mounting/torque link **(see illustration)**.

16 If necessary, unbolt the bracket from the transmission. **Note:** *The bracket bolts and link bolts are of different lengths.*

17 Refit the bracket to the transmission and tighten the bolts to the specified torque.

18 Locate the new mounting/link in position ensuring that the lug on the top of the mounting engages with the slot in the transmission bracket. Insert the bolts, screw on the nut and tighten to the specified torque.

19 On completion, lower the vehicle to the ground.

Right-hand mounting

20 Apply the handbrake, then jack up the front of the vehicle and support it on axle stands (see *Jacking and vehicle support*).

21 Remove the air cleaner as described in Chapter 4B Section 3.

22 Place a trolley jack beneath the right-hand end of the engine with a block of wood on the jack head. Raise the jack until it is supporting the weight of the engine.

23 Mark the position of the three bolts securing the mounting bracket to the engine bracket and undo the bolts. Undo the three bolts securing the mounting to the body and remove the mounting assembly **(see illustration)**.

24 Place the mounting assembly in position and refit the three bolts securing the mounting to the body. Tighten the bolts to the specified torque. Align the mounting in its original

18.15 Unscrew the two rear mounting/ torque link retaining bolts

18.31 Left-hand mounting bracket-to- transmission bracket retaining bolts (arrowed)

position, then tighten the three mounting bracket bolts to the specified torque.

25 Remove the support jack, then refit the air cleaner as described in Chapter 4B Section 3.

26 On completion, lower the vehicle to the ground.

Left-hand mounting

27 Apply the handbrake, then jack up the front of the vehicle and support it on axle stands (see *Jacking and vehicle support*). Remove the left-hand roadwheel and the plastic wheel arch liner.

28 Remove the battery and battery tray as described in Chapter 5A Section 4.

29 Attach a suitable hoist and lifting tackle to the engine lifting brackets on the cylinder head, and support the weight of the engine.

30 Working under the wheel arch undo the nut securing the lower rear corner of the mounting to the body, then withdraw the bolt from within the engine compartment.

31 Undo the three bolts securing the

18.23 Right-hand mounting retaining bolts (arrowed)

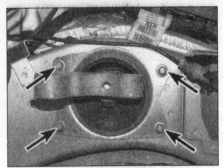

18.32 Left-hand mounting-to-body retaining bolts (arrowed) – shown with engine/transmission removed

mounting bracket to the transmission bracket **(see illustration)**.

32 Undo the three remaining bolts securing the mounting to the body **(see illustration)**.

33 Where applicable, unclip the clutch hydraulic line from the mounting bracket. Remove the mounting assembly from the car.

34 If necessary, undo the through-bolt and separate the rubber mounting from the mounting bracket.

35 If removed, refit the rubber mounting to the mounting bracket and tighten the through-bolt to the specified torque.

36 Locate the mounting brackets in position and, where applicable, clip the clutch hydraulic line onto the bracket.

37 Insert the bolts/nut, then tighten them to the specified torque.

38 Disconnect the hoist and lifting tackle.

39 Refit the wheel arch liner and roadwheel, then lower the vehicle to the ground.

40 Refit the battery tray and battery as described in Chapter 5A Section 4.

Chapter 2 Part D
1.9 litre DOHC diesel engine in-car repair procedures

Contents

Section number

Camshaft followers and hydraulic tappets – removal, inspection and
   refitting 11
Camshaft housing – removal and refitting 9
Camshaft oil seal – renewal 8
Camshafts – removal, inspection and refitting 10
Compression and leakdown tests – description and interpretation . . 2
Crankshaft oil seals – renewal 16
Crankshaft pulley/vibration damper – removal and refitting 5
Cylinder head – removal and refitting 12
Engine/transmission mountings – inspection and renewal 18

Section number

Flywheel/driveplate – removal, inspection and refitting 17
General Information 1
Oil filter housing – removal and refitting 15
Oil pump – removal, overhaul and refitting 14
Sump – removal and refitting 13
Timing belt – removal and refitting 6
Timing belt sprockets, tensioner and idler pulley – removal and
   refitting 7
Top Dead Centre (TDC) for No 1 piston – locating 3
Valve timing – checking and adjustment 4

Degrees of difficulty

Easy, suitable for novice with little experience	**Fairly easy,** suitable for beginner with some experience	**Fairly difficult,** suitable for competent DIY mechanic	**Difficult,** suitable for experienced DIY mechanic	**Very difficult,** suitable for expert DIY or professional

Specifications

General

Engine type	Four-cylinder, in-line, water-cooled. Double overhead camshaft, belt-driven
Manufacturer's engine code	Z19DTH
Bore	82.0 mm
Stroke	90.4 mm
Capacity	1910 cc
Compression ratio	17.5: 1
Firing order	1-3-4-2 (No 1 cylinder at timing belt end of engine)
Direction of crankshaft rotation	Clockwise (viewed from timing belt end of engine)

Compression pressures

Maximum difference between any two cylinders	1.5 bar

Lubrication system

Minimum oil pressure at 100ºC	1.0 bar at idle speed
Oil pump type	Rotor-type, driven by crankshaft pulley/vibration damper from crankshaft

Torque wrench settings	Nm	lbf ft
Air conditioning compressor mounting bracket to cylinder block/sump	50	37
Auxiliary drivebelt idler pulley bolt	50	37
Auxiliary drivebelt tensioner assembly bolts	50	37
Camshaft drive gear bolts	120	89
Camshaft housing bolts	25	18
Camshaft housing closure bolts	16	12
Camshaft sprocket bolt*	120	89
Connecting rod big-end bearing cap bolt: *		
Stage 1	25	18
Stage 2	Angle-tighten a further 60°	
Crankshaft oil seal housing	9	7
Crankshaft pulley/vibration damper bolts	25	18
Crankshaft sprocket bolt*†	340	251
Cylinder head bolts: *		
Stage 1	20	15
Stage 2	65	48
Stage 3	Angle-tighten a further 90°	
Stage 4	Angle-tighten a further 90°	
Stage 5	Angle-tighten a further 90°	
Driveplate bolts*	160	118
Engine/transmission mountings:		
Front mounting/torque link:		
Mounting to subframe bracket	55	41
Bracket to transmission	80	59
Left-hand mounting:		
Mounting-to-body bolts	25	18
Mounting bracket to transmission bracket	80	59
Rubber mounting through-bolt	55	41
Transmission bracket to transmission	55	41
Rear mounting/torque link:		
Mounting to subframe	55	41
Mounting-to-transmission bracket through-bolt	55	41
Transmission bracket to transmission	80	59
Right-hand mounting:		
Engine bracket-to-engine bolts:		
Lower bolts (M8)	25	18
Upper bolts (M10)	50	37
Mounting-to-body bolts	35	26
Mounting-to-engine bracket bolts	55	41
Engine-to-transmission unit bolts:		
M10 bolts	40	30
M12 bolts	60	44
Flywheel bolts*	160	118
High-pressure fuel pump sprocket nut*	50	37
Intermediate shaft bearing housing support bracket bolts	55	41
Main bearing cap bolts: *		
Stage 1	25	18
Stage 2	Angle-tighten a further 100°	
Oil filler housing bolts	9	7
Oil filter housing to cylinder block	50	37
Oil pump housing to cylinder block	9	7
Oil pump pick-up/strainer bolts	9	7
Roadwheel bolts	110	81
Sump bolts:		
M6 bolts	9	7
M8 bolts	25	18
M10 bolts	40	30
Timing belt idler pulley bolt	50	37
Timing belt tensioner bolt	30	22
Timing belt upper cover bolts:		
M6 bolts	9	7
M8 bolts	25	18

*Use new fasteners
† Left-hand thread

1 General Information

How to use this Chapter

1 This Part of Chapter 2 describes the repair procedures which can reasonably be carried out on the engine while it remains in the vehicle. If the engine has been removed from the vehicle and is being dismantled as described in Chapter 2E, any preliminary dismantling procedures can be ignored.

2 Note that, while it may be possible physically to overhaul items such as the piston/connecting rod assemblies while the engine is in the vehicle, such tasks are not usually carried out as separate operations, and usually require the execution of several additional procedures (not to mention the cleaning of components and of oil ways); for this reason, all such tasks are classed as major overhaul procedures, and are described in Chapter 2E.

3 Chapter 2E describes the removal of the engine/transmission unit from the vehicle, and the full overhaul procedures which can then be carried out.

Engine description

4 The 1.9 litre DOHC diesel engine is of the sixteen-valve, in-line four-cylinder, double overhead camshaft type, mounted transversely at the front of the car, with the transmission on its left-hand end.

5 The crankshaft is supported within the cylinder block on five shell-type main bearings. Thrustwashers are fitted to number 3 main bearing, to control crankshaft endfloat.

6 The connecting rods rotate on horizontally-split bearing shells at their big-ends. The pistons are attached to the connecting rods by gudgeon pins, which are retained by circlips. The aluminium-alloy pistons are fitted with three piston rings – two compression rings and scraper-type oil control ring.

7 The camshafts are situated in a separate housing bolted to the top of the cylinder head. The exhaust camshaft is driven by the crankshaft via a toothed composite rubber timing belt (which also drives the

high-pressure fuel pump and the coolant pump). The exhaust camshaft drives the intake camshaft via a spur gear. Each cylinder has four valves (two intake and two exhaust), operated via followers which are supported at their pivot ends by hydraulic self-adjusting tappets. One camshaft operates the intake valves, and the other operates the exhaust valves.

8 The intake and exhaust valves are each closed by a single valve spring, and operate in guides pressed into the cylinder head.

9 Lubrication is by pressure-feed from a rotor-type oil pump, which is mounted on the right-hand end of the crankshaft. The pump draws oil through a strainer located in the sump, and then forces it through an externally mounted full-flow cartridge-type filter. The oil flows into galleries in the cylinder block/crankcase, from where it is distributed to the crankshaft (main bearings) and camshafts. The big-end bearings are supplied with oil via internal drillings in the crankshaft, while the camshaft bearings also receive a pressurised supply. The camshaft lobes and valves are lubricated by splash, as are all other engine components.

10 A semi-closed crankcase ventilation system is employed; crankcase fumes are drawn from the oil separator attached to the cylinder block via a hose to the camshaft housing. The fumes are then passed via a hose to the intake manifold.

Operations with engine in car

11 The following operations can be carried out without having to remove the engine from the vehicle.

a) Removal and refitting of the cylinder head.
b) Removal and refitting of the timing belt, tensioner, idler pulleys and sprockets.
c) Renewal of the camshaft oil seal.
d) Removal and refitting of the camshaft housing.
e) Removal and refitting of the camshafts and followers.
f) Removal and refitting of the sump.
g) Removal and refitting of the connecting rods and pistons.*
h) Removal and refitting of the oil pump.
i) Removal and refitting of the oil filter housing.

j) Renewal of the crankshaft oil seals.
k) Renewal of the engine mountings.
l) Removal and refitting of the flywheel/driveplate.

Note: *Although the operation marked with an asterisk can be carried out with the engine in the car (after removal of the sump), it is preferable for the engine to be removed, in the interests of cleanliness and improved access. For this reason, the procedure is described in Chapter 2E Section 9.

2 Compression and leakdown tests – description and interpretation

Compression test

Note: A compression tester specifically designed for diesel engines must be used for this test.

Note: The battery must be in a good state of charge, the air filter must be clean, and the engine should be at normal operating temperature.

1 When engine performance is down, or if misfiring occurs which cannot be attributed to the fuel system, a compression test can provide diagnostic clues as to the engine's condition. If the test is performed regularly, it can give warning of trouble before any other symptoms become apparent.

2 The tester is connected to an adapter which screws into the glow plug holes. It is unlikely to be worthwhile buying such a tester for occasional use, but it may be possible to borrow or hire one – if not, have the test performed by a Vauxhall/Opel dealer, or suitably-equipped garage. If the necessary equipment is available, proceed as follows.

3 Remove the glow plugs as described in Chapter 5A Section 17, then open the cover on the engine compartment fuse/relay box and remove the fuel pump relay **(see illustrations)**.

4 Screw the compression tester adapter in to the glow plug hole of No 1 cylinder.

5 With the help of an assistant, crank the engine on the starter motor; after one or two revolutions, the compression pressure should build-up to a maximum figure, and then stabilise. Record the highest reading obtained.

6 Repeat the test on the remaining cylinders, recording the pressure in each.

7 All cylinders should produce very similar pressures; any difference greater than the maximum figure given in the Specifications indicates the existence of a fault. Note that the compression should build-up quickly in a healthy engine; low compression on the first stroke, followed by gradually-increasing pressure on successive strokes, indicates worn piston rings. A low compression reading on the first stroke, which does not build-up during successive strokes, indicates leaking valves or a blown head gasket (a cracked

2.3a Open the cover on the fuse/relay box ...

2.3b ... and remove the fuel pump relay (arrowed)

head could also be the cause). **Note:** *The cause of poor compression is less easy to establish on a diesel engine than on a petrol one. The effect of introducing oil into the cylinders ('wet' testing) is not conclusive, because there is a risk that the oil will sit in the recess on the piston crown instead of passing to the rings.*

8 On completion of the test, refit the fuel pump relay, then refit the glow plugs as described in Chapter 5A Section 17.

Leakdown test

9 A leakdown test measures the rate at which compressed air fed into the cylinder is lost. It is an alternative to a compression test, and in many ways it is better, since the escaping air provides easy identification of where pressure loss is occurring (piston rings, valves or head gasket).

10 The equipment needed for leakdown testing is unlikely to be available to the home mechanic. If poor compression is suspected, have the test performed by a Vauxhall/Opel dealer, or suitably-equipped garage.

3 Top Dead Centre (TDC) for No 1 piston – locating

Note: *To accurately determine the TDC position for No 1 piston, it will be necessary to use Vauxhall/Opel special tool EN-46788 (or suitable equivalent) to set the crankshaft at*

3.5 Undo the central mounting bolt (arrowed), and remove the auxiliary drivebelt tensioner assembly

3.9 Engine breather pipe retaining bolts (arrowed)

3.0a Vauxhall/Opel special tool EN-46788 (or equivalent) is required to set the TDC position for No 1 piston...

the TDC position, together with the camshaft positioning tool, Vauxhall/Opel special tool EN-46789 (or suitable equivalent) (**see illustrations**).

1 In its travel up and down its cylinder bore, Top Dead Centre (TDC) is the highest point that each piston reaches as the crankshaft rotates. While each piston reaches TDC both at the top of the compression stroke and again at the top of the exhaust stroke, for the purpose of timing the engine, TDC refers to the piston position of No 1 cylinder at the top of its compression stroke.

2 Number 1 piston (and cylinder) is at the right-hand (timing belt) end of the engine, and its TDC position is located as follows. Note that the crankshaft rotates clockwise when viewed from the right-hand side of the car.

3.8 Undo the retaining bolts and remove the right-hand engine mounting

3.10 Undo the bolt (arrowed) and release the engine oil dipstick guide tube from the coolant pipe

3.0b ... together with Vauxhall/Opel special tool EN-46789 (or equivalent) to set the camshaft position

3 Disconnect the battery negative terminal (refer to Chapter 5A Section 4), then lift off the plastic cover over the top of the engine.

4 Remove the crankshaft pulley/vibration damper as described in Section 5.

5 Undo the central mounting bolt, and remove the auxiliary drivebelt tensioner assembly from the engine (**see illustration**).

6 Remove the air cleaner assembly and air intake duct as described in Chapter 4B Section 3.

7 Place a trolley jack beneath the right-hand end of the engine with a block of wood on the jack head. Raise the jack until it is supporting the weight of the engine.

8 Mark the bolt positions for correct refitting, then undo the three bolts securing the right-hand engine mounting to the engine bracket, and the three bolts securing the mounting to the body. Remove the mounting (**see illustration**).

9 Release the retaining clip securing the engine breather hose to the breather pipe adjacent to the engine oil dipstick. Undo the two bolts securing the breather pipe to the cylinder head, and disconnect the pipe from the hose (**see illustration**).

10 Undo the bolt and release the engine oil dipstick guide tube from the coolant pipe (**see illustration**).

11 Unscrew the closure bolt from the valve timing checking hole in the camshaft housing (**see illustration**).

12 Screw the camshaft positioning tool

3.11 Unscrew the closure bolt from the valve timing checking hole in the camshaft housing

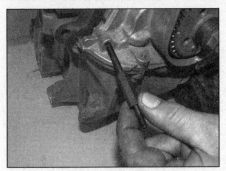

3.14 Screw the fastening stud of special tool EN-46788 into the oil pump housing

3.15 Positioning ring of tool EN-46788 (arrowed) attached to the fastening stud and crankshaft sprocket

(Vauxhall/Opel special tool EN-46789) into the valve timing checking hole.

13 Using a socket and extension bar on the crankshaft sprocket bolt, rotate the crankshaft in the normal direction of rotation until the spring-loaded plunger of the positioning tool slides into engagement with the slot in the camshaft. There will be an audible click from the tool when this happens.

14 Unscrew the bolt from the lower left-hand side of the oil pump housing and screw in the fastening stud of Vauxhall/Opel special tool EN-46788 **(see illustration)**.

15 Fit the positioning ring of tool EN-46788 over the fastening stud and engage it with the crankshaft sprocket. Ensure that the hole in the positioning ring engages with the lug on the sprocket. Secure the tool in position with the retaining bolt and nut **(see illustration)**.

16 With the crankshaft positioning ring in place and the camshaft positioning tool engaged with the slot in the camshaft, the engine is positioned with No 1 piston at TDC on compression.

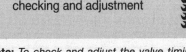

4 Valve timing – checking and adjustment

Note: *To check and adjust the valve timing, it will be necessary to use Vauxhall/Opel special tool EN-46788 (or suitable equivalent) to set the crankshaft at the TDC position. Additionally, it will be necessary to use Vauxhall/Opel special tools EN-46789 and EN46789-100 (or suitable equivalents) to lock the camshafts in the TDC position.*

Checking

1 Disconnect the battery negative terminal (refer to Chapter 5A Section 4), then lift off the plastic cover over the top of the engine.

2 Release the retaining clip securing the engine breather hose to the breather pipe adjacent to the engine oil dipstick. Undo the two bolts securing the breather pipe to the cylinder head, and disconnect the pipe from the hose **(see illustration 3.9)**.

3 Undo the bolt and release the engine oil

dipstick guide tube from the coolant pipe **(see illustration 3.10)**.

4 Unscrew the closure bolt from the valve timing checking hole in the exhaust side of camshaft housing **(see illustration 3.11)**.

5 Screw the exhaust camshaft positioning tool (Vauxhall/Opel special tool EN-46789) into the valve timing checking hole.

6 Unscrew the closure bolt from the valve timing checking hole in the intake side of the camshaft housing. The closure bolt is located below the fuel pressure regulating valve on the fuel rail.

7 Screw the intake camshaft positioning tool (Vauxhall/Opel special tool EN-46789-100) into the valve timing checking hole.

8 Using a socket and extension bar on the crankshaft sprocket bolt, rotate the crankshaft in the normal direction of rotation until the spring-loaded plungers of the positioning tools slide into engagement with the slots in the camshafts. There will be an audible click from the tools when this happens.

9 Remove the crankshaft pulley/vibration damper as described in Section 5.

10 Unscrew the bolt from the lower left-hand side of the oil pump housing and screw in the fastening stud of Vauxhall/Opel special tool EN-46788 **(see illustration 3.14)**.

11 Fit the positioning ring of tool EN-46788 over the fastening stud and engage it with the crankshaft sprocket. Ensure that the hole in the positioning ring engages with the lug on the sprocket. Secure the tool in position with the retaining bolt and nut **(see illustration 3.15)**.

12 If it is not possible to fit the positioning ring of tool EN-46788 as described, or if the camshaft positioning tools did not engage with the camshaft slots, adjust the valve timing as follows.

Adjustment

13 Remove the timing belt as described in Section 6.

14 Using a socket and extension bar on the crankshaft sprocket bolt, rotate the crankshaft anti-clockwise by 90°. This will position all the pistons half-way down their bores, and prevent any chance of the valves touching the piston crowns during the following procedure.

15 Remove the intake and exhaust camshaft

positioning tools from the valve timing checking holes.

16 Using a suitable tool engaged with the timing belt sprocket on the exhaust camshaft, rotate the sprocket approximately 90° clockwise. Vauxhall/Opel special tools EN-46787 and KM-956-1 are available for this purpose, however, a home-made tool can easily be fabricated (see Tool Tip in Section 7). Take care not to damage the camshaft sensor with the tool as the sprocket is rotated.

17 Screw the intake camshaft positioning tool (Vauxhall/Opel special tool EN-46789-100) into the valve timing checking hole.

18 Rotate the camshaft sprocket clockwise until the spring-loaded plunger of the positioning tool slides into engagement with the slot in the intake camshaft. There will be an audible click from the tool when this happens.

19 Release the two retaining clips and disconnect the charge air hose from the throttle body/housing, and intercooler charge air pipe.

20 Release the clip and disconnect the crankcase ventilation hose from the engine oil filler housing.

21 Disconnect the wiring connector from the coolant temperature sensor, then undo the three retaining bolts and remove the oil filler housing.

22 Remove the braking system vacuum pump as described in Chapter 9 Section 19.

23 Working through the oil filler housing aperture, and using the holding tool to prevent rotation of the camshaft, slacken the intake camshaft drive gear retaining bolt. Working through the vacuum pump aperture, slacken the exhaust camshaft drive gear retaining bolt in the same way.

24 Screw the exhaust camshaft positioning tool (Vauxhall/Opel special tool EN-46789) into the valve timing checking hole.

25 Rotate the camshaft sprocket clockwise until the spring-loaded plunger of the positioning tool slides into engagement with the slot in the exhaust camshaft. There will be an audible click from the tool when this happens.

26 Hold the camshaft sprocket with the tool and tighten both drive gear retaining bolts to the specified torque.

27 Remove the positioning tool from the intake camshaft housing and refit the closure bolt. Tighten the bolt to the specified torque.

28 Refit the oil filler housing to the camshaft housing using a new gasket, refit the retaining bolts and tighten the bolts to the specified torque. Reconnect the coolant temperature sensor wiring connector, and reconnect the crankcase ventilation hose.

29 Refit the braking system vacuum pump as described in Chapter 9 Section 19.

30 Refit the charge air hose to the throttle body/housing, and intercooler charge air pipe and secure with the retaining clips.

31 Refit the timing belt as described in Section 6.

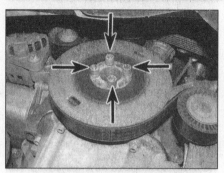

5.3 Crankshaft pulley/vibration damper retaining bolts (arrowed)

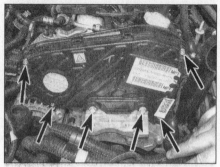

6.2 Upper timing belt cover retaining bolts (arrowed)

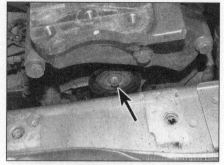

6.3 Undo the bolt (arrowed) and remove the auxiliary drivebelt idler pulley from the engine bracket

5 Crankshaft pulley/vibration damper – removal and refitting

Removal

1 Apply the handbrake, then jack up the front of the vehicle and support it on axle stands (see *Jacking and vehicle support*). Remove the right-hand front roadwheel.

2 Remove the auxiliary drivebelt as described in Chapter 1B Section 24. Prior to removal, mark the direction of rotation on the belt to ensure the belt is refitted the same way around.

3 Undo the four bolts securing the pulley to the crankshaft sprocket and remove the pulley from the sprocket **(see illustration)**.

Refitting

4 Locate the crankshaft pulley on the sprocket, ensuring that the hole on the rear face of the pulley engages with the lug on the sprocket.

5 Refit the four retaining bolts and tighten them progressively to the specified torque.

6 Refit the auxiliary drivebelt as described in Chapter 1B Section 24 using the mark made prior to removal to ensure the belt is fitted the correct way around.

7 Refit the roadwheel, then lower the car to the ground and tighten the wheel bolts to the specified torque.

6 Timing belt – removal and refitting

Note: *The timing belt must be removed and refitted with the engine cold.*

Removal

1 Position No 1 cylinder at TDC on its compression stroke as described in Section 3.

2 Unclip the wiring harness from the side of the upper timing belt cover. Unscrew the seven retaining bolts and lift off the upper timing belt cover **(see illustration)**.

3 Undo the retaining bolt and remove the auxiliary drivebelt idler pulley from the engine bracket **(see illustration)**.

4 Undo the two lower bolts, and the three upper bolts, and remove the engine bracket from the engine **(see illustrations)**.

5 Undo the nut and bolt and remove the crankshaft positioning tool (EN-46788) from the crankshaft sprocket.

6 Slacken the timing belt tensioner retaining bolt and allow the tensioner to retract, relieving the tension on the timing belt.

7 Slide the timing belt from its sprockets and remove it from the engine. If the belt is to be re-used, use white paint or similar to mark the direction of rotation on the belt. Do not rotate the crankshaft or camshafts until the timing belt has been refitted.

8 Check the timing belt carefully for any signs of uneven wear, splitting or oil contamination, and renew it if there is the slightest doubt about its condition. If the engine is undergoing an overhaul and is approaching the manufacturer's specified interval for belt renewal (see Chapter 1B Section 2) renew the belt as a matter of course, regardless of its apparent condition. If signs of oil contamination are found, trace the source of the oil leak and rectify it, then wash down the engine timing belt area and all related components to remove all traces of oil.

Refitting

9 On reassembly, thoroughly clean the timing belt sprockets and tensioner/idler pulleys.

10 Place the timing belt in position over the crankshaft sprocket. If the original belt is being refitted, ensure that the arrow mark made on removal points in the normal direction of rotation, as before.

11 Check that the camshaft and crankshaft are still positioned with No 1 piston at TDC on compression as described in Section 3, and with the camshaft positioning tool still in place. Now refit the crankshaft positioning tool.

12 Fit the timing belt over the crankshaft, camshaft and fuel pump sprockets and around the idler pulleys, ensuring that the belt front run is taut (ie, all slack is on the tensioner side of the belt), then fit the belt over the coolant pump sprocket and tensioner pulley. Do not twist the belt sharply while refitting it.

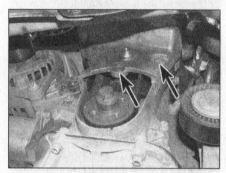

6.4a Undo the two lower bolts (arrowed) …

6.4b … and the three upper bolts (arrowed) …

6.4c … and remove the engine bracket from the engine

6.13a Using a screwdriver resting on a pivot bolt (arrowed), move the adjusting lever on the tensioner ...

6.13b ... until the tensioner pointer (arrowed) is aligned with the mark on the backplate

Ensure that the belt teeth are correctly seated centrally in the sprockets.

13 Screw a suitable bolt, approximately 50 mm in length, into the threaded hole directly below the timing belt tensioner. Using a screwdriver resting on the bolt as a pivot, move the adjusting lever on the tensioner until the tensioner pointer is aligned with the mark on the backplate. Hold the tensioner in this position and tighten the tensioner retaining bolt **(see illustrations)**.

14 Remove the crankshaft and camshaft positioning tools.

15 Using a socket on the crankshaft sprocket bolt, rotate the crankshaft smoothly through two complete turns (720°) in the normal direction of rotation to settle the timing belt in position. Stop rotating the crankshaft just before completing the second turn.

16 Refit the camshaft positioning tool and continue turning the crankshaft until the camshaft positioning tool engages.

17 Refit the positioning ring of tool EN-46788 over the fastening stud and engage it with the crankshaft sprocket. Ensure that the hole in the positioning ring engages with the lug on the sprocket. Secure the tool in position with the retaining bolt and nut.

18 Slacken the timing belt tensioner retaining bolt and, using a screwdriver resting on the pivot bolt as before, move the adjusting lever on the tensioner until the tensioner pointer is once again aligned with the mark on the backplate. Hold the tensioner in this position and tighten the tensioner retaining bolt to the specified torque.

19 Remove all the positioning tools and again rotate the crankshaft smoothly through two complete turns (720°) in the normal direction of rotation. Check that the timing belt tensioner pointer is still aligned with the mark on the backplate. If not, repeat the procedure described in paragraph 18.

20 When all is correct, remove the tensioner position pivot bolt. Refit the bolt removed from the oil pump housing and tighten it to the specified torque. Refit the closure plug to the camshaft housing and tighten to the specified torque.

21 Place the engine bracket in position and refit the two lower bolts, and the three upper bolts. Tighten the bolts to the specified torque. Refit the auxiliary drivebelt idler pulley to the engine bracket and tighten the retaining bolt to the specified torque.

22 Refit the upper timing belt cover and tighten the retaining bolts to the specified torque. Clip the wiring harness back into position.

23 Place the right-hand engine mounting assembly in position and refit the three bolts securing the mounting to the body. Tighten the bolts to the specified torque. Align the mounting in its original position, then fit and tighten the three mounting bracket bolts to the specified torque. Remove the jack from under the engine.

24 Refit the air cleaner assembly and air intake duct as described in Chapter 4B Section 3.

25 Place the auxiliary drivebelt tensioner assembly in position ensuring that the locating peg on the tensioner mounting surface engages correctly with the corresponding hole in the mounting bracket. Tighten the tensioner central mounting bolt to the specified torque.

26 Refit the crankshaft pulley/vibration damper as described in Section 5, then refit the auxiliary drivebelt as described in Chapter 1B Section 24.

27 Move the engine oil dipstick guide tube back into position. Refit the bolt securing the guide tube to the coolant pipe and tighten the bolt securely.

28 Attach the engine breather hose to the breather pipe and secure with the retaining clip. Secure the breather pipe to the cylinder head with the two bolts securely tightened.

29 Refit the plastic cover to the top of the engine.

30 Refit the roadwheel, then lower the car to the ground and tighten the wheel bolts to the specified torque.

7 Timing belt sprockets, tensioner and idler pulley – removal and refitting

Note: *Certain special tools will be required for the removal and refitting of the sprockets. Read through the entire procedure to familiarise yourself with the work involved, then either obtain the manufacturer's special tools, or use the alternatives described.*

Camshaft sprocket

Note: *A new sprocket retaining bolt will be required for refitting.*

Removal

1 Remove the timing belt as described in Section 6, then remove camshaft positioning tool from the valve timing checking hole.

2 It will now be necessary to hold the camshaft sprocket to enable the retaining bolt to be removed. Vauxhall/Opel special tools EN-46787 and KM-956-1 are available for this purpose, however, a home-made tool can easily be fabricated (see **Tool Tip**).

3 Engage the tool with the holes in the camshaft sprocket, taking care not to damage the camshaft sensor located behind the sprocket

HAYNES HINT

To make a sprocket holding tool, obtain two lengths of steel strip about 6 mm thick by about 30 mm wide or similar, one 600 mm long, the other 200 mm long (all dimensions are approximate). Bolt the two strips together to form a forked end, leaving the bolt slack so that the shorter strip can pivot freely. At the other end of each 'prong' of the fork, drill a suitable hole and fit a nut and bolt to allow the tool to engage with the spokes in the sprocket.

7.14a Remove the bolt and washer ...

7.14b ... and slide the sprocket off the end of the crankshaft

7.20 Engage the holding tool with the holes in the fuel pump sprocket and undo the retaining nut

4 Unscrew the retaining bolt and remove the sprocket from the end of the camshaft.

Refitting

5 Prior to refitting check the oil seal for signs of damage or leakage. If necessary, renew as described in Section 8.

6 Refit the sprocket to the camshaft end, aligning its cut-out with the locating peg, and fit the new retaining bolt finger-tight only at this stage. Final tightening is carried out after the timing belt has been fitted and tensioned.

7 Refit the camshaft positioning tool to the valve timing checking hole. If necessary, rotate the camshaft slightly, by means of the sprocket, until the tool audibly engages.

8 Proceed with the timing belt refitting procedure as described in Section 6, paragraphs 9 to 14.

9 Retain the camshaft sprocket using the holding tool, and tighten the retaining bolt to the specified torque.

10 Continue with the timing belt refitting procedure as described in Section 6, paragraphs 15 to 30.

Crankshaft sprocket

Note: *The crankshaft sprocket retaining bolt is extremely tight. Ensure that the holding tool used to prevent rotation as the bolt is slackened is of sturdy construction and securely attached.*

Note: *A new sprocket retaining bolt will be required for refitting.*

Removal

11 Remove the timing belt as described in Section 6.

12 It will now be necessary to hold the crankshaft sprocket to enable the retaining bolt to be removed. Vauxhall special tools EN-47630 and KM-956-1 are available for this purpose, however, a home-made tool similar to that described in paragraph 2, can easily be fabricated.

13 Using the crankshaft pulley retaining bolts, securely attach the tool to the crankshaft sprocket. With the help of an assistant, hold the sprocket stationary and unscrew the retaining bolt. **Note:** *The sprocket retaining bolt has a left-hand thread and is unscrewed by turning it clockwise.*

14 Remove the bolt and washer and slide the sprocket off the end of the crankshaft **(see illustrations)**. Note that a new bolt will be required for refitting.

Refitting

15 Align the sprocket location key with the crankshaft groove and slide the sprocket into position. Fit the new retaining bolt and washer.

16 Hold the sprocket stationary using the holding tool and tighten the retaining bolt to the specified torque. Remove the holding tool.

17 Refit the timing belt as described in Section 6.

High-pressure fuel pump sprocket

Note: *A new sprocket retaining nut will be required for refitting.*

Removal

18 Remove the timing belt as described in Section 6.

19 It will now be necessary to hold the fuel pump sprocket to enable the retaining nut to be removed. Vauxhall special tools KM-6347 and KM-956-1 are available for this purpose, however, a home-made tool similar to that described in paragraph 2, can easily be fabricated.

20 Engage the tool with the holes in the fuel pump sprocket and undo the sprocket retaining nut **(see illustration)**. Note that a new nut will be required for refitting.

21 Attach a suitable puller to the threaded holes in the fuel pump sprocket using bolts and washers similar to the arrangement shown **(see illustration)**.

22 Tighten the puller centre bolt to release the sprocket from the taper on the pump shaft. Once the taper releases, remove the puller and withdraw the sprocket. Collect the Woodruff key from the pump shaft **(see illustrations)**.

Refitting

23 Clean the fuel pump shaft and the sprocket hub ensuring that all traces of oil or grease are removed.

24 Refit the Woodruff key to the pump shaft, then locate the sprocket in position. Fit the new retaining nut.

25 Hold the sprocket stationary using the holding tool and tighten the retaining nut to the specified torque. Remove the holding tool.

7.22a Once the taper releases, withdraw the sprocket ...

7.22b ... and collect the Woodruff key from the pump shaft

7.21 Use a suitable puller to release the fuel pump sprocket taper

7.28a Slacken and remove the retaining bolt ...

7.28b ... and remove the timing belt tensioner assembly

7.29 The slot on the tensioner backplate must locate over the peg (arrowed) on the engine bracket

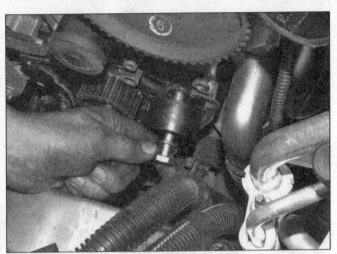

7.33 Slacken and remove the retaining bolt and remove the idler pulley from the engine

26 Refit the timing belt as described in Section 6.

Tensioner assembly

Removal

27 Remove the timing belt as described in Section 6.
28 Slacken and remove the retaining bolt and remove the tensioner assembly from the engine (see illustrations).

Refitting

29 Fit the tensioner to the engine, making sure that the slot on the tensioner backplate is correctly located over the peg on the engine bracket (see illustration).
30 Clean the threads of the retaining bolt and apply thread-ocking compound to the bolt threads. Screw in the retaining bolt, set the tensioner in the retracted position and tighten the retaining bolt.
31 Refit the timing belt as described in Section 6.

Idler pulley

Removal

32 Remove the timing belt as described in Section 6.
33 Slacken and remove the retaining bolt and remove the idler pulley from the engine (see illustration).

Refitting

34 Refit the idler pulley and tighten the retaining bolt to the specified torque.
35 Refit the timing belt as described in Section 6.

8 Camshaft oil seal – renewal

1 Remove the camshaft sprocket as described in Section 7.
2 Carefully punch or drill a small hole in the oil

seal. Screw in a self-tapping screw, and pull on the screw with pliers to extract the seal.
3 Clean the seal housing, and polish off any burrs or raised edges which may have caused the seal to fail in the first place.
4 Press the new seal into position using a suitable tubular drift (such as a socket) which bears only on the hard outer edge of the seal. Take care not to damage the seal lips during fitting; note that the seal lips should face inwards.
5 Refit the camshaft sprocket as described in Section 7.

9 Camshaft housing – removal and refitting

Removal

1 Remove the timing belt as described in Section 6.

9.2a Disconnect the wiring connectors at the fuel injectors …

9.2b … fuel pressure regulating valve …

9.2c … fuel pressure sensor …

9.2d … camshaft sensor …

9.2e … and air conditioning compressor (arrowed)

2 Disconnect the wiring harness connectors from the following components **(see illustrations):**

3 Release the air conditioning compressor wiring harness from the clip on the oil dipstick guide tube. Undo the two bolts securing the plastic wiring harness guide to the camshaft housing and move the disconnected wiring harness to one side **(see illustrations)**.

4 Disconnect the two vacuum hoses from the vacuum pipe assembly on top of the camshaft housing. Undo the two retaining bolts and move the pipe assembly to one side **(see illustrations)**.

5 Remove the fuel injectors and the fuel rail as described in Chapter 4B.

6 Release the two retaining clips and disconnect the charge air hose from the throttle body/housing, and intercooler charge air pipe **(see illustration)**.

7 Disconnect the vacuum hose quick-release fitting from the braking system vacuum pump **(see illustration)**.

8 Release the clip and disconnect the

9.3a Undo the two bolts (arrowed) securing the wiring harness guide to the camshaft housing …

9.3b … and move the disconnected wiring harness to one side

9.4a Disconnect the two vacuum hoses from the vacuum pipe assembly …

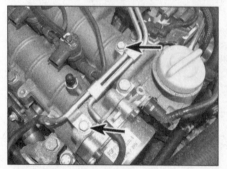

9.4b … then undo the two retaining bolts (arrowed) and move the pipe assembly to one side

9.6 Release the retaining clips and remove the charge air hose

9.7 Depress the clip and disconnect the vacuum hose quick-release fitting

crankcase ventilation hose from the engine oil filler housing (see illustration).

9 Undo the retaining bolts and remove the two engine lifting brackets from the left-hand end of the camshaft housing. Undo the bolt securing the turbocharger charge air pipe to the right-hand end of the camshaft housing.

10 Working in a spiral pattern from the outside inwards, progressively slacken, then remove, the sixteen bolts, securing the camshaft housing to the cylinder head. Ensure that the housing releases evenly from the cylinder block.

11 Lift the camshaft housing off the cylinder head and recover the gasket (see illustration).

12 Thoroughly clean the mating faces of the cylinder head, camshaft housing and vacuum pump and obtain a new gasket for refitting.

Refitting

13 Check that all the hydraulic tappets and rocker arms are correctly positioned in the cylinder head and none have been disturbed.

14 Commence refitting by turning the crankshaft anti-clockwise by 90°. This will position all the pistons half-way down their bores, and prevent any chance of the valves touching the piston crowns as the camshaft housing is being fitted.

15 Place a new gasket on the cylinder head, then locate the camshaft housing in position aligning it with the locating dowels.

16 Refit the sixteen camshaft housing retaining bolts. Progressively screw in the bolts to gradually draw the housing down and into contact with the cylinder head.

17 Working in a spiral pattern from the inside outwards, progressively tighten the sixteen bolts to the specified torque.

18 Refit the two engine lifting brackets to the left-hand end of the camshaft housing and tighten the retaining bolts securely. Refit and tighten the charge air pipe retaining bolt.

19 Reconnect the crankcase ventilation hose to the engine oil filler housing.

20 Reconnect the vacuum hose quick-release fitting to the braking system vacuum pump ensuring that the fitting audibly engages.

21 Refit the charge air hose to the throttle body/housing, and intercooler charge air pipe and secure with the retaining clips.

22 Refit the fuel rail and fuel injectors as described in Chapter 4B.

9.8 Disconnect the crankcase ventilation hose from the engine oil filler housing

23 Place the vacuum pipe assembly in position on the top of the camshaft housing and refit the two retaining bolts. Tighten the bolts securely, then reconnect the two vacuum hoses.

24 Lay the plastic wiring harness guide in position on the camshaft housing, then refit and tighten the two retaining bolts.

25 Reconnect the wiring harness connectors to the components listed in paragraph 2, ensuring that the harness is secured by all the relevant retaining clips.

26 Turn the crankshaft clockwise by 90° to bring No 1 and 4 pistons to approximately the TDC position.

27 Refit the timing belt as described in Section 6.

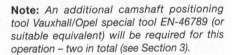

10 Camshafts – removal, inspection and refitting

Note: *An additional camshaft positioning tool Vauxhall/Opel special tool EN-46789 (or suitable equivalent) will be required for this operation – two in total (see Section 3).*

Removal

1 Carry out the operations described in Section 9, paragraphs 1 to 8.

2 Remove the braking system vacuum pump as described in Chapter 9 Section 19.

3 Disconnect the wiring connector from the coolant temperature sensor, then undo the three retaining bolts and remove the oil filler housing (see illustration).

9.11 Lift the camshaft housing off the cylinder head and recover the gasket

4 Undo the retaining bolt and remove the camshaft sensor from the right-hand end of the camshaft housing.

5 Before removing the camshaft housing completely, the retaining bolts for the camshaft drive gears and sprocket should be slackened as follows.

6 Remove the exhaust camshaft positioning tool from the valve timing checking hole.

7 It will be necessary to hold the camshaft sprocket to enable the drive gear and sprocket retaining bolts to be slackened. Vauxhall special tools EN-46787 and KM-956-1 are available for this purpose, however, a home-made tool can easily be fabricated (see **Tool Tip** in Section 7).

8 Working through the oil filler housing aperture, and using the holding tool to prevent rotation of the camshaft, slacken the intake camshaft drive gear retaining bolt. Working through the vacuum pump aperture, slacken the exhaust camshaft drive gear retaining bolt in the same way (see illustrations).

9 Again, using the holding tool, slacken the camshaft sprocket retaining bolt.

10 Continue with the camshaft housing removal procedure as described in Section 9, paragraphs 9 to 11.

11 With the camshaft housing placed upside down on the bench, unscrew and remove the previously-slackened retaining bolt, and remove the timing belt sprocket from the exhaust camshaft.

12 At the other end of the housing, unscrew and remove the two previously-slackened retaining bolts, and lift off the drive gears

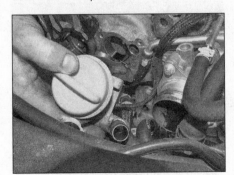

10.3 Undo the three retaining bolts and remove the oil filler housing

10.8a Slacken the intake camshaft drive gear retaining bolt ...

10.8b ... and the exhaust camshaft drive gear retaining bolt

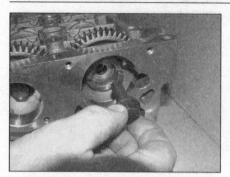

10.12a Unscrew and remove the two previously-slackened retaining bolts ...

10.12b ... then lift out the exhaust camshaft drive gear ...

10.12c ... and the intake camshaft drive gear

10.13 Withdraw the exhaust camshaft ...

10.14 ... and intake camshaft from the camshaft housing

10.22 Refit the camshaft positioning tool to the valve timing checking hole of the exhaust camshaft

from the intake and exhaust camshafts **(see illustrations)**.

13 Carefully prise out the exhaust camshaft oil seal with a screwdriver or similar hooked tool. Carefully withdraw the exhaust camshaft out from the timing belt end of the camshaft housing **(see illustration)**.

14 Using a wooden dowel or similar, carefully tap the end of the intake camshaft toward the timing belt end of the housing, to release the blanking cap. Remove the cap, then carefully withdraw the intake camshaft from the housing **(see illustration)**.

Inspection

15 Examine the camshaft bearing surfaces and cam lobes for signs of wear ridges and scoring. Renew the camshaft(s) if any of these conditions are apparent. Examine the condition of the bearing surfaces in the camshaft housing. If the any wear or scoring is evident,

the camshaft housing will need to be renewed.
16 If either camshaft is being renewed, it will be necessary to renew all the rocker arms and tappets for that particular camshaft also (see Section 11).
17 Check the condition of the camshaft drive gears and sprocket for chipped or damaged teeth, wear ridges and scoring. Renew any components as necessary.

Refitting

18 Prior to refitting, thoroughly clean all components and dry with a lint-free cloth. Ensure that all traces of oil and grease are removed from the contact faces of the drive gears, sprocket and camshafts.
19 Lubricate the camshaft bearing journals in the camshaft housing and carefully insert the intake and exhaust camshafts.
20 Ensuring that the contact faces are clean

and dry, refit the drive gear to each camshaft. Note that the gear with the vacuum pump drive dogs is fitted to the exhaust camshaft, and the plain gear is fitted to the intake camshaft.
21 Screw in a new drive gear retaining bolt for each camshaft and tighten both bolts finger-tight only at this stage.
22 Refit the camshaft positioning tool to the valve timing checking hole of the exhaust camshaft. If necessary, rotate the exhaust camshaft slightly, until the tool audibly engages **(see illustration)**.
23 Unscrew and remove the closure bolt from the intake camshaft side of the camshaft housing and fit a second camshaft positioning tool **(see illustrations)**. If necessary, rotate the camshaft slightly, until the tool audibly engages.
24 With both camshafts locked by means of the positioning tools, tighten both drive gear retaining bolts to the specified torque **(see illustration)**. It

10.23a Unscrew the closure bolt from the intake camshaft side of the camshaft housing ...

10.23b ... and fit a camshaft positioning tool for the intake camshaft

10.24 With both camshafts locked, tighten both drive gear retaining bolts to the specified torque

10.26a Fit a new intake camshaft blanking cap to the camshaft housing …

10.26b … and tap it into position until it is flush with the outer face of the housing

10.27 Similarly, fit a new exhaust camshaft oil seal to the camshaft housing

may be beneficial to have an assistant securely support the camshaft housing as the bolts are tightened.

25 Remove the positioning tool from the intake camshaft housing and refit the closure bolt. Tighten the bolt to the specified torque.

26 Fit a new intake camshaft blanking cap to the timing belt end of the camshaft housing and tap it into position until it is flush with the outer face of the housing, using a suitable socket or tube, or a wooden block **(see illustrations)**.

27 Similarly, fit a new exhaust camshaft oil seal to the timing belt end of the camshaft housing and tap it into position until it is flush with the outer face of the housing, using a suitable socket or tube, or a wooden block **(see illustration)**.

28 Refit the timing belt sprocket to the

exhaust camshaft, aligning its cut-out with the locating peg, and fit the new retaining bolt finger-tight only at this stage. Final tightening is carried out after the timing belt has been fitted and tensioned.

29 Refit the camshaft sensor to the camshaft housing and tighten the retaining bolt securely.

30 Refit the oil filler housing to the camshaft housing using a new gasket, refit the retaining bolts and tighten the bolts to the specified torque. Reconnect the coolant temperature sensor wiring connector.

31 Refit the braking system vacuum pump as described in Chapter 9 Section 19.

32 Thoroughly clean the mating faces of the cylinder head and camshaft housing.

33 Refit the camshaft housing to the cylinder head as described in Section 9, paragraphs 13 to 26.

34 Commence refitting of the timing belt as described in Section 6, paragraphs 9 to 14.

35 Retain the camshaft sprocket using the holding tool, and tighten the retaining bolt to the specified torque.

36 Continue refitting of the timing belt as described in Section 6, paragraphs 15 to 30.

11 Camshaft followers and hydraulic tappets – removal, inspection and refitting

Removal

1 Remove the camshaft housing as described in Section 9.

2 Obtain sixteen small, oil tight clean plastic containers, and number them intake 1 to 8 and exhaust 1 to 8; alternatively, divide a larger container into sixteen compartments and number each compartment accordingly.

3 Withdraw each camshaft follower and hydraulic tappet in turn, unclip the follower from the tappet, and place them in their respective container **(see illustrations)**. Do not interchange the followers and tappets, or the rate of wear will be much increased. Fill each container with clean engine oil and ensure that the tappet is submerged.

11.3a Withdraw each camshaft follower …

11.3b … and hydraulic tappet in turn, and place them in their respective container

Inspection

4 Examine the followers and hydraulic tappet bearing surfaces for wear ridges and scoring. Renew any follower or tappet on which these conditions are apparent.

5 If any new hydraulic tappets are obtained, they should be immersed in a container of clean engine oil prior to refitting.

Refitting

6 Liberally oil the cylinder head hydraulic tappet bores and the tappets. Working on one assembly at a time, clip the follower back onto the tappet, then refit the tappet to the cylinder head, ensuring that it is refitted to its original bore. Lay the follower over its respective valve **(see illustrations)**.

7 Refit the remaining tappets and followers in the same way.

8 With all the tappets and followers in place, refit the camshaft housing as described in Section 9.

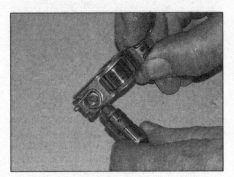

11.6a Clip the follower back onto the tappet …

11.6b … then refit the tappet to its original bore, and lay the follower over its respective valve

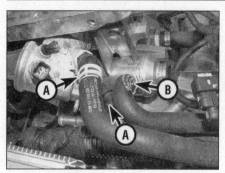

12.6 Disconnect the coolant hoses at the thermostat housing (A), and at the EGR valve heat exchanger (B)

12.7 Release the coolant pipe from the stud (arrowed) at the base of the thermostat housing

12.8 Undo the bolt (arrowed) securing the high-pressure fuel pump mounting bracket to the cylinder head

12 Cylinder head – removal and refitting

Note: *New cylinder head bolts will be required for refitting.*

Removal

1 Disconnect the battery negative terminal (refer to Chapter).

2 Drain the cooling system as described in Chapter 1B Section 30.

3 Remove the camshaft housing as described in Section 9.

4 Remove the camshaft followers and hydraulic tappets as described in Section 11.

5 Remove the intake and exhaust manifolds as described in Chapter 4B.

6 Release the clips and disconnect the remaining two coolant hoses at the thermostat housing, and the coolant hose at the EGR valve heat exchanger (see illustration).

7 Release the coolant pipe from the stud at the base of the thermostat housing (see illustration).

8 Undo the bolt securing the high-pressure fuel pump mounting bracket to the cylinder head (see illustration).

9 Make a final check to ensure that all relevant hoses, pipes and wires have been disconnected.

10 Working in the reverse of the tightening sequence (see illustration 12.27), progressively slacken the cylinder head bolts

by half a turn at a time, until all bolts can be unscrewed by hand. Note that an M14 RIBE socket bit will be required to unscrew the bolts. Remove the cylinder head bolts and recover the washers.

11 Engage the help of an assistant, if necessary, and lift the cylinder head from the cylinder block (see illustration).

Caution: Do not lay the head on its lower mating surface; support the head on wooden blocks, ensuring each block only contacts the head mating surface.

12 Remove the gasket and keep it for identification purposes (see paragraph 19).

13 If the cylinder head is to be dismantled for overhaul, then refer to Part E of this Chapter.

Preparation for refitting

14 The mating faces of the cylinder head and cylinder block/crankcase must be perfectly clean before refitting the head. Use a hard plastic or wood scraper to remove all traces of gasket and carbon; also clean the piston crowns. Take particular care, as the surfaces are damaged easily. Also, make sure that the carbon is not allowed to enter the oil and water passages – this is particularly important for the lubrication system, as carbon could block the oil supply to any of the engine's components. Using adhesive tape and paper, seal the water, oil and bolt holes in the cylinder block/crankcase. To prevent carbon entering the gap between the pistons and bores, smear a little grease in the gap. After cleaning each piston, use a small brush to

remove all traces of grease and carbon from the gap, then wipe away the remainder with a clean rag. Clean all the pistons in the same way.

15 Check the mating surfaces of the cylinder block/crankcase and the cylinder head for nicks, deep scratches and other damage. If slight, they may be removed carefully with a file, but if excessive, machining may be the only alternative to renewal.

16 Ensure that the cylinder head bolt holes in the crankcase are clean and free of oil. Syringe or soak up any oil left in the bolt holes. This is most important in order that the correct bolt tightening torque can be applied and to prevent the possibility of the block being cracked by hydraulic pressure when the bolts are tightened.

17 The cylinder head bolts must be discarded and renewed, regardless of their apparent condition.

18 If warpage of the cylinder head gasket surface is suspected, use a straight-edge to check it for distortion. Refer to Part E of this Chapter if necessary.

19 On this engine, the cylinder head-to-piston clearance is controlled by fitting different thickness head gaskets. The gasket thickness can be determined by looking at the holes stamped on the edge of the gasket (see illustration).

Number of holes	Gasket thickness
No holes	0.77 to 0.87 mm
One hole	0.87 to 0.97 mm
Two holes	0.97 to 1.07 mm

20 The correct thickness of gasket required is selected by measuring the piston protrusions as follows.

21 Mount a dial test indicator securely on the block so that its pointer can be easily pivoted between the piston crown and block mating surface. Turn the crankshaft to bring No 1 piston roughly to the TDC position. Move the dial test indicator probe over and in contact with No 1 piston. Turn the crankshaft back-and-forth slightly until the highest reading is shown on the gauge, indicating that the piston is at TDC.

12.11 Lift the cylinder head from the cylinder block

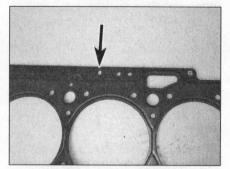

12.19 Cylinder head gasket thickness identification hole (arrowed)

12.22 Using a dial test indicator to measure piston protrusion

12.25 Place the new gasket in position with the words ALTO/TOP uppermost

12.28 Cylinder head bolt tightening sequence

22 Zero the dial test indicator on the gasket surface of the cylinder block then carefully move the indicator over No 1 piston. Measure its protrusion at the highest point between the valve cut-outs, and then again at its highest point between the valve cut-outs at 90° to the first measurement **(see illustration)**. Repeat this procedure with No 4 piston.

23 Rotate the crankshaft half a turn (180°) to bring No 2 and 3 pistons to TDC. Ensure the crankshaft is accurately positioned then measure the protrusions of No 2 and 3 pistons at the specified points. Once all pistons have been measured, rotate the crankshaft to position all the pistons at their mid-stroke.

24 Select the correct thickness of head gasket required by determining the largest amount of piston protrusion, and using the following table.

Piston protrusion measurement (mm)	Gasket thickness required
0.020 to 0.100	0.77 to 0.87 (no holes)
0.101 to 0.200	0.87 to 0.97 (one hole)
0.201 to 0.295	0.97 to 1.07 (two holes)

Refitting

25 Wipe clean the mating surfaces of the cylinder head and cylinder block/ crankcase. Place the new gasket in position with the words ALTO/TOP uppermost **(see illustration)**.

26 Carefully refit the cylinder head assembly to the block, aligning it with the locating dowels.

27 Apply a thin film of engine oil to the bolt threads and the underside of the bolt heads. Carefully enter each new cylinder head bolt into its relevant hole (do not drop them in). Screw all bolts in, by hand only, until finger-tight.

28 Working progressively in sequence, tighten the cylinder head bolts to their Stage 1 torque setting, using a torque wrench and suitable socket **(see illustration)**. Working again in the same sequence, go around and tighten all bolts through the specified Stage 2 torque setting.

29 Once all bolts have been tightened to the Stage 2 torque, working again in the same sequence, go around and tighten all bolts through the specified Stage 3 angle, then through the specified Stage 4 angle, and finally through the specified Stage 5 angle using an angle-measuring gauge.

30 Refit the bolt securing the high-pressure fuel pump mounting bracket to the cylinder head and tighten the bolt securely.

31 Engage the coolant pipe with the stud on the thermostat housing, then reconnect the coolant hoses to the thermostat housing and EGR valve heat exchanger.

32 Refit the intake and exhaust manifolds as described in Chapter 4B.

33 Refit the camshaft followers and hydraulic tappets as described in Section 11.

34 Refit the camshaft housing as described in Section 9.

35 On completion, reconnect the battery negative terminal, then refill the cooling system as described in Chapter 1B Section 30.

13 Sump – removal and refitting

Removal

1 Disconnect the battery negative terminal (refer to Chapter 5A Section 4).

2 Apply the handbrake, then jack up the front of the vehicle and support it on axle stands (see *Jacking and vehicle support*). Remove the right-hand front roadwheel.

3 Remove the right-hand driveshaft and the intermediate shaft as described in Chapter 8.

4 Undo the three bolts securing the intermediate shaft bearing housing support bracket to the cylinder block and remove the support bracket **(see illustration)**.

5 Remove the exhaust system as described in Chapter 4B Section 20.

6 Undo the three bolts and remove the support bracket from the catalytic converter and sump.

7 Remove the crankshaft pulley/vibration damper as described in Section 5.

8 Disconnect the wiring connector from the air conditioning compressor. Undo the three bolts securing the air conditioning compressor to the mounting bracket and suitably support the compressor on the front subframe.

9 Undo the four bolts securing the compressor mounting bracket to the cylinder block and sump **(see illustration)**. Unclip the wiring harness and remove the mounting bracket.

10 Drain the engine oil as described in Chapter 1B Section 6. When the oil has completely drained, refit the drain plug with new sealing washer, and tighten to the specified torque.

11 Undo the upper bolt securing the oil dipstick guide tube to the coolant pipe. Undo the lower bolt securing the guide tube to the sump flange, then unclip the wiring harness and withdraw the tube from the sump flange sealing grommet.

12 Disconnect the wiring connector from the oil level sensor, then release the retaining clip and disconnect the oil return hose.

13 Undo the two bolts securing the sump flange to the transmission bellhousing.

14 Using a socket and extension on the crankshaft pulley bolt, rotate the crankshaft in the normal direction of rotation (clockwise when viewed from the right-hand end of the

13.4 intermediate shaft bearing housing support bracket retaining bolts (arrowed)

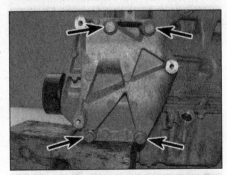

13.9 Air conditioning compressor mounting bracket retaining bolts (arrowed)

13.17 Removing the oil baffle plate from inside the sump

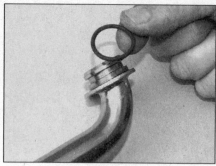

13.18 Renew the pick-up/strainer sealing ring

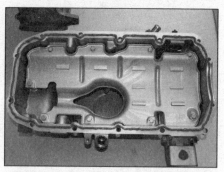

13.21 Apply a continuous bead of silicone sealing compound to the sump flange

engine) until the opening in the flywheel is positioned to allow access to one of the rear sump retaining bolts. Undo and remove the bolt, then rotate the crankshaft again until the flywheel allow access to the second rear retaining bolt. Undo and remove the bolt.

15 Progressively slacken and remove the remaining twelve bolts securing the sump to the base of the cylinder block and oil pump housing. Using a wide-bladed scraper or similar tool inserted between the sump and cylinder block, carefully break the joint to release the sump.

16 Manoeuvre the sump out from under the car. Clearance is extremely limited between the sump and subframe, and it may be necessary to release the oil pump pick-up/strainer, by undoing its two retaining bolts, to enable the sump to be removed.

17 If required, undo the retaining bolts and remove the oil baffle plate from inside the sump **(see illustration)**.

18 While the sump is removed, take the opportunity to check the oil pump pick-up/strainer for signs of clogging or splitting. If not already done, unbolt the oil pump pick-up/strainer and remove it from the engine along with its sealing ring. The strainer can then be cleaned easily in solvent or renewed. Renew the pick-up/strainer sealing ring prior to refitting **(see illustration)**.

Refitting

19 Thoroughly clean the sump and remove all traces of silicone sealer and oil from the mating surfaces of the sump and cylinder block. If removed, refit the oil baffle plate and tighten its retaining bolts securely.

20 If clearance allows, refit the oil pump pick-up/strainer using a new sealing ring, and tighten its two retaining bolts securely. If it was necessary to unbolt the pick-up/strainer to allow the sump to be removed, place the unit in position and loosely screw in the bolt securing it to the main bearing cap. It must still be possible for the forward end of the pipe to be moved to the rear as the sump is refitted.

21 Apply a continuous bead of silicone sealing compound (available from your Vauxhall/Opel dealer) at approximately 1.0 mm from the inner edge of the sump **(see illustration)**. The bead of sealant should be between 2.0 and 2.5 mm in diameter.

22 Locate the sump over the pick-up/strainer then, where applicable, fit the forward end of the pick-up/strainer to the oil pump housing and fit the retaining bolt. Tighten both retaining bolts securely.

23 Engage the sump with the cylinder block and loosely refit all the retaining bolts.

24 Working out from the centre in a diagonal sequence, progressively tighten the bolts securing the sump to the cylinder block and oil pump housing. Tighten all the bolts to their specified torque setting.

25 Tighten the two bolts securing the sump flange to the transmission bellhousing to their specified torque settings.

26 Reconnect the wiring connector to the oil level sensor, then refit the oil return hose and secure with the retaining clip.

27 Refit the oil dipstick guide tube and secure with the two bolts tightened securely.

28 Locate the air conditioning compressor mounting bracket in position and refit the four retaining bolts. Tighten the bolts to the specified torque. Clip the wiring harness back into position on the bracket.

29 Position the air conditioning compressor on the mounting bracket. Fit and tighten the three retaining bolts to the specified torque (see Chapter 3 specifications), then reconnect the compressor wiring connector.

30 Refit the crankshaft pulley/vibration damper as described in Section 5.

31 Refit the catalytic converter support bracket and securely tighten the three bolts.

32 Refit the exhaust system as described in Chapter 4B Section 20.

33 Position the intermediate shaft bearing

housing support bracket on the cylinder block and secure with the three retaining bolts tightened to the specified torque.

34 Refit the intermediate shaft and right-hand driveshaft as described in Chapter 8.

35 Refit the roadwheel, then lower the car to the ground and tighten the wheel bolts to the specified torque.

36 Fill the engine with fresh engine oil as described in Chapter 1B Section 6.

37 On completion, reconnect the battery negative terminal.

14 Oil pump –
removal, overhaul and refitting

Removal

1 Remove the timing belt as described in Section 6.

2 Remove the crankshaft sprocket as described In Section 7.

3 Remove the sump and oil pump pick-up/strainer as described in Section 13.

4 Slacken and remove the seven retaining bolts then slide the oil pump housing assembly off of the end of the crankshaft **(see illustration)**. Remove the housing gasket and discard it.

Overhaul

5 Undo the retaining screws and lift off the pump cover from the rear of the housing **(see illustration)**.

6 Check the inner and outer rotors for

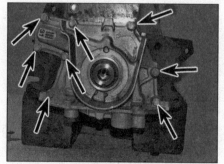

14.4 Oil pump housing retaining bolts (arrowed)

14.5 Undo the retaining screws and lift off the oil pump cover

identification dots indicating which way round they are fitted **(see illustration)**. If no marks are visible, use a suitable marker pen to mark the surface of both the pump inner and outer rotors.

7 Lift out the inner and outer rotors from the pump housing.

8 Unscrew the oil pressure relief valve bolt from the base of the housing and withdraw the spring and plunger, noting which way around the plunger is fitted **(see illustrations)**. Remove the sealing washer from the valve bolt.

9 Clean the components, and carefully examine the rotors, pump body and relief valve plunger for any signs of scoring or wear. If any damage or wear is noticed, it will be necessary to renew the complete pump assembly.

10 If the pump is satisfactory, reassemble the components in the reverse order of removal, noting the following.

a) Ensure both rotors are fitted the correct way around.

b) Fit a new sealing ring to the pressure relief valve bolt and securely tighten the bolt.

c) Apply a little locking compound to the threads, and securely tighten the pump cover screws.

d) On completion prime the oil pump by filling it with clean engine oil whilst rotating the inner rotor **(see illustration)**.

Refitting

11 Prior to refitting, carefully lever out the crankshaft oil seal using a flat-bladed screwdriver. Fit the new oil seal, ensuring its sealing lip is facing inwards, and press it squarely into the housing using a tubular drift which bears only on the hard outer edge of the seal. Press the seal into position so that it is flush with the housing and lubricate the oil seal lip with clean engine oil.

12 Ensure the mating surfaces of the oil pump and cylinder block are clean and dry.

13 Fit a new gasket to the oil pump housing and bend down the tabs on the edge of the gasket to retain it on the pump housing **(see illustration)**.

14 Locate the pump housing over the end of the crankshaft and into position on the cylinder block.

15 Refit the pump housing retaining bolts and tighten them to the specified torque.

16 Refit the oil pump pick-up/strainer and sump as described in Section 13.

14.6 Oil pump inner and outer rotor identification dots (arrowed)

14.8b ... and withdraw the spring ...

14.8a Unscrew the oil pressure relief valve bolt ...

14.8c ... and plunger

17 Refit the crankshaft sprocket as described in Section 7.

18 Refit the timing belt as described in Section 6.

19 On completion, fit a new oil filter and fill the engine with clean oil as described in Chapter 1B Section 6.

---

15 Oil filter housing – removal and refitting

Removal

1 The oil filter housing with integral oil cooler is located at the rear of the cylinder block, above the right-hand driveshaft.

2 Disconnect the battery negative terminal (refer to Chapter 5A Section 4).

3 Apply the handbrake, then jack up the front

of the vehicle and support it on axle stands (see *Jacking and vehicle support*). Remove the right-hand front roadwheel.

4 Drain the cooling system and remove the engine oil filter element as described in Chapter 1B.

5 Remove the exhaust system as described in Chapter 4B Section 20.

6 Remove the right-hand driveshaft and the intermediate shaft as described in Chapter 8.

7 Undo the three bolts securing the intermediate shaft bearing housing support bracket to the cylinder block and remove the support bracket **(see illustration 13.4)**.

8 Disconnect the wiring connector from the oil pressure switch.

9 Release the retaining clips and disconnect the two coolant hoses from the oil cooler on the oil filter housing.

10 Undo the three retaining bolts and remove the oil filter housing from the cylinder block **(see illustration)**. Recover the two rubber

14.10a Prime the oil pump by filling it with clean engine oil whilst rotating the inner rotor

14.13 Bend down the tabs on the edge of the gasket to retain it on the oil pump housing

15.10 Oil filter housing retaining bolts (arrowed)

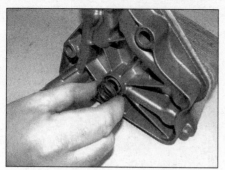

15.11a Fit a new sealing ring to the oil filter housing supply channel ...

15.11b ... and to the return channel

16.2 Screw in a self-tapping screw and pull on the screw with pliers to extract the oil seal

seals from the rear of the housing. Note that new seals will be required for refitting.

Refitting

11 Thoroughly clean the oil filter housing, then fit the two new sealing rings **(see illustrations)**.

12 Position the oil filter housing on the cylinder block and refit the retaining bolts. Tighten the bolts to the specified torque.

13 Refit the two coolant hoses and secure with their retaining clips. Reconnect the oil pressure switch wiring connector.

14 Position the intermediate shaft bearing housing support bracket on the cylinder block and secure with the three retaining bolts tightened to the specified torque.

15 Refit the intermediate shaft and right-hand driveshaft as described in Chapter 8.

16 Add new oil and fit a new oil filter element as described in Chapter 1B Section 6.

17 Refit the exhaust system as described in Chapter 4B Section 20.

18 Refit the roadwheel, then lower the car to the ground and tighten the wheel bolts to the specified torque.

19 Refill the cooling system as described in Chapter 1B Section 30.

20 On completion, reconnect the battery negative terminal.

16 Crankshaft oil seals – renewal

Right-hand (timing belt end)

1 Remove the crankshaft sprocket as described in Section 7.

2 Carefully punch or drill a small hole in the oil seal. Screw in a self-tapping screw and pull on the screw with pliers to extract the seal **(see illustration)**.

3 Clean the seal housing and polish off any burrs or raised edges which may have caused the seal to fail in the first place.

4 Ease the new seal into position on the end of the crankshaft. Press the seal squarely into position until it is flush with the housing. If necessary, a suitable tubular drift which bears only on the hard outer edge of the seal can be used to tap the seal into position **(see illustration)**. Take great care not to damage the seal lips during fitting and ensure that the seal lips face inwards.

5 Wash off any traces of oil, then refit the crankshaft sprocket as described in Section 7.

Left-hand (flywheel/driveplate end)

6 Remove the flywheel/driveplate as described in Section 17.

7 Remove the sump as described in Section 13.

8 Undo the five bolts and remove the oil seal housing. Note that the oil seal and the housing are a single assembly.

9 Clean the crankshaft and polish off any burrs or raised edges which may have caused the seal to fail in the first place.

10 Position the new oil seal housing, complete with seal, over the crankshaft and into position on the cylinder block **(see illustration)**. Note that the new oil seal housing is supplied with a protector sleeve over the oil seal. Leave the sleeve in position as the housing is fitted.

11 Refit the five retaining bolts and tighten to the specified torque.

12 Remove the protector sleeve from the housing **(see illustration)**.

13 Refit the sump as described in Section 13.

14 Refit the flywheel/driveplate as described in Section 17.

17 Flywheel/driveplate – removal, inspection and refitting

1 Refer to Chapter 2C, Section 17.

18 Engine/transmission mountings – inspection and renewal

1 Refer to Chapter 2C, Section 18.

16.4 Using a socket as a tubular drift to fit the new oil seal

16.10 Fitting the new oil seal housing, with integral oil seal, over the crankshaft

16.12 After fitting, remove the protector sleeve from the housing

Chapter 2 Part E
Engine removal and overhaul procedures

Contents

Section number

Crankshaft – inspection 13
Crankshaft – refitting 17
Crankshaft – removal 10
Cylinder block – cleaning and inspection. 11
Cylinder head – dismantling. 6
Cylinder head – reassembly. 8
Cylinder head and valves – cleaning and inspection 7
Engine – initial start-up after overhaul 19
Engine and transmission unit – removal and refitting. 4
Engine overhaul – dismantling sequence. 5

Section number

Engine overhaul – general information. 2
Engine overhaul – reassembly sequence. 15
Engine removal – methods and precautions 3
General Information 1
Main and big-end bearings – inspection 14
Piston rings – refitting. 16
Pistons/connecting rods – inspection 12
Pistons/connecting rods – refitting. 18
Pistons/connecting rods – removal 9

Degrees of difficulty

Easy, suitable for novice with little experience	**Fairly easy,** suitable for beginner with some experience	**Fairly difficult,** suitable for competent DIY mechanic	**Difficult,** suitable for experienced DIY mechanic	**Very difficult,** suitable for expert DIY or professional

Specifications

Engine identification

Engine type.	Manufacturer's engine code
1.6 litre (1598 cc) DOHC 16-valve petrol engine	Z16XEP, Z16XE1, Z16XER and A16XER
1.8 litre (1796 cc) DOHC 16-valve petrol engine	Z18XER and A18XER
1.7 litre (1686 cc) DOHC 16-valve petrol engine	A17DTR and A17DTJ
1.9 litre (1910 cc) SOHC 8-valve diesel engine	Z19DT and Z19DTL
1.9 litre (1910 cc) DOHC 16-valve diesel engine	Z19DTH

1.6 litre petrol engines

Note: *Where specifications are given as N/A, no information was available at the time of writing. Refer to your Vauxhall/Opel dealer for the latest information available.*

Cylinder head

Maximum gasket face distortion	0.05 mm
Cylinder head height	N/A
Valve seat angle in cylinder head.	90° 30'
Valve seat width in cylinder head:	
Intake valve.	1.0 to 1.4 mm
Exhaust valve	1.4 to 1.8 mm
Maximum permissible valve stem play in guide:	
Intake valve.	0.030 to 0.061 mm
Exhaust valve	0.050 to 0.081 mm

1.6 litre petrol engines (continued)

Valves and guides

Stem diameter:
Intake valve	4.955 to 4.970 mm
Exhaust valve	4.935 to 4.950 mm

Valve head diameter:
Intake valve	30.70 to 30.80 mm
Exhaust valve	27.10 to 27.20 mm

Valve length:
Intake valve	117.10 to 117.30 mm
Exhaust valve	116.16 to 116.36 mm

Valve clearances (cold):
Intake valve	0.21 to 0.29 mm
Exhaust valve	0.26 to 0.35 mm

Cylinder block

Maximum gasket face distortion	0.05 mm
Cylinder bore diameter	78.992 to 79.058 mm (nominal)
Maximum cylinder bore ovality and taper	0.013 mm

Crankshaft and bearings

Number of main bearings	5
Main bearing journal diameter	54.980 to 54.997 mm
Big-end bearing journal diameter	42.971 to 42.987 mm
Crankshaft endfloat	0.100 to 0.202 mm

Piston rings

Number of rings (per piston)	2 compression, 1 oil control

Ring end gap:
Compression	0.25 to 0.50 mm
Oil control	0.25 to 0.75 mm

Torque wrench settings

Refer to Chapter 2A Specifications

1.8 litre petrol engines

Note: *Where specifications are given as N/A, no information was available at the time of writing. Refer to your Vauxhall/Opel dealer for the latest information available.*

Cylinder head

Maximum gasket face distortion	0.05 mm
Cylinder head height	N/A
Valve seat angle in cylinder head	90° 30'

Valve seat width in cylinder head:
Intake	1.0 to 1.4 mm
Exhaust	1.4 to 1.8 mm

Maximum permissible valve stem play in guide:
Intake	0.030 to 0.061 mm
Exhaust	0.050 to 0.081 mm

Valves and guides

Stem diameter:
Intake valve	4.955 to 4.970 mm
Exhaust valve	4.935 to 4.950 mm

Valve head diameter:
Intake valve	30.70 to 30.80 mm
Exhaust valve	27.10 to 27.20 mm

Valve length:
Intake valve	117.10 to 117.30 mm
Exhaust valve	116.16 to 116.36 mm

Valve clearances (cold):
Intake valve	0.21 to 0.29 mm
Exhaust valve	0.27 to 0.35 mm

Cylinder block

Maximum gasket face distortion	0.05 mm
Cylinder bore diameter	80.492 to 80.558 mm (nominal)
Maximum cylinder bore ovality and taper	0.013 mm

1.8 litre petrol engines (continued)

Crankshaft and bearings
Number of main bearings 5
Main bearing journal diameter . . . . 54.980 to 54.997 mm
Big-end bearing journal diameter. . . . . 42.971 to 42.987 mm
Crankshaft endfloat . . . . 0.100 to 0.202 mm

Pistons
Piston diameter . . . . 80.455 to 80.515 mm (nominal)

Piston rings
Number of rings (per piston). . . . . 2 compression, 1 oil control
Ring end gap:
   Top compression . . . . 0.20 to 0.40 mm
   Second compression . . . . 0.40 to 0.60 mm
   Oil control. . . . . 0.25 to 0.75 mm

Torque wrench settings
Refer to Chapter 2A Specifications

1.7 litre diesel engines

Note: *Where specifications are given as N/A, no information was available at the time of writing. Refer to your Vauxhall/Opel dealer for the latest information available.*

Cylinder head
Maximum gasket face distortion . . . . 0.10 mm
Cylinder head height . . . . 94.95 to 95.05 mm
Valve seat angle . . . . 89.5°
Valve seat width:
   Inlet . . . . 1.6 to 1.8 mm
   Exhaust. . . . . 1.4 to 1.6 mm

Valves and guides
Stem diameter (inlet and exhaust) . . . . 5.96 to 5.97 mm
Valve head diameter:
   Inlet . . . . 27.5 mm
   Exhaust. . . . . 25.5 mm
Valve length:
   Inlet . . . . 102.5 mm
   Exhaust. . . . . 102.2 mm
Maximum permissible valve stem play in guide:
   Inlet . . . . 0.019 mm
   Exhaust. . . . . 0.021 mm
Valve clearances (cold):
   Inlet and exhaust . . . . 0.40 ± 0.05 mm

Cylinder block
Maximum gasket face distortion . . . . N/A
Cylinder bore diameter. . . . . 79.000 to 79.010 mm (nominal)
Maximum cylinder bore ovality. . . . . N/A
Maximum cylinder bore taper. . . . . N/A

Crankshaft and bearings
Number of main bearings. 5
Main bearing journal diameter:
   Standard size . . . . 51.928 to 51.938 mm (nominal)
Big-end bearing journal (crankpin) diameter . . . . N/A
Crankshaft endfloat . . . . 0.030 to 0.120 mm

Pistons
Piston diameter . . . . 78.930 to 78.939 mm (nominal)

Piston rings
Number of rings (per piston). . . . . 2 compression, 1 oil control
Ring end gap:
   Upper compression . . . . 0.20 to 0.30 mm
   Lower compression . . . . 0.20 to 0.30 mm
   Oil control. . . . . 0.20 to 0.40 mm

1.9 litre SOHC diesel engines

Note: *Where specifications are given as N/A, no information was available at the time of writing. Refer to your Vauxhall/Opel dealer for the latest information available.*

Cylinder head

Maximum gasket face distortion	0.10 mm
Cylinder head height	140.85 to 141.15 mm
Valve seat angle in cylinder head	N/A
Valve seat width in cylinder head	N/A
Maximum permissible valve stem play in guide	N/A

Valves and guides

Stem diameter (intake and exhaust)	7.974 to 7.992 mm
Valve head diameter	N/A
Valve length	N/A
Valve clearances (cold):	
Intake valve	0.25 to 0.35 mm
Exhaust valve	0.30 to 0.40 mm

Cylinder block

Maximum gasket face distortion	0.15 mm
Cylinder bore diameter	82.000 to 82.030 mm
Maximum cylinder bore ovality	0.050 mm
Maximum cylinder bore taper	0.005 mm

Crankshaft and bearings

Number of main bearings	5
Main bearing journal diameter	59.855 to 60.000 mm
Big-end bearing journal diameter	50.660 to 50.805 mm
Crankshaft endfloat	0.049 to 0.211 mm

Pistons

Piston diameter	81.920 to 81.950 mm

Piston rings

Number of rings (per piston)	2 compression, 1 oil control
Ring end gap:	
Top compression	0.25 to 0.40 mm
Second compression	0.25 to 0.50 mm
Oil control	0.25 to 0.50 mm

Torque wrench settings

Refer to Chapter 2C Specifications

1.9 litre DOHC diesel engines

Note: *Where specifications are given as N/A, no information was available at the time of writing. Refer to your Vauxhall/Opel dealer for the latest information available.*

Cylinder head

Maximum gasket face distortion	0.10 mm
Cylinder head height	106.95 to 107.05 mm
Valve seat angle in cylinder head	N/A
Valve seat width in cylinder head	N/A
Maximum permissible valve stem play in guide	N/A

Valves and guides

Stem diameter:	
Intake valve	5.982 to 6.000 mm
Exhaust valve	5.972 to 5.990 mm
Valve head diameter	N/A
Valve length	N/A
Valve clearances	Automatic adjustment by hydraulic cam followers

Cylinder block

Maximum gasket face distortion	0.15 mm
Cylinder bore diameter	82.000 to 82.030 mm
Maximum cylinder bore ovality	0.050 mm
Maximum cylinder bore taper	0.005 mm

1.9 litre DOHC diesel engines (continued)

Crankshaft and bearings
Number of main bearings. 5
Main bearing journal diameter . . . . 59.855 to 60.000 mm
Big-end bearing journal diameter. . . . . 50.660 to 50.805 mm
Crankshaft endfloat . . . . 0.049 to 0.211 mm

Pistons
Piston diameter . . . . 81.920 to 81.950 mm

Piston rings
Number of rings (per piston). . . . . 2 compression, 1 oil control
Ring end gap:
   Top compression . . . . 0.20 to 0.35 mm
   Second compression . . . . 0.60 to 0.80 mm
   Oil control . . . . 0.25 to 0.50 mm

Torque wrench settings
Refer to Chapter 2D Specifications

1 General Information

1 Included in this Part of Chapter 2 are details of removing the engine/transmission from the car and general overhaul procedures for the cylinder head, cylinder block/crankcase and all other engine internal components.

2 The information given ranges from advice concerning preparation for an overhaul and the purchase of parts, to detailed step-by-step procedures covering removal, inspection, renovation and refitting of engine internal components.

3 After Section 5, all instructions are based on the assumption that the engine has been removed from the car. For information concerning in-car engine repair, as well as the removal and refitting of those external components necessary for full overhaul, refer to Part A, B, C or D of this Chapter (as applicable) and to Section 5. Ignore any preliminary dismantling operations described in Part A, B, C or D that are no longer relevant once the engine has been removed from the car.

4 Apart from torque wrench settings, which are given at the beginning of Part A, B, C or D (as applicable), all specifications relating to engine overhaul are at the beginning of this Part of Chapter 2.

2 Engine overhaul –
general information

1 It is not always easy to determine when, or if, an engine should be completely overhauled, as a number of factors must be considered.

2 High mileage is not necessarily an indication that an overhaul is needed, while low mileage does not preclude the need for an overhaul. Frequency of servicing is probably the most important consideration. An engine which has had regular and frequent oil and filter changes, as well as other required maintenance, should give many thousands of miles of reliable service. Conversely, a neglected engine may require an overhaul very early in its life.

3 Excessive oil consumption is an indication that piston rings, valve seals and/or valve guides are in need of attention. Make sure that oil leaks are not responsible before deciding that the rings and/or guides are worn. Have a compression test performed (refer to Part A of this Chapter for petrol engines and to Part B, C or D for diesel engines), to determine the likely cause of the problem.

4 Check the oil pressure with a gauge fitted in place of the oil pressure switch, and compare it with that specified. If it is extremely low, the main and big-end bearings, and/or the oil pump, are probably worn out.

5 Loss of power, rough running, knocking or metallic engine noises, excessive valve gear noise, and high fuel consumption may also point to the need for an overhaul, especially if they are all present at the same time. If a complete service does not cure the situation, major mechanical work is the only solution.

6 A full engine overhaul involves restoring all internal parts to the specification of a new engine. During a complete overhaul, the pistons and the piston rings are renewed, and the cylinder bores are reconditioned. New main and big-end bearings are generally fitted; if necessary, the crankshaft may be reground, to compensate for wear in the journals. The valves are also serviced as well, since they are usually in less-than-perfect condition at this point. Always pay careful attention to the condition of the oil pump when overhauling the engine, and renew it if there is any doubt as to its serviceability. The end result should be an as-new engine that will give many trouble-free miles.

7 Critical cooling system components such as the hoses, thermostat and coolant pump should be renewed when an engine is overhauled. The radiator should also be checked carefully, to ensure that it is not clogged or leaking.

8 Before beginning the engine overhaul, read through the entire procedure, to familiarise yourself with the scope and requirements of the job. Check on the availability of parts and make sure that any necessary special tools and equipment are obtained in advance. Most work can be done with typical hand tools, although a number of precision measuring tools are required for inspecting parts to determine if they must be renewed.

9 The services provided by an engineering machine shop or engine reconditioning specialist will almost certainly be required, particularly if major repairs such as crankshaft regrinding or cylinder reboring are necessary. Apart from carrying out machining operations, these establishments will normally handle the inspection of parts, offer advice concerning reconditioning or renewal and supply new components such as pistons, piston rings and bearing shells. It is recommended that the establishment used is a member of the Federation of Engine Re-Manufacturers, or a similar society.

10 Always wait until the engine has been completely dismantled, and until all components (especially the cylinder block/crankcase and the crankshaft) have been inspected, before deciding what service and repair operations must be performed by an engineering works. The condition of these components will be the major factor to consider when determining whether to overhaul the original engine, or to buy a reconditioned unit. Do not, therefore, purchase parts or have overhaul work done on other components until they have been thoroughly inspected. As a general rule, time is the primary cost of an overhaul, so it does not pay to fit worn or sub-standard parts.

11 As a final note, to ensure maximum life and minimum trouble from a reconditioned engine, everything must be assembled with care, in a spotlessly-clean environment.

3 Engine removal –
methods and precautions

1 If you have decided that the engine must be removed for overhaul or major repair work, several preliminary steps should be taken.
2 Engine/transmission removal is extremely complicated and involved on these vehicles. It must be stated, that unless the vehicle can be positioned on a ramp, or raised and supported on axle stands over an inspection pit, it will be very difficult to carry out the work involved.
3 Cleaning the engine compartment and engine/transmission before beginning the removal procedure will help keep tools clean and organised.
4 An engine hoist will also be necessary. Make sure the equipment is rated in excess of the combined weight of the engine and transmission. Safety is of primary importance, considering the potential hazards involved in removing the engine/transmission from the car.
5 The help of an assistant is essential. Apart from the safety aspects involved, there are many instances when one person cannot simultaneously perform all of the operations required during engine/transmission removal.
6 Plan the operation ahead of time. Before starting work, arrange for the hire of or obtain all of the tools and equipment you will need. Some of the equipment necessary to perform engine/transmission removal and installation safely (in addition to an engine hoist) is as follows: a heavy duty trolley jack, complete sets of spanners and sockets as described in the rear of this manual, wooden blocks, and plenty of rags and cleaning solvent for mopping-up spilled oil, coolant and fuel. If the hoist must be hired, make sure that you arrange for it in advance, and perform all of the operations possible without it beforehand. This will save you money and time.
7 Plan for the car to be out of use for quite a while. An engineering machine shop or engine reconditioning specialist will be required to perform some of the work which cannot be accomplished without special equipment. These places often have a busy schedule, so it would be a good idea to consult them before removing the engine, in order to accurately estimate the amount of time required to rebuild or repair components that may need work.
8 During the engine/transmission removal procedure, it is advisable to make notes of the locations of all brackets, cable ties, earthing points, etc, as well as how the wiring harnesses, hoses and electrical connections are attached and routed around the engine and engine compartment. An effective way of doing this is to take a series of photographs of the various components before they are disconnected or removed; the resulting photographs will prove invaluable when the engine/transmission is refitted.
9 Always be extremely careful when removing and refitting the engine/transmission. Serious

injury can result from careless actions. Plan ahead and take your time, and a job of this nature, although major, can be accomplished successfully.
10 On all Zafira models, the engine must be removed complete with the transmission as an assembly. There is insufficient clearance in the engine compartment to remove the engine leaving the transmission in the vehicle. The assembly is removed by raising the front of the vehicle, and lowering the assembly from the engine compartment.

4 Engine and transmission unit
– removal and refitting

Note: *The engine can be removed from the car only as a complete unit with the transmission; the two are then separated for overhaul. The engine/transmission unit is lowered out of position, and withdrawn from under the vehicle. Bearing this in mind, and also bearing in mind the information contained in Section 3, ensure the vehicle is raised sufficiently so that there is enough clearance between the front of the vehicle and the floor to allow the engine/transmission unit to be slid out once it has been lowered out of position.*
Note: *Such is the complexity of the power unit arrangement on these vehicles, and the variations that may be encountered according to model and optional equipment fitted, that the following should be regarded as a guide to the work involved, rather than a step-by-step procedure. Where differences are encountered, or additional component disconnection or removal is necessary, make notes of the work involved as an aid to refitting.*

Removal

1 On models equipped with air conditioning, have the air conditioning system fully discharged by an air conditioning specialist.
2 Position the vehicle as described in Section 3, paragraph 2, and remove both front road-wheels. On petrol engine models, remove the right-hand wheel arch liner inner cover. On diesel engine models, remove the engine undertray.
3 Remove the bonnet, the front bumper and the windscreen cowl panel as described in Chapter 11.
4 Where fitted, remove the plastic cover from the top of the engine.
5 Remove the battery and battery tray as described in Chapter 5A Section 4.
6 Undo the retaining nuts, remove the bolts and disconnect the positive and negative secondary leads from the main battery positive and negative terminals.
7 Release the retaining clips and disconnect the three coolant hoses from the coolant expansion tank. Remove the expansion tank by pulling it forward out of its mounting bracket.
8 Lift off the cover from the wiring junction box at the left-hand rear corner of the

engine compartment. Undo the two nuts and disconnect the two positive cables from the junction box terminals **(see illustration)**.
9 Disconnect the wiring harness connector at the side of the junction box. Release the wiring harness from the retaining clips and cable ties so that it is free to be removed with the engine.
10 Disconnect the wiring harness connector located in front of the engine compartment fuse/relay box. Undo the nut securing the earth lead to the stud below the battery box location. Release the disconnected wiring harness from the retaining clips and cable ties so that it is free to be removed with the engine.
11 Carry out the following operations as described in Chapter 1A or Chapter 1B, as applicable:
a) Drain the engine oil.
b) Drain the cooling system.
c) Remove the auxiliary drivebelt.
12 Remove the air cleaner assembly and intake ducts as described in Chapter 4A or Chapter 4B, as applicable.
13 Disconnect the wiring block connector from the cooling fan module below the cooling fans. Release the wiring harness from the retaining clips so that it is free to be removed with the engine.
14 Remove the air conditioning system compressor as described in Chapter 3 Section 11.

Petrol engine models

15 Depressurise the fuel system with reference to Chapter 4A Section 5, then disconnect the fuel supply pipe from the fuel rail and support bracket. Be prepared for fuel spillage, and take adequate precautions. Clamp or plug the open unions, to minimise further fuel loss.
16 Disconnect the brake vacuum servo hose, and fuel evaporation purge hose.
17 Disconnect the wiring connector(s) from the engine management ECU.

Diesel engine models

18 Disconnect the brake vacuum servo hose from the vacuum pump.
19 Detach the fuel supply hose quick-release connector and remove the hose from the high-pressure fuel pump. A Vauxhall/Opel special tool (KM-796-A) is available

4.8 Disconnect the two positive cables (arrowed) from the junction box terminals

4.24a Release the selector inner cable end fittings from the transmission selector levers ...

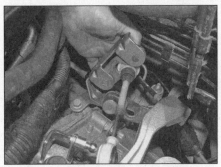

4.24b ... then pull back the retaining sleeves and detach the outer cables from the transmission mounting bracket

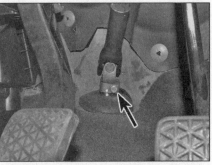

4.29 Unscrew the nut and remove the bolt (arrowed) securing the steering column intermediate shaft to the steering gear pinion shaft

to disconnect the hose connectors, but provided care is taken, the connections can be released using two screwdrivers, a pair of long-nosed pliers, or similar, to depress the retaining tangs. Suitably cover or plug the open hose connections to prevent dirt entry. Similarly disconnect the fuel return hose from the damping chamber.

20 Working under the front, right-hand side of the car, release the locking lever catch, then lift the locking levers and disconnect the two wiring connectors from the engine management system ECU.

21 Again, working under the front, right-hand side of the car, disconnect the two vacuum hoses and the wiring connector from the turbocharger wastegate solenoid valve.

All models

22 Loosen the clips and remove the upper and lower radiator hoses.

23 Release the quick-release connectors by sliding them forward, and disconnect the two heater hoses from the heater matrix pipe stubs.

24 On manual transmission models, using a suitable forked tool, release the gear-change selector cable end fittings from the transmission selector levers. Pull back the retaining sleeves and detach the outer

cables from the mounting bracket on the transmission **(see illustrations)**.

25 On automatic transmission models, use a forked tool or flat-bladed screwdriver, and carefully lever the gear selector inner cable end fitting off the balljoint on the selector lever position switch. Pull back the retaining sleeve and detach the outer cable from the mounting bracket on the transmission.

26 Drain the manual transmission oil or automatic transmission fluid as described in Chapter 7A Section 2 or Chapter 7B Section 2, as applicable.

27 Remove both driveshafts as described in Chapter 8 Section 2.

28 Position the steering with the front road-wheels straight-ahead, and lock the steering by removing the ignition key.

29 Unscrew the nut and remove the bolt securing the steering column intermediate shaft to the steering gear pinion shaft. Separate the intermediate shaft from the pinion shaft by pulling the intermediate shaft upwards **(see illustration)**.

Caution: To prevent damage to the airbag wiring contact unit, the steering lock must remain locked until the intermediate shaft is re-attached to the pinion shaft.

30 On manual transmission models, remove

the filler cap from the brake/clutch fluid reservoir on the bulkhead, then tighten it onto a piece of polythene. This will reduce the loss of fluid when the clutch hydraulic hose is disconnected. Alternatively, fit a hose clamp to the flexible hose next to the clutch hydraulic connection on the transmission housing.

31 Place some cloth rags beneath the hose, then prise out the retaining clip securing the clutch hydraulic hose to the end fitting on top of the transmission bellhousing. Detach the hose from the end fitting **(see illustrations)**. Gently squeeze the two legs of the retaining clip together and re-insert the retaining clip back into position in the end fitting. Discard the sealing ring from the hose end; a new sealing ring must be used on refitting. Plug/ cover both the end fitting and hose end to minimise fluid loss and prevent the entry of dirt into the hydraulic system. **Note:** *Whilst the hose is disconnected, do not depress the clutch pedal.*

32 On automatic transmission models, unscrew the central retaining bolt (or nut) and detach the fluid cooler pipes from the transmission. Suitably cover the pipe ends and plug the transmission orifices to prevent dirt entry.

33 Attach a suitable hoist and lifting tackle to the engine lifting brackets on the cylinder

4.31a Prise out the clip securing the clutch hydraulic hose to the end fitting on the transmission bellhousing ...

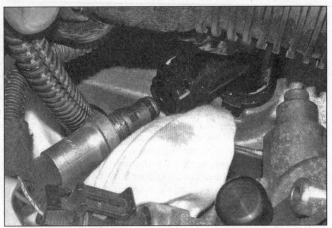

4.31b ... then detach the hose from the end fitting

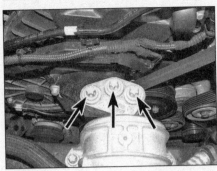

4.35 Right-hand engine mounting bracket-to-engine bracket retaining bolts (arrowed)

4.36 Left-hand engine mounting-to-transmission bracket retaining bolts (arrowed)

head, and support the weight of the engine/transmission.

34 Remove the front subframe as described in Chapter 10 Section 7.

35 Mark the position of the three bolts securing the right-hand engine mounting bracket to the engine bracket and undo the bolts **(see illustration)**. Note: *There is no need to remove the mounting, since the engine/transmission is lowered from the engine compartment.*

36 Mark the position of the three bolts securing the left-hand engine mounting to the transmission bracket **(see illustration)**.

37 Make a final check to ensure that all relevant pipes, hoses, wires, etc, have been disconnected, and that they are positioned clear of the engine and transmission.

38 With the help of an assistant, carefully lower the engine/transmission assembly to the ground. Make sure that the surrounding components in the engine compartment are not damaged. Ideally, the assembly should be lowered onto a trolley jack or low platform with castors, so that it can easily be withdrawn from under the car.

39 Ensure that the assembly is adequately supported, then disconnect the engine hoist and lifting tackle, and withdraw the engine/transmission assembly from under the front of the vehicle.

40 Clean away any external dirt using paraffin or a water-soluble solvent and a stiff brush.

41 With reference to Chapter 7A Section 7 or Chapter 7B Section 13, unbolt the transmission from the engine. Carefully withdraw the transmission from the engine. On manual transmission models, ensure that its weight is not allowed to hang on the input shaft while engaged with the clutch friction disc. On automatic transmission models, ensure that the torque converter is removed together with the transmission so that it remains engaged with the oil pump. Note that the transmission locates on dowels positioned in the rear of the cylinder block.

Refitting

42 With reference to Chapter 7A Section 7 or Chapter 7B Section 13, refit the transmission

to the engine and tighten the bolts to the specified torque.

43 With the front of the vehicle raised and supported on axle stands, move the engine/transmission assembly under the vehicle, ensuring that the assembly is adequately supported.

44 Reconnect the hoist and lifting tackle to the engine lifting brackets, and carefully raise the engine/transmission assembly up into the engine compartment with the help of an assistant.

45 Reconnect the right- and left-hand engine/transmission mountings and tighten the bolts to the specified torque given in Chapter 2A, Chapter 2B, Chapter 2C or Chapter 2D, as applicable. Ensure that the marks made on removal are correctly aligned when tightening the retaining bolts.

46 Refit the front subframe as described in Chapter 10 Section 7.

47 Disconnect the hoist and lifting tackle from the engine lifting brackets.

48 Refit the driveshafts as described in Chapter 8 Section 2.

49 On manual transmission models, refill the transmission with correct quantity and type of oil, as described in Chapter 7A Section 2.

50 Reconnect the steering column intermediate shaft to the steering gear pinion shaft and tighten the bolt and nut with reference to Chapter 10 Specifications.

51 On automatic transmission models, reconnect the fluid cooler pipes together with new O-ring seals to the transmission.

52 On manual transmission models, reconnect and bleed the clutch hydraulic connection at the transmission with reference to Chapter 6 Section 2.

53 Refit the gearchange/selector outer cable(s) to the mounting bracket on the transmission. Engage the inner cable end fitting(s) with the selector lever balljoint, squeezing them together with pliers if necessary.

54 Push the heater hoses back onto the matrix pipe stubs. Ensure that the quick-release connectors securely lock the hoses in position.

55 Refit the cooling system expansion tank, and reconnect the wiring connector and the coolant hoses.

56 Reconnect the upper and lower radiator hoses.

Petrol engine models

57 Reconnect the brake vacuum servo hose, and fuel evaporation purge hose and fuel supply pipe.

58 Reconnect the wiring connector(s) from the engine management ECU.

Diesel engine models

59 Reconnect the brake vacuum servo hose to the vacuum pump, and the fuel hoses and wiring connectors at the fuel filter.

60 Reconnect the fuel supply and return hoses.

61 Reconnect the two wiring connectors to the engine management system ECU.

62 Reconnect the two vacuum hoses and the wiring connector at the turbocharger wastegate solenoid valve.

All models

63 Refit the air conditioning system compressor as described in Chapter 3 Section 11, then refit the auxiliary drivebelt as described in Chapter 1A Section 23 or Chapter 1B Section 24, as applicable.

64 Reconnect the wiring block connector to the cooling fan module.

65 Refit the air cleaner assembly and intake ducts as described in Chapter 4A Section 2 or Chapter 4B Section 3, as applicable.

66 Reconnect the wiring harness connector located in front of the engine compartment fuse/relay box and reconnect the earth lead.

67 Reconnect the wiring harness connector at the side of the junction box.

68 Reconnect all remaining wiring connectors and secure the wiring and harness with the cable clips or new cable ties.

69 Reconnect the positive and negative wiring terminals to the battery positive and negative terminal clamps.

70 Refit the battery box and battery as described in Chapter 5A Section 4.

71 Refit the bonnet, the front bumper and the windscreen cowl panel as described in Chapter 11.

72 Refit the right-hand wheel arch liner inner cover, or engine undertray, and both front roadwheels, then lower the vehicle to the ground.

73 Make a final check to ensure that all relevant hoses, pipes and wires have been correctly reconnected.

74 Refill the engine with oil with reference to Chapter 1A Section 6 or Chapter 1B Section 6, as applicable.

75 On automatic transmission models, refill the transmission with correct quantity and type of fluid, as described in Chapter 7B Section 2.

76 Refill and bleed the cooling system with reference to Chapter 1A Section 28 or Chapter 1B Section 30, as applicable.

77 On models equipped with air conditioning, have the air conditioning system evacuated, charged and leak-tested by the specialist who discharged it.

5 Engine overhaul – dismantling sequence

1 It is much easier to dismantle and work on the engine if it is mounted on a portable engine stand. These stands can often be hired from a tool hire shop. Before the engine is mounted on a stand, the flywheel/driveplate should be removed, so that the stand bolts can be tightened into the end of the cylinder block/crankcase.

2 If a stand is not available, it is possible to dismantle the engine with it blocked up on a sturdy workbench, or on the floor. Be extra careful not to tip or drop the engine when working without a stand.

3 If you are going to obtain a reconditioned engine, all the external components must be removed first, to be transferred to the new engine (just as they will if you are doing a complete engine overhaul yourself). These components include the following:

a) Engine wiring harness and supports.
b) Alternator and air conditioning compressor mounting brackets (as applicable).
c) Coolant pump (where applicable) and inlet/outlet housings.
d) Dipstick tube.
e) Fuel system components.
f) All electrical switches and sensors.
g) Intake and exhaust manifolds.
h) Oil filter and oil cooler/heat exchanger.
i) Flywheel/driveplate.

4 Note: When removing the external components from the engine, pay close attention to details that may be helpful or important during refitting. Note the fitted position of gaskets, seals, spacers, pins, washers, bolts, and other small items.

5 If you are obtaining a 'short' engine (which consists of the engine cylinder block/crankcase, crankshaft, pistons and connecting rods all assembled), then the cylinder head, sump, oil pump, and timing belt/chains (as applicable) will have to be removed also.

6 If you are planning a complete overhaul, the engine can be dismantled, and the internal components removed, in the order given below.

Petrol engines

a) Intake and exhaust manifolds (see Chapter 4A).
b) Timing belt, sprockets, tensioner and idler pulleys (see Chapter 2A Section 7).
c) Coolant pump (see Chapter 3 Section 7).
d) Cylinder head (see Chapter 2A Section 13).
e) Flywheel/driveplate (see Chapter 2A Section 18).
f) Sump (see Chapter 2A Section 14).
g) Oil pump (see Chapter 2A Section 15).
h) Pistons/connecting rod assemblies (see Section 9).
i) Crankshaft (see Section 10).

Diesel engines

a) Intake and exhaust manifolds (see Chapter 4B).
b) Timing belt, sprockets, tensioner and idler pulleys (see Chapter 2B, Chapter 2C or Chapter 2D).
c) Coolant pump (see Chapter 3 Section 7).
d) Cylinder head (see Chapter 2B, Chapter 2C or Chapter 2D).
e) Flywheel/driveplate (see Chapter 2B, Chapter 2C or Chapter 2D).
f) Sump (see Chapter 2B, Chapter 2C or Chapter 2D).
g) Oil pump (see Chapter 2B, Chapter 2C or Chapter 2D).
h) Piston/connecting rod assemblies (see Section 9).
i) Crankshaft (see Section 10).

7 Before beginning the dismantling and overhaul procedures, make sure that you have all of the correct tools necessary. See Tools and working facilities for further information.

6 Cylinder head – dismantling

Note: New and reconditioned cylinder heads maybe available from the manufacturer, and from engine overhaul specialists. Due to the fact that some specialist tools are required for the dismantling and inspection procedures, and new components may not be readily available, it may be more practical and economical for the home mechanic to purchase a reconditioned head rather than to dismantle, inspect and recondition the original head. A valve spring compressor tool will be required for this operation.

1 With the cylinder head removed as described in the relevant Part of this Chapter, clean away all external dirt, and remove the following components as applicable, if not already done:

a) Manifolds (see Chapter 4A or Chapter 4B).
b) Spark plugs (petrol engines – see Chapter 1A Section 31).
c) Glow plugs (diesel engines – see Chapter 5A Section 17).
d) Camshafts and and associated valve train components (see Chapter 2A, Chapter 2B, Chapter 2C or Chapter 2D).
e) Fuel injectors (see Chapter 4A or Chapter 4B).
f) Engine lifting brackets.

2 To remove a valve, fit a valve spring compressor tool. Ensure that the arms of the compressor tool are securely positioned on the head of the valve and the spring cap (see illustration). The valves are often deeply-recessed, and a suitable extension piece may be required for the spring compressor.

3 Compress the valve spring to relieve the pressure of the spring cap acting on the collets.

HAYNES HINT *If the spring cap sticks to the valve stem, support the compressor tool, and give the end a light tap with a soft-faced mallet to help free the spring cap.*

4 Extract the two split collets by hooking them out using a small screwdriver, then slowly release the compressor tool (see illustration).

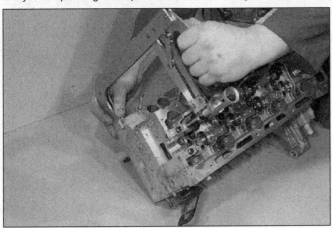

6.2 Using a valve spring compressor, compress the valve spring to relieve the pressure on the collets

6.4 Extract the two split collets by hooking them out using a small screwdriver

6.5a Remove the valve spring cap ...

6.5b ... and the spring ...

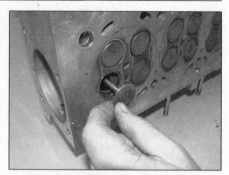

6.5c ... then withdraw the valve through the combustion chamber

6.5d Using pliers, remove the valve stem oil seal, which also incorporates the spring seat on most engines

5 Remove the valve spring cap and the spring, then withdraw the valve through the combustion chamber. Using pliers, remove the valve stem oil seal, which also incorporates the spring seat on most engines **(see illustrations)**. If the spring seat is not part of the valve stem oil seal, hook it out using a small screwdriver.

6 Repeat the procedure for the remaining valves, keeping all components in strict order so that they can be refitted in their original positions, unless all the components are to be renewed. If the components are to be kept and used again, place each valve assembly in a labelled polythene bag or a similar small container **(see illustration)**. Note that as with cylinder numbering, the valves are normally

numbered from the timing belt (or chain) end of the engine. Make sure that the valve components are identified as intake and exhaust, as well as numbered.

7 Cylinder head and valves – cleaning and inspection

1 Thorough cleaning of the cylinder head and valve components, followed by a detailed inspection, will enable you to decide how much valve service work must be carried out during the engine overhaul. **Note:** *If the engine has been severely overheated, it is best to assume that the cylinder head is warped – check carefully for signs of this.*

Cleaning

2 Scrape away all traces of old gasket material from the cylinder head.
3 Scrape away the carbon from the combustion chambers and ports, then wash the cylinder head thoroughly with paraffin or a suitable solvent.
4 Scrape off any heavy carbon deposits that may have formed on the valves, then use a power-operated wire brush to remove deposits from the valve heads and stems.

Inspection

5 Note: *Be sure to perform all the following inspection procedures before concluding*

that the services of a machine shop or engine overhaul specialist are required. Make a list of all items that require attention.

Cylinder head

6 Inspect the head very carefully for cracks, evidence of coolant leakage, and other damage. If cracks are found, a new cylinder head should be obtained.
7 Use a straight-edge and feeler gauge blade to check that the cylinder head surface is not distorted **(see illustration)**. If it is, it may be possible to resurface it, provided that the cylinder head is not reduced to less than the minimum specified height.
8 Examine the valve seats in each of the combustion chambers. If they are severely pitted, cracked or burned, then they will need to be recut by an engine overhaul specialist. If they are only slightly pitted, this can be removed by grinding-in the valve heads and seats with fine valve-grinding compound, as described below.
9 If the valve guides are worn, indicated by a side-to-side motion of the valve, oversize valve guides are available, and valves with oversize stems can be fitted. This work is best carried out by an engine overhaul specialist. A dial gauge may be used to determine whether the amount of side play of a valve exceeds the specified maximum.
10 Check the tappet bores in the cylinder head for wear. If excessive wear is evident, the cylinder head must be renewed. Also

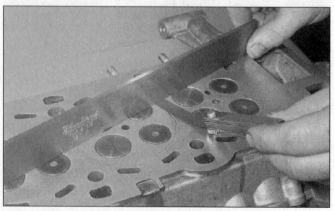

6.6 Place each valve assembly in a labelled polythene bag or similar container

7.7 Using a straight-edge and feeler gauge to check cylinder head surface distortion

7.12 Using a micrometer to measure valve stem diameter

check the tappet oil holes in the cylinder head for obstructions.

Valves

11 Examine the head of each valve for pitting, burning, cracks and general wear, and check the valve stem for scoring and wear ridges. Rotate the valve, and check for any obvious indication that it is bent. Look for pitting and excessive wear on the tip of each valve stem. Renew any valve that shows any such signs of wear or damage.

12 If the valve appears satisfactory at this stage, measure the valve stem diameter at several points using a micrometer **(see illustration)**. Any significant difference in the readings obtained indicates wear of the valve stem. Should any of these conditions be apparent, the valve(s) must be renewed.

13 If the valves are in satisfactory condition, they should be ground (lapped) into their respective seats, to ensure a smooth gas-tight seal. If the seat is only lightly pitted, or if it has been recut, fine grinding compound only should be used to produce the required finish. Coarse valve-grinding compound should not be used unless a seat is badly burned or deeply pitted; if this is the case, the cylinder head and valves should be inspected by an expert to decide whether seat recutting, or even the renewal of the valve or seat insert, is required.

14 Valve grinding is carried out as follows. Place the cylinder head upside-down on a bench, with a block of wood at each end to give clearance for the valve stems.

7.15 Grinding-in a valve

15 Smear a trace of the appropriate grade of valve-grinding compound on the seat face, and press a suction grinding tool onto the valve head. With a semi-rotary action, grind the valve head to its seat, lifting the valve occasionally to redistribute the grinding compound **(see illustration)**. A light spring placed under the valve head will greatly ease this operation.

16 If coarse grinding compound is being used, work only until a dull, matt even surface is produced on both the valve seat and the valve, then wipe off the used compound and repeat the process with fine compound. When a smooth unbroken ring of light grey matt finish is produced on both the valve and seat, the grinding operation is complete. Do not grind in the valves any further than absolutely necessary, or the seat will be prematurely sunk into the cylinder head.

17 When all the valves have been ground-in,

8.1 Lubricate the valve stem with engine oil and insert the valve into the correct guide

carefully wash off all traces of grinding compound using paraffin or a suitable solvent before reassembly of the cylinder head.

Valve components

18 Examine the valve springs for signs of damage and discoloration; if possible; also compare the existing spring free length with new components.

19 Stand each spring on a flat surface, and check it for squareness. If any of the springs are damaged, distorted or have lost their tension, obtain a complete new set of springs.

8 Cylinder head – reassembly

1 Lubricate the stems of the valves, and insert them into their original locations **(see illustration)**. If new valves are being fitted, insert them into the locations to which they have been ground.

2 Working on the first valve, refit the spring seat if it is not an integral part of the valve stem oil seal. Dip the new valve stem seal in fresh engine oil, then carefully locate it over the valve and onto the guide. Take care not to damage the seal as it is passed over the valve stem. Use a suitable socket or metal tube to press the seal firmly onto the guide. **Note:** *If genuine seals are being fitted, use the oil seal protector which is supplied with the seals; the protector fits over the valve stem and prevents the oil seal lip being damaged on the valve* **(see illustrations)**.

8.2a Fit the spring seat ...

8.2b ... then fit the seal protector (where supplied) to the valve ...

8.2c ... and install the new valve stem oil seal ...

8.2d ... pressing it onto the valve guide with a suitable socket

8.3 Refit the valve spring and fit the spring cap

8.4 Compress the valve and locate the collets in the recess on the valve stem

Use a little dab of grease to hold the collets in position on the valve stem while the spring compressor is released.

3 Locate the spring on the seat and fit the spring cap **(see illustration)**.

4 Compress the valve spring, and locate the split collets in the recess in the valve stem **(see illustration and Haynes Hint)**. Release the compressor, then repeat the procedure on the remaining valves.

5 With all the valves installed, support the cylinder head on blocks on the bench and, using a hammer and interposed block of wood, tap the end of each valve stem to settle the components.

6 Refit the components removed in Section 6, paragraph 1.

---

9 Pistons/connecting rods – removal

Note: *New connecting rod big-end cap bolts will be needed on refitting.*

1 Referring to the relevant Part of this Chapter, remove the cylinder head and sump. Where fitted, unbolt the pick-up/strainer from the base of the oil pump.

2 If there is a pronounced wear ridge at the top of any bore, it may be necessary to remove it with a scraper or ridge reamer, to avoid piston damage during removal. Such a ridge indicates excessive wear of the cylinder bore.

3 If the connecting rods and big-end caps are not marked to indicate their positions in the cylinder block (ie, marked with cylinder

numbers), suitably mark both the rod and cap with quick-drying paint or similar. Note which side of the engine the marks face and accurately record this also. There may not be any other way of identifying which way round the cap fits on the rod, when refitting.

4 Turn the crankshaft to bring pistons 1 and 4 to BDC (bottom dead centre).

5 Unscrew the nuts/bolts from No 1 piston big-end bearing cap, then take off the cap and recover the bottom half-bearing shell. If the bearing shells are to be re-used, tape the cap and the shell together.

Caution: On some engines, the connecting rod/bearing cap mating surfaces are not machined flat; the big-end bearing caps are 'cracked' off from the rod during production and left untouched to ensure the cap and rod mate perfectly. Where this type of connecting rod is fitted, great care must be taken to ensure the mating surfaces of the cap and rod are not marked or damaged in anyway. Any damage to the mating surfaces will adversely affect the strength of the connecting rod and could lead to premature failure.

6 Using a hammer handle, push the piston up through the bore, and remove it from the top of the cylinder block. Recover the bearing shell, and tape it to the connecting rod for safe-keeping.

7 Loosely refit the big-end cap to the connecting rod, and secure with the nuts/bolts – this will help to keep the components in their correct order.

8 Remove No 4 piston assembly in the same way.

9 Turn the crankshaft through 180° to bring pistons 2 and 3 to BDC, and remove them in the same way.

---

10 Crankshaft – removal

Note: *New main bearing cap bolts will be required on refitting.*

Petrol engines

1 Working as described in Part A of this Chapter, remove the flywheel and the oil pump.

2 Remove the piston and connecting rod assemblies as described in Section 9. If no work is to be done on the pistons and connecting rods, unbolt the caps and push the pistons far enough up the bores that the connecting rods are positioned clear of the crankshaft journals.

3 Before removing the crankshaft, check the endfloat using a dial gauge in contact with the end of the crankshaft. Push the crankshaft fully one way, and then zero the gauge. Push the crankshaft fully the other way, and check the endfloat **(see illustration)**. The result should be compared with the specified limit, and will give an indication as to the size of the main bearing shell thrust journal width which will be required for reassembly.

4 If a dial gauge is not available, a feeler gauge can be used to measure crankshaft endfloat. Push the crankshaft fully towards one end of the crankcase, and insert a feeler gauge between the thrust flange of the main bearing shell and the machined surface of the crankshaft web **(see illustration)**. Before measuring, ensure that the crankshaft is fully forced towards one end of the crankcase, to give the widest possible gap at the measuring location. **Note:** *Measure at the bearing with the thrustwasher* (see Section 17).

5 The main bearing caps should be numbered

10.3 Check the crankshaft endfloat using a dial gauge ...

10.4 ... or a feeler gauge

10.5 Main bearing cap identification marks (arrowed)

10.13a Main bearing cap identification marks (arrowed) …

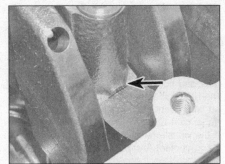

10.13b … and the lug at the base of the cap (arrowed) is used to identify the intake manifold side of the engine

1 to 5 from the timing belt end of the engine and all identification numbers should be the right way up when read from the rear of the cylinder block **(see illustration)**. If the bearing caps are not marked, using a hammer and punch or a suitable marker pen, number the caps from 1 to 5 from the timing belt end of the engine and mark each cap to indicate its correct fitted direction to avoid confusion on refitting.

6 Working in a diagonal sequence, evenly and progressively slacken the ten main bearing cap retaining bolts by half a turn at a time until all bolts are loose. Remove all the bolts.

7 Carefully remove each cap from the cylinder block, ensuring that the lower main bearing shell remains in position in the cap.

8 Carefully lift out the crankshaft, taking care not to displace the upper main bearing shells. Remove the oil seal and discard it.

9 Recover the upper bearing shells from the cylinder block, and tape them to their respective caps for safe-keeping.

Diesel engines

10 Working as described in Part B, C or D of this Chapter (as applicable), remove the flywheel/driveplate, oil pump and the crankshaft left-hand oil seal housing.

11 Remove the piston and connecting rod assemblies as described in Section 9. If no work is to be done on the pistons and connecting rods, unbolt the caps and push the pistons far enough up the bores that the connecting rods are positioned clear of the crankshaft journals.

12 Before removing the crankshaft, check the endfloat as described in paragraphs 3 and 4.

13 Check the main bearing caps for identification markings. Normally, No 1 bearing cap (timing belt end) is not marked and the remaining caps are numbered I, II, III, IIII. The lug at the base of the cap is used to identify the intake manifold side of the engine **(see illustrations)**. If the bearing caps are not marked, using a hammer and punch or a suitable marker pen, number the caps from 1 to 5 from the timing belt end of the engine and mark each cap to indicate its correct fitted direction to avoid confusion on refitting.

14 Working in a diagonal sequence, evenly

and progressively slacken the ten main bearing cap retaining bolts by half a turn at a time until all bolts are loose. Remove all the bolts.

15 Carefully remove each cap from the cylinder block, ensuring that the lower main bearing shell remains in position in the cap.

16 Carefully lift out the crankshaft, taking care not to displace the upper main bearing shells.

17 Recover the upper bearing shells and the thrustwashers from the cylinder block, and tape them to their respective caps for safe-keeping.

11 Cylinder block – cleaning and inspection

Cleaning

1 For complete cleaning, remove all external components (senders, sensors, brackets, oil pipes, coolant pipes, etc) from the cylinder block.

2 Scrape all traces of gasket and/or sealant from the cylinder block and lower casing (where applicable), taking particular care not to damage the cylinder head and sump mating faces.

3 Remove all oil gallery plugs, where fitted. The plugs are usually very tight – they may have to be drilled out and the holes retapped. Use new plugs when the engine is reassembled. On diesel engines, undo the

11.3 Unscrew the retaining bolts and remove the piston oil spray nozzles from the cylinder block

retaining bolts and remove the piston oil spray nozzles from inside the cylinder block **(see illustration)**.

4 If the block and lower casing (where applicable) are extremely dirty, they should be steam-cleaned.

5 If the components have been steam-cleaned, clean all oil holes and oil galleries one more time on completion. Flush all internal passages with warm water until the water runs clear. Dry the block and, where necessary, the lower casing thoroughly and wipe all machined surfaces with a light oil. If you have access to compressed air, use it to speed-up the drying process, and to blow out all the oil holes and galleries.

⚠️ *Warning: Wear eye protection when using compressed air.*

6 If the block and lower casing are relatively clean, an adequate cleaning job can be achieved with hot soapy water and a stiff brush. Take plenty of time, and do a thorough job. Regardless of the cleaning method used, be sure to clean all oil holes and galleries very thoroughly, dry everything completely, and coat all cast-iron machined surfaces with light oil.

7 The threaded holes in the cylinder block must be clean, to ensure accurate torque readings when tightening fixings during reassembly. Run the correct-size tap (which can be determined from the size of the relevant bolt) into each of the holes to remove rust, corrosion, thread sealant or other contamination, and to restore damaged threads. If possible, use compressed air to clear the holes of debris produced by this operation. Do not forget to clean the threads of all bolts and nuts which are to be re-used, as well.

8 Where applicable, apply suitable sealant to the new oil gallery plugs, and insert them into the relevant holes in the cylinder block. Tighten the plugs securely. On diesel engines, refit the oil spray nozzles into the block and secure with the retaining bolts tightened securely.

9 If the engine is to be left dismantled for some time, cover the cylinder block with a large plastic bag to keep it clean and prevent

corrosion. Where applicable, refit the lower casing and tighten the bolts finger-tight.

Inspection

10 Visually check the block for cracks, rust and corrosion. Look for stripped threads in the threaded holes. It's also a good idea to have the block checked for hidden cracks by an engine reconditioning specialist that has the equipment to do this type of work, especially if the vehicle had a history of overheating or using coolant. If defects are found, have the block repaired, if possible, or renewed.

11 If in any doubt as to the condition of the cylinder block, have it inspected and measured by an engine reconditioning specialist. If the bores are worn or damaged, they will be able to carry out any necessary reboring (where possible), and supply appropriate oversized pistons, etc.

12 Pistons/connecting rods – inspection

1 Before the inspection process can begin, the piston/connecting rod assemblies must be cleaned, and the original piston rings removed from the pistons. **Note:** *Always use new piston rings when the engine is reassembled.*

2 Carefully expand the old rings over the top of the pistons. The use of two or three old feeler gauges will be helpful in preventing the rings dropping into empty grooves **(see illustration)**. Take care, however, as piston rings are sharp.

3 Scrape away all traces of carbon from the top of the piston. A hand-held wire brush, or a piece of fine emery cloth, can be used once the majority of the deposits have been scraped away.

4 Remove the carbon from the ring grooves in the piston, using an old ring. Break the ring in half to do this (be careful not to cut your fingers – piston rings are sharp). Be very careful to remove only the carbon deposits – do not remove any metal, and do not nick or scratch the sides of the ring grooves.

5 Once the deposits have been removed, clean the piston/connecting rod assembly with paraffin or a suitable solvent, and dry thoroughly. Make sure that the oil return holes in the ring grooves are clear.

12.2 Using a feeler blade to remove a piston ring

6 If the pistons and cylinder bores are not damaged or worn excessively, and if the cylinder block does not need to be rebored, the original pistons can be refitted. Normal piston wear shows up as even vertical wear on the piston thrust surfaces, and slight looseness of the top ring in its groove. New piston rings should always be used when the engine is reassembled.

7 Carefully inspect each piston for cracks around the skirt, at the gudgeon pin bosses, and at the piston ring lands (between the ring grooves).

8 Look for scoring and scuffing on the thrust faces of the piston skirt, holes in the piston crown, and burned areas at the edge of the crown. If the skirt is scored or scuffed, the engine may have been suffering from overheating, and/or abnormal combustion ('pinking') which caused excessively-high operating temperatures. The cooling and lubrication systems should be checked thoroughly. A hole in the piston crown, or burned areas at the edge of the piston crown indicates that abnormal combustion (pre-ignition, 'pinking', knocking or detonation) has been occurring. If any of the above problems exist, the causes must be investigated and corrected, or the damage will occur again.

9 Corrosion of the piston, in the form of pitting, indicates that coolant has been leaking into the combustion chamber and/or the crankcase. Again, the cause must be corrected, or the problem may persist in the rebuilt engine.

10 If in any doubt as to the condition of the pistons and connecting rods, have them inspected and measured by an engine reconditioning specialist. If new parts are required, they will be able to supply and fit appropriate-sized pistons/rings, and rebore (where possible) or hone the cylinder block.

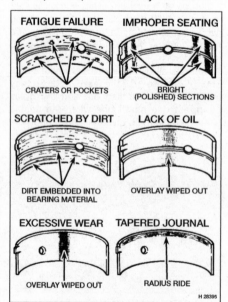

14.2 Typical bearing failures

13 Crankshaft – inspection

1 Clean the crankshaft using paraffin or a suitable solvent, and dry it, preferably with compressed air if available. Be sure to clean the oil holes with a pipe cleaner or similar probe, to ensure that they are not obstructed.

> ⚠ **Warning: Wear eye protection when using compressed air.**

2 Check the main and big-end bearing journals for uneven wear, scoring, pitting and cracking.

3 Big-end bearing wear is accompanied by distinct metallic knocking when the engine is running (particularly noticeable when the engine is pulling from low revs), and some loss of oil pressure.

4 Main bearing wear is accompanied by severe engine vibration and rumble – getting progressively worse as engine revs increase – and again by loss of oil pressure.

5 Check the bearing journal for roughness by running a finger lightly over the bearing surface. Any roughness (which will be accompanied by obvious bearing wear) indicates that the crankshaft requires regrinding.

6 If the crankshaft has been reground, check for burrs around the crankshaft oil holes (the holes are usually chamfered, so burrs should not be a problem unless regrinding has been carried out carelessly). Remove any burrs with a fine file or scraper, and thoroughly clean the oil holes as described previously.

7 Have the crankshaft journals measured by an engine reconditioning specialist. If the crankshaft is worn or damaged, they may be able to regrind the journals and supply suitable undersize bearing shells. If no undersize shells are available and the crankshaft has worn beyond the specified limits, it will have to be renewed. Consult your Vauxhall/Opel dealer or engine reconditioning specialist for further information on parts availability.

8 If a new crankshaft is to be fitted, undo the screws securing the crankshaft speed/position sensor pulse pick-up ring to the crankshaft, and transfer the ring to the new crankshaft.

14 Main and big-end bearings – inspection
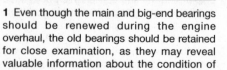

1 Even though the main and big-end bearings should be renewed during the engine overhaul, the old bearings should be retained for close examination, as they may reveal valuable information about the condition of the engine.

2 Bearing failure occurs because of lack of lubrication, the presence of dirt or other foreign particles, overloading the engine, or corrosion **(see illustration)**. If a bearing fails, the cause must be found and eliminated before the engine is reassembled, to prevent the failure from happening again.

3 To examine the bearing shells, remove them from the cylinder block, the main bearing caps or cylinder block lower casing, the connecting rods and the big-end bearing caps, and lay them out on a clean surface in the same order as they were fitted to the engine. This will enable any bearing problems to be matched with the corresponding crankshaft journal.

4 Dirt and other foreign particles can enter the engine in a variety of ways. Contamination may be left in the engine during assembly, or it may pass through filters or the crankcase ventilation system. Normal engine wear produces small particles of metal, which can eventually cause problems. If particles find their way into the lubrication system, it is likely that they will eventually be carried to the bearings. Whatever the source, these foreign particles often end up embedded in the soft bearing material, and are easily recognised. Large particles will not embed in the bearing, and will score or gouge the bearing and journal. To prevent possible contamination, clean all parts thoroughly, and keep everything spotlessly-clean during engine assembly. Once the engine has been installed in the vehicle, ensure that engine oil and filter changes are carried out at the recommended intervals.

5 Lack of lubrication (or lubrication breakdown) has a number of interrelated causes. Excessive heat (which thins the oil), overloading (which squeezes the oil from the bearing face), and oil leakage (from excessive bearing clearances, worn oil pump or high engine speeds) all contribute to lubrication breakdown. Blocked oil passages, which may be the result of misaligned oil holes in a bearing shell, will also starve a bearing of oil and destroy it. When lack of lubrication is the cause of bearing failure, the bearing material is wiped or extruded from the steel backing of the bearing. Temperatures may increase to the point where the steel backing turns blue from overheating.

6 Driving habits can have a definite effect on bearing life. Full-throttle, low-speed operation (labouring the engine) puts very high loads on bearings, which tends to squeeze out the oil film. These loads cause the bearings to flex, which produces fine cracks in the bearing face (fatigue failure). Eventually the bearing material will loosen in places, and tear away from the steel backing. Regular short journeys can lead to corrosion of bearings, because insufficient engine heat is produced to drive off the condensed water and corrosive gases which form inside the engine. These products collect in the engine oil, forming acid and sludge. As the oil is carried to the bearings, the acid attacks and corrodes the bearing material.

7 Incorrect bearing installation during engine assembly will also lead to bearing failure. Tight-fitting bearings leave insufficient bearing

lubrication clearance, and will result in oil starvation. Dirt or foreign particles trapped behind a bearing shell results in high spots on the bearing which can lead to failure.

8 Do not touch any shell's bearing surface with your fingers during reassembly; there is a risk of scratching the delicate surface, or of depositing particles of dirt on it.

9 As mentioned at the beginning of this Section, the bearing shells should be renewed as a matter of course during engine overhaul; to do otherwise is false economy.

15 Engine overhaul – reassembly sequence

1 Before reassembly begins, ensure that all necessary new parts have been obtained (particularly gaskets, and various bolts which must be renewed), and that all the tools required are available. Read through the entire procedure to familiarise yourself with the work involved, and to ensure that all items necessary for reassembly of the engine are to hand. In addition to all normal tools and materials, a thread-locking compound will be required. A tube of suitable sealant will be required to seal certain joint faces which are not fitted with gaskets.

2 In order to save time and avoid problems, engine reassembly can be carried out in the following order:

Petrol engines

a) *Piston rings (see Section 16).*
b) *Crankshaft (see Section 17).*
c) *Piston/connecting rod assemblies (see Section 18).*
d) *Oil pump (see Chapter 2A Section 15).*
e) *Sump (see Chapter 2A Section 14).*
f) *Flywheel (see Chapter 2A Section 18).*
g) *Cylinder head (see Chapter 2A Section 13).*
h) *Coolant pump (see Chapter 3 Section 7).*
i) *Timing belt and sprockets (see Chapter 2A Section 7).*
j) *Intake and exhaust manifolds (see Chapter 4A).*

Diesel engines

a) *Piston rings (see Section 16).*
b) *Crankshaft (see Section 17).*
c) *Pistons/connecting rod assemblies (see Section 18).*
d) *Cylinder head.*
e) *Oil pump.*
f) *Sump.*
g) *Flywheel/driveplate.*
h) *Coolant pump.*
i) *Timing belt, sprockets, tensioner and idler pulleys.*
j) *Intake and exhaust manifolds.*

3 At this stage, all engine components should be absolutely clean and dry, with all faults repaired. The components should be laid out (or in individual containers) on a completely clean work surface.

16 Piston rings – refitting

1 Before refitting the new piston rings, the ring end gaps must be checked as follows.

2 Lay out the piston/connecting rod assemblies and the new piston ring sets, so that the ring sets will be matched with the same piston and cylinder during the end gap measurement and subsequent engine reassembly.

3 Insert the top ring into the first cylinder, and push it down the bore slightly using the top of the piston. This will ensure that the ring remains square with the cylinder walls. Push the ring down into the bore until it is positioned 15 to 20 mm down from the top edge of the bore, then withdraw the piston.

4 Measure the end gap using feeler gauges, and compare the measurements with the figures given in the Specifications **(see illustration)**.

5 If the gap is too small (unlikely if genuine Vauxhall/Opel parts are used), it must be enlarged or the ring ends may contact each other during engine operation, causing serious damage. Ideally, new piston rings providing the correct end gap should be fitted, but as a last resort, the end gap can be increased by filing the ring ends very carefully with a fine file. Mount the file in a vice equipped with soft jaws, slip the ring over the file with the ends contacting the file face, and slowly move the ring to remove material from the ends – take care, as piston rings are sharp, and are easily broken.

6 With new piston rings, it is unlikely that the end gap will be too large. If they are too large, check that you have the correct rings for your engine and for the particular cylinder bore size.

7 Repeat the checking procedure for each ring in the first cylinder, and then for the rings in the remaining cylinders. Remember to keep rings, pistons and cylinders matched up.

8 Once the ring end gaps have been checked and if necessary corrected, the rings can be fitted to the pistons.

9 The oil control ring (lowest one on the piston) is composed of three sections, and

16.4 Measuring a piston ring end gap using a feeler gauge

16.9 Fitting the oil control spreader ring

should be installed first. Fit the lower steel ring, then the spreader ring, followed by the upper steel ring **(see illustration)**.

10 With the oil control ring components installed, the second (middle) ring can be fitted. It is usually stamped with a mark (TOP) which must face up, towards the top of the piston. **Note:** *Always follow the instructions supplied with the new piston ring sets – different manufacturers may specify different procedures. Do not mix up the top and middle rings, as they have different cross-sections. Using two or three old feeler blades, as for removal of the old rings, carefully slip the ring into place in the middle groove.*

11 Fit the top ring in the same manner, ensuring that, where applicable, the mark on the ring is facing up. If a stepped ring is being fitted, fit the ring with the smaller diameter of the step uppermost.

12 Repeat the procedure for the remaining pistons and rings.

17 Crankshaft – refitting

Note: *It is recommended that new main bearing shells are fitted regardless of the condition of the original ones.*

1 Refitting the crankshaft is the first step in the engine reassembly procedure. It is assumed at this point that the cylinder block, cylinder block lower casing (where applicable) and crankshaft have been cleaned, inspected and repaired or reconditioned as necessary.

2 Position the cylinder block with the sump/ lower casing mating face uppermost.

3 Clean the bearing shells and the bearing recesses in both the cylinder block and the lower casing/caps. If new shells are being fitted, ensure that all traces of the protective grease are cleaned off using paraffin. Wipe the shells dry with a clean lint-free cloth.

4 Note that the crankshaft endfloat is controlled by thrustwashers located on one of the main bearing shells. The thrustwashers may be separate or incorporated into, or attached to, the bearing shells themselves.

5 If the original bearing shells are being re-used, they must be refitted to their original locations in the block and lower casing, or caps.

6 Fit the upper main bearing shells in place in the cylinder block, ensuring that the tab on each shell engages in the notch in the cylinder block **(see illustration)**. Where separate thrustwashers are fitted, use a little grease to stick them to each side of their respective bearing upper location; ensure that the oilway grooves on each thrustwasher face outwards (away from the block).

Petrol engines

7 Liberally lubricate each bearing shell in the cylinder block, and lower the crankshaft into position **(see illustration)**.

8 If necessary, seat the crankshaft using light taps from a soft-faced mallet on the crankshaft balance webs.

9 Fit the bearing shells into the bearing caps.

10 Lubricate the bearing shells in the bearing caps, and the crankshaft journals, then fit Nos 1, 2, 3 and 4 bearing caps, and tighten the new bolts as far as possible by hand **(see illustration)**.

11 Ensure the No 5 bearing cap is clean and dry then fill the groove on each side of the cap with sealing compound (Vauxhall/Opel recommend the use of sealant part no 90485251, available from your dealer) **(see illustration)**. Fit the bearing cap to the engine, ensuring it is fitted the correct way around, and tighten the new bolts as far as possible by hand.

12 Working in a diagonal sequence from the centre outwards, tighten the main bearing cap bolts to the specified Stage 1 torque setting **(see illustration)**.

13 Once all bolts are tightened to the specified Stage 1 torque, go around again and tighten

17.6 Fitting a main bearing shell to the cylinder block

17.7 Liberally lubricate each bearing shell in the cylinder block and lower the crankshaft into position

17.10 Lubricate the crankshaft journals then refit bearing caps Nos 1 to 4

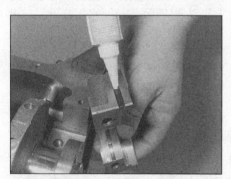

17.11 Fill the side grooves of the No 5 bearing cap with sealant prior to refitting it to the engine

17.12 Tighten the bolts to the specified Stage 1 torque setting ...

17.13 ... and then through the specified Stages 2 and 3 angles – 1.6 and 1.8 litre petrol engines

all bolts through the specified Stage 2 angle then go around for once more and tighten all bolts through the specified Stage 3 angle. It is recommended that an angle-measuring gauge is used during the final stages of the tightening, to ensure accuracy (see illustration). If a gauge is not available, use white paint to make alignment marks between the bolt head and cap prior to tightening; the marks can then be used to check that the bolt has been rotated through the correct angle.

14 Once all the bolts have been tightened, inject more sealant down the grooves in the No 5 main bearing cap until sealant is seen to be escaping through the joints. Once you are sure the cap grooves are full of sealant, wipe off all excess sealant using a clean cloth.

15 Check that the crankshaft is free to rotate smoothly; if excessive force is required to turn the crankshaft, investigate the cause before proceeding further.

16 Check the crankshaft endfloat with reference to Section 10.

17 Refit/reconnect the piston connecting rod assemblies to the crankshaft as described in Section 18.

18 Referring to Part A of this Chapter, fit a new left-hand crankshaft oil seal, then refit the oil pump, sump, flywheel, cylinder head, timing belt sprocket(s) and fit a new timing belt.

Diesel engines

19 Liberally lubricate each bearing shell in the cylinder block, and lower the crankshaft into position.

20 If necessary, seat the crankshaft using light taps from a soft-faced mallet on the crankshaft balance webs.

21 Fit the bearing shells into the bearing caps.

22 Lubricate the bearing shells in the bearing caps, and the crankshaft journals, then fit the caps ensuring they are fitted to their correct locations and the right way around. Fit and tighten the new bolts as far as possible by hand.

23 Working in a spiral pattern from the centre outwards, tighten the main bearing cap bolts to the specified Stage 1 torque setting.

24 Once all bolts are tightened to the specified Stage 1 torque, go around again and tighten all bolts through the specified Stage 2 angle. It is recommended that an angle-

18.2 Press the bearing shells into the connecting rods and caps in their correct positions

measuring gauge is used during the final stages of the tightening, to ensure accuracy. If a gauge is not available, use white paint to make alignment marks between the bolt head and cap prior to tightening; the marks can then be used to check that the bolt has been rotated through the correct angle.

25 Check that the crankshaft is free to rotate smoothly; if excessive force is required to turn the crankshaft, investigate the cause before proceeding further.

26 Check the crankshaft endfloat with reference to Section 10.

27 Refit/reconnect the piston connecting rod assemblies to the crankshaft as described in Section 18.

28 Referring to Part B, C or D (as applicable) of this Chapter, fit a new left-hand crankshaft oil seal/housing, then refit the oil pump, sump, flywheel/driveplate, cylinder head, timing belt sprocket(s) and fit a new timing belt.

18 Pistons/connecting rods – refitting

Note: *It is recommended that new big-end bearing shells are fitted regardless of the condition of the original ones.*

1 Clean the backs of the big-end bearing shells and the recesses in the connecting rods and big-end caps. If new shells are being fitted, ensure that all traces of the protective grease are cleaned off using paraffin. Wipe the

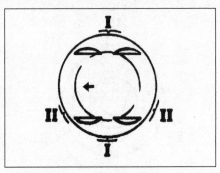

18.4 Piston ring end gap positions – petrol engines

I Top and second compression rings
II Oil control ring side rails

shells, caps and connecting rods dry with a lint-free cloth.

2 Press the bearing shells into their locations, ensuring that the tab on each shell engages in the notch in the connecting rod and cap (see illustration). If there is no tab on the bearing shell (and no notch in the rod or cap) position the shell equidistant from each side of the rod and cap. If the original bearing shells are being refitted ensure they are refitted in their original locations.

3 Lubricate the bores, the pistons and piston rings then lay out each piston/connecting rod assembly in its respective position.

Petrol engines

4 Lubricate No 1 piston and piston rings, and check that the ring gaps are correctly positioned. The gaps in the upper and lower steel rings of the oil control ring should be offset by 25 to 50 mm to the right and left of the spreader ring gap. The two upper compression ring gaps should be offset by 180° to each other (see illustration).

5 Fit a ring compressor to No 1 piston, then insert the piston and connecting rod into the cylinder bore so that the base of the compressor stands on the block. With the crankshaft big-end bearing journal positioned at its lowest point, tap the piston carefully into the cylinder bore using the wooden handle of a hammer, and at the same time guide the connecting rod onto the bearing journal. Note that the arrow on the piston crown must point towards the timing chain/belt end of the engine (see illustrations).

18.5a Ensure the piston ring end gaps are correctly spaced then fit the ring compressor – petrol engines

18.5b Ensuring the arrow on the piston crown (circled) is pointing towards the timing belt end of the engine – petrol engines

18.5c Tap the piston gently into the bore using handle of a hammer – petrol engines

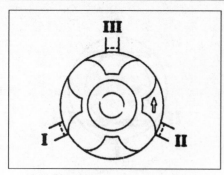

**18.11 Piston ring end gap positions –
diesel engines**

*I Top compression ring
II Second compression ring
III Oil control ring*

**18.12a Position the piston with the arrow
or notch (as applicable) pointing towards
the timing belt of the engine – 1.7 litre
engines**

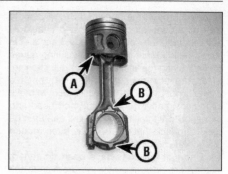

**18.12b The cut-out on the piston skirt (A)
must be on the same side as the oil spray
jet, and the lugs on the cap and rod (B)
must be toward the timing belt end of the
engine – 1.9 litre engines**

6 Liberally lubricate the bearing journals and bearing shells, and fit the bearing cap in its original location (the lug on the bearing cap base should be facing the flywheel/driveplate end of the engine).

7 Screw in the new bearing cap retaining bolts, and tighten both bolts to the specified Stage 1 torque setting then tighten the bolts through the specified angles. It is recommended that an angle-measuring gauge is used during the final stages of the tightening, to ensure accuracy. If a gauge is not available, use white paint to make alignment marks between the bolt head and cap prior to tightening; the marks can then be used to check that the bolt has been rotated through the correct angle.

8 Refit the remaining three piston and connecting rod assemblies in the same way.

9 Rotate the crankshaft, and check that it turns freely, with no signs of binding or tight spots.

10 Refit the oil pump pick-up/strainer, sump and the cylinder head as described in Part A of this Chapter.

Diesel engines

11 Lubricate No 1 piston and piston rings, and space the ring gaps uniformly around the piston at 120° intervals **(see illustration)**.

12 Fit a ring compressor to No 1 piston, then insert the piston and connecting rod into the cylinder bore so that the base of the compressor stands on the block. On 1.7 litre engines, ensure that the arrow or dot on the piston crown is toward the timing belt end

of the engine. On 1.9 litre engines, ensure that the piston/connecting rod assembly is positioned with the cut-out on the piston skirt on the same side as the the oil spray jet, and the lugs on the cap and rod are be toward the timing belt end of the engine **(see illustrations)**.

13 With the crankshaft big-end bearing journal positioned at its lowest point, tap the piston carefully into the cylinder bore with the wooden handle of a hammer, and at the same time guide the connecting rod onto the bearing journal.

14 Liberally lubricate the bearing journals and bearing shells, and fit the bearing cap in its original location.

15 Screw in the new bearing cap retaining bolts, and tighten both bolts to the specified Stage 1 torque setting then tighten them through the specified Stage 2 angle. It is recommended that an angle-measuring gauge is used during the final stages of the tightening, to ensure accuracy. If a gauge is not available, use white paint to make alignment marks between the bolt head and cap prior to tightening; the marks can then be used to check that the bolt has been rotated through the correct angle.

16 Refit the remaining three piston and connecting rod assemblies in the same way.

17 Rotate the crankshaft, and check that it turns freely, with no signs of binding or tight spots.

18 Refit the oil pump pick-up/strainer, sump and the cylinder head as described in Part B, C or D (as applicable) of this Chapter.

19 Engine –
initial start-up after overhaul

1 With the engine refitted in the vehicle, double-check the engine oil and coolant levels. Make a final check that everything has been reconnected, and that there are no tools or rags left in the engine compartment.

2 On diesel engines, prime and bleed the fuel system as described in Chapter 4B Section 5.

3 Start the engine, noting that this may take a little longer than usual. Make sure that the oil pressure warning light goes out.

4 While the engine is idling, check for fuel, water and oil leaks. Don't be alarmed if there are some odd smells and smoke from parts getting hot and burning off oil deposits.

5 Assuming all is well, run the engine until it reaches normal operating temperature, then switch off the engine.

6 After a few minutes, recheck the oil and coolant levels as described in *Weekly checks*, and top-up as necessary.

7 Note that there is no need to retighten the cylinder head bolts once the engine has first run after reassembly.

8 If new pistons, rings or crankshaft bearings have been fitted, the engine must be treated as new, and run-in for the first 600 miles. Do not operate the engine at full-throttle, or allow it to labour at low engine speeds in any gear. It is recommended that the oil and filter be changed at the end of this period.

Chapter 3
Cooling, heating and air conditioning systems

Contents

Section number

Air conditioning system – general information and precautions 10
Air conditioning system components – removal and refitting 11
Coolant pump – removal and refitting 7
Coolant temperature sensor – testing, removal and refitting....... 6
Cooling system hoses – disconnection and renewal............. 2
Electric cooling fan – removal and refitting 5

Section number

General information and precautions........................ 1
Heater/ventilation system components – removal and refitting..... 9
Heating and ventilation system – general information 8
Radiator – removal, inspection and refitting.................. 3
Thermostat – removal and refitting......................... 4

Degrees of difficulty

Easy, suitable for novice with little experience	**Fairly easy,** suitable for beginner with some experience	**Fairly difficult,** suitable for competent DIY mechanic	**Difficult,** suitable for experienced DIY mechanic	**Very difficult,** suitable for expert DIY or professional

Specifications

Thermostat
Opening temperature:
  Petrol engine models:
    Electric element .... 90°C
    Wax capsule .... 105°C
  1.7 litre diesel engines .... 82°C
  1.9 litre diesel engines .... 88°C

Air conditioning compressor
Lubricant capacity:
  Petrol engine models .... 150 cc
  Diesel engine models .... 135 cc
Lubricant type (synthetic PAG fluid) .... Vauxhall part number 90 509 933/19 49 873

Torque wrench settings	Nm	lbf ft
Air conditioning compressor mounting bolts.....................	22	16
Air conditioning refrigerant pipe block connections...............	20	15
Coolant pump pulley bolts...................................	20	15
Coolant pump retaining bolts:		
Petrol engine models....................................	8	6
Diesel engine models....................................	25	18
Coolant temperature sensor..................................	20	15
Radiator mounting brackets to subframe.......................	15	11
Thermostat housing/cover:		
Petrol engine models....................................	8	6
Diesel engine models....................................	25	18

1 General information and precautions

General information

1 The cooling system is of pressurised type, comprising a coolant pump, a crossflow radiator, electric cooling fan, and thermostat.
2 The coolant pump is driven by the auxiliary drivebelt on petrol engines and 1.7 litre diesel engines. On 1.9 litre diesel engines, the coolant pump is driven by the timing belt.
3 The system functions as follows. Cold coolant from the radiator passes through the bottom hose to the coolant pump, where it is pumped around the cylinder block, head passages and heater matrix. After cooling the cylinder bores, combustion surfaces and valve seats, the coolant reaches the underside of the thermostat, which is initially closed. The coolant passes through the heater, and is returned to the coolant pump.
4 When the engine is cold, the coolant circulates only through the cylinder block, cylinder head and heater. When the coolant reaches a predetermined temperature, the thermostat opens and the coolant also passes through to the radiator. As the coolant circulates through the radiator, it is cooled by the inrush of air when the car is in forward motion. Airflow is supplemented by the action of the electric cooling fan when necessary. Once the coolant has passed through the radiator, and has cooled, the cycle is repeated.
5 On petrol engines, an electrically-assisted thermostat is fitted. Engine coolant temperature is monitored by the engine management system electronic control unit, via the coolant temperature sensor. In conjunction with information received from various other engine sensors, the thermostat opening temperature can be controlled according to engine speed and load. During normal engine operation the thermostat operates conventionally. Under conditions of high engine speed and load, an electric heating element within the thermostat is energised, to cause the thermostat to open at a lower temperature (typically 90°).
6 The electric cooling fan, mounted on the rear of the radiator, is controlled by the engine management system electronic control unit, in conjunction with a cooling fan module. At a predetermined coolant temperature, the fan is actuated.
7 An expansion tank is fitted to the left-hand side of the engine compartment to accommodate expansion of the coolant when hot.

Precautions

 Warning: Do not attempt to remove the expansion tank filler cap, or disturb any part of the cooling system, while the engine is hot; there is a high risk of scalding. If the cap must be removed before the engine and radiator have fully cooled (even though this is not recommended) the pressure in the cooling system must first be relieved. Cover the cap with a thick layer of cloth, to avoid scalding, and slowly unscrew the filler cap until a hissing sound can be heard. When the hissing has stopped, indicating that the pressure has reduced, slowly unscrew the filler cap until it can be removed; if more hissing sounds are heard, wait until they have stopped before unscrewing the cap completely. At all times, keep well away from the filler cap opening.

 Warning: Do not allow antifreeze to come into contact with the skin, or with the painted surfaces of the vehicle. Rinse off spills immediately, with plenty of water. Never leave antifreeze lying around in an open container, or in a puddle on the driveway or garage floor. Children and pets are attracted by its sweet smell, but antifreeze can be fatal if ingested.

 Warning: If the engine is hot, the electric cooling fan may start rotating even if the engine is not running; be careful to keep hands, hair and loose clothing well clear when working in the engine compartment.

 Warning: Refer to Section 10 for precautions to be observed when working on models equipped with air conditioning.

2 Cooling system hoses – disconnection and renewal

Note: Refer to the warnings given in Section 1 of this Chapter before proceeding. Do not attempt to disconnect any hose while the system is still hot.

1 If the checks described in Chapter 1A Section 7 or Chapter 1B Section 7 reveal a faulty hose, it must be renewed as follows.
2 First drain the cooling system (see Chapter 1A Section 28 or Chapter 1B Section 30). If the coolant is not due for renewal, it may be re-used if it is collected in a clean container.
3 Before disconnecting a hose, first note its routing in the engine compartment, and whether it is secured by any additional retaining clips or cable ties. Use a pair of pliers to release the clamp-type clips, or a screwdriver to slacken the screw-type clips, then move the clips along the hose, clear of the relevant inlet/outlet union. Carefully work the hose free.
4 Note that the radiator inlet and outlet unions are fragile; do not use excessive force when attempting to remove the hoses. If a hose proves to be difficult to remove, try to release it by rotating the hose ends before attempting to free it.
5 When fitting a hose, first slide the clips onto the hose, then work the hose into position. If clamp-type clips were originally fitted, it is a good idea to use screw-type clips when refitting the hose. If the hose is stiff, use a little soapy water (washing-up liquid is ideal) as a lubricant, or soften the hose by soaking it in hot water.
6 Work the hose into position, checking that it is correctly routed and secured. Slide each clip along the hose until it passes over the flared end of the relevant inlet/outlet union, before tightening the clips securely.
7 Refill the cooling system with reference to Chapter 1A Section 28 or Chapter 1B Section 30.
8 Check thoroughly for leaks as soon as possible after disturbing any part of the cooling system.

3 Radiator – removal, inspection and refitting

Petrol engine models

Removal

1 Disconnect the battery negative terminal (refer to Chapter 5A Section 4).
2 Remove the front bumper as described in Chapter 11 Section 6.
3 Drain the cooling system as described in Chapter 1A Section 28.
4 Disconnect the cooling fan wiring harness connector from the base of the fan housing. Free the wiring harness from the cable ties.
5 Disconnect the wiring connector at the coolant temperature sensor in the radiator side tank. Free the wiring harness from the cable ties.
6 On models with an auxiliary cooling fan mounted in front of the radiator, unclip the two relays from the top of the fan housing. Disconnect the fan wiring harness connector from the base of the fan housing, then undo the bolt securing the harness to the housing. Free the wiring harness from the cable ties.
7 Release the retaining clips and disconnect the top and bottom hoses and expansion tank hose from the radiator. Release the hoses from the radiator and fan housing supports.
8 Undo the bolt each side securing the fan housing to the top of the radiator. Lift the fan housing up and out of the lower mounting brackets and remove the fan housing from the car.
9 On models with automatic transmission, undo the union bolts and disconnect the upper and lower fluid cooler pipe unions at the radiator. Recover the seals.
10 Retain the radiator in position by inserting a drill bit or similar, through the holes provided on each of the radiator upper mounting brackets **(see illustration)**.

3.10 Insert a drill bit (arrowed) or similar, through the holes provided on the radiator mounting brackets (shown with radiator removed)

3.11a Condenser right-hand upper retaining bolt (arrowed) ...

3.11b ... and right-hand lower retaining bolt (arrowed)

3.12a Undo the two bolts (arrowed) each side ...

3.12b ... and remove the radiator mounting brackets, noting their orientation

3.35a Undo the fan housing right-hand mounting bolt (arrowed) ...

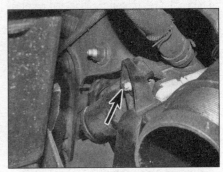

3.35b ... and left-hand mounting bolt (arrowed)

11 On models with air conditioning, secure the condenser to the bonnet crossmember with cable ties. Undo the upper and lower bolts securing the right-hand side of the condenser to the radiator **(see illustrations)**. Similarly undo the upper and lower bolts securing the left-hand side of the condenser to the radiator.

12 Undo the two bolts each side securing the radiator left-hand and right-hand mounting brackets to the subframe. Remove the brackets, noting their orientation **(see illustrations)**.

13 Remove the drill bits, or similar tools used to retain the radiator in position and carefully lower the radiator out from under the car.

Inspection

14 If the radiator has been removed due to suspected blockage, reverse-flush it as described in Chapter 1A Section 28.

15 Clean dirt and debris from the radiator fins, using an airline (in which case, wear eye protection) or a soft brush.
Caution: Be careful, as the fins are easily damaged, and are sharp.

16 If necessary, a radiator specialist can perform a 'flow test' on the radiator, to establish whether an internal blockage exists.

17 A leaking radiator must be referred to a specialist for permanent repair. Do not attempt to weld or solder a leaking radiator.

18 In an emergency, minor leaks from the radiator can be cured by using a suitable radiator sealant (in accordance with its manufacturer's instructions) with the radiator fitted in the vehicle.

19 Inspect the radiator mounting rubbers, and renew them if necessary.

Refitting

20 Refitting is a reversal of removal, bearing in mind the following points.
a) Ensure that all hoses are correctly reconnected, and their retaining clips securely tightened.
b) On completion, refill the cooling system as described in Chapter 1A Section 28.
c) On models with automatic transmission, check and if necessary top-up the automatic transmission fluid level with reference to the 'Transmission fluid – draining and refilling' procedures contained in Chapter 7B Section 2.

Diesel engine models

Removal

21 Remove the battery and battery tray as described in Chapter 5A Section 4.

22 Where fitted, remove the plastic cover from the top of the engine.

23 On models with automatic transmission, remove the air cleaner assembly and intake ducts as described in Chapter 4B Section 3.

24 Apply the handbrake, then jack up the front of the vehicle and support it on axle stands (see *Jacking and vehicle support*).

25 Remove the front bumper as described in Chapter 11 Section 6.

26 Drain the cooling system as described in Chapter 1B Section 30.

27 Disconnect the cooling fan wiring harness connector from the base of the fan housing. Free the wiring harness from the cable ties.

28 On models with air conditioning, open the retaining clip and detach the air conditioning refrigerant pipe from the right-hand side of the radiator. Release the air conditioning compressor wiring harness from the retaining clip.

29 Where applicable, release the two vacuum hoses from the clips on the right-hand side of the radiator.

30 Release the clamp and disconnect the bottom hose from the radiator.

31 Retain the radiator in position by inserting a drill bit or similar, through the holes provided on each of the radiator upper mounting brackets **(see illustration 3.10)**.

32 Undo the two bolts each side securing the radiator left-hand and right-hand mounting brackets to the subframe. Remove the brackets, noting their orientation **(see illustrations 3.12a and 3.12b)**.

33 Release the clamps and disconnect the top hose and expansion tank hose from the right-hand side of the radiator.

34 Release the retaining clip and disconnect the turbocharger charge air hose from the charge air pipe.

35 Undo the bolt each side securing the fan housing to the top of the radiator **(see illustrations)**. Unclip the charge air pipe, lift the fan housing up and out of the lower mounting brackets and move it to one side.

36 On models with automatic transmission, detach the protective ring (where fitted) over the fluid cooler pipe unions at the radiator. Using a small screwdriver, release the quick-release fitting retaining lugs and disconnect the fitting from the radiator. Suitably cover the open unions after disconnection.

37 On models with air conditioning, secure the condenser to the bonnet crossmember with cable ties. Undo the upper and lower bolts securing the right-hand side of the condenser to the radiator (see illustrations 3.11a and 3.11b). Similarly undo the upper and lower bolts securing the left-hand side of the condenser to the radiator.

38 Undo the bolt securing the upper charge air pipe to the radiator, then release the intercooler from the attachment bracket at the left-hand side of the radiator.

39 Remove the drill bits, or similar tools used to retain the radiator in position and carefully lower the radiator out from under the car.

Inspection

40 Refer to the information contained in paragraphs 14 to 19.

Refitting

41 Refitting is a reversal of removal, bearing in mind the following points.
a) *Ensure that all hoses are correctly reconnected, and their retaining clips securely tightened.*
b) *On completion, refill the cooling system as described in Chapter 1B Section 30.*
c) *On models with automatic transmission, check and if necessary top-up the automatic transmission fluid level with reference to the 'Transmission fluid – draining and refilling' procedures contained in Chapter 7B Section 2.*

4 Thermostat – removal and refitting

Removal

1 Disconnect the battery negative lead as described in Chapter 5A Section 4.

Petrol models

2 Drain the cooling system (see Chapter 1A Section 28).

3 Where applicable, undo the retaining nut and detach the wiring harness bracket from the thermostat housing.

4.19 Lift the thermostat from its housing

4.14 Disconnect the charge air hose from the throttle housing, and intercooler charge air pipe – 1.9 litre models

4 Loosen the clip and disconnect the radiator hose from the thermostat housing cover.

5 Where applicable, undo the three bolts and free the heat shield from the exhaust manifold.

6 Disconnect the thermostat wiring connector.

7 Unscrew the four bolts and remove the thermostat cover from the housing. Note that the thermostat is an integral part of the housing cover, and cannot be renewed separately.

8 Remove the sealing ring from the housing cover and discard it; a new one should be used on refitting. Thoroughly clean the housing contact surfaces.

Diesel models

9 Apply the handbrake, then jack up the front of the vehicle and support it on axle stands (see *Jacking and vehicle support*). Remove the engine undertray.

10 Drain the cooling system (see Chapter 1B Section 30).

11 On 1.9 litre models, remove the windscreen cowl panel as described in Chapter 11 Section 20.

12 Remove the plastic cover over the top of the engine.

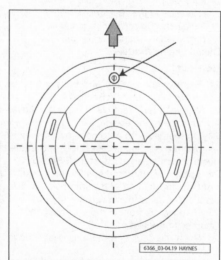

4.20 The bleed hole in the flange must point upwards – 1.7 litre engines

4.15 Release the clips and disconnect the hoses from the housing – 1.7 litre model shown

13 Remove the battery and battery box as described in Chapter 5A Section 4.

14 On 1.9 litre models, release the two retaining clips and disconnect the charge air hose from the throttle housing, and intercooler charge air pipe (see illustration).

15 Release the clips and disconnect the hoses from the thermostat housing, located at the left-hand end of the cylinder head (see illustration).

16 Disconnect the coolant temperature sensor wiring connector.

17 Unscrew the nut and release the coolant pipes from the stud at the base of the thermostat housing.

18 Unbolt the thermostat housing from the cylinder head. Clean away all traces of gasket from the housing and cylinder head.

19 On 1.7 litre engines, lift the thermostat from its housing and recover the sealing ring (see illustration). Discard the sealing ring, a new one should be fitted. Thoroughly clean the cover and housing contact surfaces.

Refitting

20 On 1.7 litre engines, when refitting the thermostat, the bleed hole in the flange must point upwards (see illustration).

21 Refitting is a reversal of removal, but fit a new gasket/seal and tighten the retaining bolts to the specified torque. Refill the cooling system as described in the relevant Part of Chapter 1.

5 Electric cooling fan – removal and refitting

> **Warning: If the engine is hot, the cooling fan may start up at any time. Take extra precautions when working in the vicinity of the fan.**

Removal

Petrol models

1 Disconnect the battery negative terminal (refer to Chapter 5A Section 4).

2 On VVT (variable valve timing) models, remove the air cleaner assembly as described in Chapter 4A Section 2. Detach the air cleaner intake from the duct on the bonnet crossmember. Undo the two retaining bolts, slide the intake duct sideways and remove it from the crossmember.

3 Release the clips and detach the radiator hoses from the fan housing brackets.

4 Disconnect the cooling fan wiring harness connector from the base of the fan housing. Free the wiring harness from the cable ties.

5 Undo the bolt each side securing the fan housing to the top of the radiator. Lift the fan housing up and out of the lower mounting brackets and remove the fan housing from the car.

6 To remove the fan motor, undo the three bolts and lift off the fan.

7 Undo the bolt securing the fan motor resistor to the housing, then undo the three bolts and remove the motor from the housing **(see illustrations)**.

Diesel models

8 Remove the radiator as described in Section 3, then lift the fan housing out of the engine compartment.

9 To remove the fan motor, undo the three bolts and lift off the fan.

10 Undo the bolt securing the fan motor resistor to the housing, then undo the three bolts and remove the motor from the housing **(see illustrations 5.7a and 5.7b)**.

Refitting

11 Refitting is a reversal of removal.

---

6 Coolant temperature sensor – testing, removal and refitting

Testing

1 Testing of the coolant temperature sensor must be entrusted to a Vauxhall/Opel dealer, who will have the necessary specialist diagnostic equipment.

Removal

2 Partially drain the cooling system with reference to Chapter 1A Section 28 or Chapter 1B Section 30, as applicable. Alternatively, it is possible to change the sensor quickly with minimal loss of coolant by first releasing

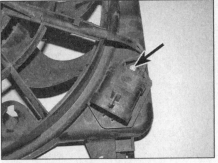

5.7a Undo the bolt (arrowed) securing the fan motor resistor to the housing ...

any pressure from the cooling system. With the engine cold, temporarily remove the expansion tank cap.

3 Where fitted, remove the plastic cover over the top of the engine.

Non-VVT (variable valve timinging) petrol models

4 The coolant temperature sensor is located in the thermostat housing at the left-hand end of the cylinder head.

5 Remove the battery and battery tray as described in Chapter 5A Section 4.

6 Disconnect the wiring from the temperature sensor, then unscrew and remove it from the thermostat housing. If the cooling system has not been drained, either insert the new sensor or fit a blanking plug to prevent further loss of coolant.

VVT (variable valve timing) petrol models

7 The coolant temperature sensor is located in the thermostat housing at the left-hand end of the cylinder head.

8 Disconnect the wiring from the temperature sensor, then unlock the retaining clamp and remove it from the thermostat housing **(see illustration)**. If the cooling system has not been drained, either insert the new sensor or fit a blanking plug to prevent further loss of coolant.

Diesel models

9 The coolant temperature sensor is located in the thermostat housing at the left-hand end of the cylinder head **(see illustrations)**.

5.7b ... then undo the three bolts (arrowed) and remove the motor from the housing

10 Slacken the two retaining clips and disconnect the upper charge air hose from the throttle housing, and intercooler left-hand charge air pipe.

11 Disconnect the wiring from the temperature sensor, then unscrew and remove it from the thermostat housing. If the cooling system has not been drained, either insert the new sensor or fit a blanking plug to prevent further loss of coolant.

Refitting

12 Fit the new sensor using a reversal of the removal procedure and using a new seal (where applicable). Tighten the sensor to the specified torque and refill the cooling system with reference to Chapter 1A Section 28 or Chapter 1B Section 30, as applicable.

---

7 Coolant pump – removal and refitting

Removal

Petrol models

1 Remove the air cleaner assembly and air intake ducts as described in Chapter 4A Section 2.

2 Slacken the three coolant pump pulley retaining bolts.

3 Remove the auxiliary drivebelt as described in Chapter 1A Section 23.

4 Drain the cooling system as described in Chapter 1A Section 28.

6.8 Coolant temperature sensor location (arrowed)

6.9a Coolant temperature sensor location – 1.7 litre diesel engine models

6.9b Coolant temperature sensor location (arrowed) – 1.9 litre diesel engine models

7.11 Remove the pulley from the coolant pump drive flange

7.12 Unscrew the pump retaining bolts

5 Unscrew the previously-slackened coolant pump pulley retaining bolts and remove the pulley from the pump flange.

6 Undo the five retaining bolts and remove the pump from the oil pump housing.

7 Note that it is not possible to overhaul the pump. If it is faulty, the unit must be renewed complete.

1.7 litre diesel engines

8 Drain the cooling system as described in Chapter 1B Section 30.

9 Slacken the three coolant pump pulley retaining bolts.

10 Remove the auxiliary drivebelt as described in Chapter 1B Section 24.

11 Completely unscrew the retaining bolts and remove the pump pulley (see illustration).

12 Undo the five retaining bolts and remove the coolant pump (see illustration). It may be necessary to gently tap the pump with a soft-faced hammer to release it.

13 Recover the gasket and discard it – a new one must be fitted (see illustration).

1.9 litre diesel models

14 Remove the plastic cover from the top of the engine.

15 Drain the cooling system as described in Chapter 1B Section 30.

16 Remove the timing belt as described in

Chapter 2C Section 7 or Chapter 2D Section 6 as applicable. **Note:** *The timing belt must not come into contact with coolant.*

17 Unscrew and remove the three coolant pump securing bolts (see illustration).

18 Withdraw the coolant pump from the cylinder block, noting that it may be necessary to tap the pump lightly with a soft-faced mallet to free it from the cylinder block (see illustration).

19 Recover the pump sealing ring, and discard it; a new one must be used on refitting.

20 Note that it is not possible to overhaul the pump. If it is faulty, the unit must be renewed complete.

Refitting

21 Refitting is a reversal of removal, noting the following points:
a) *Ensure that the pump and cylinder head/block mating surfaces are clean and dry, then fit a new seal/gasket to the pump.*
b) *Tighten all nuts/bolts to the specified torque where given.*
c) *On 1.9 litre engines, refit the timing belt as described in Chapter 2C Section 7 or Chapter 2D Section 6.*
d) *Refit the auxiliary drivebelt, and refill the cooling system as described in Chapter 1A or Chapter 1B.*

8 Heating and ventilation system – general information

1 The heater/ventilation system consists of a four-speed blower motor (housed behind the facia), face-level vents in the centre and at each end of the facia, and air ducts to the front and rear footwells.

2 The heater controls are located in the centre of the facia, and the controls operate flap valves to deflect and mix the air flowing through the various parts of the heater/ventilation system. The flap valves are contained in the air distribution housing, which acts as a central distribution unit, passing air to the various ducts and vents.

3 Cold air enters the system through the grille at the rear of the engine compartment. A pollen filter is fitted to the ventilation intake, to filter out dust, soot, pollen and spores from the air entering the vehicle.

4 The air (boosted by the blower fan if required) then flows through the various ducts, according to the settings of the controls. Stale air is expelled through ducts at the rear of the vehicle. If warm air is required, the cold air is passed through the heater matrix, which is heated by the engine coolant.

7.13 Renew the gasket

7.17 Undo the coolant pump retaining bolts (arrowed) ...

7.18 ... and remove the pump from the cylinder head – diesel engine models

5 A recirculation switch enables the outside air supply to be closed off, while the air inside the vehicle is recirculated. This can be useful to prevent unpleasant odours entering from outside the vehicle, but should only be used briefly, as the recirculated air inside the vehicle will soon deteriorate.

9 Heater/ventilation system components – removal and refitting

Heater blower motor

Removal

1 Remove the glovebox as described in Chapter 11 Section 26.
2 Prise up the centre pin, extract the plastic rivet and remove the footwell air duct on the passenger's side **(see illustrations)**.
3 Reach up to the top of the blower motor housing and disconnect the recirculating air valve actuating rod.
4 Trace the wiring from the blower motor up to the resistor and disconnect the two wires at the resistor.
5 Disconnect the wiring connector on the recirculating air valve and on the blower motor **(see illustration)**.
6 Undo the three Torx bolts securing the blower motor housing to the base of the recirculating air valve housing. Release the two retaining clips and remove the blower motor down and out from under the fascia **(see illustrations)**.

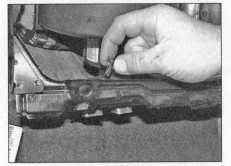

9.2a Extract the plastic rivet ...

Refitting

7 Refitting is a reversal of removal.

Heater blower motor resistor

Removal

8 Remove the glovebox as described in Chapter 11 Section 26.
9 Prise up the centre pin, extract the plastic rivet and remove the footwell air duct on the passenger's side **(see illustrations 9.2a and 9.2b)**.
10 Carefully prise free the blower motor resistor from the air distribution housing **(see illustration)**.
11 Disconnect the main wiring connector and the two heater blower motor wiring connectors and remove the resistor.

Refitting

12 Refitting is a reversal of removal.

9.2b ... and remove the footwell air duct on the passenger's side

Recirculating air valve servo motor

Removal

13 Remove the heater blower motor as described previously.
14 Undo the three retaining bolts and remove the motor from the heater blower motor housing **(see illustration)**.

Refitting

15 Refitting is a reversal of removal.

Mixed air valve servo motor

Removal

16 Remove the glovebox and the gear lever console as described in Chapter 11.
17 Disconnect the wiring connector, then undo the three bolts and remove the servo motor from the side of the air distribution housing **(see illustration)**.

9.5 Disconnect the wiring connector on the recirculating air valve and on the blower motor

9.6a Undo the three retaining bolts ...

9.6b ... and remove the blower motor from the recirculating air valve housing

9.10 Carefully prise free the heater blower motor resistor

9.14 Recirculating air valve servo motor retaining bolts (arrowed)

9.17 Mixed air valve servo motor located on the side of the air distribution housing

9.21 Release the quick-release connectors (arrowed) and disconnect the heater hoses from the matrix pipe stubs

9.23 Extract the securing clips and remove the lower cover from the air distribution housing

9.25 Pull the heater matrix from its location and remove it from the car

Refitting

18 Refitting is a reversal of removal.

Heater matrix

Removal

19 Drain the cooling system as described in Chapter 1A Section 28 or Chapter 1B Section 30.
20 Remove the glovebox and the gear lever console as described in Chapter 11.
21 Release the quick-release connectors by sliding them forward, and disconnect the two heater hoses from the heater matrix pipe stubs **(see illustration)**.
22 Undo the two bolts securing the condensation drain tube to the engine compartment bulkhead.
23 Extract the eight securing clips and remove the lower cover from the air distribution housing **(see illustration)**.
24 Be prepared for coolant spillage as the matrix is removed and place some cloths or absorbent material over the carpet.
25 Undo the two clamps and release the heater pipes from the matrix. Pull the heater matrix from its location and remove it from the car **(see illustration)**.

Refitting

26 Refitting is a reversal of removal, bearing in mind the following:
a) Push the heater hoses back onto the matrix pipe stubs, ensuring that the

quick-release connectors securely lock the hoses in position.
b) Refill the cooling system as described in Chapter 1A Section 28 or Chapter 1B Section 30.

Heater control assembly

Removal

27 Remove the radio/CD player as described in Chapter 12 Section 17.
28 Lift up the two upper retaining catches and withdraw the heater control assembly from the facia. Disconnect the two wiring connectors and remove the unit from the car **(see illustrations)**.

Refitting

29 Refitting is a reversal of removal.

Air distribution housing

Note: *On models with air conditioning, it is not possible to remove the air distribution housing without opening the refrigerant circuit (see Sections 10 and 11). Have the refrigerant discharged at a dealer service department or an automotive air conditioning repair facility before proceeding.*

Removal

30 Drain the cooling system as described in Chapter 1A Section 28 or Chapter 1B Section 30.
31 Remove the windscreen cowl panel as described in Chapter 11 Section 20.

32 On diesel engine models, undo the three bolts and release the fuel filter crash box from the engine compartment bulkhead.
33 On models with air conditioning, undo the bolt securing the refrigerant pipe block connection to the expansion valve and withdraw the refrigerant pipes from the valve **(see illustration)**. Note that new seals for the refrigerant pipes will be required for refitting. Suitably plug or cover the disconnected pipes.
34 Refit the bolt used to secure the refrigerant pipe block connection to the expansion valve and draw off the expansion valve.
35 Remove the expansion valve retaining plate.
36 Release the quick-release connectors by sliding them forward, and disconnect the two heater hoses from the heater matrix pipe stubs **(see illustration 9.21)**.
37 Undo the two bolts securing the condensation drain tube to the engine compartment bulkhead.
38 Remove the complete facia assembly and the facia crossmember as described in Chapter 11 Section 26.
39 Release the retaining clips and remove the air distribution ducts in the vicinity of the centre console.
40 Working in the windscreen cowl panel aperture and around the engine compartment bulkhead, undo the eight bolts securing the air distribution housing to the bulkhead.
41 Carefully withdraw the air distribution

9.28a Lift up the two upper retaining catches and withdraw the heater control assembly ...

9.28b ... then disconnect the two wiring connectors

9.33 Undo the bolt (arrowed) securing the refrigerant pipe block connection to the expansion valve

housing from the bulkhead. **Note:** *Keep the matrix unions uppermost as the housing is removed, to prevent coolant spillage. Mop-up any spilt coolant immediately, and wipe the affected area with a damp cloth to prevent staining.*

Refitting

42 Refitting is the reverse of removal. On completion, refill the cooling system as described in Chapter 1A Section 28 or Chapter 1B Section 30. On models with air conditioning, have the system evacuated, charged and leak-tested by the specialist who discharged it.

10 Air conditioning system – general information and precautions

General information

1 Air conditioning is standard on top of the range models, and optional on certain other models. It enables the temperature of incoming air to be lowered, and also dehumidifies the air, which makes for rapid demisting and increased comfort.

2 The cooling side of the system works in the same way as a domestic refrigerator. Refrigerant gas is drawn into a belt-driven compressor, and passes into a condenser mounted in front of the radiator, where it loses heat and becomes liquid. The liquid passes through an expansion valve to an evaporator, where it changes from liquid under high pressure to gas under low pressure. This change is accompanied by a drop in temperature, which cools the evaporator. The refrigerant returns to the compressor, and the cycle begins again.

3 Air blown through the evaporator passes to the heater assembly, where it is mixed with hot air blown through the heater matrix, to achieve the desired temperature in the passenger compartment.

4 The heating side of the system works in the same way as on models without air conditioning (see Section 8).

5 The operation of the system is controlled electronically. Any problems with the system should be referred to a Vauxhall/Opel dealer or an air conditioning specialist.

Air conditioning service ports

Note: *The air conditioning service port location varies slightly according to model. The following is a general description of service port location.*

6 The high-pressure service port is the larger of the two service port connections and is located in front of the radiator. Remove the radiator grille as described in Chapter 11 Section 20 for access **(see illustration)**.

7 The low-pressure service port is located at the rear right-hand side of the engine compartment **(see illustration)**.

10.6 Air conditioning system high-pressure service port (arrowed) …

Precautions

8 It is necessary to observe special precautions whenever dealing with any part of the system, its associated components, and any items which necessitate disconnection of the system.

 Warning: The refrigeration circuit contains a liquid refrigerant. This refrigerant is potentially dangerous, and should only be handled by qualified persons. If it is splashed onto the skin, it can cause frostbite. It is not itself poisonous, but in the presence of a naked flame it forms a poisonous gas; inhalation of the vapour through a lighted cigarette could prove fatal. Uncontrolled discharging of the refrigerant is dangerous, and potentially damaging to the environment. Do not disconnect any part of the system unless it has been discharged by a Vauxhall/Opel dealer or an air conditioning specialist.
Caution: Do not operate the air conditioning system if it is known to be short of refrigerant, as this may damage the compressor.

11 Air conditioning system components – removal and refitting

 Warning: The air conditioning system is under high pressure. Do not loosen any fittings or remove any components until after the system has been discharged. Air conditioning refrigerant should be properly discharged into an approved type of container at a dealer service department or an automotive air conditioning repair facility capable of handling R134a refrigerant. Cap or plug the pipe lines as soon as they are disconnected to prevent the entry of moisture. Always wear eye protection when disconnecting air conditioning system fittings.
Note: *This Section refers to the components of the air conditioning system itself – refer to Sections 8 and 9 for details of components common to the heating/ventilation system.*

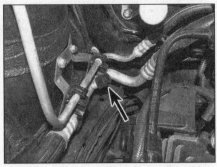

10.7 … and low-pressure service port (arrowed)

Compressor

Removal

1 Have the refrigerant discharged at a dealer service department or an automotive air conditioning repair facility.

2 Firmly apply the handbrake, then jack up the front of the car and support it securely on axle stands (see *Jacking and vehicle support*).

3 On 1.7 litre diesel models, remove the radiator grille as described in Chapter 11 Section 20.

4 Remove the auxiliary drivebelt as described in Chapter 1A Section 23 or Chapter 1B Section 24.

5 With the system discharged, undo the retaining bolt(s) and disconnect the refrigerant pipes from the compressor. Discard the O-ring seals – new ones must be used when refitting. Suitably cap the open fittings immediately to keep moisture and contamination out of the system.

6 Disconnect the compressor wiring connector.

7 Unbolt the compressor from the cylinder block/crankcase/sump, then withdraw the compressor from the vehicle.

Refitting

8 Refit the compressor in the reverse order of removal; renew all seals disturbed.

9 If you are installing a new compressor, refer to the compressor manufacturer's instructions for adding refrigerant oil to the system.

10 Have the system evacuated, charged and leak-tested by the specialist that discharged it.

11 After installing a new compressor, always observe the following running-in procedure:

a) Open all instrument panel air outlet flaps.
b) Start vehicle engine and stabilise idle speed for approximately 5 seconds.
c) Switch fan to maximum speed.
d) Switch on the air conditioning and let it run for at least 2 minutes without interruption at engine speed under 1500 rpm.

Evaporator

12 Removal of the evaporator entails extensive dismantling of the vehicle interior in the area of the facia, drilling out structural rivets and physically deforming the facia

11.16 Unclip the relays from the auxiliary cooling fan housing

11.18 Undo the two upper retaining nuts (arrowed), then lift the fan and housing up and off the condenser

11.25a Undo the upper retaining bolt (arrowed) ...

11.25b ... and lower retaining bolt (arrowed) and disconnect the refrigerant pipe connector blocks from thecondenser

structural panels. For this reason, removal and refitting of the evaporator is considered beyond the scope of the DIY enthusiast and should be entrusted to a Vauxhall/Opel dealer.

Auxiliary cooling fan

Removal

13 Disconnect the battery negative terminal (refer to Chapter 5A Section 4).
14 Apply the handbrake, then jack up the front of the vehicle and support it on axle stands (see *Jacking and vehicle support*).
15 Remove the front bumper as described in Chapter 11 Section 6.
16 Unclip the relays, then release the cable ties securing the wiring harness to the auxiliary cooling fan housing **(see illustration)**.
17 Release and disconnect the wiring harness connector at the base of the fan housing.

18 Undo the two upper retaining nuts, then lift the fan and housing up and off the condenser **(see illustration)**. Remove the fan and housing from under the car.

Refitting

19 Refitting is the reverse of removal.

Condenser

Removal

20 Have the refrigerant discharged at a dealer service department or an automotive air conditioning repair facility.
21 Disconnect the battery negative terminal (refer to Chapter 5A Section 4).
22 Apply the handbrake, then jack up the front of the vehicle and support it on axle stands (see *Jacking and vehicle support*).
23 Remove the front bumper as described in Chapter 11 Section 6.
24 Remove the auxiliary cooling fan (where fitted) as described previously in this Section.
25 Undo the retaining bolts and disconnect the upper and lower refrigerant pipe connector blocks from the right-hand side of the condenser **(see illustrations)**. Discard the seals – new ones must be used when refitting. Suitably cap the open fittings immediately to keep moisture and contamination out of the system.
26 Disconnect the wiring connector from the pressure sensor on the right-hand side of the condenser.
27 Undo the four bolts securing the condenser to the radiator **(see illustrations 3.11a and 3.11b)**. Carefully lower the condenser and remove it from under the car.

Refitting

28 Refitting is the reverse of removal ensuring that all disturbed pipe seals are renewed.
29 Have the system evacuated, charged and leak-tested by the specialist who discharged it.

Chapter 4 Part A
Fuel and exhaust systems – petrol engine

Contents

Section number

Accelerator pedal/position sensor – removal and refitting. 3
Air cleaner assembly and intake ducts – removal and refitting 2
Exhaust manifold (non-VVT engines) – removal and refitting. 16
Exhaust manifold (VVT engines) – removal and refitting 17
Exhaust system – general information, removal and refitting 18
Fuel gauge sender unit – removal and refitting 6
Fuel injection system – depressurisation 5
Fuel injection system components – testing 11
Fuel injection systems – general information 10

Section number

Fuel supply pump – removal and refitting 7
Fuel tank – removal and refitting 8
General information and precautions. 1
Intake manifold (non-VVT engines) – removal and refitting 14
Intake manifold (VVT engines) – removal and refitting 15
Multec-S injection system components – removal and refitting 12
Simtec 75.1 injection system components – removal and refitting . . 13
Throttle housing – removal and refitting. 9
Unleaded petrol – general information and usage 4

Degrees of difficulty

Easy, suitable for novice with little experience	Fairly easy, suitable for beginner with some experience	Fairly difficult, suitable for competent DIY mechanic	Difficult, suitable for experienced DIY mechanic	Very difficult, suitable for expert DIY or professional

Specifications

System type
1.6 litre non-VVT engines	Multec-S multipoint injection
All other petrol engines.	Simtec 75.1 multipoint injection

Fuel system data
Fuel supply pump type.	Electric, immersed in tank
Fuel pump regulated constant pressure.	3.8 bar
Specified idle speed.	Not adjustable – controlled by ECU
Idle mixture CO content	Not adjustable – controlled by ECU

Recommended fuel
Minimum octane rating.	95 RON unleaded (UK premium unleaded) Leaded fuel or LRP must NOT be used

Torque wrench settings
	Nm	lbf ft
Accelerator pedal position sensor nuts	12	9
Camshaft sensor retaining bolt	6	4
Crankshaft speed/position sensor retaining bolt:		
Non-VVT engines	10	7
VVT engines	5	4
Exhaust front pipe to manifold*	20	15
Exhaust manifold securing nuts: *		
Non-VVT engines	15	11
VVT engines	20	15
Exhaust system clamp bolts*	50	37
Fuel rail bolts	9	7
Fuel tank retaining strap bolts	23	17
Intake manifold retaining bolts/nuts:		
Non-VVT engines:		
Lower manifold to cylinder head	20	15
Upper manifold to lower manifold	8	6
VVT engines	20	15
Knock sensor	20	15
Manifold pressure sensor bolt	8	6
Throttle housing retaining bolts	8	6

*Use new fasteners

1 General information and precautions

General information

1 The fuel supply system consists of a fuel tank (which is mounted under the rear of the car, with an electric fuel pump immersed in it), and fuel feed lines. The fuel pump supplies fuel to the fuel rail, which acts as a reservoir for the fuel injectors which inject fuel into the intake tracts.

2 The electronic control unit controls both the fuel injection system and the ignition system, integrating the two into a complete engine management system. Refer to Section 10 for further information on the operation of the fuel injection system and to Chapter 5B for details of the ignition side of the system.

3 1.6 litre non-VVT (variable valve timing) engines utilise a 'Twinport' intake manifold configuration. Vacuum-operated flap valves located in the intake manifold are opened or closed according to engine operating conditions, to create a variable venturi manifold arrangement. This layout has significant advantages in terms of engine power, fuel economy and reduced exhaust emissions. VVT engines (1.6 and 1.8 litre) utilise a similar arrangement, but a switching drum operated by an electric motor is used instead of flap valves, to create the variable venturi manifold arrangement.

4 The exhaust manifold incorporates an integral catalytic converter to reduce harmful exhaust gas emissions. Further details can be found in Section 18 and in Part C of this Chapter, along with details of the other emission control systems and components.

Precautions

Note: *Refer to Part C of this Chapter for general information and precautions relating to the catalytic converter.*

● Before disconnecting any fuel lines, or working on any part of the fuel system, the system must be depressurised as described in Section 5.

● Care must be taken when disconnecting the fuel lines. When disconnecting a fuel union or hose, loosen the union or clamp screw slowly, to avoid sudden uncontrolled fuel spillage. Take adequate fire precautions.

● When working on fuel system components, scrupulous cleanliness must be observed, and care must be taken not to introduce any foreign matter into fuel lines or components.

● After carrying out any work involving disconnection of fuel lines, it is advisable to check the connections for leaks; pressurise the system by switching the ignition on and off several times.

● Electronic control units are very sensitive components, and certain precautions must be taken to avoid damage to these units as follows:

a) When carrying out welding operations on the vehicle using electric welding equipment, the battery and alternator should be disconnected.

b) Although the underbonnet-mounted control units will tolerate normal underbonnet conditions, they can be adversely affected by excess heat or moisture. If using welding equipment or pressure-washing equipment in the vicinity of an electronic control unit, take care not to direct heat, or jets of water or steam, at the unit. If this cannot be avoided, remove the control unit from the vehicle, and protect its wiring plug with a plastic bag.

c) Before disconnecting any wiring, or removing components, always ensure that the ignition is switched off.

d) After working on fuel injection/engine management system components, ensure that all wiring is correctly reconnected before reconnecting the battery or switching on the ignition.

⚠ **Warning: Many of the procedures in this Chapter require the removal of fuel lines and connections, which may result in some fuel spillage. Before carrying out any operation on the fuel system, refer to the precautions given in 'Safety first!' at the beginning of this manual, and follow them implicitly. Petrol is a highly-dangerous and volatile liquid, and the precautions necessary when handling it cannot be overstressed.**

Note: *Residual pressure will remain in the fuel lines long after the vehicle was last used. Before disconnecting any fuel line, first depressurise the fuel system as described in Section 5.*

2 Air cleaner assembly and intake ducts – removal and refitting

Removal

1 Disconnect the wiring connector from the side of the inlet air temperature sensor or airflow meter **(see illustration)**.

2 Slacken the clamp screws and detach the intake duct from the air cleaner lid and, where applicable, from the throttle housing intake duct **(see illustration)**.

3 Slacken the clamp screw and detach the intake duct from the throttle housing **(see illustration)**. Where applicable, release the clip and disconnect the crankcase ventilation hose from the duct. Remove the intake duct from the engine compartment.

4 Undo the retaining bolt and release the mounting bracket at the rear of the air cleaner housing **(see illustration)**.

2.1 Disconnect the wiring connector from the side of the inlet air temperature sensor

2.2 Slacken the clamp screws and detach the intake duct

2.3 Slacken the clamp screw (arrowed) and lift the intake duct from the throttle housing

2.4 Undo the retaining bolt (arrowed) and release the air cleaner housing mounting bracket

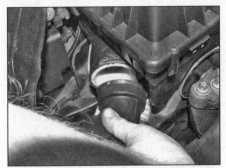

2.5 Detach the air intake duct at the front of the air cleaner housing

5 Detach the air intake duct at the front of the air cleaner housing **(see illustration)**.

6 Lift the housing upwards at the rear, then disengage the front mounting rubber from the body bracket.

7 To remove the intake pipe from the crossmember, undo the retaining screws, and slide the intake pipe to one side to release it from the radiator crossmember.

Refitting

8 Refitting is the reverse of removal, making sure all the air intake ducts are securely reconnected.

3 Accelerator pedal/position sensor – removal and refitting

Removal

1 Undo the two quick-release catches and remove the facia lower panel on the driver's side.

2 Working in the driver's footwell under the facia, disconnect the wiring connector from the top of the accelerator pedal/position sensor **(see illustration)**.

3 Unscrew the three mounting nuts, and withdraw the sensor from the bulkhead.

Refitting

4 Refitting is a reversal of removal.

4 Unleaded petrol – general information and usage

Note: *The information given in this Chapter is correct at the time of writing. If updated information is thought to be required, check with a Vauxhall/Opel dealer. If travelling abroad, consult one of the motoring organisations (or a similar authority) for advice on the fuel available.*

1 All models are designed to run on fuel with a minimum octane rating of 95 RON. However, if unavailable, 91 octane may be used on 1.6 and 1.8 litre engines, although a reduction in engine power and torque will be noticed.

2 All models have a catalytic converter, and so must be run on unleaded fuel only. Under no circumstances should leaded fuel or LRP be used, as this will damage the converter.

3 Super unleaded petrol (97/98 octane) can also be used in all models if wished, though there is no advantage in doing so.

5 Fuel injection system – depressurisation

⚠ **Warning: Refer to the warning note in Section 1 before proceeding. The following procedure will merely relieve the pressure in the fuel system – remember that fuel will still be present in the system components, and take precautions accordingly before disconnecting any of them.**

1 The fuel system referred to in this Section is defined as the tank-mounted fuel pump, the fuel injectors and the metal pipes and flexible hoses of the fuel lines between these components. All these contain fuel which will be under pressure while the engine is running, and/or while the ignition is switched on. The pressure will remain for some time after the ignition has been switched off, and it must be relieved in a controlled fashion when any of these components are disturbed for servicing work.

2 Where fitted, remove the plastic cover over the top of the engine.

3 Locate the fuel pressure connection valve which is fitted to the fuel rail. On non-VVT engines, the valve is located at the top right-hand end of the fuel rail. On VVT engines it can be found on the top left-hand end of the fuel rail **(see illustration)**.

4 Unscrew the cap from the valve and position a container beneath the valve. Hold a wad of rag over the valve and relieve the pressure in the fuel system by depressing the valve core with a suitable screwdriver. Be prepared for the squirt of fuel as the valve core is depressed and catch it with the rag. Hold the valve core down until no more fuel is expelled from the valve.

5 Once all pressure is relieved, securely refit the valve cap.

6 Fuel gauge sender unit – removal and refitting

Note: *Vauxhall/Opel special tool KM-797 (or suitable alternative) will be required to remove and refit the fuel pump cover locking ring, and special tool KM-6391 (or suitable alternative) will be required to remove the in-tank module from the fuel tank.*

Note: *A new fuel pump cover sealing ring will be required on refitting.*

Removal

1 Remove the fuel tank as described in Section 8.

2 Compress the clips located on each side of the fuel hose end fitting and ease the fitting off of its union. Plug the hose end to minimise fuel loss.

3 Using the Vauxhall/Opel special tool, unscrew the locking ring and remove it from the tank.

4 Make identification marks on the fuel pump cover and the body to ensure that the cover is refitted in its original position. There may be an arrow stamped on the cover; if so note its direction.

5 Carefully lift the fuel pump cover away from tank and remove the cover sealing ring **(see illustration)**.

3.2 Disconnect the wiring connector (arrowed) from the accelerator pedal/ position sensor

5.3 Fuel pressure connection valve (arrowed) on the fuel rail – VVT engines shown

6.5 Lift the fuel pump cover away from tank and remove the cover sealing ring

6.6 Disconnect the wiring connector(s)
from the underside of the fuel pump cover

6.7 Depress the retaining tabs and lift the
fuel pump out of the in-tank module

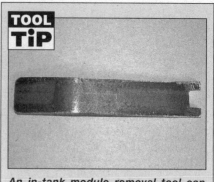

An in-tank module removal tool can
be made from 3 mm thick steel strip,
approximately 150 mm long and 26 mm
wide. Cut or file a 12 mm slot in one end
of the tool and put a slight bend in the
tool at the other end, approximately 100
mm from the slotted end. Note that 4 of
these tools will be required to remove
the module.

6 Disconnect the wiring connector(s) from the underside of the fuel pump cover **(see illustration)**.

7 Depress the retaining tabs and lift the fuel pump out of the in-tank module **(see illustration)**. Place the assembly to one side.

8 To remove the in-tank module (containing the gauge sender unit) from the fuel tank, Vauxhall/Opel special tool KM-6391, or a suitable alternative will be required. The special tool consists of four metal strips that are inserted down the sides of the in-tank module, to release the module from the four tabs of the mounting bracket, which remains in the tank. In the absence of the special tool a suitable alternative can be easily made (see **Tool Tip**).

9 Carefully insert the four tools down through

the slots on the side of the in-tank module until they engage and release the four retaining tabs in the tank mounting bracket **(see illustrations)**. Move the float arm on the sender unit slightly when inserting the tool adjacent to the sender unit.

10 Once the tabs in the tank mounting bracket are released, carefully lift the in-tank module up and out of the fuel tank **(see illustration)**.

11 With the assembly on the bench, release the two retaining tabs and lift the fuel gauge sender unit up and out of the in-tank module **(see illustrations)**.

Refitting

12 Refit the gauge sender unit to the in-tank module ensuring that the retaining tabs positively engage.

13 Manoeuvre the in-tank module carefully in through the tank aperture and push it down onto the retaining tabs of the tank mounting bracket. Ensure that the retaining tabs audibly engage with the module.

14 Locate the fuel pump or fuel filter into the in-tank module and engage the retaining tabs.

15 Reconnect the wiring connector(s) to the fuel pump cover, and place a new sealing

6.9a Carefully insert the removal tools
down through the slots on the side of the
in-tank module ...

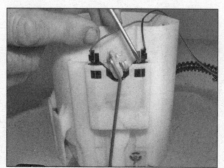

6.9b ... push the tools down into the
slots ...

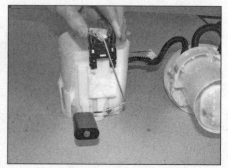

6.9c ... until they release the four retaining
tabs (arrowed) in the tank mounting bracket
(shown with in-tank module removed)

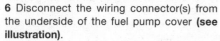

6.10 With the tabs in the mounting bracket
released, lift the in-tank module up and out
of the fuel tank

6.11a Release the two retaining tabs ...

6.11b ... and lift the fuel gauge sender unit
up and out of the in-tank module

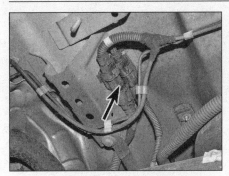

8.4 Disconnect the wiring for the gauge sender unit and fuel pump at the underbody connector (arrowed)

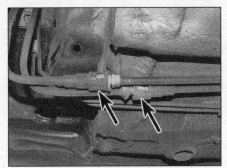

8.5 Disconnect the fuel and vapour lines at the underbody quick-release connectors (arrowed)

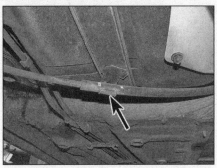

8.6 Unclip the handbrake cables from the fuel tank retaining straps (arrowed)

ring in position on the tank. Locate the cover on the tank and align the marks, or direction arrow in the position noted during removal.

16 Refit the locking ring and tighten it with the special tool until it locks in place.

17 Reconnect the fuel hose to the pump cover, using the marks made on removal, then reconnect the wiring connector.

18 Refit the fuel tank as described in Section 8.

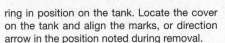

7 Fuel supply pump – removal and refitting

1 The fuel pump is located in the in-tank module in the fuel tank. The removal and refitting procedures are the same as for the fuel gauge sender unit described in Section 6. The pump is integral with the in-tank module and cannot be renewed separately.

8 Fuel tank – removal and refitting

Note: *Refer to the information contained in Section 1 before proceeding.*
Note: *The fuel tank should be as empty as possible when carrying out this procedure.*

Removal

1 Disconnect the battery negative terminal (refer to Chapter 5A Section 4), then depressurise the fuel system as described in Section 5.

2 Before removing the fuel tank, all fuel must be drained from the tank. Since a fuel tank drain plug is not provided, it is therefore preferable to carry out the removal operation when the tank is nearly empty. The remaining fuel can then be syphoned or hand-pumped from the tank.

3 Chock the front wheels then jack up the rear of the car and securely support it on axle stands (see *Jacking and vehicle support*).

4 Disconnect the wiring for the gauge sender unit and fuel pump at the underbody

connector adjacent to the fuel tank **(see illustration)**. Unclip the wiring harness from the retaining clips.

5 Disconnect the fuel and vapour lines at the underbody quick-release connectors on the left-hand side of the tank **(see illustration)**. Be prepared for some loss of fuel. A Vauxhall/Opel special tool is available to release the fuel line connectors, but provided care is taken, the connectors can be released using a pair of long-nosed pliers, or a similar tool, to depress the retaining tangs. Suitably plug the disconnected fuel and vent hoses to prevent entry of dust and dirt.

6 Unclip the handbrake cables from the fuel tank and fuel tank retaining straps **(see illustration)**.

7 Place a suitable container under the tank, then release the retaining clamp and disconnect the fuel filler pipe connection hose from the fuel tank. Collect the escaping fuel in the container.

8 Support the weight of the fuel tank on a jack with interposed block of wood.

9 Undo the five bolts and remove the three securing straps from the fuel tank.

10 Slowly lower the tank while at the same time guiding the filler pipe over the rear axle.

11 Continue to lower the tank until it can be removed from under the vehicle.

12 If necessary, remove the fuel lines and vent hoses, heat shield and wiring from the tank for transfer to the new tank. This will entail cutting off the cable ties and cutting the vent hose end fittings with a sharp knife to allow removal from the tank connections. New hoses will be required for refitting as the end fittings will be destroyed during removal. Take care when doing this not to damage the tank connections.

13 If the tank contains sediment or water, it may cleaned out with two or three rinses of clean fuel. Remove the fuel pump and fuel gauge sender unit as described in Section 6. Shake the tank vigorously, and change the fuel as necessary to remove all contamination from the tank.

14 Any repairs to the fuel tank should be carried out by a professional. Do not under any circumstances attempt any form of DIY repair to a fuel tank.

Refitting

15 Refitting is the reverse of the removal procedure, noting the following points:
a) *When lifting the tank back into position, take care to ensure that none of the hoses become trapped between the tank and vehicle body. Refit the retaining straps and tighten the bolts securely.*
b) *Ensure all pipes and hoses are correctly routed and all hoses unions are securely joined.*
c) *On completion, refill the tank with a small amount of fuel, and check for signs of leakage prior to taking the vehicle out on the road.*

9 Throttle housing – removal and refitting

Removal

1 Disconnect the battery negative terminal (refer to Chapter 5A Section 4).

2 Remove the air cleaner assembly and intake ducts as described in Section 2.

3 Disconnect the wiring connector from the throttle housing **(see illustration)**.

4 Partially drain the cooling system as described in Chapter 1A Section 28 (drain sufficient coolant to empty the coolant expansion tank).

5 Release the retaining clips and disconnect

9.3 Disconnect the wiring connector from the throttle housing

9.7 Throttle housing retaining bolts (arrowed)

11.3a Unclip and remove the ashtray insert ...

11.3b ... for access to the diagnostic socket (arrowed)

the two coolant hoses from the rear of the throttle housing.

6 On VVT (variable valve timing) engines, release the retaining clip and disconnect the crankcase ventilation hose from the throttle housing.

7 Undo the four bolts and lift the throttle housing off the intake manifold **(see illustration)**. Recover the gasket.

8 It is not possible to obtain the throttle valve control motor or throttle valve position sensor separately, so if either is faulty, the complete throttle housing must be renewed.

Refitting

9 Refitting is a reversal of removal, but thoroughly clean the mating faces and use a new gasket. Tighten the bolts progressively to the specified torque. Top-up the coolant level as described in *Weekly checks*. Finally, switch on the ignition for 30 seconds without starting the engine to allow ECU matching.

10 Fuel injection systems – general information

1 The fuel injection system is integrated with the emissions control system and ignition system to form a combined engine management system under the control of one electronic control unit (ECU).

2 All the systems operate in a similar manner and comply with the latest emission control standards. The fuel injection side of the systems operate as follows. Refer to Chapter 4C for information on the emissions control systems, and to Chapter 5B for information on the ignition system.

3 Fuel is pumped from the rear-mounted tank, via a pressure regulator to the fuel rail. The fuel rail acts as a reservoir for the fuel injectors, which inject fuel into the cylinder intake tracts, upstream of the intake valves.

4 All systems are of the 'sequential' injection type, which means that each of the four fuel injectors is triggered individually, just before the intake valve on the relevant cylinder opens.

5 The duration of the electrical pulses to the fuel injectors determines the quantity of fuel injected. The pulse duration is computed by the ECU on the basis of information received from the following sensors:

a) *Accelerator pedal position sensor – informs the ECU of accelerator pedal position, and the rate of throttle opening/ closing.*

b) *Throttle potentiometer (integral with the throttle housing) – informs the ECU of the throttle position, and confirms the signals received from the accelerator pedal position sensor.*

c) *Coolant temperature sensor – informs the ECU of engine temperature.*

d) *Inlet air temperature sensor – informs the ECU of the temperature of the air entering the inlet tract.*

e) *Oxygen sensors (two) – inform the ECU of the oxygen content of the exhaust gases (explained in greater detail in Part C of this Chapter).*

f) *Manifold pressure sensor – informs the ECU of the engine load by monitoring the pressure in the intake manifold.*

g) *Crankshaft speed/position sensor – informs the ECU of the crankshaft speed and position.*

h) *Camshaft sensor (two sensors on VVT engines – inform the ECU of speed and position of the camshaft(s).*

i) *Knock sensor – informs the ECU when pre-ignition ('pinking') is occurring.*

j) *ABS control unit – informs the ECU of the vehicle speed, based on wheel speed sensor signals (explained in greater detail in Chapter 9 Section 17).*

6 The signals from the various sensors are processed by the ECU, and the optimum fuelling and ignition settings are selected for the prevailing engine operating conditions.

7 Idle speed and throttle position is controlled by the throttle valve control motor, which is an integral part of the throttle housing. The motor is controlled by the ECU, in conjunction with signals received from the accelerator pedal position sensor.

8 A catalytic converter is incorporated in the exhaust manifold or in the exhaust system front pipe, to reduce harmful exhaust gas

emissions. Details of this and other emissions control system equipment are given in Chapter 4C.

9 If certain sensors fail, and send abnormal signals to the ECU, the ECU has a back-up programme. In this event, the abnormal signals are ignored, and a pre-programmed value is substituted for the sensor signal, allowing the engine to continue running, albeit at reduced efficiency. If the ECU enters its back-up mode, a warning light on the instrument panel will illuminate, and a fault code will be stored in the ECU memory. This fault code can be read using suitable specialist test equipment.

11 Fuel injection system components – testing

1 If a fault appears in the engine management system, first ensure that all the system wiring connectors are securely connected and free of corrosion. Ensure that the fault is not due to poor maintenance; ie, check that the air cleaner filter element is clean, the spark plugs are in good condition and correctly gapped, the cylinder compression pressures are correct and that the engine breather hoses are clear and undamaged, referring to Chapters 1A, 2A and for further information.

2 If these checks fail to reveal the cause of the problem, the vehicle should be taken to a Vauxhall/Opel dealer or suitably-equipped engine management diagnostic specialist for testing.

3 A diagnostic socket is located in the lower centre of the facia, behind the ashtray insert, to which a fault code reader or other suitable test equipment can be connected **(see illustrations)**. By using the code reader or test equipment, the engine management ECU (and the various other vehicle system ECUs) can be interrogated, and any stored fault codes can be retrieved. This will allow the fault to be quickly and simply traced, alleviating the need to test all the system components individually, which is a time-consuming operation that carries a risk of damaging the ECU.

12 Multec-S injection system components – removal and refitting

Inlet air temperature sensor

Removal

1 Disconnect the wiring connector from the inlet air temperature sensor at the right-hand rear corner of the engine compartment (see illustration 2.1).
2 On Z16XEP engines, slacken the retaining clamps and remove the inlet air temperature sensor from the air intake ducts. On Z16XE1 engines, pull the sensor out of the grommet in the air cleaner intake duct.

Refitting

3 Refitting is a reversal of removal.

Fuel injectors and fuel rail

Note: Refer to the precautions given in Section 1 before proceeding. The seals at both ends of the fuel injectors must be renewed on refitting.

Removal

4 Disconnect the battery negative terminal (refer to Chapter 5A Section 4).
5 Remove the air cleaner assembly and air intake duct as described in Section 2.
6 Depressurise the fuel system as described in Section 5.
7 Disconnect the fuel feed hose quick-release connector at the fuel rail. Be prepared for some loss of fuel. A Vauxhall/Opel special tool is available to release the connector, but provided care is taken, it can be released using a pair of long-nosed pliers, or a similar tool, to depress the retaining tangs. Clamp or plug the open end of the hose, to prevent dirt ingress and further fuel spillage.
8 Lift up the locking bars and disconnect the two wiring connectors from the ECU.
9 Disconnect the wiring connector from the throttle housing.
10 Undo the bolt securing the earth lead to the top of the ECU, then undo the three retaining bolts and remove the ECU from the intake manifold.
11 Disconnect the wiring connector from the manifold pressure sensor on the side of the intake manifold.
12 Release the two clips and move the wiring harness clear of the fuel rail.
13 Disconnect the wiring connector from each fuel injector.
14 Unscrew the two mounting bolts, then lift the fuel rail complete with the injectors off of the intake manifold.
15 To remove an injector from the fuel rail, prise out the metal securing clip using a screwdriver or a pair of pliers, and pull the injector from the fuel rail. Remove and discard the injector sealing rings; new ones must be fitted on refitting.
16 Overhaul of the fuel injectors is not possible, as no spares are available. If faulty, an injector must be renewed.

Refitting

17 Before refitting, clean thoroughly the mating surfaces of the throttle housing and intake manifold.
18 Commence refitting by fitting new O-ring seals to both ends of the fuel injectors. Coat the seals with a thin layer of petroleum jelly before fitting.
19 Refitting is a reversal of removal, bearing in mind the following points:
a) When refitting the injectors to the fuel rail, note that the groove in the metal securing clip must engage with the lug on the injector body.
b) Make sure that the quick-release connector audibly engages on the fuel rail.
c) Ensure that all wiring connectors are securely reconnected, and that the wiring is secured in the relevant clips and brackets.

Crankshaft speed/ position sensor

Note: A new O-ring seal must be used on refitting.

Removal

20 The crankshaft sensor is mounted on the front of the cylinder block below the oil filter.
21 Firmly apply the handbrake, then jack up the front of the car and support it securely on axle stands (see Jacking and vehicle support).
22 Disconnect the wiring connector, then unscrew the retaining bolt and remove the sensor from the front of the cylinder block. Discard the sealing ring, a new one should be used on refitting.

Refitting

23 Refitting is a reversal of removal using a new sealing ring and tightening the sensor bolt to the specified torque.

Camshaft sensor

Removal

24 The camshaft position sensor is located behind the timing belt rear cover, on the exhaust camshaft side.
25 Remove the air cleaner assembly and intake duct as described in Section 2.
26 Undo the two retaining bolts then unclip and remove the timing belt upper cover from the rear cover.
27 Disconnect the camshaft sensor wiring connector.
28 Using a spanner or socket on the crankshaft pulley retaining bolt, turn the crankshaft until the camshaft sensor retaining bolt is accessible through the spokes in the exhaust camshaft sprocket.
29 Undo the sensor retaining bolt, then turn the sensor and remove it from the rear of the timing belt cover.

Refitting

30 Refitting is a reversal of removal, tightening the sensor retaining bolt to the specified torque.

Coolant temperature sensor

31 Refer to Chapter 3 Section 6 for removal and refitting details.

Manifold pressure sensor

Removal

32 On Z16XEP engines, remove the engine management ECU as described later in this Section. On Z16XE1 engines, remove the throttle housing as described in Section 9.
33 Disconnect the pressure sensor wiring connector.
34 Undo the sensor retaining bolt, then remove the sensor from the intake manifold.

Refitting

35 Refitting is a reversal of removal, tightening the sensor retaining bolt to the specified torque.

Knock sensor

Removal

36 The knock sensor is located on the rear of the cylinder block, just above the starter motor.
37 Apply the handbrake, then jack up the front of the vehicle and support it on axle stands (see Jacking and vehicle support).
38 Release the vacuum hose from the intake manifold support bracket, then undo the two bolts and remove the support bracket from the cylinder block and manifold.
39 Disconnect the wiring connector from the knock sensor.
40 Note its position, then unscrew the bolt and remove the knock sensor from the block.

Refitting

41 Clean the contact surfaces of the sensor and block. Also clean the threads of the sensor mounting bolt.
42 Locate the sensor on the block and insert the mounting bolt. Position the sensor as previously noted, then tighten the bolt to the specified torque. Note that the torque setting is critical for the sensor to function correctly.
43 Refit the intake manifold support bracket and attach the vacuum hose, then lower the vehicle to the ground.

Electronic control unit (ECU)

Note: If a new ECU is to be fitted, this work must be entrusted to a Vauxhall/Opel dealer or suitably-equipped specialist as it is necessary to programme the new ECU after installation. This work requires the use of dedicated Vauxhall/Opel diagnostic equipment or a compatible alternative.

Removal

44 The engine management ECU is located on the left-hand side of the intake manifold.
45 Disconnect the battery negative terminal (refer to Chapter 5A Section 4).
46 Lift up the locking bars and disconnect the two wiring connectors from the ECU.
47 Undo the bolt securing the earth lead to the top of the ECU, then undo the three

retaining bolts and remove the ECU from the intake manifold.

Refitting

48 Refitting is a reversal of removal.

Oxygen sensors

49 Refer to Chapter 4C for removal and refitting details.

13 Simtec 75.1 injection system components – removal and refitting

Fuel injectors and fuel rail

Note: *Refer to the precautions given in Section 1 before proceeding. The seals at both ends of the fuel injectors must be renewed on refitting.*

Removal

1 Disconnect the battery negative terminal (refer to Chapter 5A Section 4).
2 Depressurise the fuel system as described in Section 5.
3 Remove the air cleaner assembly and intake duct as described in Section 2.
4 Unclip the wiring harness trough from the rear of the camshaft cover **(see illustration)**.
5 Pull out the retaining wire clip and disconnect the breather hose from the camshaft cover **(see illustration)**.
6 Disconnect the wiring connectors from the following components, labelling each connector to avoid confusion when refitting:
a) *Engine management ECU.*
b) *Evaporative emission control system purge valve.*
c) *Throttle housing.*
d) *Intake camshaft VVT oil control valve.*
e) *Fuel injectors.*
7 Unclip the wiring harness from the support brackets and move the harness to one side.
8 Disconnect the fuel feed hose quick-release connector at the fuel rail **(see illustration)**. Be prepared for some loss of fuel. A Vauxhall/Opel special tool is available to release the connector, but provided care is taken, it can be released using a pair of long-nosed pliers, or a similar tool, to depress the retaining tangs. Clamp or plug the open end of the hose, to prevent dirt ingress and further fuel spillage.
9 Unscrew the two mounting bolts, then lift the fuel rail complete with the injectors off of the intake manifold.
10 To remove an injector from the fuel rail, prise out the metal securing clip using a screwdriver or a pair of pliers, and pull the injector from the fuel rail. Remove and discard the injector sealing rings; new ones must be fitted on refitting.
11 Overhaul of the fuel injectors is not possible, as no spares are available. If faulty, an injector must be renewed.

Refitting

12 Commence refitting by fitting new O-ring seals to both ends of the fuel injectors. Coat

13.4 Unclip the wiring harness trough from the rear of the camshaft cover

the seals with a thin layer of petroleum jelly before fitting.
13 Refitting is a reversal of removal, bearing in mind the following points:
a) *When refitting the injectors to the fuel rail, note that the groove in the metal securing clip must engage with the lug on the injector body.*
b) *Make sure that the quick-release connector audibly engages on the fuel rail.*
c) *Ensure that all wiring connectors are securely reconnected, and that the wiring is secured in the relevant clips and brackets.*

Crankshaft speed/ position sensor

Note: *A new O-ring seal must be used on refitting.*

Removal

14 The crankshaft speed/position sensor is located at the rear left-hand end of the cylinder block, below the starter motor
15 Apply the handbrake, then jack up the front of the vehicle and support it on axle stands (see *Jacking and vehicle support*).
16 Remove the starter motor as described in Chapter 5A Section 11.
17 Disconnect the sensor wiring connector, then undo the retaining bolt and withdraw the sensor from the cylinder block.

Refitting

18 Refitting is a reversal of removal, but

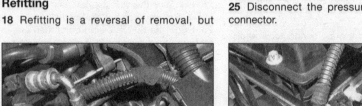

13.8 Disconnect the fuel feed hose quick-release connector (arrowed) at the fuel rail

13.5 Pull out the retaining wire clip and disconnect the breather hose from the camshaft cover

ensure that the mating surfaces of the sensor and baseplate are clean and fit a new O-ring seal to the sensor before refitting. Tighten the bolt to the specified torque.

Camshaft sensor

Removal

19 Two sensors are fitted, one for each camshaft. Both sensors are located at the left-hand end of the cylinder head.
20 Disconnect the wiring connector from the relevant sensor **(see illustration)**. If removing the exhaust camshaft sensor, unclip the oxygen sensor wiring harness from the support bracket.
21 Undo the retaining bolt and remove the sensor from the cylinder head.

Refitting

22 Refitting is a reversal of removal, tightening the sensor retaining bolt to the specified torque.

Coolant temperature sensor

23 Refer to Chapter 3 Section 6 for removal and refitting details.

Manifold pressure sensor

Removal

24 Remove the engine management ECU as described later in this Section.
25 Disconnect the pressure sensor wiring connector.

13.20 Disconnect the wiring connector (arrowed) from the camshaft sensor (exhaust sensor shown)

13.38 Lift up the locking bars and disconnect the two ECU wiring connectors

26 Undo the sensor retaining bolt, then remove the sensor from the intake manifold.

Refitting

27 Refitting is a reversal of removal, tightening the sensor retaining bolt to the specified torque.

Knock sensor

Removal

28 The knock sensor is located on the rear of the cylinder block, just above the starter motor.

29 Apply the handbrake, then jack up the front of the vehicle and support it on axle stands (see *Jacking and vehicle support*).

30 Disconnect the oxygen sensor wiring connector, then unclip the connector from the support bracket.

31 Unscrew the two retaining bolts and remove the intake manifold support bracket.

32 Disconnect the knock sensor wiring connector, then unscrew the retaining bolt and remove the sensor from the cylinder block.

Refitting

33 Clean the contact surfaces of the sensor and block. Also clean the threads of the sensor mounting bolt.

34 Locate the sensor on the block and insert the mounting bolt. Tighten the bolt to the specified torque. Note that the torque setting is critical for the sensor to function correctly.

35 Refit the intake manifold support bracket and oxygen sensor wiring connector, then lower the vehicle to the ground.

Electronic control unit (ECU)

Note: *If a new ECU is to be fitted, this work must be entrusted to a Vauxhall/Opel dealer or suitably-equipped specialist as it is necessary to programme the new ECU after installation. This work requires the use of dedicated Vauxhall/Opel diagnostic equipment or a compatible alternative.*

Removal

36 The ECU is located on the left-hand side of the intake manifold.

37 Disconnect the battery negative terminal (refer to Chapter 5A Section 4).

38 Lift up the locking bars and disconnect the

two ECU wiring connectors **(see illustration)**.

39 Undo the retaining bolt and detach the earth lead from the ECU.

40 Undo the four retaining bolts and remove the ECU from the engine.

Refitting

41 Refitting is a reversal of removal.

Oxygen sensors

42 Refer to Chapter 4C for removal and refitting details.

Inlet air temperature sensor

Removal

43 Disconnect the wiring connector from the inlet air temperature sensor in the air cleaner intake duct.

44 Pull the sensor out of the grommet in the air cleaner intake duct.

Refitting

45 Refitting is a reversal of removal.

14 Intake manifold (non-VVT engines) – removal and refitting

Removal

1 Remove the windscreen cowl panel as described in Chapter 11 Section 20.

2 Apply the handbrake, then jack up the front of the vehicle and support it on axle stands (see *Jacking and vehicle support*).

3 Disconnect the battery negative terminal (refer to Chapter 5A Section 4).

4 Drain the cooling system as described in Chapter 1A Section 28.

5 Release the vacuum hose from the intake manifold support bracket, then undo the two bolts and remove the support bracket from the cylinder block and manifold.

6 Disconnect the wiring connector from the evaporative emission control system purge valve. Release the quick-release connector and disconnect the hose from the valve.

7 Remove the air cleaner assembly and air intake duct as described in Section 2.

8 Depressurise the fuel system as described in Section 5.

9 Disconnect the fuel supply line from the fuel rail and release it from the support clip. A quick-release connector is fitted and Vauxhall technicians use a special tool to release it, however, provided care is taken, the connector can be released using a pair of long-nosed pliers, or a similar tool, to depress the retaining tangs.

10 Release the clips and disconnect the coolant hose from the throttle housing and thermostat housing.

11 Remove the engine management ECU from the intake manifold as described in Section 12.

12 Disconnect the wiring connectors from the intake manifold pressure sensor and throttle housing.

13 Disconnect the brake servo vacuum hose from the intake manifold.

14 Unclip the wiring harness trough from the rear of the camshaft cover. Release the harness from the two support clips and move the harness to one side.

15 Pull out the retaining wire clip and disconnect the breather hose from the camshaft cover.

16 Unscrew the retaining bolts and withdraw the upper intake manifold from the lower intake manifold. Discard the seals; new ones must be used for refitting.

17 To remove the lower manifold, disconnect the wiring connector at the flap valve vacuum unit.

18 Disconnect the wiring connectors from the fuel injectors.

19 Unscrew the eight bolts and two nuts and withdraw the lower manifold from the cylinder head. Discard the seals; new ones must be used for refitting.

Refitting

20 Refitting is the reverse of removal noting the following.

a) *Ensure the manifold and cylinder head mating surfaces are clean and dry and fit the new seals. Refit the manifold and tighten the retaining bolts evenly and progressively to the specified torque.*

b) *Ensure that all relevant hoses are reconnected to their original positions, and are securely held (where necessary) by their retaining clips.*

c) *Refit the windscreen cowl panel as described in Chapter 11 Section 20.*

d) *On completion, refill the cooling system as described in Chapter 1A Section 28.*

15 Intake manifold (VVT engines) – removal and refitting

Removal

1 Remove the windscreen cowl panel as described in Chapter 11 Section 20.

2 Disconnect the battery negative terminal (refer to Chapter 5A Section 4).

3 Firmly apply the handbrake, then jack up the front of the car and support it securely on axle stands (see *Jacking and vehicle support*).

4 Drain the cooling system as described in Chapter 1A Section 28.

5 Remove the air cleaner assembly and air intake duct as described in Section 2.

6 Depressurise the fuel system as described in Section 5.

7 Remove the throttle housing as described in Section 9.

8 From under the car, disconnect the oxygen sensor wiring connector, then unclip connector from the support bracket.

9 Unscrew the two retaining bolts and remove the intake manifold support bracket.

10 Unclip the wiring harness from the base of the intake manifold.

15.11 Disconnect the wiring connector (arrowed) from the evaporative emission control system purge valve

15.17 Disconnect the wiring harness block connector on the left-hand side of the inlet manifold

11 Disconnect the wiring connector from the evaporative emission control system purge valve **(see illustration)**.

12 Slide the purge valve rubber mounting off the mounting bracket, then disconnect the vapour hose from the intake manifold. Place the valve to one side.

13 Unclip the wiring harness trough from the rear of the camshaft cover **(see illustration 13.7)**.

14 Pull out the retaining wire clip and disconnect the breather hose from the camshaft cover **(see illustration 13.8)**.

15 Remove the engine management ECU as described in Section 13.

16 Disconnect the wiring connectors from the intake camshaft VVT oil control valve and the four fuel injectors. Release the wiring harness from the support brackets and place it to one side.

17 Disconnect the wiring harness block connector on the left-hand side of the intake manifold **(see illustration)**.

18 Release the throttle housing coolant hoses from their clips and supports on the intake manifold and disconnect the hoses from the coolant expansion tank and thermostat housing. Move the hoses to one side.

19 Disconnect the wiring connectors at the manifold switchover valve diaphragm and solenoid.

20 Undo the retaining bolt and detach the wiring harness support bracket from the engine lifting bracket.

21 Disconnect the quick-release fitting and detach the brake servo vacuum hose from the intake manifold.

22 Slacken and remove the seven retaining bolts and manoeuvre the manifold assembly away from the cylinder head. Remove the gasket and discard it. **Note:** *The manifold assembly must be treated as a sealed unit; do not attempt to dismantle it as no components, other than the switchover diaphragm and solenoid, are available separately.*

Refitting

23 Refitting is the reverse of removal noting the following.

a) *Ensure the manifold and cylinder head mating surfaces are clean and dry and fit the new gasket. Refit the manifold and tighten the retaining bolts evenly and progressively to the specified torque.*

b) *Ensure that all relevant hoses are reconnected to their original positions, and are securely held (where necessary) by their retaining clips.*

c) *Refit the windscreen cowl panel as described in Chapter 11 Section 20.*

d) *On completion, refill the cooling system as described in Chapter 1A Section 28.*

16 Exhaust manifold (non-VVT engines) – removal and refitting

Note: *New manifold and exhaust front pipe retaining nuts, a new manifold gasket and exhaust front pipe gasket must be used on refitting.*

Removal

1 Apply the handbrake, then jack up the front of the vehicle and support it on axle stands (see *Jacking and vehicle support*).

2 Disconnect the battery negative lead (refer to Chapter 5A Section 4).

3 Disconnect the wiring from the oxygen sensor, then unbolt the exhaust front pipe from the exhaust manifold, taking care to support the flexible section. **Note:** *Angular movement in excess of 10° can cause permanent damage to the flexible section.* Recover the gasket.

4 Release the mounting rubbers and support the front of the exhaust pipe to one side.

5 Undo the two lower exhaust manifold support bolts.

6 Remove the engine oil dipstick from the

guide tube, then unbolt and remove the guide tube.

7 Remove the oxygen sensor from the exhaust manifold as described in Chapter 4C Section 2.

8 Undo the two bolts and remove the heat shield from the exhaust manifold.

9 Undo the eleven retaining nuts and withdraw the exhaust manifold from the cylinder head studs. Recover the gasket.

Refitting

10 Thoroughly clean the mating face of the exhaust manifold and cylinder head, then locate a new gasket over the studs.

11 Locate the exhaust manifold over the cylinder head studs and secure with the (new) nuts tightened progressively to the specified torque.

12 Refit the heat shield and tighten the retaining bolts finger-tight only at this stage.

13 Using a new O-ring seal, refit the dipstick guide tube and tighten the retaining bolt securely. Now fully-tighten the manifold heat shield retaining bolts.

14 Refer to Chapter 4C Section 2 and refit the oxygen sensor to the manifold. Tighten to the specified torque.

15 Refit the two lower exhaust manifold support bolts.

16 Refit the exhaust front pipe to the manifold together with a new gasket, then tighten the (new) nuts to the specified torque. Reconnect the oxygen sensor wiring connector.

17 Lower the vehicle to the ground, then reconnect the battery negative lead.

17 Exhaust manifold (VVT engines) – removal and refitting

Note: *New manifold and exhaust front pipe retaining nuts, a new manifold gasket, exhaust front pipe gasket and oil dipstick guide tube O-rings must be used on refitting.*

Removal

1 Disconnect the battery negative terminal (refer to Chapter 5A Section 4).

2 Remove the air cleaner assembly and air intake ducts as described in Section 2.

3 Unbolt and remove the oil dipstick guide tube, and withdraw it from the cylinder block. Remove and discard the O-ring seals.

4 Trace the wiring back from the manifold oxygen sensor and disconnect its wiring connector. Free the wiring from the support bracket so the sensor is free to be removed with the manifold.

5 Apply the handbrake, then jack up the front of the vehicle and support it on axle stands (see *Jacking and vehicle support*).

6 Disconnect the wiring from the oxygen sensor, then unbolt the exhaust front pipe from the exhaust manifold, taking care to support the flexible section. **Note:** *Angular movement in excess of 10° can cause permanent damage to the flexible section.* Recover the gasket.

7 Release the mounting rubbers and support the front of the exhaust pipe to one side.

8 Undo the two lower bolts securing the heat shield to the exhaust manifold.

9 Undo the two bolts securing the manifold to the lower support bracket, and the two bolts securing the support bracket to the cylinder block. Remove the bracket.

10 On models with air conditioning, unbolt the compressor from the front of the engine with reference to Chapter 3 Section 11, and support it to one side. Do not disconnect the refrigerant lines from the compressor.

11 Unbolt the two engine lifting brackets from the exhaust manifold.

12 Undo the bolt securing the wiring harness support bracket, then remove the bracket and the exhaust manifold heat shield.

13 Slacken and remove the nine retaining nuts, and manoeuvre the manifold out of the engine compartment. Recover the gasket.

Refitting

14 Examine all the exhaust manifold studs for signs of damage and corrosion; remove all traces of corrosion, and repair or renew any damaged studs.

15 Ensure that the manifold and cylinder head sealing faces are clean and flat, and fit the new gasket.

16 Refit the manifold then fit the new retaining nuts and tighten them progressively, in a diagonal sequence, to the specified torque.

17 Align the heat shield with the manifold, then refit the wiring harness support bracket and tighten the retaining bolt securely.

18 On air conditioning models, refit the compressor with reference to Chapter 3 Section 11.

19 Refit the lower support bracket to the cylinder block and manifold and tighten the retaining bolts securely.

20 Refit and tighten the two lower bolts securing the heat shield to the exhaust manifold.

21 Reconnect the exhaust front pipe, using a new gasket. Tighten the new nuts to the specified torque. Reconnect the oxygen sensor wiring connector.

22 Reconnect the exhaust manifold oxygen sensor wiring connector making sure the wiring is correctly routed and retained by the support bracket.

23 Fit the new O-ring seals to the oil dipstick guide tube, then insert the tube in the cylinder block. Insert and tighten the retaining bolt.

24 Refit the air cleaner assembly and air intake ducts as described in Section 2.

25 Lower the vehicle to the ground, then reconnect the battery negative lead.

18 Exhaust system – general information, removal and refitting

General information

1 The exhaust system consists of three main sections comprising a front pipe including the oxygen sensor (catalytic converter control), an intermediate pipe incorporating the front silencer and a tailpipe incorporating the rear silencer.

2 The front pipe is attached to the catalytic converter by a flange joint secured by nuts. All other exhaust sections are joined by overlap joints which are secured by clamps.

3 The front pipe is fitted with a flexible section to allow for exhaust system movement, and the system is suspended throughout its entire length by rubber mountings.

Removal

4 To remove the various parts of the system, first jack up the front or rear of the car, and support it on axle stands. Alternatively, position the car over an inspection pit, or on car ramps.

Front pipe and intermediate pipe

Note: *The front pipe and intermediate pipe are removed from the car together as an assembly, then separated after removal.*

5 Remove the tailpipe as described later in this Section.

6 Trace the wiring back from the oxygen sensor, noting its correct routing, and disconnect its wiring connector. Free the wiring from its retaining clips so the sensor is free to be removed with the front pipe.

7 Undo the three nuts securing the front pipe to the exhaust manifold, then free the front pipe from the manifold and recover the gasket **(see illustration)**. While doing this, take care to support the flexible section. **Note:** *Angular movement in excess of 10° can cause permanent damage to the flexible section.*

8 Spray some penetrating oil over the exhaust rubber mounting blocks so that the mounting blocks will slide easily on the exhaust and underbody hangers.

9 Slide the front rubber mounting blocks as far forward as possible. Move the exhaust system to the rear and disengage the intermediate pipe front hangers from the mounting blocks.

10 Move the exhaust system forward and

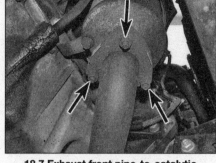

18.7 Exhaust front pipe-to-catalytic converter retaining nuts (arrowed)

disengage the intermediate pipe rear hangers from the rubber mounting blocks. Lower the front pipe and intermediate pipe to the ground and slide them out from under the car.

11 Loosen the clamp securing the front pipe to the intermediate pipe. Support the front pipe and slide out the intermediate pipe. If the intermediate pipe is rusted onto the front pipe, apply liberal amounts of penetrating oil and tap around the joint with a hammer to free it. Twist the intermediate pipe in both directions until free.

Tailpipe

12 Loosen the clamp securing the tail pipe to the intermediate pipe.

13 Unhook the tailpipe from its rubber mountings and slide the tailpipe from the intermediate pipe. If the tailpipe is rusted onto the intermediate pipe, apply liberal amounts of penetrating oil and tap around the joint with a hammer to free it. Twist the tailpipe in both directions until free.

Heat shield(s)

14 The heat shields are secured to the underside of the body by various nuts and bolts. Each shield can be removed once the relevant exhaust section has been removed. If a shield is being removed to gain access to a component located behind it, it may prove sufficient in some cases to remove the retaining nuts and/or bolts, and simply lower the shield, without disturbing the exhaust system.

Refitting

15 Each section is refitted by reversing the removal sequence, noting the following points:

a) *Ensure that all traces of corrosion have been removed from the system joints.*

b) *When refitting the front pipe to the exhaust manifold flange joint, use a new gasket and new retaining nuts, and tighten the nuts to the specified torque.*

c) *Inspect the rubber mountings for signs of damage or deterioration, and renew as necessary.*

d) *Prior to tightening the exhaust system fasteners, ensure that all rubber mountings are correctly located, and that there is adequate clearance between the exhaust system and vehicle underbody.*

Chapter 4 Part B
Fuel and exhaust systems – diesel engines

Contents

Section number

Accelerator pedal/position sensor – removal and refitting. 4
Air cleaner assembly and intake ducts – removal and refitting 3
Diesel injection system electrical components –
   removal and refitting. 11
Diesel injection system electrical components – testing 10
Exhaust manifold and turbocharger – removal and refitting 19
Exhaust system – general information, removal and refitting 20
Fuel filter crash box – removal and refitting. 9
Fuel gauge sender unit – removal and refitting 6
Fuel injectors – removal and refitting 14
Fuel rail – removal and refitting 13

Section number

Fuel supply pump – removal and refitting 7
Fuel system – priming and bleeding. 5
Fuel tank – removal and refitting 8
General information and precautions. 1
High-pressure diesel injection system – special information 2
High-pressure fuel pump – removal and refitting. 12
Intake manifold – removal and refitting 15
Intake manifold changeover flap actuator drive –
   removal and refitting. 16
Intercooler – removal and refitting 17
Turbocharger – description and precautions 18

Degrees of difficulty

Easy, suitable for novice with little experience	**Fairly easy,** suitable for beginner with some experience	**Fairly difficult,** suitable for competent DIY mechanic
Difficult, suitable for experienced DIY mechanic	**Very difficult,** suitable for expert DIY or professional	

Specifications

System type

1.7 litre engines	Denso DECe01 high-pressure direct injection 'common-rail' system, electronically controlled
SOHC (Z19DT and Z19DTL) engines.	Bosch EDC 16C9 high-pressure direct injection 'common-rail' system, electronically-controlled
DOHC (Z19DTH) engines:	Bosch EDC 16C39 high-pressure direct injection 'common-rail' system, electronically-controlled

Fuel system data

Firing order.	1–3–4–2 (No 1 at timing belt end of engine)
Fuel system operating pressure	1400 to 1600 bar at 2200 rpm
Idle speed.	Controlled by ECU
Maximum speed.	Controlled by ECU
High-pressure fuel pump:	
1.7 litre engines	Denso HP3
1.9 litre engines	Bosch CP1H
Fuel supply pump:	
Type	Electric, mounted in fuel tank
Delivery pressure	3.3 bar (maximum)
Injectors:	
1.7 litre engines	Denso DLL-P
1.9 litre engines	Bosch CRIP 2-MI

Torque wrench settings

	Nm	lbf ft
Camshaft sensor retaining bolt(s)...............................	9	7
Catalytic converter-to-turbocharger (1.7 litre engines)...............	45	33
Catalytic converter clamp bolt (1.9 litre engines)...................	20	15
Charge (boost) pressure sensor-to-manifold (1.7 litre engines)........	5	3
Charge (boost) pressure sensor retaining bolts (1.9 litre engines).....	9	7
Crankshaft speed/position sensor retaining bolt....................	9	7
EGR valve pipe to exhaust manifold.............................	25	18
Exhaust manifold nuts:		
1.7 litre engines*..	70	52
1.9 litre engines*..	25	18
Exhaust front pipe-to-catalytic converter nuts*....................	20	15
Exhaust front pipe-to-intermediate pipe nuts*.....................	20	15
Exhaust system clamp nuts....................................	50	37
Fuel injector clamp bolts (1.7 litre engines):		
Stage 1...	40	30
Stage 2...	Fully slacken	
Stage 3...	32	24
Fuel injector clamp bracket nuts:		
SOHC (Z19DT and DTL) engines...........................	32	24
DOHC (Z19DTH) engines.................................	25	18
Fuel pressure regulator to fuel rail (1.9 litre engines only)..........	60	44
Fuel pressure sensor to fuel rail (1.9 litre engines only)............	70	52
Fuel rail retaining nuts/bolts..................................	25	18
High-pressure fuel pipe unions	23	17
High-pressure fuel pump mountings:		
1.7 litre engines:		
High-pressure fuel pump mounting nuts...................	18	13
1.9 litre engines:		
High-pressure fuel pump bracket bolts....................	25	18
High-pressure fuel pump mounting nuts...................	25	18
Intake manifold nuts...	25	18
Temperature sensor to diesel particulate filter...................	45	33
Turbocharger-to-manifold nuts (1.7 litre engines): *		
Stage 1...	25	18
Stage 2...	48	36
Turbocharger oil return pipe bolts (1.9 litre engines only):		
M6 bolts..	9	7
M8 bolts..	25	18
Turbocharger oil supply pipe banjo bolt:		
1.7 litre engines	20	15
1.9 litre engines	15	11

*Use new fasteners

1 General information and precautions

General information

1 All engines are fitted with a high-pressure direct injection system which incorporates the very latest in diesel injection technology. On this system, a high-pressure fuel pump is used purely to provide the pressure required for the injection system and has no control over the injection timing (unlike conventional diesel injection systems). The injection timing is controlled by the electronic control unit (ECU) via the electrically-operated injectors. The system operates as follows.

2 The fuel system consists of a fuel tank (which is mounted under the rear of the car), an electric fuel supply pump mounted inside the fuel tank, a fuel filter with integral water separator, a high-pressure fuel pump, injectors and associated components.

3 Fuel is supplied to the fuel filter housing which is located in the engine compartment. The fuel filter removes all foreign matter and water and ensures that the fuel supplied to the pump is clean.

4 The fuel is heated to ensure no problems occur when the ambient temperature is very low. This is achieved by an electrically-operated fuel heater incorporated in the filter housing, the heater is controlled by the ECU.

5 The high-pressure fuel pump is driven at half-crankshaft speed by the timing belt. The high-pressure required in the system (up to 1600 bar) is produced by the three pistons in the pump. The high-pressure pump supplies high-pressure fuel to the fuel rail, which acts as a reservoir for the four injectors.

6 The electrical control system consists of the ECU, along with the following sensors:

a) *Accelerator pedal position sensor –*
    informs the ECU of the accelerator pedal
    position, and the rate of throttle opening/
    closing.

b) *Coolant temperature sensor – informs the*
    ECU of engine temperature.

c) *Airflow meter – informs the ECU of the*
    amount of air passing through the intake
    duct.

d) *Crankshaft sensor – informs the ECU*
    of the crankshaft position and speed of
    rotation.

e) *Camshaft sensor – informs the ECU of the*
    positions of the pistons.

f) *Charge (boost) pressure sensor – informs*
    ECU of the pressure in the intake manifold.

g) *Fuel pressure sensor – informs the ECU of*
    the fuel pressure present in the fuel rail.

h) *ABS control unit – informs the ECU of the*
    vehicle speed.

7 All the above signals are analysed by the ECU which selects the fuelling response appropriate to those values. The ECU controls the fuel injectors (varying the pulse width – the length of time the injectors are held open – to provide a richer or weaker mixture, as appropriate). The mixture is constantly varied by the ECU, to provide the best setting for cranking, starting (with either a hot or cold engine), warm-up, idle, cruising and acceleration.

8 The ECU also has full control over the fuel pressure present in the fuel rail via the high-pressure fuel regulator and third piston deactivator solenoid valve which are fitted to the high-pressure pump. To reduce the pressure, the ECU opens the high-pressure fuel regulator which allows the excess fuel to return direct to the tank from the pump. The third piston deactivator is used mainly to reduce the load on the engine, but can also be used to lower the fuel pressure. The deactivator solenoid valve relieves the fuel pressure from the third piston of the pump which results in only two of the pistons pressurising the fuel system.

9 The ECU also controls the exhaust gas recirculation (EGR) system, described in detail in Part C of this Chapter, the pre/post-heating system (see Chapter 5A), and the engine cooling fan.

10 A variable-vane turbocharger is fitted to increases engine efficiency. It does this by raising the pressure in the intake manifold above atmospheric pressure. Instead of the air simply being sucked into the cylinders, it is forced in.

11 Between the turbocharger and the intake manifold, the compressed air passes through an intercooler. This is an air-to-air heat exchanger mounted in front of the radiator, and supplied with cooling air from the front of the vehicle. The purpose of the intercooler is to remove some of the heat gained in being compressed from the intake air. Because cooler air is denser, removal of this heat further increases engine efficiency.

12 Energy for the operation of the turbocharger comes from the exhaust gas. The gas flows through a specially-shaped housing (the turbine housing) and in so doing, spins the turbine wheel. The turbine wheel is attached to a shaft, at the end of which is another vaned wheel known as the compressor wheel. The compressor wheel spins in its own housing, and compresses the intake air on the way to the intake manifold. The turbo shaft is pressure-lubricated by an oil feed pipe from the main oil gallery. The shaft 'floats' on a cushion of oil. A drain pipe returns the oil to the sump. Boost pressure (the pressure in the intake manifold) is limited by a wastegate, which diverts the exhaust gas away from the turbine wheel in response to a pressure-sensitive actuator.

13 If certain sensors fail, and send abnormal signals to the ECU, the ECU has a back-up programme. In this event, the abnormal signals are ignored, and a pre-programmed value is substituted for the sensor signal, allowing the engine to continue running, albeit at reduced

efficiency. If the ECU enters its back-up mode, a warning light on the instrument panel will illuminate, and a fault code will be stored in the ECU memory. This fault code can be read using suitable specialist test equipment plugged into the system's diagnostic socket.

Precautions

⚠️ *Warning: It is necessary to take certain precautions when working on the fuel system components, particularly the high-pressure side of the system. Before carrying out any operations on the fuel system, refer to the precautions given in 'Safety first!' at the beginning of this manual, and to any additional warning notes at the start of the relevant Sections. Also refer to the additional information contained in Section 2.*

Caution: Do not operate the engine if any of air intake ducts are disconnected or the filter element is removed. Any debris entering the engine will cause severe damage to the turbocharger.

Caution: To prevent damage to the turbocharger, do not race the engine immediately after start-up, especially if it is cold. Allow it to idle smoothly to give the oil a few seconds to circulate around the turbocharger bearings. Always allow the engine to return to idle speed before switching it off – do not blip the throttle and switch off, as this will leave the turbo spinning without lubrication.

Caution: Observe the recommended intervals for oil and filter changing, and use a reputable oil of the specified quality. Neglect of oil changing, or use of inferior oil, can cause carbon formation on the turbo shaft, leading to subsequent failure.

---

2 High-pressure diesel injection system – special information

---

Warnings and precautions

1 It is essential to observe strict precautions when working on the fuel system components, particularly the high-pressure side of the system. Before carrying out any operations on the fuel system, refer to the precautions given in *Safety first!* at the beginning of this manual, and to the following additional information.

● Do not carry out any repair work on the high-pressure fuel system unless you are competent to do so, have all the necessary tools and equipment required, and are aware of the safety implications involved.

● Before starting any repair work on the fuel system, wait at least 30 seconds after switching off the engine to allow the fuel circuit to return to atmospheric pressure.

● Never work on the high-pressure fuel system with the engine running.

● Keep well clear of any possible source of fuel leakage, particularly when starting the

engine after carrying out repair work. A leak in the system could cause an extremely high-pressure jet of fuel to escape, which could result in severe personal injury.

● Never place your hands or any part of your body near to a leak in the high-pressure fuel system.

● Do not use steam cleaning equipment or compressed air to clean the engine or any of the fuel system components.

Repair procedures and general information

1 Strict cleanliness must be observed at all times when working on any part of the fuel system. This applies to the working area in general, the person doing the work, and the components being worked on.

2 Before working on the fuel system components, they must be thoroughly cleaned with a suitable degreasing fluid. Cleanliness is particularly important when working on the fuel system connections at the following components:

a) Fuel filter.
b) High-pressure fuel pump.
c) Fuel rail.
d) Fuel injectors.
e) High-pressure fuel pipes.

3 After disconnecting any fuel pipes or components, the open union or orifice must be immediately sealed to prevent the entry of dirt or foreign material. Plastic plugs and caps in various sizes are available in packs from motor factors and accessory outlets, and are particularly suitable for this application (**see illustration**). Fingers cut from disposable rubber gloves should be used to protect components such as fuel pipes, fuel injectors and wiring connectors, and can be secured in place using elastic bands. Suitable gloves of this type are available at no cost from most petrol station forecourts.

4 Whenever any of the high-pressure fuel pipes are disconnected or removed, a new pipe(s) must be obtained for refitting.

5 The torque wrench settings given in the Specifications must be strictly observed when tightening component mountings and connections. This is particularly important when tightening the high-pressure fuel pipe

2.3 Typical plastic plug and cap set for sealing disconnected fuel pipes and components

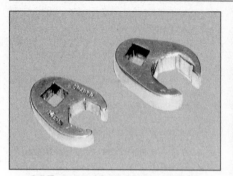

2.5 Two crow-foot adapters will be necessary for tightening the fuel pipe unions

3.1 Disconnect the wiring connector from the airflow meter

3.2 Slacken the clips (arrowed) and detach the intake duct from the charge air pipe and airflow meter

unions. To enable a torque wrench to be used on the fuel pipe unions, two crow-foot adapters are required. Suitable types are available from motor factors and accessory outlets **(see illustration)**.

3 Air cleaner assembly and intake ducts – removal and refitting

Removal

1 Disconnect the wiring connector from the side of the airflow meter **(see illustration)**.
2 Slacken the retaining clips and detach the flexible air intake duct from the turbocharger charge air pipe and airflow meter **(see illustration)**.
3 Where applicable, unclip the vacuum hose or wiring harness from the side of the air cleaner housing.
4 Undo the retaining bolt and release the mounting bracket at the rear of the air cleaner housing **(see illustration)**.
5 Detach the air intake duct at the front of the air cleaner housing **(see illustration)**.
6 Lift the housing upwards at the rear, then disengage the front mounting rubber from the body bracket.
7 When sufficient clearance exists, release the retaining clip and disconnect the water drain tube from the base of the air cleaner housing **(see illustration)**. Remove the assembly from the engine compartment.

3.7 Release the clip and disconnect the water drain tube from the base of the air cleaner housing

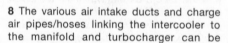

3.4 Undo the retaining bolt (arrowed) and release the air cleaner housing mounting bracket

3.5 Detach the air intake duct at the front of the air cleaner housing

8 The various air intake ducts and charge air pipes/hoses linking the intercooler to the manifold and turbocharger can be disconnected and removed once the retaining clips have been slackened **(see illustration)**. In some cases it will be necessary to

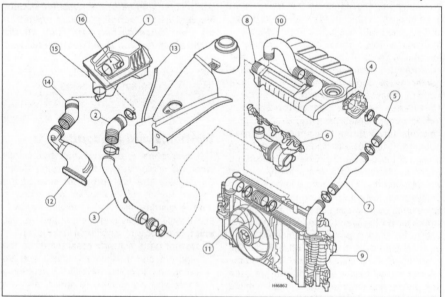

3.8 Typical air intake duct arrangement

1 Air cleaner lid
2 Upper intake duct
3 Turbocharger charge air pipe
4 Throttle housing
5 Charge air pipe elbow

6 Exhaust manifold and turbocharger
7 Intake manifold charge air pipe hose connection
8 Intercooler charge air pipe
9 Intercooler
10 Charge air hose

11 Intercooler charge air pipe hose connection
12 Resonator
13 Water drain tube
14 Air cleaner intake duct
15 Air cleaner housing
16 Airflow meter

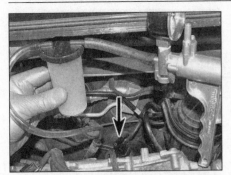

5.6 Disconnect the rubber hose from the return pipe at the engine compartment bulkhead, and connect a hand-held pump

disconnect breather hoses, vacuum pipes and wiring connectors to allow the pipe/duct to be removed; the pipe/duct may also be bolted to a support bracket.

Refitting

9 Refitting is the reverse of removal, making sure all the air intake ducts and charge air pipes/hoses are securely reconnected.

4 Accelerator pedal/position sensor – removal and refitting

1 Refer to Chapter 4A, Section 3.

5 Fuel system – priming and bleeding

1 After disconnecting part of the fuel supply system or running out of fuel, it is necessary to prime the fuel system and bleed off any air which may have entered the system components, as follows.
2 Prime the system by switching on the ignition three times for approximately 15 seconds each time. Operate the starter for a maximum of 30 seconds. If the engine does not start within this time, wait 5 seconds and repeat the procedure.
3 When the engine starts, run it at a fast idle speed for a minute or so to purge any trapped air from the fuel lines. After this time the engine should idle smoothly at a constant speed.
4 If the engine idles roughly, then there is still some air trapped in the fuel system. Increase the engine speed again for another minute or so then allow it to idle. Repeat this procedure as necessary until the engine is idling smoothly.
5 If the above procedure fails to start the engine, it may be necessary to manually draw the fuel through the system as follows.
6 Release the clamp, disconnect the rubber hose from the fuel return pipe at the engine compartment bulkhead, then connect a hand-held vacuum pump to the hose. Operate the pump until air-free fuel emerges (see

illustration). Note that this process may take several minutes.
7 Reconnect the hose to the return pipe, and secure it with the clamp.
8 Start the engine, and run it at a fast idle speed for a minute or so. After this time the engine should idle smoothly at a constant speed.

6 Fuel gauge sender unit – removal and refitting

1 Refer to Chapter 4A, Section 6.

7 Fuel supply pump – removal and refitting

1 The diesel fuel supply pump is located in the same position as the fuel supply pump on petrol engine models, and the removal and refitting procedures are virtually identical. Refer to Chapter 4A, Section 7. On completion, bleed the fuel system as described in Section 5.

8 Fuel tank – removal and refitting

1 Refer to Chapter 4A, Section 8. On completion, bleed the fuel system as described in Section 5.

9.4a Depress the clips above and below each connector...

9.6a Unclip the hoses...

9 Fuel filter crash box – removal and refitting

Removal

1 The fuel filter and crash box are located at the rear of the engine compartment, in the centre of the bulkhead.
2 Remove the windscreen cowl panel as described in Chapter 11 Section 20.

1.7 litre models

3 Release the clip and disconnect the wiring plug from the top of the filter housing.
4 Detach the two fuel hose quick-release connectors and remove the hoses from the fuel filter housing. A Vauxhall/Opel special tool (KM-796-A) is available to disconnect the hose connectors, but provided care is taken, the connections can be released using two screwdrivers, a pair of long-nosed pliers, or similar, to depress the retaining tangs (see illustrations). Suitably cover or plug the open hose connections to prevent dirt entry.
5 Pull the filter housing upwards from the crash box.
6 Unclip the fuel hoses from the bracket, then undo the 2 mounting nuts and remove the crash box (see illustrations).

1.9 litre models

7 Release the fuel supply and return hoses from the clips on the crash box cover.
8 Undo the three bolts and detach the cover from the crash box.

9.4b ...and pull the connectors from the housing

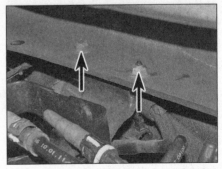

9.6b ...then undo the nuts and remove the crash box

10.3a Unclip and remove the ashtray insert …

10.3b … for access to the diagnostic socket (arrowed)

11.1 Disconnect the air intake duct from the airflow meter

9 Detach the two fuel hose quick-release connectors and remove the hoses from the fuel filter housing and cover. A Vauxhall/Opel special tool (KM-796-A) is available to disconnect the hose connectors, but provided care is taken, the connections can be released using two screwdrivers, a pair of long-nosed pliers, or similar, to depress the retaining tangs. Suitably cover or plug the open hose connections to prevent dirt entry.

10 Disconnect the heater element wiring connector from the fuel filter cover and, where fitted, the water level sensor wiring connector from the base of the filter housing.

11 Pull the fuel filter upwards and remove it from the crash box.

12 Unclip the wiring harness and wiring harness connector from the side of the crash box.

13 Undo the retaining nut and detach the differential pressure sensor from the side of the crash box.

14 Undo the three nuts and remove the crash box from the bulkhead.

Refitting

15 Refitting is the reverse of the removal procedure.

10 Diesel injection system electrical components – testing

1 If a fault is suspected in the electronic control side of the system, first ensure that all the wiring connectors are securely connected and free of corrosion. Ensure that the suspected problem is not of a mechanical nature, or due to poor maintenance; ie, check that the air cleaner filter element is clean, the engine breather hoses are clear and undamaged, and that the cylinder compression pressures are correct, referring to Chapter 1B and the relevant Parts of Chapter 2.

2 If these checks fail to reveal the cause of the problem, the vehicle should be taken to a Vauxhall/Opel dealer or suitably-equipped engine management diagnostic specialist for testing.

3 A diagnostic socket is located in the lower centre of the facia, behind the ashtray insert, to which a fault code reader or other suitable test equipment can be connected (see illustrations). By using the code reader or test equipment, the engine management ECU (and the various other vehicle system ECUs) can be interrogated, and any stored fault codes can be retrieved. This will allow the fault to be quickly and simply traced, alleviating the need to test all the system components individually, which is a time-consuming operation that carries a risk of damaging the ECU.

11 Diesel injection system electrical components – removal and refitting

Airflow meter

1 Slacken the retaining clip securing the air intake duct to the airflow meter and disconnect the duct (see illustration).

2 Disconnect the airflow meter wiring connector, then slacken the retaining clip and remove the airflow meter from the air cleaner housing lid.

3 Refitting is a reversal of removal, but ensure that the arrow on the airflow meter points toward the throttle housing when fitted.

Throttle housing

1.7 litre engines

4 Remove the battery as described in Chapter 5A Section 4.

5 Slacken the clamp and disconnect the outlet hose from the intercooler (see illustration).

6 Disconnect the throttle housing wiring plug.

7 Undo the four Allen bolts securing the throttle housing/flange to the inlet manifold and remove the flange along with the hose (see illustration).

8 Detach the housing from the manifold (see illustration). Renew the O-ring seal each side of the housing.

9 Refitting is a reversal of removal, but thoroughly clean the mating faces and use new seals. Tighten the retaining bolts to the specified torque.

1.9 litre engines

10 Remove the plastic cover over the top of the engine.

11 Slacken the two retaining clips and disconnect the charge air hose from the intercooler and throttle housing.

12 Undo the two bolts and remove the charge air pipe elbow from the throttle housing. Recover the seal.

11.5 Slacken the intercooler outlet hose clamp

11.7 Undo the Allen bolts securing the housing/flange to the manifold

11.8 Renew the seal each side of the housing

11.13 EGR pipe to EGR valve retaining bolts (arrowed)

11.16 The crankshaft speed/position sensor (arrowed) is located below the starter motor

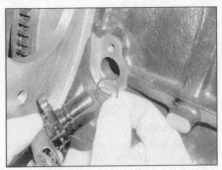

11.19 Renew the sealing ring

13 On SOHC (Z19DT and DTL) engines, undo the four bolts and disconnect the metal EGR pipe from the EGR valve and throttle housing, noting its correct fitted position **(see illustration)**. Recover the two gaskets.

14 Undo the three retaining bolts and remove the throttle housing from the intake manifold. Note the location of any wiring harness support brackets also secured by the retaining bolts.

15 Refitting is a reversal of removal, but thoroughly clean the mating faces and use a new gasket/seal and new EGR pipe gaskets. Tighten the throttle housing retaining bolts securely.

Crankshaft speed/ position sensor

16 The sensor is located at the rear of the cylinder block, below the starter motor **(see illustration)**. To gain access, firmly apply the handbrake, then jack up the front of the car and support it securely on axle stands (see *Jacking and vehicle support*).

17 Undo the retaining bolts and plastic rivets and remove the engine undertray.

18 Wipe clean the area around the crankshaft sensor then disconnect the wiring connector.

19 Slacken and remove the retaining bolt and remove the sensor from the cylinder block. Recover the sealing ring **(see illustration)**.

20 Refitting is the reverse of removal, using a new sealing ring. Tighten the sensor retaining bolt to the specified torque.

Camshaft position sensor

1.7 litre engines

21 Remove the plastic cover from the top of the engine.

22 The camshaft position sensor is located on the front right-hand side of the camshaft housing, adjacent to the camshaft sprocket.

23 Disconnect the camshaft position sensor wiring plug, then undo the retaining bolt and remove the sensor from the mounting bracket **(see illustration)**.

SOHC (Z19DT and DTL) engines

24 The camshaft sensor is located at the right-hand end of the cylinder head, behind the camshaft sprocket.

25 Remove the timing belt and camshaft sprocket as described in Chapter 2C Section 8.

11.23 Disconnect the camshaft position sensor wiring plug

26 Undo the two bolts securing the camshaft sensor bracket to the cylinder head.

27 Disconnect the sensor wiring connector, undo the two bolts and remove the sensor.

28 Refit the sensor using the reverse of removal, tightening the retaining bolts to the specified torque. Refit the camshaft sprocket and timing belt as described in Chapter 2C Section 8.

DOHC (Z19DTH) engines

29 The camshaft sensor is located at the right-hand end of the camshaft housing **(see illustration)**. To gain access, remove the plastic cover over the top of the engine.

30 Wipe clean the area around the camshaft sensor then disconnect the wiring connector. Unclip the wiring harness from the support bracket.

11.36a Charge pressure sensor – 1.7 litre engines

11.29 Camshaft sensor location (arrowed) – Z19DTH engines

31 Slacken and remove the retaining bolt and remove the sensor from the camshaft cover. Recover the sealing ring.

32 Refitting is the reverse of removal, using a new sealing ring. Tighten the sensor retaining bolt to the specified torque.

Coolant temperature sensor

33 Refer to the procedures contained in Chapter 3 Section 6.

Charge (boost) pressure sensor

34 Remove the windscreen cowl panel as described in Chapter 11 Section 20.

35 Remove the plastic cover over the top of the engine.

36 Disconnect the wiring connector from the charge pressure sensor located in intake manifold **(see illustrations)**.

11.36b Disconnect the wiring connector (arrowed) from the charge pressure sensor – 1.9 litre engines

37 Slacken and remove the retaining bolt and remove the sensor from the manifold. Recover the sealing ring.

38 Refitting is the reverse of removal, using a new sealing ring. Tighten the sensor retaining bolt to the specified torque.

Fuel pressure regulator

1.7 litre models

39 According to the manufacturer, on these engines, the regulator must not be detached from the common fuel rail.

1.9 litre models

40 Disconnect the battery negative terminal (refer to Chapter 5A Section 4).

41 Remove the plastic cover over the top of the engine.

42 On SOHC (Z19DT and DTL) engines, remove the fuel rail as described in Section 13.

43 On DOHC (Z19DTH) engines, disconnect the wiring connector from the fuel pressure regulator **(see illustration)**.

44 Remove the regulator from the fuel rail by unscrewing the inner nut (nearest the fuel rail) while counter-holding the regulator body with a second spanner. Be prepared for some loss of fuel.

45 Refitting is the reverse of removal, tightening the regulator to the specified torque.

Electronic control unit (ECU)

Note: *If a new ECU is to be fitted, this work must be entrusted to a Vauxhall/Opel dealer or suitably-equipped specialist. It is necessary to initialise the new ECU after installation, which requires the use of dedicated diagnostic equipment.*

46 Disconnect the battery negative terminal (refer to Chapter 5A Section 4).

47 Firmly apply the handbrake, then jack up the front of the car and support it securely on axle stands (see *Jacking and vehicle support*). Remove the left-hand roadwheel.

48 Undo the two bolts, remove the three plastic rivets and detach the front part of the wheel arch liner from the bumper and underbody.

49 Withdraw the locking plates, lift the locking levers and disconnect the two wiring connectors from the ECU.

50 Undo the four nuts securing the ECU to its mounting frame and remove the ECU from under the bumper **(see illustration)**.

51 Refitting is a reversal of removal, ensuring that the wiring connectors are securely connected and locked with the locking levers.

Turbocharger wastegate solenoid

1.7 litre models

52 The wastegate (charge pressure) solenoid valve is located at the rear of the engine below the high-pressure fuel pump.

53 Firmly apply the handbrake, then jack up the front of the vehicle and support it securely on axle stands (see *Jacking and vehicle support*).

54 Undo the fasteners and remove the engine undertray.

55 Undo the fasteners and remove the engine undertray.

56 Disconnect the wiring plug and two vacuum hoses from the valve, then undo the two retaining bolts and remove the valve from its location.

57 Refitting is a reversal of removal.

1.9 litre models

58 The wastegate (charge pressure) solenoid valve is located under the front bumper on the right-hand side.

59 Firmly apply the handbrake, then jack up the front of the car and support it securely on axle stands (see *Jacking and vehicle support*).

60 Disconnect the wiring connector and the two vacuum hoses from the valve then undo the retaining nuts and remove the valve from its mounting bracket.

61 Refitting is the reverse of removal.

Wheel speed sensors

62 Refer to the anti-lock braking system information contained in Chapter 9 Section 18.

12 High-pressure fuel pump – removal and refitting

⚠️ *Warning: Refer to the information contained in Section 2 before proceeding.*

1.7 litre engines

Removal

Note: *A new fuel pump-to-fuel rail high-pressure fuel pipe and new fuel return pipe banjo union sealing washers will be required for refitting.*

1 Disconnect the battery negative terminal (refer to Chapter 5A Section 4).

2 Remove the engine oil filler cap, then lift off the plastic cover over the top of the engine. Refit the oil filler cap.

3 Remove the windscreen cowl panel as described in Chapter 11 Section 20.

4 Remove the timing belt as described in Chapter 2B Section 7.

5 Remove the high-pressure fuel pump sprocket as described in Chapter 2B Section 8.

6 Disconnect the fuel feed and return hose quick-release connectors at the fuel pump. Be prepared for some loss of fuel. Clamp or plug the open unions, to prevent dirt ingress and further fuel spillage.

7 Unscrew the fuel return pipe banjo union bolt from the side of the fuel pump and collect the two sealing washers.

8 Thoroughly clean the fuel pipe unions on the fuel pump and fuel rail. Using an open-ended spanner, unscrew the union nuts securing the high-pressure fuel pipe to the fuel pump and fuel rail. Counterhold the union on the pump with a second spanner, while unscrewing the union nut. Undo the bolt securing the high-pressure fuel pipe to the support bracket and withdraw the pipe. Plug or cover the open unions to prevent dirt entry.

9 Disconnect the wiring connector from the fuel pump.

10 Unscrew the two retaining nuts and remove the pump from the engine bracket.

Caution: The high-pressure fuel pump is manufactured to extremely close tolerances and must not be dismantled in any way. No parts for the pump are available separately and if the unit is in any way suspect, it must be renewed.

Refitting

11 Refit the pump to the engine bracket and tighten the two retaining nuts to the specified torque.

12 Remove the blanking plugs from the fuel pipe unions on the pump and fuel rail. Locate a new high-pressure fuel pipe over the unions and screw on the union nuts finger tight at this stage.

13 Using a torque wrench and crow-foot adaptor, tighten the fuel pipe union nuts to the specified torque. Counterhold the union on the pump with an open-ended spanner, while

11.43 Disconnect the wiring connector from the fuel pressure regulator – Z19DTH engines

11.50 ECU location (bumper removed for clarity)

tightening the union nut. Refit and tighten the bolt securing the high-pressure fuel pipe to the support bracket.

14 Reconnect the pump wiring connector.

15 Fit new sealing washers to the fuel return pipe pipe banjo union, then screw the banjo union bolt into the fuel pump Tighten the banjo union bolt to the specified torque.

16 Reconnect the fuel feed and return hose quick-release connectors at the fuel pump.

17 Refit the high-pressure fuel pump sprocket as described in Chapter 2B Section 8.

18 Refit the timing belt as described in Chapter 2B Section 7.

19 Refit the windscreen cowl panel as described in Chapter 11 Section 20.

20 Reconnect the battery negative terminal.

21 Observing the precautions listed in Section 2, prime the fuel system as described in Section 5, then start the engine and allow it to idle. Check for leaks at the high-pressure fuel pipe unions with the engine idling. If satisfactory, increase the engine speed to 4000 rpm and check again for leaks. Take the car for a short road test and check for leaks once again on return. If any leaks are detected, obtain and fit a new high-pressure fuel pipe.

22 Refit the engine cover on completion.

SOHC (Z19DT and DTL) engines

Note: *A complete new set of high-pressure fuel pipes will be required for refitting.*

Removal

23 Disconnect the battery negative terminal (refer to Chapter 5A Section 4).

24 Remove the windscreen cowl panel as described in Chapter 11 Section 20.

25 Remove the plastic cover over the top of the engine.

26 Remove the timing belt and the high-pressure fuel pump sprocket as described in Chapter 2C Section 8.

27 Remove the fuel rail as described in Section 13.

28 Disconnect the fuel return hose quick-release fitting on the top of the high-pressure fuel pump. Suitably plug or cover the open unions to prevent dirt entry.

29 Disconnect the wiring connector from the high-pressure fuel pump.

30 Unscrew the three retaining nuts and

12.30a Unscrew the three retaining nuts (arrowed) ...

remove the pump from the engine bracket **(see illustrations)**.

Caution: The high-pressure fuel pump is manufactured to extremely close tolerances and must not be dismantled in any way. No parts for the pump are available separately and if the unit is in any way suspect, it must be renewed.

Refitting

31 Refit the pump to the engine bracket and tighten the retaining nuts to the specified torque.

32 Reconnect the pump wiring connector and the fuel return hose quick-release fitting.

33 Refit the fuel rail as described in Section 13.

34 Refit the high-pressure fuel pump sprocket and the timing belt as described in Chapter 2C Section 8.

35 Reconnect the battery negative terminal.

36 Observing the precautions listed in Section 2, prime the fuel system as described in Section 5, then start the engine and allow it to idle. Check for leaks at the high-pressure fuel pipe unions with the engine idling. If satisfactory, increase the engine speed to 4000 rpm and check again for leaks. If any leaks are detected, obtain and fit a new high-pressure fuel pipe(s).

37 Refit the windscreen cowl panel as described in Chapter 11 Section 20.

38 Refit the engine cover on completion.

DOHC (Z19DTH) engines

Note: *A new fuel pump-to-fuel rail high-pressure fuel pipe will be required for refitting.*

12.30b ... and remove the high-pressure fuel pump from the engine bracket

Removal

39 Disconnect the battery negative terminal (refer to Chapter 5A Section 4).

40 Remove the windscreen cowl panel as described in Chapter 11 Section 20.

41 Remove the plastic cover over the top of the engine.

42 Remove the timing belt and the high-pressure fuel pump sprocket as described in Chapter 2D Section 7.

43 Release the retaining clips and disconnect the two fuel return hoses at the fuel return damping chamber **(see illustrations)**. Suitably plug or cover the open unions to prevent dirt entry.

44 Disconnect the injector leak-off pipe and the fuel return quick-release fitting, then undo the two bolts and remove the damping chamber. Suitably plug or cover the open unions to prevent dirt entry.

45 Disconnect the fuel return hose quick-release fitting on the top of the high-pressure fuel pump. Suitably plug or cover the open unions to prevent dirt entry.

46 Disconnect the wiring connector from the high-pressure fuel pump.

47 Thoroughly clean the fuel pipe unions on the pump and fuel rail. Using an open-ended spanner, unscrew the union nuts securing the high-pressure fuel pipe to the fuel pump and fuel rail. Counter-hold the union on the pump with a second spanner, while unscrewing the union nut **(see illustration)**. Withdraw the high-pressure fuel pipe and plug or cover the open unions to prevent dirt entry.

12.43a Release the clips and disconnect the upper (arrowed) ...

12.43b ... and lower (arrowed) fuel return hoses at the damping chamber

12.47 Counter-hold the fuel pipe union on the pump with a second spanner while unscrewing the union nut

13.4a Open the retaining clip securing the fuel leak-off hose to the fuel rail banjo union...

13.4b ...then disconnect the hose from the banjo union

48 Unscrew the three retaining nuts and remove the pump from the engine bracket (see illustrations 12.8a and 12.8b).
Caution: The high-pressure fuel pump is manufactured to extremely close tolerances and must not be dismantled in any way. No parts for the pump are available separately and if the unit is in any way suspect, it must be renewed.

Refitting

49 Refit the pump to the engine bracket and tighten the retaining bolts to the specified torque.
50 Remove the blanking plugs from the fuel pipe unions on the pump and fuel rail. Locate a new high-pressure fuel pipe over the unions and screw on the union nuts finger tight at this stage.
51 Using a torque wrench and crow-foot adapter, tighten the fuel pipe union nuts to the specified torque. Counter-hold the union on the pump with an open-ended spanner, while tightening the union nut.
52 Reconnect the pump wiring connector and the fuel return hose quick-release fitting.
53 Refit the damping chamber and tighten the retaining bolts securely. Reconnect the injector leak-off pipe, and the two remaining fuel return hoses.
54 Refit the high-pressure fuel pump sprocket and the timing belt as described in Chapter 2D Section 7.
55 Reconnect the battery negative terminal.
56 Observing the precautions listed in Section 2, prime the fuel system as described

in Section 5, then start the engine and allow it to idle. Check for leaks at the high-pressure fuel pipe unions with the engine idling. If satisfactory, increase the engine speed to 4000 rpm and check again for leaks. If any leaks are detected, obtain and fit a new high-pressure fuel pipe(s).
57 Refit the windscreen cowl panel as described in Chapter 11 Section 20.
58 Refit the engine cover on completion.

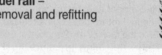

13 Fuel rail –
removal and refitting

> **Warning: Refer to the information contained in Section 2 before proceeding.**

1.7 litre engines

Removal

Note: *A complete new set of high-pressure fuel pipes will be required for refitting.*
1 Disconnect the battery negative terminal (refer to Chapter 5A Section 4).
2 Remove the windscreen cowl panel as described in Chapter 11 Section 20.
3 Remove the engine oil filler cap, then lift off the plastic cover over the top of the engine. Refit the oil filler cap.
4 Open the retaining clip securing the fuel leak-off hose to the banjo union on the fuel rail, then disconnect the hose from the banjo

union **(see illustrations)**. Plug or cover the banjo union and hose to prevent dirt entry.
5 Undo the bolt securing the fuel leak-off hose support clip to the inlet manifold and move the hose to one side **(see illustration)**.
6 Thoroughly clean the fuel pipe unions on the fuel injectors and fuel rail. Using an open-ended spanner, unscrew the union nuts securing the high-pressure fuel pipes to the injectors and fuel rail. Counterhold the union on the fuel rail with a second spanner, while unscrewing the union nut. Withdraw the high-pressure fuel pipes and plug or cover the open unions to prevent dirt entry **(see illustration)**.
7 Thoroughly clean the fuel pipe unions on the fuel pump and fuel rail. Using an open-ended spanner, unscrew the union nuts securing the high-pressure fuel pipe to the fuel pump and fuel rail. Counterhold the union on the pump with a second spanner, while unscrewing the union nut. Undo the bolt securing the high-pressure fuel pipe to the support bracket and withdraw the pipe. Plug or cover the open unions to prevent dirt entry.
8 Disconnect the wiring connector from the fuel pressure sensor on the end of the fuel rail.
9 Unscrew and remove the two fuel rail retaining bolts. Lift away the fuel rail and remove it from the engine.

Refitting

10 Locate the fuel rail in position and refit the two retaining bolts. Tighten the bolts finger tight only at this stage.
11 Reconnect the wiring connector to the fuel pressure sensor.
12 Remove the blanking plugs from the fuel pipe unions on the fuel rail and fuel injectors. Locate the new high-pressure fuel pipes over the unions and screw on the union nuts finger tight.
13 Similarly, fit a new high-pressure fuel pipe to the fuel pump and fuel rail, and tighten the union nuts finger tight. Refit and tighten the bolt securing the high-pressure fuel pipe to the support bracket.
14 Tighten the two fuel rail retaining bolts to the specified torque.
15 Using a torque wrench and crow-foot adaptor, tighten the fuel pipe unions on the injectors and fuel rail to the specified torque **(see illustration)**. Similarly tighten the fuel

13.5 Undo the bolt (arrowed) securing the fuel leak-off hose support clip to the inlet manifold and move the hose to one side

13.6 Unscrew the union nuts and remove the high-pressure fuel pipes from the injectors and fuel rail

13.15 Tighten the fuel pipe union nuts using a torque wrench and crow-foot adaptor

13.26a Undo the two bolts at the top (arrowed) ...

13.26b ... and the two bolts at the front (arrowed) and move the wiring trough and harness to one side

13.44 Unscrew the union nuts securing the high-pressure fuel pipes to the fuel rail and injectors

pipe unions on the fuel pump and fuel rail while counterholding the unions with an open-ended spanner.

16 Refit the bolt securing the leak-off hose support clip to the inlet manifold and tighten it securely.

17 Reconnect the leak-off hose to the banjo union on the fuel rail and secure the hose with a new retaining clip.

18 Reconnect the vacuum hose to the EGR vacuum valve and secure the hose with the retaining clips.

19 Refit the windscreen cowl panel as described in Chapter 11 Section 20.

20 Observing the precautions listed in Section 2, prime the fuel system as described in Section 5, then start the engine and allow it to idle. Check for leaks at the high-pressure fuel pipe unions with the engine idling. If satisfactory, increase the engine speed to 4000 rpm and check again for leaks. Take the car for a short road test and check for leaks once again on return. If any leaks are detected, obtain and fit a new high-pressure fuel pipe(s).

21 Refit the engine cover on completion.

SOHC (Z19DT and DTL) engines

Note: *A complete new set of high-pressure fuel pipes will be required for refitting.*

Removal

22 Disconnect the battery negative terminal (refer to Chapter 5A Section 4).

23 Remove the windscreen cowl panel as described in Chapter 11 Section 20.

24 Remove the plastic cover over the top of the engine.

25 Release the locking catches securing the wiring connectors to the four injectors, then disconnect the injector wiring.

26 Undo the two bolts at the top and the two bolts at the front, securing the plastic wiring trough to the intake manifold **(see illustrations)**. Move the wiring trough and injector wiring harness to one side.

27 Release the retaining clips and disconnect the two fuel return hoses at the fuel return damping chamber. Suitably plug or cover the open unions to prevent dirt entry.

28 Disconnect the injector leak-off pipe and the fuel return quick-release fitting, then undo the two bolts and remove the damping chamber. Suitably plug or cover the open unions to prevent dirt entry.

29 Thoroughly clean the fuel pipe unions on the fuel pump and fuel rail. Using an open-ended spanner, unscrew the union nuts securing the high-pressure fuel pipe to the fuel pump and fuel rail. Counter-hold the unions on the pump with a second spanner, while unscrewing the union nuts. Withdraw the high-pressure fuel pipe and plug or cover the open unions to prevent dirt entry.

30 Using two spanners, hold the unions and unscrew the union nuts securing the high-pressure fuel pipes to the fuel injectors. Unscrew the union nuts securing the high-pressure fuel pipes to the fuel rail, withdraw the pipes and plug or cover the open unions to prevent dirt entry.

31 Disconnect the wiring connectors at the fuel pressure regulator and fuel pressure sensor, then undo the two nuts and remove the fuel rail.

Refitting

32 Refit the fuel rail and tighten the retaining nuts to the specified torque. Reconnect the fuel pressure regulator and fuel pressure sensor wiring connectors.

33 Working on one fuel injector at a time, remove the blanking plugs from the fuel pipe unions on the fuel rail and the relevant injector. Locate the new high-pressure fuel pipe over the unions and screw on the union nuts finger-tight. Tighten the union nuts to the specified torque using a torque wrench and crow-foot adapter. Counter-hold the union on the injector with an open-ended spanner, while tightening the union nut. Repeat this operation for the remaining three injectors.

34 Similarly, fit the new high-pressure fuel pipe to the fuel pump and fuel rail, and tighten the union nuts to the specified torque. Counter-hold the union on the pump with an open-ended spanner, while tightening the union nut.

35 Refit the damping chamber and tighten the retaining bolts securely. Reconnect the

injector leak-off pipe, and the fuel return hoses.

36 Refit the wiring trough, and secure with the four retaining bolts. Reconnect the wiring connectors to the fuel injectors.

37 Reconnect the battery negative terminal.

38 Observing the precautions listed in Section 2, prime the fuel system as described in Section 5, then start the engine and allow it to idle. Check for leaks at the high-pressure fuel pipe unions with the engine idling. If satisfactory, increase the engine speed to 4000 rpm and check again for leaks. If any leaks are detected, obtain and fit a new high-pressure fuel pipe(s).

39 Refit the windscreen cowl panel as described in Chapter 11 Section 20.

40 Refit the engine cover on completion.

DOHC (Z19DTH) engines

Note: *A complete new set of high-pressure fuel pipes will be required for refitting.*

Removal

41 Disconnect the battery negative terminal (refer to Chapter 5A Section 4).

42 Remove the windscreen cowl panel as described in Chapter 11 Section 20.

43 Remove the plastic cover over the top of the engine.

44 Thoroughly clean all the high-pressure fuel pipe unions on the fuel rail, fuel pump and injectors. Using two spanners, hold the unions and unscrew the union nuts securing the high-pressure fuel pipes to the fuel injectors. Unscrew the union nuts securing the high-pressure fuel pipes to the fuel rail, withdraw the pipes and plug or cover the open unions to prevent dirt entry **(see illustration)**.

45 Using an open-ended spanner, unscrew the union nuts securing the high-pressure fuel pipe to the fuel pump and fuel rail **(see illustration)**. Counter-hold the unions on the pump with a second spanner, while unscrewing the union nuts. Withdraw the high-pressure fuel pipe and plug or cover the open unions to prevent dirt entry.

46 Disconnect the wiring connectors at the fuel pressure regulator and fuel pressure sensor, then release the clip and disconnect

13.45 Unscrew the union nuts securing the high-pressure fuel pipe to the fuel pump and fuel rail

13.46a Disconnect the fuel return hose ...

13.46b ... then undo the two bolts (arrowed) and remove the fuel rail

the fuel return hose. Undo the two bolts and remove the fuel rail **(see illustrations)**.

Refitting

47 Refit the fuel rail and tighten the retaining bolts to the specified torque. Reconnect the fuel pressure regulator and fuel pressure sensor wiring connectors, and reconnect the fuel return hose.

48 Working on one fuel injector at a time, remove the blanking plugs from the fuel pipe unions on the fuel rail and the relevant injector. Locate the new high-pressure fuel pipe over the unions and screw on the union nuts finger tight. Tighten the union nuts to the specified torque using a torque wrench and crow-foot adapter. Counter-hold the union on the injector with an open-ended spanner, while tightening the union nut. Repeat this operation for the remaining three injectors.

49 Similarly, fit the new high-pressure fuel pipe to the fuel pump and fuel rail, and tighten the union nuts to the specified torque. Counter-hold the union on the pump with an open-ended spanner, while tightening the union nut.

50 Reconnect the battery negative terminal.

51 Observing the precautions listed in Section 2, prime the fuel system as described in Section 5, then start the engine and allow it to idle. Check for leaks at the high-pressure fuel pipe unions with the engine idling. If satisfactory, increase the engine speed to 4000 rpm and check again for leaks. If any leaks are detected, obtain and fit a new high-pressure fuel pipe(s).

52 Refit the windscreen cowl panel as described in Chapter 11 Section 20.

53 Refit the engine cover on completion.

14 Fuel injectors – removal and refitting

⚠️ *Warning: Refer to the information contained in Section 2 before proceeding.*

1.7 litre engines

Removal

Note: *A new copper washer, O-ring seal and high-pressure fuel pipe will be required for each removed injector when refitting.*

1 Remove the camshaft cover as described in Chapter 2B Section 4.

2 Before removing the injectors it is advisable to mark their fitted position in relation to the camshaft housing. This will ensure that the injector extension will fit centrally through the seal rings in the camshaft cover and will also prevent any difficulties when screwing on the fuel pipe union nuts. Place a square or similar tool on the camshaft housing and in contact with the injector extension. Using a permanent ink marker pen, mark the position of the edge of the square on the camshaft housing surface **(see illustration)**.

3 Starting with injector No 1, unscrew the

retaining bolt then remove the injector clamp bracket **(see illustration)**.

4 Using pointed-nose pliers, lift out the clamp bracket locating dowel from the camshaft housing **(see illustration)**.

5 Withdraw the injector from the cylinder head, twisting it from side-to-side if it is initially tight.

6 Once the injector has been withdrawn, remove the copper washer from the injector base **(see illustration 14.30)**. The copper washer may have remained in place at the base of the injector orifice in the cylinder head. If so, hook it out with a length of wire.

7 Remove the remaining injectors in the same way. Label the injectors (1 to 4) so they can be refitted in their original cylinders (unless new injectors are to be fitted).

8 Examine the injector visually for any signs of obvious damage or deterioration. If any defects are apparent, renew the injector. *Caution: The injectors are manufactured to extremely close tolerances and must not be dismantled in any way. Do not unscrew the fuel pipe union on the side of the injector, or separate any parts of the injector body. Do not attempt to clean carbon deposits from the injector nozzle or carry out any form of ultra-sonic or pressure testing.*

9 If the injectors are in a satisfactory condition, plug the fuel pipe union (if not already done) and suitably cover the electrical element and the injector nozzle.

10 Prior to refitting, obtain a new copper

14.2 Mark the position of the injectors on the camshaft housing surface

14.3 Unscrew the retaining bolt (arrowed) then remove the injector clamp bracket

14.4 Lift out the clamp bracket locating dowel from the camshaft housing

washer and high-pressure fuel pipe for each injector.

Refitting

11 Thoroughly clean the injector seat in the cylinder head, ensuring all traces of carbon and other deposits are removed.

12 Locate a new copper washer on the base of the injector.

13 Place the injector in position in the cylinder head.

14 Refit the clamp bracket locating dowel to the camshaft housing, then engage the clamp bracket over the injector. Refit the clamp bracket retaining bolt finger tight only at this stage.

15 Using the square, align the injector with the marks made on the camshaft housing during removal. To be absolutely sure that the injector is correctly aligned, temporarily refit the high-pressure fuel pipe to the injector and fuel rail and lightly tighten the union nuts.

16 Tighten the clamp bracket retaining bolt to the specified torque in the three stages given in the specifications. Remove the high-pressure fuel pipe.

17 Repeat this procedure for the remaining injectors.

18 Once all the injectors are installed, refit the camshaft cover as described in Chapter 2B Section 4.

19 Observing the precautions listed in Section 2, prime the fuel system as described in Section 5, then start the engine and allow it to idle. Check for leaks at the high-pressure fuel pipe unions with the engine idling. If satisfactory, increase the engine speed to 4000 rpm and check again for leaks. Take the car for a short road test and check for leaks once again on return. If any leaks are detected, obtain and fit a new high-pressure fuel pipe(s).

20 Refit the engine cover on completion.

SOHC (Z19DT and DTL) engines

Note: *A new copper washer, retaining nut and high-pressure fuel pipe will be required for each removed injector when refitting.*

Note: *The injector is an extremely tight fit in the cylinder head, and it is likely that the special Vauxhall/Opel puller (KM-328-B) and adapter (EN-46786) or suitable alternatives, will be needed.*

Removal

21 Disconnect the battery negative terminal (refer to Chapter 5A Section 4).

22 Remove the windscreen cowl panel as described in Chapter 11 Section 20.

23 Remove the plastic cover over the top of the engine.

24 Release the locking catches securing the wiring connectors to the four injectors, then disconnect the injector wiring.

25 Undo the two bolts at the top and the two bolts at the front, securing the plastic wiring trough to the intake manifold **(see illustrations 13.26a and 13.26b)**. Move the

wiring trough and injector wiring harness to one side.

26 Thoroughly clean the fuel pipe unions on the fuel rail and injector. Using two spanners, hold the unions and unscrew the union nut securing the high-pressure fuel pipe to the fuel injector. Unscrew the union nut securing the high-pressure fuel pipe to the fuel rail, withdraw the pipe and plug or cover the open unions to prevent dirt entry.

27 Disconnect the fuel leak-off hose connection at each injector by pushing in the locking clip and lifting out the hose fitting. Suitably plug or cap the leak-off hose union on each injector, and slip a plastic bag over the disconnected leak-off hose to prevent dirt entry.

28 Unscrew the retaining nut then remove the washer from the injector clamp bracket.

29 Withdraw the injector together with the clamp bracket from the cylinder head. If difficulty is experienced removing the injector, liberally apply penetrating oil to the base of the injector and allow time for the oil to penetrate. If the injector is still reluctant to free, it will be necessary to use a small slide hammer engaged under the flange of the injector body casting, and gently tap free. If available, use Vauxhall/Opel special tools EN-46786 and KM-328-B for this purpose. Note that it is not possible to twist the injector from side-to-side to free them due to the design of the clamp bracket.

30 Once the injector has been removed, separate it from the clamp bracket and remove the copper washer from the injector base **(see illustration)**. The copper washer may have remained in place at the base of the injector orifice in the cylinder head. If so, hook it out with a length of wire.

31 Remove the remaining injectors in the same way. Label the injectors (1 to 4) so they can be refitted in their original cylinders (unless new injectors are to be fitted).

32 Examine the injector visually for any signs of obvious damage or deterioration. If any defects are apparent, renew the injector.

Caution: The injectors are manufactured to extremely close tolerances and must not be dismantled in any way. Do not unscrew the fuel pipe union on the side of the injector, or separate any parts of the injector body.

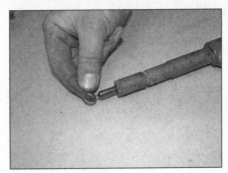

14.30 Remove the copper washer from the injector base

Do not attempt to clean carbon deposits from the injector nozzle or carry out any form of ultrasonic or pressure testing.

33 If the injectors are in a satisfactory condition, plug the fuel pipe union (if not already done) and suitably cover the electrical element and the injector nozzle.

34 Prior to refitting, obtain a new copper washer a new retaining nut and new high-pressure fuel pipe for each injector.

Refitting

35 Thoroughly clean the injector seat in the cylinder head, ensuring all traces of carbon and other deposits are removed.

36 Locate a new copper washer on the base of the injector.

37 Place the injector clamp bracket in the slot on the injector body and refit the injector to the cylinder head.

38 Fit the washer and the new injector clamp bracket retaining nut and tighten the nut to the specified torque.

39 Remove the blanking plug from the fuel pipe union on the fuel rail and the injector. Locate the new high-pressure fuel pipe over the unions and screw on the union nuts. Take care not to cross-thread the nuts or strain the fuel pipe as it is fitted.

40 Tighten the fuel pipe union nuts to the specified torque using a torque wrench and crow-foot adapter **(see illustration 14.66)**. Counter-hold the union on the injector with an open-ended spanner, while tightening the union nut.

41 Repeat this procedure for the remaining injectors.

42 Refit the wiring trough, and secure with the four retaining bolts. Reconnect the wiring connectors to the fuel injectors.

43 Reconnect the leak-off hose fittings to the injectors by pushing in the locking clip, attaching the fitting, then releasing the locking clip. Ensure that each fitting is securely connected and retained by the clip.

44 Reconnect the battery negative terminal.

45 Observing the precautions listed in Section 2, prime the fuel system as described in Section 5, then start the engine and allow it to idle. Check for leaks at the high-pressure fuel pipe unions with the engine idling. If satisfactory, increase the engine speed to 4000 rpm and check again for leaks. If any leaks are detected, obtain and fit a new high-pressure fuel pipe(s).

46 Refit the windscreen cowl panel as described in Chapter 11 Section 20.

47 Refit the engine cover on completion.

DOHC (Z19DTH) engines

Note: *A new copper washer, retaining nut and high-pressure fuel pipe will be required for each removed injector when refitting.*

Note: *The injector is an extremely tight fit in the cylinder head, and it is likely that the special Vauxhall/Opel puller (KM-328-B) and adapter (EN-46786) or suitable alternatives, will be needed.*

14.50 Undo the two bolts (arrowed) and remove the breather pipe from the cylinder head

14.51a Release the locking catches ...

14.51b ... and disconnect the injector wiring connectors

Removal

48 Disconnect the battery negative terminal (refer to Chapter 5A Section 4).

49 Remove the plastic cover over the top of the engine.

50 Release the retaining clip securing the engine breather hose to the breather pipe adjacent to the engine oil dipstick. Undo the two bolts securing the breather pipe to the cylinder head, and disconnect the pipe from the hose **(see illustration)**.

51 Release the locking catches securing the wiring connectors to the four injectors, then disconnect the injector wiring **(see illustrations)**.

52 Disconnect the fuel leak-off hose connection at each injector by pushing in the locking clip and lifting out the hose fitting.

Suitably plug or cap the leak-off hose union on each injector, and slip a plastic bag over the disconnected leak-off hose to prevent dirt entry **(see illustrations)**.

53 Thoroughly clean the fuel pipe unions on the fuel rail and injector. Using two spanners, hold the unions and unscrew the union nut securing the high-pressure fuel pipe to the fuel injector **(see illustration)**. Unscrew the union nut securing the high-pressure fuel pipe to the fuel rail, withdraw the pipe and plug or cover the open unions to prevent dirt entry.

54 Starting with injector No 1, unscrew the retaining nut then remove the washer from the injector clamp bracket **(see illustration)**.

55 Withdraw the injector together with the clamp bracket from the cylinder head. If difficulty is experienced removing the injector,

liberally apply penetrating oil to the base of the injector and allow time for the oil to penetrate. If the injector is still reluctant to free, it will be necessary to use a small slide hammer engaged under the flange of the injector body casting, and gently tap it free **(see illustration)**. If available, use Vauxhall/Opel special tools EN-46786 and KM-328-B for this purpose. Note that it is not possible to twist the injector from side-to-side to free them due to the design of the clamp bracket.

56 Once the injector has been removed, separate it from the clamp bracket and remove the copper washer from the injector base **(see illustration)**. The copper washer may have remained in place at the base of the injector orifice in the cylinder head. If so, hook it out with a length of wire.

14.52a Disconnect the fuel leak-off hose connection at each injector ...

14.52b ... then plug or cap the leak-off hose union on each injector

14.53 Counter-hold the injector union when unscrewing the high-pressure fuel pipe unions

14.54 Unscrew the injector clamp bracket retaining nut then remove the washer

14.55 Using a small slide hammer to free the injector body from the cylinder head

14.56 Once the injector has been removed, separate it from the clamp bracket

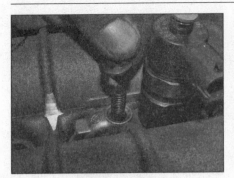

14.64a Fit the washer …

14.64b … and the injector clamp bracket retaining nut

57 Remove the remaining injectors in the same way. Label the injectors (1 to 4) so they can be refitted in their original cylinders (unless new injectors are to be fitted).
58 Examine the injector visually for any signs of obvious damage or deterioration. If any defects are apparent, renew the injector.
Caution: The injectors are manufactured to extremely close tolerances and must not be dismantled in any way. Do not unscrew the fuel pipe union on the side of the injector, or separate any parts of the injector body. Do not attempt to clean carbon deposits from the injector nozzle or carry out any form of ultrasonic or pressure testing.
59 If the injectors are in a satisfactory condition, plug the fuel pipe union (if not already done) and suitably cover the electrical element and the injector nozzle.
60 Prior to refitting, obtain a new set of copper washers, retaining nuts and high-pressure fuel pipes.

Refitting

61 Thoroughly clean the injector seat in the cylinder head, ensuring all traces of carbon and other deposits are removed.
62 Starting with injector No 4, locate a new copper washer on the base of the injector.
63 Place the injector clamp bracket in the slot on the injector body and refit the injector to the cylinder head.
64 Fit the washer and the injector clamp bracket retaining nut and tighten the nut to the specified torque **(see illustrations)**.
65 Remove the blanking plug from the fuel

pipe union on the fuel rail and the injector. Locate the new high-pressure fuel pipe over the unions and screw on the union nuts. Take care not to cross-thread the nuts or strain the fuel pipe as it is fitted.
66 Tighten the fuel pipe union nuts to the specified torque using a torque wrench and crow-foot adapter **(see illustration)**. Counter-hold the union on the injector with an open-ended spanner, while tightening the union nut.
67 Repeat this procedure for the remaining injectors.
68 Reconnect the leak-off hose fittings to the injectors by pushing in the locking clip, attaching the fitting, then releasing the locking clip. Ensure that each fitting is securely connected and retained by the clip.
69 Reconnect the wiring connectors to the fuel injectors.
70 Attach the engine breather hose to the breather pipe and secure with the retaining clip. Secure the breather pipe to the cylinder head with the two bolts securely tightened.
71 Reconnect the battery negative terminal.
72 Observing the precautions listed in Section 2, prime the fuel system as described in Section 5, then start the engine and allow it to idle. Check for leaks at the high-pressure fuel pipe unions with the engine idling. If satisfactory, increase the engine speed to 4000 rpm and check again for leaks. If any leaks are detected, obtain and fit a new high-pressure fuel pipe(s).
73 Refit the engine cover on completion.

15 Intake manifold – removal and refitting

1.7 litre engnes
Removal

1 Remove the battery and battery tray as described in Chapter 5A Section 4.
2 Remove the windscreen cowl panel as described in Chapter 11 Section 20.
3 Drain the cooling system as described in Chapter 1B Section 30.
4 Remove the fuel rail as described in Section 13.
5 Remove the EGR valve as described in Chapter 4C Section 3.
6 Undo the three bolts securing the wiring harness trough to the top of the camshaft cover **(see illustration)**.
7 Disconnect the wiring connectors from the following components:
a) Coolant temperature sensor.
b) Throttle housing.
c) Fuel injectors.
d) Glow plugs.
e) Camshaft sensor.
f) Airflow meter.
g) Inlet manifold vacuum solenoid valves.
h) Charge (boost) pressure sensor.
i) Pre/post heating system control unit.
j) Wiring harness connection plug.
8 Release the wiring harness from the cable ties and retaining clips and move the harness to one side.
9 Spread the sides of the wire retaining clip and disconnect the intercooler outlet air duct from the throttle housing.
10 Remove the oil filter housing as described in Chapter 2B Section 17.
11 Disconnect the vacuum hoses from the two solenoid valves on the underside of the inlet manifold. Release the vacuum hoses from the retaining clips.
12 Undo the bolt securing the underside of the inlet manifold front section to the thermostat housing bracket.
13 Undo the two bolts securing the inlet manifold rear support bracket to the cylinder head.
14 Undo the eight bolts and two nuts, then remove the inlet manifold from the cylinder head **(see illustration)**. Recover the gasket.

14.66 Tighten the fuel pipe union nuts to the specified torque using a torque wrench and crow-foot adapter

15.6 Undo the three bolts (arrowed) securing the wiring harness trough to the camshaft cover

15.14 Undo the eight bolts and two nuts, then remove the inlet manifold from the cylinder head

Refitting

15 Thoroughly clean the inlet manifold and cylinder head mating faces.

16 Place a new gasket on the inlet manifold flange, then position the manifold over the cylinder head studs.

17 Refit the manifold retaining bolts and nuts and tighten them finger tight only at this stage.

18 Refit the two bolts securing the inlet manifold rear support bracket to the cylinder head and tighten them finger tight only at this stage.

19 Refit the bolt securing the underside of the inlet manifold front section to the thermostat housing bracket and tighten it finger tight only at this stage.

20 Working in a diagonal sequence, progressively, tighten the manifold retaining bolts and nuts to the specified torque.

21 Tighten the three manifold support bracket bolts to the specified torque.

22 Reconnect the vacuum hoses to the two solenoid valves on the underside of the inlet manifold. Secure the vacuum hoses in the retaining clips.

23 Refit the oil filter housing as described in Chapter 2B Section 17.

24 Reconnect the intercooler outlet air duct to the throttle housing.

25 Reconnect the wiring connectors to the components listed in paragraph 5.

26 Refit and tighten the three bolts securing the wiring harness trough to the top of the camshaft cover. Secure the wiring harness with the cable ties and retaining clips.

27 Refit the EGR valve as described in Chapter 4C Section 3.

28 Refit the fuel rail as described in Section 13.

29 Refill the cooling system as described in Chapter 1B Section 30.

30 Refit the windscreen cowl panel as described in Chapter 11 Section 20.

31 Refit the battery and battery tray as described in Chapter 5A Section 4.

32 Observing the precautions listed in Section 2, prime the fuel system as described in Section 5, then start the engine and allow it to idle. Check for leaks at the high-pressure fuel pipe unions with the engine idling. If satisfactory, increase the engine speed to 4000 rpm and check again for leaks. If any leaks are detected, obtain and fit a new high-pressure fuel pipe.

33 Refit the engine cover on completion.

SOHC (Z19DT and DTL) engines

Removal

34 Disconnect the battery negative terminal (refer to Chapter 5A Section 4).

35 Remove the plastic cover over the top of the engine.

36 Drain the cooling system as described in Chapter 1B Section 30.

37 Remove the exhaust gas recirculation (EGR) valve as described in Chapter 4C Section 3.

38 Remove the high-pressure fuel pump as described in Section 12.

39 Undo the retaining bolt(s) to release the

vacuum lines running over the top of the camshaft cover **(see illustration)**.

40 Remove the throttle housing as described in Section 11.

41 Disconnect the wiring connectors at the four glow plugs.

42 Undo the three retaining bolts and detach the vacuum reservoir from the rear of the cylinder block.

43 Release the retaining clips and disconnect the two coolant hoses at the EGR heat exchanger, and the adjacent hose at the thermostat housing.

44 Unscrew the nut and two bolts securing the coolant pipes to the starter motor bracket.

45 Release the clamp and disconnect the metal pipe from the EGR heat exchanger. Undo the retaining nut and bolt and remove the heat exchanger.

46 Remove the alternator as described in Chapter 5A Section 8.

47 Undo the six bolts securing the alternator and high-pressure fuel pump mounting bracket to the cylinder block and cylinder head. There are five bolts securing the bracket to the block at the rear, and one securing the bracket to the head at the front.

48 Undo the nine retaining nuts and remove the intake manifold from the cylinder head studs. Recover the gasket.

Refitting

49 Thoroughly clean the intake manifold and cylinder head mating faces, then locate a new gasket on the intake manifold flange.

50 Locate the manifold in position and refit the retaining nuts. Diagonally and progressively, tighten the nuts to the specified torque.

51 Refit the alternator and high-pressure fuel pump bracket and tighten the retaining bolts to the specified torque.

52 Refit the alternator as described in Chapter 5A Section 8.

53 Refit the EGR heat exchanger and securely tighten the retaining nut and bolt. Reconnect the metal EGR pipe and secure with the retaining clamp.

54 Locate the coolant pipe on the starter motor bracket. Refit and securely tighten the retaining nut and bolts.

55 Reconnect the coolant hoses to the EGR

heat exchanger and thermostat housing and secure with the retaining clips.

56 Attach the vacuum reservoir to the cylinder block, refit the three retaining bolts and tighten securely.

57 Reconnect the wiring connectors to the glow plugs.

58 Refit the throttle housing as described in Section 11.

59 Refit the vacuum lines running over the top of the camshaft cover and reconnect the vacuum hoses.

60 Refit the high-pressure fuel pump as described in Section 12.

61 Refit the exhaust gas recirculation (EGR) valve as described in Chapter 4C Section 3.

62 Refill the cooling system as described in Chapter 1B Section 30.

63 Reconnect the battery negative terminal.

64 Observing the precautions listed in Section 2, prime the fuel system as described in Section 5, then start the engine and allow it to idle. Check for leaks at the high-pressure fuel pipe unions with the engine idling. If satisfactory, increase the engine speed to 4000 rpm and check again for leaks. If any leaks are detected, obtain and fit a new high-pressure fuel pipe.

65 Refit the engine cover on completion.

DOHC (Z19DTH) engines

Removal

66 Disconnect the battery negative terminal (refer to Chapter 5A Section 4).

67 Remove the plastic cover over the top of the engine.

68 Remove the fuel filter crash box as described in Section 9.

69 Remove the throttle housing as described in Section 11.

70 Remove the high-pressure fuel pump as described in Section 12.

71 Remove the exhaust gas recirculation (EGR) valve as described in Chapter 4C Section 3.

72 Disconnect the four vacuum hoses then undo the bolt(s) and remove the two vacuum pipes over the top of the intake manifold.

73 Unscrew the two nuts securing the wiring harness and coolant pipes to the starter motor bracket. Free the harness and pipes from the bracket **(see illustration)**.

15.39 Undo the retaining bolt(s) to release the vacuum lines from the camshaft cover

15.73 Unscrew the two nuts and free the wiring harness and coolant pipes from the starter motor bracket

15.75a Undo the two nuts (arrowed) above the vacuum reservoir ...

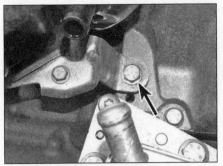

15.75b ... the bolt at the base of the vacuum reservoir ...

15.75c ... and the bolt at the right-hand side of the oil separator ...

15.75d ... then remove the mounting bracket complete with oil separator and vacuum reservoir

15.77 Lock two nuts together and unscrew the fuel pump stud from the engine bracket

15.79 Intake manifold retaining nuts (arrowed)

74 Release the clips and disconnect the crankcase breather hoses from the top and bottom of the oil separator.

75 Remove the oil separator and vacuum reservoir mounting bracket by undoing the two nuts above the vacuum reservoir, the bolt at the base of the vacuum reservoir, and the bolt at the right-hand side of the oil separator. Remove the mounting bracket complete with oil separator and vacuum reservoir **(see illustrations)**.

76 Undo the three bolts, release the hose clip, free the wiring harness and detach the coolant pipe from the intake manifold.

77 Screw two nuts onto the inner high-pressure fuel pump mounting stud. Lock the two nuts together and unscrew the stud from the engine bracket **(see illustration)**.

78 Disconnect the wiring connectors at the throttle housing and charge (boost) pressure sensor.

79 Undo the nine retaining nuts and remove the intake manifold from the cylinder head studs **(see illustration)**. Recover the gasket.

80 The changeover flap actuator drive can be removed by disconnecting the drive motor actuating rod ball socket, and undoing the two stud bolts.

Refitting

81 If removed, refit the changeover flap actuator drive.

82 Thoroughly clean the intake manifold and cylinder head mating faces, then locate a new gasket on the intake manifold flange.

83 Locate the manifold in position and

refit the retaining nuts. Diagonally and progressively, tighten the nuts to the specified torque.

84 Reconnect the wiring connectors at the throttle housing and charge (boost) pressure sensor.

85 Refit the high-pressure fuel pump mounting stud, then remove the two nuts used to remove/refit the stud.

86 Refit the coolant pipe to the manifold, and secure with the three bolts tightened securely. Reconnect the coolant pipe and attach the wiring harness.

87 Refit the oil separator and vacuum reservoir mounting bracket. Refit and tighten the two bolts and two nuts, then reconnect the crankcase breather hoses.

88 Refit the coolant pipe and wiring harness to the starter motor bracket, then refit and tighten the two nuts.

89 Refit the vacuum pipes over the manifold and reconnect the four vacuum pipes.

90 Refit the exhaust gas recirculation (EGR) valve as described in Chapter 4C Section 3.

91 Refit the high-pressure fuel pump as described in Section 12.

92 Refit the throttle housing as described in Section 11.

93 Refit the fuel filter crash box as described in Section 9.

94 Reconnect the battery negative terminal.

95 Observing the precautions listed in Section 2, prime the fuel system as described in Section 5, then start the engine and allow it to idle. Check for leaks at the high-pressure

fuel pipe unions with the engine idling. If satisfactory, increase the engine speed to 4000 rpm and check again for leaks. If any leaks are detected, obtain and fit a new high-pressure fuel pipe.

96 Refit the engine cover on completion.

16 Intake manifold changeover flap actuator drive – removal and refitting

Note: *The intake manifold changeover flap actuator drive is only fitted to DOHC (Z19DTH) engines.*

Removal

1 Disconnect the battery negative terminal (refer to Chapter 5A Section 4).

2 Remove the plastic cover over the top of the engine.

3 Remove the fuel filter crash box as described in Section 9.

4 Disconnect the four vacuum hoses then undo the bolt(s) and remove the two vacuum pipes over the top of the intake manifold.

5 Unscrew the two nuts securing the wiring harness and coolant pipes to the starter motor bracket. Free the harness and pipes from the bracket **(see illustration 15.73)**.

6 Release the clips and disconnect the crankcase breather hoses from the top and bottom of the oil separator.

7 Remove the oil separator and vacuum reservoir mounting bracket by undoing the two nuts above the vacuum reservoir, the bolt at the base of the vacuum reservoir, and the bolt at the right-hand side of the oil separator. Remove the mounting bracket complete with oil separator and vacuum reservoir **(see illustrations 15.75a to 15.75d)**.

8 Disconnect the drive motor actuating rod ball socket, and undoing the two stud bolts **(see illustration)**.

9 Withdraw the assembly from the intake manifold and disconnect the wiring connector.

Refitting

10 Refitting is the reverse of removal.

17 Intercooler –
removal and refitting

Removal

1 Disconnect the battery negative lead as described in Chapter 5A Section 4.

1.7 litre engines

2 Slacken the clamps and disconnect the two charge air hoses **(see illustration)**.

3 Remove the front bumper as described in Chapter 11 Section 6.

4 Undo the two nuts securing the windscreen washer fluid reservoir **(see illustrations)**.

5 Undo and remove the two bolts/nuts securing the left-hand end of the bumper support bar, then slacken the right-hand bolts/nuts **(see illustration)**.

6 Release the wiring harness, undo the three bolts, move the washer fluid reservoir to one side, pull the bumper support bar forwards

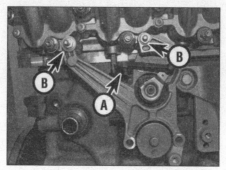

16.8 Disconnect the actuating rod ball socket (A), undo the two stud bolts (B) and remove the actuator drive

a little, then lower the intercooler from place **(see illustrations)**.

1.9 litre engines

7 Remove the plastic cover from the top of the engine.

8 Remove the radiator as described in Chapter 3 Section 3.

9 Slacken the retaining clip, undo the mounting bolt and remove the charge air pipe from the top of the intercooler.

10 Undo the two retaining nuts and lift the auxiliary cooling fan off the intercooler bracket.

11 Undo the three bolts securing intercooler to the radiator.

12 Unclip the charge air pipe from the radiator bracket and remove the intercooler from the radiator.

Refitting

13 Refitting is the reverse of removal.

18 Turbocharger –
description and precautions

Description

1 The turbocharger increases engine efficiency by raising the pressure in the intake manifold above atmospheric pressure. Instead of the air simply being sucked into the cylinders, it is forced in.

2 Energy for the operation of the turbocharger comes from the exhaust gas. The gas flows through a specially-shaped housing (the turbine housing) and, in so doing, spins the turbine wheel. The turbine wheel is attached to a shaft, at the end of which is another vaned wheel known as the compressor wheel. The compressor wheel spins in its own housing, and compresses the intake air on the way to the intake manifold.

3 The turbocharger operates on the principle of variable vane geometry. At low engine speeds the vanes close to give less flow cross-section, then as the speed increases the vanes open to give an increased flow cross-section. This helps improve the efficiency of the turbocharger.

4 Boost pressure (the pressure in the intake manifold) is limited by a wastegate, which diverts the exhaust gas away from the turbine wheel in response to a pressure-sensitive actuator.

5 The turbo shaft is pressure-lubricated by an oil feed pipe from the main oil gallery. The shaft 'floats' on a cushion of oil. A drain pipe returns the oil to the sump.

17.2 Charge air hose clamps

17.4a Washer fluid reservoir upper nut...

17.4b ...and lower nut

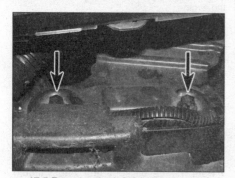

17.5 Remove the left-hand bolts, and slacken the right-hand ones

17.6a Intercooler upper mounting bolt...

17.6b ...and lower mounting bolts

Precautions

6 The turbocharger operates at extremely high speeds and temperatures. Certain precautions must be observed, to avoid premature failure of the turbo, or injury to the operator.

● Do not operate the turbo with any of its parts exposed, or with any of its hoses removed. Foreign objects falling onto the rotating vanes could cause excessive damage, and (if ejected) personal injury.

● Do not race the engine immediately after start-up, especially if it is cold. Give the oil a few seconds to circulate.

● Always allow the engine to return to idle speed before switching it off – do not blip the throttle and switch off, as this will leave the turbo spinning without lubrication.

● Allow the engine to idle for several minutes before switching off after a high-speed run.

● Observe the recommended intervals for oil and filter changing, and use a reputable oil of the specified quality. Neglect of oil changing, or use of inferior oil, can cause carbon formation on the turbo shaft, leading to subsequent failure.

---

19 Exhaust manifold and turbocharger – removal and refitting

Note: *New manifold retaining nuts, new gaskets for all disturbed joints, and new copper washers for the turbocharger oil supply pipe banjo union will be required for refitting.*

1.7 litre engines

Turbocharger

Removal

1 Remove the exhaust manifold as described later in this Section.

2 With the manifold on the bench, undo the three bolts and remove the catalytic converter heat shield **(see illustration)**.

3 Undo the three bolts, remove the catalytic converter from the turbocharger, and recover the gasket **(see illustrations)**. Note that new bolts will be required for refitting.

19.8 Release the retaining clip (arrowed) and disconnect the coolant hose from the right-hand side coolantpipe

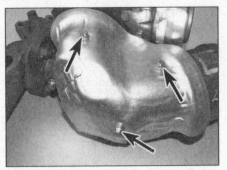

19.2 Undo the three bolts and remove the catalytic converter heat shield

19.3b ...then remove the catalytic converter from the turbocharger

4 Undo the three nuts, detach the turbocharger from the manifold and recover the gasket **(see illustration)**. Note that new nuts will be required.

Refitting

5 Refitting is the reverse of removal, noting the following points:

a) *Ensure all mating surfaces are clean and dry, and renew all gaskets.*

b) *Tighten all fasteners to their specified torque where given.*

c) *Refit the exhaust manifold as described later in this Section.*

Exhaust manifold

Removal

Note: *The exhaust manifold is removed complete with the catalytic converter and*

19.9 Undo the two bolts and remove the exhaust manifold heat shield on the left-hand side

19.3a Undo the three bolts...

19.4 Turbocharger retaining nuts

turbocharger. The three components are then separated on the bench.

Note: *New exhaust manifold retaining nuts/ bolts will be required for refitting.*

6 Disconnect the battery negative terminal (refer to Chapter 5A Section 4).

7 Remove the EGR valve cooler as described in Chapter 4C Section 3.

8 Release the retaining clip and disconnect the coolant hose from the right-hand side coolant pipe **(see illustration)**.

9 Undo the two bolts and remove the exhaust manifold heat shield on the left-hand side **(see illustration)**.

10 Release the retaining clip and disconnect the coolant hose from the left-hand side coolant pipe **(see illustration)**.

11 Unscrew the turbocharger oil supply pipe banjo union from the top of the turbocharger and collect the two sealing washers.

19.10 Release the retaining clip (arrowed) and disconnect the coolant hose from the left-hand side coolantpipe

19.12 Disconnect the vacuum hose (arrowed) from the turbocharger wastegate actuator

19.13 Release the retaining clip (arrowed) and disconnect the exhaust pressure sensor hose from the pressure sensorpipe

19.14 Disconnect the oxygen sensor wiring connector (arrowed)

19.15a Undo the three nuts (arrowed) securing the exhaust system front pipe to the catalytic converter...

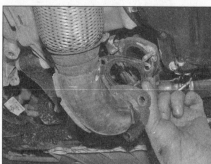
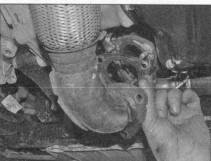
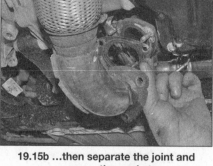

19.15b ...then separate the joint and recover the gasket

12 Disconnect the vacuum hose from the turbocharger wastegate actuator **(see illustration)**.

13 Release the retaining clip and disconnect the exhaust pressure sensor hose from the pressure sensor pipe **(see illustration)**.

14 Disconnect the oxygen sensor wiring connector and release the wiring harness retaining clip from the support bracket **(see illustration)**.

15 Undo the three nuts securing the exhaust system front pipe to the catalytic converter. Separate the joint taking care to support the flexible section. **Note:** *Angular movement in excess of 10° can cause permanent damage to the flexible section. Recover the gasket* **(see illustrations)**.

16 Undo the two bolts securing the catalytic converter to the support bracket **(see illustration)**.

17 Undo the two bolts and separate the intercooler intake air duct flange from the turbocharger **(see illustration)**. Collect the gasket.

18 Release the two turbocharger oil return hose retaining clips. Slide the hose down and release it from the turbocharger pipe **(see illustration)**.

19 Disconnect the exhaust temperature sensor wiring connector and release the wiring harness from the support clip above the alternator **(see illustration)**.

20 Undo the seven nuts and two bolts securing the exhaust manifold to the cylinder head and collect the washers **(see illustration)**.

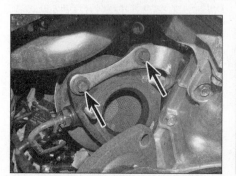

19.16 Undo the two bolts (arrowed) securing the catalytic converter to the support bracket

19.17 Undo the two bolts (arrowed) and separate the intercooler intake air duct flange from the turbocharger

19.18 Release the two retaining clips (arrowed) then slide the oil return hose down and release it from theturbocharger pipe

19.19 Disconnect the exhaust temperature sensor wiring connector (arrowed)

19.20 Undo the exhaust manifold retaining nuts and bolts and collect the washers

19.21 Withdraw the exhaust manifold complete with turbocharger and catalytic converter

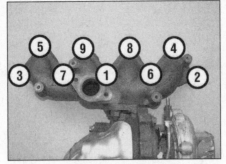

19.23a Exhaust manifold retaining nut/bolt tightening sequence

19.30 Insert a drill bit (arrowed) or similar, through the holes provided on the radiator mounting brackets (shown withradiator removed)

21 Withdraw the exhaust manifold complete with turbocharger and catalytic converter and lift it up and out of the engine compartment **(see illustration)**.

22 If required, the catalytic converter and turbocharger can now be removed from the manifold as described previously in this Section.

Refitting

23 Refitting is the reverse of removal, noting the following points.

a) *If removed, refit the turbocharger and catalytic converter to the manifold as described previously in this Section.*

b) *Ensure all mating surfaces are clean and dry and renew all gaskets and sealing washers.*

c) *Tighten the new manifold nuts and bolts evenly and progressively to the specified torque, working in the sequence shown* **(see illustration)**.

d) *Tighten all other retaining nuts and bolts to the specified torque (where given).*

e) *Refit the EGR valve cooler as described in Chapter 4C Section 3.*

1.9 litre engines

Removal

24 Disconnect the battery negative terminal (refer to Chapter 5A Section 4).

25 Remove the plastic cover from the top of the engine.

26 Firmly apply the handbrake, then jack up the front of the car and support it securely on axle stands (see *Jacking and vehicle support*).

27 Drain the cooling system as described in Chapter 1B Section 30.

28 On models equipped with air conditioning, remove the auxiliary drivebelt as described in Chapter 1B Section 24.

Automatic transmission models

29 Remove the front bumper as described in Chapter 11 Section 6.

30 Retain the radiator in position by inserting a drill bit or similar through the holes provided on each of the radiator upper mounting brackets **(see illustration)**.

31 Undo the two bolts each side securing the radiator left-hand and right-hand mounting brackets to the subframe. Remove the brackets, noting their orientation **(see illustrations)**.

32 Taking care to avoid damaging the attached parts and surrounding components, pull the radiator assembly forward at the bottom and retain it in that position by inserting a suitable block of wood between the base of the radiator and the subframe.

33 Undo the bolt and remove the clamp securing the fluid cooler pipes to the front of the engine mounting.

All models

34 Remove the exhaust system front pipe as described in Section 20.

35 Remove the air cleaner assembly and air intake duct as described in Section 3.

36 On DOHC (Z19DTH) engines, release the retaining clip securing the engine breather hose to the breather pipe adjacent to the engine oil dipstick. Undo the two bolts securing the breather pipe to the cylinder head, and disconnect the pipe from the hose **(see illustration 14.50)**.

37 Unclip the vacuum hose from the engine oil dipstick guide tube, then undo the bolt and remove the dipstick guide tube.

38 Slacken the retaining clip and disconnect the charge air pipe from the turbocharger.

39 Release the retaining clips and remove the charge air pipe above the right-hand side of the radiator. Suitably cover the turbocharger air intake to prevent the entry of dirt and foreign material.

40 Release the two retaining clips and disconnect the charge air hose from the throttle housing, and intercooler.

41 Undo the three nuts and three bolts securing the heat shield to the exhaust manifold and catalytic converter **(see illustration)**. Manipulate the heat shield off the studs and remove it from the engine.

42 On SOHC (Z19DT and DTL) engines, undo the retaining bolt(s) to release the vacuum lines running over the top of the camshaft cover **(see illustration 15.39)**.

43 Slacken the retaining clips and remove the charge air pipe from the intercooler.

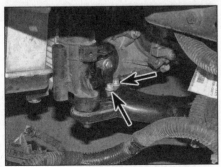

19.31a Undo the two bolts (arrowed) each side ...

19.31b ... and remove the radiator mounting brackets, noting their orientation

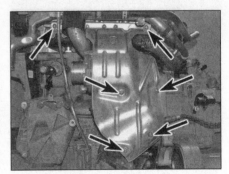

19.41 Heat shield retaining nuts and bolts (arrowed)

19.44 Release the retaining clip and disconnect the breather hose from the front of the camshaft cover

19.45a Undo the turbocharger charge air pipe upper retaining bolt (arrowed) …

19.45b … then slacken the clip (arrowed) and move the pipe to one side

44 Release the retaining clip and disconnect the breather hose from the front of the camshaft cover **(see illustration)**.

45 Undo the bolt securing the turbocharger charge air pipe to the right-hand end of the camshaft housing or support bracket, as applicable. Slacken the retaining clip securing the charge air pipe to the turbocharger and move the pipe to one side **(see illustrations)**.

46 Release the clip and disconnect the radiator top hose from the thermostat housing.

47 Release the retaining clip and disconnect the radiator hose from the coolant pipe, then undo the two bolts securing the coolant pipe flange to the right-hand end of the cylinder head.

48 Release the retaining clips securing the heater hose and EGR valve heat exchanger hose at the left-hand end of the pipe assembly. Undo the bolt securing the heater pipe to the left-hand end of the cylinder head, and the nut securing the pipe to the thermostat housing stud. Remove the pipe assembly from the engine and recover the flange gasket.

49 Undo the retaining nut and bolt and release the metal EGR pipe clamp from the EGR valve heat exchanger. Separate the pipe from the heat exchanger and recover the gasket from the pipe fitting **(see illustration)**.

50 Undo the two bolts securing the other end of the pipe to the exhaust manifold. Remove the pipe and recover the gasket **(see illustration)**.

51 Unscrew the two bolts and one nut and remove the catalytic converter lower support bracket.

52 Disconnect the pre-catalytic converter temperature sensor wiring connector, then unscrew the clamp bolt nut and remove the catalytic converter **(see illustrations)**.

53 Unscrew the four bolts securing the oil return pipe to the turbocharger and cylinder block **(see illustration)**. Remove the pipe and recover the gaskets.

54 Unscrew the turbocharger oil supply pipe banjo union from the cylinder block and collect the two copper washers **(see illustration)**.

55 Disconnect the vacuum hose from the turbocharger wastegate actuator.

56 On models equipped with air conditioning,

19.49 Release the EGR pipe clamp from the heat exchanger, separate the pipe and recover the gasket

19.50 Disconnect the other end of the pipe from the exhaust manifold, then remove the pipe and recover the gasket

19.52a Unscrew the clamp bolt nut (arrowed) …

19.52b … and remove the catalytic converter

19.53 Unscrew the bolts (arrowed) securing the oil return pipe to the turbocharger and cylinder block

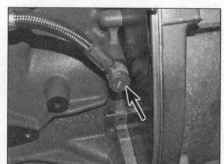

19.54 Unscrew the turbocharger oil supply pipe banjo union (arrowed) and collect the two copper washers

19.57 Exhaust manifold retaining nuts (arrowed)

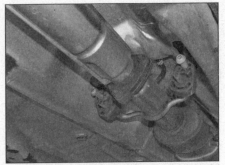

20.5 Undo the three nuts securing the front pipe flange to the intermediate pipe flange

undo the three bolts securing the compressor to the mounting bracket. Move the compressor to one side and suitably support it without straining the refrigerant pipes.

57 Unscrew the eight nuts securing the exhaust manifold to the cylinder head **(see illustration)**. Note that new nuts will be required for refitting. Withdraw the manifold and turbocharger assembly from the mounting studs, manipulate it sideways, and remove from under the car. Recover the gasket.

Refitting

58 Refitting is the reverse of removal, noting the following points.
a) *Ensure all mating surfaces are clean and dry and renew all gaskets, seals and copper washers.*
b) *Fit the new manifold nuts and tighten them evenly and progressively to the specified torque, working in a diagonal sequence.*
c) *Tighten all other retaining nuts and bolts to the specified torque (where given).*
d) *Refit the exhaust system front pipe as described in Section 20.*
e) *On automatic transmission models, refit the front bumper as described in Chapter 11 Section 6.*
f) *On completion refill the cooling system as described in Chapter 1B Section 30 and, if necessary, top-up the oil level as described in 'Weekly checks'.*
g) *On starting the engine for the first time, allow the engine to idle for a few minutes*

before increasing the engine speed; this will allow oil to be circulated around the turbocharger bearings.

20 Exhaust system – general information, removal and refitting

General information

1 The exhaust system consists of three main sections comprising a front pipe, an intermediate pipe incorporating the diesel particulate filter and a tailpipe incorporating the rear silencer. A primary catalytic converter is fitted between the exhaust manifold and front pipe.
2 The front pipe is attached to the catalytic converter by a flange joint secured by nuts. The intermediate pipe is attached to the front pipe by a flange joint secured by nuts, and the tailpipe is attached to the intermediate pipe by an overlap joint secured by a clamp.
3 The front pipe is fitted with a flexible section to allow for exhaust system movement and the system is suspended throughout its entire length by rubber mountings.

Removal

4 To remove the various parts of the system, first jack up the front or rear of the car, and support it on axle stands. Alternatively, position the car over an inspection pit, or

on car ramps. Where necessary, undo the retaining screws, release the clips and remove the engine undertray.

Front pipe

5 Undo the three nuts securing the front pipe flange to the intermediate pipe flange **(see illustration)**.
6 Undo the three nuts securing the front pipe to the catalytic converter, and the two bolts securing the support clamp to the transmission bracket **(see illustrations)**. Free the front pipe from the converter and recover the gasket. While doing this, take care to support the flexible section. **Note:** *Angular movement in excess of 10° can cause permanent damage to the flexible section.*
7 Slide the front pipe off the intermediate pipe studs and remove the front pipe from under the car.

Intermediate pipe

8 Remove the tailpipe as described later in this Section.
9 Release the retaining clips and disconnect the two differential pressure sensor vacuum hoses from the two pipes just forward of the diesel particulate filter.
10 Unscrew the retaining nut and remove the temperature sensor from the diesel particulate filter **(see illustration)**.
11 Suitably support the front pipe on blocks or secure it to the underbody with wire, to avoid damage to the flexible section.
12 Undo the three nuts securing the front pipe flange to the intermediate pipe flange **(see illustration 20.5)**.
13 Spray some penetrating oil over the exhaust rubber mounting blocks so that the mounting blocks will slide easily on the exhaust and underbody hangers.
14 Slide the front rubber mounting blocks as far forward as possible. Move the intermediate pipe to the rear to separate the flange joint, then disengage the front hangers from the mounting blocks.
15 Move the intermediate pipe forward and disengage the rear hangers from the rubber mounting blocks. Lower the intermediate pipe to the ground and slide it out from under the car.

20.6a Undo the three nuts (two arrowed) securing the front pipe to the catalytic converter ...

20.6b ... and the two bolts (arrowed) securing the support clamp to the transmission bracket

20.10 Unscrew the retaining nut (arrowed) and remove the temperature sensor from the diesel particulate filter

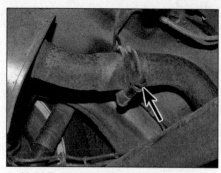

20.16 Exhaust tailpipe retaining clamp (arrowed)

Tailpipe

16 Loosen the clamp securing the tail pipe to the intermediate pipe **(see illustration)**.

17 Unhook the tailpipe from its rubber mountings and slide the tailpipe from the intermediate pipe. If the tailpipe is rusted onto the intermediate pipe, apply liberal amounts of penetrating oil and tap around the joint with a hammer to free it. Twist the tailpipe in both directions until free.

Catalytic converter/particulate filter

18 Remove the front pipe as described previously in this Section.

19 Remove the plastic cover from the top of the engine

20 Undo the three nuts and three bolts securing the heat shield to the exhaust manifold and catalytic converter **(see illustration 19.18)**. Manipulate the heat shield off the studs and remove it from the engine.

21 Unscrew the two bolts and one nut and remove the catalytic converter lower support bracket.

22 Disconnect the pre-catalytic converter temperature sensor wiring connector, then unscrew the clamp bolt nut and remove the catalytic converter.

Heat shield(s)

23 The heat shields are secured to the under- side of the body by various nuts and bolts. Each shield can be removed once the relevant exhaust section has been removed.

If a shield is being removed to gain access to a component located behind it, it may prove sufficient in some cases to remove the retaining nuts and/or bolts, and simply lower the shield, without disturbing the exhaust system.

Refitting

24 Each section is refitted by reversing the removal sequence, noting the following points:

a) *Ensure that all traces of corrosion have been removed from the system joints.*

b) *When refitting the front pipe to the catalytic converter flange joint, use a new gasket and new retaining nuts, and tighten the nuts to the specified torque.*

c) *Inspect the rubber mountings for signs of damage or deterioration, and renew as necessary.*

d) *Prior to tightening the exhaust system fasteners, ensure that all rubber mountings are correctly located, and that there is adequate clearance between the exhaust system and vehicle underbody.*

Chapter 4 Part C
Emissions control systems

Contents

	Section number			Section number
Catalytic converter – general information and precautions	4	General information and precautions		1
Diesel engine emissions control systems – testing and component renewal	3	Petrol engine emissions control systems – testing and component renewal		2

Degrees of difficulty

Easy, suitable for novice with little experience	Fairly easy, suitable for beginner with some experience	Fairly difficult, suitable for competent DIY mechanic	Difficult, suitable for experienced DIY mechanic	Very difficult, suitable for expert DIY or professional

Specifications

Torque wrench settings	Nm	lbf ft
Petrol engines		
Catalytic converter control oxygen sensor	40	30
Mixture regulation oxygen sensor:		
Non-VVT (variable valve timing) engines	30	22
VVT-engines (variable valve timing) engines	40	30
Diesel engines		
EGR valve cooler mounting bolt	25	18
EGR valve cooler pipe flange bolts	25	18
EGR valve mounting bolts	25	18
Particulate filter temperature sensor	45	33
Pre-catalytic converter temperature sensor	45	33
Vacuum reservoir mounting bracket bolts	25	18

1 General information and precautions

1 All petrol engine models use unleaded petrol and have various features built into the fuel/exhaust system to help minimise harmful emissions. All models are equipped with a crankcase emission control system, an evaporative emission control system and a catalytic converter. Additionally, 1.6 non-VVT engines are equipped with an exhaust gas recirculation (EGR) system to keep exhaust gas emissions down to a minimum.

2 All diesel engine models are also designed to meet strict emission requirements. The engines are fitted with a crankcase emission control system, a catalytic converter and a diesel particulate filter to keep exhaust emissions down to a minimum. An exhaust gas recirculation (EGR) system is also fitted to further decrease exhaust emissions.

3 The emissions control systems function as follows.

Petrol engines

Crankcase emissions control

4 To reduce the emission of unburned hydrocarbons from the crankcase into the atmosphere, the engine is sealed and the blow-by gases and oil vapour are drawn from the camshaft cover into the intake manifold to be burned by the engine during normal combustion.

5 The gases are forced out of the crankcase by the relatively higher crankcase pressure; if the engine is worn, the raised crankcase pressure (due to increased blow-by) will cause some of the flow to return under all manifold conditions.

Exhaust emission control

6 To minimise the amount of pollutants which escape into the atmosphere, all models are fitted with a catalytic converter which is either integral with the exhaust manifold, or incorporated into the exhaust system front pipe. The system is of the closed-loop type, in which oxygen sensors in the exhaust system provide the engine management system ECU with constant feedback, enabling the ECU to adjust the mixture to provide the best possible conditions for the converter to operate.

7 On all petrol engines covered by this manual, there are two heated oxygen sensors fitted to the exhaust system. The sensor on the top of the exhaust manifold/catalytic converter determines the residual oxygen content of the exhaust gases for mixture correction. The sensor in the exhaust front pipe (after the catalytic converter) monitors the function of the catalytic converter to give the driver a warning signal if there is a fault.

8 The oxygen sensor's tip is sensitive to oxygen and sends the ECU a varying voltage signal depending on the amount of oxygen in the exhaust gases. Peak conversion efficiency of all major pollutants occurs if the intake air/fuel mixture is maintained at the chemically-correct ratio for the complete combustion of petrol of 14.7 parts (by weight) of air to 1 part of fuel (the 'stoichiometric' ratio). The sensor output voltage alters in a large step at this point, the ECU using the signal change as a reference point and correcting the intake air/fuel mixture accordingly by altering the fuel injector pulse width.

Fuel evaporation emission control

9 To minimise the escape into the atmosphere of unburned hydrocarbons, a fuel evaporation emission control system is fitted. The fuel tank filler cap is sealed and a charcoal canister is mounted behind the right-hand front wing. The canister collects the petrol vapours generated in the tank when the car is parked and stores them until they can be cleared from the canister (under the control of the engine management system ECU) via the purge valve into the intake manifold to be burned by the engine during normal combustion.

10 To ensure that the engine runs correctly when it is cold and/or idling and to protect the catalytic converter from the effects of an over-rich mixture, the purge control valve is not opened by the ECU until the engine has warmed-up, and the engine is under load; the valve solenoid is then modulated on and off to allow the stored vapour to pass into the intake manifold.

Exhaust gas recirculation system

11 This system is designed to recirculate small quantities of exhaust gas into the intake manifold, and therefore into the combustion process. This reduces the level of unburnt hydrocarbons present in the exhaust gas before it reaches the catalytic converter. The system is controlled by the engine management ECU, using the information from its various sensors, via the electrically-operated EGR solenoid valve mounted on a housing bolted to the left-hand end of the cylinder head.

Diesel engines

Crankcase emission control

12 To reduce the emission of unburned hydrocarbons from the crankcase into the atmosphere, the engine is sealed and the blow-by gases and oil vapour are drawn from inside the crankcase, through an oil separator, into the intake tract to be burned by the engine during normal combustion.

13 Under all conditions the gases are forced out of the crankcase by the (relatively) higher crankcase pressure; if the engine is worn, the raised crankcase pressure (due to increased blow-by) will cause some of the flow to return under all manifold conditions.

Exhaust emission control

14 To minimise the level of exhaust pollutants released into the atmosphere, a catalytic converter and a diesel particulate filter are fitted in the exhaust system.

15 The catalytic converter consists of a canister containing a fine mesh impregnated with a catalyst material, over which the hot exhaust gases pass. The catalyst speeds up the oxidation of harmful carbon monoxide, unburned hydrocarbons, effectively reducing the quantity of harmful products released into the atmosphere via the exhaust gases.

16 The diesel particulate filter is incorporated in the exhaust system intermediate pipe and contains a silicon carbide honeycomb block containing microscopic channels in which the exhaust gases flow. As the gases flow through the honeycomb channels, soot particles are deposited on the channel walls. To prevent clogging of the honeycomb channels, the soot particles are burned off at regular intervals during what is known as a 'regeneration phase'. Under the control of the injection system ECU, the injection characteristics are altered to raise the temperature of the exhaust gases to approximately 600°C. At this temperature, the soot particles are effectively burned off the honeycomb walls as the exhaust gases pass through. A differential pressure sensor and two temperature sensors are used to inform the ECU of the condition of the particulate filter, and the temperature of the exhaust gases during the regeneration phase. When the ECU detects that soot build-up is

reducing the efficiency of the particulate filter, it will instigate the regeneration process. This occurs at regular intervals under certain driving conditions and will normally not be detected by the driver.

Exhaust gas recirculation system

17 This system is designed to recirculate small quantities of exhaust gas into the intake tract, and therefore into the combustion process. This process reduces the level of unburnt hydrocarbons present in the exhaust gas before it reaches the catalytic converter. The system is controlled by the injection system ECU, using the information from its various sensors, via the electrically-operated EGR valve.

2 Petrol engine emissions control systems – testing and component renewal

Crankcase emission control

1 The components of this system require no attention other than to check that the hose(s) are clear and undamaged at regular intervals.

Evaporative emission control

Testing

2 If the system is thought to be faulty, disconnect the hoses from the charcoal canister and purge control valve and check that they are clear by blowing through them. Full testing of the system can only be carried out using specialist electronic equipment which is connected to the engine management system diagnostic wiring connector (see Chapter 4A). If the purge control valve or charcoal canister are thought to be faulty, they must be renewed.

Charcoal canister renewal

3 At the right-hand rear corner of the engine compartment, disconnect the quick-release connectors connecting the charcoal canister to the intake manifold and fuel vapour hose **(see illustration)**. A Vauxhall special tool is available to release the connectors, but provided care is taken, the connectors can be released using a pair of long-nosed pliers, or a similar tool, to depress the retaining tangs.

4 Apply the handbrake, then jack up the front of the vehicle and support it on axle stands (see *Jacking and vehicle support*). Remove the right-hand front roadwheel.

5 Remove the wheel arch liner for access to the charcoal canister which is located on the inner wing.

6 Unbolt the charcoal canister from the mounting bracket.

7 Withdraw the canister, together with the vapour hoses from the inner wing **(see illustration)**.

8 Refitting is a reversal of the removal procedure. Make sure the hoses are correctly and securely reconnected.

2.3 Disconnect the charcoal canister quick-release connectors

2.7 Withdraw the canister, together with the vapour hoses from the inner wing

2.9 Typical purge valve location (arrowed)

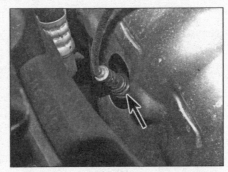

2.16 Mixture regulation oxygen sensor (arrowed)

2.21 Catalytic converter control oxygen sensor (arrowed)

Purge valve renewal

9 Disconnect the wiring from the purge valve mounted on the intake manifold (see illustration).

10 Release the purge valve from its mounting bracket, or undo the bracket retaining bolt, as applicable.

11 Disconnect the vapour hoses and remove the purge valve.

12 Refitting is a reversal of the removal procedure, ensuring the valve is fitted the correct way around and the hoses are securely connected. Check the hoses carefully for cracking and damage, and where evident, renew them. **Note:** *A cracked ventilation hose is potentially a fire hazard.*

Exhaust emission control

Testing

13 The performance of the catalytic converter can be checked only by measuring the exhaust gases using a good-quality, carefully-calibrated exhaust gas analyser.

14 If the CO level at the tailpipe is too high, the vehicle should be taken to a Vauxhall/Opel dealer so that the complete fuel injection and ignition systems, including the oxygen sensors, can be thoroughly checked using the special diagnostic equipment. Once these have been checked and are known to be free from faults, the fault must be in the catalytic converter, which must be renewed.

Catalytic converter renewal

15 The catalytic converter is either integral with the exhaust manifold, or incorporated into the exhaust system front pipe. Removal and refitting procedures are described in Chapter 4A.

Mixture regulation oxygen sensor renewal

Caution: The sensor will be very hot if the engine has been running within 10 or 15 minutes.

16 The mixture regulation oxygen sensor is located on the exhaust manifold (see illustration). First, trace the wiring back from the sensor to the connector on the left-hand side of the cylinder head and disconnect it. Release the wiring from the clip.

17 Unscrew the sensor from the exhaust manifold or front pipe. Ideally, a special 'split' socket should be used, as this will locate over the sensor wiring.

18 Clean the threads of the sensor then coat them with Vauxhall/Opel special grease for oxygen sensors. If a new sensor is being fitted, it will be supplied with the threads already coated with the special grease to prevent it seizing in the manifold.

19 Screw the sensor into the exhaust manifold and tighten to the specified torque.

20 Reconnect the wiring and clip it in place.

Catalytic converter control oxygen sensor renewal

Caution: The sensor will be very hot if the engine has been running within 10 or 15 minutes.

21 The catalytic converter control oxygen sensor is located in the exhaust front pipe, just behind the flexible section (see illustration). First, apply the handbrake, then jack up the front of the vehicle and support it on axle stands (see *Jacking and vehicle support*).

22 Trace the wiring back from the sensor to the and disconnect it. Release the wiring from the clips.

23 Unscrew the sensor from the exhaust front pipe. Ideally, a special 'split' socket should be used, as this will locate over the sensor wiring.

24 Clean the threads of the sensor then coat them with Vauxhall/Opel special grease for oxygen sensors. If a new sensor is being fitted, it will be supplied with the threads already coated with the special grease to prevent it seizing in the pipe.

25 Screw the sensor into the exhaust front pipe and tighten to the specified torque.

26 Reconnect the wiring and clip it in place.

Exhaust gas recirculation system

Testing

27 Comprehensive testing of the system can only be carried out using specialist electronic equipment which is connected to the engine management system diagnostic wiring connector (see Chapter 4A). If the EGR valve is thought to be faulty, it must be renewed.

EGR valve renewal – 1.6 litre non-VVT engines

28 The exhaust gas recirculation valve is an integral part of the coolant housing attached to the left-hand end of the cylinder head. First drain the cooling system as described in Chapter 1A Section 28.

29 Remove the battery and battery tray as described in Chapter 5A Section 4.

30 Disconnect the wiring connectors at the thermostat, coolant temperature sensor and EGR valve.

31 Release the retaining clips and disconnect the four coolant hoses from the coolant housing.

32 Undo the two bolts and detach the oxygen sensor wiring harness support bracket.

33 Undo the two bolts and remove the coolant pipe from the front of the coolant housing.

34 Undo the four bolts and remove the coolant housing from the cylinder head. Recover the gasket.

35 Refitting is a reversal of removal, but clean the mating surfaces, fit new gaskets, and tighten all bolts securely. Refill the cooling system with reference to Chapter 1A Section 28.

3 Diesel engine emissions control systems – testing and component renewal

Crankcase emission control

1 The components of this system require no attention other than to check that the hose(s) are clear and undamaged at regular intervals.

Exhaust emission control

Testing

2 The performance of the catalytic converter and diesel particulate filter can only be checked using special diagnostic equipment. If a system fault is suspected, the vehicle should be taken to a Vauxhall/Opel dealer so that the complete fuel injection system can be thoroughly checked.

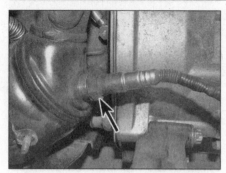

3.8 Unscrew the temperature sensor (arrowed) and remove it from the exhaust manifold – typical location

3.12 Unscrew the retaining nut and remove the temperature sensor from the particulate filter

Catalytic converter/ particulate filter renewal

3 Refer to Chapter 4B, for removal and refitting details.

Pre-catalytic converter temperature sensor renewal

4 Warm the engine up to normal operating temperature then stop the engine and disconnect the battery negative terminal (refer to Chapter 5A Section 4). Remove the plastic cover from the top of the engine.

5 Firmly apply the handbrake, then jack up the front of the car and support it securely on axle stands (see *Jacking and vehicle support*).

6 Disconnect the temperature sensor wiring connector, then unclip the wiring plug from the bracket on the front of the transmission.

7 Trace the wiring back to the sensor and release the wiring from the cable clips.

Caution: Take great care not burn yourself on the hot manifold/sensor.

8 Unscrew the sensor and remove it from the exhaust manifold **(see illustration)**.

9 Refitting is a reverse of the removal procedure. Prior to installing the sensor, apply a smear of high temperature grease to the sensor threads (Vauxhall/Opel recommend the use of a special grease available from your dealer). Tighten the sensor to the specified torque and ensure that the wiring is correctly routed and in no danger of contacting either

the exhaust system or engine.

Particulate filter temperature sensor renewal

10 Firmly apply the handbrake, then jack up the front of the car and support it securely on axle stands (see *Jacking and vehicle support*). Undo the retaining screws, release the clips and remove the engine undertray.

11 Trace the wiring from the sensor back to the connector in the engine compartment. Disconnect the wiring connector, then release the wiring from the clips on the underbody.

1.9 litre engines

12 Unscrew the retaining nut and remove the temperature sensor from the particulate filter **(see illustration)**.

13 Refitting is the reverse of removal tightening the sensor retaining nut to the specified torque.

1.7 litre engines

14 On 1.7 litre engines, two temperature sensors are fitted; one located in the catalytic converter, and one located in the diesel particulate filter in the exhaust system front pipe. To renew the sensor located in the catalytic converter, proceed as described previously in paragraphs 13 to 16 **(see illustrations)**.

15 Unscrew the sensor and remove it from the particulate filter **(see illustration)**.

Caution: Take great care not burn yourself on the hot filter/sensor.

16 Refitting is a reverse of the removal procedure. Prior to installing the sensor, apply a smear of high temperature grease to the sensor threads (Vauxhall/Opel recommend the use of a special grease available from your dealer). Tighten the sensor to the specified torque and ensure that the wiring is correctly routed and in no danger of contacting either the exhaust system or engine.

Differential pressure sensor renewal

17 The differential pressure sensor is located on the side of the fuel filter crash box in the engine compartment. To gain access, remove the windscreen cowl panel as described in Chapter 11 Section 20.

18 Disconnect the pressure sensor wiring connector.

19 Undo the retaining nut and withdraw the sensor from the fuel filter crash box.

20 Noting their correct fitted positions, release the retaining clips and disconnect the two vacuum hoses from the sensor. Remove the sensor from the engine compartment.

21 Refitting is the reverse of removal.

Exhaust gas recirculation system

Testing

22 Comprehensive testing of the system can only be carried out using specialist electronic equipment which is connected to the injection system diagnostic wiring connector.

EGR valve renewal – 1.7 litre engines

23 Disconnect the battery negative terminal (refer to Chapter 5A Section 4).

24 Unclip the engine management ECU wiring harness from the side of the battery tray.

25 Release the retaining tab and carefully lift the engine management ECU mounting bracket off the side of the battery tray. Position the ECU and mounting bracket to one side.

26 Undo the two bolts securing the EGR valve pipe to the EGR valve. Withdraw the

3.14a Particulate filter temperature sensor wiring connector (arrowed) – 1.7 litre engines

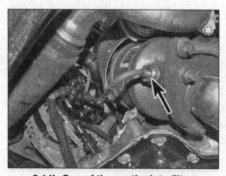

3.14b One of the particulate filter temperature sensors is located in the catalytic converter (arrowed) – 1.7 litre engines

3.15 Unscrew the sensor (arrowed) and remove it from the particulate filter – 1.7 litre engines

3.26a Undo the two bolts (arrowed) securing the EGR valve pipe to the EGR valve – 1.7 litre engines

3.26b Withdraw the pipe slightly and collect the gasket – 1.7 litre engines

3.27 Undo the four retaining bolts (arrowed) and remove the EGR valve – 1.7 litre engines

pipe slightly and collect the gasket (see illustrations).

27 Disconnect the EGR valve wiring connector, then undo the four retaining bolts (noting the location of the coolant hose support bracket) and remove the valve (see illustration). Collect the EGR valve gasket.

28 Refitting is the reverse of removal using a new gasket and tightening the retaining bolts to the specified torque.

EGR valve renewal – SOHC (Z19DT and DTL) engines

29 Disconnect the battery negative terminal (refer to Chapter 5A Section 4). Remove the plastic cover over the top of the engine.

30 Remove the windscreen cowl panel as described in Chapter 11 Section 20.

31 Disconnect the EGR valve wiring connector.

32 Undo the two bolts and disconnect the metal EGR pipe from the throttle housing. Recover the gasket.

33 Undo the two bolts securing the EGR heat exchanger metal pipe to the base of the valve.

34 Undo the three bolts securing the EGR valve to the intake manifold (see illustration). Remove the valve together with the engine lifting bracket and recover the gasket fitted on each side of the lifting bracket.

35 Refitting is the reverse of removal using new gaskets and tightening the retaining bolts to the specified torque.

EGR valve renewal – DOHC (Z19DTH) engines

36 Remove the battery and battery tray as described in Chapter 5A Section 4.

37 Remove the windscreen cowl panel as described in Chapter 11 Section 20.

38 Remove the plastic cover over the top of the engine.

39 Disconnect the quick-release fitting and detach the brake servo vacuum hose from the vacuum pump. Release the hose from the support clip.

40 Release the two retaining clips and disconnect the charge air hose from the throttle housing, and intercooler.

41 Disconnect the EGR valve wiring connector.

42 Unscrew the two bolts on the top of the valve and detach the metal EGR pipe flange from the base of the valve. Recover the gasket (see illustration).

43 Unscrew the two nuts and two bolts securing the EGR valve to the intake manifold and lift off the engine cover bracket (see illustration).

44 To provide sufficient clearance to remove the valve, it will be necessary to unscrew the two mounting studs from the manifold. To do this, lock two nuts together on each stud and remove the studs by unscrewing the inner nut.

45 With the studs removed, lift off the valve and recover the gasket (see illustration).

46 Refitting is the reverse of removal using new gaskets and tightening the retaining nuts and bolts to the specified torque.

EGR valve cooler renewal – 1.7 litre engines

47 Disconnect the battery negative terminal (refer to Chapter 5A Section 4).

48 Firmly apply the handbrake, then jack up the front of the vehicle and support it securely on axle stands (see *Jacking and vehicle support*).

49 Remove the engine undertray.

50 Drain the cooling system as described in Chapter 1B Section 30.

51 Drain the engine oil as described in Chapter 1B Section 6.

52 Remove the auxiliary drivebelt as described in Chapter 1B Section 24.

53 Remove the air cleaner assembly and the outlet air duct as described in Chapter 4B Section 3.

3.34 EGR valve retaining bolts (arrowed)

3.42 Unscrew the two bolts, detach the metal EGR pipe flange and recover the gasket

3.43 Unscrew the two nuts and two bolts (arrowed) securing the EGR valve to the intake manifold

3.45 Lift off the valve and recover the gasket

3.55 Unbolt the compressor and secure it to the front body panel using cable ties or similar – 1.7 litre engines

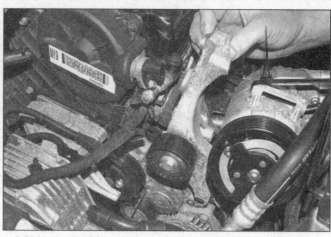

3.56 Undo the five retaining bolts and remove the compressor mounting bracket – 1.7 litre engines

54 Undo the oil level dipstick guide tube upper retaining bolt. Undo the two lower bolts securing the dipstick tube flange to the sump and remove the dipstick tube. Collect the O-ring seal.

55 Undo the three bolts securing the air conditioning compressor to the compressor mounting bracket. Lift the compressor off the mounting bracket and secure it to the front body panel using cable ties or similar **(see illustration)**. Do not disconnect the refrigerant lines from the compressor.

56 Undo the three upper bolts and two lower bolts securing the compressor mounting bracket to the cylinder head and cylinder block. Withdraw the mounting bracket from the engine, release the wiring harness retaining clip and remove the mounting bracket **(see illustration)**.

57 Undo the three bolts and remove the exhaust manifold heat shield on the right-hand side **(see illustrations)**.

58 Undo the two bolts securing the EGR valve pipe to the EGR valve. Withdraw the pipe slightly and collect the gasket **(see illustrations 3.26a and 3.26b).**

59 Undo the bolt securing the EGR valve cooler mounting bracket to the cylinder head on the left-hand side **(see illustration)**.

60 Undo the bolt securing the EGR valve cooler coolant pipe to the thermostat housing **(see illustration)**.

61 Release the retaining clip securing the EGR valve cooler pipe to the bypass hose **(see illustration)**.

62 Undo the two EGR valve cooler flange bolts **(see illustration)**. Withdraw the EGR cooler pipe from the bypass hose and collect the cooler flange gasket.

3.57a Undo the three bolts (arrowed)…

3.57b …and remove the exhaust manifold heat shield on the right-hand side – 1.7 litre engines

3.59 Undo the bolt securing the EGR valve cooler bracket – 1.7 litre engines

3.60 Undo the bolt (arrowed) securing the EGR valve cooler coolant pipe – 1.7 litre engines

3.61 Release the retaining clip (arrowed) securing the EGR valve cooler pipe to the bypass hose

3.62 Undo the two EGR valve cooler flange bolts (arrowed) – 1.7 litre engines

3.63a Undo the EGR valve cooler upper mounting bolt (arrowed)...

3.63b ...and remove the cooler assembly from the engine – 1.7 litre engines

63 Undo the EGR valve cooler upper mounting bolt and remove the cooler assembly from the engine **(see illustrations)**.

64 Refitting is the reverse of removal, bearing in mind the following points:

a) *Renew all disturbed gaskets and seals.*

b) *Tighten the retaining bolts/nuts to the specified torque (where given).*

c) *Refit the auxiliary drivebelt as described in Chapter 1B Section 24.*

d) *Refit the air cleaner assembly and outlet air duct as described in Chapter 4B Section 3.*

e) *Fill the engine with fresh oil as described in Chapter 1B Section 6.*

f) *Refit the engine undertray.*

g) *Refill the cooling system as described in Chapter 1B Section 30.*

EGR valve cooler enewal – SOHC (Z19DT and DTL) engines

65 Drain the cooling system as described in Chapter 1B Section 30.

66 Remove the plastic cover over the top of the engine.

67 Remove the windscreen cowl panel as described in Chapter 11 Section 20.

68 Remove the battery and battery tray as described in Chapter 5A Section 4.

69 Slacken the retaining clips and remove the charge air hose from the throttle housing and intercooler.

70 Slacken the retaining clips and disconnect the two coolant hoses from the metal coolant pipe assembly at the rear of the engine.

71 Unscrew the two nuts securing the wiring harness and coolant pipe assembly to the starter motor bracket and the nut securing the pipes to the thermostat housing stud. Free the harness and pipes from the bracket.

72 Slacken the retaining clips securing the remaining coolant hoses to the coolant pipe assembly and manoeuvre the pipe assembly from the engine.

73 Undo the two bolts securing the rear metal EGR pipe to the EGR valve. Undo the retaining nut and bolt and release the metal EGR pipe clamp from the EGR valve heat exchanger. Separate the pipe from the heat exchanger and recover the gasket from the pipe fitting.

74 Similarly, undo the retaining nut and bolt and release the front metal EGR pipe clamp from the EGR valve heat exchanger.

75 Free the vacuum reservoir mounting bracket from the rear of the cylinder block by undoing the three mounting bracket retaining bolts.

76 Slacken the retaining clips and disconnect the two coolant hoses from the EGR valve heat exchanger. Undo the retaining nut and bolt securing the heat exchanger to the cylinder head and remove the heat exchanger from the engine.

77 Refitting is the reverse of removal, bearing in mind the following points:

a) *Renew all disturbed gaskets and seals.*

b) *Tighten the retaining bolts/nuts to the specified torque.*

c) *Refit the battery tray and battery as described in Chapter 5A Section 4.*

d) *Refill the cooling system as described in Chapter 1B Section 30.*

EGR valve heat exchanger renewal – DOHC (Z19DTH) engines

78 Drain the cooling system as described in Chapter 1B Section 30.

79 Remove the plastic cover over the top of the engine.

80 Remove the battery and battery tray as described in Chapter 5A Section 4.

81 Remove the windscreen cowl panel as described in Chapter 11 Section 20.

82 Release the two retaining clips and disconnect the charge air hose from the throttle housing, and intercooler.

83 Slacken the retaining clips and disconnect the two coolant hoses from the metal coolant pipe assembly at the rear of the engine.

84 Unscrew the two nuts securing the wiring harness and coolant pipe assembly to the starter motor bracket and the nut securing the pipes to the thermostat housing stud. Free the harness and pipes from the bracket.

85 Slacken the retaining clips securing the remaining coolant hoses to the coolant pipe assembly and manoeuvre the pipe assembly from the engine.

86 Remove the thermostat housing as described in Chapter 3 Section 4.

87 Slacken the retaining clips and remove the charge air hose from the turbocharger and intercooler.

88 Release the retaining clip and disconnect the coolant hose from the metal coolant pipe at the front of the engine.

89 Release the retaining clips and disconnect the coolant hoses from the EGR valve heat exchanger.

90 Undo the two bolts securing the rear metal EGR pipe to the EGR valve. Undo the retaining nut and bolt and release the metal EGR pipe clamp from the EGR valve heat exchanger. Separate the pipe from the heat exchanger and recover the gasket from the pipe fitting.

91 Similarly, undo the two bolts securing the front metal EGR pipe to the exhaust manifold. Undo the retaining nut and bolt and release the metal EGR pipe clamp from the EGR valve heat exchanger. Separate the pipe from the heat exchanger and recover the gasket from the pipe fitting.

92 Undo the two bolts and remove the heat exchanger from the engine.

93 Refitting is the reverse of removal, bearing in mind the following points:

a) *Renew all disturbed gaskets and seals.*

b) *Tighten the retaining bolts to the specified torque.*

c) *Refit the thermostat housing as described in Chapter 3 Section 4.*

d) *Refit the battery tray and battery as described in Chapter 5A Section 4.*

e) *Refill the cooling system as described in Chapter 1B Section 30.*

4 Catalytic converter – general information and precautions

1 The catalytic converter is a reliable and simple device which needs no maintenance in itself, but there are some facts of which an owner should be aware if the converter is to function properly for its full service life.

Petrol engines

a) DO NOT use leaded petrol or LRP in a car equipped with a catalytic converter – the lead will coat the precious metals, reducing their converting efficiency and will eventually destroy the converter.

b) Always keep the ignition and fuel systems well-maintained in accordance with the manufacturer's schedule.

c) If the engine develops a misfire, do not drive the car at all (or at least as little as possible) until the fault is cured.

d) DO NOT push- or tow-start the car – this will soak the catalytic converter in unburned fuel, causing it to overheat when the engine does start.

e) DO NOT switch off the ignition at high engine speeds.

f) DO NOT use fuel or engine oil additives – these may contain substances harmful to the catalytic converter.

g) DO NOT continue to use the car if the engine burns oil to the extent of leaving a visible trail of blue smoke.

h) Remember that the catalytic converter operates at very high temperatures. DO NOT, therefore, park the car in dry undergrowth, over long grass or piles of dead leaves after a long run.

i) Remember that the catalytic converter is FRAGILE – do not strike it with tools during servicing work.

j) In some cases a sulphurous smell (like that of rotten eggs) may be noticed from the exhaust. This is common to many catalytic converter-equipped cars and once the car has covered a few thousand miles the problem should disappear – it could also be the brand of fuel used; try using a different filling station.

k) The catalytic converter, used on a well-maintained and well-driven car, should last for between 50 000 and 100 000 miles – if the converter is no longer effective it must be renewed.

Diesel engines

2 Refer to the information given in parts f, g, h, i and k of the petrol engines information given above.

Chapter 5 Part A
Starting and charging systems

Contents

Section number

Alternator – removal and refitting 8
Alternator – testing and overhaul 9
Auxiliary drivebelt – removal and refitting. 6
Auxiliary drivebelt tensioner – removal and refitting. 7
Battery – testing and charging 3
Battery disconnection, replacement and battery tray
 removal and refitting. 4
Charging system – testing 5
Electrical fault finding – general information 2
General information, precautions and battery disconnection 1
Glow plugs (diesel engine models) – removal, inspection and
 refitting 17

Section number

Ignition switch – removal and refitting 13
Oil level sensor – removal and refitting. 15
Oil pressure warning light switch – removal and refitting. 14
Pre/post-heating system (diesel engine models) – description
 and testing 16
Pre/post-heating system control unit (diesel engine models) –
 removal and refitting. 18
Starter motor – removal and refitting 11
Starter motor – testing and overhaul 12
Starting system – testing 10

Degrees of difficulty

Easy, suitable for novice with little experience	**Fairly easy,** suitable for beginner with some experience	**Fairly difficult,** suitable for competent DIY mechanic	**Difficult,** suitable for experienced DIY mechanic	**Very difficult,** suitable for expert DIY or professional

Specifications

General
Electrical system type . . . . 12 volt negative earth

Battery
Type . . . . Lead-acid, 'maintenance-free' (sealed for life)
Charge condition:
  Poor . . . . 12.5 volts
  Normal . . . . 12.6 volts
  Good. . . . . 12.7 volts

Torque wrench settings

	Nm	lbf ft
Petrol engine models		
Alternator:		
Alternator to mounting bracket	35	26
Auxiliary drivebelt tensioner	50	37
Oil level sensor	8	6
Oil pressure warning light switch	20	15
Roadwheel bolts	110	81
Starter motor:		
Intake manifold support bracket bolts	8	6
Starter motor mounting bolts	25	18
Diesel engine models		
Alternator mounting bolts:		
1.7 litre engines:		
Upper bolt	20	15
Lower bolt	45	33
1.9 litre engines	70	52
Auxiliary drivebelt tensioner	50	37
Glow plugs:		
1.7 litre engines	14	10
1.9 litre engines	8	6
Oil pressure warning light switch:		
1.7 litre engines	21	16
1.9 litre engines	25	18
Roadwheel bolts	110	81
Starter motor mounting bolts:		
1.7 litre engines:		
Upper bolt	60	44
Lower bolt	38	28
1.9 litre engines	25	18

1 General information, precautions and battery disconnection

General information

1 The engine electrical system consists mainly of the charging and starting systems, and the diesel engine pre/post-heating system. Because of their engine-related functions, these components are covered separately from the body electrical devices such as the lights, instruments, etc (which are covered in Chapter 12). On petrol engine models refer to Part B for information on the ignition system.

2 The electrical system is of 12 volt negative earth type.

3 The battery is of the maintenance-free (sealed for life) type, and is charged by the alternator, which is belt-driven from the crankshaft pulley.

4 The starter motor is of pre-engaged type incorporating an integral solenoid. On starting, the solenoid moves the drive pinion into engagement with the flywheel/driveplate ring gear before the starter motor is energised. Once the engine has started, a one-way clutch prevents the motor armature being driven by the engine until the pinion disengages.

5 Further details of the various systems are given in the relevant Sections of this Chapter. While some repair procedures are given, the usual course of action is to renew the component concerned.

Precautions

6 It is necessary to take extra care when working on the electrical system to avoid damage to semi-conductor devices (diodes and transistors), and to avoid the risk of personal injury. In addition to the precautions given in *Safety first!* at the beginning of this manual, observe the following when working on the system:

- Always remove rings, watches, etc, before working on the electrical system. Even with the battery disconnected, capacitive discharge could occur if a component's live terminal is earthed through a metal object. This could cause a shock or nasty burn.

- Do not reverse the battery connections. Components such as the alternator, electronic control units, or any other components having semi-conductor circuitry could be irreparably damaged.

- If the engine is being started using jump leads and a slave battery, connect the batteries positive-to-positive and negative-to-negative (see *Jump starting*). This also applies when connecting a battery charger but in this case both of the battery terminals should first be disconnected.

- Never disconnect the battery terminals, the alternator, any electrical wiring or any test instruments when the engine is running.

- Do not allow the engine to turn the alternator when the alternator is not connected.

- Never test for alternator output by flashing the output lead to earth.

- Never use an ohmmeter of the type incorporating a hand-cranked generator for circuit or continuity testing.

- Always ensure that the battery negative lead is disconnected when working on the electrical system.

- Before using electric-arc welding equipment on the car, disconnect the battery, alternator and components such as the fuel injection/ignition electronic control unit to protect them from the risk of damage.

2 Electrical fault finding – general information

1 Refer to Chapter 12 Section 2.

3 Battery – testing and charging

Testing

Traditional and low maintenance battery

1 If the vehicle covers a small annual mileage, it is worthwhile checking the specific gravity of the electrolyte every three months to determine the state of charge of the battery. Use a hydrometer to make the check and compare the results with the following table. Note that the specific gravity readings assume an electrolyte temperature of 15°C; for every 10°C below 15°C subtract 0.007. For every 10°C above 15°C add 0.007.

	Ambient temperature above 25°C	Ambient temperature below 25°C
Fully-charged	1.210 to 1.230	1.270 to 1.290
70% charged	1.170 to 1.190	1.230 to 1.250
Discharged	1.050 to 1.070	1.110 to 1.130

2 If the battery condition is suspect, first check the specific gravity of electrolyte in each cell. A variation of 0.040 or more between any cells indicates loss of electrolyte or deterioration of the internal plates.

3 If the specific gravity variation is 0.040 or more, the battery should be renewed. If the cell variation is satisfactory but the battery is discharged, it should be charged as described later in this Section.

Maintenance-free battery

4 Where a 'sealed for life' maintenance-free battery is fitted, topping-up and testing of the electrolyte in each cell is not possible. The condition of the battery can therefore only be tested using a battery condition indicator or a voltmeter.

5 Some models are fitted with a maintenance-free battery with a built-in 'magic-eye' charge condition indicator. The indicator is located in the top of the battery casing, and indicates the condition of the battery from its colour **(see illustration)**. If the indicator shows green, then the battery is in a good state of charge. If the indicator turns darker, eventually to black, then the battery requires charging, as described later in this Section. If the indicator shows clear/yellow, then the electrolyte level in the battery is too low to allow further use, and the battery should be renewed. Do not attempt to charge, load or jump start a battery when the indicator shows clear/yellow.

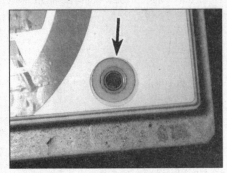

3.5 Battery charge condition indicator – 'Delco' type battery

All battery types

6 If testing the battery using a voltmeter, connect the voltmeter across the battery and compare the result with those given in the Specifications under 'charge condition'. The test is only accurate if the battery has not been subjected to any kind of charge for the previous six hours. If this is not the case, switch on the headlights for 30 seconds, then wait four to five minutes before testing the battery after switching off the headlights. All other electrical circuits must be switched off, so check that the doors and tailgate are fully shut when making the test.

7 If the voltage reading is less than 12.2 volts, then the battery is discharged, whilst a reading of 12.2 to 12.4 volts indicates a partially-discharged condition.

8 If the battery is to be charged, remove it from the vehicle (Section 4) and charge it as described later in this Section.

Charging

Note: *The following is intended as a guide only. Always refer to the manufacturer's recommendations (often printed on a label attached to the battery) before charging a battery.*

Traditional and low maintenance battery

9 Charge the battery at a rate of 3.5 to 4 amps and continue to charge the battery at this rate until no further rise in specific gravity is noted over a four hour period.

10 Alternatively, a trickle charger charging at the rate of 1.5 amps can safely be used overnight.

11 Specially rapid 'boost' charges which are claimed to restore the power of the battery in 1 to 2 hours are not recommended, as they can cause serious damage to the battery plates through overheating.

12 While charging the battery, note that the temperature of the electrolyte should never exceed 38°C.

Maintenance-free battery

13 This battery type takes considerably longer to fully recharge than the standard type, the time taken being dependent on the extent of discharge, but it will take anything up to three days.

14 A constant voltage type charger is required, to be set, when connected, to 13.9 to 14.9 volts with a charger current below 25 amps. Using this method, the battery should be usable within three hours, giving a voltage reading of 12.5 volts, but this is for a partially-discharged battery and, as mentioned, full charging can take considerably longer.

15 If the battery is to be charged from a fully-discharged state (condition reading less than 12.2 volts), have it recharged by your Vauxhall/Opel dealer or local automotive electrician, as the charge rate is higher and constant supervision during charging is necessary.

4 Battery disconnection, replacement and battery tray removal and refitting

Battery

Disconnection

1 Numerous systems fitted to the vehicle require battery power to be available at all times, either to ensure their continued operation (such as the clock) or to maintain control unit memories which would be erased if the battery were to be disconnected. Whenever the battery is to be disconnected therefore, first note the following, to ensure that there are no unforeseen consequences of this action:

a) *First, on any vehicle with central locking, it is a wise precaution to remove the key from the ignition, and to keep it with you, so that it does not get locked in, if the central locking should engage accidentally when the battery is reconnected.*

b) *Depending on model and specification, the Vauxhall anti-theft alarm system may be of the type which is automatically activated when the vehicle battery is disconnected and/or reconnected. To prevent the alarm sounding on models so equipped, switch the ignition on, then off, and disconnect the battery within 15 seconds. If the alarm is activated when the battery is reconnected, switch the ignition on then off to deactivate the alarm.*

c) *If a security-coded audio unit is fitted, and the unit and/or the battery is disconnected, the unit will not function again on reconnection until the correct security code is entered. Details of this procedure, which varies according to the unit fitted, are given in the vehicle audio system operating instructions. Ensure you have the correct code before you disconnect the battery. If you do not have the code or details of the correct procedure, but can supply proof of ownership and a legitimate reason for wanting this information, a Vauxhall dealer may be able to help.*

d) *The engine management electronic control unit is of the 'self-learning' type, meaning that as it operates, it also monitors and stores the settings which give optimum engine performance under all operating conditions. When the battery is disconnected, these settings are lost and the ECU reverts to the base settings programmed into its memory at the factory. On restarting, this may lead to the engine running/idling roughly for a short while, until the ECU has relearned the optimum settings. This process is best accomplished by taking the vehicle on a road test (for approximately 15 min- utes), covering all engine speeds and loads, concentrating mainly in the 2500 to 3500 rpm region*

4.3 Unscrew the battery negative (–) terminal retaining nut, then lift the terminal clamp off the batterypost

4.6 Unscrew the retaining bolt (arrowed) and remove the battery clamp

4.10 Release the wiring harness retaining clip from the battery tray

4.11 Unclip the coolant hose(s) and release it from the battery tray

4.12 On diesel engine models, unclip the pre/post-heating system control unit from the front of the batterytray

4.13 Undo the three retaining bolts (arrowed) and remove the battery tray from the engine compartment

e) *On models equipped with automatic transmission, the transmission selector lever assembly incorporates an electrically-operated selector lever lock mechanism that prevents the lever being moved out of the P position unless the ignition is switched on and the brake pedal is depressed. If the selector lever is in the P position and the battery is disconnected, it will not be possible to move the selector lever out of position P by the normal means. Although it is possible to manually override the system (see Chapter 7B), it is sensible to move the selector lever to the N position before disconnecting the battery.*

f) *On models with electric windows, it will be necessary to reprogramme the motors to restore the one-touch function of the buttons, after reconnection of the battery. To do this, fully close both front windows. With the windows closed, depress the up button of the driver's side window for approximately 5 seconds, then release it and depress the passenger side window up button for approximately 5 seconds.*

g) *On models with an electric sliding sunroof, it will be necessary to fully open and fully close the sunroof after battery reconnection, to recalibrate the sensors.*

h) *On all models, when reconnecting the battery after disconnection, switch on the ignition and wait 10 seconds to allow the*

electronic vehicle systems to stabilise and re-initialise.

2 The battery is located at the front, left-hand side of the engine compartment.

3 Open the battery jacket (where fitted) and disconnect the lead at the negative (–) terminal by unscrewing the retaining nut and removing the terminal clamp **(see illustration)**. Note that the battery negative (–) and positive (+) terminal connections are stamped on the battery case.

4 Disconnect the lead at the positive (+) terminal by lifting the plastic terminal cover, unscrewing the retaining nut and removing the terminal clamp. If necessary, the auxiliary lead may also be unbolted from the terminal.

Removal

5 Disconnect the leads from the battery terminals as described previously in this Section.

6 On the inner side of the battery, unscrew the bolt and remove the retaining clamp **(see illustration)**.

7 Carefully lift the battery from its location and remove it from the car. Make sure the battery is kept upright at all times.

Refitting

Note: *As a precaution, before refitting, the battery check that all doors are unlocked.*

8 Refitting is a reversal of removal, but smear petroleum jelly on the terminals after reconnecting the leads to reduce corrosion,

and always reconnect the positive lead first, followed by the negative lead.

Battery tray

Removal

9 Remove the battery as described previously. Where fitted, remove the battery jacket.

10 Release the wiring harness retaining clip from the battery tray and move the harness to one side **(see illustration)**.

11 Unclip the coolant hose(s) and release it from the battery tray **(see illustration)**.

12 Unclip the pre/post-heating system control unit from the front of the battery tray and move it to one side **(see illustration)**.

13 Undo the three retaining bolts and remove the battery tray from the engine compartment **(see illustration)**.

Refitting

14 Refitting is a reversal of removal.

---

5   Charging system – testing

Note: *Refer to the precautions given in 'Safety first!' and in Section 1 of this Chapter before starting work.*

1 If the ignition no-charge warning light fails to illuminate when the ignition is switched on, first check the alternator wiring connections. If satisfactory, check the condition of all related fuses, fusible links, wiring connections and earthing points. If this fails to reveal the fault, the vehicle should be taken to a Vauxhall/Opel dealer or auto-electrician, as further testing entails the use of specialist diagnostic equipment.

2 If the ignition warning light illuminates when the engine is running, stop the engine and check the condition of the auxiliary drivebelt (see the relevant Part of Chapter 1) and the security of the alternator wiring connections. If satisfactory, have the alternator checked by a Vauxhall/Opel dealer or auto-electrician.

3 If the alternator output is suspect even though the warning light functions correctly, the regulated voltage may be checked as follows.

4 Connect a voltmeter across the battery terminals, and start the engine.

5 Increase the engine speed until the voltmeter reading remains steady; the reading should be approximately 12 to 13 volts, and no more than 14 volts.

6 Switch on as many electrical accessories (eg, the headlights, heated rear window and heater blower) as possible, and check that the alternator maintains the regulated voltage at around 13.5 to 14.5 volts.

7 If the regulated voltage is not as stated, the fault may be due to worn brushes, weak brush springs, a faulty voltage regulator, a faulty diode, a severed phase winding, or worn or damaged slip-rings. The alternator should be renewed or taken to a Vauxhall/Opel dealer or auto-electrician for testing and repair.

6 Auxiliary drivebelt – removal and refitting

1 Refer to Chapter 1A Section 23 or Chapter 1B Section 24.

7 Auxiliary drivebelt tensioner – removal and refitting

Petrol engine models

Removal

1 Firmly apply the handbrake, then jack up the front of the car and support it securely on axle stands (see *Jacking and vehicle support*). Remove the right-hand front roadwheel.

2 Remove the air cleaner assembly and air intake duct as described in Chapter 4A Section 2.

3 Remove the auxiliary drivebelt as described in Chapter 1A Section 23.

4 Undo the central mounting bolt, and remove the tensioner assembly from the engine **(see illustration)**.

Refitting

5 Place the tensioner assembly in position and tighten the tensioner central mounting bolt to the specified torque.

6 Refit the auxiliary drivebelt as described in Chapter 1A Section 23.

7 Refit the air cleaner assembly and air intake duct as described in Chapter 4A Section 2.

8 Refit the roadwheel then lower the car to the ground. Tighten the roadwheel bolts to the specified torque.

Diesel engine models

Removal

9 Firmly apply the handbrake, then jack up the front of the car and support it securely on axle stands (see *Jacking and vehicle support*). Remove the right-hand front roadwheel.

10 Remove the auxiliary drivebelt as described in Chapter 1B Section 24.

11 Undo the central mounting bolt, and remove the tensioner assembly from the engine **(see illustration)**.

Refitting

12 Place the tensioner assembly in position ensuring that the locating peg on the tensioner mounting surface engages correctly with the corresponding hole in the mounting bracket. Tighten the tensioner central mounting bolt to the specified torque.

13 Refit the auxiliary drivebelt as described in Chapter 1B Section 24.

14 Refit the roadwheel then lower the car to the ground. Tighten the roadwheel bolts to the specified torque.

8 Alternator – removal and refitting

Petrol engines

Removal

1 Disconnect the battery negative terminal (refer to Section 4).

2 Firmly apply the handbrake, then jack up the front of the car and support it securely on axle stands (see *Jacking and vehicle support*). Remove the right-hand front roadwheel.

3 Remove the air cleaner assembly and air intake duct as described in Chapter 4A Section 2.

4 On non-VVT (variable valve timing) engines, disconnect the wiring connector and the operating rod from the port deactivation vacuum valve on the intake manifold. Unscrew the two mounting bolts and move the valve to one side.

5 Remove the auxiliary drivebelt as described in Chapter 1A Section 23.

6 Unscrew the nuts and disconnect the two wires from the rear of the alternator.

7 Unscrew the upper and lower mounting bolts and withdraw the alternator upwards from the block.

7.4 Auxiliary drivebelt tensioner mounting bolt (arrowed)

7.11 Undo the central mounting bolt (arrowed) and remove the tensioner assembly – 1.9 litre engine shown

8.18 Alternator mounting bolts

8.22 Alternator lower front mounting bolt (arrowed)

8.26 Alternator upper rear mounting bolts (arrowed)

Refitting

8 Manoeuvre the alternator into position and refit the upper and lower mounting bolts. Tighten the bolts to the specified torque.

9 Reconnect the wiring to the alternator terminals and tighten the retaining nuts securely.

10 Refit the auxiliary drivebelt as described in Chapter 1A Section 23.

11 On non-VVT engines, locate the port deactivation vacuum valve back into position and secure with the two mounting bolts securely tightened. Reconnect the wiring connector and the operating rod to the valve.

12 Refit the air cleaner assembly and air intake duct as described in Chapter 4A Section 2.

13 Refit the roadwheel then lower the car to the ground. Tighten the roadwheel bolts to the specified torque.

14 On completion, reconnect the battery negative terminal.

Diesel engine models

Removal

15 Disconnect the battery negative lead as described in Section 4.

1.7 litre engines

16 Remove the auxiliary drivebelt as described in Chapter 1B Section 24.

17 Unscrew the retaining nut and disconnect the wiring terminal, then unplug the wiring block connector from the rear of the alternator.

18 Undo the mounting bolts and manoeuvre the alternator upwards and out of position **(see illustration)**.

1.9 litre engines

19 Remove the windscreen cowl panel as described in Chapter 11 Section 20.

20 Firmly apply the handbrake, then jack up the front of the car and support it securely on axle stands (see *Jacking and vehicle support*). Remove the right-hand front roadwheel.

21 Remove the auxiliary drivebelt as described in Chapter 1B Section 24.

22 Undo the alternator lower front mounting bolt **(see illustration)**.

23 Remove the fuel filter crash box as described in Chapter 4B Section 9.

24 Release the engine management wiring

harness from the support brackets at the rear of the alternator.

25 Unscrew the three retaining nuts and disconnect the wiring connectors from the alternator terminals.

26 Undo the alternator upper rear mounting bolts and manoeuvre the alternator upwards and out of position **(see illustration)**.

Refitting

27 Refitting is a reversal of removal.

9 Alternator – testing and overhaul

1 If the alternator is thought to be suspect, it should be removed from the vehicle and taken to an auto-electrician for testing. Most auto-electricians will be able to supply and fit brushes at a reasonable cost. However, check on the cost of repairs before proceeding as it may prove more economical to obtain a new or exchange alternator.

10 Starting system – testing

Note: *Refer to the precautions given in 'Safety first!' and in Section 1 of this Chapter before starting work.*

1 If the starter motor fails to operate during the normal starting procedure, the possible causes are as follows:
a) *The engine immobiliser is faulty.*
b) *The battery is faulty.*
c) *The electrical connections between the switch, solenoid, battery and starter motor are somewhere failing to pass the necessary current from the battery through the starter to earth.*
d) *The solenoid is faulty.*
e) *The starter motor is mechanically or electrically defective.*

2 To check the battery, switch on the headlights. If they dim after a few seconds, this indicates that the battery is discharged – recharge (see Section 3) or renew the battery. If the headlights glow brightly, operate the starter switch while watching the headlights. If they dim, then this

indicates that current is reaching the starter motor, therefore the fault must lie in the starter motor. If the lights continue to glow brightly (and no clicking sound can be heard from the starter motor solenoid), this indicates that there is a fault in the circuit or solenoid – see the following paragraphs. If the starter motor turns slowly when operated, but the battery is in good condition, then this indicates either that the starter motor is faulty, or there is considerable resistance somewhere in the circuit.

3 If a fault in the circuit is suspected, disconnect the battery leads (including the earth connection to the body), the starter/solenoid wiring and the engine/transmission earth strap. Thoroughly clean the connections, and reconnect the leads and wiring. Use a voltmeter or test light to check that full battery voltage is available at the battery positive lead connection to the solenoid. Smear petroleum jelly around the battery terminals to prevent corrosion – corroded connections are among the most frequent causes of electrical system faults.

4 If the battery and all connections are in good condition, check the circuit by disconnecting the ignition switch supply wire from the solenoid terminal. Connect a voltmeter or test lamp between the wire end and a good earth (such as the battery negative terminal), and check that the wire is live when the ignition switch is turned to the 'start' position, or the 'start/stop' button is depressed. If it is, then the circuit is sound – if not the circuit wiring can be checked as described in Chapter 12 Section 2.

5 The solenoid contacts can be checked by connecting a voltmeter or test light between the battery positive feed connection on the starter side of the solenoid and earth. When the ignition switch is turned to the 'start' position, or the 'start/stop' button is depressed, there should be a reading or lighted bulb, as applicable. If there is no reading or lighted bulb, the solenoid is faulty and should be renewed.

6 If the circuit and solenoid are proved sound, the fault must lie in the starter motor. In this event, it may be possible to have the starter motor overhauled by a specialist, but check on the cost of spares before proceeding, as it may prove more economical to obtain a new or exchange motor.

11 Starter motor – removal and refitting

Petrol engines

Removal

1 Disconnect the battery negative terminal (refer to Section 4).

2 Firmly apply the handbrake, then jack up the front of the vehicle and support it securely on axle stands (see *Jacking and vehicle support*).

3 Where applicable, detach the vacuum hose and the oxygen sensor wiring harness from the intake manifold support bracket.

4 Unscrew the two retaining bolts and remove the support bracket from the underside of the intake manifold.

5 Unscrew the two nuts and disconnect the battery positive cable and the starter trigger wire from the starter.

6 Unscrew the nut and disconnect the earth cable from the starter mounting bolt.

7 Unscrew the two mounting bolts and withdraw the starter motor from the engine.

Refitting

8 Refitting is a reversal of removal, tightening the retaining bolts to the specified torque. Ensure all wiring is correctly routed and its retaining nuts are securely tightened.

Diesel engine models

Removal

9 Disconnect the battery negative terminal (refer to Section 4).

10 Remove the windscreen cowl panel as described in Chapter 11 Section 20.

11 Firmly apply the handbrake, then jack up the front of the car and support it securely on axle stands (see *Jacking and vehicle support*).

1.7 litre models

12 Remove the battery and battery tray as described in Section 4.

13 Unscrew and remove the starter motor upper mounting bolt.

14 Remove the engine undertray.

11.19a Remove the oil filler cap …

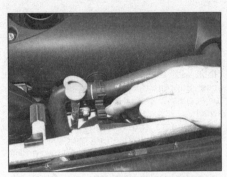

11.19c … release the engine breather hose …

15 Unscrew the union and withdraw the exhaust pressure sensor from the diesel particulate filter. Release the hose clip and remove the exhaust pressure sensor and connecting hose.

16 Unscrew the retaining nut and bolt, then disconnect the wiring from the starter motor solenoid.

17 Undo the retaining nut and disconnect the earth lead from the starter motor lower stud bolt.

18 Unscrew the lower stud bolt and withdraw the starter motor from the engine.

1.9 litre models

19 On SOHC (Z19DT and Z19DTL) engines, remove the oil filler cap and unscrew the two bolts securing the plastic cover over the top of the engine. Release the engine breather hose, then lift off the cover and refit the oil filler

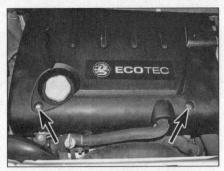

11.19b … unscrew the two bolts (arrowed) …

11.19d … and lift off the plastic engine cover – Z19DT and DTL diesel engines

cap **(see illustrations)**. On DOHC (Z19DTH) engines, remove the plastic cover by pulling it upwards off the mounting studs.

20 Undo the retaining bolts and plastic rivets and remove the undertray from beneath the engine.

21 Slacken and remove the two retaining nuts and disconnect the wiring from the starter motor solenoid **(see illustration)**. Recover the washers under the nuts.

22 Unscrew the retaining nut and disconnect the earth lead from the starter motor lower stud bolt **(see illustration)**.

23 Open the retaining clips and release the two heater hoses from the coolant pipe support bracket.

24 Undo the two nuts and release the wiring harness from the support bracket above the starter motor **(see illustration)**.

11.21 Undo the nuts (arrowed) and disconnect the starter solenoid wiring connectors

11.22 Unscrew the nut (arrowed) and disconnect the earth lead from the starter motor stud bolt

11.24 Undo the nuts and release the wiring harness from the support bracket

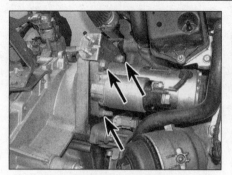

11.25 Unscrew the bolts (arrowed), collect the wiring harness bracket and remove the starter from above

14.16 Oil pressure warning light switch (arrowed)

15.2 Slide off the retaining clip (arrowed) and free the oil level sensor wiring connector from the sump

25 Unscrew the starter motor lower stud bolt and the two upper mounting bolts **(see illustration)**. Collect the wiring harness support bracket then manoeuvre the starter motor upwards and out of position.

Refitting

26 Refitting is a reversal of removal, tightening the retaining bolts to the specified torque. Ensure all wiring is correctly routed and its retaining nuts are securely tightened.

12 Starter motor –
testing and overhaul

1 If the starter motor is thought to be suspect, it should be removed from the vehicle and taken to an auto-electrician for testing. Most auto-electricians will be able to supply and fit brushes at a reasonable cost. However, check on the cost of repairs before proceeding as it may prove more economical to obtain a new or exchange motor.

13 Ignition switch –
removal and refitting

1 The switch is integral with the steering column lock, and removal and refitting is described in Chapter 10 Section 14.

14 Oil pressure warning light
switch – removal and refitting

Petrol engines

Removal

1 The oil pressure warning light switch is screwed into the front of the cylinder block.
2 Firmly apply the handbrake, then jack up the front of the car and support it securely on axle stands (see *Jacking and vehicle support*).

3 On models equipped with air conditioning, refer to Chapter 3 Section 11 and unbolt the air conditioning compressor from the cylinder block without disconnecting the refrigerant lines. Support the compressor to one side for access to the oil pressure warning light switch.
4 Disconnect the wiring connector then unscrew the switch and recover the sealing washer. Be prepared for oil spillage, and if the switch is to be left removed from the engine for any length of time, plug the switch aperture.

Refitting

5 Examine the sealing washer (where fitted) for signs of damage or deterioration and if necessary renew.
6 Refit the switch and washer (where fitted), tightening it to the specified torque, and reconnect the wiring connector.
7 Where applicable, refit the air conditioning compressor as described in Chapter 3 Section 11.
8 Lower the vehicle to the ground then check and, if necessary, top-up the engine oil as described in *Weekly checks*.

Diesel engine models

1.7 litre engines

Removal

9 The oil pressure warning light switch is screwed into the oil filter housing at the rear of the engine.
10 Remove the plastic cover over the top of the engine.
11 Remove the starter motor as described in Section 11.
12 Disconnect the switch wiring connector, then unscrew the switch and collect the O-ring seal. Be prepared for oil spillage, and if the switch is to be left removed from the engine for any length of time, plug the switch aperture.

Refitting

13 Examine the O-ring seal for signs of damage or deterioration, and renew it if necessary.

14 Refit the switch, tightening it to the specified torque, and reconnect the wiring.
15 The remainder of refitting is a reversal of removal.

1.9 litre engines

Removal

16 The oil pressure warning light switch is screwed into the oil filter housing at the rear of the engine **(see illustration)**.
17 Firmly apply the handbrake, then jack up the front of the car and support it securely on axle stands (see *Jacking and vehicle support)*.
18 Undo the retaining bolts and plastic rivets and remove the undertray from beneath the engine.
19 Disconnect the wiring connector then unscrew the switch and recover the sealing washer. Be prepared for oil spillage, and if the switch is to be left removed from the engine for any length of time, plug the switch aperture.

Refitting

20 Examine the sealing washer for signs of damage or deterioration and if necessary renew.
21 Refit the switch and washer, tightening it to the specified torque, and reconnect the wiring connector.
22 Refit the engine undertray.
23 Lower the vehicle to the ground then check and, if necessary, top-up the engine oil as described in *Weekly checks*.

15 Oil level sensor –
removal and refitting

Removal

1 The oil level sensor is located inside the sump which must first be removed (see the relevant Part of Chapter 2).
2 With the sump removed, slide off the retaining clip and free the sensor wiring connector from the sump **(see illustration)**.
3 Undo the retaining bolts and remove the

15.3 Where fitted, undo the retaining bolts and remove the oil baffle plate

15.4 Undo the two bolts (arrowed) and remove the oil level sensor from the sump

17.7 Disconnect the wiring connector (arrowed) at the charge (boost) pressure sensor

oil baffle plate from inside the sump **(see illustration).**

4 Note the correct routing of the wiring then undo the retaining bolts and remove the sensor assembly from the sump **(see illustration).** Check the wiring connector seal for signs or damage and renew if necessary.

Refitting

5 Prior to refitting remove all traces of locking compound from the sensor retaining bolt and sump threads. Apply a drop of fresh locking compound to the bolt threads and lubricate the wiring connector seal with a smear of engine oil.

6 Fit the sensor, making sure the wiring is correctly routed, and securely tighten its retaining bolts. Ease the wiring connector through the sump, taking care not to damage its seal, and secure it in position with the retaining clip.

7 Ensure the sensor is correctly refitted then refit the oil baffle plate.

8 Refit the sump as described in the relevant Part of Chapter 2.

16 Pre/post-heating system (diesel engine models) – description and testing

Description

1 Each cylinder of the engine is fitted with a heater plug (commonly called a glow plug) screwed into it. The plugs are electrically-operated before and during start-up when the engine is cold. Electrical feed to the glow plugs is controlled via the pre/post-heating system control unit.

2 A warning light in the instrument panel tells the driver that pre/post-heating is taking place. When the light goes out, the engine is ready to be started. The voltage supply to the glow plugs continues for several seconds after the light goes out. If no attempt is made to start, the timer then cuts off the supply, in order to avoid draining the battery and overheating the glow plugs.

3 The glow plugs also provide a 'post-heating' function, whereby the glow plugs

remain switched on after the engine has started. The length of time 'post-heating' takes place is also determined by the control unit, and is dependent on engine temperature.

4 The fuel filter is fitted with a heating element to prevent the fuel 'waxing' in extreme cold temperature conditions and to improve combustion. The heating element is an integral part of the fuel filter housing and is controlled by the pre/post-heating system control unit.

Testing

5 If the system malfunctions, testing is ultimately by substitution of known good units, but some preliminary checks may be made as follows.

6 Connect a voltmeter or 12 volt test lamp between the glow plug supply cable and earth (engine or vehicle metal). Make sure that the live connection is kept clear of the engine and bodywork.

7 Have an assistant switch on the ignition, and check that voltage is applied to the glow plugs. Note the time for which the warning light is lit, and the total time for which voltage is applied before the system cuts out. Switch off the ignition.

8 At an underbonnet temperature of 20°C, typical times noted should be approximately 3 seconds for warning light operation. Warning light time will increase with lower temperatures and decrease with higher temperatures.

9 If there is no supply at all, the control unit or associated wiring is at fault.

10 To locate a defective glow plug, disconnect the wiring connector from each plug.

11 Use a continuity tester, or a 12 volt test lamp connected to the battery positive terminal, to check for continuity between each glow plug terminal and earth. The resistance of a glow plug in good condition is very low (less than 1 ohm), so if the test lamp does not light or the continuity tester shows a high resistance, the glow plug is certainly defective.

12 If an ammeter is available, the current draw of each glow plug can be checked. After an initial surge of 15 to 20 amps, each plug should draw 12 amps. Any plug which

draws much more or less than this is probably defective.

13 As a final check, the glow plugs can be removed and inspected as described in the following Section.

17 Glow plugs (diesel engine models) – removal, inspection and refitting

Caution: If the pre/post-heating system has just been energised, or if the engine has been running, the glow plugs will be very hot.

Removal

1.7 litre engines

1 The glow plugs are located at the rear of the cylinder head above the inlet manifold. To improve access, remove the windscreen cowl panel as described in Chapter 11 Section 20.

2 Lift off the plastic cover over the top of the engine by pulling it upwards off the mounting studs.

3 Disconnect the wiring from the glow plugs by squeezing the connectors with thumb and forefinger, and pulling them from the plug.

4 Unscrew the glow plugs and remove them from the cylinder head.

SOHC (Z19DT and Z19DTL) engines

5 The glow plugs are located at the rear of the cylinder head above the intake manifold. To gain access, remove the windscreen cowl panel as described in Chapter 11 Section 20.

6 Remove the oil filler cap and unscrew the two bolts securing the plastic cover over the top of the engine. Release the engine breather hose, then lift off the cover and refit the oil filler cap **(see illustrations 11.19a to 11.19d).**

7 Disconnect the wiring connector at the EGR valve and at the charge (boost) pressure sensor **(see illustration).**

8 Undo the two retaining bolts, disconnect the four vacuum hoses and remove the vacuum pipe assembly from the top of the camshaft cover.

9 Disconnect the fuel leak-off hose connection at each fuel injector by pushing in the locking clip and lifting out the hose fitting.

17.13 Unscrew the glow plugs and remove them from the cylinder head

Suitably plug or cap the leak-off hose union on each injector, and slip a plastic bag over the disconnected leak-off hose to prevent dirt entry. Release the leak-off hose from the plastic support bracket on the intake manifold.
10 Release the retaining clips and disconnect the two fuel return hoses at the fuel return damping chamber. Suitably plug or cover the open unions to prevent dirt entry.
11 Disconnect the fuel return hose quick-release fitting, then undo the two bolts and remove the damping chamber. Suitably plug or cover the open unions to prevent dirt entry.
12 Disconnect the wiring from the glow plugs by squeezing the connectors with thumb and forefinger, and pulling them from the plugs.
13 Unscrew the glow plugs and remove them from the cylinder head **(see illustration)**.

DOHC (Z19DTH) engines

14 The glow plugs are located at the rear of the cylinder head above the intake manifold. To gain access, remove the windscreen cowl panel as described in Chapter 11.
15 Remove the plastic engine cover by pulling it upwards off the mounting studs.
16 Disconnect the wiring from the glow plugs by squeezing the connectors with thumb and forefinger, and pulling them from the plugs.
17 Unscrew the glow plugs and remove them from the cylinder head **(see illustration 17.13)**.

Inspection

18 Inspect each glow plug for physical damage. Burnt or eroded glow plug tips can be caused by a bad injector spray pattern. Have the injectors checked if this type of damage is found.
19 If the glow plugs are in good physical condition, check them electrically using a 12 volt test lamp or continuity tester as described in the previous Section.
20 The glow plugs can be energised by applying 12 volts to them to verify that they heat up evenly and in the required time. Observe the following precautions.
a) *Support the glow plug by clamping it carefully in a vice or self-locking pliers. Remember it will become red-hot.*
b) *Make sure that the power supply or test lead incorporates a fuse or overload trip to protect against damage from a short-circuit.*
c) *After testing, allow the glow plug to cool for several minutes before attempting to handle it.*

21 A glow plug in good condition will start to glow red at the tip after drawing current for 5 seconds or so. Any plug which takes much longer to start glowing, or which starts glowing in the middle instead of at the tip, is defective.

Refitting

22 Carefully refit the plugs and tighten to the specified torque. Do not overtighten, as this can damage the glow plug element. Push the electrical connectors firmly onto the glow plugs.
23 The remainder of refitting is a reversal of removal, checking the operation of the glow plugs on completion.

18 Pre/post-heating system control unit (diesel engine models) – removal and refitting

Removal

1 The pre/post-heating system control unit is located on the left-hand side of the engine compartment where it is mounted onto the front of the battery tray.
2 Remove the battery as described in Section 4.
3 Unclip the control unit and slide it up and off the battery tray **(see illustration 4.12)**.
4 Disconnect the wiring connector from the base of the control unit and remove the unit from the engine compartment.

Refitting

5 Refitting is a reversal of removal.

Chapter 5 Part B
Ignition system – petrol engines

Contents

	Section number		Section number
Ignition module – removal and refitting	3	Ignition timing – checking and adjustment	4
Ignition system – general information	1	Knock sensor – removal and refitting	5
Ignition system – testing	2		

Degrees of difficulty

Easy, suitable for novice with little experience | **Fairly easy,** suitable for beginner with some experience | **Fairly difficult,** suitable for competent DIY mechanic | **Difficult,** suitable for experienced DIY mechanic | **Very difficult,** suitable for expert DIY or professional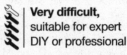

Specifications

General
System type	Distributorless ignition system
System application:	
Non-VVT (variable valve timing) engines	Multec-S
VVT (variable valve timing) engines	Simtec 75.1
Location of No 1 cylinder	Timing chain/timing belt end of engine
Firing order	1-3-4-2

Torque wrench setting	Nm	lbf ft
Ignition module retaining bolts	8	6

1 Ignition system – general information

1 The ignition system is integrated with the fuel injection system to form a combined engine management system under the control of one electronic control unit (ECU) – see Chapter 4A for further information. The ignition side of the system is of the distributorless type, and consists of the ignition module and the knock sensor.

2 The ignition module consists of four ignition coils, one per cylinder, in one casing mounted directly above the spark plugs. This module eliminates the need for any HT leads as the coils locate directly onto the relevant spark plug. The ECU uses its inputs from the various sensors to calculate the required ignition advance setting and coil charging time.

3 The knock sensor is mounted onto the cylinder block and informs the ECU when the engine is 'pinking' under load. The sensor is sensitive to vibration and detects the knocking which occurs when the engine starts to 'pink' (pre-ignite). The knock sensor sends an electrical signal to the ECU which in turn retards the ignition advance setting until the 'pinking' ceases.

4 The ignition systems fitted to the engines covered by this manual all operate in a similar fashion under the overall control of the engine management ECU. The systems comprise various sensors (whose inputs also provide data to control the fuel injection system) and

the ECU, in addition to the ignition module and spark plugs. Further details of the system sensors and the ECU are given in Chapter 4A.

5 The ECU selects the optimum ignition advance setting based on the information received from the various sensors, and fires the relevant ignition coil accordingly. The degree of advance can thus be constantly varied to suit the prevailing engine operating conditions.

 Warning: Due to the high voltages produced by the electronic ignition system, extreme care must be taken when working on the system with the ignition switched on. Persons with surgically-implanted cardiac pacemaker devices should keep well clear of the ignition circuits, components and test equipment.

2.2a Unclip and remove the ashtray insert ...

2.2b ... for access to the diagnostic socket (arrowed)

3.2 Disconnect the wiring connector from the ignition module

2 Ignition system – testing

1 If a fault appears in the engine management system, first ensure that all the system wiring connectors are securely connected and free of corrosion. Ensure that the fault is not due to poor maintenance; ie, check that the air cleaner filter element is clean, the spark plugs are in good condition and correctly gapped, the cylinder compression pressures are correct and that the engine breather hoses are clear and undamaged, referring to Chapters 1A, 2A and for further information.
2 If these checks fail to reveal the cause of the problem, the vehicle should be taken to a suitably-equipped Vauxhall/Opel dealer or engine management diagnostic specialist for testing. A diagnostic socket is located in the lower centre of the facia, behind the ashtray insert, to which a fault code reader or other suitable test equipment can be connected **(see illustrations)**. By using the code reader or test equipment, the engine management ECU can be interrogated, and any stored fault codes can be retrieved. This will allow the fault to be quickly and simply traced, alleviating the need to test all the system components individually, which is a time-consuming

operation that carries a risk of damaging the ECU.
3 The only ignition system checks which can be carried out by the home mechanic are those described in Chapter 1A relating to the spark plugs. If necessary, the system wiring and wiring connectors can be checked as described in Chapter 12 Section 2, ensuring that the ECU wiring connector(s) have first been disconnected.

3 Ignition module – removal and refitting

Removal

1 Unclip the wiring trough from the left-hand end of the cylinder head.
2 Disconnect the wiring connector at the left-hand end of the module **(see illustration)**.
3 Remove the cover from the ignition module by sliding it towards the transmission and lifting off **(see illustration)**.
4 Undo the two retaining bolts, and lift the module up and out of position **(see illustration)**. If the module proves reluctant to separate from the spark plugs, insert two long 8 mm bolts into the threaded holes in the top of the module, and pull up on the bolts to free the module from the plugs.

5 With the module removed, check the condition of the sealing grommets and renew if necessary **(see illustration)**.

Refitting

6 Refitting is the reversal of removal, tightening the retaining bolts to the specified torque.

4 Ignition timing – checking and adjustment

1 Due to the nature of the ignition system, the ignition timing is constantly being monitored and adjusted by the engine management ECU.
2 The only way in which the ignition timing can be checked is by using specialist diagnostic test equipment, connected to the engine management system diagnostic socket. No adjustment of the ignition timing is possible. Should the ignition timing be incorrect, then a fault is likely to be present in the engine management system.

5 Knock sensor – removal and refitting

1 Refer to the procedures contained in Chapter 4A Section 12, 13.

3.3 Slide the cover towards the transmission

3.4 Undo the two retaining bolts, and lift the module up and out of position

3.5 Check the condition of the sealing grommets and renew if necessary

Chapter 6
Clutch

Contents

	Section number			Section number
Clutch assembly – removal, inspection and refitting	6	General Information		1
Clutch hydraulic system – bleeding	2	Master cylinder – removal and refitting		3
Clutch pedal – removal and refitting	5	Release cylinder – removal and refitting		4

Degrees of difficulty

Easy, suitable for novice with little experience	**Fairly easy,** suitable for beginner with some experience	**Fairly difficult,** suitable for competent DIY mechanic	**Difficult,** suitable for experienced DIY mechanic	**Very difficult,** suitable for expert DIY or professional

Specifications

Type . . . . Single dry plate with diaphragm spring, hydraulically-operated

Friction disc
Diameter:
  Petrol engine models:
    1.6 litre engines . . . . 200 mm
    1.8 litre engines . . . . 205 mm
  Diesel engine models . . . . 239 mm
New lining thickness:
  Petrol engine models:
    1.6 and 1.8 litre engines . . . . 7.65 mm
  Diesel engine models . . . . 7.80 mm

Torque wrench settings	Nm	lbf ft
ABS hydraulic modulator mounting bracket bolts	20	15
Clutch master cylinder retaining nuts*	20	15
Clutch pedal bracket nut/bolts*	20	15
Pressure plate retaining bolts*	15	11
Release cylinder mounting bolts	5	4

*Use new fasteners

1 General Information

1 The clutch consists of a friction disc, a pressure plate assembly, and the hydraulic release cylinder (which incorporates the release bearing); all of these components are contained in the large cast-aluminium alloy bellhousing, sandwiched between the engine and the transmission.

2 The friction disc is fitted between the engine flywheel and the clutch pressure plate, and is allowed to slide on the transmission input shaft splines.

3 The pressure plate assembly is bolted to the engine flywheel. When the engine is running, drive is transmitted from the crankshaft, via the flywheel, to the friction disc (these components being clamped securely together by the pressure plate assembly) and from the friction disc to the transmission input shaft.

4 To interrupt the drive, the spring pressure must be relaxed. This is achieved using a hydraulic release mechanism which consists of the master cylinder, the release cylinder and the pipe/hose linking the two components. Depressing the clutch pedal pushes on the master cylinder pushrod which hydraulically forces the release cylinder piston against the pressure plate spring fingers. This causes the springs to deform and releases the clamping force on the friction disc.

5 The clutch is self-adjusting and requires no manual adjustment.

Semi-automatic clutch

6 Models equipped with the Easytronic MTA (Manual Transmission with Automatic shift), are fitted with a semi-automatic clutch. The clutch may be operated either fully-automatically or semi-automatically by means of the gear selector lever. There is no conventional clutch pedal fitted.

7 The Easytronic system essentially consists of a conventional manual gearbox and clutch fitted with electrical and hydraulic controls, the clutch being operated by a clutch module attached to the side of the transmission casing. Refer to Chapter 7C for more information. The clutch component removal and refitting procedures are included in this Chapter as they are very similar to those for the standard manual transmission.

2 Clutch hydraulic system – bleeding

Note: *On models equipped with the Easytronic transmission, the following manual method of bleeding the clutch is not possible since the hydraulic control unit is integral with the transmission. On these models, bleeding is carried out using the Vauxhall/Opel TECH2 diagnostic instrument, therefore this work should be entrusted to a Vauxhall/Opel dealer.*

Warning: Hydraulic fluid is poisonous; wash off immediately and thoroughly in the case of skin contact, and seek immediate medical advice if any fluid is swallowed or gets into the eyes. Certain types of hydraulic fluid are flammable, and may ignite when allowed into contact with hot components; when servicing any hydraulic system, it is safest to assume that the fluid is flammable, and to take precautions against the risk of fire as though it is petrol that is being handled. Hydraulic fluid is also an effective paint stripper, and will attack plastics; if any is spilt, it should be washed off immediately, using copious quantities of fresh water. Finally, it is hygroscopic (it absorbs moisture from the air) – old fluid may be contaminated and unfit for further use. When topping-up or renewing the fluid, always use the recommended type, and ensure that it comes from a freshly-opened sealed container.

General information

1 The correct operation of any hydraulic system is only possible after removing all air from the components and circuit; this is achieved by bleeding the system.

2 The manufacturer's stipulate that the system must be initially bled by the 'back-bleeding' method using Vauxhall/Opel special bleeding equipment. This entails connecting a pressure bleeding unit containing fresh brake fluid to the release cylinder bleed screw, with a collecting vessel connected to the brake fluid master cylinder reservoir. The pressure bleeding unit is then switched on, the bleed screw is opened and hydraulic fluid is delivered under pressure, backwards, to be expelled from the reservoir into the collecting vessel. Final bleeding is then carried out in the conventional way.

3 In practice, this method would normally only be required if new hydraulic components have been fitted, or if the system has been completely drained of hydraulic fluid. If the system has only been disconnected to allow component removal and refitting procedures to be carried out, such as removal and refitting of the transmission (for example for clutch renewal) or engine removal and refitting, then it is quite likely that normal bleeding will be sufficient.

4 Our advice would therefore be as follows:

a) *If the hydraulic system has only been partially disconnected, try bleeding by the conventional methods described in paragraphs 10 to 15, or 16 to 19.*

b) *If the hydraulic system has been completely drained and new components have been fitted, try bleeding by using the pressure bleeding method described in paragraphs 20 to 22.*

c) *If the above methods fail to produce a firm pedal on completion, it will be necessary to 'back-bleed' the system using Vauxhall/Opel bleeding equipment, or suitable alternative equipment as described in paragraphs 23 to 28.*

5 During the bleeding procedure, add only clean, unused hydraulic fluid of the recommended type; never re-use fluid that has already been bled from the system. Ensure that sufficient fluid is available before starting work.

6 If there is any possibility of incorrect fluid being already in the system, the hydraulic circuit must be flushed completely with uncontaminated, correct fluid.

7 If hydraulic fluid has been lost from the system, or air has entered because of a leak, ensure that the fault is cured before continuing further.

8 The bleed screw is located in the hose end fitting which is situated on the top of the transmission housing **(see illustration)**. On some models access to the bleed screw is limited and it may be necessary to jack up the front of the vehicle and support it on axle stands so that the screw can be reached from below, or remove the battery and battery tray as described in Chapter 5A Section 4, so that the screw can be reached from above.

9 Check that all pipes and hoses are secure, unions tight and the bleed screw is closed. Clean any dirt from around the bleed screw.

Bleeding procedure

Conventional method

10 Collect a clean glass jar, a suitable length of plastic or rubber tubing which is a tight fit over the bleed screw, and a ring spanner to fit the screw. The help of an assistant will also be required.

11 Unscrew the master cylinder fluid reservoir cap (the clutch shares the same fluid reservoir as the braking system), and top the master

2.8 Clutch bleed screw (arrowed)

cylinder reservoir up to the upper (MAX) level line. Ensure that the fluid level is maintained at least above the lower level line in the reservoir throughout the procedure.

12 Remove the dust cap from the bleed screw. Fit the spanner and tube to the screw, place the other end of the tube in the jar, and pour in sufficient fluid to cover the end of the tube.

13 Have the assistant fully depress the clutch pedal several times to build-up pressure, then maintain it on the final down stroke.

14 While pedal pressure is maintained, unscrew the bleed screw (approximately one turn) and allow the compressed fluid and air to flow into the jar. The assistant should maintain pedal pressure and should not release it until instructed to do so. When the flow stops, tighten the bleed screw again, have the assistant release the pedal slowly, and recheck the reservoir fluid level.

15 Repeat the steps given in paragraphs 13 and 14 until the fluid emerging from the bleed screw is free from air bubbles. If the master cylinder has been drained and refilled allow approximately five seconds between cycles for the master cylinder passages to refill.

Using a one-way valve kit

16 As their name implies, these kits consist of a length of tubing with a one-way valve fitted, to prevent expelled air and fluid being drawn back into the system; some kits include a translucent container, which can be positioned so that the air bubbles can be more easily seen flowing from the end of the tube.

17 The kit is connected to the bleed screw, which is then opened.

18 The user returns to the driver's seat, depresses the clutch pedal with a smooth, steady stroke, and slowly releases it; this is repeated until the expelled fluid is clear of air bubbles.

19 Note that these kits simplify work so much that it is easy to forget the clutch fluid reservoir level; ensure that this is maintained at least above the lower level line at all times.

Pressure-bleeding method

20 These kits are usually operated by the reservoir of pressurised air contained in the spare tyre. However, note that it will probably be necessary to reduce the pressure to a lower level than normal; refer to the instructions supplied with the kit.

21 By connecting a pressurised, fluid-filled container to the clutch fluid reservoir, bleeding can be carried out simply by opening the bleed screw and allowing the fluid to flow out until no more air bubbles can be seen in the expelled fluid.

22 This method has the advantage that the large reservoir of fluid provides an additional safeguard against air being drawn into the system during bleeding.

'Back-bleeding' method

23 The following procedure describes the bleeding method using Vauxhall/Opel equipment. Alternative equipment is available and should be used in accordance with the maker's instructions.

24 Connect the pressure hose (MKM-6174-1) to the bleed screw located in the hose end fitting situated on the top of the transmission housing **(see illustration 2.8)**. Connect the other end of the hose to a suitable pressure bleeding device set to operate at approximately 2.0 bar.

25 Attach the cap (MKM-6174-2) to the master cylinder reservoir, and place the hose in a collecting vessel.

26 Switch on the pressure bleeding equipment, open the bleed screw, and allow fresh hydraulic fluid to flow from the pressure bleeding unit, through the system and out through the top of the reservoir and into the collecting vessel. When fluid free from air bubbles appears in the reservoir, close the bleed screw and switch off the bleeding equipment.

27 Disconnect the bleeding equipment from the bleed screw and reservoir.

28 Carry out a final conventional bleeding pro- cedure as described in paragraphs 10 to 15, or 16 to 19.

All methods

29 When bleeding is complete, no more bubbles appear and correct pedal feel is restored, tighten the bleed screw securely (do not overtighten). Remove the tube and spanner, and wash off any spilt fluid. Refit the dust cap to the bleed screw.

30 Check the hydraulic fluid level in the master cylinder reservoir, and top-up if necessary (see *Weekly checks*).

31 Discard any hydraulic fluid that has been bled from the system; it will not be fit for re-use.

32 Check the operation of the clutch pedal. If the clutch is still not operating correctly, air must still be present in the system, and further bleeding is required. Failure to bleed satisfactorily after a reasonable repetition of the bleeding procedure may be due to worn master cylinder/release cylinder seals.

3 Master cylinder – removal and refitting

Note: *New master cylinder retaining nuts will be required for refitting.*
Note: *This procedure does not apply to models fitted with the Easytronic transmission.*

Removal

Right-hand drive models

1 For access to the clutch master cylinder, remove the windscreen cowl panel as described in Chapter 11 Section 20.

2 Unscrew the brake/clutch hydraulic fluid reservoir filler cap, and top-up the reservoir to the MAX mark (see *Weekly checks*). Place a piece of polythene over the filler neck,

3.4 Extract the retaining clip (arrowed) and disconnect the hydraulic pipe from the master cylinder connector

3.5 Disconnect the fluid supply hose (arrowed) from the reservoir

and secure the polythene with the filler cap. This will minimise brake fluid loss during subsequent operations.

3 Remove all traces of dirt from the outside of the master cylinder and the brake/clutch hydraulic fluid reservoir, then position some cloth beneath the cylinder to catch any spilt fluid.

4 Extract the retaining clip and disconnect the hydraulic pipe from the connector on the end of the master cylinder **(see illustration)**. Plug the pipe end and master cylinder port to minimise fluid loss and prevent the entry of dirt. Gently squeeze the two legs of the retaining clip together, and re-insert the clip into the master cylinder connector.

5 Release the retaining clip (where fitted) and disconnect the fluid supply hose from the brake/clutch hydraulic fluid reservoir **(see illustration)**.

6 From inside the car, remove the lower facia panel on the driver's side as described in Chapter 11 Section 26.

7 Disconnect the return spring from the clutch pedal, then slide off the spring clip and withdraw the clevis pin securing the master cylinder pushrod to the clutch pedal.

8 Unscrew the two nuts securing the master cylinder to the pedal support bracket, then return to the engine compartment and remove the master cylinder from the vehicle. If the master cylinder is faulty it must be renewed; overhaul of the unit is not possible.

Left-hand drive models

9 Remove the windscreen cowl panel as described in Chapter 11 Section 20.

10 Remove the battery and battery tray as described in Chapter 5A Section 4.

11 Lift the coolant expansion tank up and out of its mounting bracket and place it to one side.

12 Undo the two bolts securing the ABS hydraulic modulator mounting bracket to the bulkhead and body. Taking great care not to strain the hydraulic brake pipes, carefully move the assembly to one side as far as the brake pipes will allow and support it in this position.

13 Continue with the removal procedure as described in paragraphs 2 to 8.

Refitting

Right-hand drive models

14 Manoeuvre the master cylinder into position whilst ensuring that the pushrod aligns correctly with the pedal. Fit two new master cylinder retaining nuts and tighten them to the specified torque.

15 Refit the master cylinder pushrod-to-clutch pedal clevis pin, and secure it in position with the spring clip.

16 Refit the return spring to the clutch pedal.

17 Refit the lower facia panel on the driver's side as described in Chapter 11 Section 26.

18 Connect the fluid supply hose to the brake/clutch hydraulic fluid reservoir and, where applicable, secure with the retaining clip.

19 Press the hydraulic pipe back into the connector on the end of the master cylinder ensuring that the pipe audibly engages and is securely retained.

20 Bleed the clutch hydraulic system as described in Section 2.

21 Refit the windscreen cowl panel as described in Chapter 11 Section 20.

Left-hand drive models

22 Carry out the operations described in paragraphs 14 to 19.

23 Carefully locate the ABS hydraulic modulator mounting bracket back into position and secure with the two bolts, tightened to the specified torque.

24 Refit the coolant expansion tank back into its mounting bracket.

25 Refit the battery tray and battery described in Chapter 5A Section 4.

26 Bleed the clutch hydraulic system as described in Section 2.

27 Refit the windscreen cowl panel as described in Chapter 11 Section 20.

4 Release cylinder – removal and refitting

Note: *Due to the amount of work necessary to remove and refit clutch components, it is usually considered good practice to renew the clutch friction disc, pressure plate assembly and release cylinder as a matched set, even*

4.2 Clutch release cylinder hydraulic pipe union nut (arrowed)

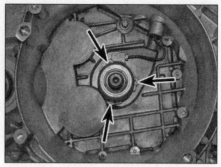

4.3 Clutch release cylinder retaining bolts (arrowed)

if only one of these is actually worn enough to require renewal. It is also worth considering the renewal of the clutch components on a preventative basis if the engine and/or transmission have been removed for some other reason.

Note: *Refer to the warning concerning the dangers of asbestos dust at the beginning of Section 6.*

Note: *On models equipped with the Easytronic transmission, Vauxhall/Opel TECH2 diagnostic equipment will be required to bleed the clutch hydraulic system and carry out a clutch Contact Point Determination program. If this equipment is not available, the following procedure should be entrusted to a Vauxhall/Opel dealer.*

Removal

1 Unless the complete engine/transmission unit is to be removed from the car and separated for major overhaul (see the relevant Part of Chapter 2), the clutch release cylinder can be reached by removing the transmission only, as described in Chapter 7A or Chapter 7C.

2 Wipe clean the outside of the release cylinder then slacken the union nut and disconnect the hydraulic pipe **(see illustration)**. Wipe up any spilt fluid with a clean cloth.

3 Unscrew the three retaining bolts and slide the release cylinder off from the transmission input shaft **(see illustration)**. Remove the sealing ring which is fitted between the cylinder and transmission housing and discard

it; a new one must be used on refitting. Whilst the cylinder is removed, take care not to allow any debris to enter the transmission unit.

4 The release cylinder is a sealed unit and cannot be overhauled. If the cylinder seals are leaking or the release bearing is noisy or rough in operation, then the complete unit must be renewed.

5 To remove the hydraulic pipe, extract the retaining clip and remove the hydraulic hose end fitting from the fastening sleeve on top of the transmission housing **(see illustration)**. Gently squeeze the legs of the retaining clip together and re-insert the clip back into position in the end fitting.

6 Using a small screwdriver, carefully spread the retaining lugs of the fastening sleeve to release the hydraulic pipe connection, and remove the pipe from inside the transmission housing. Check the condition of the sealing ring on the hydraulic pipe and renew if necessary.

7 If required, the fastening sleeve can be removed by squeezing the lower retaining lugs together with pointed-nose pliers, then withdrawing the sleeve upwards and out of the transmission. Note that if the fastening sleeve is removed, a new one must be obtained for refitting.

Refitting

8 Ensure the release cylinder and transmission mating surfaces are clean and dry and fit the new sealing ring to the transmission recess.

9 Lubricate the release cylinder seal with a smear of transmission oil then carefully ease the cylinder along the input shaft and into position. **Note:** *Vauxhall/Opel technicians use a special tapered sleeve on the input shaft to prevent damage to the seal. If necessary, wrap suitable tape around the end of the shaft. Ensure the sealing ring is still correctly seated in its groove then refit the release cylinder retaining bolts and tighten them to the specified torque.*

10 If removed, fit the new fastening sleeve, engaging the lug on the sleeve with the cut-out in the housing **(see illustration)**. Ensure that the sleeve can be felt to positively lock in position.

11 Insert the hydraulic pipe into the fastening sleeve until the end fitting can be felt to positively lock in position.

12 Reconnect the hydraulic pipe to the release cylinder, tightening its union nut securely.

13 Refit the hydraulic hose end fitting to the fastening sleeve ensuring that it is positively retained by its clip.

14 Refit the transmission unit as described in Chapter 7A or Chapter 7C.

15 On models equipped with a conventional transmission, bleed the clutch hydraulic system as described in Section 2.

16 On models equipped with the Easytronic transmission, bleed the clutch hydraulic system and carry out a clutch Contact Point Determination program using Vauxhall/Opel TECH2 diagnostic equipment.

5 Clutch pedal – removal and refitting

Note: *New master cylinder retaining nuts and pedal bracket retaining nut/bolts will be required for refitting.*

Removal

1 Remove the lower facia panel on the driver's side, and the steering column lower shroud, as described in Chapter 11 Section 26.

2 Where fitted (according to model), remove the clutch switch from the pedal bracket.

3 Disconnect the return spring from the clutch pedal, then slide off the spring clip and withdraw the clevis pin securing the master cylinder pushrod to the clutch pedal.

4 Unscrew the upper nut (right-hand drive models), or the two upper bolts (left-hand drive models), securing the pedal bracket to the facia crossmember.

5 Unscrew the two nuts securing the clutch master cylinder to the pedal bracket, then carefully withdraw the clutch pedal and bracket from inside the vehicle. Make sure that all wiring is moved to one side as the pedal and bracket are removed.

6 Check the pedal and bracket for excessive wear and damage. It is not possible to renew the pedal pivot bushes separately, so if they are worn, the complete assembly must be renewed.

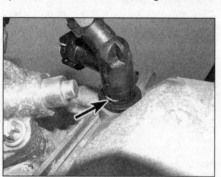

4.5 Extract the retaining clip (arrowed) and remove the hydraulic hose end fitting from the fastening sleeve

4.10 Make sure the lug (arrowed) on the fastening sleeve is located correctly in the transmission housing

Refitting

7 Manoeuvre the pedal and bracket assembly into position, making sure that the surrounding wiring is not trapped. Screw on the new retaining nuts/bolts, including those for the master cylinder, and tighten to the specified torque.

8 Refit the master cylinder pushrod-to-clutch pedal clevis pin, and secure it in position with the spring clip.

9 Refit the return spring to the clutch pedal then, where applicable, refit the clutch switch.

10 Refit the steering column lower shroud and the lower facia panel as described in Chapter 11 Section 26.

---

6 Clutch assembly – removal, inspection and refitting

Warning: Dust created by clutch wear and deposited on the clutch components may contain asbestos, which is a health hazard. DO NOT blow it out with compressed air, or inhale any of it. DO NOT use petrol or petroleum-based solvents to clean off the dust. Brake system cleaner or methylated spirit should be used to flush the dust into a suitable receptacle. After the clutch components are wiped clean with rags, dispose of the contaminated rags and cleaner in a sealed, marked container.

Note: *To prevent possible damage to the ends of the pressure plate diaphragm spring fingers, Vauxhall/Opel recommend the use of a special jig (KM-6263) to remove the clutch assembly, however, with care it is possible to carry out the work without the jig.*

Note: *On models equipped with the Easytronic transmission, Vauxhall/Opel TECH2 diagnostic equipment will be required to carry out a clutch Contact Point Determination program after the transmission has been refitted. If this equipment is not available, the following procedure should be entrusted to a Vauxhall/Opel dealer.*

Removal

1 Unless the complete engine/transmission unit is to be removed from the car and separated for major overhaul (see the relevant Part of Chapter 2E), the clutch can be reached by removing the transmission as described in Chapter 7A or Chapter 7C Section 7.

2 Before disturbing the clutch, use chalk or a marker pen to mark the relationship of the pressure plate assembly to the flywheel.

3 At this stage, Vauxhall/Opel technicians fit the special jig KM-6263 to the engine and compress the diaphragm spring fingers until the friction disc is released **(see illustrations)**. The pressure plate mounting bolts are then unscrewed, and the jig spindle backed off.

4 If the jig is not available, progressively unscrew the pressure plate retaining bolts in diagonal sequence by half a turn at a time,

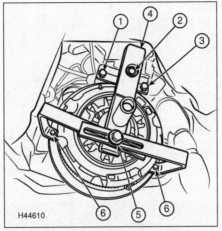

6.3a Vauxhall special jig KM-6263 for removing the clutch pressure plate and friction disc

1, 3 and 6 Bolts securing the jig to the engine
2 and 5 Bolts for adjusting the jig to the
 centre of the crankshaft

until spring pressure is released and the bolts can be unscrewed by hand.

5 Remove the pressure plate assembly and collect the friction disc, noting which way round the disc is fitted. It is recommended that new pressure plate retaining bolts are obtained.

Inspection

Note: *Due to the amount of work necessary to remove and refit clutch components, it is usually considered good practice to renew the clutch friction disc, pressure plate assembly and release cylinder as a matched set, even if only one of these is actually worn enough to require renewal. It is also worth considering the renewal of the clutch components on a preventative basis if the engine and/or transmission have been removed for some other reason.*

6 When cleaning clutch components, read first the warning at the beginning of this Section; remove dust using a clean, dry cloth, and working in a well-ventilated atmosphere.

7 Check the friction disc facings for signs of wear, damage or oil contamination. If the friction material is cracked, burnt, scored or damaged, or if it is contaminated with oil or grease (shown by shiny black patches), the friction disc must be renewed.

8 If the friction material is still serviceable, check that the centre boss splines are unworn, that the torsion springs are in good condition and securely fastened, and that all the rivets are tight. If any wear or damage is found, the friction disc must be renewed.

9 If the friction material is fouled with oil, this must be due to an oil leak from the crankshaft oil seal, from the sump-to-cylinder block joint, or from the release cylinder assembly (either the main seal or the sealing ring). Renew the crankshaft oil seal or repair the sump joint as described in the appropriate Part of Chapter 2,

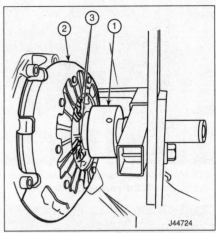

6.3b Thrust piece (1) in contact with the diaphragm spring fingers (3) of the pressure plate (2)

before installing the new friction disc. The clutch release cylinder is covered in Section 4.

10 Check the pressure plate assembly for obvious signs of wear or damage; shake it to check for loose rivets, or worn or damaged fulcrum rings, and check that the drive straps securing the pressure plate to the cover do not show signs of overheating (such as a deep yellow or blue discoloration). If the diaphragm spring is worn or damaged, or if its pressure is in any way suspect, the pressure plate assembly should be renewed.

11 Examine the machined bearing surfaces of the pressure plate and of the flywheel; they should be clean, completely flat, and free from scratches or scoring. If either is discoloured from excessive heat, or shows signs of cracks, it should be renewed – although minor damage of this nature can sometimes be polished away using emery paper.

12 Check that the release cylinder bearing rotates smoothly and easily, with no sign of noise or roughness. Also check that the surface itself is smooth and unworn, with no signs of cracks, pitting or scoring. If there is any doubt about its condition, the clutch release cylinder should be renewed (it is not possible to renew the bearing separately).

Refitting

13 On diesel engine models, and petrol engine models equipped with the Easytronic transmission, the clutch pressure plate is unusual, as there is a pre-adjustment mechanism to compensate for wear in the friction disc (this is termed by Vauxhall/Opel as a self-adjusting clutch (SAC), which is slightly ambiguous as all clutches fitted to these models are essentially self-adjusting). However, this mechanism must be reset before refitting the pressure plate. A new plate may be supplied preset, in which case this procedure can be ignored.

14 A large diameter bolt (M14 at least) long enough to pass through the pressure plate, a matching nut, and several large diameter

6.15 Mount a large bolt and washer into a vice, then fit the pressure plate over it

6.16 Fit large washers and a nut to the bolt and hand-tighten

6.17a Tighten the nut until the spring adjuster is free to turn ...

6.17b ... then open up the jaws of suitable pliers to compress the springs

washers, will be needed for this procedure. Mount the bolt head in the jaws of a sturdy bench vice, with one large washer fitted.

15 Offer the plate over the bolt, friction disc surface facing down, and locate it centrally over the bolt and washer – the washer should bear on the centre hub (**see illustration**).

16 Fit several further large washers over the bolt, so that they bear on the ends of the spring fingers, then add the nut and tighten by hand to locate the washers (**see illustration**).

17 The purpose of the procedure is to turn the plate's internal adjuster disc so that the three small coil springs visible on the plate's outer surface are fully compressed. Tighten the nut just fitted until the adjuster disc is free to turn. Using a pair of thin-nosed, or circlip pliers, in one of the three windows in the top surface, open the jaws of the pliers to turn the adjuster

disc anti-clockwise, so that the springs are fully compressed (**see illustrations**).

18 Hold the pliers in this position, then unscrew the centre nut. Once the nut is released, the adjuster disc will be gripped in position, and the pliers can be removed. Take the pressure plate from the vice, and it is ready to fit.

19 On reassembly, ensure that the friction surfaces of the flywheel and pressure plate are completely clean, smooth, and free from oil or grease. Use solvent to remove any protective grease from new components.

20 Lightly grease the teeth of the friction disc hub with high melting-point grease. Do not apply too much, otherwise it may eventually contaminate the friction disc linings.

Using the Vauxhall jig

21 Fit the special Vauxhall guide bush to the centre of the crankshaft, and locate the friction

disc on it, making sure that the lettering 'transmission side' or 'Getriebeseite' points towards the transmission (**see illustration**).

22 Locate the pressure plate on the special centring pins on the flywheel, then compress the diaphragm spring fingers with the jig, until the friction disc is in full contact with the flywheel.

23 Insert new pressure plate retaining bolts, and progressively tighten them to the specified torque. If necessary, hold the flywheel stationary while tightening the bolts, using a screwdriver engaged with the teeth of the starter ring gear.

24 Back off the jig spindle so that the diaphragm spring forces the pressure plate against the friction disc and flywheel, then remove the jig and guide bush from the engine.

25 Refit the transmission as described in Chapter 7A or Chapter 7C.

Without using the Vauxhall jig

26 Locate the friction disc on the flywheel, making sure that the lettering 'transmission side' or 'Getriebeseite' points towards the transmission (**see illustration 6.21**).

27 Refit the pressure plate assembly, aligning the marks made on dismantling (if the original pressure plate is re-used). Fit new pressure plate bolts, but tighten them only finger-tight so that the friction disc can still be moved (**see illustration**).

28 The friction disc must now be centralised so that, when the transmission is refitted, its input shaft will pass through the splines at the centre of the friction disc.

29 Centralisation can be achieved by passing a screwdriver or other long bar through the friction disc and into the hole in the crankshaft. The friction disc can then be moved around until it is centred on the crankshaft hole. Alternatively, a clutch-aligning tool can be used to eliminate the guesswork; these can be obtained from most accessory shops (**see illustration**).

30 When the friction disc is centralised, tighten the pressure plate bolts evenly and in a diagonal sequence to the specified torque setting.

31 Refit the transmission as described in Chapter 7A or Chapter 7C.

6.21 The lettering 'transmission side' or 'Getriebeseite' on the friction disc must point towards the transmission

6.27 Fit the pressure plate assembly over the friction disc

6.29 Centralise the friction disc using a clutch aligning tool or similar

Chapter 7 Part A
Manual transmission

Contents

Section number

Gearchange mechanism – adjustment. 3
Gearchange mechanism – removal and refitting 4
General Information 1
Oil seals – renewal 5
Reversing light switch – testing, removal and refitting. 6

Section number

Transmission – removal and refitting 7
Transmission oil – draining and refilling 2
Transmission oil level check. 9
Transmission overhaul – general information 8

Degrees of difficulty

Easy, suitable for novice with little experience 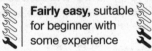	**Fairly easy,** suitable for beginner with some experience	**Fairly difficult,** suitable for competent DIY mechanic	**Difficult,** suitable for experienced DIY mechanic	**Very difficult,** suitable for expert DIY or professional

Specifications

General
Type:
    Petrol engine models . . . . Five forward speeds and reverse. Synchromesh on all forward speeds
    Diesel engine models . . . . Six forward speeds and reverse. Synchromesh on all forward speeds
Manufacturer's designation:
    Petrol engine models . . . . F17+
    Diesel engine models M32

Lubrication
Lubricant type . . . . See *Lubricants and fluids*
Lubricant capacity . . . . See Chapter 1A Section 1 or Chapter 1B Section 1

Torque wrench settings

	Nm	lbf ft
Differential lower cover plate bolts (F17+ transmission).	18	13
Engine/transmission mountings.	See the relevant Part of Chapter 2	
Engine-to-transmission bolts.	See the relevant Part of Chapter 2	
Oil drain plug (M32 transmission).	20	15
Oil filler plug (M32 transmission)	30	22
Oil level plug (F17+ transmission):		
Stage 1.	4	3
Stage 2.	Angle-tighten a further 45° to 135°	
Oil seal carrier to differential (M32 transmission):		
Stage 1.	20	15
Stage 2.	Angle-tighten a further 45°	
Reversing light switch	20	15
Roadwheel bolts.	110	81

1 General Information

1 The transmission is contained in a cast-aluminium alloy casing bolted to the engine's left-hand end, and consists of the gearbox and final drive differential – often called a transaxle.

2 Drive is transmitted from the crankshaft via the clutch to the input shaft, which has a splined extension to accept the clutch friction disc, and rotates in sealed ball-bearings. From the input shaft, drive is transmitted to the output shaft, which rotates in a roller bearing at its right-hand end, and a sealed ball-bearing at its left-hand end. From the output shaft, the drive is transmitted to the differential crownwheel, which rotates with the differential case and planetary gears, thus driving the sun gears and driveshafts. The rotation of the planetary gears on their shaft allows the inner roadwheel to rotate at a slower speed than the outer roadwheel when the car is cornering.

3 The input and output shafts are arranged side-by-side, parallel to the crankshaft and driveshafts, so that their gear pinion teeth are in constant mesh. In the neutral position, the output shaft gear pinions rotate freely, so that drive cannot be transmitted to the crownwheel.

4 Gear selection is via a floor-mounted lever and a cable-operated selector linkage mechanism. The selector linkage cause the appropriate selector fork to move its respective synchro-sleeve along the shaft, to lock the gear pinion to the synchro-hub. Since the synchro-hubs are splined to the output shaft, this locks the pinion to the shaft, so that drive can be transmitted. To ensure that gearchanging can be made quickly and quietly, a synchromesh system is fitted to all forward gears, consisting of baulk rings and spring-loaded fingers, as well as the gear pinions and synchro-hubs. The synchromesh cones are formed on the mating faces of the baulk rings and gear pinions.

2 Transmission oil – draining and refilling

1 This operation is much more efficient if the car is first taken on a journey of sufficient length to warm the engine/transmission up to normal operating temperature.

Note: *If the procedure is to be carried out on a hot transmission unit, take care not to burn yourself on the hot exhaust or the transmission/engine unit.*

2 Position the vehicle over an inspection pit, on vehicle ramps, or jack it up and support it securely on axle stands (see *Jacking and vehicle support*), but make sure that it is level. Where fitted, remove the clips and bolts and remove the undertray from beneath the engine.

2.5 Differential cover plate securing bolts (arrowed) – F17+ transmission

F17+ transmission

Note: *A new differential lower cover plate gasket will be required for this operation.*

Draining

3 Since the transmission oil is not renewed as part of the manufacturer's maintenance schedule, no drain plug is fitted to the transmission. If for any reason the transmission needs to be drained, the only way of doing so is to remove the differential lower cover plate.

4 Wipe clean the area around the differential cover plate and position a suitable container underneath the cover.

5 Evenly and progressively slacken and remove the retaining bolts then withdraw the cover plate and allow the transmission oil to drain into the container (see illustration). Remove the gasket and discard it; a new one should be used on refitting.

6 Allow the oil to drain completely into the container. If the oil is hot, take precautions against scalding. Remove all traces of dirt and oil from the cover and transmission mating surfaces and wipe clean the inside of the cover plate.

7 Once the oil has finished draining, ensure the mating surfaces are clean and dry then refit the cover plate to the transmission unit, complete with a new gasket. Refit the retaining bolts and evenly and progressively tighten them to the specified torque.

Refilling

8 Wipe clean the area around the level plug. The level plug is located behind the driveshaft

2.9 Fill the transmission through the reversing light switch aperture – F17+ transmission

2.8 Transmission oil level plug (arrowed) – F17+ transmission

inner joint on the left-hand side of the transmission (see illustration). Unscrew the plug and clean it.

9 The transmission is refilled via the reversing light switch aperture (see illustration). Wipe clean the area around the reversing light switch, and remove the switch as described in Section 6. Refill the transmission with the specified grade of oil given in Lubricants and fluids, until it reaches the bottom of the level plug aperture. Allow any excess oil to drain, then refit and tighten the level plug to the specified torque.

10 Refit the reversing light switch with reference to Section 6, then lower the vehicle to the ground.

M32 transmission

Note: *A new transmission oil drain plug will be required.*

Draining

11 Wipe clean the area around the drain plug, located on the lower left-hand side of the differential housing, and position a suitable container under the plug.

12 Undo the drain plug and allow the oil to drain.

13 Once the oil has finished draining, fit the new drain plug and tighten the plug to the specified torque.

Refilling

14 The transmission is refilled via the oil filler plug on the top of the casing (see illustration). To gain access to the plug, remove the battery

2.14 Transmission oil filler plug (arrowed) – M32 transmission

and battery tray as described in Chapter 5A Section 4.

15 Wipe clean the area around the plug and unscrew it. Refill the transmission with exactly 2.4 litres of the specified grade of oil given in Lubricants and fluids, then refit and tighten the oil filler plug to the specified torque **(see illustration)**.

16 Where applicable, refit the engine undertray, then lower the vehicle to the ground.

17 Refit the battery tray and battery as described in Chapter 5A Section 4.

3 Gearchange mechanism – adjustment

Note: *A 5 mm drill or metal rod will be required to carry out this procedure.*

1 Adjustment of the gearchange mechanism should only be needed if any part of the mechanism has been disconnected or removed. Adjustment is carried out at the clamping pieces located at the gear lever end of the each selector cable, with the transmission and gear lever set and locked in the neutral position.

2 Disconnect the battery negative terminal (refer to Chapter 5A Section 4).

3 Remove the centre console as described in Chapter 11 Section 25.

4 Remove the ashtray insert then unclip the ashtray housing from the base of the facia **(see illustration)**.

5 Undo the two gear lever gaiter trim panel retaining screws, then lift the panel up at the rear and disengage it from the facia at the front **(see illustrations)**.

6 Release the gear lever gaiter from the trim panel and remove the panel **(see illustration)**.

7 Unscrew the two quick-release catches and remove the lower facia panel on the passenger's side **(see illustrations)**. Remove the lower facia panel on the driver's side in the same way.

8 Release the retaining clips (three on each panel) and remove the footwell trim panels on the left- and right-hand sides of the facia **(see illustration)**.

2.15 Use a graduated container to fill the transmission with the specified quantity of oil – M32 transmission

3.4 Unclip the ashtray housing from the base of the facia

3.5a Undo the two gear lever gaiter trim panel retaining screws (arrowed) ...

3.5b ... then lift the panel up at the rear ...

3.5c ... and disengage it from the facia at the front

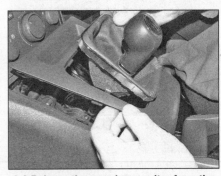

3.6 Release the gear lever gaiter from the trim panel and remove the panel

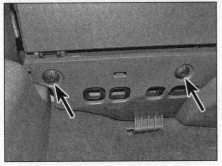

3.7a Unscrew the two quick-release catches (arrowed) ...

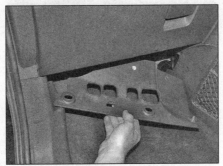

3.7b ... and remove the lower facia panel on the passenger's side

3.8 Release the retaining clips and remove the footwell trim panels

3.9a Undo the gear lever console trim retaining frame lower screw (arrowed) on each side …

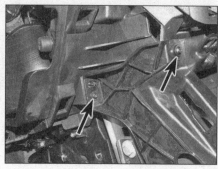

3.9b … the two upper screws (arrowed) on each side …

3.9c … and the two centre screws …

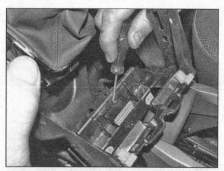

3.9d … then lift off the frame and unclip the diagnostic socket

3.10a Using a small screwdriver, open the clamping piece (arrowed) on the end of each selector cable …

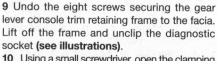
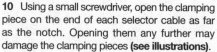
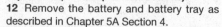

9 Undo the eight screws securing the gear lever console trim retaining frame to the facia. Lift off the frame and unclip the diagnostic socket **(see illustrations)**.

10 Using a small screwdriver, open the clamping piece on the end of each selector cable as far as the notch. Opening them any further may damage the clamping pieces **(see illustrations)**.

11 Push the gear lever to the left in neutral until the special hole in the lever base is aligned with the locking peg in the lever housing. Push the locking peg up to engage with the hole and lock the lever in the adjustment position **(see illustrations)**.

12 Remove the battery and battery tray as described in Chapter 5A Section 4.

13 If working on the F17+ (5-speed) transmission, set the gearchange selector on the transmission to the 'neutral' position. Push the selector down and lock it in the adjustment position by inserting a 5 mm drill bit or dowel rod through the hole in the rear of the housing **(see illustration)**. Ensure that the drill bit or dowel rod fully engages with the selector.

14 If working on the M32 (6-speed) transmission, set the gearchange selector on the transmission to the 'neutral' position. Pull the selector up and lock it in the adjustment position by inserting a 5 mm drill bit or dowel rod through the hole in the side of the housing **(see illustration)**. Ensure that the drill bit or dowel rod fully engages with the selector.

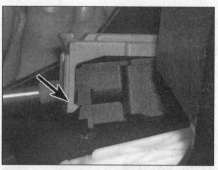

3.10b … until the lug (arrowed) rests on the notch

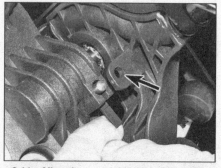

3.11a Align the special hole (arrowed) in the gear lever base with the locking peg …

3.11b … then push the locking peg up to engage with the hole

3.13 Insert a 5 mm drill bit (arrowed) through the hole in the rear of the housing to lock the selector mechanism – F17+ transmission

3.14 Insert a 5 mm drill bit (arrowed) through the hole in the front of the housing to lock the selector mechanism – M32 transmission

15 Working back inside the car, lock both gearshift cable clamping pieces by pushing them down.

16 Remove the drill bit or dowel rod used to lock the gearchange selector on the transmission.

17 Push the gear lever locking peg down to disengage it from the hole in the lever base.

18 Refit the battery tray and battery as described in Chapter 5A Section 4.

19 Check that all gears can be engaged easily, first with the engine off, then with the engine running and the clutch disengaged.

20 On completion, refit the gear lever console trim retaining frame, the footwell trim panels, lower facia panels, gear lever gaiter trim panel and ashtray insert, then refit the centre console as described in Chapter 11 Section 25.

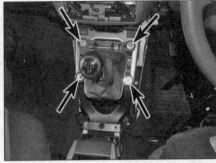

4.2 Gear lever housing retaining bolts (arrowed)

4.4 Depress the lugs on the sides of the outer cable ends and lift the cables from the gear lever housing

---

4   Gearchange mechanism – removal and refitting

Gear lever housing

Removal

1 Carry out the operations described in Section 3, paragraphs 2 to 10.

2 Undo the four bolts securing the gear lever housing to the mounting bracket **(see illustration)**.

3 Lift the gear lever housing off the mounting bracket and turn it through 180° to gain access to the selector cable attachments.

4 Note the fitted locations of the two cables, then depress the lugs on the sides of the outer cable ends and lift the outer cables from the gear lever housing **(see illustration)**.

5 Disengage the inner cable ends from the clamping pieces and remove the gear lever housing from the car.

6 If required, the cable clamping pieces attached to the gear lever can be carefully prised from their position using a forked tool. No further dismantling of the assembly is recommended.

Refitting

7 If previously removed, attached the cable clamping pieces to the base of the lever using a pair of pliers.

8 Engage the selector inner cables with the clamping pieces, then refit the outer cables to the gear lever housing. Do not lock the clamping pieces at this stage.

9 Position the gear lever housing on the mounting bracket, insert the securing bolts and tighten securely.

10 Carry out the gearchange mechanism adjustment procedure, as described in Section 3, paragraphs 11 to 20.

Selector cables

Removal

11 Carry out the operations described in paragraphs 1 to 4 above.

12 Remove the battery and battery tray as described in Chapter 5A Section 4.

13 Working in the engine compartment, note the fitted locations of the cables at their transmission attachments.

14 Using a suitable forked tool, release the inner cable end fittings from the transmission selector levers **(see illustration)**.

15 Pull back the retaining sleeves and detach the outer cables from the mounting bracket on the transmission **(see illustration)**.

16 Apply the handbrake, then jack up the front of the vehicle and support it on axle stands (see *Jacking and vehicle support*). Where fitted, remove the engine undertray.

17 Release the rubber grommet at the cable entry point on the engine compartment bulkhead, then pull the cables (complete with grommet) out of the bulkhead and into the engine compartment.

Refitting

18 Push the selector cables through the bulkhead passage from the engine compartment and locate the rubber grommet back into position in the bulkhead. Note that the coloured marking on the grommet must face upward.

19 Refit the engine undertray (where applicable) and lower the vehicle to the ground.

20 Refit the outer cables to the mounting bracket on the transmission.

21 Engage the inner cable end fittings with the transmission selector levers, squeezing them together with pliers if necessary.

4.14 Release the inner cable end fittings from the transmission selector levers

4.15 Pull back the retaining sleeves and detach the outer cables from the transmission mounting bracket

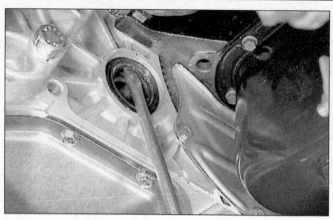

5.4 Prising out a driveshaft oil seal

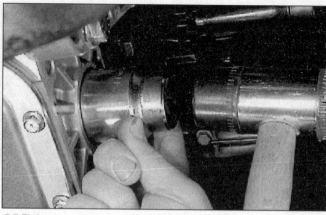

5.5 Fitting a new driveshaft oil seal using a socket as a tubular drift

22 Refit the battery tray and battery as described in Chapter 5A Section 4.

23 Engage the selector inner cables with the clamping pieces, then refit the outer cables to the gear lever housing. Do not lock the clamping pieces at this stage.

24 Position the gear lever housing on the mounting bracket, insert the securing bolts and tighten securely.

25 Carry out the gearchange mechanism adjustment procedure, as described in Section 3, paragraphs 11 to 20.

5 Oil seals – renewal

Driveshaft oil seals

F17+ transmission

1 Firmly apply the handbrake, then jack up the front of the car and support it securely on axle stands (see *Jacking and vehicle support*). Where fitted, remove the engine undertray.

2 Drain the transmission oil as described in Section 2.

3 Remove the driveshaft/intermediate shaft as described in Chapter 8.

4 Note the correct fitted depth of the seal in its housing then carefully prise it out of position using a large flat-bladed screwdriver **(see illustration)**.

5 Remove all traces of dirt from the area around the oil seal aperture, then apply a smear of grease to the outer lip of the new oil seal. Ensure the seal is correctly positioned, with its sealing lip facing inwards, and tap it squarely into position, using a suitable tubular drift (such as a socket) which bears only on the hard outer edge of the seal **(see illustration)**. Ensure the seal is fitted at the same depth in its housing that the original was.

6 Refit the driveshaft/intermediate shaft as described in Chapter 8.

7 Refill the transmission with the specified type and amount of oil, as described in Section 2.

M32 transmission right-hand oil seal

8 Proceed as described above in paragraphs 1 to 7.

M32 transmission left-hand oil seal

Note: *A hydraulic press, together with tubes and mandrels of suitable diameters will be needed for this operation.*

9 Firmly apply the handbrake, then jack up the front of the car and support it securely on axle stands (see *Jacking and vehicle support*). Where fitted, remove the engine undertray.

10 Drain the transmission oil as described in Section 2.

11 Remove the driveshaft as described in Chapter 8 Section 2.

12 Undo the four bolts and remove the oil seal carrier from the side of the differential housing.

13 Place the oil seal carrier on the press bed with its outer surface facing down. Using a suitable mandrel, press the oil seal out of the carrier.

14 Using a small screwdriver, remove the sealing O-ring from the oil seal carrier.

15 Support the inner surface of the oil seal carrier on the press bed. Lubricate the new oil seal with transmission oil, then press it fully into position in the carrier using a suitable tube which bears only on the hard outer edge of the seal.

16 Fit a new O-ring to the oil seal carrier, then refit the carrier to the differential housing, tightening the retaining bolts to the specified torque.

17 Refit the driveshaft as described in Chapter 8 Section 2.

18 Refill the transmission with the specified type and amount of oil, as described in Section 2.

Input shaft oil seal

19 The input shaft oil seal is an integral part of the clutch release cylinder; if the seal is leaking, the complete release cylinder assembly must be renewed. Before condemning the release cylinder, check that the leak is not coming from the sealing ring which is fitted between the cylinder and the transmission housing; the sealing ring can be renewed once the release cylinder assembly has been removed. Refer to Chapter 6 Section 4 for removal and refitting details.

6 Reversing light switch – testing, removal and refitting

1 The reversing light circuit is controlled by a plunger-type switch screwed into the top of the transmission towards the front of the housing.

2 To gain access to the switch, firmly apply the handbrake, then jack up the front of the car and support it securely on axle stands (see *Jacking and vehicle support*). Where fitted, remove the engine undertray.

Testing

3 If a fault develops in the circuit, first ensure that the circuit fuse has not blown and that the reversing light bulbs are sound.

4 To test the switch, disconnect the wiring connector. Use a multimeter (set to the resistance function) or a battery-and-bulb test circuit to check that there is continuity between the switch terminals only when reverse gear is selected. If this is not the case, and there are no obvious breaks or other damage to the wires, the switch is faulty, and must be renewed.

Removal

5 Disconnect the wiring connector, then unscrew the switch and remove it from the transmission casing along with its sealing washer **(see illustration)**.

6.5 Unscrew and remove the reversing light switch together with its sealing washer

Refitting

6 Fit a new sealing washer to the switch, then screw it back into position in the top of the transmission housing and tighten it to the specified torque. Reconnect the wiring connector, then test the operation of the circuit.
7 On completion, refit the engine undertray (where applicable) and lower the vehicle to the ground.

---

7 Transmission – removal and refitting

Removal

1 Apply the handbrake, then jack up the front of the vehicle and support it on axle stands (see *Jacking and vehicle support*). Allow sufficient working room to remove the transmission from under the left-hand side of the engine compartment. Remove both front roadwheels then, where necessary, undo the retaining clips/screws and remove the engine undertray. Also remove the engine top cover where fitted.
2 Remove the battery and battery tray as described in Chapter 5A Section 4, and the windscreen cowl panel as described in Chapter 11 Section 20.
3 Drain the transmission oil as described in Section 2.
4 Disconnect the wiring connectors from the reversing light switch and oxygen sensor and free the wiring from the transmission unit and retaining brackets.
5 Remove the filler cap from the brake/clutch fluid reservoir on the bulkhead, then tighten it onto a piece of polythene. This will reduce the loss of fluid when the clutch hydraulic hose is disconnected. Alternatively, fit a hose clamp to the flexible hose next to the clutch hydraulic connection on the transmission housing.
6 Place some cloth rags beneath the hose, then prise out the retaining clip securing the clutch hydraulic pipe/hose end fitting to the top of the transmission bellhousing and detach the end fitting from the transmission **(see illustration)**. Gently squeeze the two legs of the retaining clip together and re-insert the retaining clip back into position in the end fitting. Discard the sealing ring from the pipe end; a new sealing ring must be used on refitting. Plug/cover both the union and pipe ends to minimise fluid loss and prevent the entry of dirt into the hydraulic system. **Note:** *Whilst the hose/pipe is disconnected, do not depress the clutch pedal.*
7 Refer to Section 4 and disconnect the gearchange selector cables at their transmission attachments.
8 On the M32 transmission, remove the EGR valve cooler as described in Chapter 4C Section 3.
9 Working as described in Chapter 8, disconnect the inner ends of both driveshafts

7.6 Prise out the clip to disconnect the clutch hydraulic hose from the release cylinder pipe

from the differential and intermediate shaft, then remove the intermediate shaft. There is no need to disconnect the driveshafts from the swivel hub. Support the driveshafts by suspending them with wire or string – do not allow the driveshafts to hang down under their own weight, or the joints may be damaged.
10 Remove the front subframe assembly as described in Chapter 10 Section 7, ensuring that the engine unit is securely supported by connecting a hoist to the engine assembly. If available, the type of support bar which locates in the engine compartment side channels is to be preferred.
11 Unscrew and remove the upper bolts securing the transmission to the rear of the engine. Where necessary, pull up the coolant hoses and secure them away from the transmission using plastic cable ties. On the M32 transmission, undo and remove the starter motor lower mounting bolt.
12 Place a jack with a block of wood beneath the transmission, and raise the jack to take the weight of the transmission.
13 Unbolt the left-hand engine/transmission mounting bracket from the transmission with reference to the relevant Part of Chapter 2.
14 Lower the left-hand side of the engine/transmission making sure that the coolant hoses and wiring harnesses are not stretched.
15 Slacken and remove the remaining bolts securing the transmission to the engine and sump flange. Note the correct fitted positions of each bolt, and the relevant brackets, as they are removed to use as a reference on refitting. Make a final check that all components have been disconnected, and are positioned clear of the transmission so that they will not hinder the removal procedure.
16 With the bolts removed, move the trolley jack and transmission, to free it from its locating dowels. Once the transmission is free, lower the jack and manoeuvre the unit out from under the car. Remove the locating dowels from the transmission or engine if they are loose, and keep them in a safe place.

Refitting

17 The transmission is refitted by a reversal of the removal procedure, bearing in mind the following points.

a) Ensure the locating dowels are correctly positioned prior to installation.
b) Tighten all nuts and bolts to the specified torque (where given).
c) Renew the driveshaft oil seals (see Section 5) before refitting the driveshafts/intermediate shaft.
d) Refit the front subframe assembly as described in Chapter 10 Section 7.
e) Fit a new sealing ring to the clutch hydraulic hose before clipping the hose into the end fitting. Ensure the hose is securely retained by its clip then bleed the hydraulic system as described in Chapter 6 Section 2.
f) On the M32 transmission, refit the EGR valve cooler as described in Chapter 4C Section 3.
g) Refill the transmission with the specified type and quantity of oil, as described in Section 2.
h) On completion, adjust the gearchange mechanism as described in Section 3.

---

8 Transmission overhaul – general information

1 Overhauling a manual transmission unit is a difficult and involved job for the DIY home mechanic. In addition to dismantling and reassembling many small parts, clearances must be precisely measured and, if necessary, changed by selecting shims and spacers. Internal transmission components are also often difficult to obtain, and in many instances, extremely expensive. Because of this, if the transmission develops a fault or becomes noisy, the best course of action is to have the unit overhauled by a specialist repairer, or to obtain an exchange reconditioned unit.
2 Nevertheless, it is not impossible for the more experienced mechanic to overhaul the transmission, provided the special tools are available, and the job is done in a deliberate step-by-step manner, so that nothing is overlooked.
3 The tools necessary for an overhaul include internal and external circlip pliers, bearing pullers, a slide hammer, a set of pin punches, a dial test indicator, and possibly a hydraulic press. In addition, a large, sturdy workbench and a vice will be required.
4 During dismantling of the transmission, make careful notes of how each component is fitted, to make reassembly easier and more accurate.
5 Before dismantling the transmission, it will help if you have some idea what area is malfunctioning. Certain problems can be closely related to specific areas in the transmission, which can make component examination and renewal easier. Refer to the Fault finding Section of this manual for more information.

9 Transmission oil level check

1 Position the vehicle over an inspection pit, on vehicle ramps, or jack it up and support it securely on axle stands (see *Jacking and vehicle support*), but make sure that it is level. The oil must be checked before the car is driven, or at least 5 minutes after the engine has been switched off. If the oil is checked immediately after driving the car, some of the oil will remain distributed around the transmission components, resulting in an inaccurate level reading.

F17+ transmission

2 Where fitted, undo the retaining clips/screws and remove the engine undertray.
3 Wipe clean the area around the level plug. The level plug is located behind the driveshaft inner joint on the left-hand side of the transmission **(see illustration 2.8)**. Unscrew the plug and clean it.
4 The oil level should reach the lower edge of the level plug aperture. If topping-up is necessary, wipe clean the area around the reversing light switch, and remove the switch as described in Section 6.
5 Add the specified grade of oil given in Lubricants and fluids, through the reversing light switch aperture, until it reaches the bottom of the level plug aperture. Allow any excess oil to drain, then refit and tighten the level plug to the specified torque.
6 Refit the reversing light switch with reference to Section 6.
7 Where applicable, refit the engine undertray, then lower the vehicle to the ground.

M32 transmission

8 On the M32 transmission, there is no provision for oil level checking once the transmission has been initially filled. If for any reason it is thought that the oil level may be low, the transmission oil must be completely drained, then refilled with an exact specified quantity of oil as described in Section 2.

Chapter 7 Part B
Automatic transmission

Contents

Section number

Automatic transmission – removal and refitting 13
Automatic transmission overhaul – general information 14
Electronic control unit – removal and refitting 12
Fluid cooler – general information 9
General Information 1
Mode switches – removal and refitting. 7
Oil seals – renewal 8

Section number

Selector cable – adjustment. 3
Selector cable – removal and refitting 4
Selector lever assembly – removal and refitting. 5
Selector lever assembly components – removal and refitting 6
Selector lever position switch – adjustment, removal and refitting . . 10
Transmission fluid – draining and refilling. 2
Transmission input/output speed sensors – removal and refitting. . . 11

Degrees of difficulty

Easy, suitable for novice with little experience	Fairly easy, suitable for beginner with some experience	Fairly difficult, suitable for competent DIY mechanic	Difficult, suitable for experienced DIY mechanic	Very difficult, suitable for expert DIY or professional

Specifications

General
Type:
   1.9 litre diesel engine models . . . .   Electronically-controlled adaptive automatic, six forward speeds and reverse, with sequential manual gear selection capability

Manufacturer's designation:
   1.9 litre diesel engine models AF40

Lubrication
Lubricant type . . . .   See *Lubricants and fluids*
Lubricant capacity . . . .   See Chapter 1B Section 1

Torque wrench settings

	Nm	lbf ft
Automatic transmission fluid drain/filler plugs:		
Drain plug	50	37
Filler plug	40	30
Level checking plug	8	6
Electronic control unit mounting bolts	25	18
Engine/transmission mountings	See the relevant Part of Chapter 2	
Engine-to-transmission bolts	See the relevant Part of Chapter 2	
Fluid cooler pipes to transmission	7	5
Input shaft speed sensor bolt	6	4
Output shaft speed sensor bolt	6	4
Roadwheel bolts.	110	81
Selector lever assembly mounting bolts	8	6
Selector lever position switch:		
Lever to selector shaft	15	11
Selector shaft main nut.	7	5
Switch retaining bolts	25	18
Torque converter-to-driveplate bolts*	30	22

*Use new bolts

1 General Information

1 A six-speed, electronically-controlled automatic transmission was optionally available on certain models covered by this manual. The transmission consists of a torque converter, an epicyclic geartrain, and hydraulically-operated clutches and brakes. The unit is controlled by the electronic control unit (ECU) via electrically-operated solenoid valves. On six-speed transmissions, in addition to the fully-automatic operation, the transmission can also be operated manually with six-speed sequential gear selection.

2 Both transmission types have three driving modes; economy, sport and winter modes. The economy mode is the standard mode for driving in which the transmission shifts up at relatively low engine speeds to combine reasonable performance with economy. If the transmission unit is switched into sport mode, using the button on the facia, the transmission shifts up only at high engine speeds, giving improved acceleration and overtaking performance. When the transmission is in sport mode, the indicator light in the instrument panel is illuminated. If the transmission is switched into winter mode, using the button on the selector lever indicator panel, the transmission will select second or third gear (depending on transmission type) as the vehicle pulls away from a standing start; this helps to maintain traction on very slippery surfaces.

3 The torque converter provides a fluid coupling between engine and transmission, which acts as an automatic clutch, and also provides a degree of torque multiplication when accelerating. The torque converter incorporates a lock-up function whereby the engine and transmission can be directly coupled by means of a clutch unit inside the torque converter. The lock-up function is controlled by the ECU according to operating conditions.

4 The epicyclic geartrain provides six forward, or one reverse gear ratios, according to which of its component parts are held stationary or allowed to turn. The components of the geartrain are held or released by hydraulically actuated brakes and clutches. A fluid pump within the transmission provides the necessary hydraulic pressure to operate the brakes and clutches.

5 In automatic mode, the transmission is fully-adaptive, whereby the shift points are dependant on driver input, roadspeed, engine speed and vehicle operating conditions. The ECU receives inputs from various engine and drive train related sensors, and determines the appropriate shift point for each gear.

6 Driver control of the transmission is by a floor-mounted selector lever. The drive D position, allows automatic changing throughout the range of forward gear ratios. An automatic kickdown facility shifts the transmission down a gear if the accelerator pedal is fully depressed. If the selector lever is moved to the left from the D position, the transmission enters manual mode. In manual mode the gear selector lever can be used to shift the transmission up or down each gear sequentially.

7 Due to the complexity of the automatic transmission, any repair or overhaul work must be left to a Vauxhall/Opel dealer or transmission specialist with the necessary special equipment for fault diagnosis and repair. The contents of the following Sections are therefore confined to supplying general information, and any service information and instructions that can be used by the owner.

2 Transmission fluid – draining and refilling

Draining

1 Position the vehicle over an inspection pit, on vehicle ramps, or jack it up and support it securely on axle stands (see *Jacking and vehicle support*), but make sure that it is level. Remove the bolts and clips and remove the undertray from beneath the engine.

2 Position a container under the combined drain plug/level checking plug at the base of the transmission. Note that the drain plug and level checking plug are incorporated into one unit – the drain plug is the larger of the two plugs, with the level checking plug screwed into the centre of it **(see illustration)**.

3 Unscrew the level checking plug and remove it, along with its sealing washer, from the centre of the drain plug. Now unscrew the drain plug and remove it, along with its sealing washer, from the transmission. Allow the fluid to drain completely into the container.

4 When the fluid has finished draining, clean the drain plug threads and those of the transmission casing, fit a new sealing washer and refit the drain plug, tightening it to the specified torque.

Refilling

5 Wipe clean the area around the transmission fluid filler plug, located on the top of the transmission housing, adjacent to the selector cable **(see illustration)**. Unscrew and remove the filler plug along with its sealing washer.

6 Slowly refill the transmission with the specified type of fluid, via the filler plug aperture until fluid just starts to drip out of the level checking plug aperture. Use a funnel

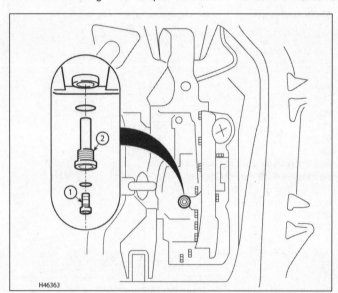

2.2 Transmission fluid level checking plug (1) and drain plug (2) – AF40 transmission

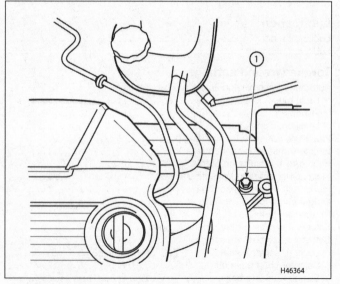

2.5 Transmission fluid filler plug (1) – AF40 transmission

with a fine mesh gauze to avoid spillage, and to ensure that no foreign matter enters the transmission.

7 Refit the level checking plug and tighten it securely.

8 Add a further 0.5 litre of fluid via the filler plug aperture.

9 Start the engine and allow it to idle. With the footbrake firmly applied, slowly move the selector lever from position P to position D and back to position P, stopping at each position for at least two seconds. Repeat this procedure twice.

10 With the engine still idling, unscrew the fluid level checking plug once more. Allow the excess fluid to run from the level checking plug aperture until it is only dripping out. Refit the level checking plug with a new sealing washer, and tighten the plug to the specified torque.

11 If no fluid runs from the level checking plug aperture, switch the engine off and repeat paragraphs 8 to 10.

12 Once the fluid level is correct, refit the filler plug with a new sealing washer, and tighten the plug to the specified torque.

13 On completion, refit the engine undertray and lower the vehicle to the ground.

3 Selector cable – adjustment

Note: *If the battery is disconnected with the selector lever in the P (park) position, the lever will be locked in position. To manually release the lever, remove the ashtray insert then unclip the ashtray housing from the base of the facia. Pull the emergency release lever loop in the ashtray aperture, whilst moving the selector lever to the N (neutral) position (see illustration).*

1 Operate the selector lever throughout its entire range and check that the transmission engages the correct gear indicated on the selector lever position indicator. If adjustment is necessary, continue as follows.

2 Position the selector lever in the P (park) position.

3 Remove the ashtray insert then unclip the

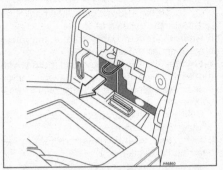

3.0 Pull the emergency release lever loop in the direction of the arrow to unlock the selector lever

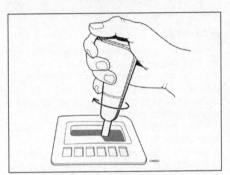

3.4 Rotate the engaging sleeve clockwise to release the selector lever knob

ashtray housing from the base of the facia **(see illustration).**

4 Rotate the engaging sleeve, located directly beneath the selector lever knob, clockwise **(see illustration).** Press the selector lever locking button on the lever knob, then withdraw the knob from the selector lever.

5 Undo the two selector lever trim panel retaining screws, then lift the panel up at the rear and disengage it from the facia at the front **(see illustration).** Lift the panel up and off the selector lever.

6 Release the retaining clips (three on each panel) and remove the footwell trim panels on the left- and right-hand sides of the facia, below the selector lever **(see illustration).**

7 Remove the selector lever frame by pulling it rearwards, away from the facia to release.

3.3 Unclip the ashtray housing from the base of the facia

3.5 Selector lever trim panel retaining screws (arrowed)

8 Unclip the selector lever cover at the rear on each side. Lift the cover up and off the selector lever and position it to one side without disconnecting the wiring.

9 Release the selector cable by turning the cable lock, located to the left of the lever, 90° anti-clockwise **(see illustration).**

10 To gain access to the transmission end of the selector cable, remove the battery and battery tray as described in Chapter 5A Section 4.

11 Ensure that the selector lever is still in the P position and move the lever on the trans- mission selector mechanism fully forwards so that the transmission is also positioned in the Park position **(see illustration).** With both the selector lever and transmission correctly positioned, turn the selector cable lock 90° clockwise.

3.6 Release the retaining clips and remove the footwell trim panels

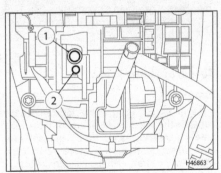

3.9 Turn the selector cable lock (1) 90° anti-clockwise to release the cable (2)

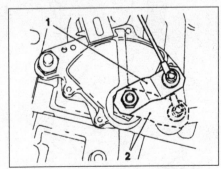

3.11 Move the transmission selector lever (1) fully forwards so that it is in the P position (2)

12 Refit the selector lever cover and selector lever frame.

13 Refit the lower trim panels on each side of the facia.

14 Refit the selector lever trim panel and secure with the two retaining screws.

15 Ensure that the actuating rod for the selector lever lock protrudes from the top of the lever, then with the locking button depressed, refit the knob to the selector lever. Rotate the engaging sleeve on the selector lever anti-clockwise to secure the knob.

16 Refit the ashtray housing to the base of the facia, then refit the ashtray.

17 Refit the battery tray and battery as described in Chapter 5A Section 4.

4 Selector cable – removal and refitting

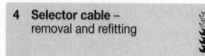

Removal

1 Remove the selector lever assembly as described in Section 5.

2 To gain access to the transmission end of the selector cable, remove the battery and battery tray as described in Chapter 5A Section 4.

3 Working in the engine compartment, use a forked tool or flat-bladed screwdriver and carefully lever the selector inner cable end fitting off the balljoint on the selector lever position switch. Pull back the retaining sleeve and detach the outer cable from the mounting bracket on the transmission **(see illustration)**.

4 Release the rubber grommet at the cable entry point on the engine compartment bulkhead, then pull the cable (complete with grommet) out of the bulkhead and into the engine compartment.

Refitting

5 Push the selector cable through the bulkhead passage from the engine compartment

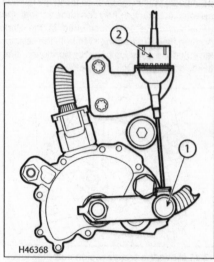

4.3 Selector inner cable end fitting (1) and outer cable retaining sleeve (2)

and locate the rubber grommet back into position in the bulkhead.

6 Refit the outer cable to the mounting bracket on the transmission.

7 Engage the inner cable end fitting with the balljoint on the selector lever position switch, squeezing them together with pliers if necessary.

8 Refit the battery and tray as described in Chapter 5A Section 4.

9 Refit the selector lever assembly as described in Section 5.

5 Selector lever assembly – removal and refitting

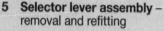

Removal

1 Disconnect the battery negative terminal (refer to Chapter 5A Section 4).

2 Carry out the operations described in Section 3, paragraphs 2 to 9.

3 Disconnect the selector lever assembly wiring harness connector.

4 Undo the four bolts securing the selector lever assembly to the mounting bracket.

5 Using a small screwdriver inserted through the left-hand side of the lever assembly, release the outer selector cable by pushing the guide clip forward **(see illustration)**.

6 Lift the selector lever assembly upwards and remove it from the car.

Refitting

7 Place the selector lever assembly in position and insert the selector cable fully into the lever from below. Lock the outer cable in position by pulling the guide clip rearward with a small screwdriver.

8 Secure the selector inner cable by turning the cable lock, located to the left of the lever, 90° clockwise.

9 Refit the four bolts securing the selector lever assembly to the mounting bracket and tighten the bolts securely.

10 Reconnect the selector lever assembly wiring harness connector.

11 Carry out the operations described in Section 3, paragraphs 12 to 17.

6 Selector lever assembly components – removal and refitting

Selector lever knob

Removal

1 Rotate the engaging sleeve, located directly beneath the selector lever knob, clockwise **(see illustration 3.4)**. Press the selector lever locking button on the lever knob, then withdraw the knob from the selector lever.

Refitting

2 Ensure that the actuating rod for the selector lever lock protrudes from the top

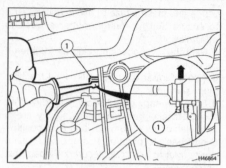

5.5 Using a small screwdriver, release the outer selector cable by pushing the guide clip (1) forward

of the lever, then with the locking button depressed, refit the knob to the selector lever. Rotate the engaging sleeve on the selector lever anti-clockwise to secure the knob.

Selector lever cover

Removal

3 Remove the selector lever assembly as described in Section 5.

4 Carefully disconnect the wiring connector from the selector lever control unit on the side of the selector lever assembly.

5 Note the routing of the wiring harness then remove the selector lever cover and wiring harness from the lever assembly.

Refitting

6 Feed the wiring harness back into its correct position as noted during removal.

7 Reconnect the wiring connector, then refit the selector lever assembly as described in Section 5.

Selector lever control unit

Removal

8 Remove the selector lever assembly as described in Section 5.

9 Disconnect the three wiring harness connectors then unclip and remove the control unit from the side of the selector lever assembly.

Refitting

10 Clip the control unit back into position and reconnect the wiring connectors.

11 Refit the selector lever assembly as described in Section 5.

Selector lever lock switch

Removal

12 Remove the selector lever assembly as described in Section 5.

13 Carefully unclip the selector emergency release lever from the three guides on the side of the selector lever assembly. Pivot the release lever downwards by 90°.

14 Disconnect the wiring harness connector then unclip and remove the switch from the selector lever assembly.

Refitting

15 Clip the switch back into position and reconnect the wiring connector.

16 Pivot the emergency release lever back into place and engage the lever with the three guides.
17 Refit the selector lever assembly as described in Section 5.

7 Mode switches – removal and refitting

Winter mode switch

1 The winter mode switch is an integral part of the selector lever cover and cannot be individually removed. If the switch is faulty, the complete selector lever cover must be renewed. Removal and refitting procedures for the selector lever cover are contained in Section 6.

Sport mode switch

2 The sport mode switch is an integral part of the facia centre switch panel and cannot be individually removed. If the switch is faulty, the complete switch panel must be renewed. Removal and refitting procedures for the facia centre switch panel are contained in Chapter 12 Section 4.

8 Oil seals – renewal

Driveshaft oil seals

1 Firmly apply the handbrake, then jack up the front of the car and support it securely on axle stands (see Jacking and vehicle support).
2 Drain the transmission fluid as described in Section 2.
3 Remove the driveshaft as described in Chapter 8.
4 Note the correct fitted depth of the seal in its housing then carefully prise it out of position using a large flat-bladed screwdriver.
5 Remove all traces of dirt from the area around the oil seal aperture, then lubricate the new oil seal with automatic transmission fluid. Ensure the seal is correctly positioned, with its sealing lip facing inwards, and tap it squarely into position, using a suitable tubular drift (such as a socket) which bears only on the hard outer edge of the seal. Ensure the seal is fitted at the same depth in its housing that the original was.
6 Refit the driveshaft as described in Chapter 8.
7 Refill the transmission with fresh fluid as described in Section 2.

Torque converter oil seal

8 Remove the transmission as described in Section 13.
9 Carefully slide the torque converter off of the transmission shaft whilst being prepared for fluid spillage.
10 Note the correct fitted position of the seal in the oil pump housing then carefully lever

the seal out of position taking care not to mark the housing or input shaft.
11 Remove all traces of dirt from the area around the oil seal aperture then press the new seal into position, ensuring its sealing lip is facing inwards.
12 Lubricate the seal with clean transmission fluid then carefully ease the torque converter into position. On the AF40 transmission, slide the torque converter onto the transmission shaft by turning it until it fully engages with the oil pump.
13 Refit the transmission as described in Section 13.

9 Fluid cooler – general information

1 The transmission fluid cooler is an integral part of the radiator assembly. Refer to Chapter 3 Section 3 for removal and refitting details; if the cooler is damaged the complete radiator assembly must be renewed.

10 Selector lever position switch – adjustment, removal and refitting

1 On the AF40 transmission, the selector lever position switch is an integral part of the transmission electronic control unit and cannot be separated. Removal and refitting procedures for the electronic control unit are contained in Section 12.

11 Transmission input/output speed sensors – removal and refitting

1 On the AF40 transmission, the input and output shaft speed sensors are located internally within the transmission and are not individually available. If one or both speed sensors are diagnosed as faulty, it will be necessary to obtain a complete new transmission.

12 Electronic control unit – removal and refitting

Note: If a new ECU is to be fitted, this work must be entrusted to a Vauxhall/Opel dealer or suitably-equipped specialist. It is necessary to reset the transmission electronic control system prior to removal, and to programme the new ECU after installation. This work requires the use of dedicated Vauxhall/Opel diagnostic equipment or a compatible alternative.

Removal

1 The combined ECU and selector lever position switch are located on the top of the transmission housing.
2 Ensure the handbrake is fully applied, then

move the gear selector lever to the N (neutral) position.
3 Remove the battery and battery tray as described in Chapter 5A Section 4.
4 Unclip the pre/post-heating system control unit wiring harness from the battery tray support.
5 Release the ECU wiring harness from its retaining clips, then disconnect the wiring harness connector from the ECU.
6 Using a forked tool or flat-bladed screwdriver, carefully lever the selector inner cable end fitting off the balljoint on the selector lever position switch. Pull back the retaining sleeve and detach the outer cable from the mounting bracket on the transmission (see illustration 4.3).
7 Unscrew the retaining nut and remove the lever from the transmission selector shaft.
8 Unscrew and remove the three mounting bolts, then carefully lift the ECU upwards and remove it from the transmission (see illustration). Take great care not to damage the wiring connector pins on the underside of the ECU as it is lifted off.

Refitting

9 Prior to refitting, first make sure that the transmission selector shaft is still in the N (neutral) position. If there is any doubt, temporarily engage the selector shaft lever with the transmission selector shaft and move the lever fully forwards (to the P position) then move it two notches backwards.
10 Set the selector lever position switch on the ECU to the N position by turning the switch until the two arrows are aligned.
11 Check that the transmission wiring harness is correctly located, then carefully place the ECU in position. Take great care not to damage the wiring connector pins as the ECU is fitted.
12 Refit the three bolts and tighten to the specified torque.
13 Refit the selector lever to the shaft and tighten its retaining nut to the specified torque.
14 Refit the selector outer cable to the mounting bracket on the transmission. Engage the selector inner cable end fitting with the

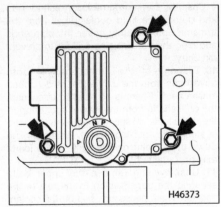

12.8 Electronic control unit mounting bolts (arrowed) – AF40 transmission

balljoint on the selector lever, squeezing them together with pliers if necessary.

15 Reconnect the ECU wiring harness connector, then secure the harness in its retaining clips.

16 Clip the pre/post-heating system control unit wiring harness to the battery tray support.

17 Refit the battery tray and battery as described in Chapter 5A Section 4.

13 Automatic transmission – removal and refitting

Note: *New torque converter-to-driveplate bolts will be required for refitting.*

Removal

1 Apply the handbrake, then jack up the front of the vehicle and support it on axle stands (see *Jacking and vehicle support*). Allow sufficient working room to remove the transmission from under the left-hand side of the engine compartment. Remove both front roadwheels then, on diesel engine models, undo the bolts and plastic rivets and remove the undertray from beneath the engine. Also remove the engine top cover where fitted.

2 Remove the battery, battery tray, and the starter motor as described in Chapter 5A.

3 Remove the air cleaner housing and intake ducts as described in Chapter 4B Section 3.

4 Remove the front bumper and the windscreen cowl panel as described in Chapter 11.

5 Drain the transmission fluid as described in Section 2.

6 Using a forked tool or flat-bladed screwdriver, carefully lever the selector inner cable end fitting off the balljoint on the selector lever position switch. Pull back the retaining sleeve and detach the outer cable from the mounting bracket on the transmission.

7 Unclip the pre/post-heating system control unit wiring harness from the battery tray support. Release the ECU wiring harness from its retaining clips, then disconnect the wiring harness connector from the ECU.

8 Disconnect the breather hose (where fitted) from the top of the transmission unit.

9 Unscrew the central retaining bolt (or nut) and detach the fluid cooler pipes from the transmission. Suitably cover the pipe ends and plug the transmission orifices to prevent dirt entry.

10 Disconnect the inner ends of both driveshafts from the differential as described in Chapter 8. There is no need to disconnect the driveshafts from the swivel hub. Support the driveshafts by suspending them with wire or string – do not allow the driveshafts to hang down under their own weight, or the joints may be damaged.

11 Unscrew and remove the upper bolts securing the transmission to the rear of the engine. Where necessary, pull up the coolant hoses and secure them away from the transmission using plastic cable ties.

12 Remove the front subframe assembly as described in Chapter 10 Section 7, ensuring that the engine unit is securely supported by connecting a hoist to the engine assembly. If available, the type of support bar which locates in the engine compartment side channels is to be preferred.

13 Unbolt and remove the front and rear engine/transmission mounting torque link brackets with reference to Chapter 2C Section 18 or Chapter 2D Section 18.

14 Using a socket and extension bar, turn the crankshaft pulley until one of the bolts securing the torque converter to the driveplate becomes accessible through the starter motor aperture. Slacken and remove the bolt, then turn the crankshaft pulley as necessary, and undo the remaining bolts as they become accessible. There are six. Discard the bolts, new ones must be used on refitting.

15 Place a jack with a block of wood beneath the transmission, and raise the jack to take the weight of the transmission.

16 Unbolt and remove the left-hand engine/transmission mounting bracket from the transmission with reference to the relevant Part of Chapter 2.

17 Lower the engine and transmission by approximately 5 cm making sure that the coolant hoses and wiring harnesses are not stretched.

18 Slacken and remove the remaining bolts securing the transmission to the engine and sump flange. Note the correct fitted positions of each bolt, and the relevant brackets, as they are removed to use as a reference on refitting. Make a final check that all components have been disconnected, and are positioned clear of the transmission so that they will not hinder the removal procedure.

19 With all the bolts removed, move the trolley jack and transmission, to free it from its locating dowels. Once the transmission is free, lower the jack and manoeuvre the unit out from under the car, taking care to ensure that the torque converter does not fall off. Remove the locating dowels from the transmission or engine if they are loose, and keep them in a safe place. Retain the torque converter while the transmission is removed by bolting a strip of metal across the transmission bellhousing end face.

Refitting

20 The transmission is refitted by a reversal of the removal procedure, bearing in mind the following points:

a) *Prior to refitting, remove all traces of old locking compound from the torque converter threads by running a tap of the correct thread diameter and pitch down the holes. In the absence of a suitable tap, use one of the old bolts with slots cut in its threads.*

b) *Ensure the engine/transmission locating dowels are correctly positioned and apply a smear of molybdenum disulphide grease*

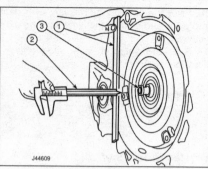

13.20a Check that the torque converter is fully entered

1 Straight-edge
2 Vernier calipers on bolt hole
3 Torque converter centre stub

to the torque converter locating pin and its centering bush in the crankshaft end.

c) *Check that the torque converter is fully entered inside the transmission bellhousing by measuring the distance from the flange to the bolt holes in the torque converter, using a straight-edge and vernier calipers* **(see illustration)**. *The distance must measure approximately 20.0 mm.*

d) *Once the transmission and engine are correctly joined, refit the securing bolts, tightening them to the specified torque setting.*

e) *Fit the new torque converter-to-driveplate bolts and tighten them lightly only to start then go around and tighten them to the specified torque setting in a diagonal sequence.*

f) *Tighten all nuts and bolts to the specified torque (where given).*

g) *Renew the driveshaft oil seals (see Section 8) and refit the driveshafts to the transmission as described in Chapter 8.*

h) *Refit the front subframe assembly as described in Chapter 10 Section 7.*

i) *On completion, refill the transmission with the specified type and quantity of fluid as described in Section 2 and adjust the selector cable as described in Section 3.*

14 Automatic transmission overhaul – general information

1 In the event of a fault occurring with the transmission, it is first necessary to determine whether it is of a mechanical, electrical or hydraulic nature, and to do this, special test equipment is required. It is therefore essential to have the work carried out by a Vauxhall/Opel dealer or suitably-equipped specialist if a transmission fault is suspected.

2 Do not remove the transmission from the car for possible repair before professional fault diagnosis has been carried out, since most tests require the transmission to be in the vehicle.

Chapter 7 Part C
Easytronic transmission

Contents

Section number

Clutch module with MTA control unit – removal and refitting. 5
Driveshaft oil seals – renewal 6
Easytronic transmission – removal and refitting. 7
Easytronic transmission overhaul – general information 8

Section number

General Information 1
Selector lever assembly – removal and refitting. 3
Transmission oil – draining and refilling 2
Transmission shift module – removal and refitting 4

Degrees of difficulty

Easy, suitable for novice with little experience	Fairly easy, suitable for beginner with some experience	Fairly difficult, suitable for competent DIY mechanic	Difficult, suitable for experienced DIY mechanic	Very difficult, suitable for expert DIY or professional

Specifications

General
Type . . . . Five forward speeds and one reverse, automatic or manual selection. Integral differential

Manufacturer's designation . . . . F17+ MTA

Gear ratios
1st. 3.72: 1
2nd 2.13: 1
3rd 1.41: 1
4th 1.12: 1
5th 0.89: 1
Reverse 3.30: 1
Final drive. 4.19: 1

Lubrication
Lubricant type . . . . See *Lubricants and fluids*
Lubricant capacity . . . . See Chapter 1A Section 1

Torque wrench settings

	Nm	lbf ft
Clutch module with MTA control unit	11	8
Differential lower cover plate bolts.	18	13
Engine/transmission mountings.	See Chapter 2A Section 0	
Transmission oil filler/level plug:		
Stage 1	4	3
Stage 2	Angle-tighten a further 45° to 135°	
Transmission shift module	11	8
Transmission-to-engine bolts.	See Chapter 2A Specifications	

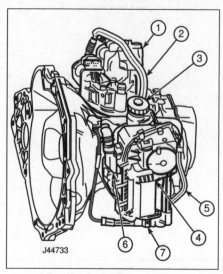

1.1 Easytronic (MTA) transmission

1 Transmission shift module
2 Wiring harness
3 Hydraulic fluid reservoir
4 Clutch control module
5 Hydraulic supply line to clutch control module
6 Wiring harness for clutch control module
7 Hydraulic pressure line to clutch release cylinder

1 General Information

1 The Easytronic MTA transmission (Manual Transmission Automatic-shift) is essentially a conventional manual transmission with the addition of a clutch module and shift module, used in conjunction with a self-adjusting clutch plate **(see illustration)**.
2 The description of the MTA transmission is basically as for the manual transmission given in Chapter 7A, but with an electronically-operated hydraulic clutch control module and gear selection module. The transmission can be switched between fully-automatic and manual mode, even while driving.
3 The clutch control module incorporates its

own master cylinder and pushrod, which is operated electrically by a worm gear.
4 The gear selection module is fitted with a shifting motor and a selector motor, which together position the selector lever to move the selector forks in the transmission. It is located in exactly the same position as the gear selection cover fitted to the conventional manual transmission.
5 Since the transmission is electronically-controlled, in the event of a problem, in the first instance the vehicle should be taken to a Vauxhall/Opel dealer or diagnostic specialist who will have the TECH2 diagnostic equipment (or equivalent) necessary to pin-point the faulty area. Note also that if the transmission assembly, shift module or clutch module are renewed, the vehicle must be taken to a Vauxhall/Opel dealer or diagnostic specialist in order to have the fault memory erased and new parameters programmed into the ECU.

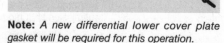

2 Transmission oil – draining and refilling

Note: *A new differential lower cover plate gasket will be required for this operation.*

Draining

1 This operation is much more efficient if the car is first taken on a journey of sufficient length to warm the engine/transmission up to normal operating temperature.
Caution: If the procedure is to be carried out on a hot transmission unit, take care not to burn yourself on the hot exhaust or the transmission/engine unit.
2 Position the vehicle over an inspection pit, on vehicle ramps, or jack it up and support it securely on axle stands (see *Jacking and vehicle support*), but make sure that it is level. Where fitted, remove the clips and bolts and remove the undertray from beneath the engine.
3 Since the transmission oil is not renewed as part of the manufacturer's maintenance schedule, no drain plug is fitted to the transmission. If for any reason the transmission needs to be drained, the only

way of doing so is to remove the differential lower cover plate.
4 Wipe clean the area around the differential lower cover plate and position a suitable container underneath the cover plate.
5 Evenly and progressively slacken and remove the retaining bolts then withdraw the cover plate and allow the transmission oil to drain into the container **(see illustration)**. Remove the gasket and discard it; a new one should be used on refitting.
6 Allow the oil to drain completely into the container. If the oil is hot, take precautions against scalding. Remove all traces of dirt and oil from the cover plate and transmission mating surfaces and wipe clean the inside of the cover plate.
7 Once the oil has finished draining, ensure the mating surfaces are clean and dry then refit the cover plate to the transmission unit, complete with a new gasket. Refit the retaining bolts and evenly and progressively tighten them to the specified torque.

Refilling

8 Wipe clean the area around the filler/level plug. The filler/level plug is located behind the driveshaft inner joint on the left-hand side of the transmission **(see illustration)**. Unscrew the plug and clean it.
9 Refill the transmission via the filler/level plug orifice with the specified type of oil until it begins to trickle out of the orifice. Once the oil level is correct, refit the filler/level plug and tighten to the specified torque.
10 Refit the engine undertray (where fitted) and lower the vehicle to the ground.

3 Selector lever assembly – removal and refitting

Removal

1 Disconnect the battery negative terminal (refer to Chapter 5A Section 4).
2 Remove the ashtray insert then unclip the ashtray housing from the base of the facia **(see illustration)**.
3 Undo the two selector lever trim panel retaining screws, then lift the panel up at the

2.5 Differential cover plate securing bolts (arrowed)

2.8 Transmission oil filler/level plug (arrowed)

3.2 Unclip the ashtray housing from the base of the facia

3.3 Undo the two selector lever trim panel retaining screws (arrowed)

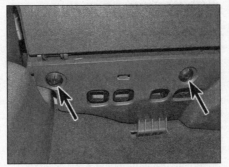

3.5a Unscrew the two quick-release catches (arrowed) ...

3.5b ... and remove the lower facia panel on the passenger's side

rear and disengage it from the facia at the front **(see illustration)**.

4 Unclip the winter programme push-button switch from the selector console and disconnect the wiring connector.

5 Unscrew the two quick-release catches and remove the lower facia panel on the passenger's side **(see illustrations)**. Remove the lower facia panel on the driver's side in the same way.

6 Release the retaining clips (three on each panel) and remove the footwell trim panels on the left- and right-hand sides of the facia **(see illustration)**.

7 Release the retaining clips and remove the selector lever console trim retaining frame.

8 Disconnect the wiring harness connector, then undo the four selector lever assembly retaining bolts. Lift the assembly from its location and remove it from the car.

Refitting

9 Refitting is a reversal of removal.

4	Transmission shift module – removal and refitting

Removal

1 Switch on the ignition, then depress the footbrake pedal and move the selector lever to position N. Switch off the ignition.

2 Remove the battery and battery tray as described in Chapter 5A Section 4.

3 Remove the ABS hydraulic modulator as described in Chapter 9 Section 18.

4 Disconnect the two wiring plugs and release the harness from the support cable ties on the top of the transmission.

5 Unbolt and remove the transmission shift module from the top of the transmission. To do this, lift it and tilt it slightly forwards before removing. Recover the gasket.

6 If the module cannot be removed because of internal jamming, unbolt the selector motor followed by the shifting motor **(see illustration)**, and use a screwdriver to move the selector lever to its neutral position first. The selector motor is the uppermost unit. **Note:** *The manufacturers recommend that the shift module assembly is never re-used if dismantled.*

Refitting

7 Clean the gasket faces of the module and transmission, and obtain a new gasket.

8 Make sure that the selector lever is in neutral by checking that the mark on the segment is aligned with the pinion tooth. Check also that the lever is fully extended so that the annular groove is visible. The shift forks in the transmission must also be in neutral – use a screwdriver to move them if necessary **(see illustrations)**.

9 Refit the shift module together with a new

3.6 Release the retaining clips and remove the footwell trim panels

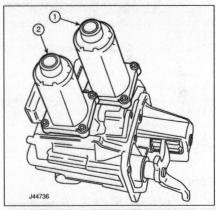

4.6 Shift motor (1) and selector motor (2) on the transmission shift module

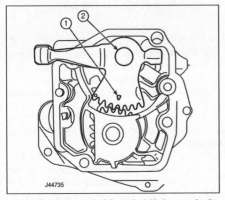

4.8a Neutral mark (1) and shift lever shaft (2) on the transmission shift module

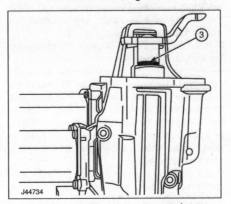

4.8b Groove (3) visible when the shift module is in neutral

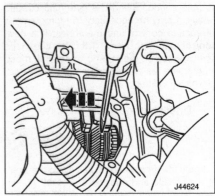

4.8c Using a screwdriver to move the transmission shift forks into neutral

gasket, then insert the bolts and tighten to the specified torque.

10 Reconnect the wiring and secure with new cable ties.

11 Refit the ABS hydraulic modulator as described in Chapter 9 Section 18.

12 Refit the battery tray and battery as described in Chapter 5A Section 4.

13 Finally, it may be necessary to have a Vauxhall/Opel dealer or diagnostic specialist reprogramme all volatile control unit memories. If a new control unit has been fitted, a Vauxhall/Opel dealer or diagnostic specialist must programme the unit specifically for the model to which it is fitted.

5 Clutch module with MTA control unit – removal and refitting

Note: *Bleeding the module is carried out using the Vauxhall/Opel TECH2 diagnostic instrument, therefore this work should be entrusted to a Vauxhall/Opel dealer or diagnostic specialist.*

Removal

1 Apply the handbrake, then jack up the front of the vehicle and support it on axle stands (see *Jacking and vehicle support*). Where necessary, remove the engine undertray.

2 Disconnect the wiring from the Easytronic transmission and release it from the cable tie supports.

3 Place a suitable container beneath the front of the transmission to catch spilt hydraulic fluid.

4 Fit a hose clamp to the hydraulic hose leading from the hydraulic fluid reservoir to the clutch control unit, then disconnect the hose.

5 Disconnect the hydraulic quick-release pressure hose from the clutch control unit.

6 Unscrew the mounting bolts and remove the clutch module with MTA control unit from the transmission.

Refitting

7 Refitting is a reversal of removal, but tighten the mounting bolts to the specified torque. Make sure that the quick-release pressure hose is fully engaged – it must make an audible sound. Bleed the hydraulic circuit. Finally, it may be necessary to reprogramme all volatile control unit memories. If a new control unit has been fitted, a Vauxhall/Opel dealer or diagnostic specialist must programme the unit specifically for the model to which it is fitted.

6 Driveshaft oil seals – renewal

1 Apply the handbrake, then jack up the front of the vehicle and support it on axle stands (see *Jacking and vehicle support*). Remove the relevant front roadwheel.

2 Drain the transmission oil as described in Section 2 or be prepared for oil loss as the seal is changed.

3 Disconnect the inner end of the relevant driveshaft from the differential as described in Chapter 8. There is no need to disconnect the driveshaft from the swivel hub. Support the driveshaft by suspending it with wire or string – do not allow the driveshaft to hang down under its own weight, or the joints may be damaged.

4 Prise the now-exposed oil seal from the differential housing, using a screwdriver or similar instrument.

5 Smear the sealing lip of the new oil seal with a little transmission oil, then using a metal tube or socket of suitable diameter, drive the new seal into the differential casing until the outer surface of the seal is flush with the outer surface of the differential casing.

6 Reconnect the driveshaft to the differential as described in Chapter 8.

7 Refill or top-up the transmission oil level with reference to Section 2.

8 Refit the roadwheel, then lower the vehicle to the ground.

7 Easytronic transmission – removal and refitting

Removal

1 Apply the handbrake, then jack up the front of the vehicle and support it on axle stands (see *Jacking and vehicle support*). Allow sufficient working room to remove the transmission from under the left-hand side of the engine compartment. Remove both front roadwheels then, where necessary, undo the retaining clips/screws and remove the engine undertray. Also remove the engine top cover where fitted.

2 Remove the transmission shift module as described in Section 4.

3 Drain the transmission oil as described in Section 2 or be prepared for oil loss as the transmission is removed.

4 Attach a suitable hoist and lifting tackle to the lifting bracket(s) located on the left-hand side of the cylinder head, and support the weight of the engine/transmission.

5 Refer to Chapter 10 Section 7 and remove the front subframe.

6 Disconnect the inner ends of both driveshafts from the differential as described in Chapter 8. There is no need to disconnect the driveshafts from the swivel hub. Support the driveshafts by suspending them with wire or string – do not allow the driveshafts to hang down under their own weight, or the joints may be damaged.

7 Disconnect the wiring from the transmission clutch module, and release the wiring from the support cables.

8 Place a jack with a block of wood beneath the transmission, and raise the jack to take the weight of the transmission.

9 Unbolt the left-hand engine/transmission mounting bracket from the transmission with reference to Chapter 2A Section 19.

10 Lower the engine and transmission by approximately 5 cm making sure that the coolant hoses and wiring harnesses are not stretched.

11 Unscrew and remove the upper bolts securing the transmission to the rear of the engine. Where necessary, pull up the coolant hoses and secure them away from the transmission using plastic cable ties.

12 Slacken and remove the remaining bolts securing the transmission to the engine and sump flange. Note the correct fitted positions of each bolt, and the relevant brackets, as they are removed to use as a reference on refitting. Make a final check that all components have been disconnected, and are positioned clear of the transmission so that they will not hinder the removal procedure.

13 With the bolts removed, move the trolley jack and transmission to free it from its locating dowels. Once the transmission is free, lower the jack and manoeuvre the unit out from under the car. Remove the locating dowels from the transmission or engine if they are loose, and keep them in a safe place.

Refitting

14 The transmission is refitted by a reversal of the removal procedure, bearing in mind the following points.

a) Tighten all nuts and bolts to the specified torque (where given).

b) Renew the driveshaft oil seals (see Section 6) before refitting the driveshafts.

c) Refit the front subframe assembly with reference to Chapter 10 Section 7.

d) Refill or top-up the transmission with the specified type and quantity of oil, as described in Section 2.

e) Finally, it may be necessary to have a dealer or diagnostic specialist reprogramme all volatile control unit memories.

8 Easytronic transmission overhaul – general information

1 In the event of a fault occurring on the transmission, it is first necessary to determine whether it is of an electrical, mechanical or hydraulic nature, and to achieve this, special test equipment is required. It is therefore essential to have the work carried out by a Vauxhall/Opel dealer if a transmission fault is suspected.

2 Do not remove the transmission from the car for possible repair before professional fault diagnosis has been carried out, since most tests require the transmission to be in the vehicle.

Chapter 8
Driveshafts

Contents

Section number

Driveshaft – removal and refitting. 2
Driveshaft joint gaiters – renewal 5
Driveshaft overhaul – general information 6

Section number

General Information 1
Intermediate shaft – removal and refitting 3
Intermediate shaft bearing – renewal 4

Degrees of difficulty

Easy, suitable for novice with little experience	Fairly easy, suitable for beginner with some experience	Fairly difficult, suitable for competent DIY mechanic	Difficult, suitable for experienced DIY mechanic	Very difficult, suitable for expert DIY or professional

Specifications

General
Driveshaft type . . . . Solid steel shafts with inner and outer constant velocity (CV) joints. Right-hand driveshaft incorporating intermediate shaft on some models

Lubrication (overhaul only – see text)
Lubricant type/specification. . . . . Use only special grease supplied in sachets with gaiter kits – joints are otherwise pre-packed with grease and sealed

Torque wrench settings

	Nm	lbf ft
Anti-roll bar connecting link retaining nut*	55	41
Driveshaft retaining nut*:		
Stage 1	150	111
Stage 2	Slacken the nut by 45°	
Stage 3	250	185
Intermediate shaft bearing housing to support bracket	18	13
Lower arm balljoint clamp bolt nut*	50	37
Roadwheels	110	81
Track rod end-to-swivel hub: *		
Stage 1	30	22
Stage 2	Angle-tighten a further 90°	
Stage 3	Angle-tighten a further 15°	

*Use new nuts/bolts

1 General Information

1 Drive is transmitted from the differential to the front wheels by means of two, solid steel driveshafts.

2 Both driveshafts are splined at their outer ends to accept the wheel hubs, and are threaded so that each hub can be fastened by a large nut. The inner end of each driveshaft is splined to accept the intermediate shaft and is held in place by an internal circlip.

3 Constant velocity (CV) joints are fitted to each end of the driveshafts, to ensure the smooth and efficient transmission of drive at all the angles possible as the roadwheels move up-and-down with the suspension, and as they turn from side-to-side under steering. On petrol engine models, both inner and outer constant velocity joints are of the ball-and-cage type. On all diesel engine models, the outer constant velocity joints are of the ball-and-cage type and the inner joints are of the tripod type.

4 The right-hand driveshaft on diesel engine models has an intermediate shaft attached to the rear of the cylinder block.

TOOL TiP

A tool to hold the wheel hub stationary whilst the driveshaft retaining nut is slackened can be fabricated from two lengths of steel strip (one long, one short) and a nut an bolt; the nut and bolt forming the pivot of a forked tool.

2 Driveshaft – removal and refitting

Note: *A new driveshaft retaining nut, inner joint circlip, lower arm balljoint clamp bolt and nut, anti-roll bar connecting link retaining nut and a new track rod end retaining nut will be needed for refitting. The driveshaft outer joint splines may be a tight fit in the hub and it is possible that a puller/extractor will be required to draw the hub assembly off the driveshaft during removal.*

Removal

1 Firmly apply the handbrake, then jack up the front of the car and support it securely on axle stands (see *Jacking and vehicle support*). Remove the relevant front roadwheel then, where fitted, remove the screws and clips and remove the engine undertray.

2 To prevent rotation of the wheel hub as the driveshaft retaining nut is slackened, make up a holding tool and bolt the tool to the wheel hub using two wheel bolts (see **Tool Tip**).

3 With the holding tool in place, slacken and remove the driveshaft retaining nut using a socket and long bar. Where necessary, support the socket on an axle stand to prevent it slipping off the nut. This nut is very tight; make sure that there is no risk of pulling the

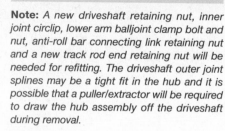

2.4 Unscrew the retaining nut, then use a balljoint separator tool to remove the track rod end from the swivel hub

car off the axle stands as the nut is slackened.

4 Unscrew the nut securing the track rod end to the steering arm on the swivel hub, then use a balljoint separator tool to remove the track rod end **(see illustration)**.

5 Unscrew and remove the nut securing the anti-roll bar connecting link to the suspension strut, while holding the link stub on the flats provided with a further spanner **(see illustration)**. Release the link from the strut to one side.

6 Unscrew the nut and remove the clamp bolt securing the front suspension lower arm to the swivel hub. Note that the bolt head faces the front of the vehicle **(see illustration)**.

7 Use a chisel or screwdriver as a wedge to expand the lower portion of the swivel hub **(see illustration)**.

8 Using a lever, push down on the suspension lower arm to free the balljoint from the swivel hub, then move the swivel hub to one side and release the arm, taking care not to damage the balljoint rubber boot **(see illustration)**. It is advisable to place a protective cover over the rubber boot such as the plastic cap from an aerosol can, suitably cut to fit.

9 The hub must now be freed from the end of the driveshaft. It may be possible to pull the hub off the driveshaft, but if the end of the driveshaft is tight in the hub, temporarily refit the driveshaft retaining nut to protect the driveshaft threads, then tap the end of the driveshaft with a soft-faced hammer while

2.5 Unscrew the nut securing the connecting link to the anti-roll bar, while holding the link stub with a further spanner

2.6 Unscrew the retaining nut and withdraw the clamp bolt from the swivel hub

2.7 Use a chisel or screwdriver as a wedge to expand the lower portion of the swivel hub

2.8 Push down the lower suspension arm to free the balljoint from the swivel hub

2.9a Use a soft-faced hammer to drive the driveshaft from the hub splines ...

2.9b ... then pull the swivel hub outwards

2.12 Using a stout bar, release the inner end of the driveshaft from the differential or intermediate shaft

pulling outwards on the swivel hub **(see illustrations)**. Alternatively, use a suitable puller to press the driveshaft through the hub.
10 With the driveshaft detached from the swivel hub, tie the suspension strut to one side and support the driveshaft on an axle stand.
11 If working on the left-hand driveshaft, place a suitable container beneath the differential, to collect escaping transmission oil/fluid when the driveshaft is withdrawn.
12 Using a stout bar, release the inner end of the driveshaft from the differential or intermediate shaft. Lever between the constant velocity joint and differential housing, or between the constant velocity joint and intermediate shaft bearing housing, to release the driveshaft retaining circlip **(see illustration)**.
13 Withdraw the driveshaft, ensuring that the constant velocity joints are not placed under excessive strain, and remove the driveshaft from beneath the vehicle. Whilst the driveshaft is removed, plug or tape over the differential aperture to prevent dirt entry.
Caution: Do not allow the vehicle to rest on its wheels with one or both driveshafts removed, as damage to the wheel bearings(s) may result. If the vehicle must be moved on its wheels, clamp the wheel bearings using spacers and a long threaded rod to take the place of the driveshaft.

Refitting

14 Before refitting the driveshaft, examine the oil seal in the transmission housing and renew it if necessary as described in the relevant Part of Chapter 7.
15 Remove the circlip from the end of the driveshaft inner joint splines or intermediate shaft and discard it. Fit a new circlip, making sure it is correctly located in the groove.
16 Thoroughly clean the driveshaft splines, intermediate shaft splines (where applicable), and the apertures in the transmission and hub assembly. Apply a thin film of grease to the oil seal lips, and to the driveshaft splines and shoulders. Check that all gaiter clips are securely fastened.
17 Offer up the driveshaft, and engage the inner joint splines with those of the differential sun gear or intermediate shaft, taking care not to damage the oil seal. Push the joint

fully into position, then check that the circlip is correctly located and securely holds the joint in position. If necessary, use a soft-faced mallet or drift to drive the driveshaft inner joint fully into position.
18 Align the outer constant velocity joint splines with those of the hub, and slide the joint back into position in the hub.
19 Using a lever, push down on the lower suspension arm, then relocate the balljoint and release the arm. Make sure that the balljoint stub is fully entered in the swivel hub.
20 Insert a new lower arm balljoint clamp bolt with its head facing the front of the vehicle, fit a new retaining nut and tighten the nut to the specified torque.
21 Refit the track rod end to the steering arm on the swivel hub and tighten the new nut to the specified torque in the stages given in the Specifications.
22 Locate the anti-roll bar connecting link on the suspension strut, fit a new retaining nut and tighten the nut to the specified torque.
23 Lubricate the inner face and threads of the new driveshaft retaining nut with clean engine oil, and refit it to the end of the driveshaft. Use the method employed on removal to prevent the hub from rotating, and tighten the driveshaft retaining nut to the specified torque in the stages given in the Specifications. Check that the hub rotates freely.
24 Refit the roadwheel and engine undertray (where fitted), then lower the vehicle to the ground and tighten the roadwheel bolts to the specified torque.

3.3 Intermediate shaft bearing housing retaining bolts (arrowed)

25 Check and if necessary top-up the transmission oil/fluid level, using the information given in the relevant Part of Chapter 7.

3 Intermediate shaft – removal and refitting

Note: *An intermediate shaft is not fitted petrol engine models.*

Removal

1 Remove the right-hand driveshaft as described in Section 2.
2 Place a suitable container beneath the differential, to collect escaping transmission oil/fluid when the intermediate shaft is withdrawn.
3 Undo the three bolts securing the intermediate shaft bearing housing to the support bracket on the cylinder block **(see illustration)**. Pull the intermediate shaft out of the transmission, slide it through the support bracket and remove the shaft from under the car.

Refitting

4 Before refitting the intermediate shaft, examine the oil seal in the transmission housing and renew it if necessary as described in the relevant Part of Chapter 7.
5 Remove the circlip from the end of the intermediate shaft and discard it. Fit a new circlip, making sure it is correctly located in the groove.
6 Thoroughly clean the driveshaft splines, intermediate shaft splines, and the aperture in the transmission. Apply a thin film of grease to the oil seal lips, and to the driveshaft and intermediate shaft splines and shoulders.
7 Insert the intermediate shaft into the transmission, engaging the splines with the differential sun gear, taking care not to damage the oil seal.
8 Refit the three bolts securing the intermediate shaft bearing housing to the support bracket on the cylinder block. Tighten the bolts to the specified torque.
9 Refit the right-hand driveshaft as described in Section 2.

4.3 Extract the circlip (arrowed) securing the intermediate shaft in the bearing

4 Intermediate shaft bearing – renewal

Note: *A hydraulic press, together with tubes and mandrels of suitable diameters will be needed for this operation. A new intermediate shaft circlip and, where fitted, a new O-ring will also be required.*

1 Remove the intermediate shaft as described in Section 3.

2 Where fitted, remove the O-ring from the end of the intermediate shaft.

3 Using circlip pliers, or a small screwdriver, extract the circlip securing the intermediate shaft in the bearing **(see illustration)**.

4 Support the underside of the bearing housing on the press bed and press the intermediate shaft downwards out of the bearing.

5 With the intermediate shaft removed, press the bearing out of the housing using a suitable mandrel.

6 Locate the new bearing in the housing and press it fully into position using a suitable tube in contact with the bearing outer race.

7 With the bearing supported on its inner race, press the intermediate shaft back into the bearing until it is fully engaged.

8 Secure the intermediate shaft with a new circlip then, where applicable, fit a new O-ring to the end of the shaft.

9 On completion, refit the intermediate shaft as described in Section 3.

5 Driveshaft joint gaiters – renewal

Outer CV joint

1 Remove the driveshaft from the car as described in Section 2, then secure the shaft in a vice equipped with soft jaws.

2 Release the rubber gaiter inner and outer retaining clips by cutting through them using a junior hacksaw **(see illustration)**. Spread the clips and remove them from the gaiter.

3 Slide the rubber gaiter down the shaft to expose the CV joint or, alternatively, cut the gaiter open using a suitable knife and remove it from the driveshaft **(see illustration)**.

4 Using old rags, clean away as much of the old grease as possible from the CV joint. It is advisable to wear disposable rubber gloves during this operation.

5 The outer CV joint will be retained on the driveshaft either by an external snap-ring, or by an internal circlip **(see illustration)**. If an external snap-ring is fitted, use circlip pliers to expand the snap-ring as the CV joint is removed.

6 Using a mallet, sharply strike the edge of the outer joint to drive it off the end of the shaft **(see illustrations)**.

7 Once the joint has been removed, extract the snap-ring from the joint, or remove the circlip from the groove in the driveshaft splines **(see illustration)**. A new snap-ring or circlip must be fitted on reassembly.

8 If still in place, withdraw the rubber gaiter from the driveshaft.

9 With the CV joint removed from the driveshaft, wipe away the remaining grease (do not use any solvent) to allow the joint components to be inspected.

10 Move the inner splined driving member from side-to-side, to expose each ball in turn at the top of its track. Examine the balls for cracks, flat spots, or signs of surface pitting.

11 Inspect the ball tracks on the inner and outer members. If the tracks have widened, the balls will no longer be a tight fit. At the same time, check the ball cage windows for wear or cracking between the windows.

12 If on inspection any of the constant velocity joint components are found to be

5.2 Release the rubber gaiter retaining clips by cutting through them using a hacksaw

5.3 Cut the gaiter open using a suitable knife and remove it from the driveshaft

5.5 Outer CV joint snap-ring in driveshaft groove (arrowed)

5.6a Sharply strike the edge of the outer joint to drive it off the end of the shaft

5.6b If an external snap-ring is fitted, use circlip pliers to expand the snap-ring as the joint is removed

5.7 Removing the circlip from the groove in the driveshaft splines

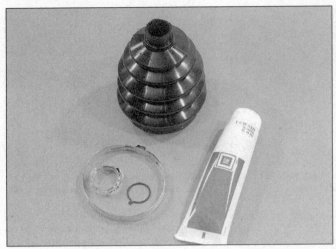

5.12 Components required for driveshaft gaiter renewal

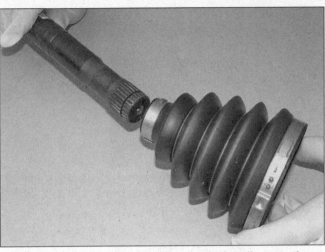

5.13 Slide the new rubber gaiter and retaining clips onto the driveshaft

worn or damaged, it will be necessary to renew the complete joint assembly. If the joint is in satisfactory condition, obtain a repair kit consisting of a new gaiter and retaining clips, a constant velocity joint snap-ring or circlip, and the correct type and quantity of grease **(see illustration)**.

13 Slide the new rubber gaiter and retaining clips onto the driveshaft **(see illustration)**.

14 Fit a new snap-ring to the constant velocity joint, or a new circlip to the groove in the driveshaft, as applicable **(see illustrations)**.

15 Pack the joint with the grease supplied in the repair kit **(see illustration)**. Work the grease well into the bearing tracks whilst twisting the joint, and fill the rubber gaiter with any excess.

16 Screw on the driveshaft retaining nut two or three turns to protect the threads, then engage the joint with the driveshaft splines. Tap the joint onto the driveshaft until the snap-ring or circlip engages in its groove **(see illustration)**. Make sure that the joint is securely retained, by pulling on the joint, not the shaft.

17 Ease the gaiter over the joint, and ensure that the gaiter lips are correctly located in the grooves on both the driveshaft and constant velocity joint. Lift the outer sealing lip of the gaiter, to equalise air pressure within the gaiter.

18 Pull the large gaiter retaining clip as tight as possible, and locate the hooks on the clip in their slots. Remove any slack in the gaiter retaining clip by carefully compressing the raised section of the clip. In the absence of the special tool, a pair of side-cutters may be used. Secure the small retaining clip using the same procedure **(see illustrations)**.

19 Check that the constant velocity joint moves freely in all directions, then refit the driveshaft to the car as described in Section 2.

5.14a Fit a new snap-ring to the constant velocity joint ...

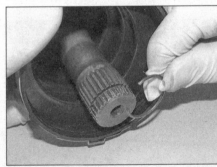

5.14b ... or a new circlip to the groove in the driveshaft

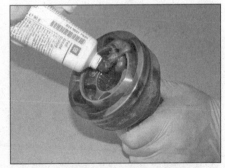

5.15 Pack the joint with the grease supplied in the repair kit

5.16 Tap the joint onto the driveshaft until the snap-ring or circlip engages in its groove

5.18a Secure the large gaiter retaining clip in position by compressing the raised section of the clip

5.18b The small inner retaining clip is secured in the same way

5.21a Remove the circlip from the groove in the inner CV joint splines ...

5.21b ... then, where fitted, slide off the rubber dust cover

5.22 Cut off the rubber gaiter retaining clips, then slide the gaiter down the shaft

Inner CV joint

Note: *On diesel engine models the inner tripod type CV joint cannot be detached from the driveshaft. If inner CV joint gaiter renewal is required, it will be necessary to remove the outer CV joint as described previously and slide the inner joint gaiter off the outer end of the driveshaft.*

20 Remove the driveshaft from the car as described in Section 2, then secure the shaft in a vice equipped with soft jaws.

21 Remove the circlip from the groove in the CV joint splines then, where fitted, slide off the rubber dust cover **(see illustrations)**. Note that a new circlip must be fitted on reassembly.

22 Release the rubber gaiter inner and outer retaining clips by cutting through them using a junior hacksaw **(see illustration)**. Spread the clips and remove them from the gaiter.

23 Slide the rubber gaiter down the shaft to expose the CV joint.

24 Using old rags, clean away as much of the old grease as possible from the CV joint **(see illustration)**. It is advisable to wear disposable rubber gloves during this operation.

25 Expand the CV joint retaining snap-ring using circlip pliers, then remove the joint by tapping it off the driveshaft with a hammer and punch in contact with the joint inner member **(see illustrations)**.

26 Once the joint has been removed, extract the snap-ring noting that a new one must be fitted on reassembly.

27 Withdraw the rubber gaiter from the driveshaft.

28 With the CV joint removed from the driveshaft, wipe away the remaining grease (do not use any solvent) and inspect the joint components as described previously in paragraphs 10 and 11.

29 If on inspection any of the constant velocity joint components are found to be worn or damaged, it will be necessary to renew the complete joint assembly. If the joint is in satisfactory condition, obtain a repair kit consisting of a new gaiter and retaining clips, a constant velocity joint snap-ring and circlip, and the correct type and quantity of grease.

30 Slide the new rubber gaiter and retaining clips onto the driveshaft **(see illustration)**.

31 Fit a new snap-ring to the constant velocity joint, then engage the joint with the driveshaft splines. Tap the joint onto the driveshaft until the snap-ring engages in its groove **(see illustration)**. Make sure that the joint is securely retained, by pulling on the joint, not the shaft.

32 Pack the joint with the grease supplied in the repair kit **(see illustration)**. Work the grease well into the bearing tracks whilst twisting the joint, and fill the rubber gaiter with any excess.

5.24 Clean away as much of the old grease as possible from the CV joint

5.25a Expand the joint retaining snap-ring using circlip pliers ...

5.25b ... then remove the joint by tapping it off the driveshaft with a hammer and punch

5.30 Slide the new rubber gaiter and retaining clips onto the driveshaft

5.31 Tap the joint onto the driveshaft until the snap-ring engages in its groove

5.32 Pack the joint with the grease supplied in the repair kit

5.34a Secure the large gaiter retaining clip in position by compressing the raised section of the clip

5.34b The small inner retaining clip is secured in the same way

33 Ease the gaiter over the joint, and ensure that the gaiter lips are correctly located in the grooves on both the driveshaft and constant velocity joint. Lift the outer sealing lip of the gaiter, to equalise air pressure within the gaiter.

34 Pull the large gaiter retaining clip as tight as possible, and locate the hooks on the clip in their slots. Remove any slack in the gaiter retaining clip by carefully compressing the raised section of the clip. In the absence of the special tool, a pair of side-cutters may be used. Secure the small retaining clip using the same procedure **(see illustrations)**.

35 Where applicable, slide the rubber dust cover onto the CV joint, then fit a new circlip to the groove in the joint splines.

36 Check that the constant velocity joint moves freely in all directions, then refit the driveshaft to the car as described in Section 2.

6 Driveshaft overhaul – general information

1 If any of the checks described in Chapter 1A Section 13 or Chapter 1B Section 13 reveal possible wear in any driveshaft joint, carry out the following procedures to identify the source of the problem.

2 Firmly apply the handbrake, then jack up the front of the vehicle and support it securely on axle stands (see *Jacking and vehicle support*).

3 Referring to the information contained in Section 2, make up a tool to hold the wheel hub, and bolt the tool to the hub. Use a torque wrench to check that the driveshaft retaining nut is securely fastened, then

repeat this check on the remaining driveshaft nut.

4 Road test the vehicle, and listen for a metallic clicking from the front as the vehicle is driven slowly in a circle on full-lock. If a clicking noise is heard, this indicates wear in the outer constant velocity joint.

5 If vibration, consistent with roadspeed, is felt through the car when accelerating, there is a possibility of wear in the inner constant velocity joints.

6 To check the joints for wear, remove the driveshafts, then dismantle them as described in Section 3 ; if any wear or free play is found, the affected joint must be renewed. Note that if renewal of the inner joint on 2.2 litre petrol engine or diesel engine models is required, it will be necessary to obtain a new inner joint complete with driveshaft, then transfer the existing outer joint to the new driveshaft.

Chapter 9
Braking system

Contents

Section number

Anti-lock Braking and Traction Control system components –
    removal and refitting................................... 18
Anti-lock Braking and Traction Control systems –
    general information................................... 17
Brake pedal – removal and refitting......................... 10
Front brake caliper – removal, overhaul and refitting........... 7
Front brake pads – renewal 4
Front/rear brake disc – inspection, removal and refitting......... 6
General Information 1
Handbrake cables – removal and refitting 14
Handbrake lever – removal and refitting..................... 13

Section number

Handbrake warning light switch – removal and refitting 16
Hydraulic pipes and hoses – renewal........................ 3
Hydraulic system – bleeding 2
Master cylinder – removal, overhaul and refitting 9
Rear brake caliper – removal, overhaul and refitting 8
Rear brake pads – renewal................................ 5
Stop-light switch – removal, refitting and adjustment 15
Vacuum pump (diesel engine models) – removal and refitting...... 19
Vacuum servo unit – testing, removal and refitting 11
Vacuum servo unit check valve and hose –
    removal, testing and refitting 12

Degrees of difficulty

Easy, suitable for novice with little experience 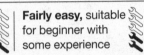	Fairly easy, suitable for beginner with some experience	Fairly difficult, suitable for competent DIY mechanic	Difficult, suitable for experienced DIY mechanic	Very difficult, suitable for expert DIY or professional

Specifications

Front brakes

Type .... Ventilated disc, with single-piston sliding caliper
Disc diameter:
   All petrol models, and 1.7 litre diesel models.................. 280.0 mm
   1.9 litre diesel models................................ 308.0 mm
Disc thickness:
   New .... 25.0 mm
   Minimum... 22.0 mm
Maximum disc run-out................................. 0.11 mm
Brake pad friction material minimum thickness................. 2.0 mm
Brake caliper piston diameter .... 57.0 mm

Rear brakes

Type .... Solid disc, with single-piston sliding caliper
Disc diameter....................................... 264.0 mm
Disc thickness:
   New .... 10.0 mm
   Minimum... 8.0 mm
Maximum disc run-out................................. 0.13 mm
Brake pad friction material minimum thickness................. 2.0 mm
Brake caliper piston diameter .... 41.0 mm

ABS system type

Standard ABS system .... ATE Mk 70
ABS with traction control and electronic stability program .... ATE Mk 60 ESP

Torque wrench settings

	Nm	lbf ft
ABS hydraulic modulator mounting bracket bolts	20	15
ABS hydraulic modulator to mounting bracket	8	6
Brake caliper bleed screws	10	7
Brake caliper guide bolts:		
Front caliper	28	21
Rear caliper	25	18
Brake caliper mounting bracket bolts	100	74
Brake fluid pipe unions.	14	10
Brake hydraulic hose banjo union bolts.	40	30
Brake pedal mounting bracket bolts/nuts	20	15
Handbrake lever retaining nuts	10	7
High-pressure fuel pump mounting bracket bolts	25	18
Master cylinder retaining nuts:		
Petrol engine models	15	11
Diesel engine models	21	15
Roadwheel bolts.	110	81
Vacuum pump mounting bolts: *		
Stage 1	6	4
Stage 2	Angle-tighten a further 50°	
Vacuum servo unit mounting nuts	20	15

Use new fasteners

1 General Information

1 The braking system is of servo-assisted, dual-circuit hydraulic type split diagonally. The arrangement of the hydraulic system is such that each circuit operates one front and one rear brake from a tandem master cylinder. Under normal circumstances, both circuits operate in unison. However, in the event of hydraulic failure in one circuit, full braking force will still be available at two wheels.

2 All models are fitted with front and rear disc brakes. The disc brakes are actuated by single-piston sliding type calipers, which ensure that equal pressure is applied to each disc pad.

3 An Anti-lock Braking System (ABS) is fitted as standard equipment to all vehicles covered in this manual. On higher specification models, the ABS may also incorporate traction control or an electronic stability program. Refer to Section 17 for further information on ABS operation.

4 The cable-operated handbrake provides an independent mechanical means of rear brake application.

5 On diesel engines, since there is no throttling as such of the intake manifold, the manifold is not a suitable source of vacuum to operate the vacuum servo unit. The servo unit is therefore connected to a separate, engine-mounted vacuum pump bolted to the left-hand end of the cylinder head and driven by the camshaft.

Warning: When servicing any part of the system, work carefully and methodically; also observe scrupulous cleanliness when overhauling any part of the hydraulic system. Always renew components (in axle sets, where applicable) if in doubt about their condition, and use only genuine Vauxhall/Opel parts, or at least those of known good quality. Note the warnings given in 'Safety first!' and at relevant points in this Chapter concerning the dangers of asbestos dust and hydraulic fluid.

2 Hydraulic system – bleeding

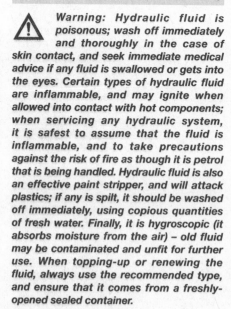

Warning: Hydraulic fluid is poisonous; wash off immediately and thoroughly in the case of skin contact, and seek immediate medical advice if any fluid is swallowed or gets into the eyes. Certain types of hydraulic fluid are inflammable, and may ignite when allowed into contact with hot components; when servicing any hydraulic system, it is safest to assume that the fluid is inflammable, and to take precautions against the risk of fire as though it is petrol that is being handled. Hydraulic fluid is also an effective paint stripper, and will attack plastics; if any is spilt, it should be washed off immediately, using copious quantities of fresh water. Finally, it is hygroscopic (it absorbs moisture from the air) – old fluid may be contaminated and unfit for further use. When topping-up or renewing the fluid, always use the recommended type, and ensure that it comes from a freshly-opened sealed container.

General

1 The correct operation of any hydraulic system is only possible after removing all air from the components and circuit; this is achieved by bleeding the system.

2 During the bleeding procedure, add only clean, unused hydraulic fluid of the recommended type; never re-use fluid that has already been bled from the system. Ensure that sufficient fluid is available before starting work.

3 If there is any possibility of incorrect fluid being already in the system, the brake components and circuit must be flushed completely with uncontaminated, correct fluid, and new seals should be fitted to the various components.

4 If hydraulic fluid has been lost from the system, or air has entered because of a leak, ensure that the fault is cured before proceeding further.

5 Park the vehicle over an inspection pit or on car ramps. Alternatively, apply the handbrake then jack up the front and rear of the vehicle and support it on axle stands (see *Jacking and vehicle support*). For improved access with the vehicle jacked up, remove the roadwheels.

6 Check that all pipes and hoses are secure, unions tight and bleed screws closed. Clean any dirt from around the bleed screws.

7 Unscrew the master cylinder reservoir cap, and top the master cylinder reservoir up to the MAX level line; refit the cap loosely, and remember to maintain the fluid level at least above the MIN level line throughout the procedure, otherwise there is a risk of further air entering the system.

8 There are a number of one-man, do-it-yourself brake bleeding kits currently available from motor accessory shops. It is recommended that one of these kits is used whenever possible, as they greatly simplify the bleeding operation, and also reduce the risk of expelled air and fluid being drawn back into the system. If such a kit is not available, the basic (two-man) method must be used, which is described in detail below.

Caution: Vauxhall recommend using a pressure bleeding kit for this operation (see paragraphs 24 to 27).

9 If a kit is to be used, prepare the vehicle as described previously, and follow the kit manufacturer's instructions, as the procedure may vary slightly according to the type being used; generally, they are as outlined below in the relevant sub-section.

10 Whichever method is used, the same sequence should be followed (paragraphs 11 and 12) to ensure the removal of all air from the system.

Bleeding sequence

11 If the system has been only partially disconnected, and suitable precautions were taken to minimise fluid loss, it should only be necessary to bleed that part of the system (ie, the primary or secondary circuit). If the master cylinder or main brake lines have been disconnected, then the complete system must be bled.

12 If the complete system is to be bled, then it should be done in the following sequence:

Right-hand drive models

a) *Left-hand rear brake.*
b) *Right-hand rear brake.*
c) *Left-hand front brake.*
d) *Right-hand front brake.*

Left-hand drive models

a) *Right-hand rear brake.*
b) *Left-hand rear brake.*
c) *Right-hand front brake.*
d) *Left-hand front brake.*

Bleeding

Basic (two-man) method

13 Collect together a clean glass jar, a suitable length of plastic or rubber tubing which is a tight fit over the bleed screw, and a ring spanner to fit the screw. The help of an assistant will also be required.

14 Remove the dust cap from the first bleed screw in the sequence **(see illustrations)**. Fit the spanner and tube to the screw, place the other end of the tube in the jar, and pour in sufficient fluid to cover the end of the tube.

15 Ensure that the master cylinder reservoir fluid level is maintained at least above the MIN level line throughout the procedure.

16 Have the assistant fully depress the brake pedal several times to build-up pressure, then maintain it on the final downstroke.

17 While pedal pressure is maintained, unscrew the bleed screw (approximately one turn) and allow the compressed fluid and air to flow into the jar. The assistant should maintain pedal pressure, following it down to the floor if necessary, and should not release it until instructed to do so. When the flow stops, tighten the bleed screw again, have the assistant release the pedal slowly, and recheck the reservoir fluid level.

18 Repeat the steps given in paragraphs 16 and 17 until the fluid emerging from the bleed screw is free from air bubbles. If the master cylinder has been drained and refilled, and air is being bled from the first screw in the sequence, allow approximately five seconds between cycles for the master cylinder passages to refill.

19 When no more air bubbles appear, securely tighten the bleed screw, remove the tube and spanner, and refit the dust cap. Do not overtighten the bleed screw.

20 Repeat the procedure on the remaining screws in the sequence, until all air is removed from the system and the brake pedal feels firm again.

Using a one-way valve kit

21 As the name implies, these kits consist of a length of tubing with a one-way valve fitted, to prevent expelled air and fluid being drawn back into the system; some kits include a translucent container, which can be positioned so that the air bubbles can be more easily seen flowing from the end of the tube.

22 The kit is connected to the bleed screw, which is then opened. The user returns to the driver's seat, depresses the brake pedal with a smooth, steady stroke, and slowly releases it; this is repeated until the expelled fluid is clear of air bubbles.

23 Note that these kits simplify work so much that it is easy to forget the master cylinder reservoir fluid level; ensure that this is maintained at least above the MIN level line at all times.

Using a pressure-bleeding kit

24 These kits are usually operated by a reservoir of pressurised air contained in the spare tyre. However, note that it will probably be necessary to reduce the pressure to a lower level than normal; refer to the instructions supplied with the kit.

25 By connecting a pressurised, fluid-filled container to the master cylinder reservoir, bleeding can be carried out simply by opening each screw in turn (in the specified sequence), and allowing the fluid to flow out until no more air bubbles can be seen in the expelled fluid.

26 This method has the advantage that the large reservoir of fluid provides an additional

safeguard against air being drawn into the system during bleeding.

27 Pressure-bleeding is particularly effective when bleeding 'difficult' systems, or when bleeding the complete system at the time of routine fluid renewal.

All methods

28 When bleeding is complete, and firm pedal feel is restored, wash off any spilt fluid, securely tighten the bleed screws, and refit the dust caps.

29 Check the hydraulic fluid level in the master cylinder reservoir, and top-up if necessary (see *Weekly checks*).

30 Discard any hydraulic fluid that has been bled from the system; it will not be fit for re-use.

31 Check the feel of the brake pedal. If it feels at all spongy, air must still be present in the system, and further bleeding is required. Failure to bleed satisfactorily after a reasonable repetition of the bleeding procedure may be due to worn master cylinder seals.

---

3 Hydraulic pipes and hoses – renewal

Note: *Before starting work, refer to the note at the beginning of Section 2 concerning the dangers of hydraulic fluid.*

1 If any pipe or hose is to be renewed, minimise fluid loss by first removing the master cylinder reservoir cap and screwing it down onto a piece of polythene. Alternatively, flexible hoses can be sealed, if required, using a proprietary brake hose clamp. Metal brake pipe unions can be plugged (if care is taken not to allow dirt into the system) or capped immediately they are disconnected. Place a wad of rag under any union that is to be disconnected, to catch any spilt fluid.

2 If a flexible hose is to be disconnected, unscrew the brake pipe union nut before removing the spring clip which secures the hose to its mounting bracket. Where applicable, unscrew the banjo union bolt securing the hose to the caliper and recover the copper washers. When removing the

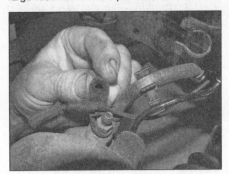

2.14a Remove the dust caps from the front ...

2.14b ... and rear bleed screws

3.2a Pull out the spring clip ...

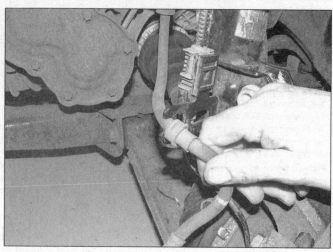

3.2b ... and disconnect the hydraulic hose from the strut bracket

front flexible hose, pull out the spring clip and disconnect it from the strut **(see illustrations)**.
3 To unscrew union nuts, it is preferable to obtain a brake pipe spanner of the correct size; these are available from most motor accessory shops. Failing this, a close-fitting open-ended spanner will be required, though if the nuts are tight or corroded, their flats may be rounded-off if the spanner slips. In such a case, a self-locking wrench is often the only way to unscrew a stubborn union, but it follows that the pipe and the damaged nuts must be renewed on reassembly. Always clean a union and surrounding area before disconnecting it. If disconnecting a component with more than one union, make a careful note of the connections before disturbing any of them.
4 If a brake pipe is to be renewed, it can be obtained, cut to length and with the union nuts and end flares in place, from Vauxhall/Opel dealers. All that is then necessary is to bend it to shape, following the line of the original, before fitting it to the car. Alternatively, most motor accessory shops can make up brake pipes from kits, but this requires very careful measurement of the original, to ensure that the new one is of the correct length. The safest answer is usually to take the original to the shop as a pattern.
5 On refitting, do not overtighten the union nuts.
6 When refitting hoses to the calipers, always use new copper washers and tighten the banjo union bolts to the specified torque. Make sure that the hoses are positioned so that they will not touch surrounding bodywork or the roadwheels.
7 Ensure that the pipes and hoses are correctly routed, with no kinks, and that they are secured in the clips or brackets provided. After fitting, remove the polythene from the reservoir, and bleed the hydraulic system as described in Section 2. Wash off any spilt fluid, and check carefully for fluid leaks.

4 Front brake pads – renewal

Warning: Renew BOTH sets of front brake pads at the same time – NEVER renew the pads on only one wheel, as uneven braking may result. Note that the dust created by wear of the pads may contain asbestos, which is a health hazard. Never blow it out with compressed air, and do not inhale any of it. An approved filtering mask should be worn when working on the brakes. DO NOT use petroleum-based solvents to clean brake parts – use brake cleaner or methylated spirit only.

1 Apply the handbrake, then jack up the front of the vehicle and support it on axle stands (see *Jacking and vehicle support*). Remove the front roadwheels.
2 Follow the accompanying photos **(illustrations 4.2a to 4.2y)** for the pad renewal procedure, bearing in mind the additional points listed below. Be sure to stay in order and read the caption under each illustration. Note that if the old pads are to be refitted, ensure that they are identified so that they can be returned to their original positions.
3 After removing the caliper from the mounting bracket, support it on top of the brake disc. Do not allow the caliper to hang unsupported on the flexible brake hose.
4 If the original brake pads are still serviceable, carefully clean them using a clean, fine wire brush or similar, paying particular attention to the sides and back of the metal backing plate. Clean out the grooves in the friction material, and pick out any large embedded particles of dirt or debris. Carefully clean the pad locations in the caliper body/mounting bracket.
5 Prior to fitting the pads, check that the guide bolts are a snug fit in the caliper mounting bracket. Inspect the dust seal around

the piston for damage, and the piston for evidence of fluid leaks, corrosion or damage. If attention to any of these components is necessary, refer to Section 7.
6 If new brake pads are to be fitted, the caliper piston must be pushed back into the cylinder to allow for the extra pad thickness. Either use a G-clamp or similar tool, or use suitable pieces of wood as levers. Clamp off the flexible brake hose leading to the caliper then connect a brake bleeding kit to the caliper bleed screw. Open the bleed screw as the piston is retracted, the surplus brake fluid will then be collected in the bleed kit vessel **(see illustration 4.2o)**. Close the bleed screw just before the caliper piston is pushed fully into the caliper. This should ensure no air enters the hydraulic system.
Note: *The ABS unit contains hydraulic components that are very sensitive to impurities in the brake fluid. Even the smallest particles can cause the system to fail through blockage. The pad retraction method described here prevents any debris in the brake fluid expelled from the caliper from being passed back to the ABS hydraulic unit, as well as preventing any chance of damage to the master cylinder seals.*

4.2a Push in the caliper piston by levering the caliper body towards the outside of the vehicle

4.2b Unclip the wiring guide from the brake hose. Where fitted, detach the pad wear warning indicator wire from the inner pad

4.2c Release the legs of the retaining spring from the caliper body ...

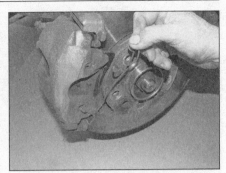

4.2d ... then remove the spring from the caliper mounting bracket

4.2e Remove the dust caps from the upper and lower guide bolts

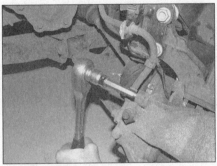

4.2f Unscrew the upper guide bolt ...

4.2g ... and remove it from the caliper

4.2h Similarly unscrew the lower guide bolt and remove it from the caliper

4.2i Lift the caliper and brake pads off the mounting bracket

4.2j Remove the outer pad from the caliper body ...

4.2k ... and the inner pad from the caliper piston, noting that it is retained by a spring clip attached to the pad backing plate

4.2l Measure the thickness of the pad friction material. If any are worn down to the specified minimum, or fouled with oil or grease, all four pads must be renewed

4.2m Brush the dust and dirt from the caliper piston and mounting bracket

4.2n Apply a little high melting-point copper brake grease to the pad backing plate contact areas on the mounting bracket

4.2o If new pads are fitted, before refitting the caliper, push back the caliper piston with the bleed screw open. This will prevent any dirt/debris being forced back up the hydraulic circuit in the ABS modulator

4.2p The brake pads are 'handed' for each side. Make sure the arrow on the backing plate points in the direction of forward rotation of the brake disc

4.2q Fit the inner pad to the caliper, ensuring that its clip is correctly located in the caliper piston

4.2r Fit the outer pad to the caliper mounting bracket, ensuring that its friction material is facing the brake disc

4.2s Slide the caliper into position in the mounting bracket

4.2t Fit the guide bolts ...

4.2u ... tighten the guide bolts to the specified torque ...

4.2v ... then refit the dust caps

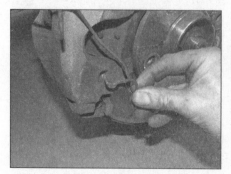

4.2w Locate the retaining spring legs into the holes in the caliper ...

4.2x ... then hold the legs in place and locate the spring behind the lugs on the mounting bracket

4.2y Clip the wiring guide back onto the brake hose. Where fitted, attach the pad wear warning indicator wire to the inner pad

7 With the brake pads installed, depress the brake pedal repeatedly, until normal (non-assisted) pedal pressure is restored, and the pads are pressed into firm contact with the brake disc.

8 Repeat the above procedure on the remaining front brake caliper.

9 Refit the roadwheels, then lower the vehicle to the ground and tighten the roadwheel bolts to the specified torque setting.

10 Check the hydraulic fluid level as described in *Weekly checks*.

Caution: New pads will not give full braking efficiency until they have bedded-in. Be prepared for this, and avoid hard braking as far as possible for the first hundred miles or so after pad renewal.

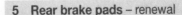

5 Rear brake pads – renewal

Warning: Renew BOTH sets of rear brake pads at the same time – NEVER renew the pads on only one wheel, as uneven braking may result. Note that the dust created by wear of the pads may contain asbestos, which is a health hazard. Never blow it out with compressed air, and do not inhale any of it. An approved filtering mask should be worn when working on the brakes. DO NOT use petroleum-based solvents to clean brake

parts – use brake cleaner or methylated spirit only.

1 Chock the front wheels then jack up the rear of the car and securely support it on axle stands (see *Jacking and vehicle support*). Remove the rear roadwheels.

2 Slacken the handbrake cable adjuster at the handbrake lever as described in Section 14, paragraphs 11 and 12.

3 Follow the accompanying photos **(illustrations 5.3a to 5.3u)** for the pad renewal procedure, bearing in mind the additional points listed below. Be sure to stay in order and read the caption under each illustration. Note that if the old pads are to be refitted, ensure that they are identified so that they can be returned to their original positions.

5.3a Using a screwdriver, push the handbrake operating lever downwards, and detach the cable end fitting from the lever

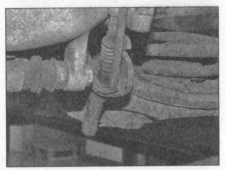
5.3b Prise out the handbrake outer cable retaining clip ...

5.3c ... and withdraw the handbrake cable from the caliper bracket

5.3d Unscrew the lower guide pin bolt whilst counter-holding the guide pin with an open-ended spanner

5.3e Pivot the caliper upwards...

5.3f ... slide the caliper and guide pin from the mounting bracket, and move it to one side. Take care to prevent straining the rubber hose

5.3g Remove the inner pad ...

5.3h ... and outer pad from the caliper mounting bracket

5.3i Remove the lower guide plate ...

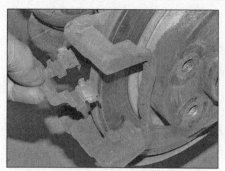

5.3j ... and upper guide plate from the caliper mounting bracket

5.3k Measure the thickness of the pad friction material. If any are worn down to the specified minimum, or fouled with oil or grease, all four pads must be renewed

5.3l Using a caliper retracting tool to retract the piston as far as the stop

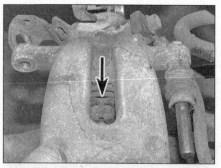

5.3m Once the piston is fully retracted, unscrew it slightly until the next piston cut-out (arrowed) is visible through the front of the caliper

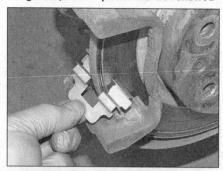

5.3n Brush the dust and dirt from the caliper, piston and mounting bracket, then fit the lower guide plate ...

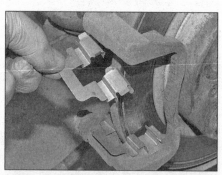

5.3o ... and upper guide plate to the caliper mounting bracket

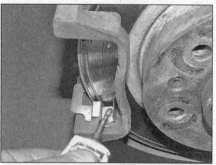

5.3p Apply a little high melting-point copper brake grease to the pad backing plate contact areas on the guide plates. Ensure the grease doesn't contact the disc face.

5.3q If present, remove the protective film from the pad backing plate, then fit the inner pad to the caliper mounting bracket ...

5.3r ... followed by the outer pad

5.3s Slide the caliper into position in the mounting bracket. Ensure the guide pin rubber boot engages correctly.

5.3t Refit the lower guide pin bolt and tighten it to the specified torque

5.3u Refit the handbrake cable to the mounting bracket and secure with the retaining clip, then reconnect the cable end to the caliper lever

4 If the original brake pads are still serviceable, carefully clean them using a clean, fine wire brush or similar, paying particular attention to the sides and back of the metal backing plate. Clean out the grooves in the friction material, and pick out any large embedded particles of dirt or debris. Carefully clean the pad locations in the caliper body/mounting bracket.

5 Prior to fitting the pads, check that the guide pins are a snug fit in the caliper mounting bracket. Brush the dust and dirt from the caliper and piston, but do not inhale it, as it is injurious to health. Inspect the dust seal around the piston for damage, and the piston for evidence of fluid leaks, corrosion or damage. If attention to any of these components is necessary, refer to Section 8.

6 If new brake pads are to be fitted, it will be necessary to retract the piston fully into the caliper bore by rotating it in a clockwise direction. This can be achieved by using sturdy circlip pliers, noting that as well as being turned, the piston has to be pressed in very firmly. Special tools are readily available to achieve this with less effort. While the caliper is being retracted, clamp off the flexible brake hose leading to the caliper then connect a brake bleeding kit to the caliper bleed screw. Open the bleed screw as the piston is retracted, the surplus brake fluid will then be collected in the bleed kit vessel **(see illustration 5.3l)**. Close the bleed screw just before the caliper piston is pushed fully into the caliper. This should ensure no air enters the hydraulic system. **Note:** *The ABS unit contains hydraulic components that are very sensitive to impurities in the brake fluid. Even the smallest particles can cause the system to fail through blockage. The pad retraction method described here prevents any debris in the brake fluid expelled from the caliper from being passed back to the ABS hydraulic unit, as well as preventing any chance of damage to the master cylinder seals.*

7 With the brake pads installed, depress the brake pedal repeatedly, until normal (non-assisted) pedal pressure is restored, and the pads are pressed into firm contact with the brake disc.

8 Repeat the above procedure on the remaining rear brake caliper.

9 Adjust the handbrake cable as described

in Chapter 1A Section 24 or Chapter 1B Section 26 after fitting both sets of brake pads.

10 Refit the roadwheels, then lower the vehicle to the ground and tighten the roadwheel bolts to the specified torque setting.

11 Check the hydraulic fluid level as described in *Weekly checks*.

Caution: New pads will not give full braking efficiency until they have bedded-in. Be prepared for this, and avoid hard braking as far as possible for the first hundred miles or so after pad renewal.

---

6 Front/rear brake disc – inspection, removal and refitting

Note: *Before starting work, refer to the warning at the beginning of Section 4 concerning the dangers of asbestos dust. If either disc requires renewal, both should be renewed at the same time together with new pads, to ensure even and consistent braking.*

Inspection

1 Remove the wheel trim, then loosen the roadwheel bolts. If checking a front disc, apply the handbrake, and if checking a rear disc, chock the front wheels and release the handbrake, then jack up the relevant end of the vehicle and support on axle stands (see *Jacking and vehicle support*). Remove the roadwheel.

2 Check that the brake disc securing screw is tight, then fit a spacer approximately 10.0 mm thick to one of the roadwheel bolts, and refit

and tighten the bolt in the hole opposite the disc securing screw.

3 Rotate the brake disc, and examine it for deep scoring or grooving. Light scoring is normal, but if excessive, the disc should be removed and either renewed or machined (within the specified limits) by an engineering works. The minimum thickness is given in the Specifications at the start of this Chapter.

4 Using a dial gauge, or a flat metal block and feeler blades, check that the disc run-out does not exceed the figure given in the Specifications. Measure the run-out 10.0 mm in from the outer edge of the disc.

5 If the disc run-out is excessive, remove the disc as described later, and check that the disc-to-hub surfaces are perfectly clean. Refit the disc and check the run-out again.

6 If the run-out is still excessive, the disc should be renewed.

7 To remove a disc, proceed as follows.

Front disc

Removal

8 Remove the roadwheel bolt and spacer used when checking the disc.

9 Unclip the ABS wheel speed sensor wiring guide from the brake hydraulic hose, then extract the retaining clip and release the hydraulic hose from the suspension strut **(see illustrations)**.

10 Unbolt and remove the front brake caliper complete with disc pads and mounting bracket and suspend it from the coil spring using a cable tie **(see illustrations)**.

6.9a Unclip the ABS wheel speed sensor wiring guide from the brake hydraulic hose ...

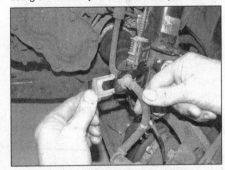

6.9b ... pull out the spring clip ...

6.9c ... and disconnect the hydraulic hose from the strut bracket

6.10a Unbolt and remove the front brake caliper complete with disc pads and mounting bracket ...

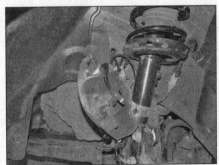

6.10b ... and suspend it from the coil spring using a cable tie

11 Remove the securing screw and withdraw the disc from the hub **(see illustrations)**.

Refitting

12 Refit the disc, making sure that the mating faces of the disc and hub are perfectly clean, and apply a little locking fluid to the threads of the securing screw.
13 Refit the caliper mounting bracket complete with caliper and pads and tighten the bolts to the specified torque.

Rear disc

Removal

14 Where applicable, remove the roadwheel bolt and spacer used when checking the disc.
15 Remove the rear brake pads as described in Section 5.
16 Undo the two bolts securing the caliper mounting bracket to the hub carrier and remove the mounting bracket.
17 Remove the securing screw and withdraw the disc from the hub **(see illustrations)**.

Refitting

18 Refit the disc, making sure that the mating faces of the disc and hub are perfectly clean, and apply a little locking fluid to the threads of the securing screw.
19 Refit the caliper mounting bracket and tighten the bolts to the specified torque.
20 Refit the brake pads as described in Section 5.

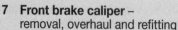

---

7 Front brake caliper –
  removal, overhaul and refitting

Note: *New brake hose copper washers will be required when refitting. Before starting work, refer to the note at the beginning of Section 2 concerning the dangers of hydraulic fluid, and to the warning at the beginning of Section 4 concerning the dangers of asbestos dust.*

Removal

1 Apply the handbrake, then jack up the front of the vehicle and support it on axle stands (see *Jacking and vehicle support*). Remove the roadwheel.
2 Minimise fluid loss by first removing the

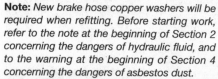

6.17a Remove the securing screw (arrowed) ...

6.11a Remove the securing screw ...

master cylinder reservoir cap and screwing it down onto a piece of polythene. Alternatively, use a brake hose clamp to clamp the flexible hose leading to the brake caliper.
3 Clean the area around the caliper brake hose union. Unscrew and remove the union bolt, and recover the copper sealing washer from each side of the hose union. Discard the washers; new ones must be used on refitting. Plug the hose end and caliper hole, to minimise fluid loss and prevent the ingress of dust and dirt into the hydraulic system.
4 Remove the brake pads as described in Section 4, then remove the caliper from the vehicle.

Overhaul

5 With the caliper on the bench, wipe it clean with a cloth rag.
6 Withdraw the partially-ejected piston from the caliper body, and remove the dust seal. The piston can be withdrawn by hand, or if necessary pushed out by applying compressed air to the brake hose union hole. Only low pressure should be required, such as is generated by a foot pump.
7 Using a small screwdriver, carefully remove the piston seal from the groove in the caliper, taking care not to mark the bore **(see illustration)**.
8 Carefully press the guide bushes out of the caliper body.
9 Thoroughly clean all components, using only methylated spirit or clean hydraulic fluid. Never use mineral-based solvents such as petrol or paraffin, which will attack the rubber

6.17b ... and withdraw the disc from the hub

6.11b ... and withdraw the disc from the hub

components of the hydraulic system. Dry the components using compressed air or a clean, lint-free cloth. If available, use compressed air to blow clear the fluid passages.

⚠️ *Warning: Wear eye protection when using compressed air.*

10 Check all components, and renew any that are worn or damaged. If the piston and/or cylinder bore are scratched excessively, renew the complete caliper body. Similarly check the condition of the guide bushes and pins; both bushes and pins should be undamaged and (when cleaned) a reasonably tight sliding fit. If there is any doubt about the condition of any component, renew it.
11 If the caliper is fit for further use, obtain the necessary components from your Vauxhall/Opel dealer. Renew the caliper seals and dust covers as a matter of course; these should never be re-used.
12 On reassembly, ensure that all components are absolutely clean and dry.
13 Dip the piston and the new piston seal in clean hydraulic fluid, and smear clean fluid on the cylinder bore surface.
14 Locate the new seal in the cylinder bore groove, using only the fingers to manipulate it into position.
15 Fit the new dust seal to the piston, then insert the piston into the cylinder bore using a twisting motion to ensure it enters the seal correctly. Locate the dust seal in the body groove, and push the piston fully into the caliper bore.
16 Insert the guide bushes into position in the caliper body.

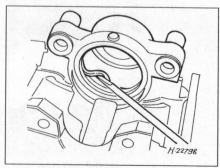

7.7 Removing the piston seal from the caliper body

Refitting

17 Refit the brake pads as described in Section 4, together with the caliper which at this stage will not have the hose attached.

18 Position a new copper sealing washer on each side of the hose union, and connect the brake hose to the caliper. Ensure that the hose is correctly positioned against the caliper body lug, then install the union bolt and tighten it to the specified torque setting.

19 Remove the brake hose clamp or polythene, and bleed the hydraulic system as described in Section 2. Note that, providing the precautions described were taken to minimise brake fluid loss, it should only be necessary to bleed the relevant front brake circuit.

20 Refit the roadwheel, then lower the vehicle to the ground and tighten the roadwheel bolts to the specified torque.

---

8 Rear brake caliper – removal, overhaul and refitting

Note: *Before starting work, refer to the note at the beginning of Section 2 concerning the dangers of hydraulic fluid, and to the warning at the beginning of Section 5 concerning the dangers of asbestos dust.*

Note: *Due to the integral handbrake operating mechanism incorporated in the caliper piston, it is not possible to fully dismantle the caliper. Only the guide bushes and dust seal can be individually renewed. Check the availability of parts before proceeding.*

Removal

1 Chock the front wheels, then jack up the rear of the vehicle and support on axle stands (see *Jacking and vehicle support*). Remove the roadwheel.

2 Minimise fluid loss by first removing the master cylinder reservoir cap and screwing it down onto a piece of polythene. Alternatively, use a brake hose clamp to clamp the flexible hose leading to the brake caliper.

3 Clean the area around the caliper brake hose union. Unscrew and remove the union bolt, and recover the copper sealing washer from each side of the hose union (see illustration). Discard the washers; new ones must be used

on refitting. Plug the hose end and caliper hole, to minimise fluid loss and prevent the ingress of dust and dirt into the hydraulic system.

4 Remove the brake pads as described in Section 5, then remove the caliper from the vehicle.

Overhaul

5 With the caliper on the bench, wipe it clean with a cloth rag.

6 Using a small screwdriver, carefully prise out the dust seal from the caliper, taking care not to damage the piston.

7 Carefully press the guide bushes out of the caliper body.

8 Further dismantling of the caliper is not possible as individual parts are not available separately.

9 Thoroughly clean all components, using only methylated spirit or clean hydraulic fluid. Dry the components using a clean, lint-free cloth.

10 Check the condition of the exposed portion of the caliper piston. If the piston and/or cylinder bore are scratched excessively or corroded, renew the complete caliper body. Similarly check the condition of the guide bushes and pins; both bushes and pins should be undamaged and (when cleaned) a reasonably tight sliding fit. If there is any doubt about the condition of any component, renew it.

11 If the caliper is fit for further use, obtain the necessary components from your Vauxhall/Opel dealer. Renew the caliper dust cover as a matter of course; it should never be re-used.

12 Fit the new dust seal to the piston, then locate the dust seal in the caliper body groove.

13 Insert the guide bushes into position in the caliper body.

Refitting

14 Refit the brake pads as described in Section 5, together with the caliper which at this stage will not have the hose attached.

15 Position a new copper sealing washer on each side of the hose union, and connect the brake hose to the caliper. Ensure that the hose is correctly positioned against the caliper body lug, then install the union bolt and tighten it to the specified torque setting.

16 Remove the brake hose clamp or

polythene, and bleed the hydraulic system as described in Section 2. Note that, providing the precautions described were taken to minimise brake fluid loss, it should only be necessary to bleed the relevant rear brake circuit.

17 Refit the roadwheel, then lower the vehicle to the ground and tighten the roadwheel bolts to the specified torque.

---

9 Master cylinder – removal, overhaul and refitting

Note: *Before starting work, refer to the warning at the beginning of Section 2 concerning the dangers of hydraulic fluid.*

Removal

1 Remove the windscreen cowl panel as described in Chapter 11 Section 20.

2 Remove the master cylinder reservoir cap, and syphon the hydraulic fluid from the reservoir. **Note:** *Do not syphon the fluid by mouth, as it is poisonous; use a syringe or an old hydrometer. Alternatively, open any convenient bleed screw in the system, and gently pump the brake pedal to expel the fluid through a plastic tube connected to the screw (see Section 2).*

3 Disconnect the wiring connector from the brake fluid level sensor at the base of the reservoir.

4 On models with manual transmission, release the clip and disconnect the clutch hydraulic pipe from the fluid reservoir **(see illustration)**. Tape over or plug the outlet.

5 Place cloth rags beneath the fluid reservoir then undo the reservoir retaining bolt and carefully prise the reservoir from the top of the master cylinder and remove it from the engine compartment. If necessary, prise the reservoir seals from the top of the cylinder.

6 Place cloth rags beneath the master cylinder to collect escaping brake fluid. Identify the brake lines for position, then unscrew the union nuts and move the lines to one side. Tape over or plug the line outlets.

7 Unscrew the mounting nuts and withdraw the master cylinder from the vacuum servo unit **(see illustration)**. Take care not to spill fluid on the vehicle paintwork.

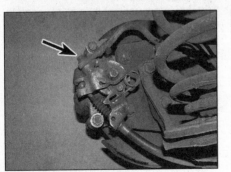

8.3 Rear caliper brake hose union bolt (arrowed)

9.4 Disconnect the clutch hydraulic pipe (arrowed) from the fluid reservoir

9.7 Master cylinder mounting nuts (arrowed)

Overhaul

8 At the time of writing, master cylinder overhaul is not possible as no spares are available.

9 The only parts available individually are the fluid reservoir and its mounting seals, and the filler cap.

10 If the master cylinder is worn excessively, it must be renewed.

11 Remove the reservoir seals from the master cylinder body and obtain new seals for reassembly.

12 Lubricate the new seals with clean brake hydraulic fluid and push the new seals into position.

Refitting

13 Fit the master cylinder to the servo unit, ensuring that the servo unit pushrod enters the master cylinder piston centrally. Fit the retaining nuts and tighten them to the specified torque setting.

14 Refit the brake lines and tighten the union nuts securely.

15 On manual transmission models, reconnect the clutch hydraulic pipe.

16 Reconnect the wiring connector to the brake fluid level sensor.

17 Remove the reservoir filler cap and polythene, then top-up the reservoir with fresh hydraulic fluid to the MAX mark (see *Weekly checks*).

18 Bleed the hydraulic systems as described in Section 2 and Chapter 6 Section 2 then refit the filler cap.

19 Refit the windscreen cowl panel as described in Chapter 11 Section 20.

20 Thoroughly check the operation of the brakes and clutch before using the vehicle on the road.

10 Brake pedal – removal and refitting

Removal

1 Disconnect the battery negative terminal (refer to Chapter 5A Section 4).

2 Unscrew the two quick-release catches and remove the facia lower panel above the pedals **(see illustrations)**.

3 Remove the steering column shrouds and the lower trim panel beneath the facia on the driver's side, as described in Chapter 11 Section 26.

4 Release the expanding rivet and remove the driver's side footwell air duct.

5 Disconnect the wiring connector at the stop-light switch and release the wiring harness from the support clips.

6 Unhook the return spring from the brake pedal, then slide off the spring clip, and withdraw the clevis pin securing the pedal to the servo unit pushrod **(see illustration)**.

7 On left-hand drive models, remove the steering column intermediate shaft as described in Chapter 10 Section 16.

8 Undo the six mounting bracket retaining

nuts (right-hand drive models) or the four nuts and two bolts (left-hand drive models) and remove the pedal and support bracket assembly from the vehicle.

9 Check the pedal and bracket for excessive wear and damage. It is not possible to renew the pedal pivot bushes separately, so if they are worn, the complete assembly must be renewed.

Refitting

10 Manoeuvre the pedal and support bracket assembly into place making sure the brake servo pushrod fits correctly over the brake pedal.

11 Refit the pedal mounting bracket bolts/nuts and tighten to the specified torque.

12 Align the pedal hole with the pushrod end, and insert the clevis pin. Secure the pin in position with the spring clip.

13 Refit the return spring to the brake pedal.

14 Reconnect the stop-light switch wiring connector.

15 On left-hand drive models, refit the steering column intermediate shaft as described in Chapter 10 Section 16.

16 Refit the driver's side footwell air duct, then refit the facia trim panels as described in Chapter 11 Section 26.

11 Vacuum servo unit – testing, removal and refitting

Testing

1 To test the operation of the servo unit, with the engine off, depress the footbrake several times to exhaust the vacuum. Now start the engine, keeping the pedal firmly depressed. As the engine starts, there should be a noticeable 'give' in the brake pedal as the vacuum builds-up. Allow the engine to run for at least two minutes, then switch it off. The brake pedal should now feel normal, but further applications should result in the pedal feeling firmer, the pedal stroke decreasing with each application.

2 If the servo does not operate as described, first inspect the servo unit check valve as described in Section 12.

3 If the servo unit still fails to operate satisfactorily, the fault lies within the unit itself. Repairs to the unit are not possible; if faulty, the servo unit must be renewed.

Removal

Note: *On petrol models equipped with air conditioning, refer to the air conditioning system precautionary information contained in Chapter 3 Section 10.*

Right-hand drive petrol models

4 On models equipped with air conditioning, have the refrigerant discharged at a dealer service department or an automotive air conditioning repair facility.

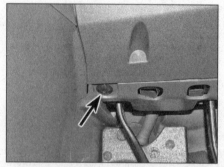

10.2a Unscrew the quick-release catch (arrowed) on the left-hand side …

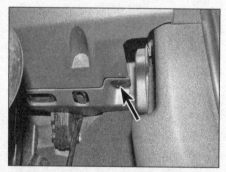

10.2b … and right-hand side (arrowed) …

10.2c … and remove the facia lower panel above the pedals

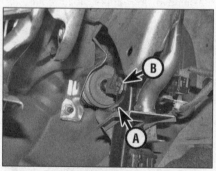

10.6 Unhook the pedal return spring (A) then slide off the spring clip (B) and withdraw the clevis pin

5 Disconnect the battery negative terminal (refer to Chapter 5A Section 4).
6 Remove the air cleaner assembly as described in Chapter 4A Section 2.
7 Remove the windscreen cowl panel as described in Chapter 11 Section 20.
8 On models equipped with air conditioning, undo the bolt securing the refrigerant pipe block connection to the expansion valve and withdraw the refrigerant pipes from the valve **(see illustration)**. Note that new seals for the refrigerant pipes will be required for refitting. Suitably plug or cover the disconnected pipes.
9 On models equipped with air conditioning, unscrew the retaining nut, release the two clips and free the refrigerant pipes from the vicinity of the servo unit.
10 Remove the master cylinder as described in Section 9.
11 Carefully ease the vacuum hose out of the servo unit, taking care not to displace the sealing grommet **(see illustration)**.
12 Unscrew the two quick-release catches and remove the facia lower panel above the pedals **(see illustrations 10.2a to 10.2c)**.
13 Unhook the return spring from the brake pedal, then slide off the spring clip, and withdraw the clevis pin securing the pedal to the servo unit pushrod **(see illustration 10.6)**.
14 Slacken and remove the two diagonally opposite nuts securing the servo unit to the pedal mounting bracket.
15 Return to the engine compartment, and lift the servo unit out of position.

Right-hand drive diesel models

16 Disconnect the battery negative terminal (refer to Chapter 5A Section 4).
17 Remove the windscreen wiper motor and linkage as described in Chapter 12 Section 13.
18 Carry out the following operations as described in the Chapters indicated:
a) *Remove the auxiliary drivebelt (Chapter 1B Section 24).*
b) *Remove the auxiliary drivebelt tensioner (Chapter 5A Section 7).*
c) *Remove the alternator (Chapter 5A Section 8).*
d) *Remove the high-pressure fuel pump (Chapter 4B Section 12).*
19 After removal of the components listed in paragraph 19, undo the six bolts, noting the different bolt lengths, securing the high-pressure fuel pump mounting bracket to the cylinder block and cylinder head. Remove the bracket from the engine.
20 Remove the master cylinder as described in Section 9.
21 Carefully ease the vacuum hose out of the servo unit, taking care not to displace the sealing grommet **(see illustration 11.11)**.
22 Unscrew the two quick-release catches and remove the facia lower panel above the pedals **(see illustrations 10.2a to 10.2c)**.
23 Unhook the return spring from the brake pedal, then slide off the spring clip, and withdraw the clevis pin securing the pedal to the servo unit pushrod **(see illustration 10.6)**.

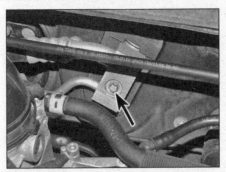

11.8 Undo the bolt (arrowed) and withdraw the refrigerant pipes from the expansion valve

24 Slacken and remove the two diagonally opposite nuts securing the servo unit to the pedal mounting bracket.
25 Return to the engine compartment, and lift the servo unit out of position.

Left-hand drive models

26 Remove the windscreen cowl panel as described in Chapter 11 Section 20.
27 Remove the battery and battery tray as described in Chapter 5A Section 4.
28 Release the locking clip, then lift up the cooling system expansion tank and remove it from the mounting bracket. Place the tank to one side.
29 Remove the ABS hydraulic modulator as described in Section 18, then undo the three retaining bolts and remove the modulator mounting bracket.
30 Remove the master cylinder as described in Section 9.
31 Carefully ease the vacuum hose out of the servo unit, taking care not to displace the sealing grommet.
32 Unscrew the two quick-release catches and remove the facia lower panel above the pedals **(see illustrations 10.2a to 10.2c)**.
33 Unhook the return spring from the brake pedal, then slide off the spring clip, and withdraw the clevis pin securing the pedal to the servo unit pushrod **(see illustration 10.6)**.
34 Slacken and remove the two diagonally opposite nuts securing the servo unit to the pedal mounting bracket.
35 Return to the engine compartment, and lift the servo unit out of position.

Refitting

Right-hand drive petrol models

36 Locate the vacuum servo unit in position on the bulkhead ensuring that the servo unit pushrod locates correctly around the brake pedal. Refit the two nuts and tighten them to the specified torque.
37 Apply a smear of multi-purpose grease to the clevis pin then align the servo unit pushrod with the brake pedal hole and insert the pin. Secure the pin in position with the retaining clip, making sure it is correctly located in the groove. Reconnect the pedal return spring.
38 Refit the facia lower panel above the pedals.

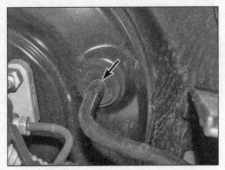

11.11 Carefully ease the vacuum hose (arrowed) out of the servo unit rubber grommet

39 Refit the vacuum hose to the servo grommet, ensuring that the hose is correctly seated.
40 Refit the brake master cylinder as described in Section 9.
41 On models equipped with air conditioning, resecure the refrigerant pipes in the vicinity of the servo unit.
42 On models equipped with air conditioning, refit the refrigerant pipe block connection to the expansion valve using new seals and secure with the retaining bolt, tightened securely.
43 Refit the windscreen cowl panel as described in Chapter 11 Section 20.
44 Refit the air cleaner assembly as described in Chapter 4A Section 2.
45 Reconnect the battery negative terminal as described in Chapter 5A Section 4.
46 On models with air conditioning, on completion, have the system evacuated, charged and leak-tested by the specialist who discharged it.

Right-hand drive diesel models

47 Locate the vacuum servo unit in position on the bulkhead ensuring that the servo unit pushrod locates correctly around the brake pedal. Refit the two nuts and tighten them to the specified torque.
48 Apply a smear of multipurpose grease to the clevis pin then align the servo unit pushrod with the brake pedal hole and insert the pin. Secure the pin in position with the retaining clip, making sure it is correctly located in the groove. Reconnect the pedal return spring.
49 Refit the facia lower panel above the pedals.
50 Refit the vacuum hose to the servo grommet, ensuring that the hose is correctly seated.
51 Refit the brake master cylinder as described in Section 9.
52 Refit the high-pressure fuel pump mounting bracket and tighten the retaining bolts to the specified torque.
53 Refit the components listed in paragraph 18, as described in the Chapters indicated.
54 Refit the windscreen wiper motor and linkage as described in Chapter 12 Section 13.
55 Reconnect the battery negative terminal as described in Chapter 5A Section 4.

12.3 Disconnect the vacuum hose quick-release fitting at the vacuum pump

Left-hand drive models

56 Locate the vacuum servo unit in position on the bulkhead ensuring that the servo unit pushrod locates correctly around the brake pedal. Refit the two nuts and tighten them to the specified torque.

57 Apply a smear of multipurpose grease to the clevis pin then align the servo unit pushrod with the brake pedal hole and insert the pin. Secure the pin in position with the retaining clip, making sure it is correctly located in the groove. Reconnect the pedal return spring.

58 Refit the facia lower panel above the pedals.

59 Refit the vacuum hose to the servo grommet, ensuring that the hose is correctly seated.

60 Refit the brake master cylinder as described in Section 9, but don't bleed the hydraulic circuits at this stage.

61 Refit the ABS hydraulic modulator mounting bracket, then refit the hydraulic modulator as described in Section 18.

62 Refit the cooling system expansion tank and secure with the locking clip.

63 Refit the battery tray and battery as described in Chapter 5A Section 4.

64 Remove the master cylinder reservoir filler cap and polythene, then top-up the reservoir with fresh hydraulic fluid to the MAX mark (see *Weekly checks*).

65 Bleed the hydraulic systems as described in Section 2 and Chapter 6 Section 2 then refit the filler cap.

66 Refit the windscreen cowl panel as described in Chapter 11 Section 20.

---

12 Vacuum servo unit check valve and hose – removal, testing and refitting

Removal

1 Carefully ease the vacuum hose out of the servo unit, taking care not to displace the sealing grommet **(see illustration 11.11)**.

2 Where applicable, remove the plastic cover over the top of the engine.

3 Disconnect the hose quick-release fitting from the intake manifold or vacuum pump **(see illustration)**.

4 Unclip the vacuum hose from its supports on the bulkhead and engine, then remove the hose and check valve from the car.

Testing

5 Examine the check valve and hose for signs of damage, and renew if necessary. The valve may be tested by blowing through it in both directions. Air should flow through the valve in one direction only – when blown through from the servo unit end. If air flows in both directions, or not at all, renew the valve and hose as an assembly.

6 Examine the servo unit rubber sealing grommet for signs of damage or deterioration, and renew as necessary.

Refitting

7 Refitting is a reversal of removal ensuring that the quick-release connector audibly locks in position, and that the hose is correctly seated in the servo grommet.

8 On completion, start the engine and check that there are no air leaks.

---

13 Handbrake lever – removal and refitting

Removal

1 Disconnect the battery negative terminal (refer to Chapter 5A Section 4).

2 Remove the centre console as described in Chapter 11 Section 25.

3 Ensure that the handbrake lever is released (off).

4 Disconnect the wiring connector from the handbrake lever warning light switch **(see illustration)**.

5 On models with ESP, disconnect the yaw rate sensor wiring connector, then undo the two nuts and remove the sensor. Undo the two nuts and remove the yaw rate sensor mounting bracket.

6 Undo the bolt each side and unclip the cable ducts from the right-hand and left-hand sides of the handbrake lever.

7 Unclip the wiring harness from the handbrake lever support plate.

8 Remove the protective cap from the end of the handbrake cable. Undo the handbrake cable adjuster nut and release the cable from the handbrake lever **(see illustration)**.

9 Undo the four retaining nuts and remove the handbrake lever assembly from inside the car **(see illustration)**.

Refitting

10 Refitting is the reverse of removal, but adjust the handbrake as described in Chapter 1A Section 24 or Chapter 1B Section 26, and refit the centre console as described in Chapter 11 Section 25.

---

14 Handbrake cables – removal and refitting

Removal

1 The handbrake cable consists of two sections, a short front (primary) section which connects the lever to the compensator plate, and the main cables (secondary) section which links the compensator plate to the rear brake calipers. Each section can be removed individually as follows.

Primary (front) cable

2 Firmly apply the handbrake, then jack up the front of the vehicle and support it securely

---

13.4 Disconnect the wiring connector (arrowed) from the handbrake lever warning light switch

13.8 Undo the handbrake cable adjuster nut (arrowed) and release the cable from the handbrake lever

13.9 Handbrake lever retaining nuts (arrowed)

on axle stands (see *Jacking and vehicle support*). Ensure that the handbrake lever is released (off).

3 Remove the centre console as described in Chapter 11 Section 25.

4 Undo the handbrake cable adjuster nut and release the cable from the handbrake lever **(see illustration 13.8)**.

5 Remove the exhaust front pipe and intermediate pipe with reference to Chapter 4A Section 18 or Chapter 4B Section 20, as applicable.

6 Unscrew the nuts and remove the exhaust heat shield from the underbody.

7 Detach the front cable from the compensator plate by twisting it through 90°.

8 Remove the handbrake lever as described in Section 13.

9 Unclip the primary cable protective sleeve from the handbrake cable carrier plate, then pull the front end of the cable out of the protective sleeve.

Secondary (main) cable

Note: *The secondary cables are supplied as one part, together with the compensator plate.*

10 Chock the front wheels then jack up the rear of the car and securely support it on axle stands (see *Jacking and vehicle support*). Remove both rear roadwheels.

11 From inside the vehicle, unclip and remove the access panel in the centre console, beneath the handbrake lever.

12 Move the handbrake lever to the fully released position, then turn the cable adjuster nut anti-clockwise to remove all tension from the cables **(see illustration)**.

13 Working on each side in turn, use a screwdriver to push the handbrake operating lever on the brake caliper downwards, and detach the cable end fitting from the lever **(see illustration)**.

14 Prise out the handbrake outer cable retaining clip and withdraw the handbrake cable from the caliper bracket **(see illustrations)**.

15 Remove the exhaust front pipe and intermediate pipe with reference to Chapter 4A Section 18 or Chapter 4B Section 20, as applicable.

16 Unscrew the nuts and remove the exhaust heat shield from the underbody.

17 Detach the front cable from the compensator plate by twisting it through 90°.

18 Release the main cable sections from the supports on the rear axle and fuel tank, and withdraw the cable from under the vehicle.

Refitting

19 Refitting is a reversal of the removal procedure, but adjust the handbrake as described in Chapter 1A Section 24 or Chapter 1B Section 26. Where applicable, make sure that the fitting on the rear of the front cable locates correctly in the compensator plate.

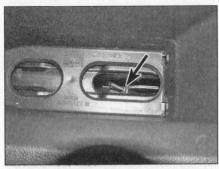

14.12 Turn the handbrake cable adjuster nut (arrowed) anti-clockwise to remove all tension from the cables

14.14a Prise out the handbrake outer cable retaining clip …

14.13 Push the handbrake operating lever on the brake caliper downwards, and detach the cable end fitting from the lever

14.14b … and withdraw the handbrake cable from the caliper bracket

15 Stop-light switch –
removal, refitting and adjustment

Removal

1 The stop-light switch is located on the brake pedal bracket in the driver's footwell.

2 Unscrew the two quick-release catches and remove the facia lower panel above the pedals **(see illustrations 10.2a to 10.2c)**.

3 Remove the lower trim panel beneath the facia on the driver's side as described in Chapter 11 Section 26.

4 Release the expanding rivet and remove the driver's side footwell air duct.

5 Disconnect the wiring connector at the stop-light switch.

6 Push the brake pedal down, pull out the

brake switch actuating pin, then unclip the locking sleeve from around the actuating pin **(see illustrations)**.

7 Release the securing clips and pull the switch to disengage it from the pedal mounting bracket.

Refitting and adjustment

8 With the actuating pin pulled out, and the locking sleeve unclipped, refit the switch to the pedal bracket.

9 Secure the switch with the locking sleeve.

10 Release the brake pedal and the pedal will automatically adjust the position of the actuating pin.

11 Reconnect the wiring connector, then refit the facia footwell trim panel as described in Chapter 11 Section 26, followed by the facia lower panel above the pedals.

15.6a Pull out the centre actuating pin arrowed (switch removed for clarity) …

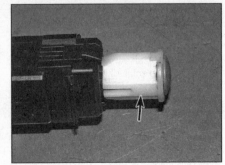

15.6b … and unclip the locking sleeve

16 Handbrake warning light switch – removal and refitting

Removal

1 Remove the centre console as described in Chapter 11 Section 25.
2 Disconnect the wiring connector from the warning light switch on the side of the handbrake lever (see illustration 13.4).
3 Unscrew the mounting bolt and remove the switch from the handbrake lever bracket.

Refitting

4 Refitting is a reversal of removal.

17 Anti-lock Braking and Traction Control systems – general information

1 ABS is fitted as standard to all models. On higher specification models, the ABS may also incorporate traction control or an electronic stability program as additional safety features.
2 The ABS system comprises a hydraulic modulator and electronic control unit together with four wheel speed sensors. The hydraulic modulator contains the electronic control unit (ECU), the hydraulic solenoid valves (one set for each brake) and the electrically-driven pump. The purpose of the system is to prevent the wheel(s) locking during heavy braking. This is achieved by automatic release of the brake on the relevant wheel, followed by re-application of the brake.
3 The solenoid valves are controlled by the ECU, which itself receives signals from the four wheel speed sensors which monitor the speed of rotation of each wheel. By comparing these signals, the ECU can determine the speed at which the vehicle is travelling. It can then use this speed to determine when a wheel is decelerating at an abnormal rate, compared to the speed of the vehicle, and therefore predicts when a wheel is about to lock. During normal operation, the system functions in the same way as a conventional braking system.
4 If the ECU senses that a wheel is about to lock, it operates the relevant solenoid valve(s) in the hydraulic unit, which then isolates from the master cylinder the relevant brake(s) on the wheel(s) which is/are about to lock, effectively sealing-in the hydraulic pressure.
5 If the speed of rotation of the wheel continues to decrease at an abnormal rate, the ECU operates the electrically-driven pump which pumps the hydraulic fluid back into the master cylinder, releasing the brake. Once the speed of rotation of the wheel returns to an acceptable rate, the pump stops, and the solenoid valves switch again, allowing the hydraulic master cylinder pressure to return to the caliper, which then re-applies the brake. This cycle can be carried out many times a second.
6 The action of the solenoid valves and return pump creates pulses in the hydraulic circuit. When the ABS system is functioning, these pulses can be felt through the brake pedal.
7 On models with traction control, the ABS hydraulic modulator incorporates an additional set of solenoid valves which operate the traction control system. The system operates at speeds up to approximately 30 mph using the signals supplied by the wheel speed sensors. If the ECU senses that a driving wheel is about to lose traction, it prevents this by momentarily applying the relevant front brake. The ABS ECU also communicates with the engine management ECU during traction control operation. In severe cases of traction loss the engine management ECU will reduce engine power to assist with traction recovery.
8 The electronic stability program (ESP) is a further development of ABS and traction control. Using additional sensors to monitor steering wheel position, vehicle yaw rate, acceleration and deceleration, in conjunction with the ABS sensors, the ECU can intervene under conditions of vehicle instability. Using the signals from the various sensors, the ECU can determine driver intent (steering wheel position, throttle position, vehicle speed and engine speed). From the sensor inputs from the wheel speed sensors, yaw rate sensors and acceleration sensors the ECU can calculate whether the vehicle is responding to driver input, or whether an unstable driving situation is occurring. If instability is detected, the ECU will intervene by applying or releasing the relevant front or rear brake, in conjunction with a power reduction, until vehicle stability returns.
9 The operation of the ABS, traction control, and stability programs is entirely dependent on electrical signals. To prevent the system responding to any inaccurate signals, a built-in safety circuit monitors all signals received by the ECU. If an inaccurate signal or low battery voltage is detected, the system is automatically shut down, and the relevant warning light on the instrument panel is illuminated, to inform the driver that the system is not operational. Normal braking is still available, however.
10 If a fault develops in the ABS/traction control/ESP system, the vehicle must be taken to a Vauxhall/Opel dealer for fault diagnosis and repair.

18.5 Disconnect the wiring harness plug (arrowed) from the ECU

18 Anti-lock Braking and Traction Control system components – removal and refitting

Note: *Faults on the ABS system can only be diagnosed using Vauxhall/Opel diagnostic equipment or compatible alternative equipment.*
Note: *Before starting work, refer to the note at the beginning of Section 2 concerning the dangers of hydraulic fluid.*

Hydraulic modulator

1 Remove the windscreen cowl panel as described in Chapter 11 Section 20.
2 Remove the battery and battery tray as described in Chapter 5A Section 4.
3 Release the locking clip, then lift up the cooling system expansion tank and remove it from the mounting bracket. Place the tank to one side.
4 Minimise fluid loss by first removing the master cylinder reservoir cap and screwing it down onto a piece of polythene.
5 Pull out the locking bar and disconnect the wiring harness plug from the ECU (see illustration).
6 Note and record the fitted position of the brake pipes at the modulator, then unscrew the union nuts and release the pipes. As a precaution, place absorbent rags beneath the brake pipe unions when unscrewing them. Suitably plug or cap the disconnected unions to prevent dirt entry and fluid loss.
7 Unscrew the three retaining bolts and remove the hydraulic modulator from the mounting bracket.
8 Refitting is the reverse of the removal procedure, noting the following points:
a) Tighten the modulator retaining bolts to the specified torque.
b) Refit the brake pipes to their respective locations, and tighten the union nuts to the specified torque.
c) Ensure that the wiring is correctly routed, and that the ECU wiring harness plug is firmly pressed into position and secured with the locking bar.
d) Refit the battery tray and battery as described in Chapter 5A Section 4.
e) Refit the windscreen cowl panel as described in Chapter 11 Section 20.
f) On completion, bleed the complete hydraulic system as described in Section 2. Ensure that the system is bled in the correct order, to prevent air entering the modulator return pump.

Electronic control unit (ECU)

Note: *At the time of writing, no information was available for removal and refitting of the ECU on systems incorporating an electronic stability program (ESP). This work should therefore be entrusted to a Vauxhall/Opel dealer.*

9 Remove the hydraulic modulator from the car as described previously in this Section.

10 Undo the three retaining bolts and carefully withdraw the ECU from the base of the hydraulic modulator. Note that new retaining bolts will be required for refitting.

11 Carefully remove the eight sealing rings from the modulator valves and obtain new sealing rings for refitting.

12 Locate the new sealing rings over the solenoid valves, then carefully place the ECU in position, keeping it square and level.

13 Fit the three new retaining bolts and tighten securely.

14 On completion, refit the hydraulic modulator as described previously in this Section.

Wheel speed sensors

15 The front and rear wheel speed sensors are an integral part of the hub bearings and cannot be separated.

16 Refer to Chapter 10 for front and rear hub bearing removal and refitting procedures.

Yaw rate/acceleration sensor

Note: *The yaw rate/acceleration sensor is only fitted to vehicles equipped with an electronic stability program (ESP).*

17 Disconnect the battery negative terminal (refer to Chapter 5A Section 4).

18 Remove the centre console as described in Chapter 11 Section 25.

19 Disconnect the yaw rate sensor wiring

connector, then undo the two nuts and remove the sensor.

20 Refitting is the reverse of the removal procedure.

Steering angle sensor

Note: *The steering angle sensor is only fitted to vehicles equipped with an electronic stability program (ESP).*

21 The steering angle sensor is an integral part of the steering column electronics module and is not available separately. Removal and refitting details for the steering column electronics module are contained in Chapter 12.

---

19 Vacuum pump (diesel engine models) – removal and refitting

Removal

1.7 litre engines

1 Remove the battery and battery tray as described in Chapter 5A Section 4.

2 Lift off the plastic cover over the top of the engine.

3 Remove the EGR valve as described in Chapter 4C Section 3.

4 Spread the sides of the wire retaining clip and disconnect the intercooler outlet duct from the throttle housing **(see illustration)**.

5 Disconnect the throttle housing wiring connector.

6 Undo the bolt securing the underside of the inlet manifold front section to the thermostat housing bracket.

7 Undo the two bolts securing the inlet manifold rear support bracket to the cylinder head.

8 Undo the three bolts securing the inlet manifold front section to the main section. Lift off the front section and collect the gasket **(see illustrations)**.

9 Disconnect the quick-release fitting and detach the vacuum servo unit vacuum hose from the pump. Disconnect the smaller vacuum hose from the outlet on the top of the pump **(see illustration)**.

10 Undo the three mounting bolts and remove the pump from the camshaft housing **(see illustration)**. Remove the sealing ring from the rear of the pump.

1.9 litre engines

11 Disconnect the battery negative terminal (refer to Chapter 5A Section 4).

12 Remove the plastic cover over the top of the engine.

13 Slacken the two retaining clips and disconnect the charge air hose from the intercooler and charge air pipe elbow.

14 Disconnect the quick-release fitting and detach the vacuum servo unit vacuum hose from the pump **(see illustration)**. Disconnect

19.4 Spread the sides of the wire retaining clip and disconnect the intercooler outlet duct from the throttle housing

19.8a Undo the three bolts securing the inlet manifold front section to the main section then lift off the front section...

19.8b ...and collect the gasket

19.9 Disconnect the two vacuum hoses (arrowed) from the pump

19.10 Undo the three mounting bolts and remove the pump from the camshaft housing

19.14 Disconnect the quick-release fitting and detach the vacuum hose from the pump

19.15a Undo the four mounting bolts (arrowed) …

19.15b … and remove the vacuum pump from the cylinder head/camshaft housing

the smaller vacuum hose from the outlet on the side of the pump.

15 Undo the four mounting bolts and remove the pump from the cylinder head/camshaft housing **(see illustrations)**. Recover the gasket. Note that new mounting bolts will be required for refitting.

Refitting

16 Refitting is a reversal of removal, but clean the mating faces of the pump and cylinder head/camshaft housing and fit a new gasket/seal. Tighten the mounting bolts to the specified torque.

Chapter 10
Suspension and steering

Contents

Section number

Electro-hydraulic power steering pump – removal and refitting 19
Front anti-roll bar – removal and refitting 8
Front hub bearings – checking and renewal 3
Front subframe – removal and refitting 7
Front suspension lower arm – removal, overhaul and refitting 5
Front suspension lower balljoint – renewal 6
Front suspension strut – removal, overhaul and refitting 4
Front swivel hub – removal and refitting. 2
General Information 1
Ignition switch/steering column lock – removal and refitting. 14
Power steering hydraulic system – bleeding 20
Rear hub bearings – checking and renewal 9

Section number

Rear shock absorber – removal, inspection and refitting. 10
Rear suspension coil spring – removal and refitting 11
Rear suspension torsion beam and trailing arms –
    removal and refitting. 12
Steering column – removal and refitting. 15
Steering column intermediate shaft – removal and refitting. 16
Steering gear – removal and refitting 18
Steering gear rubber gaiters – renewal 17
Steering wheel – removal and refitting. 13
Track rod – removal and refitting 22
Track rod end – removal and refitting. 21
Wheel alignment and steering angles – general information 23

Degrees of difficulty

Easy, suitable for novice with little experience 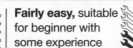	**Fairly easy,** suitable for beginner with some experience	**Fairly difficult,** suitable for competent DIY mechanic	**Difficult,** suitable for experienced DIY mechanic	**Very difficult,** suitable for expert DIY or professional

Specifications

Front suspension
Type . . . .   Independent, with MacPherson struts, gas-filled shock absorbers and anti-roll bar

Rear suspension
Type . . . .   Semi-independent torsion beam, with trailing arms, coil springs and telescopic shock absorbers

Steering
Type . . . .   Rack and pinion with electro-hydraulic power steering (EHPS)

Front and rear hub bearings
Bearing play (maximum). . . . .   0.1 mm
Bearing radial run-out. . . . .   0.04 mm
Bearing lateral run-out . . . .   0.05 mm

Wheel alignment
Front wheels:
    Camber angle . . . .   -0°55' ± 45'
    Caster angle . . . .   3°00' ± 45'
    Toe-in . . . .   +0°00' ± 10'
Rear wheel:
    Camber angle . . . .   -1°20' ± 30' not adjustable
    Toe-in . . . .   -0°08' not adjustable

Note: *These values apply with 70 kg on each front seat, and fuel tank half-full*

Torque wrench settings

	Nm	lbf ft
Front suspension		
Anti-roll bar connecting link retaining nut*	55	41
Anti-roll bar to subframe	20	15
Driveshaft retaining nut: *		
Stage 1	150	110
Stage 2	Slacken the nut by 45°	
Stage 3	250	185
Front engine mounting/torque link to subframe	55	41
Hub bearing assembly to swivel hub: *		
Stage 1	90	66
Stage 2	Angle-tighten a further 30°	
Stage 3	Angle-tighten a further 15°	
Lower arm balljoint clamp bolt nut: *	50	37
Lower arm to subframe: *		
Stage 1	90	66
Stage 2	Angle-tighten a further 75°	
Stage 3	Angle-tighten a further 15°	
Lower balljoint to lower arm	35	26
Rear engine mounting/torque link bracket to subframe	55	41
Rear engine mounting/torque link bracket to transmission	80	59
Subframe mounting bolts:		
Stage 1	90	66
Stage 2	Angle-tighten a further 45°	
Stage 3	Angle-tighten a further 15°	
Suspension strut piston rod nut*	80	59
Swivel hub to strut: *		
Stage 1	85	63
Stage 2	Angle-tighten a further 75°	
Stage 3	Angle-tighten a further 15°	
Rear suspension		
Brake hydraulic line union nuts	14	10
Hub bearing assembly to trailing arm: *		
Stage 1	50	37
Stage 2	Angle-tighten a further 30°	
Stage 3	Angle-tighten a further 15°	
Shock absorber:		
To body	90	66
To trailing arm	130	96
Torsion beam front mounting bracket: *		
Centre bolt:		
Stage 1	90	66
Stage 2	Angle-tighten a further 60°	
Stage 3	Angle-tighten a further 15°	
Bracket-to-underbody bolts:		
Stage 1	90	66
Stage 2	Angle-tighten a further 30°	
Stage 3	Angle-tighten a further 15°	
Steering		
Electro-hydraulic pump to steering gear and subframe	22	16
Hydraulic pressure and return line union nuts:		
TRW steering gear	30	22
ZF steering gear	16	12
Intermediate shaft to steering gear pinion and steering column*	24	18
Steering column mounting bolts*	22	16
Steering gear to subframe: *		
Stage 1	45	33
Stage 2	Angle-tighten a further 45°	
Stage 3	Angle-tighten a further 15°	
Steering wheel retaining bolt*	30	22
Track rod end locking nut	60	44
Track rod end to swivel hub: *		
Stage 1	30	22
Stage 2	Angle-tighten a further 90°	
Stage 3	Angle-tighten a further 15°	
Track rod to steering rack	90	66
Use new fasteners		
Roadwheels	110	81

1 General Information

1 The independent front suspension is of the MacPherson strut type, incorporating coil springs and integral telescopic shock absorbers. The MacPherson struts are located by transverse lower suspension arms, which utilise rubber inner mounting bushes, and incorporate a balljoint at the outer ends. The front swivel hubs, which carry the hub bearings, brake calipers and disc assemblies, are bolted to the MacPherson struts, and connected to the lower arms via the balljoints. A front anti-roll bar is fitted, which has link rods with balljoints at each end to connect it to the strut.

2 The rear suspension is of semi-independent type, consisting of a torsion beam and trailing arms, with double-conical coil springs and telescopic shock absorbers. The front ends of the trailing arms are attached to the vehicle underbody by horizontal bushes, and the rear ends are located by the shock absorbers, which are bolted to the underbody at their upper ends. The coil springs are mounted independently of the shock absorbers, and act directly between the trailing arms and the underbody. Each rear wheel bearing, hub and stub axle assembly is manufactured as a sealed unit, and cannot be dismantled.

3 The steering system is of the electro-hydraulic power steering (EHPS) type. This system utilises a conventional rack-and-pinion type steering gear mounted on the front subframe, with variable power assistance generated by a hydraulic pump, driven by an electric motor. The degree of power assistance available is governed by the speed of the electric motor which is controlled by the steering system electronic control unit. The ECU receives input signals on steering wheel position (from a steering angle sensor) and roadspeed (from the ABS wheel speed sensors) and calculates the amount of power assistance required. The hydraulic pump, electric motor and hydraulic fluid reservoir are mounted above the rack-and-pinion steering gear on the front subframe.

4 The steering column is linked to the steering gear by an intermediate shaft. The intermediate shaft has a universal joint fitted to its upper end, and is secured to the column by a clamp bolt. The lower end of the intermediate shaft is attached to the steering gear pinion by means of a clamp bolt.

2 Front swivel hub – removal and refitting

Caution: The front wheel camber setting is controlled by the bolts securing the swivel hub to the front suspension strut. Before removing the bolts, mark the swivel hub in relation to the strut accurately. On completion, the camber setting must be checked and adjusted by a suitably-equipped garage.

Note: *A new driveshaft retaining nut, lower arm balljoint clamp bolt and nut, suspension strut-to-swivel hub nuts and bolts and a new track rod end retaining nut will be needed for refitting. The driveshaft outer joint splines may be a tight fit in the hub and it is possible that a puller/extractor will be required to draw the hub assembly off the driveshaft during removal.*

Removal

1 Firmly apply the handbrake, then jack up the front of the car and support it securely on axle stands (see Jacking and vehicle support 13,5). Remove the relevant front roadwheel.

2 Remove the front brake disc as described in Chapter 9 Section 6.

3 On models without a front brake pad wear indicator, depress the retaining tab and release the ABS wheel speed sensor wiring connector from the suspension strut bracket. Push the locking tab downward and disconnect the wheel speed sensor wiring from the connector **(see illustrations)**.

4 On models with a front brake pad wear indicator depress the locking tab and release the wiring connector from the suspension strut. Slide the locking bar on the connector downward, then hold the upper part of the connector and twist the lower part to open the connector. Disconnect the ABS wheel speed sensor wire from the connector and also disconnect the brake pad wear warning indicator wire **(see illustrations)**.

2.3a Depress the retaining tab and release the wheel speed sensor wiring connector from the strut bracket – models without a brake pad wear indicator

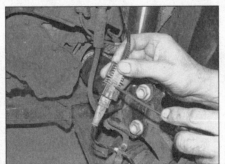

2.3b Push the locking tab downward and disconnect the wheel speed sensor wiring from the connector – models without a brake pad wear indicator

2.4a Depress the locking tab and release the wiring connector from the suspension strut

2.4b Slide the locking bar on the wiring connector downward ...

2.4c ... then hold the upper part of the connector and twist the lower part in the direction of the arrow

2.4d Disconnect the wires from the connector – models with a brake pad wear indicator

HAYNES HiNT

A tool to hold the wheel hub stationary whilst the driveshaft retaining nut is slackened can be fabricated from two lengths of steel strip (one long, one short) and a nut an bolt; the nut and bolt forming the pivot of a forked tool.

5 To prevent rotation of the wheel hub as the driveshaft retaining nut is slackened, make up a holding tool and bolt the tool to the wheel hub using two wheel bolts (see **Tool Tip**).

6 With the holding tool in place, slacken and remove the driveshaft retaining nut using a socket and long bar. Where necessary, support the socket on an axle stand to prevent it slipping off the nut. This nut is very tight; make sure that there is no risk of pulling the car off the axle stands as the nut is slackened.

7 Unscrew the nut securing the track rod end

to the steering arm on the swivel hub, then use a balljoint separator tool to remove the track rod end **(see illustration)**.

8 Unscrew the nut and remove the clamp bolt securing the front suspension lower arm balljoint to the swivel hub **(see illustration)**. Note that a new clamp bolt and nut will be required for refitting.

9 Use a chisel or screwdriver as a wedge to expand the lower portion of the swivel hub **(see illustration)**.

10 Using a lever, push down on the suspension lower arm to free the balljoint from the swivel hub, then move the swivel hub to one side and release the arm, taking care not to damage the balljoint rubber boot. It is advisable to place a protective cover over the rubber boot such as the plastic cap from an aerosol can, suitably cut to fit.

11 The hub must now be freed from the end of the driveshaft. It may be possible to pull the hub off the driveshaft, but if the end of the driveshaft is tight in the hub, temporarily refit the driveshaft retaining nut to protect the driveshaft threads, then tap the end of the driveshaft with a soft-faced hammer while pulling outwards on the swivel hub **(see illustrations)**. Alternatively, use a suitable puller to press the driveshaft through the hub.

12 Mark the position of the suspension strut on the swivel hub by drawing a circle around the heads of the two retaining bolts. **Note:** *This is important to maintain the camber setting.*

13 Slacken and remove the two nuts and bolts securing the suspension strut to the swivel hub, noting that new nuts and bolts will be required for refitting **(see illustration)**. Disengage the swivel hub from the strut and remove it from the car.

Refitting

14 Ensure that the driveshaft outer constant velocity joint and hub splines are clean, then slide the hub onto the driveshaft splines. Fit the new driveshaft retaining nut, tightening it by hand only at this stage.

15 Engage the swivel hub with the suspension strut, and insert the new bolts from the front of the strut so that their threads are facing to the rear. Fit the new nuts, tightening them by hand only at this stage.

16 Locate the lower arm balljoint in the swivel hub. Insert the new clamp bolt from the front of the swivel hub, so that its threads are facing to the rear. Fit the new nut to the clamp bolt, and tighten it to the specified torque.

17 With the hub correctly located, align the strut-to-swivel hub bolt heads with the marks made on the strut during removal. Tighten the bolts to the specified torque and through the specified angles given in the Specifications, using a torque wrench and angle-tightening gauge.

18 Engage the track rod balljoint in the swivel hub, then fit the new retaining nut and tighten it to the specified torque setting.

19 Refit the brake disc together with the

2.7 Use a balljoint separator tool to remove the track rod end

2.8 Unscrew the nut and remove the clamp bolt securing the lower arm balljoint to the swivel hub

2.9 Use a chisel or screwdriver as a wedge to expand the lower portion of the swivel hub

2.11a Tap the end of the driveshaft with a soft-faced hammer ...

2.11b ... then free the driveshaft from the swivel hub

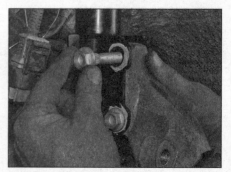

2.13 Slacken and remove the two nuts and bolts securing the suspension strut to the swivel hub

brake caliper and pads as described in Chapter 9 Section 6.

20 Reconnect the ABS wheel speed sensor wiring connector and, where applicable, the break pad wear warning indicator wire. Secure the wiring in the relevant support brackets and clips.

21 Refit the brake hydraulic hose to the suspension strut and secure with the retaining clip.

22 Using the method employed on removal to prevent rotation, tighten the driveshaft retaining nut through the stages given in the Specifications.

23 Refit the roadwheel, then lower the vehicle to the ground and tighten the roadwheel bolts to the specified torque.

3 Front hub bearings – checking and renewal

Note: *The front hub bearing and integral ABS wheel speed sensor is a sealed unit and no repairs are possible. If the bearing is worn or the speed sensor is faulty, a new bearing assembly must be obtained.*

Checking

1 Firmly apply the handbrake, then jack up the front of the car and support it securely on axle stands (see Jacking and vehicle support13,5). Remove the roadwheel.

2 A dial test indicator (DTI) will be required to measure the amount of play in the bearing. Locate the DTI on the suspension strut and zero the probe on the brake disc.

3 Lever the hub in and out and measure the amount of play in the bearing.

4 To measure the bearing lateral and radial run-out, undo the two bolts securing the brake caliper mounting bracket to the swivel hub. Slide the mounting bracket, complete with brake caliper and pads off the brake disc, and tie it to the coil spring using wire or a cable tie.

5 Undo the securing screw and remove the brake disc from the wheel hub.

6 To check the lateral run-out, locate the DTI on the suspension strut and zero the probe on the front face of the hub flange. Rotate the hub and measure the run-out.

7 To check the radial run-out, zero the DTI probe on the upper face of the extended portion at the centre of the hub. Rotate the hub and measure the run-out.

8 If the play or run-out exceeds the specified amounts, renew the hub bearing as described below.

9 If the bearing is satisfactory, refit the brake disc and tighten its retaining screw securely.

10 Slide the brake pads, caliper and mounting bracket over the disc and into position on the swivel hub. Fit the two caliper mounting bracket retaining bolts and tighten them to the specified torque (see Chapter 9 Section 0).

11 Refit the roadwheel, then lower the vehicle

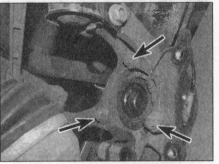

3.13 Undo the three bolts (arrowed) securing the bearing assembly to the swivel hub ...

to the ground and tighten the roadwheel bolts to the specified torque.

Renewal

Note: *New hub bearing retaining bolts will be required for refitting.*

12 Carry out the operations described in Section 2, paragraphs 1 to 11.

13 Undo the three bolts securing the bearing assembly to the swivel hub **(see illustration)**.

14 Remove the bearing and the brake shield from the swivel hub **(see illustration)**.

15 Thoroughly clean the swivel hub and brake shield, then place the shield in position on the swivel hub.

16 Locate the hub bearing over the brake shield and into the swivel hub. Position the bearing so that the wheel speed sensor wiring connector is toward the brake caliper side of the swivel hub (ie, towards the front of the vehicle). Align the retaining bolt holes and fit the three new bolts.

17 Tighten the retaining bolts progressively to the specified Stage 1 torque setting using a torque wrench, and then through the specified Stage 2 and Stage 3 angles, using an angle tightening gauge **(see illustrations)**.

18 Ensure that the driveshaft outer constant velocity joint and hub splines are clean, then slide the hub onto the driveshaft splines. Fit the new driveshaft retaining nut, tightening it by hand only at this stage.

19 Locate the lower arm balljoint in the swivel hub. Insert the clamp bolt from the front of the swivel hub, so that its threads are facing to

3.17a Tighten the retaining bolts to the Stage 1 torque setting using a torque wrench ...

3.14 ... then remove the bearing assembly and brake shield from the hub

the rear. Fit the new nut to the clamp bolt, and tighten it to the specified torque.

20 Engage the track rod balljoint in the swivel hub, then fit the new retaining nut and tighten it to the specified torque setting.

21 Refit the brake disc together with the brake caliper and pads as described in Chapter 9 Section 6.

22 Reconnect the ABS wheel speed sensor wiring connector and, where applicable, the brake pad wear warning indicator wire. Secure the wiring in the relevant support brackets and clips.

23 Refit the brake hydraulic hose to the suspension strut and secure with the retaining clip.

24 Using the method employed on removal to prevent rotation, tighten the driveshaft retaining nut through the stages given in the Specifications.

25 Refit the roadwheel, then lower the vehicle to the ground and tighten the roadwheel bolts to the specified torque.

4 Front suspension strut – removal, overhaul and refitting

Note: *New strut-to-swivel hub bolts and nuts, strut retaining clamp and strut link rod nut, will be required for refitting. Ideally, both front suspension struts should be renewed at the same time in order to maintain good steering and suspension characteristics.*

3.17b ... and then through the Stage 2 and 3 angles, using an angle tightening gauge

4.2a Unclip the ABS wheel speed sensor wiring guide from the hydraulic hose ...

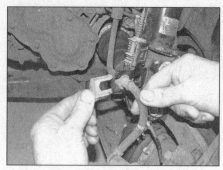

4.2b ... then extract the retaining clip ...

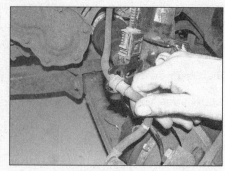

4.2c ... and release the hydraulic hose from the suspension strut

Removal

1 Apply the handbrake, then jack up the front of the vehicle and support it on axle stands (see Jacking and vehicle support13,5). Remove the front roadwheel.

2 Unclip the ABS wheel speed sensor wiring guide from the brake hydraulic hose, then extract the retaining clip and release the hydraulic hose from the suspension strut **(see illustrations)**.

3 On models without a front brake pad wear indicator, depress the retaining tab and release the ABS wheel speed sensor wiring connector from the suspension strut bracket. Push the locking tab downward and disconnect the wheel speed sensor wiring from the connector **(see illustrations 2.3a and 2.3b)**.

4 On models with a front brake pad wear indicator depress the locking tab and release the wiring connector from the suspension strut. Slide the locking bar on the connector downward, then hold the upper part of the connector and twist the lower part to open the connector. Disconnect the ABS wheel speed sensor wire from the connector and also disconnect the brake pad wear warning indicator wire **(see illustrations 2.4a to 2.4d)**.

5 Unscrew the nut and disconnect the anti-roll bar link rod from the strut. Use a spanner on the special flats to hold the link while the nut is being loosened **(see illustration)**.

6 Mark the position of the suspension strut on the swivel hub by drawing around the heads of the two retaining bolts. **Note:** *This is important to maintain the camber setting.*

7 Slacken and remove the two nuts and bolts securing the suspension strut to the swivel

hub, noting that new nuts and bolts will be required for refitting. Disengage the top of the swivel hub from the strut **(see illustrations)**.

8 To gain access to the strut upper mounting, remove the windscreen cowl panel as described in Chapter 11 Section 20.

9 Engage the help of an assistant to support the strut beneath the front wing. From within the engine compartment, prise apart the two halves of the strut retaining clamp by spreading open the serrations **(see illustration)**. Push up on the strut to relieve the tension on the clamp, and remove the two clamp halves from the strut tower. Note that the retaining clamp will be destroyed during removal and a new clamp must be obtained for refitting.

10 Lower the strut and withdraw it from under the front wing.

Overhaul

Note: *A spring compressor tool will be required for this operation. Before overhaul, mark the position of each component in relationship with each other for reassembly.*

Note: *A new piston rod nut will be required for reassembly.*

11 With the suspension strut resting on a bench, or clamped in a vice, fit a spring compressor tool, and compress the coil spring to relieve the pressure on the spring seats **(see illustration)**. Ensure that the compressor tool is securely located on the spring, in accordance with the tool manufacturer's instructions.

4.5 Unscrew the nut and disconnect the anti-roll bar link rod from the strut

4.7a Undo the two nuts and bolts securing the suspension strut to the swivel hub ...

4.7b ... then disengage the top of the swivel hub from the strut

4.9 Prise apart the two halves of the strut retaining clamp by spreading open the serations

4.11 Fit a spring compressor tool, and compress the coil spring

4.12 Prise out the plastic cap from the upper mounting

4.13 Counter-hold the strut piston rod with an Allen key or suitable bit, and unscrew the piston rod nut

4.14a Remove the strut upper mounting ...

4.14b ... upper spring seat with rubber gaiter ...

4.14c ... spring ...

4.14d ... and buffer, from the strut

12 Using a screwdriver, prise out the plastic cap from the upper mounting **(see illustration)**.

13 Mark the position of the spring relevant to the top and bottom mountings, then counter-hold the strut piston rod with an Allen key or suitable bit, and unscrew the piston rod nut **(see illustration)**.

14 Remove the strut upper mounting, upper spring seat with rubber gaiter, spring and buffer from the strut **(see illustrations)**.

15 With the strut assembly now completely dismantled, examine all the components for wear, damage or deformation. Renew any of the components as necessary.

16 Examine the strut for signs of fluid leakage. Check the strut piston for signs of pitting along its entire length, and check the strut body for signs of damage. While holding it in an upright position, test the operation of the strut by moving the piston through a full stroke, and then through short strokes of 50 to 100 mm. In both cases, the resistance felt should be smooth and continuous. If the resistance is jerky or uneven or if there is any visible sign of wear or damage to the strut, renewal is necessary.

17 If any doubt exists as to the condition of the coil spring, carefully remove the spring compressors and check the spring for distortion and signs of cracking. Renew the spring if it is damaged or distorted, or if there is any doubt as to its condition.

18 Inspect all other components for damage

or deterioration, and renew any that are suspect.

19 With the spring compressed with the compressor tool, locate the spring on the strut making sure that it is correctly seated with its lower end against the raised stop **(see illustration)**.

20 Refit the buffer, rubber gaiter, upper spring seat and the upper mounting.

21 Refit the new piston rod nut and tighten it to the specified torque while counter-holding the piston rod. Refit the plastic cap to the upper mounting.

22 Slowly slacken the spring compressor tool to relieve the tension in the spring. Check that the ends of the spring locate correctly against

the stops on the spring seats. If necessary, turn the spring and the upper seat so that the components locate correctly before the compressor tool is removed. Remove the compressor tool when the spring is fully-seated.

Refitting

23 Locate the strut in position under the front wing and engage the help of an assistant to retain it in place. Engage the two halves of the new strut retaining clamp with the strut upper mounting and push the two halves together so that the serrations engage. Using a pair of wide-opening grips or similar, squeeze the two clamp halves fully together **(see illustration)**.

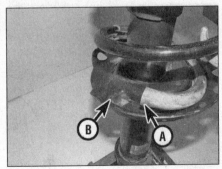

4.19 Locate the spring on the strut making sure that its lower end (A) is against the raised stop (B)

4.23 Engage the two halves of the strut retaining clamp with the strut upper mounting and squeze the two clamp halves fully together

24 Engage the swivel hub with the suspension strut, and insert the new bolts from the front of the strut so that their threads are facing to the rear. Fit the new nuts, tightening them by hand only at this stage.

25 Align the strut-to-swivel hub bolt heads with the marks made on the strut during removal. Tighten the bolts to the specified torque and through the specified angles given in the Specifications, using a torque wrench and angle-tightening gauge.

26 Locate the hydraulic hose in the strut bracket and secure with the retaining clip. Refit the ABS wheel speed sensor wiring guide to the brake hydraulic hose.

27 Reconnect the ABS wheel speed sensor wiring connector and, where applicable, the brake pad wear warning indicator wire. Secure the wiring in the relevant support brackets and clips.

28 Connect the anti-roll bar link rod to the strut and use a spanner on the flats to hold the link while tightening the nut to the specified torque.

29 Refit the roadwheel, then lower the vehicle to the ground and tighten the roadwheel bolts to the specified torque.

30 On completion, refit the windscreen cowl panel as described in Chapter 11 Section 20.

---

5 Front suspension lower arm – removal, overhaul and refitting

Note: *New lower arm inner pivot bolts and lower arm balljoint clamp bolt and nut will be needed for refitting.*

Removal

1 Firmly apply the handbrake, then jack up the front of the car and support it securely on axle stands (see Jacking and vehicle support 13,5). Remove the front roadwheel.

2 Unscrew the nut and remove the clamp bolt securing the front suspension lower arm balljoint to the swivel hub **(see illustration 2.8)**. Note that a new clamp bolt and nut will be required for refitting.

3 Use a chisel or screwdriver as a wedge to expand the lower portion of the swivel hub **(see illustration 2.9)**.

4 Using a lever, push down on the suspension lower arm to free the balljoint from the swivel hub, then move the swivel hub to one side and release the arm, taking care not to damage the balljoint rubber boot. It is advisable to place a protective cover over the rubber boot such as the plastic cap from an aerosol can, suitably cut to fit.

5 Note that the lower arm inner retaining bolt heads are facing the front of the vehicle. Unscrew and remove the bolts and withdraw the lower arm from the subframe **(see illustration)**. It will be necessary to slightly press the arms to release the rubber mountings.

5.5 Front suspension lower arm inner mounting located on the subframe

Overhaul

6 The lower balljoint may be renewed as described in Section 6. The rubber bushes are a tight fit in the arm and must be pressed out. If a press is not available, the bushes can be drawn out using a long bolt, nut, washers and a socket or length of metal tubing.

7 Prior to fitting the new bushes, coat them with silicone grease or soapy water. Press both bushes fully into the lower arm.

Refitting

8 Locate the lower arm on the subframe and fit the retaining bolts from the front of the vehicle. Hand-tighten the bolts at this stage.

9 Locate the lower arm balljoint in the swivel hub. Insert the new clamp bolt from the front of the swivel hub, so that its threads are facing to the rear. Fit the new nut to the clamp bolt, and tighten it to the specified torque.

10 Refit the front wheel and lower the vehicle to the ground.

11 With the weight of the vehicle on the suspension, tighten the lower arm inner pivot bolts to the specified torque and in the stages given.

12 Have the front wheel alignment settings checked on completion.

---

6 Front suspension lower balljoint – renewal

Note: *The original balljoint is riveted to the lower arm; service balljoints are bolted in position.*

1 Remove the front suspension lower arm as described in Section 5. **Note:** *If the fitted balljoint is a service item, it is not necessary to completely remove the arm but only disconnect the balljoint from the bottom of the swivel hub then unbolt the old balljoint.*

2 Mount the lower arm in a vice, then drill the heads from the three rivets that secure the balljoint to the lower arm, using an 8.0 mm diameter drill **(see illustration)**.

3 If necessary, tap the rivets from the lower arm, then remove the balljoint.

6.2 Front suspension lower balljoint showing rivets securing it to the lower arm

4 Clean any rust from the rivet holes, and apply rust inhibitor.

5 The new balljoint must be fitted using three special bolts, spring washers and nuts, available from a Vauxhall/Opel parts stockists.

6 Ensure that the balljoint is fitted the correct way up, noting that the securing nuts are positioned on the underside of the lower arm. Tighten the nuts to the specified torque.

7 Refit the front suspension lower arm as described in Section 5.

---

7 Front subframe – removal and refitting

Note: *Vauxhall/Opel technicians use special jigs to ensure that the subframe is correctly aligned. Without the use of these tools it is important to note the position of the subframe accurately before removal.*

Removal

1 Jack up the front and rear of the car and support it securely on axle stands (see Jacking and vehicle support 13,5). Preferably, position the car over an inspection pit, or on a lift. The help of an assistant will be needed for this procedure.

2 Set the front wheels in the straight-ahead position, then remove the ignition key and lock the column by turning the steering wheel as required. Remove both front roadwheels and remove the lower liner from the right-hand wheel arch.

3 Remove the front bumper as described in Chapter 11 Section 6.

4 Remove the battery and battery tray as described in Chapter 5A Section 4.

5 Remove the complete exhaust system as described in Chapter 4A or Chapter 4B.

6 In the driver's footwell, unscrew the bolt securing the bottom of the steering column intermediate shaft to the steering gear pinion. Use paint or a suitable marker pen to make alignment marks between the intermediate shaft and the steering gear pinion, then pull

7.6 Unscrew the clamp bolt, then disconnect the intermediate shaft from the steering gear pinion

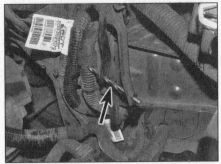

7.8 Insert a drill bit (arrowed) or similar through the holes provided on the radiator mounting brackets (shown with radiator removed)

7.9 Disconnect the power steering positive cable (arrowed) from the junction box terminal

the shaft from the pinion and position to one side (**see illustration**).

7 Release the locking clip, then lift up the cooling system expansion tank and remove it from the mounting bracket. Place the tank to one side.

8 Retain the radiator in position by inserting a drill bit or similar through the holes provided on each of the radiator upper mounting brackets (**see illustration**). This is necessary as the radiator bottom mounting rubbers are located in the subframe.

9 Lift off the cover from the wiring junction box at the left-hand rear corner of the engine compartment. Undo the nut and disconnect the electro-hydraulic power steering system positive cable from the junction box terminal (**see illustration**).

10 Disconnect the wiring connector for the electro-hydraulic power steering system at the block connector adjacent to the ABS hydraulic modulator (**see illustration**).

11 Undo the bolt and disconnect the electro-hydraulic power steering system earth cable from the battery negative terminal clamp.

12 Working under the car, release the cable ties and retaining clips and release the

power steering wiring harness from its body attachments. The wiring harness must be free to be removed with the subframe.

13 Connect a hoist to the engine/transmission assembly and support its weight. If available, the type of support bar which locates in the engine compartment side channels is to be preferred, as this will ensure correct repositioning during refitting. Connect the hoist chains to the lifting brackets on the cylinder head.

14 Unscrew the nut and disconnect the anti-roll bar link rod from the strut. Use a spanner on the special flats to hold the link while the nut is being loosened (**see illustration 4.5**).

15 Unscrew the nut securing the track rod end to the steering arm on the swivel hub, then use a balljoint separator tool to remove the track rod end (**see illustration 2.7**).

16 Unscrew the nut and remove the clamp bolt securing the front suspension lower arm ball-joint to the swivel hub (**see illustration 2.8**). Note that a new clamp bolt and nut will be required for refitting.

17 Use a chisel or screwdriver as a wedge to expand the lower portion of the swivel hub (**see illustration 2.9**).

18 Using a lever, push down on the suspension lower arm to free the balljoint from the swivel hub, then move the swivel hub to one side and release the arm, taking care not to damage the balljoint rubber boot. It is advisable to place a protective cover over the rubber boot such as the plastic cap from an aerosol can, suitably cut to fit.

19 Undo the three bolts and detach the rear engine mounting/torque link bracket from the transmission.

20 Slacken and remove the nut securing the front engine mounting/torque link to the subframe bracket. Withdraw the through-bolt (**see illustration**).

21 Support the subframe with a length of wood on a trolley jack. Ideally, a purpose-made cradle should be used. Enlist the help of an assistant.

22 Accurately mark the position of the subframe and mounting bolts to ensure correct refitting. Note that Vauxhall/Opel technicians use a special jig with guide pins located through the alignment holes in the subframe and underbody.

23 Unscrew and remove the subframe mounting bolts, noting the position of each

7.10 Disconnect the power steering wiring at the block connector (arrowed)

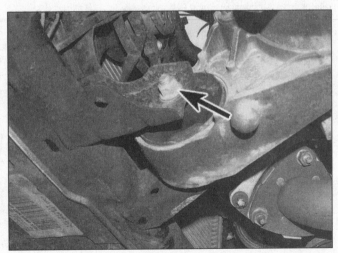

7.20 Undo the nut (arrowed) and remove the bolt securing the front engine mounting/torque link to the subframe bracket

7.23a Unscrew the subframe front mounting bolts ...

7.23b ... side mounting bolts ...

7.23c ... and rear support bracket bolts

7.24 Guide the steering gear pinion through the rubber grommet when lowering the subframe

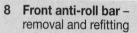

8 Front anti-roll bar – removal and refitting

Note: *It is recommended that all mounting nuts and bolts are renewed when refitting.*

Removal

1 Remove the front subframe assembly as described in Section 7.

2 Prior to removal of the anti-roll bar, mark the position of each anti-roll bar mounting clamp rubber.

3 Unscrew the retaining nut and disconnect the link rod from the ends of the anti-roll bar, discard the retaining nut; a new one should be used on refitting. Use a spanner on the flats to hold the link while the nut is being loosened.

4 Unscrew the two bolts from each mounting clamp, and remove the clamp **(see illustration)**. As the last clamp is removed, support the anti-roll bar and remove it from the subframe.

5 Inspect the mounting clamp rubbers for signs of damage and deterioration, and renew if necessary **(see illustrations)**.

Refitting

6 Align the mounting rubbers with the marks made on the anti-roll bar prior to removal.

7 Refit the anti-roll bar to the subframe, and fit the mounting clamps. Ensure that the clamp half is correctly engaged with the anti-roll bar rubbers, then tighten each clamp retaining bolt, by hand only at this stage.

8 With the two clamps loosely installed, check the position of the anti-roll bar to the marks made on removal, then tighten the clamp bolts to the specified torque setting.

9 Refit the link rods to the ends of the anti-roll bar using new retaining nuts, tighten to the specified torque setting.

10 Refit the front subframe assembly as described in Section 7.

11 Refit the roadwheels if not already done, then lower the vehicle to the ground and tighten the roadwheel bolts to the specified torque setting.

bolt, as they are of different lengths **(see illustrations)**. There are two bolts at the front, two bolts located above the lower suspension arms, and six bolts located on the triangular rear support brackets.

24 With the help of an assistant, carefully lower the subframe taking care not to damage the wiring harness for the power steering. As it is being lowered, guide the steering gear pinion through the rubber grommet in the floor **(see illustrations)**.

25 Remove the steering gear, front suspension lower arms and anti-roll bar with reference to Sections 18, 5 and 8. If necessary, the subframe mounting rubbers may be renewed, however, they must be renewed in pairs only (ie, left and right together). Use a metal tube, a long threaded bar, and two

nuts and washers to force out the rubbers. If necessary, unbolt and remove the gearchange bracket (where fitted).

Refitting

26 Refitting is a reversal of removal, bearing in mind the following points:

a) *Ensure that the radiator lower mounting pegs engage correctly in the subframe brackets as the subframe is refitted.*

b) *Tighten all nuts and bolts to the specified torque and, where necessary, in the stages given. Note that new nuts/bolts should be used on all disturbed fittings.*

c) *Make sure that the subframe is correctly aligned with the underbody before fully tightening the mounting bolts.*

8.4 Anti-roll bar clamp mounting bolts (arrowed)

8.5a Remove the clamps from the rubber bushes ...

8.5b ... then remove the bushes and inspect for wear

9 Rear hub bearings – checking and renewal

Note: *The rear hub bearing and integral ABS wheel speed sensor is a sealed unit and no repairs are possible. If the bearing is worn or the speed sensor is faulty, a new bearing assembly must be obtained.*

Checking

1 Chock the front wheels then jack up the rear of the car and securely support it on axle stands (see *Jacking and vehicle support*). Remove the roadwheel.

2 Remove the brake disc as described in Chapter 9 Section 6.

3 A dial test indicator (DTI) will be required to measure the amount of radial and lateral run-out in the bearing. Zero the indicator on the outer edge of the hub flange.

4 Lever the hub in and out and measure the amount of play in the bearing.

5 To measure lateral run-out, locate the probe on the surface of the hub which contacts the disc. To measure radial run-out, locate the probe on the outer perimeter of the hub so that it is pointing towards the centre of the hub.

6 Slowly turn the hub and note the maximum amount of run-out. If the run-out exceeds the amount given in the Specifications, renew the hub bearing unit as described below.

7 Remove the indicator and refit the brake disc with reference to Chapter 9 Section 6.

8 Refit the roadwheel, then lower the vehicle to the ground and tighten the roadwheel bolts to the specified torque.

Renewal

9 New hub bearing retaining nuts will be required for refitting.

10 Chock the front wheels then jack up the rear of the car and securely support it on axle stands (see *Jacking and vehicle support*). Remove the roadwheel.

11 Remove the rear brake disc as described in Chapter 9 Section 6.

12 Disconnect the wiring for the ABS wheel speed sensor located on the inside of the bearing assembly **(see illustration)**.

13 Attach the brake caliper carrier plate to the rear coil spring with a plastic cable tie to prevent straining the hydraulic brake line.

14 Support the bearing assembly and unscrew the four mounting nuts on the inside of the trailing arm. Withdraw the bearing and brake shield from the rear trailing arm. Note that the locating studs are spaced so that the bearing will only fit in one position.

15 Thoroughly clean the trailing arm, bearing unit and brake shield mating faces, then place the shield in position on the bearing unit.

16 Refit the bearing unit and brake shield to the trailing arm, and screw on four new retaining nuts.

17 Tighten the retaining nuts progressively to the specified Stage 1 torque setting using a torque wrench, and then through the specified Stage 2 and Stage 3 angles, using an angle tightening gauge.

18 Reconnect the ABS wheel speed sensor wiring connector.

19 Refit the rear brake disc as described in Chapter 9 Section 6.

10 Rear shock absorber – removal, inspection and refitting

Note: *Always renew shock absorbers in pairs to maintain good road handling.*

Removal

1 Chock the front wheels then jack up the rear of the car and securely support it on axle

9.12 Disconnecting the ABS wiring from the inside of the rear hub

stands (see *Jacking and vehicle support*). Remove the rear roadwheels.

2 Using a trolley jack, slightly raise the trailing arm on the relevant side.

3 Unscrew and remove the shock absorber lower mounting bolt from the trailing arm **(see illustration)**.

4 Support the shock absorber, then unscrew and remove the upper mounting bolt and withdraw the shock absorber from the underbody bracket **(see illustration)**.

Inspection

5 The shock absorber can be tested by clamping the lower mounting eye in a vice, then fully extending and compressing the shock absorber several times. Any evidence of jerky movement or lack of resistance indicates the need for renewal.

6 Examine the mounting rubbers in the shock absorber for excessive wear.

7 If the shock absorber or its mounting rubbers are worn excessively, renew the complete shock absorber.

Refitting

8 Refitting is a reversal of removal, but tighten the mounting bolts to the specified torque.

10.3 Unscrew and remove the shock absorber lower mounting bolt from the trailing arm ...

10.4 ... and the upper mounting bolt from the underbody bracket

11.5a Remove the rear coil spring, together with the spring seats ...

11.5b ... then remove the upper spring seat ...

11.5c ... and lower spring seat

11 Rear suspension coil spring – removal and refitting

Note: *Due to the design of the rear suspension, it is important to note that only one coil spring should be removed at a time. Note that the rear springs should be renewed in pairs.*

Removal

1 Chock the front wheels then jack up the rear of the car and securely support it on axle stands (see *Jacking and vehicle support*). Remove the rear roadwheels.

2 Using a trolley jack, slightly raise the trailing arm on the relevant side.

3 Unscrew and remove the shock absorber lower mounting bolt from the trailing arm **(see illustration 10.3)**.

4 Carefully lower the trailing arm as far as possible without straining the brake flexible hoses leading to the rear brakes.

5 Remove the coil spring and spring seats from the underbody and trailing arm, and withdraw from under the vehicle. Note that the upper spring seat incorporates a damper buffer **(see illustrations)**.

Refitting

6 Refitting is a reversal of removal, but note the following points.

a) *Ensure that the spring locates correctly on the upper and lower seats, as well as on the trailing arm and underbody.*

b) *Tighten the shock absorber lower mounting bolt to the specified torque.*

c) *If the springs are being renewed, repeat the procedure on the remaining side of the vehicle.*

12 Rear suspension torsion beam and trailing arms – removal and refitting

Note: *New front mounting bracket retaining bolts will be required for refitting.*

Removal

1 Chock the front wheels then jack up the rear of the car and securely support it on axle stands (see *Jacking and vehicle support*). Remove the rear roadwheels.

2 From inside the vehicle, unclip and remove the access panel in the centre console, beneath the handbrake lever.

3 Move the handbrake lever to the fully-released position.

4 Turn the handbrake cable adjuster nut anti-clockwise to remove all tension from the cables **(see illustration)**.

5 Working on each side in turn, use a screwdriver to push the handbrake operating lever on the brake caliper downwards, and detach the cable end fitting from the lever **(see illustration)**.

6 Prise out the handbrake outer cable retaining clip and withdraw the handbrake cable from the caliper bracket **(see illustrations)**.

7 Remove the clips and disconnect the handbrake outer cables from the support brackets on the trailing arms. Also release the handbrake cables from the supports on the torsion beam.

8 Disconnect the ABS rear wheel speed sensor wiring from the rear hubs, and unclip the wiring from the torsion beam.

9 Remove the filler cap from the brake hydraulic fluid reservoir in the engine compartment, then tighten the cap down onto a piece of polythene sheeting. This will help prevent the fluid from draining from the system when the rear brake flexible hoses are disconnected.

10 Unscrew the union nuts and disconnect the rear brake hydraulic pipes from the flexible hoses at the support brackets on the trailing arms on each side. Recover the retaining plates.

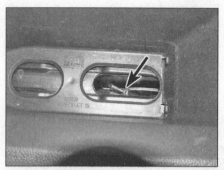

12.4 Handbrake cable adjuster nut (arrowed)

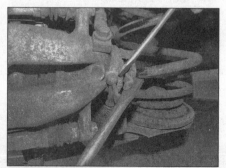

12.5 Push the handbrake operating lever on the brake caliper downwards, and detach the cable end fitting from the lever

12.6a Prise out the handbrake outer cable retaining clip ...

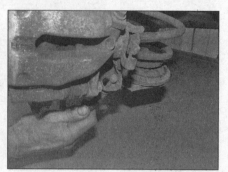

12.6b ... and withdraw the handbrake cable from the caliper bracket

Be prepared for some loss of brake fluid, and plug or tape over the ends of the lines and hoses to prevent entry of dust and dirt.

11 Support the weight of the torsion beam and trailing arms using two trolley jacks. Alternatively, one trolley jack and a length of wood may be used, but the help of an assistant will be required.

12 Unscrew the lower mounting bolts and detach both shock absorbers from the torsion beam.

13 Carefully lower the torsion beam until it is possible to remove the coil springs and spring seats. Note that the upper spring seats incorporate buffers.

14 Make sure that the torsion beam is supported, then unscrew and remove the front mounting bracket bolts from the underbody **(see illustration)**. Note that new bolts will be required for refitting.

15 Lower the torsion beam to the ground and remove it from under the vehicle.

16 The brake components can be removed from the trailing arms, referring to the relevant Sections of Chapter 9. The hub bearing units can be removed with reference to Section 9.

17 If necessary, the front mounting brackets can be removed after unscrewing the retaining nut and withdrawing the centre through-bolt. Note that a new nut and bolt will be required for refitting. Renewal of the front mounting bushes is a complex operation requiring numerous special tools and a hydraulic press. Bush renewal should therefore be entrusted to a Vauxhall/Opel dealer.

Refitting

18 Refit any components that were removed from the torsion beam, referring to the relevant Sections of this Chapter and Chapter 9, as applicable. If the front mounting brackets were removed from the trailing arms, refit the brackets using new nuts and bolts, but only tighten the nuts lightly at this stage.

19 Check the condition of the threads in the front mounting bracket captive nuts on the underbody. If necessary, use a tap to clean out the threads.

20 Support the torsion beam on the trolley jacks, and position the assembly under the rear of the vehicle.

21 Raise the jacks, and fit the new mounting

12.14 Rear suspension torsion beam front mounting bracket

bracket bolts. Do not fully-tighten the bolts at this stage.

22 If the front mounting brackets have been removed from the trailing arms, position the torsion beam so that the distance between the coil spring contact surfaces on the trailing arms and underbody is 183.0 ± 10.0 mm. With the torsion beam in this position, tighten the front mounting bracket centre bolts on each side to the specified torque and angle settings in the stages given.

23 Fully tighten the front mounting bracket-to-underbody bolts to the specified torque and angle settings in the stages given.

24 Locate the upper and lower seats on the coil springs, then refit the springs on the torsion beam.

25 Raise the torsion beam until the shock absorber lower mounting bolts can be inserted. Tighten the bolts to the specified torque.

26 Refit the brake hydraulic pipes and flexible hoses together with the retaining plates and tighten the union nuts to the specified torque.

27 Clip the wiring to the torsion beam and reconnect it to the ABS wheel speed sensors.

28 Reconnect the handbrake cables to the caliper levers and fit the cables in the supports.

29 Bleed the complete brake hydraulic system, as described in Chapter 9 Section 2.

30 Adjust the handbrake cable as described in Chapter 1A Section 24 or Chapter 1B Section 26, then refit the centre console access panel.

31 Refit the roadwheels and lower the vehicle to the ground.

13.3 Disconnect the wiring harness connector for the steering wheel switches

13 Steering wheel – removal and refitting

Warning: Make sure that the airbag safety recommendations given in Chapter 12 Section 22 are followed, to prevent personal injury.

Note: *A new steering wheel retaining bolt will be required for refitting.*

Removal

1 Remove the airbag as described in Chapter 12 Section 23.

2 Set the front wheels in the straight-ahead position, then lock the column in position after removing the ignition key.

3 Disconnect the wiring harness connector for the steering wheel switches **(see illustration)**.

4 Unscrew the Torx retaining bolt securing the steering wheel to the column **(see illustration)**.

5 Check that there are alignment marks between the steering column shaft and steering wheel **(see illustration)**. If no marks are visible, centre punch the wheel and column shaft to ensure correct alignment when refitting.

6 Grip the steering wheel with both hands and carefully rock it from side-to-side to release it from the splines on the steering column. As the steering wheel is being removed, guide the wiring for the airbag through the aperture in the wheel, taking care not to damage the wiring connectors **(see illustration)**.

13.4 Unscrew the steering wheel retaining bolt (arrowed)

13.5 Alignment marks (arrowed) between the steering column shaft and steering wheel

13.6 Guide the wiring for the airbag through the aperture in the wheel

14.4 Insert a thin rod into the lock housing hole, press the rod to release the detent spring, and pull out the lockcylinder

Refitting

7 Refit the steering wheel, aligning the marks made prior to removal. Route the airbag wiring connectors through the steering wheel aperture. **Note:** *Make sure the guide pin on the steering wheel centre hub locates correctly with the contact unit on the steering column, and that the two arrows on the contact unit are aligned.*

8 Clean the threads in the steering column, coat the new retaining bolt threads with locking compound, then fit the bolt and tighten to the specified torque.

9 Reconnect the wiring connector for the steering wheel switches.

10 Release the steering lock, and refit the airbag as described in Chapter 12 Section 23.

14 Ignition switch/steering column lock – removal and refitting

Removal

1 Disconnect the battery negative terminal (refer to Chapter 5A Section 4).

2 Remove the steering column shrouds as described in Chapter 11 Section 26.

3 Insert the ignition key into the ignition switch/lock, and turn it to position I.

4 Insert a thin rod into the hole in the lock housing, press the rod to release the detent spring, and pull out the lock cylinder using the key **(see illustration)**.

Refitting

5 Insert the ignition switch/lock into the lock housing, while the key is in position I. Remove the rod from the lock housing.

6 Refit steering column shrouds as described in Chapter 11 Section 26, then reconnect the battery.

15 Steering column – removal and refitting

Note: *It is recommended that all mounting nuts and bolts are renewed when refitting.*

Removal

1 Remove the steering wheel as described in Section 13.

2 Unscrew the two quick-release catches and remove the facia lower panel above the pedals **(see illustrations)**.

3 Remove the steering column shrouds and the lower trim panel beneath the facia on the driver's side, as described in Chapter 11 Section 26.

4 Release the expanding rivet and remove the driver's side footwell air duct.

5 Remove the steering column electronics module as described in Chapter 12 Section 16.

6 If applicable, make sure the steering column adjustment handle is in the locked position.

7 In the driver's footwell, unscrew the bolt securing the bottom of the steering column intermediate shaft to the steering gear pinion. Use paint or a suitable marker pen to make alignment marks between the intermediate shaft and the steering gear pinion, then pull the shaft from the pinion and position to one side **(see illustration 7.6)**.

8 Undo the retaining bolt and disconnect the earth cable from the column. Unscrew the plastic retainer and release the wiring harness from the side of the column.

9 Unscrew the steering column lower fastening clamp bolt, and the two upper mounting bolts. Slide the column upward to disengage the locating tongue, then withdraw the steering column from the facia crossmember, and remove the column from inside the vehicle **(see illustrations)**.

15.2a Unscrew the quick-release catch (arrowed) on the left-hand side ...

15.2b ... and right-hand side (arrowed) ...

15.2c ... and remove the facia lower panel above the pedals

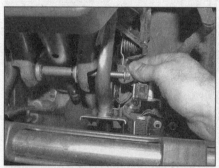

15.9a Unscrew the steering column lower fastening clamp bolt ...

15.9b ... and the two upper mounting bolts (arrowed) ...

15.9c ... then slide the column upward to disengage the locating tongue (arrowed)

16.5a Unscrew the intermediate shaft upper clamp bolt (arrowed) ...

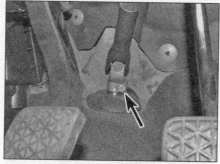

16.5b ... and lower clamp bolt (arrowed) ...

16.6a Separate the intermediate shaft from the steering column ...

Refitting

10 Refitting is a reversal of removal, bearing in mind the following points:

a) *Tighten all nuts and bolts to the specified torque. Note that new nuts/bolts should be used on all disturbed fittings.*

b) *Ensure that the marks made on the steering column and intermediate shaft are correctly aligned.*

c) *Refit the steering column electronics module as described in Chapter 12 Section 16.*

d) *Refit the steering column shrouds and facia footwell trim panel as described in Chapter 11 Section 26.*

e) *Refit the steering wheel as described in Section 13.*

16.6b ... and steering gear pinion

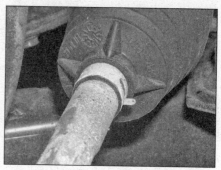

17.2 Steering gear rubber gaiter outer securing clip

16 Steering column intermediate shaft – removal and refitting

Note: *New intermediate shaft upper and lower clamp bolts will be required for refitting.*

Removal

1 Set the front wheels in the straight-ahead position. Remove the ignition key and allow the steering lock to engage.

2 Unscrew the two quick release catches and remove the facia lower panel above the pedals **(see illustrations 15.2a to 15.2c)**.

3 Remove the steering column shrouds and the lower trim panel beneath the facia on the driver's side, as described in Chapter 11 Section 26.

4 Release the expanding rivet and remove the driver's side footwell air duct.

5 Mark the steering column intermediate shaft upper and lower joints in relation to the steering column and steering gear pinion as an aid to refitting, then unscrew both clamp bolts **(see illustrations)**.

6 Compress the telescopic intermediate shaft and slide the joints from the column and pinion **(see illustration)**. Withdraw the intermediate shaft from inside the vehicle.

7 Inspect the intermediate shaft universal joints for excessive wear or damage. If either

joint is worn or damaged, the complete shaft assembly must be renewed.

Refitting

8 Check that the front wheels and steering wheel are still in the straight-ahead position, and that the steering wheel is still locked.

9 Slide the intermediate shaft lower joint onto the steering gear pinion, aligning the previously-made marks. Note that it will not be possible to insert the clamp bolt if the splines are not correctly aligned. Insert the new clamp bolt and tighten to the specified torque.

10 Slide the upper end of the intermediate shaft onto the column splines, aligning the previously-made marks. Insert the new clamp bolt and tighten to the specified torque.

11 Refit the steering column shrouds and facia footwell trim panel as described in Chapter 11 Section 26.

17 Steering gear rubber gaiters – renewal

1 Remove the relevant track rod end as described in Section 21.

2 Remove the inner and outer securing clips **(see illustration)**, then slide the gaiter off the end of the track rod.

3 Thoroughly clean the track rod, then slide the new gaiter into position. Note that a

groove is provided in the track rod for the outer end of the gaiter to locate in.

4 Fit the gaiter securing clips, using new clips if necessary, making sure that the gaiter is not twisted.

5 Refit the track rod end as described in Section 21.

6 Have the front wheel toe-setting checked and adjusted at the earliest opportunity.

18 Steering gear – removal and refitting

Note: *New steering gear mounting bolts will be required for refitting.*

Removal

1 Set the front wheels in the straight-ahead position. Remove the ignition key and allow the steering lock to engage.

2 Remove the front subframe as described in Section 7.

3 On left-hand drive models, unbolt the rear engine mounting/torque link bracket from the subframe.

4 Where fitted, unbolt the support bracket for the pressure and return lines from the subframe.

5 Position a suitable container beneath the steering gear fluid unions to catch spilt hydraulic fluid.

6 Unscrew the union nuts and disconnect the fluid pressure and return lines from the steering gear **(see illustration)**.

7 Note the routing of the wiring loom then either disconnect it from the electro-hydraulic pump (where possible) or release it from the subframe. **Note:** *On pumps supplied by TRW, the wiring loom is supplied together with the pump and cannot be separated.*

8 Unscrew the mounting nuts and withdraw the electro-hydraulic pump together with the fluid reservoir and pressure/return lines from the subframe and steering gear.

9 Unscrew the mounting bolts and remove the steering gear from the subframe **(see illustration)**. If necessary, remove the anti-roll bar first with reference to Section 8. The manufacturers recommend that the mounting bolts are renewed whenever removed.

10 If necessary, remove the track rod ends and track rods with reference to Sections 21 and 22. **Note:** *New steering gear assemblies are available from Vauxhall/Opel either with or without the track rods fitted. Also remove the rubber grommets from the pinion.*

Refitting

11 Refit the track rods and track rod ends with reference to Sections 22 and 21. Also refit the rubber grommets to the pinion.

12 Clean any dirt from the steering gear and subframe, then locate the steering gear in position. Insert the new mounting bolts and tighten to the specified torque, then through the specified angles.

13 Where removed, refit the anti-roll bar with reference to Section 8.

14 Refit the electro-hydraulic pump, together with the fluid reservoir and pressure/return lines to the subframe and steering gear, and tighten the mounting nuts to the specified torque.

15 Reconnect the wiring loom to the electro-hydraulic pump and attach it to the subframe.

16 Fit new rubber sealing rings to the pressure and return lines, then refit the lines to the steering gear and tighten the union nuts to the specified torque.

17 Where fitted, refit the support bracket for the pressure and return lines to the subframe and tighten the mounting bolts securely.

18 On left-hand drive models, refit the rear engine mounting/torque link bracket to the subframe and tighten to the specified torque.

19 Refit the front subframe as described in Section 7.

20 Bleed the power steering hydraulic system as described in Section 20.

21 Have the front wheel toe-setting checked and adjusted at the earliest opportunity.

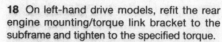

19 Electro-hydraulic power steering pump – removal and refitting

Removal

1 Remove the front subframe as described in Section 7.

2 Position a suitable container beneath the power steering pump fluid unions to catch spilt hydraulic fluid.

3 Disconnect the pressure and return lines from the power steering pump. Use a spanner to unscrew the pressure line union nut. If necessary, cut free the return line clip and replace it with a screw-type clip.

4 Note the routing of the wiring loom then either disconnect it from the electro-hydraulic pump (where possible) or release it from the subframe. **Note:** *On pumps supplied by TRW, the wiring loom is supplied together with the pump and cannot be separated.*

5 Unscrew the mounting nuts and withdraw the electro-hydraulic pump, together with the bracket, wiring and fluid reservoir from the subframe and steering gear.

6 Unscrew the mounting nuts and remove the electro-hydraulic pump and mounting bushes from the bracket. Check the rubber mounting bushes for wear and damage and renew them if necessary.

Refitting

7 Refit the pump and bushes to the bracket and tighten the mounting nuts.

8 Refit the electro-hydraulic pump and bracket on the subframe and steering gear and tighten the mounting nuts to the specified torque.

9 Reconnect the wiring loom (where applicable) and secure it to the subframe. Make sure that the loom is routed as noted during removal.

10 Fit a new rubber sealing ring to the pressure line, then reconnect the pressure and return lines to the power steering pump. Tighten the pressure line union nut securely, and fit a new clip to the return line.

11 Refit the front subframe as described in Section 7.

12 Bleed the power steering hydraulic system as described in Section 20.

20 Power steering hydraulic system – bleeding

Note: *The system must be bled at room temperature – do not bleed the system immediately after using the vehicle on the road.*

1 For improved access to the power steering fluid reservoir, remove the windscreen cowl panel as described in Chapter 11 Section 26. The reservoir is located at the left-hand side of the engine compartment bulkhead – access is limited.

2 Check and top-up the power steering fluid level in the reservoir to the MAX mark on the dipstick as described in Chapter 1A Section 8 or Chapter 1B Section 9. If the system regularly requires more fluid, check the hoses for leaks.

3 Start the engine, then switch it off again after approximately five seconds. Repeat this procedure two more times, pausing briefly between each stop/start and maintaining the fluid level in the reservoir.

4 Now start the engine again and allow it to idle. Turn the steering to full left lock, then full right lock five times. Switch the engine off.

5 Recheck the fluid level in the reservoir and top-up if necessary. Remove the funnel and tube and refit the reservoir filler cap.

6 If removed, refit the windscreen cowl panel as described in Chapter 11 Section 20.

7 It is possible that some air may still remain in the system after bleeding but this will be expelled when the car is driven on the road.

21 Track rod end – removal and refitting

Note: *A new track rod end retaining nut will be needed for refitting.*

Removal

1 Apply the handbrake, then jack up the front of the vehicle, and support securely on axle stands (see Jacking and vehicle support 13,5). Remove the relevant roadwheel.

2 Loosen the track rod end securing locknut on the track rod a quarter turn, while holding

18.6 Hydraulic fluid line connections on the steering gear

18.9 Steering gear mounting bolt retaining nut (arrowed)

the track rod stationary with a second spanner on the flats provided **(see illustration)**. If necessary, use a wire brush to remove rust from the nut and threads and lubricate the threads with penetrating oil before unscrewing the nut. As an additional check, measure the visible amount of threads on the track rod using vernier calipers. This will ensure the track rod end is refitted in the same position.

3 Unscrew and remove the balljoint nut securing the track rod end to the steering arm on the swivel hub **(see illustration)**.

4 Disconnect the track rod end balljoint from the steering arm on the swivel hub using a balljoint separator tool, taking care not to damage the balljoint boot **(see illustration)**.

5 Unscrew the track rod end from the track rod, counting the number of turns necessary to remove it and taking care not to disturb the locknut. **Note:** *The track rod ends are handed side-for-side. The right-hand track rod end is marked with an R and has a right-hand thread, whereas the left-hand one is marked with an L and has a left-hand thread.*

Refitting

6 Screw the track rod end onto the track rod the number of turns noted during removal. Check that the visible amount of threads on the track rod is as previously noted.

7 Insert the track rod end balljoint in the steering arm on the swivel hub, then fit the nut and tighten to the specified torque, then through the angles given. If the balljoint stud turns as the nut is being tightened, press down on the track rod end to force the stud into the arm.

8 Tighten the track rod end securing locknut on the track rod while holding the track rod stationary with a second spanner on the flats provided. If possible, tighten the nut to the specified torque using a special crow's-foot adapter for the torque wrench.

9 Refit the roadwheel, then lower the vehicle to the ground, and tighten the wheelbolts.

10 Have the front wheel alignment checked and adjusted at the earliest opportunity.

---

22 Track rod – removal and refitting

Removal

1 Remove the track rod end from the relevant track rod as described in Section 21. Note, however, that on right-hand drive models it is necessary to remove both track rod ends and bellows when removing the left-hand track rod. Conversely, on left-hand drive models it is necessary to remove both track rod ends and bellows when removing the right-hand track rod.

2 Where necessary, remove the wheel arch liner or trim from under the wheel arch by removing the fasteners (see Chapter 11 Section 20).

21.2 Hold the track rod stationary while loosening the track rod end securing locknut

3 Release the clips and slide the rubber bellows from the steering gear and track rod. Remove the bellows from both sides where necessary (see paragraph 1). Where metal clips are fitted, either prise them free with a screwdriver, or carefully cut them off with a hacksaw.

4 Turn the steering on full lock so that the rack protrudes from the steering gear on the relevant side. Mark the inner joint housing and rack in relation to each other to indicate how tight it is (see paragraph 6).

5 Hold the rack stationary with a spanner on the flats provided, then unscrew and remove the track rod inner joint housing. Use either a large adjustable spanner or grips.

Refitting

6 Clean the threads and apply a little locking fluid to them, then screw the track rod inner joint housing into the rack and tighten to the specified torque. Because of its size and design, using a torque wrench may be difficult, in which case the joint housing should be tightened until the previously-made marks are aligned with each other.

7 Refit the bellows making sure that the inner end is pushed fully onto the steering gear and the outer end is seated in the groove on the track rod. Use new clips if necessary.

8 Where necessary, refit the wheel arch liner or trim.

9 Refit the track rod end(s) as described in Section 21.

10 Have the front wheel alignment checked and adjusted at the earliest opportunity.

21.4 Disconnect the track rod end from the steering arm on the swivel hub using a balljoint separator tool

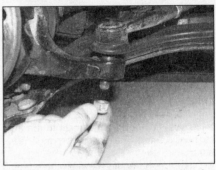

21.3 Unscrew the balljoint nut securing the track rod end to the steering arm on the swivel hub

---

23 Wheel alignment and steering angles – general information

Definitions

1 A car's steering and suspension geometry is defined in four basic settings – all angles are expressed in degrees (toe settings are also expressed as a measurement); the steering axis is defined as an imaginary line drawn through the axis of the suspension strut, extended where necessary to contact the ground **(see illustration)**.

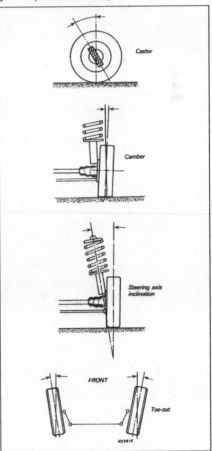

23.1 Wheel alignment details

2 Camber is the angle between each roadwheel and a vertical line drawn through its centre and tyre contact patch, when viewed from the front or rear of the car. Positive camber is when the roadwheels are tilted outwards from the vertical at the top; negative camber is when they are tilted inwards. Slight adjustment of the front camber angle is possible, by altering the position of the swivel hub at its attachment to the front suspension strut. The rear camber angle is not adjustable.

3 Castor is the angle between the steering axis and a vertical line drawn through each roadwheel's centre and tyre contact patch, when viewed from the side of the car. Positive castor is when the steering axis is tilted so that it contacts the ground ahead of the vertical; negative castor is when it contacts the ground behind the vertical. The castor angle is not adjustable.

4 Toe is the difference, viewed from above, between lines drawn through the roadwheel centres and the car's centre-line. 'Toe-in' is when the roadwheels point inwards, towards each other at the front, while 'toe-out' is when they splay outwards from each other at the front.

5 The front wheel toe setting is adjusted by screwing the track rod in or out of its balljoints, to alter the effective length of the track rod assembly. The rear wheel toe setting is not adjustable.

Checking and adjustment

6 Due to the special measuring equipment necessary to check the wheel alignment and steering angles, and the skill required to use it properly, the checking and adjustment of these settings is best left to a Vauxhall/Opel dealer or similar expert. Note that most tyre-fitting shops now possess sophisticated checking equipment.

Chapter 11
Bodywork and fittings

Contents

Section number

Body exterior fittings – removal and refitting 20
Bonnet – removal, refitting and adjustment 8
Bonnet lock spring – removal and refitting. 10
Bonnet release cable – removal and refitting 9
Centre console – removal and refitting. 25
Door – removal, refitting and adjustment 11
Door handles and lock components – removal and refitting 13
Door inner trim panel – removal and refitting 12
Door window glass and regulator – removal and refitting 14
Exterior mirrors and associated components – removal and refitting 17
Facia panel components – removal and refitting. 26
Front bumper – removal and refitting. 6
General Information 1

Section number

Interior trim – removal and refitting 24
Maintenance – bodywork and underframe. 2
Maintenance of upholstery and carpets – general 3
Major body damage repair – general 5
Minor body damage – repair 4
Rear bumper – removal and refitting 7
Seat belt components – removal and refitting 23
Seat belt tensioning mechanism – general information 22
Seats – removal and refitting 21
Sunroof – general information 19
Tailgate and support struts – removal, refitting and adjustment 15
Tailgate lock components – removal and refitting 16
Windscreen and fixed window glass – general information 18

Degrees of difficulty

Easy, suitable for novice with little experience	**Fairly easy,** suitable for beginner with some experience	**Fairly difficult,** suitable for competent DIY mechanic	**Difficult,** suitable for experienced DIY mechanic	**Very difficult,** suitable for expert DIY or professional

Specifications

Torque wrench settings	Nm	lbf ft
Front seat mounting bolts	20	15
Front seat belt:		
Anchorage bolts	20	15
Inertia reel nut	35	26
Stalk and tensioner bolt	35	26
Rear seat belt:		
Anchorage bolts	35	26
Inertia reel bolt	35	26
Stalk/buckle retaining bolts	35	26
Rear seat mounting bolts:		
2nd row rear seats	35	26
3rd row rear seats	20	15
Seat belt-to-height adjuster mounting bolts	30	22

1 General Information

1 The bodyshell is made of pressed-steel sections, and is available as a five-door MPV version. Most components are welded together, but some use is made of structural adhesives; the front wings are bolted on.

2 The bonnet is made of aluminium, whereas the doors, and some other vulnerable panels, are made of zinc-coated metal. These are further protected by being coated with an anti-chip primer, prior to being sprayed.

3 Extensive use is made of plastic materials, mainly on the interior, but also in exterior components. The front and rear bumpers are injection-moulded from a synthetic material which is very strong and yet light. Plastic components such as wheel arch liners are fitted to the underside of the vehicle, to improve the body's resistance to corrosion.

2 Maintenance –
bodywork and underframe

1 The general condition of a vehicle's body-work is the one thing that significantly affects its value. Maintenance is easy, but needs to be regular. Neglect, particularly after minor damage, can lead quickly to further deterioration and costly repair bills. It is important also to keep watch on those parts of the vehicle not immediately visible, for instance the underside, inside all the wheel arches, and the lower part of the engine compartment.

2 The basic maintenance routine for the bodywork is washing – preferably with a lot of water, from a hose. This will remove all the loose solids which may have stuck to the vehicle. It is important to flush these off in such a way as to prevent grit from scratching the finish. The wheel arches and underframe need washing in the same way, to remove any accumulated mud, which will retain moisture and tend to encourage rust. Paradoxically enough, the best time to clean the underframe and wheel arches is in wet weather, when the mud is thoroughly wet and soft. In very wet weather, the underframe is usually cleaned of large accumulations automatically, and this is a good time for inspection.

3 Periodically, except on vehicles with a wax-based underbody protective coating, it is a good idea to have the whole of the underframe of the vehicle steam-cleaned, engine compartment included, so that a thorough inspection can be carried out to see what minor repairs and renovations are necessary. Steam-cleaning is available at many garages, and is necessary for the removal of the accumulation of oily grime, which sometimes is allowed to become thick in certain areas. If steam-cleaning facilities are not available, there are some excellent grease solvents available which can be brush-applied; the dirt can then be simply hosed off. Note that these methods should not be used on vehicles with wax-based underbody protective coating, or the coating will be removed. Such vehicles should be inspected annually, preferably just prior to Winter, when the underbody should be washed down, and any damage to the wax coating repaired. Ideally, a completely fresh coat should be applied. It would also be worth considering the use of such wax-based protection for injection into door panels, sills, box sections, etc, as an additional safeguard against rust damage, where such protection is not provided by the vehicle manufacturer.

4 After washing paintwork, wipe off with a chamois leather to give an unspotted clear finish. A coat of clear protective wax polish will give added protection against chemical pollutants in the air. If the paintwork sheen has dulled or oxidised, use a cleaner/polisher combination to restore the brilliance of the shine. This requires a little effort, but such dulling is usually caused because regular washing has been neglected. Care needs to be taken with metallic paintwork, as special non-abrasive cleaner/polisher is required to avoid damage to the finish. Always check that the door and ventilator opening drain holes and pipes are completely clear, so that water can be drained out. Brightwork should be treated in the same way as paintwork. Windscreens and windows can be kept clear of the smeary film which often appears, by the use of proprietary glass cleaner. Never use any form of wax or other body or chromium polish on glass.

3 Maintenance of upholstery and carpets – general

1 Mats and carpets should be brushed or vacuum-cleaned regularly, to keep them free of grit. If they are badly stained, remove them from the vehicle for scrubbing or sponging, and make quite sure they are dry before refitting. Seats and interior trim panels can be kept clean by wiping with a damp cloth. If they do become stained (which can be more apparent on light-coloured upholstery), use a little liquid detergent and a soft nail brush to scour the grime out of the grain of the material. Do not forget to keep the headlining clean in the same way as the upholstery. When using liquid cleaners inside the vehicle, do not over-wet the surfaces being cleaned. Excessive damp could get into the seams and padded interior, causing stains, offensive odours or even rot.

2 If the inside of the vehicle gets wet accidentally, it is worthwhile taking some trouble to dry it out properly, particularly where carpets are involved. Do not leave oil or electric heaters inside the vehicle for this purpose.

4 Minor body damage – repair

Minor scratches

1 If the scratch is very superficial, and does not penetrate to the metal of the bodywork, repair is very simple. Lightly rub the area of the scratch with a paintwork renovator, or a very fine cutting paste, to remove loose paint from the scratch, and to clear the surrounding bodywork of wax polish. Rinse the area with clean water.

2 Apply touch-up paint to the scratch using a fine paint brush; continue to apply fine layers of paint until the surface of the paint in the scratch is level with the surrounding paintwork. Allow the new paint at least two weeks to harden, then blend it into the surrounding paintwork by rubbing the scratch area with a paintwork renovator or a very fine cutting paste. Finally, apply wax polish.

3 Where the scratch has penetrated right through to the metal of the bodywork, causing the metal to rust, a different repair technique is required. Remove any loose rust from the bottom of the scratch with a penknife, then apply rust-inhibiting paint to prevent the formation of rust in the future. Using a rubber or nylon applicator, fill the scratch with bodystopper paste. If required, this paste can be mixed with cellulose thinners to provide a very thin paste which is ideal for filling narrow scratches. Before the stopper-paste in the scratch hardens, wrap a piece of smooth cotton rag around the top of a finger. Dip the finger in cellulose thinners, and quickly sweep it across the surface of the stopper-paste in the scratch; this will ensure that the surface of the stopper-paste is slightly hollowed. The scratch can now be painted over as described earlier in this Section.

Dents

4 When deep denting of the vehicle's bodywork has taken place, the first task is to pull the dent out, until the affected bodywork almost attains its original shape. There is little point in trying to restore the original shape completely, as the metal in the damaged area will have stretched on impact, and cannot be reshaped fully to its original contour. It is better to bring the level of the dent up to a point which is about 3 mm below the level of the surrounding bodywork. In cases where the dent is very shallow anyway, it is not worth trying to pull it out at all. If the underside of the dent is accessible, it can be hammered out gently from behind, using a mallet with a wooden or plastic head. Whilst doing this, hold a suitable block of wood firmly against the outside of the panel, to absorb the impact from the hammer blows and thus prevent a large area of the bodywork from being 'belled-out'.

5 Should the dent be in a section of the

bodywork which has a double skin, or some other factor making it inaccessible from behind, a different technique is called for. Drill several small holes through the metal inside the area – particularly in the deeper section. Then screw long self-tapping screws into the holes, just sufficiently for them to gain a good purchase in the metal. Now the dent can be pulled out by pulling on the protruding heads of the screws with a pair of pliers.

6 The next stage of the repair is the removal of the paint from the damaged area, and from an inch or so of the surrounding 'sound' bodywork. This is accomplished most easily by using a wire brush or abrasive pad on a power drill, although it can be done just as effectively by hand, using sheets of abrasive paper. To complete the preparation for filling, score the surface of the bare metal with a screwdriver or the tang of a file, or alternatively, drill small holes in the affected area. This will provide a really good 'key' for the filler paste.

7 To complete the repair, see the Section on filling and respraying.

Rust holes or gashes

8 Remove all paint from the affected area, and from an inch or so of the surrounding 'sound' bodywork, using an abrasive pad or a wire brush on a power drill. If these are not available, a few sheets of abrasive paper will do the job most effectively. With the paint removed, you will be able to judge the severity of the corrosion, and therefore decide whether to renew the whole panel (if this is possible) or to repair the affected area. New body panels are not as expensive as most people think, and it is often quicker and more satisfactory to fit a new panel than to attempt to repair large areas of corrosion.

9 Remove all fittings from the affected area, except those which will act as a guide to the original shape of the damaged bodywork (eg headlight shells etc). Then, using tin snips or a hacksaw blade, remove all loose metal and any other metal badly affected by corrosion. Hammer the edges of the hole inwards, in order to create a slight depression for the filler paste.

10 Wire-brush the affected area to remove the powdery rust from the surface of the remaining metal. Paint the affected area with rust-inhibiting paint, if the back of the rusted area is accessible, treat this also.

11 Before filling can take place, it will be necessary to block the hole in some way. This can be achieved by the use of aluminium or plastic mesh, or aluminium tape.

12 Aluminium or plastic mesh, or glass-fibre matting, is probably the best material to use for a large hole. Cut a piece to the approximate size and shape of the hole to be filled, then position it in the hole so that its edges are below the level of the surrounding bodywork. It can be retained in position by several blobs of filler paste around its periphery.

13 Aluminium tape should be used for small or very narrow holes. Pull a piece off the roll, trim it to the approximate size and shape required, then pull off the backing paper (if used) and stick the tape over the hole; it can be overlapped if the thickness of one piece is insufficient. Burnish down the edges of the tape with the handle of a screwdriver or similar, to ensure that the tape is securely attached to the metal underneath.

Filling and respraying

14 Before using this Section, see the Sections on dent, deep scratch, rust holes and gash repairs.

15 Many types of bodyfiller are available, but generally speaking, those proprietary kits which contain a tin of filler paste and a tube of resin hardener are best for this type of repair. A wide, flexible plastic or nylon applicator will be found invaluable for imparting a smooth and well-contoured finish to the surface of the filler.

16 Mix up a little filler on a clean piece of card or board – measure the hardener carefully (follow the maker's instructions on the pack), otherwise the filler will set too rapidly or too slowly. Using the applicator, apply the filler paste to the prepared area; draw the applicator across the surface of the filler to achieve the correct contour and to level the surface. As soon as a contour that approximates to the correct one is achieved, stop working the paste – if you carry on too long, the paste will become sticky and begin to 'pick-up' on the applicator. Continue to add thin layers of filler paste at 20-minute intervals, until the level of the filler is just proud of the surrounding bodywork.

17 Once the filler has hardened, the excess can be removed using a metal plane or file. From then on, progressively-finer grades of abrasive paper should be used, starting with a 40-grade production paper, and finishing with a 400-grade wet-and-dry paper. Always wrap the abrasive paper around a flat rubber, cork, or wooden block – otherwise the surface of the filler will not be completely flat. During the smoothing of the filler surface, the wet-and-dry paper should be periodically rinsed in water. This will ensure that a very smooth finish is imparted to the filler at the final stage.

18 At this stage, the 'dent' should be surrounded by a ring of bare metal, which in turn should be encircled by the finely 'feathered' edge of the good paintwork. Rinse the repair area with clean water, until all of the dust produced by the rubbing-down operation has gone.

19 Spray the whole area with a light coat of primer – this will show up any imperfections in the surface of the filler. Repair these imperfections with fresh filler paste or bodystopper, and once more smooth the surface with abrasive paper. Repeat this spray-and-repair procedure until you are satisfied that the surface of the filler, and the feathered edge of the paintwork, are perfect.

Clean the repair area with clean water, and allow to dry fully.

20 The repair area is now ready for final spraying. Paint spraying must be carried out in a warm, dry, windless and dust-free atmosphere. This condition can be created artificially if you have access to a large indoor working area, but if you are forced to work in the open, you will have to pick your day very carefully. If you are working indoors, dousing the floor in the work area with water will help to settle the dust which would otherwise be in the atmosphere. If the repair area is confined to one body panel, mask off the surrounding panels; this will help to minimise the effects of a slight mis-match in paint colours. Bodywork fittings (eg chrome strips, door handles etc) will also need to be masked off. Use genuine masking tape, and several thicknesses of newspaper, for the masking operations.

21 Before commencing to spray, agitate the aerosol can thoroughly, then spray a test area (an old tin, or similar) until the technique is mastered. Cover the repair area with a thick coat of primer; the thickness should be built up using several thin layers of paint, rather than one thick one. Using 400-grade wet-and-dry paper, rub down the surface of the primer until it is really smooth. While doing this, the work area should be thoroughly doused with water, and the wet-and-dry paper periodically rinsed in water. Allow to dry before spraying on more paint.

22 Spray on the top coat, again building up the thickness by using several thin layers of paint. Start spraying at one edge of the repair area, and then, using a side-to-side motion, work until the whole repair area and about 2 inches of the surrounding original paintwork is covered. Remove all masking material 10 to 15 minutes after spraying on the final coat of paint.

23 Allow the new paint at least two weeks to harden, then, using a paintwork renovator, or a very fine cutting paste, blend the edges of the paint into the existing paintwork. Finally, apply wax polish.

Plastic components

24 With the use of more and more plastic body components by the vehicle manufacturers (eg bumpers. spoilers, and in some cases major body panels), rectification of more serious damage to such items has become a matter of either entrusting repair work to a specialist in this field, or renewing complete components. Repair of such damage by the DIY owner is not really feasible, owing to the cost of the equipment and materials required for effecting such repairs. The basic technique involves making a groove along the line of the crack in the plastic, using a rotary burr in a power drill. The damaged part is then welded back together, using a hot-air gun to heat up and fuse a plastic filler rod into the groove. Any excess plastic is then removed, and the area rubbed down to a smooth finish. It is important that a filler rod of the correct plastic is used, as body components can be made of a variety of different types (eg polycarbonate, ABS, polypropylene).

25 Damage of a less serious nature (abrasions, minor cracks etc) can be repaired by the DIY owner using a two-part epoxy filler repair material. Once mixed in equal proportions, this is used in similar fashion to the bodywork filler used on metal panels. The filler is usually cured in twenty to thirty minutes, ready for sanding and painting.

26 If the owner is renewing a complete component himself, or if he has repaired it with epoxy filler, he will be left with the problem of finding a suitable paint for finishing which is compatible with the type of plastic used. At one time, the use of a universal paint was not possible, owing to the complex range of plastics encountered in body component applications. Standard paints, generally speaking, will not bond to plastic or rubber satisfactorily. However, it is now possible to obtain a plastic body parts finishing kit which consists of a pre-primer treatment, a primer and coloured top coat. Full instructions are normally supplied with a kit, but basically, the method of use is to first apply the pre-primer to the component concerned, and allow it to dry for up to 30 minutes. Then the primer is applied, and left to dry for about an hour before finally applying the special-coloured top coat. The result is a correctly-coloured component, where the paint will flex with the plastic or rubber, a property that standard paint does not normally possess.

5 Major body damage repair – general

1 Where serious damage has occurred, or large areas need renewal due to neglect, it means that complete new panels will need welding-in, and this is best left to professionals. If the damage is due to impact, it will also be necessary to check completely the alignment of the bodyshell, and this can only be carried out accurately by a Vauxhall/ Opel dealer, or accident repair specialist, using special jigs. If the body is left misaligned, it is primarily dangerous as the car will not handle properly, and secondly, uneven stresses will be imposed on the steering, suspension and possibly transmission, causing abnormal wear, or complete failure, particularly to such items as the tyres.

6 Front bumper – removal and refitting

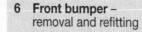

Removal

1 Remove the radiator grille as described in Section 20.

2 Working under the wheel arch, undo the four retaining screws (two on each side) securing the wheel arch liner to the bumper **(see illustrations)**.

3 Pull out the centre pins and extract the six expanding rivets securing the underside of the bumper to the mounting strip on the front subframe **(see illustration)**.

4 Pull out the centre pin and remove the expanding rivet each side in the radiator grille aperture **(see illustration)**.

5 Undo the upper retaining screw each side, adjacent to the headlights **(see illustration)**.

6 Unclip the outside temperature sensor from the centre ventilation grille.

7 Where applicable, disconnect the wiring connectors at the foglights, and the headlight washer hose at the washer pump.

8 With the aid of an assistant, pull the bumper upward and outward at the sides to disengage the guide rails, and carefully lift it off the car **(see illustration)**.

Refitting

9 Refitting is a reversal of the removal procedure, ensuring that all bumper fasteners are securely tightened.

7 Rear bumper – removal and refitting

Removal

1 Remove the rear light cluster each side as described in Chapter 12 Section 7.

2 Working under the wheel arch, undo the four retaining screws (two on each side)

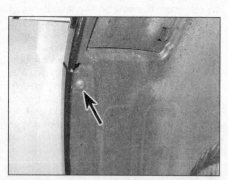

6.2a Undo the upper screw (arrowed) ...

6.2b ... and lower screw (arrowed) each side securing the wheel arch liner to the bumper

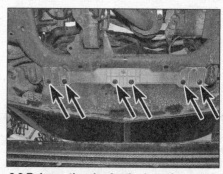

6.3 Release the six plastic rivets (arrowed) securing the bumper to the subframe mounting strip

6.4 Pull out the centre pin and extract the expanding rivet (arrowed) each side

6.5 Undo the upper retaining screw (arrowed) each side

6.8 Pull the bumper upward and outward at the sides to disengage the guide rails

7.2a Undo the upper screw (arrowed) …

7.2b … and lower screw (arrowed) each side securing the wheel arch liner to the bumper

7.3 Pull out the centre pins and extract the two expanding rivets

securing the wheel arch liner to the bumper **(see illustrations)**.

3 Pull out the centre pin and extract the two expanding rivets securing the underside of the bumper to the body **(see illustration)**.

4 On models with parking distance sensors, disconnect the distance sensor main wiring connector from the underside of the bumper.

5 With the aid of an assistant, pull the bumper upward and outward at the sides to disengage the side guide rails **(see illustration)**.

6 Pull the bumper rearwards to disengage the rear guide rails and centre guide rails, and carefully lift the bumper off the car **(see illustration)**.

Refitting

7 Refitting is a reversal of the removal procedure, ensuring that all bumper fasteners are securely tightened.

8 Bonnet – removal, refitting and adjustment

Removal

1 Open the bonnet, and have an assistant support it.

2 Using a marker pen or paint, mark around the hinge positions on the bonnet.

3 With the aid of the assistant, unscrew the two bolts securing the bonnet to the hinges on each side.

4 Lift off the bonnet taking care not to damage the vehicle paintwork.

Refitting

5 Align the marks made on the bonnet before removal with the hinges, then refit and tighten the bonnet securing bolts.

6 Check the bonnet adjustment as follows.

Adjustment

7 Close the bonnet, and check that there is an equal gap (approximately 4.0 mm) at each side, between the bonnet and the wing panels. Check also that the bonnet sits flush in relation to the surrounding body panels.

8 The bonnet should close smoothly and positively without excessive pressure. If this is not the case, adjustment will be required.

9 To adjust the bonnet alignment, loosen the bonnet-to-hinge mounting bolts, and move the bonnet on the bolts as required (the bolt

7.5 Pull the bumper upward and outward at the sides to disengage the side guide rails

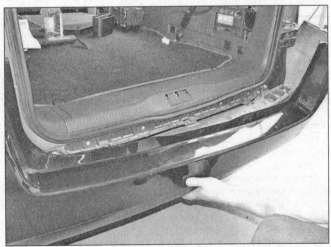

7.6 Pull the bumper rearwards to disengage the rear guide rails and centre guide rails

9.4 Undo the retaining screw (arrowed) and remove the bonnet support prop retaining plate

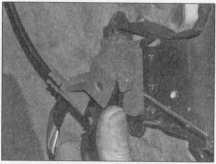

9.5a Insert a small screwdriver through the gap between the release handle and mounting bracket ...

9.5b ... to depress the detent lug (arrowed)

9.6a Detach the outer cable from the release handle frame ...

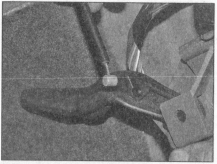

9.6b ... then slip the inner cable end fitting out of the lever

holes in the hinges are enlarged). To adjust the bonnet front height in relation to the front wings, adjustable rubber bump stops are fitted to the front corners of the bonnet. These may be screwed in or out as necessary. After making an adjustment, the bonnet striker must be adjusted so that the lock spring holds the bonnet firmly against the rubber bump stops. Loosen the locknut and screw the striker in or out as necessary.

9 Bonnet release cable – removal and refitting

Removal

1 Remove the driver's side lower trim panel as described in Section 26.
2 Remove the windscreen cowl panel as described in Section 20.
3 Remove the bonnet lock spring as described in Section 10.
4 Undo the retaining screw and remove the bonnet support prop retaining plate **(see illustration)**.
5 Insert a small screwdriver through the gap between the release handle and mounting bracket, to depress the detent lug **(see illustrations)**. With the lug depressed, lift the release handle off the mounting bracket.
6 Detach the outer cable from the release handle frame, then slip the inner cable end fitting out of the lever **(see illustrations)**.

7 Release the cable from the support clips and brackets in the engine compartment, then withdraw the cable through the rubber grommet and into the passenger compartment. As an aid to refitting, tie a length of string to the cable before removing it and leave the string in position ready for refitting.

Refitting

8 Refitting is a reversal of removal, but tie the string to the end of the cable, and use the string to pull the cable into position. Ensure that the cable is routed as noted before removal, and make sure that the grommet is correctly seated. On completion, refit the windscreen cowl panel and the interior trim panels as described in Sections 20 and 26.

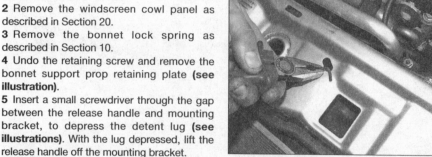

10.3a Disengage the bonnet lock spring leg from the front crossmember ...

10 Bonnet lock spring – removal and refitting

Removal

1 The bonnet is held in its locked position with a strong spring which engages with the striker on the front edge of the bonnet. The release cable is connected to the end of the spring.
2 The striker may be removed from the bonnet by unscrewing the locknut, however measure its fitted length first as a guide to refitting it.
3 To remove the lock spring, disengage the spring leg from the front crossmember, slide the other end of the spring off the release cable and remove the spring from the crossmember **(see illustrations)**.

Refitting

4 Refitting is a reversal of removal.

11 Door – removal, refitting and adjustment

Front door
Removal

1 To remove a door, open it fully and support it under its lower edge on blocks or axle stands covered with pads of rag.

10.3b ... slide the other end off the release cable and remove the spring from the crossmember

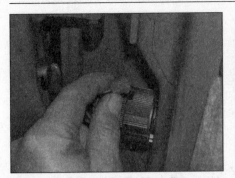

11.2a Pull out the locking clip ...

11.2b ... then twist the collar and pull the connector from the socket

11.3 The front door check arm pivot is attached to the A-pillar with a Torx bolt

2 Disconnect the wiring connector from the front edge of the door. To release the connector, pull out the locking clip, then twist the collar and pull the connector from the socket in the door **(see illustrations)**.
3 Unscrew the Torx bolt securing the door check arm pivot to the A-pillar **(see illustration)**.
4 Where applicable, remove the plastic covers from the hinge pins **(see illustration)**, then drive out the pins using a punch. Have an assistant support the door as the pins are driven out, then withdraw the door from the vehicle. If renewing a door, transfer all the serviceable fixings to the new door.

Refitting

5 Refitting is a reversal of removal.

Adjustment

6 The door hinges are welded onto the door frame and the body pillar, so that there is no provision for adjustment or alignment.

7 If the door can be moved up-and-down on its hinges due to wear in the hinge pins or their holes, it may be possible to drill out the holes and fit slightly oversize pins. Consult a Vauxhall/Opel dealer for further advice.
8 Door closure may be adjusted by altering the position of the lock striker on the body pillar, using an Allen key or a hexagon bit **(see illustration)**.

Rear door

Removal

9 Disconnect the wiring connector from the front edge of the door **(see illustration)**. To release the connector, twist the locking collar, then pull the connector from the socket in the door.
10 Unscrew the Torx bolt securing the door check arm pivot to the B-pillar **(see illustration)**.
11 Where applicable, remove the plastic

covers from the hinge pins **(see illustration)**, then drive out the pins using a punch. Have an assistant support the door as the pins are driven out, then withdraw the door from the vehicle. If renewing a door, transfer all the serviceable fixings to the new door.

Refitting

12 Refitting is a reversal of removal.

Adjustment

13 The door hinges are welded onto the door frame and the body pillar, so that there is no provision for adjustment or alignment.
14 If the door can be moved up-and-down on its hinges due to wear in the hinge pins or their holes, it may be possible to drill out the holes and fit slightly oversize pins. Consult a Vauxhall/Opel dealer for further advice.
15 Door closure may be adjusted by altering the position of the lock striker on the body pillar, using an Allen key or a hexagon bit **(see illustration)**.

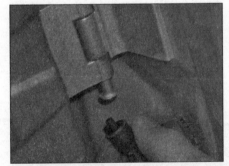

11.4 Removing the plastic covers from the front door hinge pins

11.8 Front door lock striker on the B-pillar

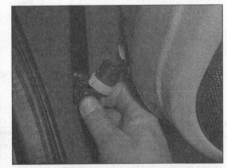

11.9 Disconnecting the wiring from the front edge of the rear door

11.10 Rear door check arm

11.11 Removing the plastic covers from the rear door hinge pins

11.15 Rear door lock striker on the C-pillar

12.1a Carefully prise off the door grab handle cover ...

12.1b ... and undo the two screws now exposed

12.2a Carefully prise off the trim plate ...

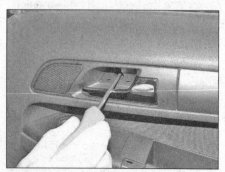

12.2b ... then undo the screw in the trim panel aperture

12.3 Carefully prise off the tweeter speaker trim panel, complete with speaker

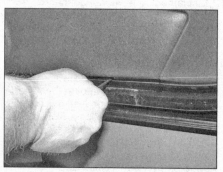

12.4a Undo the lower screw ...

12 Door inner trim panel – removal and refitting

Front door
Removal

1 Using a plastic wedge or similar tool, carefully prise off the door grab handle plastic cover and undo the two screws now exposed (see illustrations).

2 Pull open the door interior handle and prise off the trim plate using a small screwdriver. Undo the screw in the trim panel aperture (see illustrations).

3 Carefully prise off the tweeter speaker trim panel, complete with speaker, and disconnect the wiring connector (see illustration).

4 Undo the lower screw and the rear screw securing the edge of the trim panel to the door (see illustrations).

5 Using a wide-bladed screwdriver or removal tool, carefully prise the bottom and sides of the panel away from door to release the internal clips (see illustration). Lift the panel upward to release it from the window aperture.

6 Once the panel is free, reach behind and release the door lock operating cable from the

12.4b ... and the rear screw securing the edge of the trim panel to the door

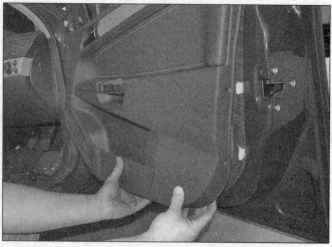

12.5 Carefully prise the bottom and sides of the panel away from door to release the internal clips

12.6 Reach behind the panel and release the door lock operating cable from the interior handle

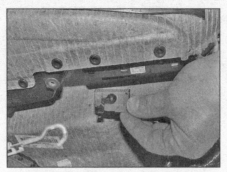

12.7a Disconnect the wiring connectors from the window control switch ...

12.7b ... and door interior handle

interior handle. Disengage the inner cable end from the handle lever **(see illustration)**.

7 Disconnect the wiring connectors from the window control switch and door interior handle, then remove the trim panel from the car **(see illustrations)**.

Refitting

8 Refitting is a reversal of removal.

Rear door

Removal

9 Where a manual window regulator is fitted, locate a cloth rag between the handle and the trim panel and pull it to one side to release the spring clip. Remove the handle from the splined shaft and refit the spring clip to the handle.

10 Using a plastic wedge or similar tool, carefully prise off the door grab handle plastic cover and undo the two screws now exposed **(see illustrations 12.1a and 12.1b)**.

11 Pull open the door interior handle and prise off the trim plate using a small screwdriver. Undo the screw in the trim panel aperture **(see illustrations 12.2a and 12.2b)**.

12 Using a wide-bladed screwdriver or removal tool, carefully prise the bottom and sides of the panel away from door to release the internal clips. Lift the panel upward to release it from the window aperture **(see illustration)**.

13 Once the panel is free, reach behind and release the door lock operating cable from the interior handle. Disengage the inner cable end from the handle lever **(see illustration 12.6)**.

14 On models with electric windows, disconnect the wiring connector from the window control switch, then remove the trim panel from the car.

Refitting

15 Refitting is a reversal of removal.

13 Door handles and lock components – removal and refitting

Door interior handle

Removal

1 The door interior handle is an integral part of the door inner trim panel and cannot be individually removed. If there are any problems with the interior handle, a new inner trim panel will be required.

Front door exterior handle

Removal

2 On vehicles with the Open and Start system, remove the door inner trim panel

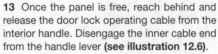

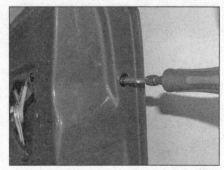

12.12 Carefully prise the bottom and sides of the panel away from door to release the internal clips

as described in Section 12, and disconnect the Open and Start wiring harness connector.

3 Open the door and remove the cover screw from the rear edge of the door to gain access to the handle locking screw **(see illustrations)**.

4 Pull the exterior door handle outwards and hold it in that position. With the exterior door handle held in the open position, turn the handle locking screw anti-clockwise until it reaches its stop **(see illustration)**. The exterior door handle should now be fixed in the open position.

5 Withdraw the fixed part of the handle,

13.3a Remove the screw (arrowed) from the rear edge of the door ...

13.3b ... to gain access to the handle locking screw (arrowed)

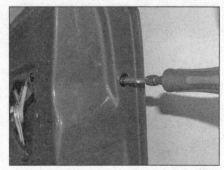

13.4 With the exterior door handle held open, turn the handle locking screw anti-clockwise until it reaches its stop

13.5 Withdraw the fixed part of the handle, containing the lock cylinder, from the door

13.6 Disengage the exterior handle front pivot from the frame and remove the handle from the door

13.12a Prise out the blanking cap from the rear edge of the door ...

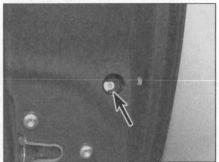

13.12b ... to gain access to the handle locking screw (arrowed)

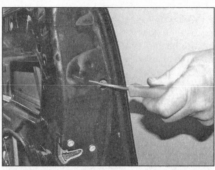

13.13 With the exterior door handle held open, turn the handle locking screw anti-clockwise until it reaches its stop

the handle locking screw anti-clockwise until it reaches its stop **(see illustration)**. The exterior door handle should now be fixed in the open position.

14 Withdraw the fixed part of the handle from the door **(see illustration)**.

15 Slide the exterior door handle to the rear, disengage the front pivot from the handle frame and remove the handle from the door **(see illustration)**.

Refitting

16 Engage the handle front pivot with the frame and move the handle back into position.

17 Refit the fixed part of the handle to the door.

18 Hold the exterior handle and turn the handle locking screw clockwise to retain the handle.

19 Check the operation of the handle then refit the blanking cap to the edge of the door.

containing the lock cylinder, from the door **(see illustration)**.

6 Slide the exterior door handle to the rear, disengage the front pivot from the handle frame and remove the handle from the door **(see illustration)**.

Refitting

7 Engage the handle front pivot with the frame and move the handle back into position.

8 Refit the fixed part of the handle with the lock cylinder to the door.

9 Hold the exterior handle and turn the handle locking screw clockwise to retain the handle.

10 Check the operation of the handle then refit the cover screw to the edge of the door.

11 On vehicles with the Open and Start system, reconnect the wiring connector then refit the door inner trim panel as described in Section 12.

Rear door exterior handle

Removal

12 Open the door and carefully prise out the blanking cap from the rear edge of the door to gain access to the handle locking screw **(see illustrations)**.

13 Pull the exterior door handle outwards and hold it in that position. With the exterior door handle held in the open position, turn

Front door lock cylinder

Removal

20 Remove the exterior handle as described previously in this Section.

21 Unclip the trim cap and remove the cap from the lock cylinder housing.

22 The lock cylinder body is an integral part of the housing and no further dismantling is possible.

Refitting

23 Refitting is a reversal of removal.

Front door exterior handle frame

Note: *A pop-rivet gun and suitable rivets will be required when refitting. The rivet heads should be approximately 4.8 mm in diameter and 11 mm in length.*

Removal

24 Disconnect the battery negative terminal (refer to Chapter 5A Section 4).

25 Remove the exterior handle as described previously in this Section.

26 Pull out the centre pin and remove the

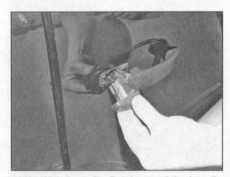

13.14 Withdraw the fixed part of the handle from the door

13.15 Disengage the exterior handle front pivot from the frame and remove the handle from the door

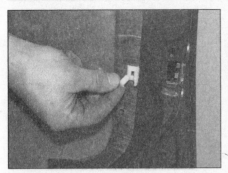

13.26 Pull out the centre pin and remove the inner trim panel plastic guides from the door panel

13.27 Release the clips (arrowed) securing the wiring harness to the door

13.28 Carefully peel back the protective plastic sheet

inner trim panel plastic guide from the door panel **(see illustration)**.

27 Release the two clips securing the wiring harness to the door **(see illustration)**.

28 Carefully peel back the protective plastic sheet and remove the sheet from the door **(see illustration)**.

29 Using an 8.5 mm drill bit, drill out the two rivets securing the window rear guide rail to the door, taking great care not to damage the door panel **(see illustrations)**.

30 Remove the guide rail through the door aperture.

31 Undo the two screws securing the security cover to the exterior handle frame and door lock, and remove the cover through the door aperture **(see illustrations)**.

32 Release the retaining clip and disconnect the lock operating rod from the lever

13.29a Drill out the upper rivet (arrowed) ...

13.29b ... and lower rivet (arrowed) securing the window rear guide rail to the door

on the exterior handle frame **(see illustration)**.

33 Slacken the exterior handle frame front retaining screw approximately five turns. Extract the rear guide clip, then slide the

handle frame forward to release the rear locating lugs. Disengage the lock cylinder operating rod and remove the frame through the door aperture **(see illustrations)**.

13.31a Undo the two screws (arrowed) securing the security cover to the exterior handle frame and door lock...

13.31b ... and remove the cover through the door aperture

13.32 Release the retaining clip (arrowed) and disconnect the lock operating rod from the lever on the exterior handle frame

13.33a Slacken the exterior handle frame front retaining screw approximately five turns ...

13.33b ... extract the rear guide clip, then slide the handle frame forward ...

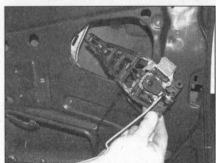

13.33c ... disengage the lock cylinder operating rod and remove the frame through the door aperture

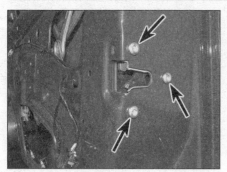

13.53 Undo the three screws (arrowed) securing the lock to the door

13.54 Disconnect the wiring connector, then remove the lock assembly through the upper door aperture

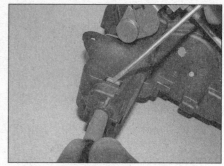

13.55a Release the locking clip and disconnect the outer cable ...

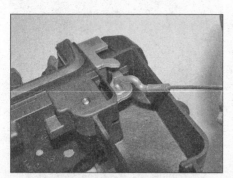

13.55b ... and inner cable from the lock

13.59 Release the retaining clip (arrowed) and disconnect the lock operating rod from the lever on the exterior handle frame

13.61 Withdraw the lock from its location, then lift the locking bar and disconnect the wiring connector

34 Clean out the remains of the old rivets from inside the door.

Refitting

35 Connect the lock cylinder operating rod, then place the exterior handle frame in position in the door. Refit the rear guide clip, then tighten the front retaining screw securely.

36 Engage the lock operating rod with the lever on the exterior handle frame and push the retaining clip back into position on the rod.

37 Refit the security cover and secure with the two screws.

38 Position the window guide rail in the door and secure the guide rail with new pop rivets.

39 Refit the protective plastic sheet to the door ensuring it is firmly stuck with no air bubbles. If the sheet was damaged during removal it should be renewed. This entails cutting a new sheet to the correct size and shape using the old sheet as a template. The new sheet can then be attached to the door with fresh adhesive.

40 Refit the wiring harness clips and inner trim panel plastic guides to the door, ensuring they are firmly attached.

41 Refit the door inner trim panel as described in Section 12.

42 Refit the exterior handle as described previously in this Section, then reconnect the battery negative terminal.

Rear door exterior handle frame

Removal

43 Disconnect the battery negative terminal (refer to Chapter 5A Section 4).

44 Remove the exterior handle as described previously in this Section.

45 Remove the door inner trim panel as described in Section 12.

46 Remove the rear door lock as described later in this Section.

47 Slacken the exterior handle frame front retaining screw approximately five turns. Extract the rear guide clip, then slide the handle frame forward to release the rear locating lugs. Disengage the lock cylinder operating rod and remove the frame through the door aperture (see illustrations 13.33a to 13.33c).

Refitting

48 Place the exterior handle frame in position in the door. Refit the rear guide clip, then tighten the front retaining screw securely.

49 Refit the rear door lock as described later in this Section.

50 Refit the door inner trim panel as described in Section 12.

51 Refit the exterior handle as described previously in this Section, then reconnect the battery negative terminal.

Front door lock

Removal

52 Remove the front door exterior handle frame as described earlier in this Section.

53 Undo the three screws securing the lock to the door (see illustration).

54 Withdraw the lock from its location, then lift the locking bar and disconnect the wiring connector. Remove the lock assembly through the upper door aperture (see illustration).

55 If required, disconnect the operating cables from the lock linkage and bracket (see illustrations).

Refitting

56 Refitting is a reversal of removal.

Rear door lock

Removal

57 Remove the door inner trim panel as described in Section 12.

58 Carefully peel back the protective plastic sheet and remove the sheet from the door (see illustration 13.28).

59 Release the retaining clip and disconnect the lock operating rod from the lever on the exterior handle frame (see illustration).

60 Undo the three screws securing the lock to the door (see illustration 13.53).

61 Withdraw the lock from its location, then lift the locking bar and disconnect the wiring connector (see illustration).

62 Remove the lock assembly through the door aperture.

63 If required, disconnect the operating cables from the lock linkage and bracket **(see illustration 13.55a and 13.55b).**

Refitting

64 If removed, reconnect the operating cables to the lock linkage and bracket.

65 Insert the lock assembly into the door and reconnect the wiring connector.

66 Position the lock assembly in its location, refit the three retaining screws and tighten securely.

67 Engage the lock operating rod with the lever on the exterior handle frame, and push the retaining clip back into position on the rod.

68 Refit the protective plastic sheet to the door ensuring it is firmly stuck with no air bubbles. If the sheet was damaged during removal it should be renewed. This entails cutting a new sheet to the correct size and shape using the old sheet as a template. The new sheet can then be attached to the door with fresh adhesive.

69 Refit the door inner trim panel as described in Section 12.

---

14 Door window glass and regulator – removal and refitting

Front door window glass

Note: *A pop-rivet gun and suitable rivets will be required when refitting. The rivet heads should be approximately 4.8 mm in diameter and 11 mm in length.*

Removal

1 Open the door window fully.

2 Remove the door inner trim panel as described in Section 12.

3 Pull out the centre pin and remove the inner trim panel plastic guide from the door panel **(see illustration 13.26).**

14.7 Tap up the door window inner waist seal from the door aperture, then lift the seal up and remove it from the door

4 Release the clips securing the wiring harness to the door **(see illustration 13.27).**

5 Carefully peel back the protective plastic sheet and remove the sheet from the door **(see illustration 13.28).**

6 Remove the exterior mirror as described in Section 17.

7 Using a plastic wedge or similar tool, starting from the rear, tap up the door window inner waist seal from the door aperture. Lift the seal up and remove it from the door **(see illustration).**

8 Similarly, tap up the door window outer waist seal from the door aperture. Lift the seal up and remove it from the door **(see illustration).**

9 Using an 8.5 mm drill bit, drill out the two rivets securing the window rear guide rail to the door, taking great care not to damage the door panel. Remove the guide rail through the door aperture **(see illustration 13.29a and 13.29b).**

10 Undo the two bolts securing the window glass lower frame to the regulator front lifting arm **(see illustration).**

11 Disengage the window glass lower frame from the regulator rear lifting arm and lift the glass up and out of the door **(see illustration).**

14.8 Similarly, tap up the outer waist seal and remove it from the door

12 Clean out the remains of the old rivets from inside the door.

Refitting

13 Carefully lower the window glass into the door and engage the lower frame with the regulator rear lifting arm.

14 Locate the regulator front lifting arm over the window glass lower frame, refit the two retaining bolts and tighten securely.

15 Refit the window rear guide rail to the door and secure the guide rail with new pop rivets.

16 Refit the window inner and outer waist seals to the door aperture, ensuring that the retaining clips securely engage.

17 Refit the exterior mirror as described in Section 17.

18 Refit the protective plastic sheet to the door ensuring it is firmly stuck with no air bubbles. If the sheet was damaged during removal it should be renewed. This entails cutting a new sheet to the correct size and shape using the old sheet as a template. The new sheet can then be attached to the door with fresh adhesive.

19 Refit the inner trim panel plastic guides and the wiring harness retaining clips.

20 Refit the door inner trim panel as described in Section 12.

14.10 Undo the two bolts (arrowed) securing the window glass lower frame to the regulator front lifting arm

14.11 Disengage the window glass lower frame from the regulator rear lifting arm (arrowed)

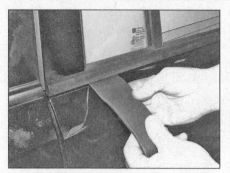

14.26a Using a plastic wedge or similar tool, starting from the rear, lift up the door window outer waist seal …

14.26b … and remove the seal from the door

14.27 Similarly remove the door window inner waist seal from the door aperture

14.28 Carefully pull away the window guide channel from the rear guide rail

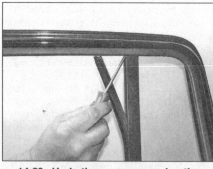

14.29a Undo the screws securing the upper …

Rear door window glass

Removal

21 Open the door window fully.

22 Remove the door inner trim panel as described in Section 12.

23 On models with manual window regulators, remove the rubber seal from the regulator shaft.

24 On models with electric window regulators, release the clips securing the wiring harness to the door.

25 Carefully peel back the protective plastic sheet and remove the sheet from the door (see illustration 13.28).

26 Using a plastic wedge or similar tool, starting from the rear, tap up the door window outer waist seal from the door aperture. Lift the seal up and remove it from the door (see illustrations).

27 Similarly, tap up the door window inner waist seal from the door aperture. Lift the seal up and remove it from the door (see illustration).

28 Carefully pull away the window guide channel from the rear guide rail (see illustration).

29 Undo the screws securing the upper and lower ends of the window rear guide rail to the door, then remove the guide rail (see illustrations).

30 Remove the fixed window glass from the door (see illustration).

31 Disengage the window glass lower frame from the regulator lifting arm and lift the glass up and out of the door (see illustrations).

14.29b … and lower ends of the window rear guide rail to the door …

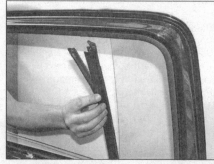

14.29c … then remove the guide rail

14.30 Remove the fixed window glass from the door

14.31a Disengage the window glass lower frame from the regulator lifting arm (arrowed) …

14.31b … and lift the glass up and out of the door

14.42 Disconnect the wiring connector from the window regulator motor

14.43a Front door window regulator securing rivets (arrowed) …

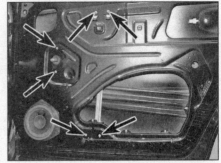

14.43b … and rear door window regulator securing rivets (arrowed)

Refitting

32 Carefully lower the window glass into the door and engage the lower frame with the regulator lifting arms.

33 Locate the fixed window glass in the guide channel.

34 Refit the window rear guide rail to the door and secure the guide rail with the three screws.

35 Refit the window inner and outer waist seals to the door aperture, ensuring that the retaining clips securely engage.

36 Refit the protective plastic sheet to the door ensuring it is firmly stuck with no air bubbles. If the sheet was damaged during removal it should be renewed. This entails cutting a new sheet to the correct size and shape using the old sheet as a template. The new sheet can then be attached to the door with fresh adhesive.

37 Refit the wiring harness retaining clips or regulator shaft rubber seal, as applicable.

38 Refit the door inner trim panel as described in Section 12.

Rear door fixed window glass

Removal

39 Carry out the operations described previously in paragraphs 21 to 30.

Refitting

40 Carry out the operations described in paragraphs 33 to 38.

Window regulator

Note: *A pop-rivet gun and suitable rivets will be required when refitting. The rivet heads should be approximately 4.8 mm in diameter and 11 mm in length.*

Removal

41 Remove the front or rear door window glass as described previously in this Section.

42 Where applicable, disconnect the wiring connector from the window regulator motor **(see illustration)**.

43 Using an 8.5 mm drill bit, drill out the rivets securing the window regulator to the door, taking great care not to damage the door panel. Five rivets are used to secure the rear window regulator on models with electric windows. On all other regulators, six rivets are used **(see illustrations)**.

44 Remove the regulator through the door aperture.

45 Clean out the remains of the old rivets from inside the door.

Refitting

46 Refit the regulator to the door and secure the regulator with new pop rivets.

47 Reconnect the regulator wiring connector, where applicable.

48 Refit the front or rear door window glass as described previously in this Section.

15.1 Carefully prise free the upper inner tailgate trim panel

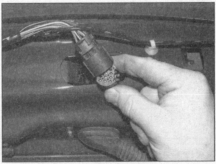

15.2a Disconnect the tailgate main wiring harness connector …

15.3 Pull the tailgate washer jet out of its grommet and disconnect the washer hose

15 Tailgate and support struts
– removal, refitting and adjustment

Tailgate

Removal

1 Open the tailgate and carefully prise free the upper inner tailgate trim panel to release the four retaining clips **(see illustration)**.

2 Disconnect the tailgate main wiring harness connector, then release the grommet and pull the wiring connector out of the tailgate **(see illustrations)**.

3 Pull the tailgate washer jet out of its grommet and disconnect the washer hose from the jet **(see illustration)**. Pull the hose out of the tailgate.

4 Have an assistant support the tailgate, then disconnect the tops of the support struts by prising out the spring clips with a small

15.2b … then release the grommet and pull the wiring connector out of the tailgate

15.4 Prise the spring clip from the top of the support struts and disconnect them from the tailgate

15.5 Extract the clips (arrowed) and carefully drive out the hinge pins, from outside to inside

screwdriver **(see illustration)**. Lower the struts to the body.

5 Extract the clips and carefully drive out the hinge pins, from outside to inside, using a small drift, while the assistant supports the tailgate **(see illustration)**. Withdraw the tailgate from the body.

Refitting

6 Refitting is a reversal of removal, but apply a little grease to the pivots, and check that when closed the tailgate is positioned centrally within the body aperture and flush with the surrounding bodywork. If necessary, adjust the position of the rubber supports so that the tailgate is flush with the surrounding bodywork. After making adjustments, check

that the striker enters the lock centrally and if necessary loosen the striker bolts to reposition it. Tighten the bolts on completion.

Support struts

Removal

7 Open the tailgate and note which way round the struts are fitted. Have an assistant support the tailgate in its open position.

8 Using a small screwdriver, prise the spring clip from the top of the strut and disconnect it from the ball on the tailgate **(see illustration 15.4)**.

9 Similarly prise the spring clip from the bottom of the strut and disconnect it from the ball on the body. Withdraw the strut.

Refitting

10 Refitting is a reversal of removal.

16 Tailgate lock components – removal and refitting

Tailgate lock

Removal

1 Undo the three screws and remove the lock cover panel from the base of the tailgate **(see illustrations)**.

2 Undo the two screws securing the lower trim panel to the tailgate. Pull the lower trim panel away from the tailgate to release the ten internal clips and remove the panel from the tailgate **(see illustrations)**.

3 Undo the three lock assembly retaining screws **(see illustration)**.

4 Withdraw the lock through the tailgate aperture and disconnect the wiring connector **(see illustration)**.

Refitting

5 Refitting is a reversal of removal.

Tailgate exterior handle

Removal

6 Carry out the operations described previously in paragraphs 1 and 2.

7 Lift off the rubber covers from the tailgate

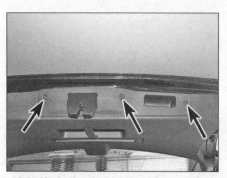

16.1a Undo the three screws (arrowed) ...

16.1b ... and remove the lock cover panel from the base of the tailgate

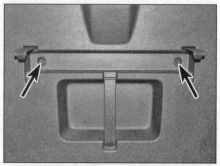

16.2a Undo the two screws (arrowed) securing the lower trim panel to the tailgate ...

16.2b ... then pull the panel away from the tailgate to release the remaining internal clips

16.3 Undo the three lock assembly retaining screws (arrowed)

16.4 Withdraw the lock through the tailgate aperture and disconnect the wiring connector

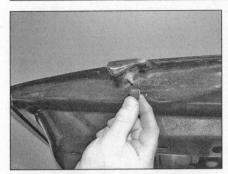

16.7 Lift off the rubber covers from the tailgate trim strip outer retaining nuts and unscrew the nut each side

16.8 Tailgate trim strip inner retaining nuts on the right-hand side

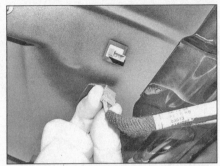

16.9 Disconnect the wiring connector and remove the trim strip from the tailgate

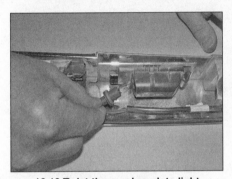

16.10 Twist the number plate light bulbholders and remove them from the two light units

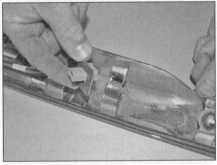

16.11 Detach the main wiring connector from the support bracket on the trim strip

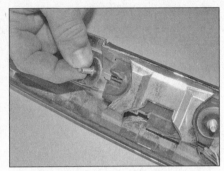

16.12 Unclip the two trim strip mounting studs from the exterior handle

trim strip outer retaining nuts and unscrew the nut each side **(see illustration)**.

8 Unscrew the remaining nuts securing the trim strip to the tailgate **(see illustration)**.

9 Disconnect the wiring connector and remove the trim strip from the tailgate **(see illustration)**.

10 Twist the number plate light bulbholders and remove them from the two light units **(see illustration)**.

11 Detach the main wiring connector from the support bracket on the trim strip **(see illustration)**.

12 Unclip the two trim strip mounting studs from the rear of the exterior handle **(see illustration)**.

13 Carefully prise the exterior handle from its

location, then withdraw the handle, complete with wiring harness, from the trim strip **(see illustrations)**.

Refitting

14 Refitting is a reversal of removal.

17 Exterior mirrors and associated components – removal and refitting

Exterior mirror

Removal

1 Remove the door inner trim panel as described in Section 12.

2 Release the clips securing the wiring harness to the door **(see illustration 13.27)**.

3 Carefully peel back the protective plastic sheet in the vicinity of the mirror wiring harness connector.

4 Disconnect the mirror wiring harness connector and release the harness rubber grommet from the door. As an aid to refitting, attach a length of string or wire to the wiring connector, to enable the connector and harness to be drawn back into position when refitting.

5 Prise out the two grommets in the door frame for access to the upper and lower mirror mounting bolts **(see illustration)**.

6 Unscrew the two mirror mounting bolts and withdraw the mirror and wiring harness from

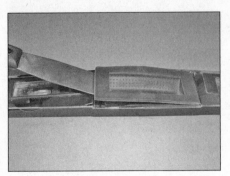

16.13a Carefully prise the exterior handle from its location ...

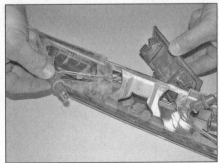

16.13b ... then withdraw the handle, complete with wiring harness, from the trim strip

17.5 Prise out the two grommets for access to the exterior mirror mounting bolts

17.6a Unscrew the two mirror mounting bolts (arrowed) ...

17.6b ... and withdraw the mirror and wiring harness from the door

17.9 Using a plastic wedge, prise the outer edge of the glass outwards to release the internal retaining clips

the door **(see illustrations)**. When the wiring connector is clear of the door frame, detach the string or wire from the connector and leave it in position for refitting.

Refitting

7 Refitting is a reversal of removal.

Mirror glass

Removal

8 Push in the upper inner (nearest the door) corner of the glass so that the lower outer corner of the glass is forced out from the centre.

9 Using a plastic wedge, prise the outer edge of the glass outwards to release the internal retaining clips **(see illustration)**.

10 Withdraw the mirror glass and, where applicable, disconnect the wiring connectors **(see illustration)**.

Refitting

11 Refitting is a reversal of removal. Carefully press the mirror glass into the housing until the centre retainer clips are engaged.

Outer cover

Removal

12 Carefully prise the upper edge of the outer cover away from the mirror body to release the four upper clips.

13 Unhook the lower clips and remove the outer cover from the mirror body.

Refitting

14 Refitting is a reversal of removal.

18 Windscreen and fixed window glass – general information

Note: *The rear door fixed window glass is covered in Section 14.*

1 The windscreen, tailgate and quarter window glasses are cemented in position with a special adhesive and require the use of specialist equipment for their removal and refitting. Renewal of such fixed glass is considered beyond the scope of the home mechanic. Owners are strongly advised to have the work carried out by one of the many specialist windscreen fitting specialists.

19 Sunroof – general information

1 An electric sunroof was offered as an optional extra on most models, and is fitted as standard equipment on some models.

2 Due to the complexity of the sunroof mechanism, considerable expertise is needed to repair, renew or adjust the sunroof components successfully. Removal of the roof first requires the headlining to be removed, which is a complex and tedious operation in

itself, and not a task to be undertaken lightly. Therefore, any problems with the sunroof should be referred to a Vauxhall/Opel dealer.

20 Body exterior fittings – removal and refitting

Radiator grille

1 Unscrew and remove the three Torx screws securing the upper edge of the radiator grille to the body panel **(see illustration)**.

2 Disengage the eight lower lugs and remove the radiator grille from the car **(see illustration)**.

Wheel arch liners and body under-panels

3 The various plastic covers fitted to the underside of the vehicle are secured in position by a mixture of screws, nuts and retaining clips, and removal will be fairly obvious on inspection. Work methodically around the liner/panel, removing its retaining screws and releasing its retaining clips until it is free to be removed from the underside of the vehicle. Most clips used on the vehicle, with the exception of the fasteners which are used to secure the wheel arch liners, are simply prised out of position. The wheel arch liner clips are released by tapping their centre pins through the clip, and then removing the outer section of

17.10 Withdraw the mirror glass and, where applicable, disconnect the wiring connectors (arrowed)

20.1 Unscrew and remove the three Torx screws

20.2 Pull the grille upwards to release the lower lugs

20.6 Pull up the rubber weatherseal from the flange at the rear of the engine compartment

20.7 Lift up the cowl centre panel to release it from the side panels and from the base of the windscreen

20.9a Extract the retaining clip each side ...

20.9b ... and remove the cowl left-hand and right-hand side panels

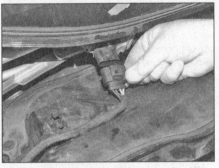

20.10a Disconnect the windscreen wiper motor wiring connector ...

20.10b ... and release the wiring harness from the clip on the cowl base panel

the clip; new clips will be required on refitting if the centre pins are not recovered.

4 When refitting, renew any retaining clips that may have been broken on removal, and ensure that the panel is securely retained by all the relevant clips, nuts and screws. Vauxhall/Opel also recommend that plastic nuts (where used) are renewed, regardless of their apparent condition, whenever they are disturbed.

Windscreen cowl panel

5 Remove the windscreen wiper arms as described in Chapter 12 Section 12.

6 Open the bonnet, and pull up the rubber weatherseal from the flange at the rear of the engine compartment **(see illustration)**.

7 Lift up the cowl centre panel to release it from the side panels and from the base of the windscreen **(see illustration)**.

8 Disconnect the windscreen washer hose and remove the cowl centre panel from the car.

9 Extract the retaining clip each side, and remove the cowl left-hand and right-hand side panels **(see illustrations)**.

10 Disconnect the windscreen wiper motor wiring connector and release the wiring harness from the clip on the cowl base panel **(see illustration)**.

11 Unclip the bonnet release cable and, where applicable, the air quality sensor from the cowl base panel **(see illustration)**.

12 Undo the two bolts each side and remove

the base panel from the engine compartment **(see illustrations)**.

13 Refit the windscreen cowl panel using a reversal of the removal procedure. Refit the wiper arms as described in Chapter 12 Section 12.

Body trim strips and badges

14 The various body trim strips and badges are held in position with a special adhesive tape. Removal requires the trim/badge to be heated, to soften the adhesive, and then cut away from the surface. Due to the high risk of damage to the vehicle's paintwork during this operation, it is recommended that this task should be entrusted to a Vauxhall/Opel dealer.

20.11 Unclip the bonnet release cable from the cowl base panel

20.12a Undo the two bolts (arrowed) on each side ...

20.12b ... and remove the base panel from the engine compartment

21.3 Unclip the cover over the seat belt mounting

21.4 Undo the seat belt retaining bolt (arrowed)

21.5 Front seat left-hand rear retaining bolt (arrowed) ...

21 Seats – removal and refitting

⚠️ **Warning: The front seats are equipped with seat belt tensioners, and side airbags may be built into the outer sides of the seats. The seat belt tensioners and side airbags may cause injury if triggered accidentally. If the tensioner has been triggered due to a sudden impact or accident, the unit must be renewed, as it cannot be reset. If a seat is to be disposed of, the tensioner must be triggered before the seat is removed from the vehicle. Due to safety considerations, tensioner renewal or seat disposal must be entrusted to a Vauxhall/Opel dealer. Where side airbags are fitted, refer to Chapter 12 Section 22 for the precautions which should be observed when dealing with an airbag system.**

1 Disconnect the battery negative terminal (refer to Chapter 5A Section 4). Wait 2 minutes for any residual energy to dissipate, before working on the seat electrics.

Front seat removal

2 Slide the seat adjustment fully forward.
3 Unclip the cover over the seat belt mounting, by releasing it at the rear then disengaging the front locating tabs (see illustration).

4 Undo the seat belt retaining bolt (see illustration).
5 Slacken and remove the seat retaining bolts from the rear of the guide rails (see illustration).
6 Slide the seat adjustment fully rearward, then slacken and remove the seat retaining bolts from the front of the guide rails (see illustration).
7 Pull out the locking bar and disconnect the wiring connector from the underside of the seat, then remove the seat from the car.

Rear seat removal

2nd row

8 Working on one side at a time, undo the retaining screw and remove the seat cushion release handle (see illustration).
9 Push the seat adjustment handle forward, depress the retaining catch with a small screwdriver, and pull the handle up and off the adjustment lever (see illustration).
10 Using a small screwdriver, push in the centre pin and remove the two plastic rivets at the rear of the seat adjuster trim panel (see illustration).
11 Unclip the seat adjuster trim panel and remove it from the seat frame (see illustration).
12 Repeat the operations described in paragraphs 8 to 11 to remove the seat adjuster trim panel on the other side.
13 Move the seat as far forward as possible to release the centre guide.

21.6 ... and left-hand front retaining bolt (arrowed)

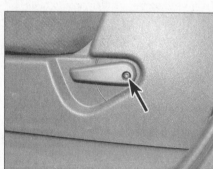

21.8 Undo the retaining screw (arrowed) and remove the seat cushion release handle

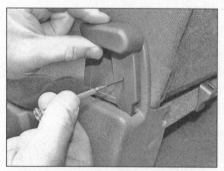

21.9 Depress the retaining catch with a small screwdriver, and pull the handle up and off the adjustment lever

21.10 Push in the centre pins and remove the two plastic rivets at the rear of the seat adjuster trim panel

21.11 Unclip the seat adjuster trim panel and remove it from the seat frame

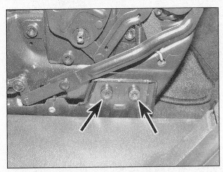

21.14a Undo the two rear bolts (arrowed) …

21.14b … and two front bolts (arrowed) each side securing the seat frame to the sliding rail

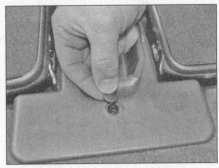

21.20a Extract the screw caps …

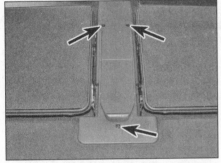

21.20b … and undo the three seat guide cover retaining screws (arrowed)

21.21a Undo the retaining bolt (arrowed) and remove the seat belt buckle …

21.21b … then lift off the seat guide cover

14 Undo the four bolts each side securing the seat frame to the sliding rail **(see illustrations)**.
15 Engage the help of an assistant and remove the seat from the car.
16 If required, the seat cushion and backrest can be removed from the seat frame after undoing the mounting bolts.

3rd row

17 Remove the centre luggage compartment cover.
18 Move the 2nd row seat bench as far forward as possible.
19 Remove the luggage compartment carpet.
20 Extract the screw caps and undo the three seat guide cover retaining screws **(see illustrations)**.
21 Undo the retaining bolt and remove the seat belt buckle, then lift off the seat guide cover **(see illustration)**.

21.22a Unclip the front trim cover …

22 Unclip the front and rear trim covers from the seat side rail on the seat to be removed **(see illustrations)**.
23 Undo the bolt securing the seat belt lower mounting to the seat side rail **(see illustration)**.

21.22b … and rear trim cover from the seat side rail

24 Undo the two seat side rail inner mounting bolts and the two outer mounting bolts **(see illustrations)**. Engage the help of an assistant and remove the seat from the car.
25 If required the backrest can be separated

21.23 Undo the bolt (arrowed) securing the seat belt lower mounting to the seat side rail

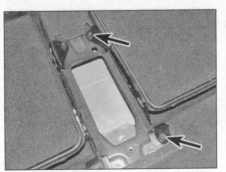

21.24a Undo the two seat side rail inner mounting bolts (arrowed) …

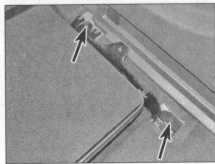

21.24b … and the two outer mounting bolts (arrowed)

from the seat cushion by undoing the two hinge retaining bolts, and driving out the centre connecting rod.

Front seat refitting

26 Refitting is a reverse of the removal procedure, noting the following points:
a) *Remove all traces of old thread-locking compound from the threads of the seat retaining bolts, and clean the threaded holes in the vehicle floor, ideally by running a tap of the correct size and pitch down them.*
b) *Apply a suitable thread-locking compound to the threads of the seat bolts. Refit the bolts, and tighten them to the specified torque setting.*
c) *Reconnect the seat wiring connector making sure it has locked securely, then reconnect the battery negative terminal.*

Rear seat refitting

27 Refitting is a reverse of the removal procedure.

22 Seat belt tensioning mechanism – general information

1 All models covered in this manual are fitted with a front seat belt pyrotechnic tensioner system. The system is designed to instantaneously take up any slack in the seat belt in the case of a sudden frontal impact, therefore reducing the possibility of injury to the front seat occupants. Each front seat is fitted with its own system, the components of which are mounted on the seat frame.
2 The seat belt tensioner is triggered by a frontal impact causing a deceleration of six times the force of gravity or greater. Lesser impacts, including impacts from behind, will not trigger the system.
3 When the system is triggered, a pretensioned spring draws back the seat belt via a cable which acts on the seat belt stalk. The cable can move by up to 80.0 mm, which therefore reduces the slack in the seat

23.4 Front seat belt upper mounting bolt

belt around the shoulders and waist of the occupant by a similar amount.
4 There is a risk of injury if the system is triggered inadvertently when working on the vehicle, and it is therefore strongly recommended that any work involving the seat belt tensioner system is entrusted to a Vauxhall/Opel dealer. Refer to the warning given at the beginning of Section 23 before contemplating any work on the front seats.

23 Seat belt components – removal and refitting

⚠ *Warning: The front seats are fitted with pyrotechnic seat belt tensioners which are triggered by the airbag control system.*
Before removing a seat belt, disconnect the battery (Chapter 5A Section 4) and wait at least 2 minutes to allow the system capacitors to discharge.

Front seat

Belt and inertia reel

1 Unclip the cover over the seat belt mounting on the front seat, by releasing it at the rear, then disengaging the front locating tabs (see illustration 21.3).

2 Undo the seat belt retaining bolt (see illustration 21.4).
3 Remove the B-pillar upper and lower trim panels as described in Section 24.
4 Undo the seat belt upper mounting bolt (see illustration).
5 Prise the cover from the lower outside of the B-pillar for access to the front seat belt reel mounting nut (see illustrations). Using a 13 mm socket, 65 mm deep on the inside, unscrew the nut taking care not to drop it inside the B-pillar. Note that an extension pin is provided to enable the nut to be removed safely.
6 With the nut removed, remove the reel from the inside of the pillar.
7 Refitting is a reversal of removal, but tighten the mounting bolts to the specified torque.

Belt stalk and tensioner

8 Remove the front seat as described in Section 21.
9 From underneath the seat, slide out the wiring connector locking bar and disconnect the wiring connector. Unclip the wiring harness from the seat.
10 Undo the retaining bolt and withdraw the tensioner from the seat (see illustration).
11 Release the cable retaining clip (where fitted) and remove the tensioner.
12 Refitting is a reverse of the removal procedure, noting the following points:
a) *Remove all traces of old thread-locking compound from the thread of the tensioner retaining bolt, and clean the threaded hole in the seat, ideally by running a tap of the correct size and pitch down it.*
b) *Apply a suitable thread-locking compound to the thread of the tensioner retaining bolt. Refit the bolt, and tighten it to the specified torque setting.*

2nd row rear seat

Outer belt and inertia reel

13 Remove the relevant luggage compartment side trim panel as described in Section 24.
14 Undo the two bolts and remove the seat belt guide from the C-pillar.

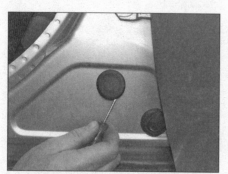

23.5a Prise the cover from the lower outside of the B-pillar ...

23.5b ... for access to the front seat belt reel mounting nut

23.10 Undo the retaining bolt (arrowed) and withdraw the tensioner from the seat

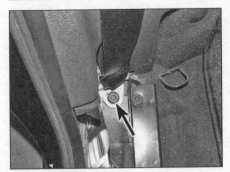

23.15 2nd row rear seat belt lower mounting bolt (arrowed)

23.16a 2nd row rear seat belt upper mounting bolt ...

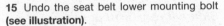

23.16b ... and inertia reel mounting bolt (arrowed)

15 Undo the seat belt lower mounting bolt (see illustration).

16 Undo the seat belt upper mounting bolt and the inertia reel mounting bolt and remove the reel and belt from the car (see illustrations).

17 Refitting is a reversal of removal, but tighten the mounting bolts to the specified torque.

Centre belt and inertia reel

18 The inertia reel for the centre rear seat belt is located internally within the 2nd row rear seat backrest. To gain access, the backrest must be removed and completely dismantled. This is a complex operation and considerable expertise is needed to remove and refit the seat upholstery and internal components without damage. Therefore, any problems with the centre seat belt and reel should be referred to a Vauxhall/Opel dealer.

Belt buckle

19 Lift up the rear seat cushion, undo the two mounting bolts each side and the centre bolt, and remove the cushion.

20 Position the seat backrest as necessary for access to the buckle retaining bolts. Undo the retaining bolt and remove the relevant buckle from the seat frame.

21 Refitting is a reversal of removal, but tighten the mounting bolts to the specified torque.

3rd row rear seat

Belt and inertia reel

22 Remove the relevant D-pillar trim panel as described in Section 24.

23 Remove the storage compartment cover from the luggage compartment side trim panel. Where applicable, remove the tyre repair kit and foam mounting box for access to the inertia reel.

24 Undo the seat belt upper mounting bolt and the inertia reel mounting bolt and remove the reel and belt out through the storage compartment aperture (see illustrations).

25 Refitting is a reversal of removal, but tighten the mounting bolts to the specified torque.

23.24a 3rd row rear seat belt upper mounting bolt ...

Belt buckle

26 Open the seat guide cover flap, undo the retaining bolt and remove the seat belt buckle (see illustration 21.21a).

27 Refitting is a reversal of removal, but tighten the retaining bolt to the specified torque.

24 Interior trim – removal and refitting

1 The interior trim panels are secured by a combination of clips and screws. Removal and refitting is generally self-explanatory, noting that it may be necessary to remove or loosen surrounding panels to allow a particular panel to be removed. The following

23.24b ... and inertia reel mounting bolt (arrowed)

paragraphs describe the general removal and refitting details of the major panels.

Door inner trim panel

2 Refer to Section 12.

A-pillar trim panel

3 Pull off the front door weather strip in the vicinity of the A-pillar trim panel.

4 Pull out the airbag positioning clip from the trim panel (see illustration).

5 Pull the trim panel away from the A-pillar and remove it from the car (see illustration).

6 Refitting is a reversal of removal.

B-pillar upper trim panel

7 Unclip the cover over the seat belt mounting on the front seat, by releasing it at the rear, then disengaging the front locating tabs (see illustration 21.3).

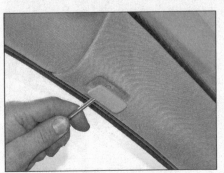

24.4 Pull out the airbag positioning clip from the trim panel

24.5 Pull the trim panel away from the A-pillar and remove it from the car

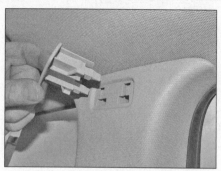

24.9 Prise out the plastic cover at the top of the panel

24.11 Unclip the upper trim panel from the B-pillar

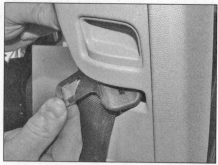

24.12 Feed the seat belt through the opening and remove the panel from the car

8 Undo the seat belt retaining bolt (**see illustration 21.4**).

9 Prise out the plastic cover at the top of the panel (**see illustration**).

10 Unclip the upper area of the B-pillar lower trim panel.

11 Unclip the upper trim panel from the B-pillar (**see illustration**).

12 Feed the seat belt through the opening and remove the panel from the car (**see illustration**).

13 Refitting is a reversal of removal, but tighten the seat belt retaining bolt to the specified torque.

B-pillar lower trim panel

14 Release the three clips and remove the storage compartment adjacent to the front seat (**see illustration**).

15 Remove the side sill rear trim panel as described later in this Section.

16 Release the two upper retaining clips and remove the B-pillar lower trim panel (**see illustration**).

17 Refitting is a reversal of removal.

Side sill front trim panel

18 Release the three clips and remove the storage compartment adjacent to the front seat (**see illustration 24.14**).

19 Lift the panel upwards to unclip it from the sill and remove the panel from the car (**see illustration**).

20 Refitting is a reversal of removal.

Side sill rear trim panel

21 Undo the retaining screw and remove the 2nd row rear seat cushion release handle (**see illustration 21.8**).

22 Push the seat adjustment handle forward, depress the retaining catch with a small screwdriver, and pull the handle up and off the adjustment lever (**see illustration 21.9**).

23 Using a small screwdriver, push in the centre pin and remove the two plastic rivets at the rear of the seat adjuster trim panel (**see illustration 21.10**).

24 Unclip the seat adjuster trim panel and remove it from the seat frame (**see illustration 21.11**).

25 Release the five retaining clips and remove the side sill rear trim panel (**see illustration**).

Tailgate aperture

Upper centre trim panel

26 Open the tailgate.

27 Pull the panel away to release the five internal clips, and remove the panel from the car (**see illustration**).

28 Refitting is a reversal of removal.

Lower centre trim panel

29 Open the tailgate.

30 Remove the luggage compartment floor covering.

24.14 Release the three clips and remove the storage compartment adjacent to the front seat

24.16 Release the two upper retaining clips and remove the B-pillar lower trim panel

24.19 Lift the side sill front trim panel upwards to unclip it from the sill

24.25 Release the five retaining clips and remove the side sill rear trim panel

24.27 Pull the tailgate aperture upper centre trim panel away to release the five internal clips

24.31 Undo the turnbuckle and remove the rear storage compartment cover

24.32 Undo the two tailgate aperture lower centre trim panel retaining screws

24.33 Pull the panel away to release the internal clips, and remove the panel from the car

31 Undo the turnbuckle and remove the rear storage compartment cover **(see illustration)**.
32 Undo the two panel retaining screws **(see illustration)**.
33 Pull the panel away to release the internal clips, and remove the panel from the car **(see illustration)**.
34 Refitting is a reversal of removal.

C-pillar trim panel

35 Remove the side sill rear trim panel as described previously.
36 Remove the D-pillar trim panel as described later in this Section.
37 Undo the seat belt lower mounting bolt **(see illustration 23.15)**.
38 Prise out the plastic cover at the top of the panel **(see illustration)**.

39 Unclip the upper area of the C-pillar trim panel and disengage its lower end from the luggage compartment side trim panel **(see illustration)**.
40 Feed the seat belt through the opening and remove the panel from the car.
41 Refitting is a reversal of removal, but tighten the seat belt retaining bolt to the specified torque.

D-pillar trim panel

42 Remove the tailgate aperture upper centre trim panel as described previously.
43 Undo the 3rd row rear seat belt lower mounting bolt.
44 Pull the panel away from the C- and D-pillars and roof to release the internal clips

(see illustrations). Feed the seat belt through the opening and remove the panel from the car.
45 Refitting is a reversal of removal.

Luggage area side trim panel

46 Remove the luggage compartment floor covering.
47 Remove the C-pillar trim panel as described previously.
48 Remove the tailgate aperture lower centre trim panel as described previously.
49 Undo the upper and lower screws securing the panel to the D-pillar **(see illustrations)**. On some models, there may be an additional D-pillar retaining screw located in the storage compartment aperture.

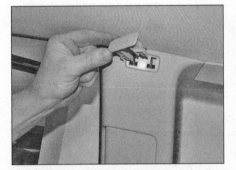

24.38 Prise out the plastic cover at the top of the C-pillar trim panel

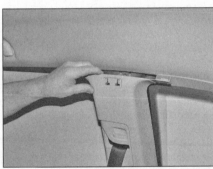

24.39 Unclip the upper area of the C-pillar trim panel

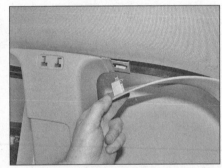

24.44a Pull the D-pillar trim panel away from the C-pillar ...

24.44b ... D-pillar and roof to release the internal clips

24.49a Undo the upper retaining screw ...

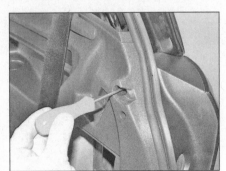

24.49b ... and lower retaining screw securing the luggage compartment side trim panel to the D-pillar

24.50 Undo the upper front retaining screw, adjacent to the C-pillar

24.51a Using a forked tool, prise out the two upper ...

24.51b ... and two lower panel retaining plates

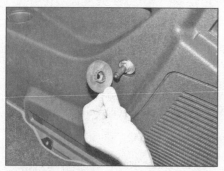

24.52 Remove the cover from the seat locking stud bolt

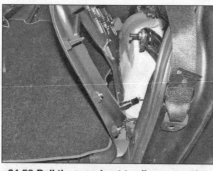

24.53 Pull the panel out to disengage the retaining clips and release the panel from the pillar

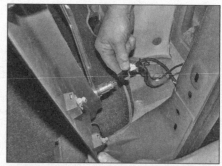

24.54a Where applicable, disconnect the wiring at the accessory socket ...

50 Undo the upper front retaining screw, adjacent to the C-pillar **(see illustration)**.

51 Using a forked tool, prise out the two upper and two lower panel retaining plates **(see illustrations)**.

52 Remove the cover from the seat locking stud bolt **(see illustration)**.

53 Pull the panel out to disengage the retaining clips and release the panel from the pillar **(see illustration)**.

54 Where applicable, disconnect the wiring at the accessory socket, then remove the panel from the car **(see illustrations)**.

55 Refitting is a reversal of removal.

Tailgate trim panels

56 Undo the three screws and remove the

lock cover panel from the base of the tailgate **(see illustrations 16.1a and 16.1b)**.

57 Undo the two screws securing the lower trim panel to the tailgate. Pull the lower trim panel away from the tailgate to release the ten internal clips and remove the panel from the tailgate **(see illustrations 16.2a and 16.2b)**.

58 Carefully prise free the upper inner tailgate trim panel to release the four retaining clips **(see illustration 15.1)**.

59 Undo the retaining screw each side, then carefully prise free the upper side trim panels **(see illustrations)**.

60 Refitting is a reversal of removal.

Interior mirror

61 On models fitted with a rain sensor,

unclip and remove the sensor trim panel, then release the retaining clip(s) and disconnect the wiring connectors from the mirror assembly.

62 Press the retaining clip at the top of the interior mirror mounting bracket, then carefully release the interior mirror in the downwards direction to remove it from the windscreen.

63 Refitting is the reverse of removal.

25 Centre console – removal and refitting

Removal

1 Disconnect the battery negative terminal (refer to Chapter 5A Section 4).

24.54b ... then remove the panel from the car

24.59a Undo the retaining screw each side (arrowed) ...

24.59b ... then carefully prise free the upper side trim panels

25.2 Apply the handbrake fully, then unclip and remove the centre console front panel

25.3 Remove the stowage box by pulling it outward at the bottom to release the retaining clips

25.4a Undo the two screws at the rear (arrowed) ...

2 Apply the handbrake fully, then unclip and remove the console front panel (see illustration).

3 At the rear of the console, remove the stowage box by pulling it outward at the bottom to release the retaining clips (see illustration). Where applicable, disconnect the wiring connectors at the rear of the panel.

4 Undo the two screws at the rear and two screws at the front securing the console to the mounting bracket (see illustrations).

5 Disconnect the wiring harness connectors at the front of the console, and remove the console from the car (see illustration).

Refitting

6 Refitting is a reversal of removal.

25.4b ... and two screws at the front (arrowed) securing the console to the mounting bracket

25.5 Disconnect the wiring harness connectors and remove the console from the car

26 Facia panel components – removal and refitting

Glovebox

Removal

1 Unscrew the two quick-release catches and remove the lower facia panel on the passenger's side (see illustrations).

2 Open the glovebox lid and undo the four screws securing the glovebox to the facia (see illustrations).

3 Withdraw the glovebox from the facia, disconnect the glovebox light wiring connector and remove the glovebox from the car.

Refitting

4 Refitting is a reversal of removal.

Gear lever console

Removal

5 Remove the centre console as described in Section 25.

6 Remove the ashtray insert then unclip the

26.1a Unscrew the two quick-release catches (arrowed) ...

26.1b ... and remove the facia lower panel on the passenger's side

26.2a Undo the glovebox upper retaining screws (arrowed) ...

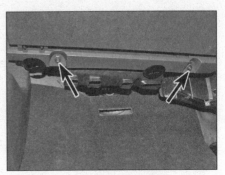

26.2b ... and lower retaining screws (arrowed)

26.6 Unclip the ashtray housing from the base of the facia

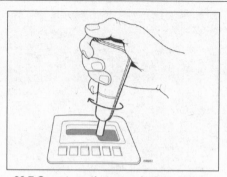

26.7 On automatic transmission models, rotate the engaging sleeve clockwise to release the selector leverknob

26.8a Undo the two gear lever gaiter trim panel retaining screws (arrowed) ...

26.8b ... then lift the panel up at the rear ...

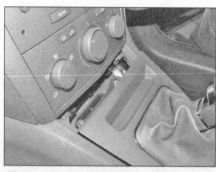

26.8c ... and disengage it from the facia at the front

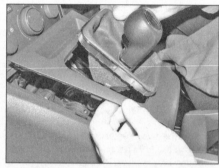

26.9 Release the gear lever gaiter from the trim panel and remove the panel

ashtray housing from the base of the facia (**see illustration**).

7 On automatic transmission models, rotate the engaging sleeve, located directly beneath the gear selector lever knob, clockwise (**see illustration**). Press the selector lever locking button on the lever knob, then withdraw the knob from the selector lever.

8 Undo the two gear lever gaiter trim panel retaining screws, then lift the panel up at the rear and disengage it from the facia at the front (**see illustrations**).

9 Release the gear lever gaiter from the trim panel and remove the panel (**see illustration**).

10 Unscrew the two quick-release catches and remove the lower facia panel on the

passenger's side (**see illustrations 26.1a and 26.1b**). Remove the lower facia panel on the driver's side in the same way.

11 Release the retaining clips (three on each panel) and remove the footwell trim panels on the left- and right-hand sides of the facia (**see illustration**).

Refitting

12 Refitting is a reversal of removal.

Facia upper centre panel

13 Using a plastic spatula or similar tool, carefully lift up the rear edges and sides of the upper centre panel, to release the retaining clips each side. Once the sides are free, slide the panel away from the windscreen to disengage

the lugs at the front (**see illustrations**). Where applicable, disconnect the wiring connector.

Refitting

14 Refitting is a reversal of removal.

Facia lower centre panel

Removal

15 Disconnect the battery negative terminal (refer to Chapter 5A Section 4).

16 Remove the facia upper centre panel as described previously in this Section.

17 Remove the radio/CD player as described in Chapter 12 Section 17.

18 Remove the heater control assembly as described in Chapter 3 Section 9.

26.11 Release the retaining clips and remove the footwell trim panels

26.13a Carefully lift up the rear edges ...

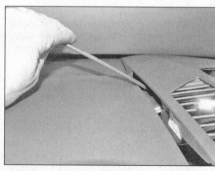

26.13b ... and sides of the upper centre panel

26.19 Disconnect the wiring connector for the facia centre switches

26.20a Undo the two upper retaining screws ...

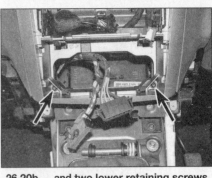

26.20b ... and two lower retaining screws (arrowed) ...

19 Disconnect the wiring connector for the facia centre switches **(see illustration)**.
20 Undo the two upper and two lower retaining screws, then remove the panel from the facia **(see illustrations)**.

Refitting

21 Refitting is a reversal of removal.

Driver's side lower trim panel

Removal

22 Unscrew the two quick-release catches and remove the lower facia panel on the driver's side **(see illustration)**.
23 Using a plastic spatula or similar tool, carefully prise free the facia end panel on the driver's side.
24 Undo the six retaining screws and remove the lower trim panel from the facia **(see illustrations)**.

Refitting

25 Refitting is a reversal of removal.

Steering column shrouds

Removal

26 Turn the steering wheel as necessary to access the left and right front retaining screws.
27 Carefully prise off the screw trim cap and undo the front retaining screw now exposed

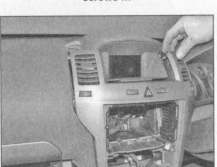

26.20c ... then remove the lower centre panel from the facia

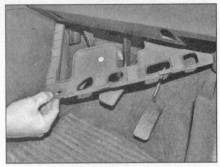

26.22 Unscrew the two quick-release catches and remove the lower facia panel on the driver's side

26.24a Undo the two screws at the right-hand side (arrowed) ...

26.24b ... the two screws at the left-hand side (arrowed) ...

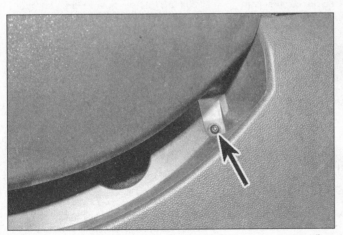

26.24c ... and the two screws in the centre (one screw arrowed) ...

26.24d ... then remove the lower trim panel from the facia

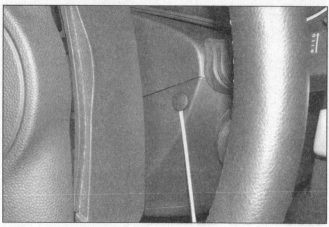

26.27a Carefully prise off the screw trim cap ...

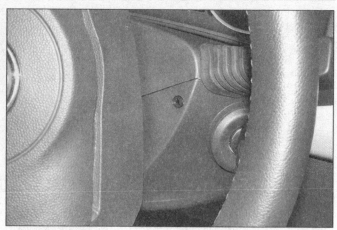

26.27b ... and undo the front retaining screw now exposed

(see illustrations). Repeat this procedure on the other side of the shroud.

28 Undo the lower shroud lower retaining screw (see illustration).

29 Carefully prise free the circular trim panel around the ignition switch (see illustration).

30 Lift up the upper column shroud and undo the two screws securing the lower shroud to the steering column (see illustrations).

31 Remove the lower shroud from the steering column (see illustration).

32 Unclip the upper shroud from the instrument panel and remove it from the car (see illustration).

Refitting

33 Refitting is a reversal of removal.

Complete facia assembly

Note: *This is an involved operation entailing the removal of numerous components and assemblies, and the disconnection of a multitude of wiring connectors. Make notes on the location of all disconnected wiring, or attach labels to the connectors, to avoid confusion when refitting.*

Removal

34 Disconnect the battery negative terminal (refer to Chapter 5A Section 4).

35 Remove the A-pillar trim panels on both sides as described in Section 24.

36 Remove the side sill front trim panel on both sides as described in Section 24.

37 Remove the centre console as described in Section 25.

38 Remove the steering wheel as described in Chapter 10 Section 13.

39 Remove the following facia panels as described previously in this Section:
a) Glovebox.
b) Gear lever console.
c) Facia upper and lower centre panels.
d) Driver's side lower trim panel.
e) Steering column shrouds.

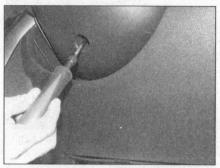

26.28 Undo the lower shroud lower retaining screw

26.29 Carefully prise free the circular trim panel around the ignition switch

26.30a Lift up the upper column shroud and undo the right-hand retaining screw (arrowed) ...

26.30b ... and left-hand retaining screw (arrowed) securing the lower shroud to the steering column

26.31 Remove the lower shroud from the steering column

26.32 Unclip the upper shroud from the instrument panel and remove it from the car

26.42a Undo the gear lever console trim retaining frame lower screw (arrowed) on each side …

40 Remove the following components as described in Chapter 12 :
a) *Steering column electronics module.*
b) *Instrument panel.*
c) *Information display.*
d) *Passenger's airbag.*
e) *Lighting switch assembly.*
41 Remove the steering column as described in Chapter 10 Section 15.
42 Undo the eight screws securing the gear lever console retaining frame to the facia. Lift off the frame and unclip the diagnostic socket **(see illustrations)**.
43 Using a plastic spatula or similar tool, carefully prise free the facia end panel on the passenger's side **(see illustration)**.
44 Again, using a plastic spatula or similar tool, carefully prise free the facia side panels adjacent to the A-pillars **(see illustration)**.
45 Where fitted, disconnect the wiring

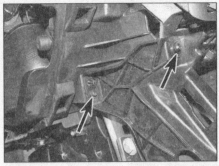

26.42b … the two upper screws (arrowed) on each side …

26.42d … then lift off the frame and unclip the diagnostic socket

connector, undo the two screws and remove the loudspeaker from the top, centre of the facia.
46 Extract the plastic rivet and remove the footwell air duct on the passenger's side **(see**

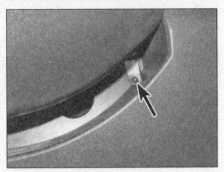

26.42c … and the two centre screws …

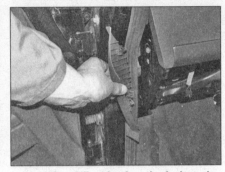

26.43 Carefully prise free the facia end panel on the passenger's side

illustrations). Similarly, remove the footwell air duct on the driver's side.
47 Undo the following fasteners securing the facia to the mounting brackets **(see illustrations)**:

26.44 Carefully prise free the facia side panels adjacent to the A-pillars

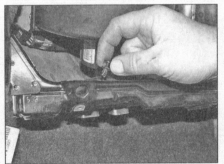

26.46a Extract the plastic rivet …

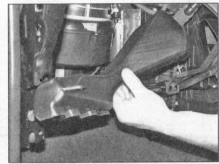

26.46b … and remove the footwell air duct on the passenger's side

26.47a Undo the facia retaining bolt (arrowed) at the top centre …

26.47b … the two bolts (arrowed) at the left-hand and right-hand sides …

26.47c … and the two screws (arrowed) at the lower centre

a) 1 bolt at the top centre.
b) 2 bolts at the left-hand and right-hand sides.
c) 2 screws at the lower centre.

48 With the help of an assistant, carefully lift the facia from its location. Check that all wiring has been disconnected, then remove the facia from the car.

Refitting

49 Refitting is a reversal of removal ensuring that all wiring is correctly reconnected and all mountings securely tightened.

Facia crossmember

Note: *This is an involved operation entailing the disconnection of a multitude of wiring connectors. Make notes on the location of all disconnected wiring, or attach labels to the connectors, to avoid confusion when refitting.*

Removal

50 Remove the facia as described previously in this Section.
51 Remove the front doors as described in Section 11.
52 Remove the brake pedal as described in Chapter 9 Section 10.
53 Remove the clutch pedal as described in Chapter 6 Section 5.
54 Remove the gear lever housing or selector lever assembly as described in Chapter 7A or Chapter 7B, as applicable.
55 Undo the six bolts securing the crossmember centre supports to the crossmember and floor brackets.
56 Disconnect all remaining earth cables and wiring connections, making careful notes as to their locations.
57 From outside the car, undo the two bolts securing the crossmember to the A-pillar on each side.
58 With the help of an assistant, check that all wiring has been disconnected, then remove the crossmember from the car.

Refitting

59 Refitting is a reversal of removal ensuring that all wiring is correctly reconnected and all mountings securely tightened.

Chapter 12
Body electrical systems

Contents

Section number

Airbag system – general information and precautions............ 22
Airbag system components – removal and refitting.............. 23
Anti-theft alarm system – general information 20
Bulbs (exterior lights) – renewal 5
Bulbs (interior lights) – renewal............................. 6
Electrical fault finding – general information 2
Exterior light units – removal and refitting 7
Fuses and relays – general information 3
General information and precautions......................... 1
Headlight beam alignment – general information............... 8
Heated seat components – general information 21
Horn – removal and refitting................................ 11

Section number

Information display unit – removal and refitting 10
Instrument panel – removal and refitting 9
Radio aerial – general information 19
Radio/CD player – removal and refitting 17
Speakers – removal and refitting 18
Steering column electronics module – removal and refitting....... 16
Switches – removal and refitting 4
Tailgate wiper motor – removal and refitting 14
Windscreen wiper motor and linkage – removal and refitting 13
Windscreen/tailgate washer system components – removal and
    refitting 15
Wiper arm – removal and refitting 12

Degrees of difficulty

Easy, suitable for novice with little experience | **Fairly easy,** suitable for beginner with some experience | **Fairly difficult,** suitable for competent DIY mechanic | **Difficult,** suitable for experienced DIY mechanic | **Very difficult,** suitable for expert DIY or professional

Specifications

System type .... 12 volt negative earth

Bulbs	**Wattage**
Direction indicator side repeater	5
Direction indicator	21
Front foglight	55
Headlight	55
Interior lights	10
Number plate light	10
Rear foglight	21
Reversing light	21
Sidelight	5
Stop/tail light	21/5

1 General information and precautions

⚠️ **Warning: Before carrying out any work on the electrical system, read through the precautions given in 'Safety first!' at the beginning of this manual, and in Chapter 5A.**

1 The electrical system is of the 12 volt negative earth type. Power for the lights and all electrical accessories is supplied by a lead-acid type battery, which is charged by the engine-driven alternator.

2 This Chapter covers repair and service procedures for the various electrical components not associated with the engine. Information on the battery, alternator and starter motor can be found in Chapter 5A.

3 It should be noted that, prior to working on any component in the electrical system, the battery negative terminal should first be disconnected, to prevent the possibility of electrical short-circuits and/or fires.

Caution: Before proceeding, refer to Chapter 5A Section 4 for further information.

2 Electrical fault finding – general information

Note: *Refer to the precautions given in 'Safety first!' and in Section 1 before starting work. The following tests relate to testing of the main electrical circuits, and should not be used to test delicate electronic circuits (such as the anti-lock braking system or fuel injection system), particularly where an electronic control unit is used.*

General

1 A typical electrical circuit consists of an electrical component, any switches, relays, motors, fuses, fusible links or circuit breakers related to that component, and the wiring and connectors which link the component to both the battery and the vehicle body. To help to pinpoint a problem in an electrical circuit, wiring diagrams are shown at the end of this Chapter.

2 Before attempting to diagnose an electrical fault, first study the appropriate wiring diagram to obtain a complete understanding of the components included in the particular circuit concerned. The possible sources of a fault can be narrowed down by noting if other components related to the circuit are operating properly. If several components or circuits fail at one time, the problem is likely to be related to a shared fuse or earth connection.

3 Electrical problems usually stem from simple causes, such as loose or corroded connections, a faulty earth connection, a blown fuse, a melted fusible link, or a faulty relay (refer to Section 3 for details of testing relays). Inspect the condition of all fuses, wires and connections in a problem circuit before testing the components. Use the wiring diagrams to determine which terminal connections will need to be checked in order to pinpoint the trouble-spot.

4 The basic tools required for electrical fault finding include a circuit tester or voltmeter (a 12 volt bulb with a set of test leads can also be used for certain tests); a self-powered test light (sometimes known as a continuity tester); an ohmmeter (to measure resistance); a battery and set of test leads; and a jumper wire, preferably with a circuit breaker or fuse incorporated, which can be used to bypass suspect wires or electrical components. Before attempting to locate a problem with test instruments, use the wiring diagram to determine where to make the connections.

5 To find the source of an intermittent wiring fault (usually due to a poor or dirty connection, or damaged wiring insulation), a 'wiggle' test can be performed on the wiring. This involves wiggling the wiring by hand to see if the fault occurs as the wiring is moved. It should be possible to narrow down the source of the fault to a particular section of wiring. This method of testing can be used in conjunction with any of the tests described in the following sub-Sections.

6 Apart from problems due to poor connections, two basic types of fault can occur in an electrical circuit – open-circuit, or short-circuit.

7 Open-circuit faults are caused by a break somewhere in the circuit, which prevents current from flowing. An open-circuit fault will prevent a component from working, but will not cause the relevant circuit fuse to blow.

8 Short-circuit faults are caused by a 'short' somewhere in the circuit, which allows the current flowing in the circuit to 'escape' along an alternative route, usually to earth. Short-circuit faults are normally caused by a breakdown in wiring insulation, which allows a feed wire to touch either another wire, or an earthed component such as the bodyshell. A short-circuit fault will normally cause the relevant circuit fuse to blow.

Finding an open-circuit

9 To check for an open-circuit, connect one lead of a circuit tester or voltmeter to either the negative battery terminal or a known good earth.

10 Connect the other lead to a connector in the circuit being tested, preferably nearest to the battery or fuse.

11 Switch on the circuit, bearing in mind that some circuits are live only when the ignition switch is turned to a particular position.

12 If voltage is present (indicated either by the tester bulb lighting or a voltmeter reading, as applicable), this means that the section of the circuit between the relevant connector and the battery is problem-free.

13 Continue to check the remainder of the circuit in the same fashion.

14 When a point is reached at which no voltage is present, the problem must lie between that point and the previous test point with voltage. Most problems can be traced to a broken, corroded or loose connection.

Finding a short-circuit

15 To check for a short-circuit, first disconnect the load(s) from the circuit (loads are the components which draw current from a circuit, such as bulbs, motors, heating elements, etc).

16 Remove the relevant fuse from the circuit, and connect a circuit tester or voltmeter to the fuse connections.

17 Switch on the circuit, bearing in mind that some circuits are live only when the ignition switch is turned to a particular position.

18 If voltage is present (indicated either by the tester bulb lighting or a voltmeter reading, as applicable), this means that there is a short-circuit.

19 If no voltage is present, but the fuse still blows with the load(s) connected, this indicates an internal fault in the load(s).

Finding an earth fault

20 The battery negative terminal is connected to 'earth' – the metal of the engine/transmission unit and the car body – and most systems are wired so that they only receive a positive feed, the current returning via the metal of the car body. This means that the component mounting and the body form part of that circuit. Loose or corroded mountings can therefore cause a range of electrical faults, ranging from total failure of a circuit, to a puzzling partial fault. In particular, lights may shine dimly (especially when another circuit sharing the same earth point is in operation), motors (eg, wiper motors or the radiator cooling fan motor) may run slowly, and the operation of one circuit may have an apparently-unrelated effect on another. Note that on many vehicles, earth straps are used between certain components, such as the engine/transmission and the body, usually where there is no metal-to-metal contact between components, due to flexible rubber mountings, etc.

21 To check whether a component is properly earthed, disconnect the battery, and connect one lead of an ohmmeter to a known good earth point. Connect the other lead to the wire or earth connection being tested. The resistance reading should be zero; if not, check the connection as follows.

22 If an earth connection is thought to be faulty, dismantle the connection, and clean back to bare metal both the bodyshell and the wire terminal or the component earth connection mating surface. Be careful to remove all traces of dirt and corrosion, then use a knife to trim away any paint, so that a clean metal-to-metal joint is made. On reassembly, tighten the joint fasteners securely; if a wire terminal is being refitted, use serrated washers between the terminal and the bodyshell, to ensure a clean and secure connection. When the connection is remade, prevent the onset of corrosion in the future by applying a coat of petroleum jelly or silicone-based grease. Alternatively, at regular intervals, spray on a proprietary ignition sealer or a water-dispersant lubricant.

3.2 Access to the fuses in the luggage compartment can be gained by opening the stowage compartment cover

3.3 Release the catches and lift off the fuse/relay box cover for access to the engine compartment fuses

3.4 Pull the fuse out of its terminals using the plastic removal tool provided

3 Fuses and relays – general information

Fuses

1 The main fuses are located behind the trim panel on the left-hand side of the luggage compartment, with additional fuses and relays located in the fuse/relay box on the left-hand side of the engine compartment.

2 To gain access to the luggage compartment fuses, turn the catches and open the cover **(see illustration)**.

3 To gain access to the engine compartment fuses, release the catches using a small screwdriver and lift off the fuse/relay box cover **(see illustration)**.

4 To remove a fuse, first switch off the circuit concerned (or the ignition), then pull the fuse out of its terminals using the plastic removal tool provided **(see illustration)**. The wire within the fuse is clearly visible; if the fuse is blown, it will be broken or melted.

5 Always renew a fuse with one of an identical rating; never use a fuse with a different rating from the original, nor substitute anything else. Never renew a fuse more than once without tracing the source of the trouble. The fuse rating is stamped on top of the fuse; note that the fuses are also colour-coded for easy recognition.

6 If a new fuse blows immediately, find the cause before renewing it again; a short to earth as a result of faulty insulation is most likely. Where a fuse protects more than one circuit, try to isolate the defect by switching on each circuit in turn (if possible) until the fuse blows again. Always carry a supply of spare fuses of each relevant rating on the vehicle, a spare of each rating should be clipped into the base of the fuse/relay box.

Relays

7 Most of the relays are located in the fuse/relay boxes in the luggage compartment and engine compartment **(see illustrations 3.2 and 3.3)**.

8 If a circuit or system controlled by a relay develops a fault and the relay is suspect, operate the system; if the relay is functioning, it should be possible to hear it click as it is energised. If this is the case, the fault lies with the components or wiring of the system. If the relay is not being energised, then either the relay is not receiving a main supply or a switching voltage, or the relay itself is faulty. Testing is by the substitution of a known good unit, but be careful; while some relays are identical in appearance and in operation, others look similar but perform different functions.

9 To renew a relay, first ensure that the ignition switch is off. The relay can then simply be pulled out from the socket and the new relay pressed in.

4 Switches – removal and refitting

Note: *Disconnect the battery negative terminal (refer to Chapter 5A Section 4) before removing any switch, and reconnect the terminal after refitting.*

Ignition switch/ steering column lock

1 Refer to Chapter 10 Section 14.

Steering column switches

2 The direction indicator and windscreen wiper switches are an integral part of the steering column electronics module, and cannot be individually renewed.

3 To remove the steering column electronics module, which also contains the airbag rotary connector, proceed as described in Section 16.

Lighting switch assembly

4 With the light switch knob in the off position, press the knob in and turn it to the AUTO position (vehicles with automatic dipped beam activation), or to the vertical position (sidelights 'on'). The switch assembly internal catch is now unlocked and the switch assembly can be withdrawn from the facia **(see illustrations)**. Once the switch is released, turn the switch off.

5 Release the locking catch and disconnect the switch wiring connector.

6 Note that the switch assembly cannot be dismantled; if any of its functions are faulty, the complete assembly must be renewed.

7 Reconnect the wiring connector and push the switch back into the facia.

Facia centre switches

8 The facia centre switches are contained in the switch strip assembly located in the facia centre panel. If an individual switch is faulty the complete switch strip must be renewed. To gain access to the switch, remove the facia centre panel as described in Chapter 11 Section 26.

4.4a Press the switch knob in and turn it to the appropriate position ...

4.4b ... then withdraw the switch assembly from the facia

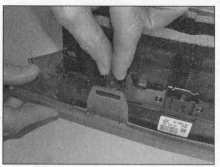

4.9a Turn the switch strip retaining catches a quarter of a turn ...

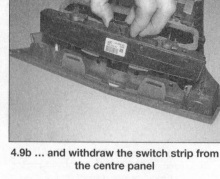

4.9b ... and withdraw the switch strip from the centre panel

9 With the facia centre panel removed, turn the switch strip retaining catches a quarter of a turn and withdraw the switch strip from the centre panel **(see illustrations)**.

10 Refit the switch strip and turn the retaining catches back a quarter of a turn to lock the assembly in position.

11 Refit the facia centre panel as described in Chapter 11 Section 26.

Heated rear window/ blower motor switches

12 The heated rear window and blower motor switches are an integral part of the heater control assembly. Removal and refitting procedures are contained in Chapter 3 Section 9.

Handbrake warning light switch

13 Refer to Chapter 9 Section 16.

Stop-light switch

14 Refer to Chapter 9 Section 15.

Electric window/mirror switches

Front door

15 Remove the front door inner trim panel as described in Chapter 11 Section 12.

16 Carefully release the retaining clip and push the rear of the switch out of the trim panel **(see illustration)**.

17 Disengage the switch front locating tab and remove the switch from the panel **(see illustration)**.

18 Refitting is the reverse of removal.

Rear door

19 Carefully prise out the switch assembly and disconnect the wiring connector **(see illustrations)**.

20 Refitting is the reverse of removal.

Air conditioning system switch

21 The air conditioning system control switch is an integral part of the heating/ventilation control unit, and cannot be removed. Should the switch become faulty, the complete control unit assembly must be renewed (see Chapter 3 Section 9).

Steering wheel switches

22 Turn the steering wheel so that the switch retaining screw opening is accessible, then undo the retaining screw from the rear of the steering wheel **(see illustration)**.

23 Unclip the switch surround from the steering wheel, then disconnect the wiring connector from the switch **(see illustration)**.

24 Refitting is the reverse of removal.

| 5 | Bulbs (exterior lights) – renewal | |

General

1 Whenever a bulb is renewed, note the following points:

a) Make sure the switch is in the OFF position, for the bulb you are working on.

4.16 Release the retaining clip and push the rear of the switch out of the trim panel

4.17 Disengage the control switch front locating tab (arrowed) and remove the switch

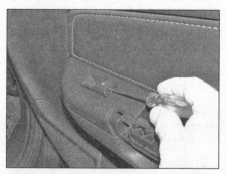

4.19a Carefully prise out the rear control switch assembly ...

4.19b ... and disconnect the wiring connector

4.22 Undo the retaining screw from the rear of the steering wheel to release the switches

4.23 Unclip the switch surround from the steering wheel, then disconnect the switch wiring connector

b) *Remember that if the light has just been in use, the bulb may be extremely hot.*

c) *Always check the bulb contacts and holder, ensuring that there is clean metal-to-metal contact between the bulb and its live(s) and earth. Clean off any corrosion or dirt before fitting a new bulb.*

d) *Wherever bayonet-type bulbs are fitted, ensure that the live contact(s) bear firmly against the bulb contact.*

e) *Always ensure that the new bulb is of the correct rating, and that it is completely clean before fitting it; this applies particularly to headlight/foglight bulbs.*

Halogen headlight unit

Note: *The outer bulb in the headlight unit is the dipped beam bulb and the inner bulb is the main beam bulb.*

Dipped beam

2 Turn the steering on to full lock for access under the wheel arch. Open the flap in the wheel arch liner for access to the rear of the headlight unit Remove the plastic cover from the rear of the headlight unit **(see illustrations)**.

3 Rotate the bulbholder anti-clockwise to release the bayonet fitting, then withdraw the bulbholder from the light unit **(see illustration)**.

4 Hold the bulb by its base and withdraw it from the bulbholder **(see illustration)**. When handling the new bulb, use a tissue or clean

5.2a Open the flap in the wheel arch liner for access to the outer bulbs in the headlight unit

cloth to avoid touching the glass with the fingers; moisture and grease from the skin can cause blackening and rapid failure of this type of bulb.

 HAYNES HINT *If the glass is accidentally touched, wipe it clean using methylated spirit.*

5 Fit the new bulb to the bulbholder, then refit the bulbholder to the headlight unit. Turn the bulbholder clockwise to lock it in position.

6 Refit the plastic cover to the rear of the headlight unit, then refit any components removed for access.

5.2b Remove the outer plastic cover from the rear of the headlight

Main beam

7 Remove the air intake duct at the front of the air cleaner housing (right-hand side) or unclip the wiring harness connector from the front of the fuse/relay box (left-hand side). Remove the plastic cover from the rear of the headlight unit **(see illustration)**.

8 Disconnect the wiring connector from the rear of the bulb **(see illustration)**.

9 Press the retaining spring clip forward and pivot the clip off the bulb. Lift the bulb out of the light unit **(see illustrations)**. When handling the new bulb, use a tissue or clean cloth to avoid touching the glass with the fingers; moisture and grease from the skin can cause blackening and rapid failure of this type of bulb.

5.3 Rotate the dipped beam bulbholder anti-clockwise to release the bayonet fitting

5.4 Hold the bulb by its base and withdraw it from the bulbholder

5.7 Remove the inner plastic cover from the rear of the headlight

5.8 Disconnect the wiring connector from the rear of the bulb

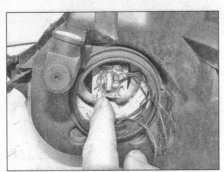

5.9a Press the retaining spring clip forward and pivot the clip off the bulb ...

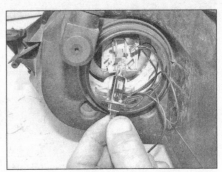

5.9b ... then lift the bulb out of the light unit

If the glass is accidentally touched, wipe it clean using methylated spirit.

10 Fit the new bulb to the headlight unit and secure with the spring clip. Reconnect the wiring connector.

11 Refit the plastic cover to the rear of the headlight unit, then refit any components removed for access.

Front sidelight

12 Remove the main beam plastic cover from the rear of the headlight unit **(see illustration 5.7)**.

13 Withdraw the sidelight bulbholder from the rear of the headlight unit. The bulb is of the capless (push-fit) type, and can be removed by simply pulling it out of the bulbholder **(see illustrations)**.

14 Refitting is the reverse of the removal procedure, ensuring that the bulbholder is fully engaged. On completion, refit any components removed for access.

Front indicator

15 Remove the plastic cover from the rear of the headlight unit, then twist the indicator bulbholder anti-clockwise, and remove it from the rear of the headlight unit **(see illustrations)**.

16 The bulb is a bayonet fit in the holder, and can be removed by pressing it and twisting in an anti-clockwise direction **(see illustration)**.

17 Refitting is a reverse of the removal procedure. On completion, refit any components removed for access.

Xenon headlight unit

 Warning: Xenon dipped beam headlights operate at very high voltage. Do not touch the associated wiring when the headlights are switched on.

Dipped beam

18 Turn the steering on to full lock for access under the wheel arch. Open the flap in the wheel arch liner for access to the rear of the headlight unit **(see illustration 5.1a)**. Disconnect the battery negative terminal (refer to Chapter 5A Section 4).

19 Remove the rubber cap at the rear of the headlight unit.

20 Release the xenon starter unit wiring harness from the lug at the side of the headlight unit.

21 Compress the legs of the retaining spring clip and pivot the clip off the xenon starter unit. Withdraw the starter unit and bulb from the rear of the headlight unit and disconnect the wiring connector. Note that the xenon starter unit and the bulb are one single component and cannot be separated.

22 When handling the new bulb, use a tissue or clean cloth to avoid touching the glass with the fingers; moisture and grease from the skin can cause blackening and rapid failure of this type of bulb.

 If the glass is accidentally touched, wipe it clean using methylated spirit.

23 Connect the wiring and install the new bulb and starter unit. Secure the starter unit with the retaining spring clip and engage the wiring harness with the lug at the side of the headlight unit.

24 Refit the rubber cap to the rear of the unit, then reconnect the battery.

Main beam

25 Renewal of the main beam bulb is as described previously in this Section for the halogen headlight unit.

Front sidelight

26 Renewal of the front sidelight bulb is as described previously in this Section for the halogen headlight unit.

Front indicator

27 Renewal of the front indicator bulb is as described previously in this Section for the halogen headlight unit.

Indicator side repeater

28 Push the light unit toward the front of the car, and release the rear edge of the unit from the wing **(see illustration)**. If necessary, assist removal using a suitable plastic wedge, taking great care not damage the painted finish of the wing.

5.13a Withdraw the sidelight bulbholder from the rear of the headlight unit

5.13b The bulb is a push-fit in the bulbholder

5.15a Remove the plastic cover from the rear of the headlight unit ...

5.15b ... then twist the indicator bulbholder anti-clockwise, and remove it from the rear of the headlightunit

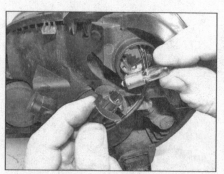

5.16 The bulb is a bayonet fit in the bulbholder

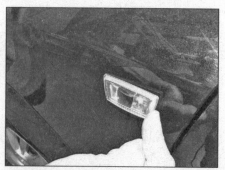

5.28 Push the light unit toward the front of the car, and release the rear edge of the unit from the wing

5.29a Withdraw the light unit from the wing ...

5.29b ... and pull the bulbholder out of the light unit

5.29c Pull the capless bulb from the bulbholder

5.31 Twist the cover and free it from the foglight unit

5.32 Release the spring clip and withdraw the foglight bulb from the light unit

5.33 Disconnect the wiring connector and remove the bulb

29 Withdraw the light unit from the wing, and pull the bulbholder out of the light unit. The bulb is of the capless (push-fit) type, and can be removed by simply pulling it out of the bulbholder **(see illustrations)**.

30 Refitting is a reverse of the removal procedure.

Front foglight

31 Reach up under the front bumper, twist the cover and free it from the foglight unit **(see illustration)**.

32 Release the spring clip and withdraw the foglight bulb from the light unit **(see illustration)**.

33 Disconnect the wiring connector and remove the bulb **(see illustration)**.

34 When handling the new bulb, use a tissue or clean cloth to avoid touching the glass with the fingers; moisture and grease from the skin can cause blackening and rapid failure of this type of bulb.

HINT: If the glass is accidentally touched, wipe it clean using methylated spirit.

35 Connect the wiring connector to the new bulb.

36 Insert the new bulb, making sure it is correctly located, and secure it in position with the spring clip.

37 Refit the cover to the rear of the unit.

Rear light cluster

38 Push the locking tabs forward and remove the access cover from the luggage compartment trim panel **(see illustration)**.

39 If working on the right-hand side, remove the tyre repair kit and the foam mounting box. If working on the left-hand side, pull out the luggage compartment cover bracket **(see illustration)**.

40 Reach in through the trim panel opening and slacken the two light cluster plastic retaining nuts **(see illustration)**.

41 Hold the light cluster from the outside and unscrew the plastic nuts by hand the rest of the way. Withdraw the light cluster from

5.38 Remove the access cover from the luggage compartment trim panel

5.39 Pull the plastic bracket from place

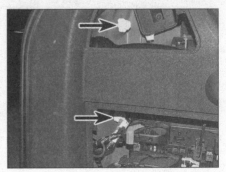

5.40 Slacken the plastic nuts

5.41a Pull the light cluster rearwards from the wing

5.41b Depress the locking clip and disconnect the wiring plug

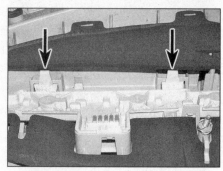

5.42 Depress the two locking tabs and withdraw the bulbholder from the light cluster

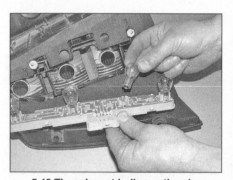

5.43 The relevant bulb can then be renewed

5.44a Pull the edge of the grommet through the hole in the light cluster

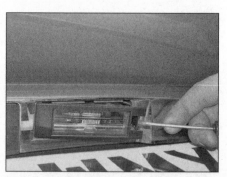

5.45 Carefully prise the number plate light unit out from its location

the rear wing and disconnect the bulbholder wiring connector **(see illustration)**.

42 Depress the two locking tabs on the side of the bulbholder and withdraw the bulbholder from the light cluster **(see illustration)**.

43 The relevant bulb can then be renewed; all bulbs have a bayonet fitting **(see illustration)**. Note that the stop/tail light bulb has offset locating pins, to prevent it being installed incorrectly.

44 Refitting is the reverse of the removal sequence, bearing in mind the following points:

a) Ensure that the bulbholder locates securely in position on the light cluster.

b) Re-engage the sealing grommet with the

top of the light cluster after refitting **(see illustration)**.

Number plate light

45 Using a small flat-bladed screwdriver, carefully prise the light unit out from its location **(see illustration)**.

46 Twist the bulbholder to remove it from the light unit, and remove the bulb **(see illustrations)**.

47 Refitting is a reverse of the removal procedure.

High-level stop-light

48 The high-level stop-light bulbs are of the LED (light emitting diode) type and cannot be individually renewed. Remove the complete light unit as described in Section 7.

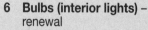

6 Bulbs (interior lights) – renewal

General

1 Refer to Section 5, paragraph 1.

Front courtesy light

Low specification models

2 Using a suitable screwdriver, carefully prise the right-hand side of the light unit out of position, and withdraw the light unit **(see illustration)**.

5.46a Twist the bulbholder to remove it from the light unit ...

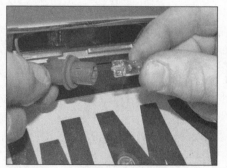

5.46b ... and remove the push-fit bulb

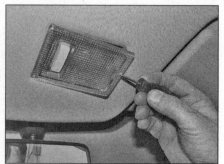

6.2 Carefully prise the right-hand side of the light unit out of position, and withdraw the light unit

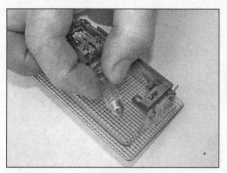

6.3 Remove the festoon bulb from the light unit contacts

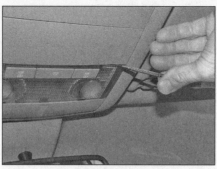

6.5 Carefully prise the light unit lens from the overhead console

6.6 Pull the relevant bulb from its socket

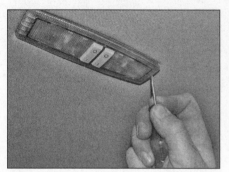

6.8 Carefully prise the centre courtesy light unit out of position

6.9 Disconnect the wiring connector and remove the light unit

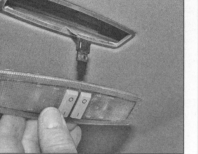

6.10 Unclip and remove the reflector from the base of the light unit

3 Remove the festoon bulb from the light unit contacts **(see illustration)**.

4 Install the new bulb, ensuring that it is securely held in position by the contacts, then clip the light unit back into position.

High specification models

5 Using a small screwdriver, carefully prise the light unit lens from the overhead console **(see illustration)**.

6 Pull the relevant bulb from its socket **(see illustration)**.

7 Install the new bulb, ensuring that it is securely held in position by the contacts, and clip the light unit lens back into position.

Centre courtesy light

8 Using a suitable screwdriver, carefully prise the right-hand side of the light unit out of position, and withdraw the light unit **(see illustration)**.

9 Disconnect the wiring connector and remove the light unit **(see illustration)**.

10 Unclip and remove the reflector from the base of the light unit **(see illustration)**.

11 Pull the relevant bulb from its socket **(see illustration)**.

12 Install the new bulb, then refit the reflector. Reconnect the wiring connector, then clip the light unit back into position.

Rear courtesy light

13 Using a suitable screwdriver, carefully prise the right-hand side of the light unit out of position, and withdraw the light unit.

14 Release the locking plate and disconnect the wiring connector. Remove the relevant bulb from the light unit.

15 Install the new bulb, ensuring that it is securely held in position by the contacts. Refit the wiring connector and locking plate, then clip the light unit back into position.

Luggage compartment, glovebox and footwell lights

16 Using a suitable screwdriver, carefully prise the light unit out of position, and release the festoon bulb from the light unit contacts **(see illustration)**.

17 Install the new bulb, ensuring that it is securely held in position by the contacts, and clip the light unit back into position.

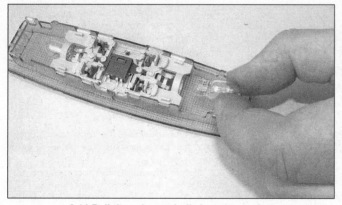

6.11 Pull the relevant bulb from its socket

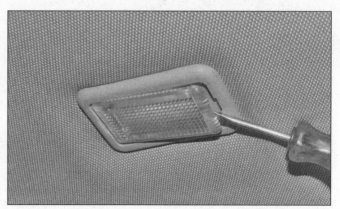

6.16 Carefully prise the light unit out of position, and release the festoon bulb from the light unit contacts

6.20 Twist and remove the relevant bulbholder from the rear of the information display

7.2a Undo the three retaining bolts (arrowed) and withdraw the headlight unit from the vehicle

7.2b Pull out the locking catch and disconnect the wiring connector

Switch illumination

18 All the switches are fitted with illumination bulbs; some are also fitted with a bulb to show when the circuit concerned is operating. These bulbs are an integral part of the switch assembly, and cannot be obtained separately.

Information display illumination

19 Remove the information display unit as described in Section 10.
20 Twist and remove the relevant bulbholder from the rear of the unit (see illustration). The bulbs are integral with the bulbholders.
21 Fit the new bulbholder and bulb, then refit the information display unit as described in Section 10.

7 Exterior light units – removal and refitting

Note: *Disconnect the battery negative terminal (refer to Chapter 5A Section 4) before removing any light unit, and reconnect the terminal after refitting.*

Headlight

 Warning: Xenon dipped beam headlights operate at very high voltage. Do not touch the associated wiring when the headlights are switched on.

1 Remove the front bumper as described in Chapter 11 Section 6.
2 Undo the three retaining bolts and withdraw the headlight unit from the vehicle. Pull out the locking catch and disconnect the wiring connector from rear of the headlight unit as it is withdrawn (see illustrations).
3 Refitting is a reverse of the removal procedure. On completion, check the headlight beam alignment using the information given in Section 8.

Front indicator

4 The front direction indicator lights are integral with the headlight units. Removal and refitting is as described above.

Indicator side repeater

5 Push the light unit toward the front of the car, and release the rear edge of the unit from the wing (see illustration 5.28). If necessary, assist removal using a suitable plastic wedge, taking great care not damage the painted finish of the wing.
6 Withdraw the light unit from the wing, and disconnect its wiring connector. Tie a piece of string to the wiring, to prevent it falling back into the wing.
7 On refitting, connect the wiring connector, and clip the light unit back into position.

Front foglight

8 Remove the front bumper as described in Chapter 11 Section 6.

9 Undo the three foglight retaining bolts and remove the light unit from the bumper.
10 Refit the light unit to the bumper, and securely tighten its retaining bolts.
11 Refit the front bumper as described in Chapter 11 Section 6.

Rear light cluster

12 Push the locking tabs forward and remove the access cover from the luggage compartment trim panel (see illustration 5.38).
13 If working on the right-hand side, remove the tyre repair kit and the foam mounting box. If working on the left-hand side, remove the luggage compartment cover bracket (see illustration 5.39).
14 Using a small screwdriver, release the sealing grommet from the top of the light cluster (see illustration 5.40).
15 Reach in through the trim panel opening and slacken the two light cluster plastic retaining nuts.
16 Hold the light cluster from the outside and unscrew the plastic nuts by hand the rest of the way. Withdraw the light cluster from the rear wing and disconnect the bulbholder wiring connector (see illustrations 5.42a and 5.42b).
17 Refitting is the reverse of the removal sequence.

Number plate light

18 Using a small flat-bladed screwdriver, carefully prise the light unit out from its location (see illustration 5.46).
19 Twist the bulbholder to remove it from the light unit.
20 Refitting is the reverse of the removal sequence.

High-level stop-light

21 Carefully prise free the upper inner tailgate trim panel to release the four retaining clips (see illustration).
22 Working through the apertures on the inside of the tailgate, depress the three retaining lugs to release the light unit from the tailgate (see illustration).
23 Withdraw the light unit from outside the

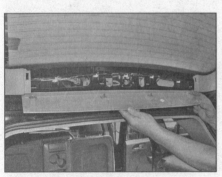

7.21 Carefully prise free the upper inner tailgate trim panel to release the four retaining clips

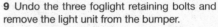

7.22 Depress the three retaining lugs (arrowed) to release the light unit from the tailgate

tailgate and disconnect the wiring connector **(see illustration)**.

24 Reconnect the wiring connector, then push the light unit into the tailgate until it locks in position.

25 Refit the tailgate trim panel.

8 Headlight beam alignment – general information

1 Accurate adjustment of the headlight beam is only possible using optical beam-setting equipment, and this work should therefore be carried out by a Vauxhall/Opel dealer or suitably-equipped workshop.

2 For reference, the headlights can be adjusted using the adjuster assemblies fitted to the top of each light unit. The inner adjuster alters the vertical position of the beam. The outer adjuster alters the horizontal aim of the beam.

3 Most models have an electrically-operated headlight beam adjustment system, controlled via a switch in the facia. The recommended settings are as follows.

a) *0 Front seat(s) occupied*
b) *1 All seats occupied*
c) *2 All seats occupied, and load in luggage compartment*
d) *3 Driver's seat occupied and load in the luggage compartment*

Note: *When adjusting the headlight aim, ensure that the switch is set to position 0.*

9 Instrument panel – removal and refitting

Note: *The instrument panel is a complete sealed assembly, and no dismantling of the instrument panel is possible.*

Removal

1 Disconnect the battery negative terminal (refer to Chapter 5A Section 4).

2 Remove the steering column shrouds as described in Chapter 11 Section 26.

3 Undo the two lower retaining screws, then pull the panel away from the facia at the bottom **(see illustrations)**.

4 Disengage the top of the panel from the facia,

7.23 Withdraw the light unit from the tailgate and disconnect the wiring connector

9.3b ... and right-hand lower retaining screw (arrowed)

disconnect the wiring connector and remove the panel from the car **(see illustration)**.

Refitting

5 Refitting is a reversal of removal.

10 Information display unit – removal and refitting

Removal

1 Disconnect the battery negative terminal (refer to Chapter 5A Section 4).

2 Remove the facia upper and lower centre panels as described in Chapter 11 Section 26.

3 Undo the two retaining screws securing the information display unit to the facia **(see illustration)**.

9.3a Undo the instrument panel left-hand lower retaining screw (arrowed) ...

9.4 Disengage the top of the panel from the facia and disconnect the wiring connector

4 Disengage the two lower retaining lugs, then withdraw the information display unit downwards from its location **(see illustration)**.

5 Disconnect the wiring connector and remove the unit from the car **(see illustration)**.

Refitting

6 Refitting is a reversal of removal.

11 Horn – removal and refitting

Removal

1 Firmly apply the handbrake, then jack up the front of the car and support it securely on axle stands (see *Jacking and vehicle support*).

10.3 Undo the two information display unit retaining screws (arrowed)

10.4 Withdraw the display unit downwards from the facia

10.5 Disconnect the wiring connector

2 Working under the front bumper on the right-hand side, undo the retaining nut/bolt and remove the horn(s), disconnecting the wiring connector as it becomes accessible.

Refitting

3 Refitting is the reverse of removal.

12 Wiper arm – removal and refitting

Removal

1 Operate the wiper motor, then switch it off so that the wiper arm returns to the at-rest (parked) position.

 HAYNES HINT *Stick a piece of masking tape along the edge of the wiper blade, to use as an alignment aid on refitting.*

2 Unclip the wiper arm spindle nut cover (windscreen wiper arm), or pivot the cover up (tailgate wiper arm), then slacken and remove the spindle nut and washer **(see illustration)**.
3 Using a suitable puller, free the wiper arm from the spindle and remove the arm **(see illustration)**. Note: *If both windscreen wiper arms are to be removed at the same time, mark them for identification.*

Refitting

4 Ensure that the wiper arm and spindle splines are clean and dry, then refit the arm to

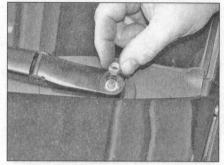

12.2 Slacken and remove the wiper arm spindle nut

the spindle, aligning the wiper blade with the tape fitted on removal. Refit the spindle nut, tightening it securely, and clip the nut cover back in position.

13 Windscreen wiper motor and linkage – removal and refitting

Removal

1 Disconnect the battery negative terminal (refer to Chapter 5A Section 4).
2 Remove the wiper arms as described in Section 12.
3 Remove the windscreen cowl panel as described in Chapter 11 Section 20.
4 Undo the three retaining bolts, and withdraw the wiper motor and linkage assembly from the scuttle **(see illustrations)**.

12.3 Using a suitable puller, free the wiper arm from the spindle

5 Disconnect the wiring connector from the wiper motor and remove the assembly from the car **(see illustration)**.
6 If necessary, free the wiper linkage from the motor crank arm, then undo the four motor retaining bolts, and separate the motor and linkage **(see illustrations)**. It may be necessary to turn the crank arm slightly to gain access to all the motor retaining bolts.

Refitting

7 Where necessary, assemble the motor and linkage, and securely tighten the motor retaining bolts. Locate the linkage arm on the motor crank arm and press it firmly on to the balljoint.
8 Reconnect the wiper motor wiring connector, then manoeuvre the motor assembly back into position in the vehicle. Refit the retaining bolts, and tighten them securely.

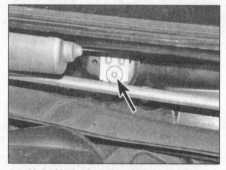

13.4a Undo the wiper linkage centre retaining bolt (arrowed) …

13.4b … left-hand retaining bolt (arrowed) …

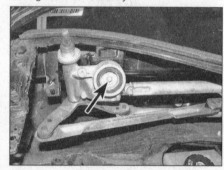

13.4c … and right-hand retaining bolt (arrowed)

13.5 Disconnect the wiring connector and remove the wiper motor and linkage assembly

13.6a Free the wiper linkage from the motor crank arm …

13.6b … then undo the four motor retaining bolts

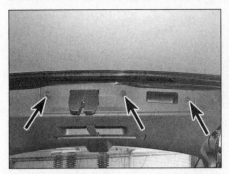

14.1a Undo the three screws (arrowed) ...

14.1b ... and remove the lock cover panel from the base of the tailgate

14.2a Undo the two screws (arrowed) securing the lower trim panel to the tailgate

9 Refit the windscreen cowl panel as described in Chapter 11 Section 20.

10 Reconnect the battery negative terminal, then switch on the ignition. Turn the windscreen wiper switch on, then switch it off again to allow the motor to return to the at-rest (parked) position.

11 Refit the wiper arms as described in Section 12.

14 Tailgate wiper motor – removal and refitting

14.2b Pull the panel away from the tailgate to release the internal clips then remove the panel

14.4 Disconnect the wiring connector, then slacken and remove the wiper motor mounting bolts (arrowed)

Removal

1 Undo the three screws and remove the lock cover panel from the base of the tailgate (see illustrations).

2 Undo the two screws securing the lower trim panel to the tailgate. Pull the lower trim panel away from the tailgate to release the ten internal clips and remove the panel from the tailgate (see illustrations).

3 Remove the wiper arm as described in Section 12.

4 Disconnect the wiring connector, then slacken and remove the three wiper motor mounting bolts and remove the wiper motor (see illustration).

Refitting

5 Refitting is the reverse of removal, ensuring the wiper motor retaining bolts are securely tightened.

15 Windscreen/tailgate washer system components – removal and refitting

Washer system reservoir

1 Remove the front bumper as described in Chapter 11 Section 6.

2 Unscrew the bolt securing the filler neck to the bonnet crossmember (see illustration).

3 Disconnect the wiring connector(s) and washer hoses at the washer pump(s), then release the wiring and hoses from the side of the reservoir (see illustration).

4 Undo the retaining bolt (two bolts on some models, according to equipment) and lower the reservoir out from under the car.

5 Refitting is the reverse of removal,

ensuring that the washer hose(s) are securely connected.

Washer pump

6 Remove the front bumper as described in Chapter 11 Section 6.

7 Disconnect the pump washer hoses, then carefully ease the pump out from the reservoir and recover its sealing grommet (see illustration).

8 Refitting is the reverse of removal, using a new sealing grommet if the original one shows signs of damage or deterioration.

Windscreen washer jets

9 Remove the windscreen cowl panel as described in Chapter 11 Section 20

10 Disconnect the fluid hose(s) from the nozzle, then depress the retaining clip and

15.2 Unscrew the bolt (arrowed) securing the filler neck to the bonnet crossmember

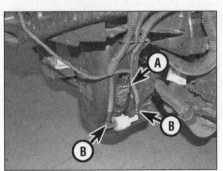

15.3 Disconnect the wiring connector (A) and washer hoses at the washer pump (B)

15.7 Ease the pump out from the reservoir and recover its sealing grommet

15.10a Depress the retaining clip …

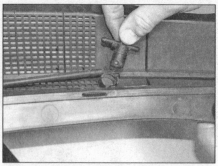

15.10b … then prise the washer nozzle from the windscreen cowl panel

15.12 Carefully extract the washer jet from the tailgate

carefully prise the nozzle from the cowl panel **(see illustrations)**.

11 On refitting, clip the nozzle into position in the cowl panel and reconnect the hose(s). Refit the windscreen cowl panel, then check the operation of the jet. If necessary, adjust the nozzle using a pin, aiming the spray to a point slightly above the centre of the swept area.

Tailgate washer jet

12 Carefully extract the washer jet from the tailgate **(see illustration)**.
13 Disconnect the fluid hose and remove the jet from the car.
14 When refitting, ensure that the jet is clipped securely in position. Check the operation of the jet. If necessary, adjust the nozzle using a pin, aiming the spray to a point slightly above the centre of the swept area.

16 Steering column electronics module – removal and refitting

Removal

Note: *If a new module is to be fitted, it must be programmed using Vauxhall's TECH2 diagnostic equipment (or equivalent). Entrust this task to a Vauxhall dealer or suitably equipped repairer.*

1 Disconnect the battery negative terminal (refer to Chapter 5A Section 4) and wait for 2 minutes to allow any residual electrical energy to dissipate.
2 Remove the driver's airbag as described in Section 23.
3 Set the roadwheels in the straight-ahead position and ensure they remain in that position during the removal and refitting procedures.
4 Remove the steering wheel as described in Chapter 10 Section 13.
Caution: Do not rotate the airbag rotary contact unit once the steering wheel has been removed. With the front wheels in the straight-ahead position, the arrow on the contact unit should align with the arrow on the casing.
5 Remove the steering column shrouds as described in Chapter 11 Section 26.
6 Undo the three bolts securing the module to the steering column **(see illustration)**.
7 Withdraw the module from the steering

column, disconnect the wiring connector and remove the module **(see illustration)**.
8 If required, the direction indicator and wiper switch stalks can be removed from the module as follows. Insert a 1.5 mm diameter rod down the slot on the side of the stalk. Push the rod in fully, to depress the internal retaining lug, and withdraw the stalk from the module **(see illustrations)**. Note that this procedure merely allows the stalks to be removed, the actual direction indicator and wiper switches themselves are an integral part of the electronics module and cannot be removed.

Refitting

9 If removed, push the switch stalks back into position in the module until they lock into place.
10 Refit the electronics module to the steering wheel using a reverse of the removal procedure.

16.6 Undo the three bolts (arrowed) securing the electronics module to the steering column

16.8a Insert a thin rod down the slot on the side of the stalk to depress the internal retaining lug …

17 Radio/CD player – removal and refitting

Note: *The following removal and refitting procedure is for the range of radio/CD units which Vauxhall/Opel fit as standard equipment. Removal and refitting procedures of non-standard units may differ slightly.*

Removal

1 All the radio/CD players fitted by Vauxhall have DIN standard fixings. Two special tools, obtainable from most car accessory shops, are required for removal. Alternatively, suitable tools can be fabricated from 3 mm diameter wire, such as welding rod.

16.7 Withdraw the module from the steering column and disconnect the wiring connector

16.8b … then withdraw the stalk from the electronics module

17.3 Removing the radio/CD player using welding rod to compress the internal clips

2 Disconnect the battery negative terminal (refer to Chapter 5A Section 4).

3 Insert the tools into the holes on the front of the unit, and push them until they snap into place. The radio/CD player can then be slid out of the facia **(see illustration)**.

4 Disconnect the wiring and aerial connections at the rear of the unit, and remove the unit from the car.

Refitting

5 To refit the radio/CD, reconnect the wiring and simply push the unit into the facia until the retaining lugs snap into place. On completion, reconnect the battery and enter the radio security code, where applicable.

18 Speakers – removal and refitting

Door small speaker (tweeter)

1 Carefully prise off the speaker trim panel, complete with speaker, to release the internal retaining clips.

2 Disconnect the wiring connector and unclip the speaker from the panel **(see illustration)**.

3 Refitting is the reverse of removal.

Door main speaker

4 Remove the door inner trim panel as described in Chapter 11 Section 12.

5 Undo the retaining screws, then free the speaker from its location **(see illustration)**. Disconnect the wiring connectors and remove the speaker.

6 Refitting is the reverse of removal.

18.2 Disconnect the wiring connector and unclip the tweeter speaker from the panel

19 Radio aerial – general information

1 Where required, the aerial mast can be unscrewed from the base unit.

2 Removal of the base unit entails removal of the headlining, which is a complicated operation, considered to be outside the scope of this manual. Therefore, any problems relating to the aerial base unit or wiring should be entrusted to a Vauxhall/Opel dealer.

20 Anti-theft alarm system – general information

Note: *This information is applicable only to the anti-theft alarm system fitted by Vauxhall/Opel as standard equipment.*

1 Most models in the range are fitted with an anti-theft alarm system as standard equipment. The alarm is automatically armed and disarmed when the deadlocks are operated using the driver's door lock or remote control key. The alarm has switches on all the doors (including the tailgate), the bonnet, the radio/CD player and the ignition and starter circuits. If the tailgate, bonnet or any of the doors are opened whilst the alarm is set, the alarm horn will sound and the hazard warning lights will flash. The alarm also has an immobiliser function which makes the ignition and starter circuits inoperable whilst the alarm is triggered.

2 The alarm system performs a self-test every time it is switched on; this test takes approximately 10 seconds. During the self-test, the LED (light emitting diode) in the hazard warning light switch will come on. If the LED flashes, then either the tailgate, bonnet or one of the doors is open, or there is a fault in the circuit. After the initial 10 second period, the LED will flash to indicate that the alarm is switched on. On unlocking the driver's door lock, the LED will illuminate for approximately 1 second, then go out, indicating that the alarm has been switched off.

3 With the alarm set, if the tailgate is unlocked, the tailgate switch sensing will automatically be switched off, but the door

18.5 Door loudspeaker retaining screws (arrowed)

and bonnet switches will still be active. Once the tailgate is shut and locked again, the tailgate switch sensing will be switched back on after approximately 10 seconds.

4 Should the alarm system develop a fault, the vehicle should be taken to a Vauxhall/Opel dealer for examination.

21 Heated seat components – general information

1 On models with heated seats, a heater mat is fitted to both the seat back and seat cushion. Renewal of either heater mat involves peeling back the upholstery, removing the old mat, sticking the new mat in position and then refitting the upholstery. Note that upholstery removal and refitting requires considerable skill and experience if it is to be carried out successfully, and is therefore best entrusted to your Vauxhall/Opel dealer. In practice, it will be very difficult for the home mechanic to carry out the job without ruining the upholstery.

22 Airbag system – general information and precautions

General information

1 A driver's airbag is fitted as standard equipment on all models. The airbag is fitted in the steering wheel centre pad. Additionally, a passenger's airbag located in the facia, side airbags located in the front seats, and curtain airbags located in the headlining are optionally available.

2 The system is armed only when the ignition is switched on, however, a reserve power source maintains a power supply to the system in the event of a break in the main electrical supply. The steering wheel and facia airbags are activated by a 'g' sensor (deceleration sensor), and controlled by an electronic control unit located under the centre console. The side airbags and curtain airbags are activated by severe side impact and operate independently of the main system. A separate electrical supply, control unit and sensor is provided for the side/curtain airbags on each side of the car.

3 The airbags are inflated by a gas generator, which forces the bag out from its location in the steering wheel, facia, seat back frame, or headlining.

Precautions

⚠ *Warning: The following precautions must be observed when working on vehicles equipped with an airbag system, to prevent the possibility of personal injury.*

General precautions

4 The following precautions must be observed when carrying out work on a vehicle equipped with an airbag:

a) Do not disconnect the battery with the engine running.
b) Before carrying out any work in the vicinity of the airbag, removal of any of the airbag components, or any welding work on the vehicle, de-activate the system as described in the following sub-Section.
c) Do not attempt to test any of the airbag system circuits using test meters or any other test equipment.
d) If the airbag warning light comes on, or any fault in the system is suspected, consult a Vauxhall/Opel dealer without delay. Do not attempt to carry out fault diagnosis, or any dismantling of the components.

Precautions when handling an airbag

a) Transport the airbag by itself, bag upward.
b) Do not put your arms around the airbag.
c) Carry the airbag close to the body, bag outward.
d) Do not drop the airbag or expose it to impacts.
e) Do not attempt to dismantle the airbag unit
f) Do not connect any form of electrical equipment to any part of the airbag circuit.

Precautions when storing an airbag

a) Store the unit in a cupboard with the airbag upward.
b) Do not expose the airbag to temperatures above 80ºC.
c) Do not expose the airbag to flames.
d) Do not attempt to dispose of the airbag – consult a Vauxhall/Opel dealer.
e) Never refit an airbag which is known to be faulty or damaged.

De-activation of airbag system

5 The system must be de-activated before carrying out any work on the airbag components or surrounding area:

a) Switch on the ignition and check the operation of the airbag warning light on the instrument panel. The light should illuminate when the ignition is switched on, then extinguish.
b) Switch off the ignition.
c) Remove the ignition key.
d) Switch off all electrical equipment.
e) Disconnect the battery negative terminal (refer to Chapter 5A Section 4).
f) Insulate the battery negative terminal and the end of the battery negative lead to prevent any possibility of contact.

23.3 Release the locking clips, then disconnect the wiring connectors

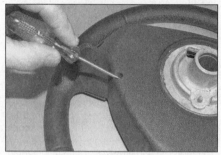

23.2a Insert a screwdriver into the holes at the rear of the steering wheel (shown with steering wheel removed) ...

g) Wait for at least two minutes before carrying out any further work. Wait at least ten minutes if the airbag warning light did not operate correctly.

Activation of airbag system

6 To activate the system on completion of any work, proceed as follows:

a) Ensure that there are no occupants in the vehicle, and that there are no loose objects around the vicinity of the steering wheel. Close the vehicle doors and windows.
b) Ensure that the ignition is switched off then reconnect the battery negative terminal.
c) Open the driver's door and switch on the ignition, without reaching in front of the steering wheel. Check that the airbag warning light illuminates briefly then extinguishes.
d) Switch off the ignition.
e) If the airbag warning light does not operate as described in paragraph c), consult a Vauxhall/Opel dealer before driving the vehicle.

23 Airbag system components – removal and refitting

⚠ **Warning: Refer to the precautions given in Section 22 before attempting to carry out work on any of the airbag components.**

1 De-activate the airbag system as described in the previous Section, then proceed as described under the relevant heading.

Driver's airbag

2 Turn the steering wheel through 90° so that

23.6 Passenger's airbag retaining bolt (arrowed)

23.2b ... to depress the airbag internal spring retainers (arrowed – shown with airbag removed)

the two holes at the rear of the steering wheel spokes are accessible. Insert a screwdriver into the holes, one at a time, to depress the internal spring retainers, and at the same time pull the airbag unit away from the steering wheel to release it **(see illustrations)**.

3 Release the locking clips, then disconnect the wiring connectors at the rear of the airbag unit **(see illustration)**. Remove the airbag unit. Note that the airbag must not be knocked or dropped, and should be stored the correct way up, with its padded surface uppermost.

4 Refitting is a reversal of the removal procedure.

Passenger's airbag

5 Remove the glovebox as described in Chapter 11 Section 26.

6 Undo the bolt securing the airbag to the facia crossmember **(see illustration)**. Withdraw the airbag and disconnect the wiring connector(s). Note that the airbag must not be knocked or dropped, and should be stored the correct way up (as mounted in the vehicle).

7 Refitting is a reversal of the removal procedure, tightening the retaining bolt securely.

Side airbags

8 The side airbags are located internally within the front seat back and no attempt should be made to remove them. Any suspected problems with the side airbag system should be referred to a Vauxhall/Opel dealer.

Curtain airbags

9 The curtain airbags are located behind the headlining above the doors on each side and no attempt should be made to remove them. Any suspected problems with the curtain airbag system should be referred to a Vauxhall/Opel dealer.

Airbag control unit

10 The airbag control unit is located beneath the centre console and no attempt should be made to remove it. Any suspected problems with the control unit should be referred to a Vauxhall/Opel dealer.

Airbag rotary connector

11 The airbag rotary connector is an integral part of the steering column electronics module. Removal and refitting procedures for the module are contained in Section 16.

ENGINE COMPARTMENT – UNDERHOOD ELECTRICAL CENTRE

FUSE/RELAY	VALUE	DESCRIPTION
F1	20 A	ABS
F2	30 A	ABS
F3	40 A	Climate control fan
F4	40 A	Blower
F5	40 A	Cooling fan
F6	40 A	Cooling fan
F7	20 A	Central locking control unit
F8	10 A	Windscreen washer
F9	25 A	Heated rear windscreen, Heated mirror
F10	7.5 A	Diagnostic connector
F11	7.5 A	Instrument
F12	7.5 A	Telephone, Infotainment control unit, Information display
F13	5 A	Courtesy light
F14	30 A	Windscreen wiper
F15	30 A	Windscreen wiper
F16	5 A	Horn, ABS, Brake light switch, Air conditioning system
F17	25 A	Fuel filter (diesel) or Air conditioning system
F18	-	Not used
F19	25 A	Starter relay
F20	10 A	Horn
F21	20 A	Engine electronics
F22	7.5 A	Engine electronics
F23	10 A	Headlight range control
F24	15 A	Fuel pump
F25	15 A	Not used
F26	10 A	Engine electronics
F27	7.5 A	Heating, Air conditioning system, Air quality sensor
F28	-	Not used
F29	5 A	Power steering
F30	10 A	Engine electronics
F31	15 A	Rear windscreen wiper
F32	5 A	Brake light switch

Fuses and relays

F33	5 A	Headlight range control, Light switch, Clutch switch, Intrument, Driver's door module
F34	7.5 A	Steering column control unit
F35	20 A	Infotainment control unit
F36	15 A	Cigarette lighter, Front power outlet
R1	-	Starter relay
R2	-	Engine control unit relay
R3	-	Terminal 15 relay
R4	-	Wiper high/low speed relay
R5	-	Windscreen wiper switch
R6	-	Headlight washer pump relay or Heated back window relay
R7	-	Air-conditioning compressor relay or Horn relay
R8	-	Fuel pump relay
R9	-	Cooling fan relay
R10	-	Cooling fan relay
R11	-	Cooling fan relay
R12	-	Fuel filter heater relay or Air conditioning compressor relay
R13	-	Blower relay
R14	-	Front fog light relay or Power cut-off relay

FUSE AND RELAY BOX IN LUGGAGE COMPARTMENT, REAR ELECTRONIC MODULE

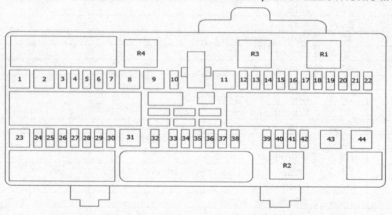

FUSE/RELAY	VALUE	DESCRIPTION
F1	25 A	Front power windows
F2	-	Not used
F3	7.5 A	Instrument
F4	5 A	Heating, Air conditioning system, Automatic climate control
F5	-	Not used
F6	-	Not used
F7	-	Not used
F8	-	Not used
F9	-	Not used
F10	-	Not used
F11	25 A	Heated rear windscreen
F12	15 A	Rear window wiper
F13	5 A	Parking assistance
F14	7.5 A	Heating, Air conditioning system
F15	-	Not used
F16	5 A	Seat occupancy sensor, Entry and start authorisation control unit

Fuses and relays (continued)

F17	5 A	Rain sensor, Air quality sensor, Tyre pressure monitoring system control unit, Interior mirror
F18	5 A	Intrument, Switches
F19	-	Not used
F20	10 A	Active damping ride control unit
F21	7.5 A	Heated mirrors
F22	-	Not used
F23	25 A	Rear power windows
F24	7.5 A	Diagnostic connector
F25	-	Not used
F26	7.5 A	Electric mirrors
F27	5 A	Ultrasonic sensor, Security alarm system
F28	-	Not used
F29	15 A	Cigarette lighter, Front power outlet
F30	15 A	Rear power outlet
F31	-	Not used
F32	-	Not used
F33	15 A	Entry and start authorisation control unit
F34	-	Not used
F35	15 A	Rear power outlet
F36	20 A	Trailer connector socket
F37	-	Not used
F38	25 A	Central locking control unit, Terminal 30
F39	15 A	Left heated seats
F40	15 A	Right heated seats
F41	-	Not used
F42	-	Not used
F43	-	Not used
F44	-	Not used
R1	-	Terminal 15 relay
R2	-	Terminal 15A
R3	-	Heated rear windscreen relay
R4	-	Not used

FUSE AND RELAY BOX IN LUGGAGE COMPARTMENT, WITHOUT REAR ELECTRONIC MODULE

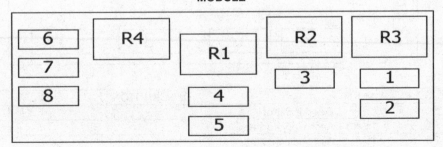

FUSE/RELAY	VALUE	DESCRIPTION
F1	30 A	Front power windows
F2	7.5 A	Exterior mirror
F3	10 A	Air conditioning
F4	7.5 A	Rear lights
F5	30 A	Rear power windows
F6	15 A	Accessory socket or front fog lights

Fuses and relays (continued)

F7	15 A	Front fog lights or Accessory socket
F8	15 A	Accessory socket
R1	-	Reversing light relay
R2	-	Air conditioning compressor relay
R3	-	Rear windscreen wiper relay
R4	-	Front fog light relay

FUSE BOX IN ENGINE COMPARTMENT

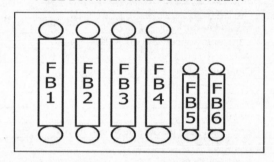

FUSE/RELAY	VALUE	DESCRIPTION
FB1	-	Not used
FB2	80 A	Glow time control unit
FB3	80 A	Electro-hydraulic power steering
FB4	100 A	Additional heater or Auxiliary heating system (30 A also used)
FB5	80 A	Fuse and relay box in luggage compartment, with rear electrical centre (REC)
FB6	80 A	Fuse and relay box in luggage compartment, with rear electrical centre (REC)

ADDITIONAL FUSES AND RELAYS IN LUGGAGE COMPARTMENT

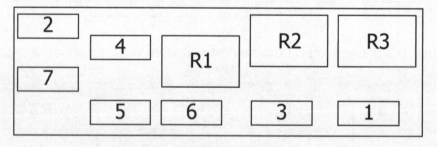

FUSE/RELAY	VALUE	DESCRIPTION
F1	7.5 A	Exterior mirror
F2	15 A	Accessory socket
F3	10 A	Air conditioning
F4	30 A	Front power windows
F5	30 A	Rear power windows
F6	7.5 A	Rear lights
F7	15 A	Accessory socket
R1	-	Reversing light relay
R2	-	Air conditioning compressor relay
R3	-	Rear windscreen wiper relay

Fuses and relays (continued)

ENGINE COMPARTMENT – RADIATOR EXCEPT Z19DT AND Z19DTL

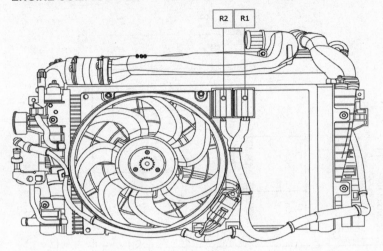

FUSE/RELAY	VALUE	DESCRIPTION
R1	-	Radiator fan relay
R2	-	Radiator fan relay

ENGINE COMPARTMENT – RADIATOR Z19DT AND Z19DTL

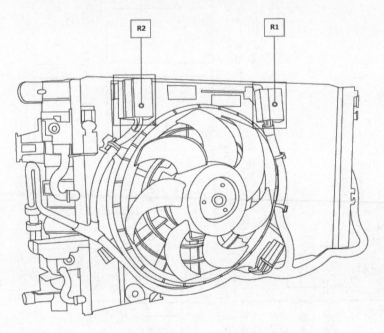

FUSE/RELAY	VALUE	DESCRIPTION
R1	-	Radiator fan relay
R2	-	Radiator fan relay

Fuses and relays (continued)

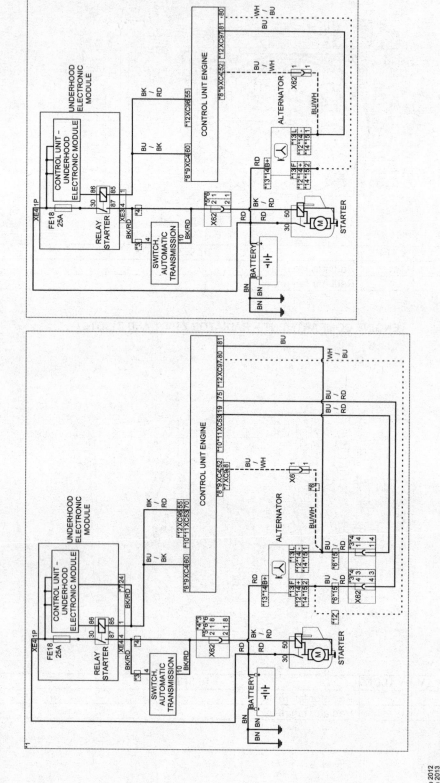

Starting and charging

*1 Up to 2012
*2 From 2013
*3 Automatic transmission
*4 Manual transmission
*5 Petrol
*6 Diesel
*7 Engine code: Z16XE1
*8 Engine code: A16XER, Z16XER
*9 Engine code: A18XER, Z18XER
*10 Engine code: Z19DT, Z19DTL
*11 Engine code: Z19DTH
*12 Engine code: A17DTJ, A17DTR
*13 Alternator 1 PIN Connector
*14 Alternator 2 PIN Connector
*15 Except 1.7 Diesel

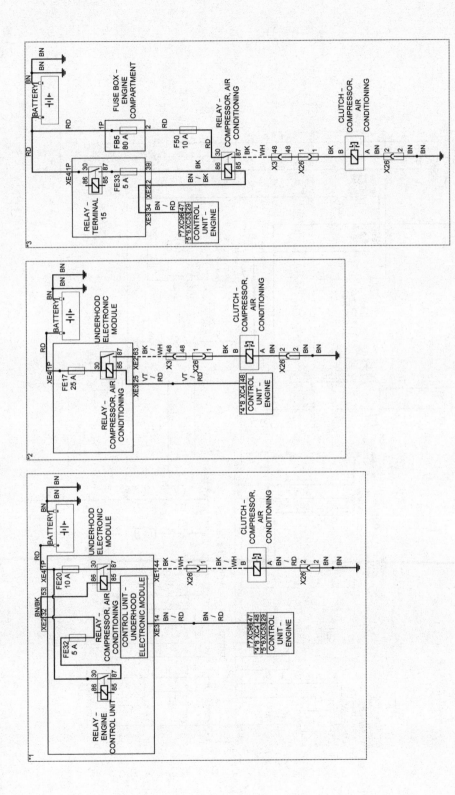

Heating and cooling – Compressor

*1 Rear electronic module
*2 Not Rear electronic module Petrol
*3 Not Rear electronic module Diesel
*4 Engine code: A16XER, Z16XER
*5 Engine code: Z19DT, Z19DTL
*6 Engine code: Z19DTH
*7 Engine code: Z19DTJ, A17DTR
*8 Engine code: A18XER, Z18XER

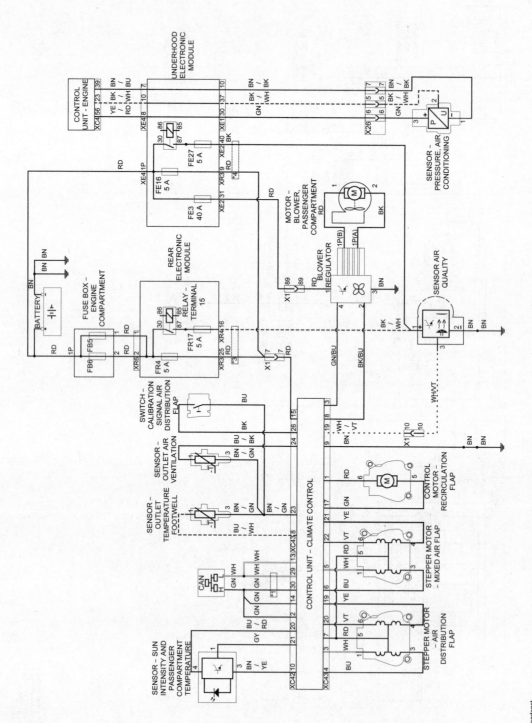

Electronic climate control

*1 Digital audio broadcast
*2 Semi automatic air conditioning
*3 Rear electronic module
*4 Not Rear electronic module
*5 Diesel
*6 Petrol

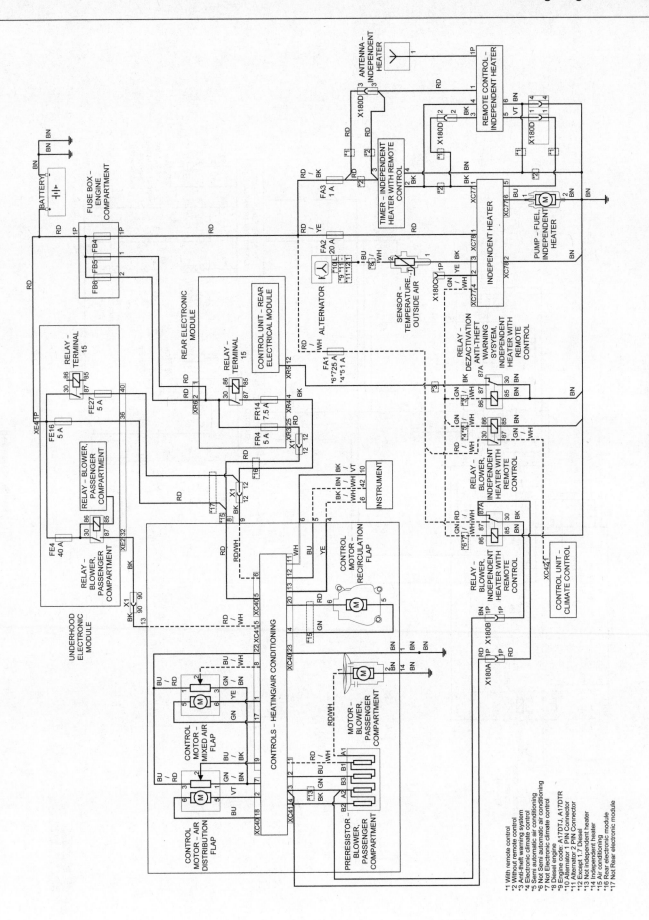

Independent Heater and Air conditioning

*1 With remote control
*2 Without remote control
*3 Anti-theft warning system
*4 Electronic climate control
*5 Semi automatic air conditioning
*6 Not Semi automatic air conditioning
*7 Not Electronic climate control
*8 Diesel engine
*9 Engine code: A17DTJ, A17DTR
*10 Alternator 1 PIN Connector
*11 Alternator 2 PIN Connector
*12 Except 1.7 Diesel
*13 Not independent heater
*14 Independent heater
*15 Air conditioning
*16 Rear electronic module
*17 Not Rear electronic module

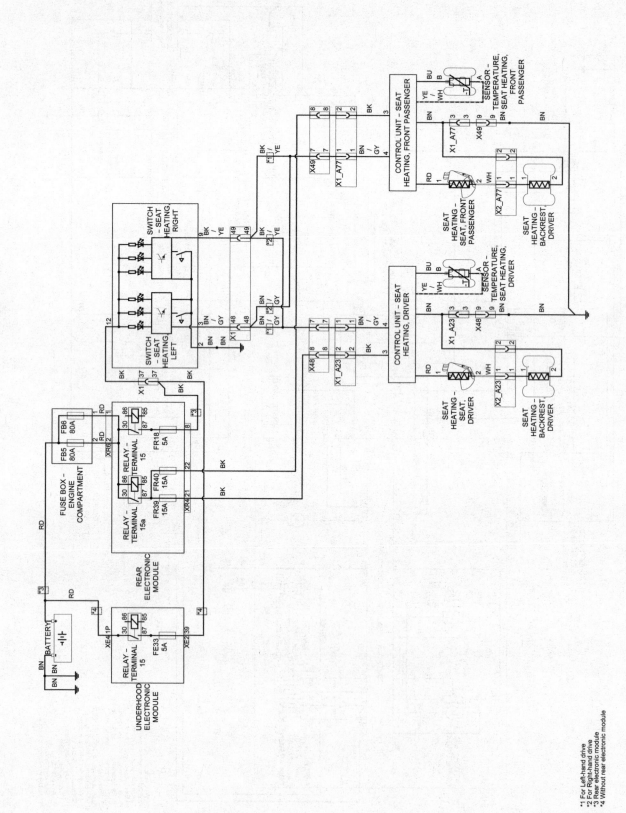

Seat heating

*1 For Left-hand drive
*2 For Right-hand drive
*3 Rear electronic module
*4 Without rear electronic module

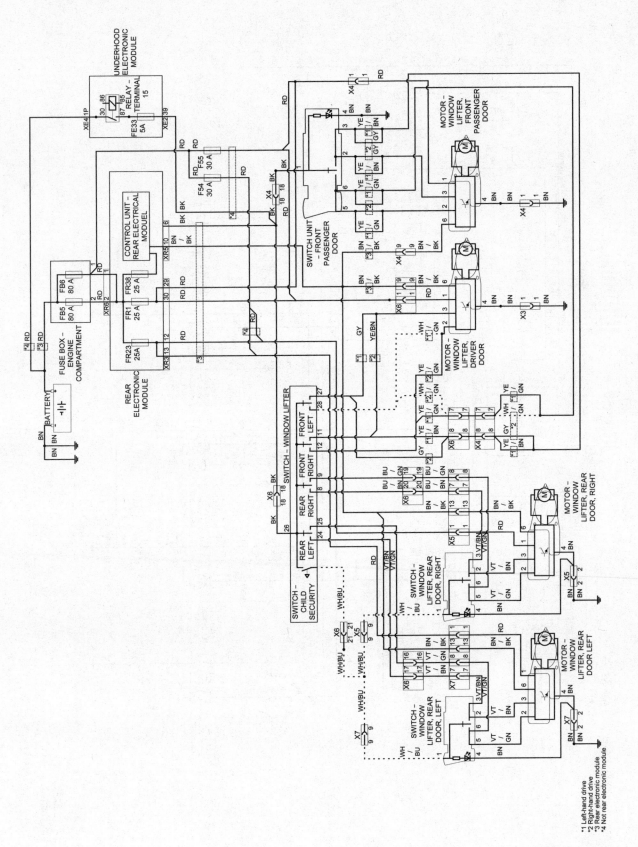

Power windows

*1 Left-hand drive
*2 Right-hand drive
*3 Rear electronic module
*4 Not rear electronic module

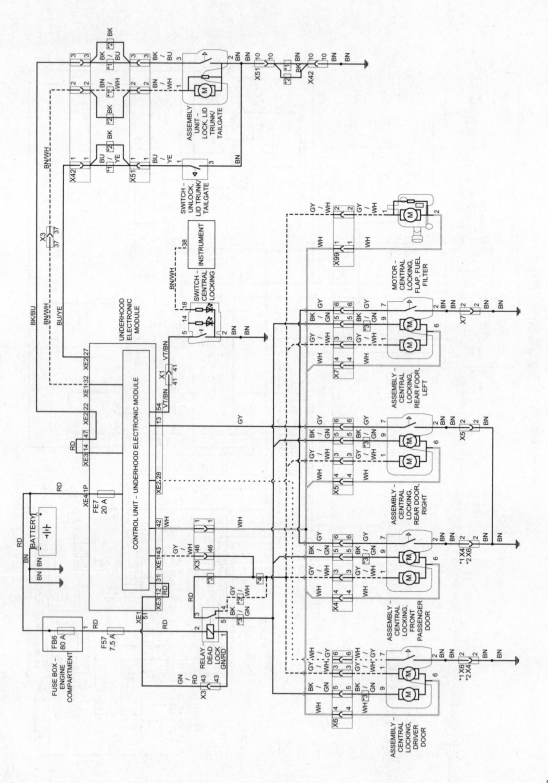

Central locking – without Keyless entry or rear electronic module

*1 Left-hand drive
*2 Right-hand drive
*3 Dead lock
*4 Not Dead lock

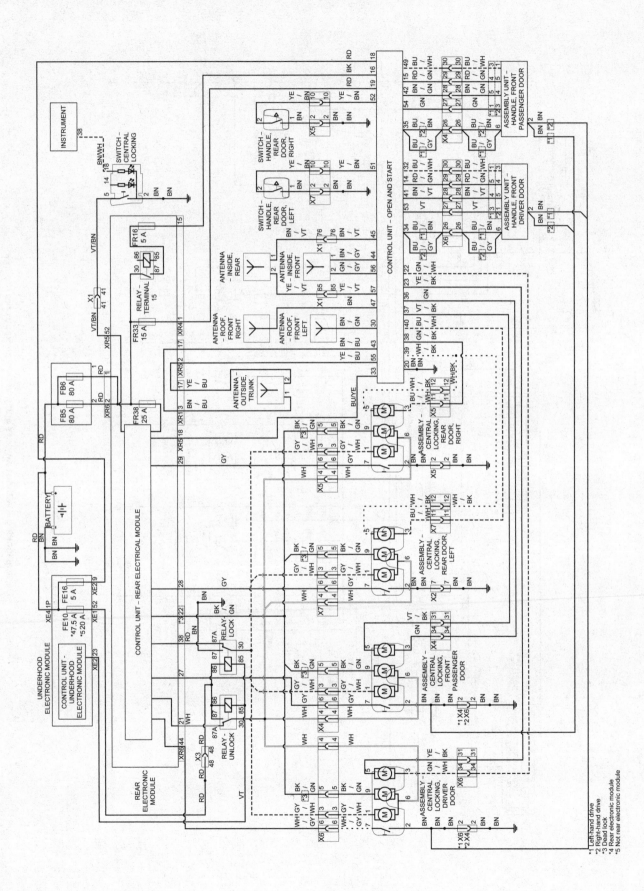

Central locking – Keyless entry

*1 Left-hand drive
*2 Right-hand drive
*3 Dead lock
*4 Rear electronic module
*5 Not rear electronic module

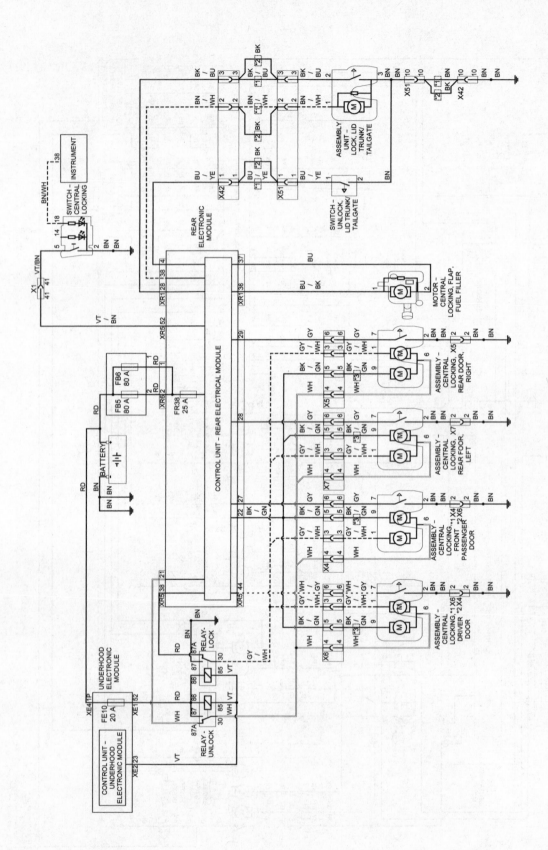

Central locking – without Keyless entry, with rear electronic module

*1 Left-hand drive
*2 Right-hand drive
*3 Dead lock

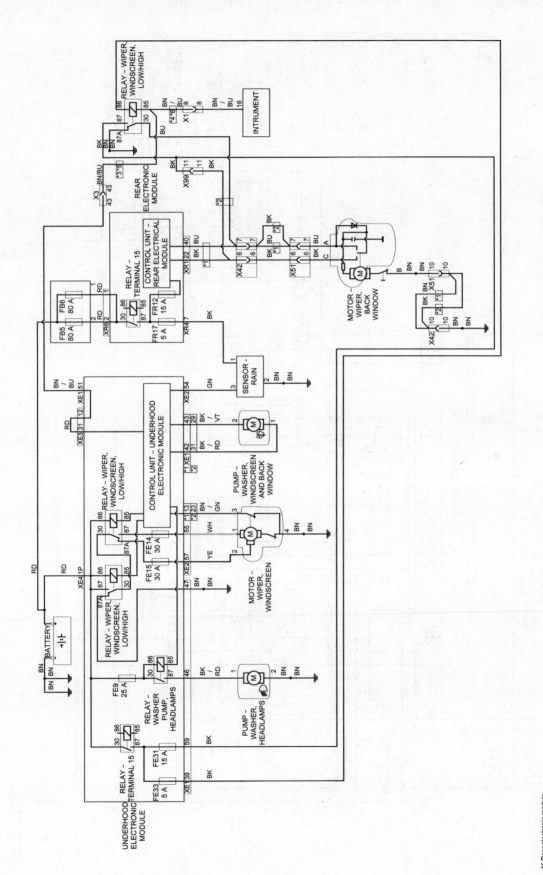

Washer and wipers

*1 Rear electronic module
*2 Not rear electronic module
*3 Left-hand drive
*4 Right-hand drive
*5 Without front fog lamps
*6 With front fog lamps

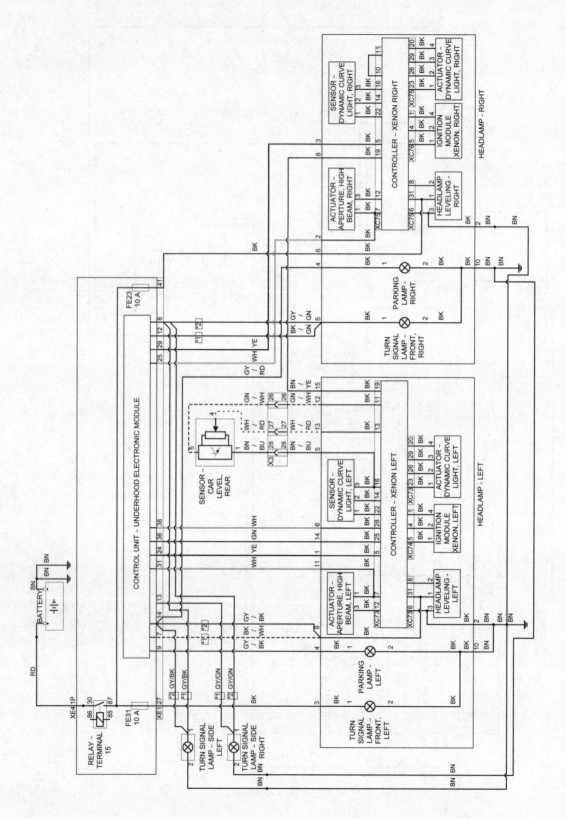

Exterior lighting – Adaptive forward lighting

*1 Rear electronic module
*2 Not Rear electronic module

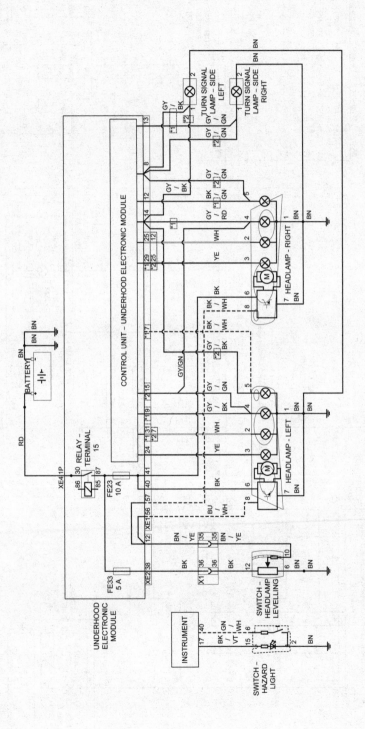

Exterior lighting – non-Adaptive forward lighting

*1 Rear electronic module
*2 Not Rear electronic module

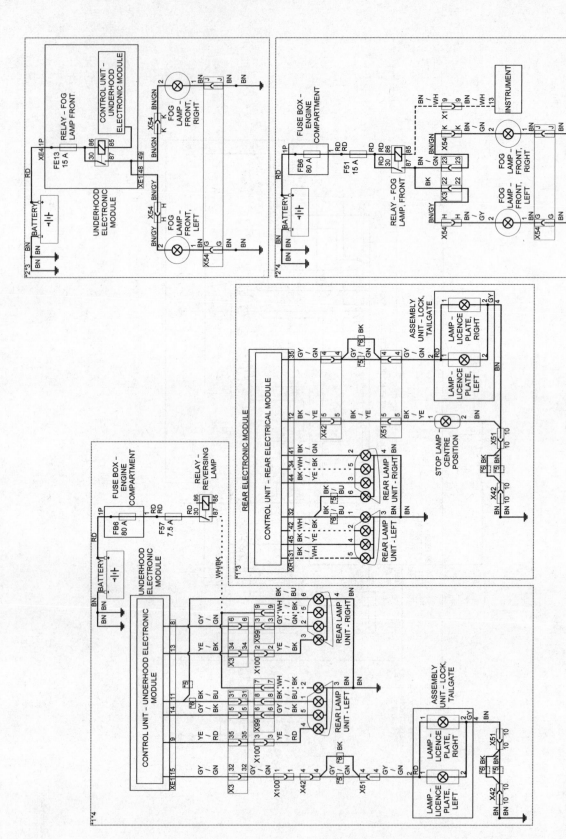

Exterior lighting – Rear lighting

*1 Lighting rear and licence plate lamps
*2 Fog lamp
*3 Rear eletronic module
*4 Not Rear eletronic module
*5 Left-hand traffic
*6 Right-hand traffic

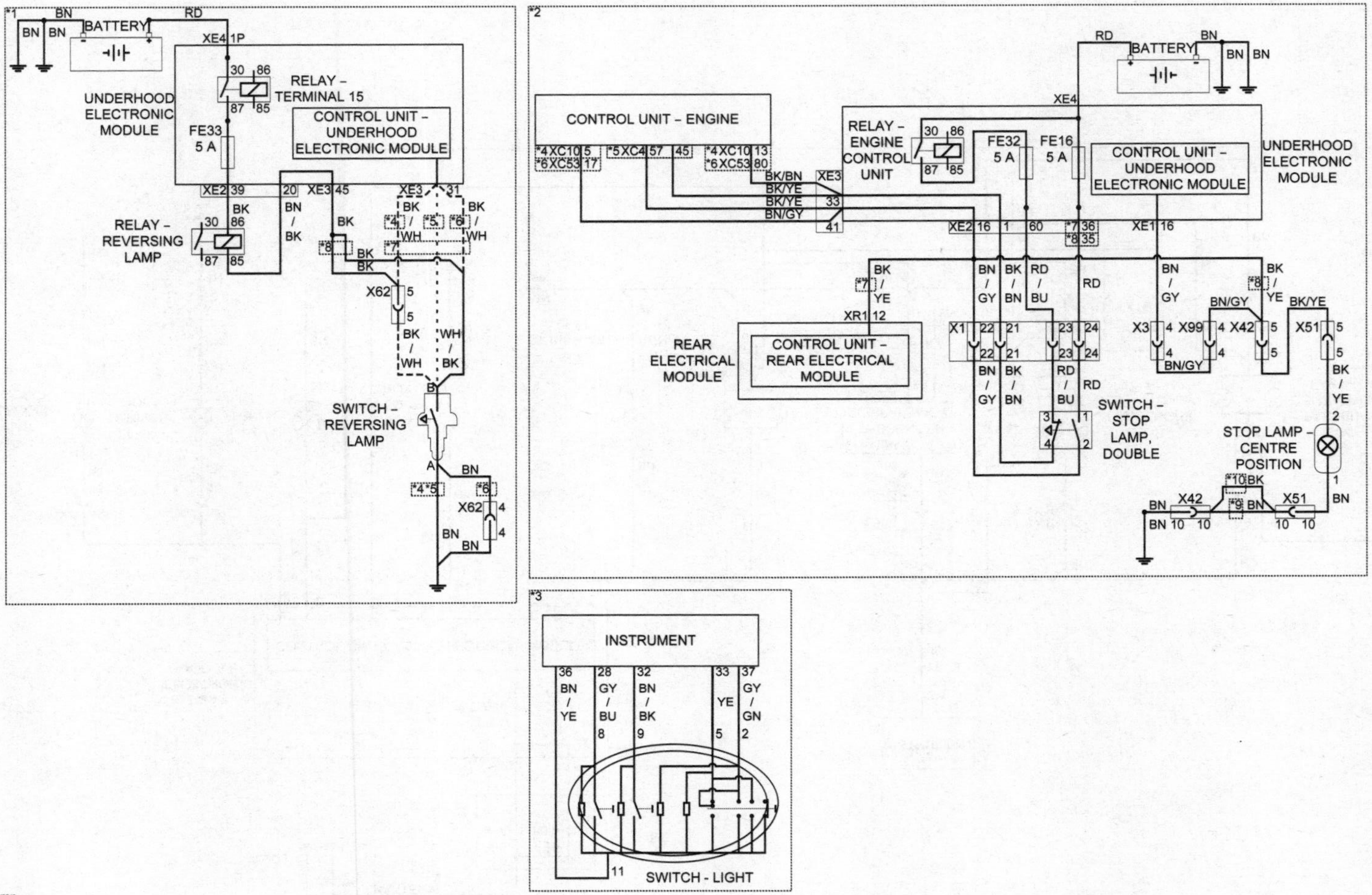

Exterior lighting – reversing light switch, brake light switch and lighting control switch

*1 Switch - Reversing lamp
*2 Switch - Stop lamp
*3 Switch - Light
*4 Engine code: Z16XE1
*5 Engine code: Z16XER, Z16XER
*6 Engine code: Z18XER, Z16XER
*7 Engine code: Z18DT, Z19DTL, Z19DTH, A17DTJ, A17DTR
*7 Rear electronic module
*8 Not Rear electronic module
*9 Left-hand traffic
*10 Right-hand traffic

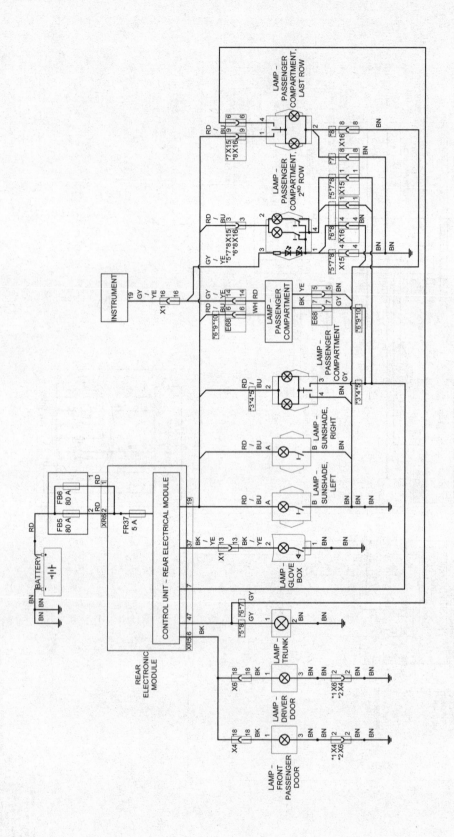

Interior lighting – with rear electronic module

*1 Left-hand drive
*2 Right-hand drive
*3 Not Anti-theft warning system
*4 Not microphone
*5 Not reading lamp, rear
*6 Reading lamp, rear
*7 Sun roof
*8 Not Sun roof
*9 Microphone
*10 Anti-theft warning system

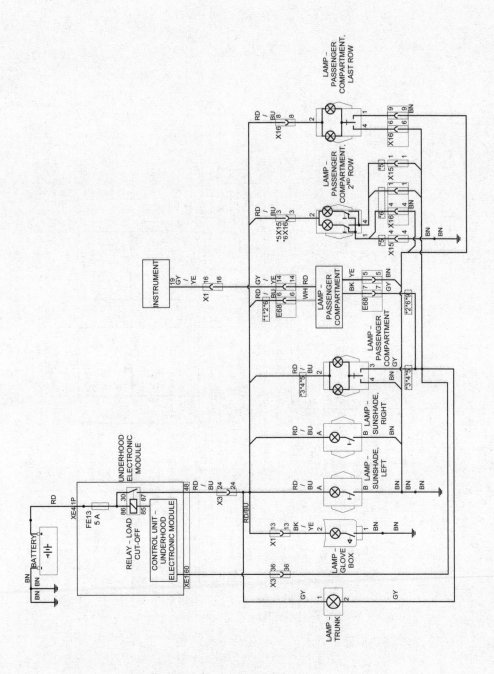

Interior lighting – without rear electronic module

*1 Microphone
*2 Anti-theft warning system
*3 Not Anti-theft warning system
*4 Not microphone
*5 Not reading lamp, rear
*6 Reading lamp, rear

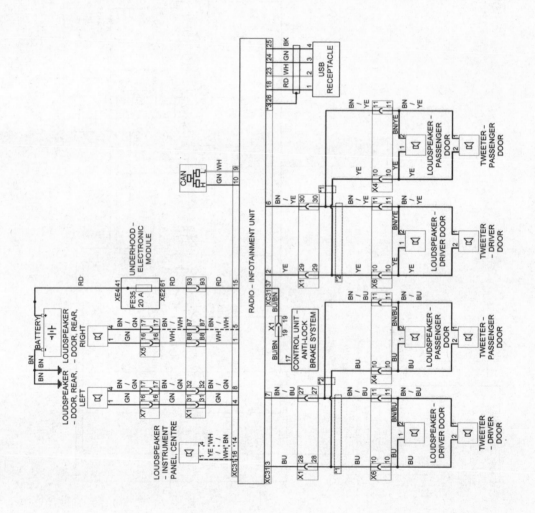

Sound system – Part 1

*1 Left-hand drive
*2 Right-hand drive

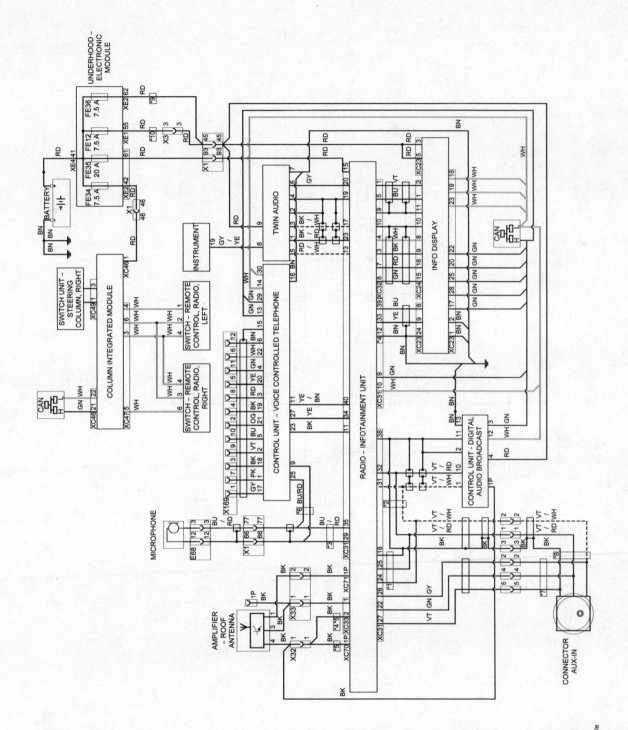

Sound system – Part 2

*1 Radio CD70
*2 Not radio CD70
*3 Radio
*4 Car phone
*5 Navigation System
*6 Telephone
*7 UFZ Radio
*8 Not UFZ Radio
*9 Rear electronic module
*10 Not Rear electronic module

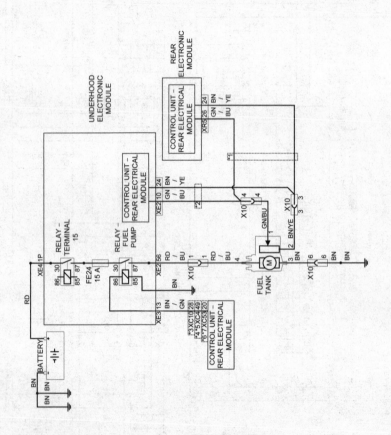

Fuel pump

*1 Rear electronic module
*2 Not Rear electronic module
*3 Engine code: Z16XE1
*4 Engine code: A16XER, Z16XER
*5 Engine code: A18XER, Z18XER
*6 Engine code: A18XER, Z19DT, Z19DTL
*7 Engine code: Z19DTH

Dimensions and weights . . . . **REF•1**
Fuel economy. . . . . **REF•2**
Conversion factors . . . . **REF•6**
Buying spare parts . . . . **REF•7**
Vehicle identification. . . . . **REF•7**
General repair procedures . . . . **REF•8**
Jacking and vehicle support . . . . **REF•9**

Disconnecting the battery . . . . **REF•9**
Tools and working facilities . . . . **REF•10**
MOT test checks . . . . **REF•12**
Fault finding . . . . **REF•16**
Glossary of technical terms . . . . **REF•26**
Index. . . . . **REF•30**

Dimensions and weights

Note: *All figures are approximate and may vary according to model. Refer to manufacturer's data for exact figures.*

Dimensions

Overall length . . . . 4467 mm
Overall width (including door mirrors) . . . . 2025 mm
Overall height (unladen):
  Without panoramic roof . . . . 1635 mm
  With panoramic roof. . . . . 1670 mm
Wheelbase . . . . 2703 mm
Turning circle diameter (wall to wall) . . . . 11.50 metres
Front track . . . . 1488 mm
Rear track. . . . . 1488 mm

Weights

Kerb weight:
  1.6 litre petrol engine models. . . . . 1505 kg
  1.8 litre petrol engine models. . . . . 1503 kg
  1.7 lite diesel engine models . . . . 1600 kg
  1.9 litre diesel engine models. . . . . 1613 kg
Gross vehicle weight . . . . Refer to information contained on the vehicle identification plate
Maximum roof load (including weight of rack) . . . . 75 kg

Fuel economy

Although depreciation is still the biggest part of the cost of motoring for most car owners, the cost of fuel is more immediately noticeable. These pages give some tips on how to get the best fuel economy.

Working it out

Manufacturer's figures

Car manufacturers are required by law to provide fuel consumption information on all new vehicles sold. These 'official' figures are obtained by simulating various driving conditions on a rolling road or a test track. Real life conditions are different, so the fuel consumption actually achieved may not bear much resemblance to the quoted figures.

How to calculate it

Many cars now have trip computers which will

display fuel consumption, both instantaneous and average. Refer to the owner's handbook for details of how to use these.

To calculate consumption yourself (and maybe to check that the trip computer is accurate), proceed as follows.

1. Fill up with fuel and note the mileage, or zero the trip recorder.
2. Drive as usual until you need to fill up again.
3. Note the amount of fuel required to refill the tank, and the mileage covered since the previous fill-up.
4. Divide the mileage by the amount of fuel used to obtain the consumption figure.

For example:

Mileage at first fill-up (a) = 27,903
Mileage at second fill-up (b) = 28,346
Mileage covered (b - a) = 443
Fuel required at second fill-up = 48.6 litres

The half-completed changeover to metric units in the UK means that we buy our fuel

in litres, measure distances in miles and talk about fuel consumption in miles per gallon. There are two ways round this: the first is to convert the litres to gallons before doing the calculation (by dividing by 4.546, or see Table 1). So in the example:

48.6 litres ÷ 4.546 = 10.69 gallons
443 miles ÷ 10.69 gallons = 41.4 mpg

The second way is to calculate the consumption in miles per litre, then multiply that figure by 4.546 (or see Table 2).

So in the example, fuel consumption is:

443 miles ÷ 48.6 litres = 9.1 mpl
9.1 mpl x 4.546 = 41.4 mpg

The rest of Europe expresses fuel consumption in litres of fuel required to travel 100 km (l/100 km). For interest, the conversions are given in Table 3. In practice it doesn't matter what units you use, provided you know what your normal consumption is and can spot if it's getting better or worse.

Table 1: conversion of litres to Imperial gallons

litres	1	2	3	4	5	10	20	30	40	50	60	70
gallons	0.22	0.44	0.66	0.88	1.10	2.24	4.49	6.73	8.98	11.22	13.47	15.71

Table 2: conversion of miles per litre to miles per gallon

miles per litre	5	6	7	8	9	10	11	12	13	14
miles per gallon	23	27	32	36	41	46	50	55	59	64

Table 3: conversion of litres per 100 km to miles per gallon

litres per 100 km	4	4.5	5	5.5	6	6.5	7	8	9	10
miles per gallon	71	63	56	51	47	43	40	35	31	28

Maintenance

A well-maintained car uses less fuel and creates less pollution. In particular:

Filters

Change air and fuel filters at the specified intervals.

Oil

Use a good quality oil of the lowest viscosity specified by the vehicle manufacturer (see *Lubricants and fluids*). Check the level often and be careful not to overfill.

Spark plugs

When applicable, renew at the specified intervals.

Tyres

Check tyre pressures regularly. Under-inflated tyres have an increased rolling resistance. It is generally safe to use the higher pressures specified for full load conditions even when not fully laden, but keep an eye on the centre band of tread for signs of wear due to over-inflation.

When buying new tyres, consider the 'fuel saving' models which most manufacturers include in their ranges.

Driving style

Acceleration

Acceleration uses more fuel than driving at a steady speed. The best technique with modern cars is to accelerate reasonably briskly to the desired speed, changing up through the gears as soon as possible without making the engine labour.

Air conditioning

Air conditioning absorbs quite a bit of energy from the engine – typically 3 kW (4 hp) or so. The effect on fuel consumption is at its worst in slow traffic. Switch it off when not required.

Anticipation

Drive smoothly and try to read the traffic flow so as to avoid unnecessary acceleration and braking.

Automatic transmission

When accelerating in an automatic, avoid depressing the throttle so far as to make the transmission hold onto lower gears at higher speeds. Don't use the 'Sport' setting, if applicable.

When stationary with the engine running, select 'N' or 'P'. When moving, keep your left foot away from the brake.

Braking

Braking converts the car's energy of motion into heat – essentially, it is wasted. Obviously some braking is always going to be necessary, but with good anticipation it is surprising how much can be avoided, especially on routes that you know well.

Carshare

Consider sharing lifts to work or to the shops. Even once a week will make a difference.

Electrical loads

Electricity is 'fuel' too; the alternator which charges the battery does so by converting some of the engine's energy of motion into electrical energy. The more electrical accessories are in use, the greater the load on the alternator. Switch off big consumers like the heated rear window when not required.

Freewheeling

Freewheeling (coasting) in neutral with the engine switched off is dangerous. The effort required to operate power-assisted brakes and steering increases when the engine is not running, with a potential lack of control in emergency situations.

In any case, modern fuel injection systems automatically cut off the engine's fuel supply on the overrun (moving and in gear, but with the accelerator pedal released).

Gadgets

Bolt-on devices claiming to save fuel have been around for nearly as long as the motor car itself. Those which worked were rapidly adopted as standard equipment by the vehicle manufacturers. Others worked only in certain situations, or saved fuel only at the expense of unacceptable effects on performance, driveability or the life of engine components.

The most effective fuel saving gadget is the driver's right foot.

Journey planning

Combine (eg) a trip to the supermarket with a visit to the recycling centre and the DIY store, rather than making separate journeys.

When possible choose a travelling time outside rush hours.

Load

The more heavily a car is laden, the greater the energy required to accelerate it to a given speed. Remove heavy items which you don't need to carry.

One load which is often overlooked is the contents of the fuel tank. A tankful of fuel (55 litres / 12 gallons) weighs 45 kg (100 lb) or so. Just half filling it may be worthwhile.

Lost?

At the risk of stating the obvious, if you're going somewhere new, have details of the route to hand. There's not much point in achieving record mpg if you also go miles out of your way.

Parking

If possible, carry out any reversing or turning manoeuvres when you arrive at a parking space so that you can drive straight out when you leave. Manoeuvering when the engine is cold uses a lot more fuel.

Driving around looking for free on-street parking may cost more in fuel than buying a car park ticket.

Premium fuel

Most major oil companies (and some supermarkets) have premium grades of fuel which are several pence a litre dearer than the standard grades. Reports vary, but the consensus seems to be that if these fuels improve economy at all, they do not do so by enough to justify their extra cost.

Roof rack

When loading a roof rack, try to produce a wedge shape with the narrow end at the front. Any cover should be securely fastened – if it flaps it's creating turbulence and absorbing energy.

Remove roof racks and boxes when not in use – they increase air resistance and can create a surprising amount of noise.

Short journeys

The engine is at its least efficient, and wear is highest, during the first few miles after a cold start. Consider walking, cycling or using public transport.

Speed

The engine is at its most efficient when running at a steady speed and load at the rpm where it develops maximum torque. (You can find this figure in the car's handbook.) For most cars this corresponds to between 55 and 65 mph in top gear.

Above the optimum cruising speed, fuel consumption starts to rise quite sharply. A car travelling at 80 mph will typically be using 30% more fuel than at 60 mph.

Supermarket fuel

It may be cheap but is it any good? In the UK all supermarket fuel must meet the relevant British Standard. The major oil companies will say that their branded fuels have better additive packages which may stop carbon and other deposits building up. A reasonable compromise might be to use one tank of branded fuel to three or four from the supermarket.

Switch off when stationary

Switch off the engine if you look like being stationary for more than 30 seconds or so. This is good for the environment as well as for your pocket. Be aware though that frequent restarts are hard on the battery and the starter motor.

Windows

Driving with the windows open increases air turbulence around the vehicle. Closing the windows promotes smooth airflow and

reduced resistance. The faster you go, the more significant this is.

And finally . . .

Driving techniques associated with good fuel economy tend to involve moderate acceleration and low top speeds. Be considerate to the needs of other road users who may need to make brisker progress; even if you do not agree with them this is not an excuse to be obstructive.

Safety must always take precedence over economy, whether it is a question of accelerating hard to complete an overtaking manoeuvre, killing your speed when confronted with a potential hazard or switching the lights on when it starts to get dark.

Conversion factors

Length (distance)

Inches (in)	x 25.4	= Millimetres (mm)	x 0.0394	= Inches (in)
Feet (ft)	x 0.305	= Metres (m)	x 3.281	= Feet (ft)
Miles	x 1.609	= Kilometres (km)	x 0.621	= Miles

Volume (capacity)

Cubic inches (cu in; in³)	x 16.387	= Cubic centimetres (cc; cm³)	x 0.061	= Cubic inches (cu in; in³)
Imperial pints (Imp pt)	x 0.568	= Litres (l)	x 1.76	= Imperial pints (Imp pt)
Imperial quarts (Imp qt)	x 1.137	= Litres (l)	x 0.88	= Imperial quarts (Imp qt)
Imperial quarts (Imp qt)	x 1.201	= US quarts (US qt)	x 0.833	= Imperial quarts (Imp qt)
US quarts (US qt)	x 0.946	= Litres (l)	x 1.057	= US quarts (US qt)
Imperial gallons (Imp gal)	x 4.546	= Litres (l)	x 0.22	= Imperial gallons (Imp gal)
Imperial gallons (Imp gal)	x 1.201	= US gallons (US gal)	x 0.833	= Imperial gallons (Imp gal)
US gallons (US gal)	x 3.785	= Litres (l)	x 0.264	= US gallons (US gal)

Mass (weight)

Ounces (oz)	x 28.35	= Grams (g)	x 0.035	= Ounces (oz)
Pounds (lb)	x 0.454	= Kilograms (kg)	x 2.205	= Pounds (lb)

Force

Ounces-force (ozf; oz)	x 0.278	= Newtons (N)	x 3.6	= Ounces-force (ozf; oz)
Pounds-force (lbf; lb)	x 4.448	= Newtons (N)	x 0.225	= Pounds-force (lbf; lb)
Newtons (N)	x 0.1	= Kilograms-force (kgf; kg)	x 9.81	= Newtons (N)

Pressure

Pounds-force per square inch (psi; lbf/in²; lb/in²)	x 0.070	= Kilograms-force per square centimetre (kgf/cm²; kg/cm²)	x 14.223	= Pounds-force per square inch (psi; lbf/in²; lb/in²)
Pounds-force per square inch (psi; lbf/in²; lb/in²)	x 0.068	= Atmospheres (atm)	x 14.696	= Pounds-force per square inch (psi; lbf/in²; lb/in²)
Pounds-force per square inch (psi; lbf/in²; lb/in²)	x 0.069	= Bars	x 14.5	= Pounds-force per square inch (psi; lbf/in²; lb/in²)
Pounds-force per square inch (psi; lbf/in²; lb/in²)	x 6.895	= Kilopascals (kPa)	x 0.145	= Pounds-force per square inch (psi; lbf/in²; lb/in²)
Kilopascals (kPa)	x 0.01	= Kilograms-force per square centimetre (kgf/cm²; kg/cm²)	x 98.1	= Kilopascals (kPa)
Millibar (mbar)	x 100	= Pascals (Pa)	x 0.01	= Millibar (mbar)
Millibar (mbar)	x 0.0145	= Pounds-force per square inch (psi; lbf/in²; lb/in²)	x 68.947	= Millibar (mbar)
Millibar (mbar)	x 0.75	= Millimetres of mercury (mmHg)	x 1.333	= Millibar (mbar)
Millibar (mbar)	x 0.401	= Inches of water (inH₂O)	x 2.491	= Millibar (mbar)
Millimetres of mercury (mmHg)	x 0.535	= Inches of water (inH₂O)	x 1.868	= Millimetres of mercury (mmHg)
Inches of water (inH₂O)	x 0.036	= Pounds-force per square inch (psi; lbf/in²; lb/in²)	x 27.68	= Inches of water (inH₂O)

Torque (moment of force)

Pounds-force inches (lbf in; lb in)	x 1.152	= Kilograms-force centimetre (kgf cm; kg cm)	x 0.868	= Pounds-force inches (lbf in; lb in)
Pounds-force inches (lbf in; lb in)	x 0.113	= Newton metres (Nm)	x 8.85	= Pounds-force inches (lbf in; lb in)
Pounds-force inches (lbf in; lb in)	x 0.083	= Pounds-force feet (lbf ft; lb ft)	x 12	= Pounds-force inches (lbf in; lb in)
Pounds-force feet (lbf ft; lb ft)	x 0.138	= Kilograms-force metres (kgf m; kg m)	x 7.233	= Pounds-force feet (lbf ft; lb ft)
Pounds-force feet (lbf ft; lb ft)	x 1.356	= Newton metres (Nm)	x 0.738	= Pounds-force feet (lbf ft; lb ft)
Newton metres (Nm)	x 0.102	= Kilograms-force metres (kgf m; kg m)	x 9.804	= Newton metres (Nm)

Power

Horsepower (hp)	x 745.7	= Watts (W)	x 0.0013	= Horsepower (hp)

Velocity (speed)

Miles per hour (miles/hr; mph)	x 1.609	= Kilometres per hour (km/hr; kph)	x 0.621	= Miles per hour (miles/hr; mph)

Fuel consumption*

Miles per gallon, Imperial (mpg)	x 0.354	= Kilometres per litre (km/l)	x 2.825	= Miles per gallon, Imperial (mpg)
Miles per gallon, US (mpg)	x 0.425	= Kilometres per litre (km/l)	x 2.352	= Miles per gallon, US (mpg)

Temperature

Degrees Fahrenheit = (°C x 1.8) + 32   Degrees Celsius (Degrees Centigrade; °C) = (°F - 32) x 0.56

It is common practice to convert from miles per gallon (mpg) to litres/100 kilometres (l/100km), where mpg x l/100 km = 282

Spare parts are available from many sources, including maker's appointed garages, accessory shops, and motor factors. To be sure of obtaining the correct parts, it will sometimes be necessary to quote the vehicle identification number. If possible, it can also be useful to take the old parts along for positive identification. Items such as starter motors and alternators may be available under a service exchange scheme – any parts returned should be clean.

Our advice regarding spare parts is as follows.

Officially appointed garages

This is the best source of parts which are peculiar to your car, and which are not otherwise generally available (eg, badges, interior trim, certain body panels, etc). It is also the only place at which you should buy parts if the vehicle is still under warranty.

Accessory shops

These are very good places to buy materials and components needed for the maintenance of your car (oil, air and fuel filters, light bulbs, drivebelts, greases, brake pads, touch-up paint, etc). Components of this nature sold by a reputable shop are of the same standard as those used by the car manufacturer.

Besides components, these shops also sell tools and general accessories, usually have convenient opening hours, charge lower prices, and can often be found close to home. Some accessory shops have parts counters where components needed for almost any repair job can be purchased or ordered.

Motor factors

Good factors will stock all the more important components which wear out comparatively quickly, and can sometimes supply individual components needed for the overhaul of a larger assembly (eg, brake seals and hydraulic parts, bearing shells, pistons, valves). They may also handle work such as cylinder block reboring, crankshaft regrinding, etc.

Tyre and exhaust specialists

These outlets may be independent, or members of a local or national chain. They frequently offer competitive prices when compared with a main dealer or local garage, but it will pay to obtain several quotes before making a decision. When researching prices, also ask what 'extras' may be added – for instance fitting a new valve and balancing the wheel are both commonly charged on top of the price of a new tyre.

Other sources

Beware of parts or materials obtained from market stalls, car boot sales or similar outlets. Such items are not invariably sub-standard, but there is little chance of compensation if they do prove unsatisfactory. In the case of safety-critical components such as brake pads, there is the risk not only of financial loss, but also of an accident causing injury or death.

Second-hand components or assemblies obtained from a car breaker can be a good buy in some circumstances, but his sort of purchase is best made by the experienced DIY mechanic.

Vehicle identification

Modifications are a continuing and unpublished process in vehicle manufacture, quite apart from major model changes. Spare parts manuals and lists are compiled upon a numerical basis, the individual vehicle numbers being essential to correct identification of the component required.

When ordering spare parts, always give as much information as possible. Quote the car model, year of manufacture and vehicle identification and/or engine numbers as appropriate.

The vehicle identification plate is attached to the front right-hand side door pillar **(see illustration)** and includes the Vehicle Identification Number (VIN), vehicle weight information and paint and trim colour codes.

The Vehicle Identification Number (VIN) is given on the vehicle identification plate and is also stamped into the body floor panel between the right-hand front seat and the door sill panel **(see illustration)**; lift the flap in the carpet to see it.

Vauxhall/Opel use a 'Car pass' scheme for vehicle identification. This is a card which is issued to the customer when the car is first purchased. It contains important information, eg, VIN number, key number and radio code. It also includes a special code for diagnostic equipment, therefore it must be kept in a secure place and not in the vehicle.

The engine number is stamped on a horizontal flat located on the front of the cylinder block, at the transmission end. The first part of the engine number gives the engine code – eg, Z16XEP.

Engine codes are as follows

1.6 litre (1796 cc) DOHC 16-valve petrol engine	Z16XEP, Z16XE1, A16XER and Z16XER
1.8 litre (1796 cc) DOHC 16-valve petrol engine	Z18XER and A18XER
1.7 litre (1686 cc) DOHC 16-valve diesel engine	A17DTR and A17DTJ
1.9 litre (1910 cc) SOHC 8-valve diesel engine	Z19DT and Z19DTL
1.9 litre (1910 cc) DOHC 16-valve diesel engine	Z19DTH

Vehicle Identification Number (VIN) plate attached to the front right-hand side door pillar

The VIN number is stamped into the body floor next to the right-hand front seat

Whenever servicing, repair or overhaul work is carried out on the car or its components, observe the following procedures and instructions. This will assist in carrying out the operation efficiently and to a professional standard of workmanship.

Joint mating faces and gaskets

When separating components at their mating faces, never insert screwdrivers or similar implements into the joint between the faces in order to prise them apart. This can cause severe damage which results in oil leaks, coolant leaks, etc upon reassembly. Separation is usually achieved by tapping along the joint with a soft-faced hammer in order to break the seal. However, note that this method may not be suitable where dowels are used for component location.

Where a gasket is used between the mating faces of two components, a new one must be fitted on reassembly; fit it dry unless otherwise stated in the repair procedure. Make sure that the mating faces are clean and dry, with all traces of old gasket removed. When cleaning a joint face, use a tool which is unlikely to score or damage the face, and remove any burrs or nicks with an oilstone or fine file.

Make sure that tapped holes are cleaned with a pipe cleaner, and keep them free of jointing compound, if this is being used, unless specifically instructed otherwise.

Ensure that all orifices, channels or pipes are clear, and blow through them, preferably using compressed air.

Oil seals

Oil seals can be removed by levering them out with a wide flat-bladed screwdriver or similar implement. Alternatively, a number of self-tapping screws may be screwed into the seal, and these used as a purchase for pliers or some similar device in order to pull the seal free.

Whenever an oil seal is removed from its working location, either individually or as part of an assembly, it should be renewed.

The very fine sealing lip of the seal is easily damaged, and will not seal if the surface it contacts is not completely clean and free from scratches, nicks or grooves. If the original sealing surface of the component cannot be restored, and the manufacturer has not made provision for slight relocation of the seal relative to the sealing surface, the component should be renewed.

Protect the lips of the seal from any surface which may damage them in the course of fitting. Use tape or a conical sleeve where possible. Where indicated, lubricate the seal lips with oil before fitting and, on dual-lipped seals, fill the space between the lips with grease.

Unless otherwise stated, oil seals must be fitted with their sealing lips toward the lubricant to be sealed.

Use a tubular drift or block of wood of the appropriate size to install the seal and, if the seal housing is shouldered, drive the seal down to the shoulder. If the seal housing is unshouldered, the seal should be fitted with its face flush with the housing top face (unless otherwise instructed).

Screw threads and fastenings

Seized nuts, bolts and screws are quite a common occurrence where corrosion has set in, and the use of penetrating oil or releasing fluid will often overcome this problem if the offending item is soaked for a while before attempting to release it. The use of an impact driver may also provide a means of releasing such stubborn fastening devices, when used in conjunction with the appropriate screwdriver bit or socket. If none of these methods works, it may be necessary to resort to the careful application of heat, or the use of a hacksaw or nut splitter device. Before resorting to extreme methods, check that you are not dealing with a left-hand thread!

Studs are usually removed by locking two nuts together on the threaded part, and then using a spanner on the lower nut to unscrew the stud. Studs or bolts which have broken off below the surface of the component in which they are mounted can sometimes be removed using a stud extractor.

Always ensure that a blind tapped hole is completely free from oil, grease, water or other fluid before installing the bolt or stud. Failure to do this could cause the housing to crack due to the hydraulic action of the bolt or stud as it is screwed in.

For some screw fastenings, notably cylinder head bolts or nuts, torque wrench settings are no longer specified for the latter stages of tightening, "angle-tightening" being called up instead. Typically, a fairly low torque wrench setting will be applied to the bolts/nuts in the correct sequence, followed by one or more stages of tightening through specified angles.

When checking or retightening a nut or bolt to a specified torque setting, slacken the nut or bolt by a quarter of a turn, and then retighten to the specified setting. However, this should not be attempted where angular tightening has been used.

Locknuts, locktabs and washers

Any fastening which will rotate against a component or housing during tightening should always have a washer between it and the relevant component or housing.

Spring or split washers should always be renewed when they are used to lock a critical component such as a big-end bearing retaining bolt or nut. Locktabs which are folded over to retain a nut or bolt should always be renewed.

Self-locking nuts can be re-used in non-critical areas, providing resistance can be felt when the locking portion passes over the bolt or stud thread. However, it should be noted that self-locking stiffnuts tend to lose their effectiveness after long periods of use, and should then be renewed as a matter of course.

Split pins must always be replaced with new ones of the correct size for the hole.

When thread-locking compound is found on the threads of a fastener which is to be re-used, it should be cleaned off with a wire brush and solvent, and fresh compound applied on reassembly.

Special tools

Some repair procedures in this manual entail the use of special tools such as a press, two or three-legged pullers, spring compressors, etc. Wherever possible, suitable readily-available alternatives to the manufacturer's special tools are described, and are shown in use. In some instances, where no alternative is possible, it has been necessary to resort to the use of a manufacturer's tool, and this has been done for reasons of safety as well as the efficient completion of the repair operation. Unless you are highly-skilled and have a thorough understanding of the procedures described, never attempt to bypass the use of any special tool when the procedure described specifies its use. Not only is there a very great risk of personal injury, but expensive damage could be caused to the components involved.

Environmental considerations

When disposing of used engine oil, brake fluid, antifreeze, etc, give due consideration to any detrimental environmental effects. Do not, for instance, pour any of the above liquids down drains into the general sewage system, or onto the ground to soak away, as this is likely to pollute your local environment. Many local council refuse tips provide a facility for waste oil disposal, as do some garages. You can find your nearest disposal point by calling the Environment Agency on 03708 506 506 or by visiting www.oilbankline.org.uk.

Note: It is illegal and anti-social to dump oil down the drain. To find the location of your local oil recycling bank, call 03708 506 506 or visit www.oilbankline.org.uk.

Jacking and vehicle support

The jack supplied with the vehicle tool kit should only be used for changing roadwheels – see Wheel changing at the front of this manual. Ensure the jack head is correctly engaged before attempting to raise the vehicle. When carrying out any other kind of work, raise the vehicle using a hydraulic jack, and always supplement the jack with axle stands positioned under the vehicle jacking points.

When jacking up the vehicle with a trolley jack, position the jack head under one of the relevant jacking points. Use a block of wood between the jack or axle stand and the sill – the block of wood should have a groove cut into it, in which the welded flange of the sill will locate. Do not jack the vehicle under the sump or any of the steering or suspension components. Supplement the jack using axle stands (see illustrations).

⚠️ **Warning: Never work under, around, or near a raised vehicle, unless it is adequately supported in at least two places.**

Front jacking point for hydraulic jack or axle stands

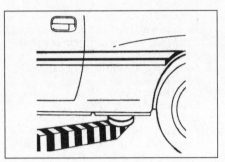

Rear jacking point for hydraulic jack or axle stands

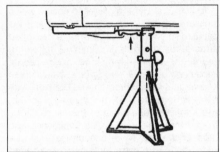

Axle stands should be placed under, or adjacent to the jacking point (arrowed)

Disconnecting the battery

Numerous systems fitted to the vehicle require battery power to be available at all times, either to ensure their continued operation (such as the clock) or to maintain control unit memories which would be erased if the battery were to be disconnected. Whenever the battery is to be disconnected therefore, first note the following, to ensure that there are no unforeseen consequences of this action:

☐ *First, on any vehicle with central locking, it is a wise precaution to remove the key from the ignition, and to keep it with you, so that it does not get locked in, if the central locking should engage accidentally when the battery is reconnected.*

☐ *Depending on model and specification, the Vauxhall anti-theft alarm system may be of the type which is automatically activated when the vehicle battery is disconnected and/or reconnected. To prevent the alarm sounding on models so equipped, switch the ignition on, then off, and disconnect the battery within 15 seconds. If the alarm is activated when the battery is reconnected, switch the ignition on then off to deactivate the alarm.*

☐ *If a security-coded audio unit is fitted, and the unit and/or the battery is disconnected, the unit will not function again on reconnection until the correct security code is entered. Details of this procedure, which varies according to the unit fitted, are given in the vehicle audio system operating instructions. Ensure you have the correct code before you disconnect the battery. If you do not have the code or details of the correct procedure, but can supply proof of ownership and a legitimate reason for wanting this information, a Vauxhall dealer may be able to help.*

☐ *The engine management electronic control unit is of the ' self-learning' type, meaning that as it operates, it also monitors and stores the settings which give optimum engine performance under all operating conditions. When the battery is disconnected, these settings are lost and the ECU reverts to the base settings programmed into its memory at the factory. On restarting, this may lead to the engine running/idling roughly for a short while, until the ECU has relearned the optimum settings. This process is best accomplished by taking the vehicle on a road test (for approximately 15 min- utes), covering all engine speeds and loads, concentrating mainly in the 2500 to 3500 rpm region*

☐ *On models equipped with automatic transmission, the transmission selector lever assembly incorporates an electrically-operated selector lever lock mechanism that prevents the lever being moved out of the P position unless the ignition is switched on and the brake pedal is depressed. If the selector lever is in the P position and the battery is disconnected, it will not be possible to move the selector lever out of position P by the normal means. Although it is possible to manually override the system (see Chapter 7B), it is sensible to move the selector lever to the N position before disconnecting the battery.*

☐ *On models with electric windows, it will be necessary to reprogramme the motors to restore the one-touch function of the buttons, after reconnection of the battery. To do this, fully close both front windows. With the windows closed, depress the up button of the driver's side window for approximately 5 seconds, then release it and depress the passenger side window up button for approximately 5 seconds.*

☐ *On models with an electric sliding sunroof, it will be necessary to fully open and fully close the sunroof after battery reconnection, to recalibrate the sensors.*

☐ *On all models, when reconnecting the battery after disconnection, switch on the ignition and wait 10 seconds to allow the electronic vehicle systems to stabilise and re-initialise.*

Introduction

A selection of good tools is a fundamental requirement for anyone contemplating the maintenance and repair of a motor vehicle. For the owner who does not possess any, their purchase will prove a considerable expense, offsetting some of the savings made by doing-it-yourself. However, provided that the tools purchased meet the relevant national safety standards and are of good quality, they will last for many years and prove an extremely worthwhile investment.

To help the average owner to decide which tools are needed to carry out the various tasks detailed in this manual, we have compiled three lists of tools under the following headings: *Maintenance and minor repair*, *Repair and overhaul*, and *Special*. Newcomers to practical mechanics should start off with the *Maintenance and minor repair* tool kit, and confine themselves to the simpler jobs around the vehicle. Then, as confidence and experience grow, more difficult tasks can be undertaken, with extra tools being purchased as, and when, they are needed. In this way, a *Maintenance and minor repair* tool kit can be built up into a *Repair and overhaul* tool kit over a considerable period of time, without any major cash outlays. The experienced do-it-yourselfer will have a tool kit good enough for most repair and overhaul procedures, and will add tools from the *Special* category when it is felt that the expense is justified by the amount of use to which these tools will be put.

Maintenance and minor repair tool kit

The tools given in this list should be considered as a minimum requirement if routine maintenance, servicing and minor repair operations are to be undertaken. We recommend the purchase of combination spanners (ring one end, open-ended the other); although more expensive than open-ended ones, they do give the advantages of both types of spanner.

☐ *Combination spanners:*
  Metric - 8 to 19 mm inclusive
☐ *Adjustable spanner - 35 mm jaw (approx.)*
☐ *Spark plug spanner (with rubber insert) - petrol models*
☐ *Spark plug gap adjustment tool - petrol models*
☐ *Set of feeler gauges*
☐ *Brake bleed nipple spanner*
☐ *Screwdrivers:*
  Flat blade - 100 mm long x 6 mm dia
  Cross blade - 100 mm long x 6 mm dia
  Torx - various sizes (not all vehicles)
☐ *Combination pliers*
☐ *Hacksaw (junior)*
☐ *Tyre pump*
☐ *Tyre pressure gauge*
☐ *Oil can*
☐ *Oil filter removal tool (if applicable)*
☐ *Fine emery cloth*
☐ *Wire brush (small)*
☐ *Funnel (medium size)*
☐ *Sump drain plug key (not all vehicles)*

Repair and overhaul tool kit

These tools are virtually essential for anyone undertaking any major repairs to a motor vehicle, and are additional to those given in the *Maintenance and minor repair* list. Included in this list is a comprehensive set of sockets. Although these are expensive, they will be found invaluable as they are so versatile - particularly if various drives are included in the set. We recommend the half-inch square-drive type, as this can be used with most proprietary torque wrenches.

The tools in this list will sometimes need to be supplemented by tools from the *Special* list:

☐ *Sockets to cover range in previous list (including Torx sockets)*
☐ *Reversible ratchet drive (for use with sockets)*
☐ *Extension piece, 250 mm (for use with sockets)*
☐ *Universal joint (for use with sockets)*
☐ *Flexible handle or sliding T "breaker bar" (for use with sockets)*
☐ *Torque wrench (for use with sockets)*
☐ *Self-locking grips*
☐ *Ball pein hammer*
☐ *Soft-faced mallet (plastic or rubber)*
☐ *Screwdrivers:*
  Flat blade - long & sturdy, short (chubby), and narrow (electrician's) types
  Cross blade – long & sturdy, and short (chubby) types
☐ *Pliers:*
  Long-nosed
  Side cutters (electrician's)
  Circlip (internal and external)
☐ *Cold chisel - 25 mm*
☐ *Scriber*
☐ *Scraper*
☐ *Centre-punch*
☐ *Pin punch*
☐ *Hacksaw*
☐ *Brake hose clamp*
☐ *Brake/clutch bleeding kit*
☐ *Selection of twist drills*
☐ *Steel rule/straight-edge*
☐ *Allen keys (inc. splined/Torx type)*
☐ *Selection of files*
☐ *Wire brush*
☐ *Axle stands*
☐ *Jack (strong trolley or hydraulic type)*
☐ *Light with extension lead*
☐ *Universal electrical multi-meter*

Sockets and reversible ratchet drive

Brake bleeding kit

Torx key, socket and bit

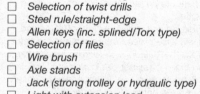
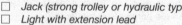
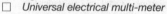

Hose clamp

Angular-tightening gauge

Special tools

The tools in this list are those which are not used regularly, are expensive to buy, or which need to be used in accordance with their manufacturers' instructions. Unless relatively difficult mechanical jobs are undertaken frequently, it will not be economic to buy many of these tools. Where this is the case, you could consider clubbing together with friends (or joining a motorists' club) to make a joint purchase, or borrowing the tools against a deposit from a local garage or tool hire specialist.

The following list contains only those tools and instruments freely available to the public, and not those special tools produced by the vehicle manufacturer specifically for its dealer network. You will find occasional references to these manufacturers' special tools in the text of this manual. Generally, an alternative method of doing the job without the vehicle manufacturers' special tool is given. However, sometimes there is no alternative to using them. Where this is the case and the relevant tool cannot be bought or borrowed, you will have to entrust the work to a dealer.

- ☐ Angular-tightening gauge
- ☐ Valve spring compressor
- ☐ Valve grinding tool
- ☐ Piston ring compressor
- ☐ Piston ring removal/installation tool
- ☐ Cylinder bore hone
- ☐ Balljoint separator
- ☐ Coil spring compressors (where applicable)
- ☐ Two/three-legged hub and bearing puller
- ☐ Impact screwdriver
- ☐ Micrometer and/or vernier calipers
- ☐ Dial gauge
- ☐ Tachometer
- ☐ Fault code reader
- ☐ Cylinder compression gauge
- ☐ Hand-operated vacuum pump and gauge
- ☐ Clutch plate alignment set
- ☐ Brake shoe steady spring cup removal tool
- ☐ Bush and bearing removal/installation set
- ☐ Stud extractors
- ☐ Tap and die set
- ☐ Lifting tackle

Buying tools

Reputable motor accessory shops and superstores often offer excellent quality tools at discount prices, so it pays to shop around.

Remember, you don't have to buy the most expensive items on the shelf, but it is always advisable to steer clear of the very cheap tools. Beware of 'bargains' offered on market stalls, on-line or at car boot sales. There are plenty of good tools around at reasonable prices, but always aim to purchase items which meet the relevant national safety standards. If in doubt, ask the proprietor or manager of the shop for advice before making a purchase.

Care and maintenance of tools

Having purchased a reasonable tool kit, it is necessary to keep the tools in a clean and serviceable condition. After use, always wipe off any dirt, grease and metal particles using a clean, dry cloth, before putting the tools away. Never leave them lying around after they have been used. A simple tool rack on the garage or workshop wall for items such as screwdrivers and pliers is a good idea. Store all normal spanners and sockets in a metal box. Any measuring instruments, gauges, meters, etc, must be carefully stored where they cannot be damaged or become rusty.

Take a little care when tools are used. Hammer heads inevitably become marked, and screwdrivers lose the keen edge on their blades from time to time. A little timely attention with emery cloth or a file will soon restore items like this to a good finish.

Working facilities

Not to be forgotten when discussing tools is the workshop itself. If anything more than routine maintenance is to be carried out, a suitable working area becomes essential.

It is appreciated that many an owner-mechanic is forced by circumstances to remove an engine or similar item without the benefit of a garage or workshop. Having done this, any repairs should always be done under the cover of a roof.

Wherever possible, any dismantling should be done on a clean, flat workbench or table at a suitable working height.

Any workbench needs a vice; one with a jaw opening of 100 mm is suitable for most jobs. As mentioned previously, some clean dry storage space is also required for tools, as well as for any lubricants, cleaning fluids, touch-up paints etc, which become necessary.

Another item which may be required, and which has a much more general usage, is an electric drill with a chuck capacity of at least 8 mm. This, together with a good range of twist drills, is virtually essential for fitting accessories.

Last, but not least, always keep a supply of old newspapers and clean, lint-free rags available, and try to keep any working area as clean as possible.

Micrometers

Dial test indicator ("dial gauge")

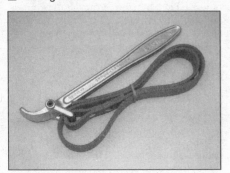

Oil filter removal tool (strap wrench type)

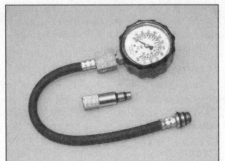

Compression tester

Bearing puller

This is a guide to getting your vehicle through the MOT test. Obviously it will not be possible to examine the vehicle to the same standard as the professional MOT tester. However, working through the following checks will enable you to identify any problem areas before submitting the vehicle for the test.

It has only been possible to summarise the test requirements here, based on the regulations in force at the time of printing. Test standards are becoming increasingly stringent, although there are some exemptions for older vehicles.

An assistant will be needed to help carry out some of these checks.

The checks have been sub-divided into four categories, as follows:

1 Checks carried out **FROM THE DRIVER'S SEAT**

2 Checks carried out **WITH THE VEHICLE ON THE GROUND**

3 Checks carried out **WITH THE VEHICLE RAISED AND THE WHEELS FREE TO TURN**

4 Checks carried out on **YOUR VEHICLE'S EXHAUST EMISSION SYSTEM**

---

1 Checks carried out **FROM THE DRIVER'S SEAT**

Handbrake (parking brake)

☐ Test the operation of the handbrake. Excessive travel (too many clicks) indicates incorrect brake or cable adjustment.

☐ Check that the handbrake cannot be released by tapping the lever sideways. Check the security of the lever mountings.

☐ If the parking brake is foot-operated, check that the pedal is secure and without excessive travel, and that the release mechanism operates correctly.

☐ Where applicable, test the operation of the electronic handbrake. The brake should engage and disengage without excessive delay. If the warning light does not extinguish when the brake is disengaged, this could indicate a fault which will need further investigation.

Footbrake

☐ Depress the brake pedal and check that it does not creep down to the floor, indicating a master cylinder fault. Release the pedal, wait a few seconds, then depress it again. If the pedal travels nearly to the floor before firm resistance is felt, brake adjustment or repair is necessary. If the pedal feels spongy, there is air in the hydraulic system which must be removed by bleeding.

☐ Check that the brake pedal is secure and in good condition. Check also for signs of fluid leaks on the pedal, floor or carpets, which would indicate failed seals in the brake master cylinder.

☐ Check the servo unit (when applicable) by operating the brake pedal several times, then keeping the pedal depressed and starting the engine. As the engine starts, the pedal will move down slightly. If not, the vacuum hose or the servo itself may be faulty.

Steering wheel and column

☐ Examine the steering wheel for fractures or looseness of the hub, spokes or rim.

☐ Move the steering wheel from side to side and then up and down. Check that the steering wheel is not loose on the column, indicating wear or a loose retaining nut. Continue moving the steering wheel as before, but also turn it slightly from left to right.

☐ Check that the steering wheel is not loose on the column, and that there is no abnormal movement of the steering wheel, indicating wear in the column support bearings or couplings.

☐ Check that the ignition lock (where fitted) engages and disengages correctly.

☐ Steering column adjustment mechanisms (where fitted) must be able to lock the column securely in place with no play evident.

Windscreen, mirrors and sunvisor

☐ The windscreen must be free of cracks or other significant damage within the driver's field of view. (Small stone chips are acceptable.) Rear view mirrors must be secure, intact, and capable of being adjusted.

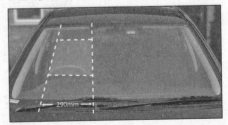

☐ The driver's sunvisor must be capable of being stored in the "up" position.

Seat belts and seats

Note: *The following checks are applicable to all seat belts, front and rear.*

☐ Examine the webbing of all the belts (including rear belts if fitted) for cuts, serious fraying or deterioration. Fasten and unfasten each belt to check the buckles. If applicable, check the retracting mechanism. Check the security of all seat belt mountings accessible from inside the vehicle, ensuring any height adjustable mountings lock securely in place.

☐ Seat belts with pre-tensioners, once activated, have a "flag" or similar showing on the seat belt stalk. This, in itself, is not a reason for test failure.

☐ The front seats themselves must be securely attached and the backrests must lock in the upright position.

Doors

☐ Both front doors must be able to be opened and closed from outside and inside, and must latch securely when closed.

Bonnet and boot/tailgate

☐ The bonnet and boot/tailgate must latch securely when closed.

2 Checks carried out WITH THE VEHICLE ON THE GROUND

Vehicle identification

☐ Number plates must be in good condition, secure and legible, with letters and numbers correctly spaced – spacing at (A) should be 33 mm and at (B) 11 mm. At the front, digits must be black on a white background and at the rear black on a yellow background. Other background designs (such as honeycomb) are not permitted.

☐ The VIN plate and/or homologation plate must be permanently displayed and legible.

Electrical equipment

☐ Switch on the ignition and check the operation of the horn.

☐ Check the windscreen washers and wipers, examining the wiper blades; renew damaged or perished blades. Also check the operation of the stop-lights.

☐ Check the operation of the sidelights and number plate lights. The lenses and reflectors must be secure, clean and undamaged.

☐ Check the operation and alignment of the headlights. The headlight reflectors must not be tarnished and the lenses must be undamaged.

☐ Switch on the ignition and check the operation of the direction indicators (including the instrument panel tell-tale) and the hazard warning lights. Operation of the sidelights and stop-lights must not affect the indicators - if it does, the cause is usually a bad earth at the rear light cluster. Indicators should flash at a rate of between 60 and 120 times per minute – faster or slower than this could indicate a fault with the flasher unit or a bad earth at one of the light units.

☐ Check the operation of the rear foglight(s), including the warning light on the instrument panel or in the switch.

☐ The warning lights must illuminate in accordance with the manufacturer's design. For most vehicles, the ABS and other warning lights should illuminate when the ignition is switched on, and (if the system is operating properly) extinguish after a few seconds. Refer to the owner's handbook.

Footbrake

☐ Examine the master cylinder, brake pipes and servo unit for leaks, loose mountings, corrosion or other damage. If ABS is fitted, this unit should also be examined for signs of leaks or corrosion.

☐ The fluid reservoir must be secure and the fluid level must be between the upper (**A**) and lower (**B**) markings.

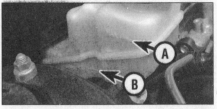

☐ Inspect both front brake flexible hoses for cracks or deterioration of the rubber. Turn the steering from lock to lock, and ensure that the hoses do not contact the wheel, tyre, or any part of the steering or suspension mechanism. With the brake pedal firmly depressed, check the hoses for bulges or leaks under pressure.

Steering and suspension

☐ Have your assistant turn the steering wheel from side to side slightly, up to the point where the steering gear just begins to transmit this movement to the roadwheels. Check for excessive free play between the steering wheel and the steering gear, indicating wear or insecurity of the steering column joints, the column-to-steering gear coupling, or the steering gear itself.

☐ Have your assistant turn the steering wheel more vigorously in each direction, so that the roadwheels just begin to turn. As this is done, examine all the steering joints, linkages, fittings and attachments. Renew any component that shows signs of wear or damage. On vehicles with power steering, check the security and condition of the steering pump, drivebelt and hoses.

☐ Check that the vehicle is standing level, and at approximately the correct ride height.

Shock absorbers

☐ Depress each corner of the vehicle in turn, then release it. The vehicle should rise and then settle in its normal position. If the vehicle continues to rise and fall, the shock absorber is defective. A shock absorber which has seized will also cause the vehicle to fail.

Exhaust system

☐ Start the engine. With your assistant holding a rag over the tailpipe, check the entire system for leaks. Repair or renew leaking sections.

3 Checks carried out
WITH THE VEHICLE RAISED AND THE WHEELS FREE TO TURN

Jack up the front and rear of the vehicle, and securely support it on axle stands. Position the stands clear of the suspension assemblies. Ensure that the wheels are clear of the ground and that the steering can be turned from lock to lock.

Steering mechanism

☐ Have your assistant turn the steering from lock to lock. Check that the steering turns smoothly, and that no part of the steering mechanism, including a wheel or tyre, fouls any brake hose or pipe or any part of the body structure.
☐ Examine the steering rack rubber gaiters for damage or insecurity of the retaining clips. If power steering is fitted, check for signs of damage or leakage of the fluid hoses, pipes or connections. Also check for excessive stiffness or binding of the steering, a missing split pin or locking device, or severe corrosion of the body structure within 30 cm of any steering component attachment point.

Front and rear suspension and wheel bearings

☐ Starting at the front right-hand side, grasp the roadwheel at the 3 o'clock and 9 o'clock positions and rock gently but firmly. Check for free play or insecurity at the wheel bearings, suspension balljoints, or suspension mount-ings, pivots and attachments.
☐ Now grasp the wheel at the 12 o'clock and 6 o'clock positions and repeat the previous inspection. Spin the wheel, and check for roughness or tightness of the front wheel bearing.

☐ If excess free play is suspected at a component pivot point, this can be confirmed by using a large screwdriver or similar tool and levering between the mounting and the component attachment. This will confirm whether the wear is in the pivot bush, its retaining bolt, or in the mounting itself (the bolt holes can often become elongated).

☐ Carry out all the above checks at the other front wheel, and then at both rear wheels.

Springs and shock absorbers

☐ Examine the suspension struts (when applicable) for serious fluid leakage, corrosion, or damage to the casing. Also check the security of the mounting points.
☐ If coil springs are fitted, check that the spring ends locate in their seats, and that the spring is not corroded, cracked or broken.
☐ If leaf springs are fitted, check that all leaves are intact, that the axle is securely attached to each spring, and that there is no deterioration of the spring eye mountings, bushes, and shackles.

☐ The same general checks apply to vehicles fitted with other suspension types, such as torsion bars, hydraulic displacer units, etc. Ensure that all mountings and attachments are secure, that there are no signs of excessive wear, corrosion or damage, and (on hydraulic types) that there are no fluid leaks or damaged pipes.
☐ Inspect the shock absorbers for signs of serious fluid leakage. Check for wear of the mounting bushes or attachments, or damage to the body of the unit.

Driveshafts (fwd vehicles only)

☐ Rotate each front wheel in turn and inspect the constant velocity joint gaiters for splits or damage. Also check that each driveshaft is straight and undamaged.

Braking system

☐ If possible without dismantling, check brake pad wear and disc condition. Ensure that the friction lining material has not worn excessively, (A) and that the discs are not fractured, pitted, scored or badly worn (B).

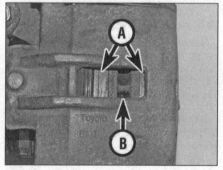

☐ Examine all the rigid brake pipes underneath the vehicle, and the flexible hose(s) at the rear. Look for corrosion, chafing or insecurity of the pipes, and for signs of bulging under pressure, chafing, splits or deterioration of the flexible hoses.
☐ Look for signs of fluid leaks at the brake calipers or on the brake backplates. Repair or renew leaking components.
☐ Slowly spin each wheel, while your assistant depresses and releases the footbrake. Ensure that each brake is operating and does not bind when the pedal is released.

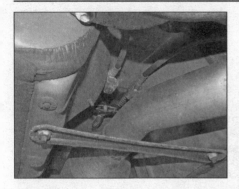

☐ Examine the handbrake mechanism, checking for frayed or broken cables, excessive corrosion, or wear or insecurity of the linkage. Check that the mechanism works on each relevant wheel, and releases fully, without binding.

☐ It is not possible to test brake efficiency without special equipment, but a road test can be carried out later to check that the vehicle pulls up in a straight line.

Fuel and exhaust systems

☐ Inspect the fuel tank (including the filler cap), fuel pipes, hoses and unions. All components must be secure and free from leaks. Locking fuel caps must lock securely and the key must be provided for the MOT test.

☐ Examine the exhaust system over its entire length, checking for any damaged, broken or missing mountings, security of the retaining clamps and rust or corrosion.

Wheels and tyres

☐ Examine the sidewalls and tread area of each tyre in turn. Check for cuts, tears, lumps, bulges, separation of the tread, and exposure of the ply or cord due to wear or damage. Check that the tyre bead is correctly seated on the wheel rim, that the valve is sound and properly seated, and that the wheel is not distorted or damaged.

☐ Check that the tyres are of the correct size for the vehicle, that they are of the same size and type on each axle, and that the pressures are correct.

☐ Check the tyre tread depth. The legal minimum at the time of writing is 1.6 mm over the central three-quarters of the tread width. Abnormal tread wear may indicate incorrect front wheel alignment or wear in steering or suspension components.

☐ If the spare wheel is fitted externally or in a separate carrier beneath the vehicle, check that mountings are secure and free of excessive corrosion.

Body corrosion

☐ Check the condition of the entire vehicle structure for signs of corrosion in load-bearing areas. (These include chassis box sections, side sills, cross-members, pillars, and all suspension, steering, braking system and seat belt mountings and anchorages.) Any corrosion which has seriously reduced the thickness of a load-bearing area (or is within 30 cm of safety-related components such as steering or suspension) is likely to cause the vehicle to fail. In this case professional repairs are likely to be needed.

☐ Damage or corrosion which causes sharp or otherwise dangerous edges to be exposed will also cause the vehicle to fail.

Towbars

☐ Check the condition of mounting points (both beneath the vehicle and within boot/hatchback areas) for signs of corrosion, ensuring that all fixings are secure and not worn or damaged. There must be no excessive play in detachable tow ball arms or quick-release mechanisms.

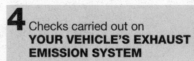

4 Checks carried out on **YOUR VEHICLE'S EXHAUST EMISSION SYSTEM**

Petrol models

☐ The engine should be warmed up, and running well (ignition system in good order, air filter element clean, etc).

☐ Before testing, run the engine at around 2500 rpm for 20 seconds. Let the engine drop to idle, and watch for smoke from the exhaust. If the idle speed is too high, or if dense blue or black smoke emerges for more than 5 seconds, the vehicle will fail. Typically, blue smoke signifies oil burning (engine wear);

black smoke means unburnt fuel (dirty air cleaner element, or other fuel system fault).

☐ An exhaust gas analyser for measuring carbon monoxide (CO) and hydrocarbons (HC) is now needed. If one cannot be hired or borrowed, have a local garage perform the check.

CO emissions (mixture)

☐ The MOT tester has access to the CO limits for all vehicles. The CO level is measured at idle speed, and at 'fast idle' (2500 to 3000 rpm). The following limits are given as a general guide:

At idle speed – Less than 0.5% CO
At 'fast idle' – Less than 0.3% CO
Lambda reading – 0.97 to 1.03

☐ If the CO level is too high, this may point to poor maintenance, a fuel injection system problem, faulty lambda (oxygen) sensor or catalytic converter. Try an injector cleaning treatment, and check the vehicle's ECU for fault codes.

HC emissions

☐ The MOT tester has access to HC limits for all vehicles. The HC level is measured at 'fast idle' (2500 to 3000 rpm). The following limits are given as a general guide:

At 'fast idle' – Less then 200 ppm

☐ Excessive HC emissions are typically caused by oil being burnt (worn engine), or by a blocked crankcase ventilation system ('breather'). If the engine oil is old and thin, an oil change may help. If the engine is running badly, check the vehicle's ECU for fault codes.

Diesel models

☐ The only emission test for diesel engines is measuring exhaust smoke density, using a calibrated smoke meter. The test involves accelerating the engine at least 3 times to its maximum unloaded speed.

Note: *On engines with a timing belt, it is VITAL that the belt is in good condition before the test is carried out.*

☐ With the engine warmed up, it is first purged by running at around 2500 rpm for 20 seconds. A governor check is then carried out, by slowly accelerating the engine to its maximum speed. After this, the smoke meter is connected, and the engine is accelerated quickly to maximum speed three times. If the smoke density is less than the limits given below, the vehicle will pass:

Non-turbo vehicles: 2.5m-1
Turbocharged vehicles: 3.0m-1

☐ If excess smoke is produced, try fitting a new air cleaner element, or using an injector cleaning treatment. If the engine is running badly, where applicable, check the vehicle's ECU for fault codes. Also check the vehicle's EGR system, where applicable. At high mileages, the injectors may require professional attention.

Engine

- ☐ Engine fails to rotate when attempting to start
- ☐ Engine rotates, but will not start
- ☐ Engine difficult to start when cold
- ☐ Engine difficult to start when hot
- ☐ Starter motor noisy or excessively-rough in engagement
- ☐ Engine starts, but stops immediately
- ☐ Engine idles erratically
- ☐ Engine misfires at idle speed
- ☐ Engine misfires throughout the driving speed range
- ☐ Engine hesitates on acceleration
- ☐ Engine stalls
- ☐ Engine lacks power
- ☐ Engine backfires
- ☐ Oil pressure warning light illuminated with engine running
- ☐ Engine runs-on after switching off
- ☐ Engine noises

Cooling system

- ☐ Overheating
- ☐ Overcooling
- ☐ External coolant leakage
- ☐ Internal coolant leakage
- ☐ Corrosion

Fuel and exhaust systems

- ☐ Excessive fuel consumption
- ☐ Fuel leakage and/or fuel odour
- ☐ Excessive noise or fumes from exhaust system

Clutch

- ☐ Pedal travels to floor – no pressure or very little resistance
- ☐ Clutch fails to disengage (unable to select gears)
- ☐ Clutch slips (engine speed increases, with no increase in vehicle speed)
- ☐ Judder as clutch is engaged
- ☐ Noise when depressing or releasing clutch pedal

Manual transmission

- ☐ Noisy in neutral with engine running
- ☐ Noisy in one particular gear
- ☐ Difficulty engaging gears
- ☐ Jumps out of gear
- ☐ Vibration
- ☐ Lubricant leaks

Automatic transmission

- ☐ Fluid leakage
- ☐ Transmission fluid brown, or has burned smell
- ☐ General gear selection problems
- ☐ Transmission will not downshift (kickdown) with accelerator pedal fully depressed
- ☐ Engine will not start in any gear, or starts in gears other than Park or Neutral
- ☐ Transmission slips, shifts roughly, is noisy, or has no drive in forward or reverse gears

Driveshafts

- ☐ Vibration when accelerating or decelerating
- ☐ Clicking or knocking noise on turns (at slow speed on full-lock)

Braking system

- ☐ Vehicle pulls to one side under braking
- ☐ Noise (grinding or high-pitched squeal) when brakes applied
- ☐ Excessive brake pedal travel
- ☐ Brake pedal feels spongy when depressed
- ☐ Excessive brake pedal effort required to stop vehicle
- ☐ Judder felt through brake pedal or steering wheel when braking
- ☐ Brakes binding
- ☐ Rear wheels locking under normal braking

Suspension and steering

- ☐ Vehicle pulls to one side
- ☐ Wheel wobble and vibration
- ☐ Excessive pitching and/or rolling around corners, or during braking
- ☐ Wandering or general instability
- ☐ Excessively-stiff steering
- ☐ Excessive play in steering
- ☐ Lack of power assistance
- ☐ Tyre wear excessive

Electrical system

- ☐ Battery will not hold a charge for more than a few days
- ☐ Ignition/no-charge warning light remains illuminated with engine running
- ☐ Ignition/no-charge warning light fails to come on
- ☐ Lights inoperative
- ☐ Instrument readings inaccurate or erratic
- ☐ Horn inoperative, or unsatisfactory in operation
- ☐ Windscreen wipers inoperative, or unsatisfactory in operation
- ☐ Windscreen washers inoperative, or unsatisfactory in operation
- ☐ Electric windows inoperative, or unsatisfactory in operation
- ☐ Window glass fails to move
- ☐ Central locking system inoperative, or unsatisfactory in operation

Introduction

The vehicle owner who does his or her own maintenance according to the recommended service schedules should not have to use this section of the manual very often. Modern component reliability is such that, provided those items subject to wear or deterioration are inspected or renewed at the specified intervals, sudden failure is comparatively rare. Faults do not usually just happen as a result of sudden failure, but develop over a period of time. Major mechanical failures in particular are usually preceded by characteristic symptoms over hundreds or even thousands of miles. Those components which do occasionally fail without warning are often small and easily carried in the vehicle.

With any fault-finding, the first step is to decide where to begin investigations. Sometimes this is obvious, but on other occasions, a little detective work will be necessary. The owner who makes half a dozen haphazard adjustments or replacements may be successful in curing a fault (or its symptoms), but will be none the wiser if the fault recurs, and ultimately may have spent more time and money than was necessary. A calm and logical approach will be found to be more satisfactory in the long run. Always take into account any warning signs or abnormalities that may have been noticed in the period preceding the fault – power loss, high or low gauge readings, unusual smells, etc – and remember that failure of components such as fuses or spark plugs may only be pointers to some underlying fault.

The pages which follow provide an easy-reference guide to the more common problems which may occur during the operation of the vehicle. These problems and their possible causes are grouped under headings denoting various components or systems, such as Engine, Cooling system,

etc. The general Chapter which deals with the problem is also shown in brackets; refer to the relevant part of that Chapter for system-specific information. Whatever the fault, certain basic principles apply. These are as follows:

Verify the fault. This is simply a matter of being sure that you know what the symptoms are before starting work. This is particularly important if you are investigating a fault for someone else, who may not have described it very accurately.

Don't overlook the obvious. For example, if the vehicle won't start, is there fuel in the tank? (Don't take anyone else's word on this particular point, and don't trust the fuel gauge either!) If an electrical fault is indicated, look for loose or broken wires before digging out the test gear.

Cure the disease, not the symptom. Substituting a flat battery with a fully-charged one will get you off the hard shoulder, but if the underlying cause is not attended to, the new battery will go the same way. Similarly, changing oil-fouled spark plugs for a new set will get you moving again, but remember that the reason for the fouling (if it wasn't simply an incorrect grade of plug) will have to be established and corrected.

Don't take anything for granted. Particularly, don't forget that a 'new' component may itself be defective (especially if it's been rattling around in the boot for months), and don't leave components out of a fault diagnosis sequence just because they are new or recently-fitted. When you do finally diagnose a difficult fault, you'll probably realise that all the evidence was there from the start.

Consider what work, if any, has recently been carried out. Many faults arise through careless or hurried work. For instance, if any work has been performed under the

bonnet, could some of the wiring have been dislodged or incorrectly routed, or a hose trapped? Have all the fasteners been properly tightened? Were new, genuine parts and new gaskets used? There is often a certain amount of detective work to be done in this case, as an apparently-unrelated task can have far-reaching consequences.

Diesel fault diagnosis

The majority of starting problems on small diesel engines are electrical in origin. The mechanic who is familiar with petrol engines but less so with diesel may be inclined to view the diesel's injectors and pump in the same light as the spark plugs and distributor, but this is generally a mistake.

When investigating complaints of difficult starting for someone else, make sure that the correct starting procedure is understood and is being followed. Some drivers are unaware of the significance of the preheating warning light – many modern engines are sufficiently forgiving for this not to matter in mild weather, but with the onset of winter, problems begin. Glow plugs in particular are often neglected – just one faulty plug will make cold-weather starting very difficult.

As a rule of thumb, if the engine is difficult to start but runs well when it has finally got going, the problem is electrical (battery, starter motor or preheating system). If poor performance is combined with difficult starting, the problem is likely to be in the fuel system. The low-pressure (supply) side of the fuel system should be checked before suspecting the injectors and high-pressure pump. The most common fuel supply problem is air getting into the system, and any pipe from the fuel tank forwards must be scrutinised if air leakage is suspected.

Engine

Engine fails to rotate when attempting to start

- ☐ Battery terminal connections loose or corroded (see *Weekly checks*)
- ☐ Battery discharged or faulty (Chapter 5A Section 3)
- ☐ Broken, loose or disconnected wiring in the starting circuit (Chapter 5A Section 10)
- ☐ Defective starter solenoid or ignition switch (Chapter 5A Section 10 or Chapter 10 Section 14)
- ☐ Defective starter motor (Chapter 5A Section 11)
- ☐ Starter pinion or flywheel ring gear teeth loose or broken
- ☐ Engine earth strap broken or disconnected (Chapter 12 Section 2)
- ☐ Engine suffering 'hydraulic lock' (eg from water drawn into the engine after traversing flooded roads, or from a serious internal coolant leak) – consult a main dealer for advice
- ☐ Automatic transmission not in position P or N

Engine rotates, but will not start

- ☐ Fuel tank empty
- ☐ Battery discharged (engine rotates slowly) (Chapter 5A Section 3)
- ☐ Battery terminal connections loose or corroded (see *Weekly checks*)
- ☐ Ignition components damp or damaged – petrol models (Chapter 1A or Chapter 5B)
- ☐ Immobiliser fault, or 'uncoded' ignition key being used
- ☐ Broken, loose or disconnected wiring in the ignition circuit – petrol models (Chapter 1A or Chapter 5B)
- ☐ Worn, faulty or incorrectly-gapped spark plugs – petrol models (Chapter 1A Section 31)
- ☐ Preheating system faulty – diesel models (Chapter 5A)
- ☐ Fuel injection/engine management system fault (Chapter 4A, or Chapter 4B)
- ☐ Air in fuel system – diesel models (Chapter 4B Section 5)
- ☐ Major mechanical failure (eg timing belt snapped)
- ☐ (Chapter 2A, Chapter 2B, Chapter 2C or Chapter 2D)

Engine difficult to start when cold

- ☐ Battery discharged (Chapter 5A Section 3)
- ☐ Battery terminal connections loose or corroded (see *Weekly checks*)
- ☐ Worn, faulty or incorrectly-gapped spark plugs – petrol models (Chapter 1A Section 31)
- ☐ Other ignition system fault – petrol models (Chapter 1A or Chapter 5B)
- ☐ Preheating system faulty – diesel models (Chapter 5A)
- ☐ Fuel injection/engine management system fault (Chapter 4A, or Chapter 4B)
- ☐ Wrong grade of engine oil used (see *Weekly checks*)
- ☐ Low cylinder compression (Chapter 2A Section 2, Chapter 2B Section 2, Chapter 2C Section 2 or Chapter 2D Section 2)

Engine difficult to start when hot

- ☐ Air filter element dirty or clogged (Chapter 1A Section 30 or Chapter 1B Section 32)
- ☐ Fuel injection/engine management system fault (Chapter 4A or Chapter 4B)
- ☐ Low cylinder compression (Chapter 2A, Chapter 2B, Chapter 2C or Chapter 2D)

Starter motor noisy or excessively-rough in engagement

- ☐ Starter pinion or flywheel ring gear teeth loose or broken
- ☐ Starter motor mounting bolts loose or missing (Chapter 5A Section 11)

- ☐ Starter motor internal components worn or damaged (Chapter 5A Section 12)

Engine starts, but stops immediately

- ☐ Loose or faulty electrical connections in the ignition circuit – petrol models (Chapter 1A or Chapter 5B)
- ☐ Vacuum leak at the throttle body or inlet manifold – petrol models (Chapter 4A)
- ☐ Blocked injectors/fuel injection system fault (Chapter 4A or Chapter 4B)

Engine idles erratically

- ☐ Air filter element clogged (Chapter 1A Section 30 or Chapter 1B Section 32)
- ☐ Vacuum leak at the throttle body, inlet manifold or associated hoses – petrol models (Chapter 4A)
- ☐ Worn, faulty or incorrectly-gapped spark plugs – petrol models (Chapter 1A Section 31)
- ☐ Uneven or low cylinder compression (Chapter 2A Section 2, Chapter 2B Section 2, Chapter 2C Section 2 or Chapter 2D Section 2)
- ☐ Camshaft lobes worn (Chapter 2A Section 12, Chapter 2B Section 11, Chapter 2C Section 11 or Chapter 2D Section 11)
- ☐ Blocked injectors/fuel injection system fault (Chapter 4A or Chapter 4B)

Engine misfires at idle speed

- ☐ Worn, faulty or incorrectly-gapped spark plugs – petrol models (Chapter 1A Section 31)
- ☐ Vacuum leak at the throttle body, inlet manifold or associated hoses – petrol models (Chapter 4A)
- ☐ Blocked injectors/fuel injection system fault (Chapter 4A or Chapter 4B)
- ☐ Faulty injector(s) – diesel models (Chapter 4B Section 14)
- ☐ Uneven or low cylinder compression (Chapter 2A Section 2, Chapter 2B Section 2, Chapter 2C Section 2 or Chapter 2D Section 2)
- ☐ Disconnected, leaking, or perished crankcase ventilation hoses (Chapter 4C)

Engine misfires throughout the driving speed range

- ☐ Fuel filter choked – diesel models (Chapter 1B Section 23)
- ☐ Fuel pump faulty, or delivery pressure low – petrol models (Chapter 4A Section 7)
- ☐ Fuel tank vent blocked, or fuel pipes restricted (Chapter 4A or Chapter 4B)
- ☐ Vacuum leak at the throttle body, inlet manifold or associated hoses – petrol models (Chapter 4A)
- ☐ Worn, faulty or incorrectly-gapped spark plugs – petrol models (Chapter 1A Section 31)
- ☐ Faulty injector(s) – diesel models (Chapter 4B Section 14)
- ☐ Faulty ignition module – petrol models (Chapter 5B Section 3)
- ☐ Uneven or low cylinder compression (Chapter 2A Section 2, Chapter 2B Section 2, Chapter 2C Section 2 or Chapter 2D Section 2)
- ☐ Blocked injector/fuel injection system fault (Chapter 4A or Chapter 4B)
- ☐ Blocked catalytic converter (Chapter 4A Section 18 or Chapter 4B Section 20)
- ☐ Engine overheating (Chapter 3)

Engine (continued)

Engine hesitates on acceleration

- ☐ Worn, faulty or incorrectly-gapped spark plugs – petrol models (Chapter 1A Section 31)
- ☐ Vacuum leak at the throttle body, inlet manifold or associated hoses – petrol models (Chapter 4A)
- ☐ Blocked injectors/fuel injection system fault (Chapter 4A or Chapter 4B)
- ☐ Faulty injector(s) – diesel models (Chapter 4B Section 14)

Engine stalls

- ☐ Vacuum leak at the throttle body, inlet manifold or associated hoses – petrol models (Chapter 4A)
- ☐ Fuel filter choked – diesel models (Chapter 1B Section 23)
- ☐ Fuel pump faulty, or delivery pressure low – petrol models (Chapter 4A Section 7)
- ☐ Fuel tank vent blocked, or fuel pipes restricted (Chapter 4A or Chapter 4B)
- ☐ Blocked injectors/fuel injection system fault (Chapter 4A or Chapter 4B)
- ☐ Faulty injector(s) – diesel models (Chapter 4B Section 14)

Engine lacks power

- ☐ Air filter element blocked (Chapter 1A Section 30 or Chapter 1B Section 32)
- ☐ Fuel filter choked – diesel models (Chapter 1B Section 23)
- ☐ Fuel pipes blocked or restricted (Chapter 4A or Chapter 4B)
- ☐ Worn, faulty or incorrectly-gapped spark plugs – petrol models (Chapter 1A Section 31)
- ☐ Engine overheating (Chapter 3)
- ☐ Accelerator pedal position sensor faulty (Chapter 4A Section 3 or Chapter 4B Section 4)
- ☐ Vacuum leak at the throttle body, inlet manifold or associated hoses – petrol models (Chapter 4A)
- ☐ Blocked injectors/fuel injection system fault (Chapter 4A or Chapter 4B)
- ☐ Faulty injector(s) – diesel models (Chapter 4B Section 14)
- ☐ Fuel pump faulty, or delivery pressure low – petrol models (Chapter 4A Section 7)
- ☐ Uneven or low cylinder compression (Chapter 2A Section 2, Chapter 2B Section 2, Chapter 2C Section 2 or Chapter 2D Section 2)
- ☐ Blocked catalytic converter (Chapter 4A Section 18 or Chapter 4B Section 20)
- ☐ Brakes binding (Chapter 1A, Chapter 1B or Chapter 9)
- ☐ Clutch slipping (Chapter 6)

Engine backfires

- ☐ Vacuum leak at the throttle body, inlet manifold or associated hoses – petrol models (Chapter 4A)
- ☐ Blocked injectors/fuel injection system fault (Chapter 4A or Chapter 4B)
- ☐ Blocked catalytic converter (Chapter 4A Section 18 or Chapter 4B Section 20)
- ☐ Faulty ignition module – petrol models (Chapter 5B Section 3)

Oil pressure warning light illuminated with engine running

- ☐ Low oil level, or incorrect oil grade (see *Weekly checks*)
- ☐ Faulty oil pressure sensor, or wiring damaged (Chapter 5A Section 14)
- ☐ Worn engine bearings and/or oil pump (Chapter 2A, Chapter 2B, Chapter 2C, Chapter 2D or Chapter 2E)

- ☐ High engine operating temperature (Chapter 3)
- ☐ Oil pump pressure relief valve defective (Chapter 2A Section 15, Chapter 2B Section 15, Chapter 2C Section 14 or Chapter 2D Section 14)
- ☐ Oil pump pick-up strainer clogged (Chapter 2A Section 14, Chapter 2B Section 14, Chapter 2C Section 13 or Chapter 2D Section 13)

Engine runs-on after switching off

- ☐ Excessive carbon build-up in engine (Chapter 2E Section 7)
- ☐ High engine operating temperature (Chapter 3)
- ☐ Fuel injection/engine management system fault (Chapter 4A or Chapter 4B)

Engine noises

Pre-ignition (pinking) or knocking during acceleration or under load

- ☐ Ignition system/engine management system fault – petrol models (Chapter 4A or Chapter 5B)
- ☐ Incorrect grade of spark plug – petrol models (Chapter 1A Section 1)
- ☐ Incorrect grade of fuel (Chapter 4A or Chapter 4B)
- ☐ Knock sensor faulty – petrol models (Chapter 4A)
- ☐ Vacuum leak at the throttle body, inlet manifold or associated hoses – petrol models (Chapter 4A)
- ☐ Excessive carbon build-up in engine (Chapter 2E Section 7)
- ☐ Fuel injection/engine management system fault (Chapter 4A or Chapter 4B)
- ☐ Faulty injector(s) – diesel models (Chapter 4B Section 14)

Whistling or wheezing noises

- ☐ Leaking inlet manifold or throttle body gasket – petrol models (Chapter 4A)
- ☐ Leaking exhaust manifold gasket or pipe-to-manifold joint (Chapter 4A Section 16, 17 or Chapter 4B Section 19)
- ☐ Leaking vacuum hose (Chapter 4A, Chapter 4B, Chapter 4C or Chapter 9)
- ☐ Blowing cylinder head gasket (Chapter 2A Section 13, Chapter 2B Section 13, Chapter 2C Section 12 or Chapter 2D Section 12)
- ☐ Partially blocked or leaking crankcase ventilation system (Chapter 4C)

Tapping or rattling noises

- ☐ Worn valve gear or camshaft (Chapter 2A Section 12, Chapter 2B Section 11, Chapter 2C Section 11 or Chapter 2D Section 11)
- ☐ Incorrect valve clearances (Chapter 2A Section 11, Chapter 2B Section 10 or Chapter 2C Section 10)
- ☐ Ancillary component fault (coolant pump, alternator, etc) (Chapter 3, Chapter 5A, etc)

Knocking or thumping noises

- ☐ Worn big-end bearings (regular heavy knocking, perhaps less under load) (Chapter 2E Section 10)
- ☐ Worn main bearings (rumbling and knocking, perhaps worsening under load) (Chapter 2E Section 14)
- ☐ Piston slap – most noticeable when cold, caused by piston/bore wear (Chapter 2E Section 12)
- ☐ Ancillary component fault (coolant pump, alternator, etc) (Chapter 3, Chapter 5A, etc)
- ☐ Engine mountings worn or defective (Chapter 2B Section 20, Chapter 2A Section 19, Chapter 2C Section 18 or Chapter 2D Section 18)
- ☐ Front suspension or steering components worn (Chapter 10)

Cooling system

Overheating

☐ Insufficient coolant in system (see *Weekly checks*)
☐ Thermostat faulty (Chapter 3 Section 4)
☐ Radiator core blocked, or grille restricted (Chapter 3 Section 3)
☐ Cooling fan or cooling module faulty (Chapter 3 Section 5)
☐ Inaccurate coolant temperature sensor (Chapter 3 Section 6)
☐ Airlock in cooling system (Chapter 1A Section 28 or Chapter 1B Section 30)
☐ Expansion tank pressure cap faulty (Chapter 1A Section 28 or Chapter 1B Section 30)
☐ Engine management system fault (Chapter 4A or Chapter 4B)

Overcooling

☐ Thermostat faulty (Chapter 3 Section 4)
☐ Inaccurate coolant temperature sensor (Chapter 3 Section 6)
☐ Cooling fan faulty (Chapter 3 Section 5)
☐ Engine management system fault (Chapter 4A or Chapter 4B)

External coolant leakage

☐ Deteriorated or damaged hoses or hose clips (Chapter 1A Section 7 or Chapter 1B Section 7)
☐ Radiator core or heater matrix leaking (Chapter 3)
☐ Expansion tank pressure cap faulty (Chapter 1A Section 28 or Chapter 1B Section 30)
☐ Coolant pump internal seal leaking (Chapter 3 Section 7)
☐ Coolant pump gasket leaking (Chapter 3 Section 7)
☐ Boiling due to overheating (Chapter 3)
☐ Cylinder block core plug leaking (Chapter 2E Section 11)

Internal coolant leakage

☐ Leaking cylinder head gasket (Chapter 2A Section 13, Chapter 2B Section 13, Chapter 2C Section 12 or Chapter 2D Section 12)
☐ Cracked cylinder head or cylinder block (Chapter 2E)

Corrosion

☐ Infrequent draining and flushing (Chapter 1A Section 28 or Chapter 1B Section 30)
☐ Incorrect coolant mixture or inappropriate coolant type (see *Weekly checks*)

Fuel and exhaust systems

Excessive fuel consumption

☐ Air filter element dirty or clogged (Chapter 1A Section 30 or Chapter 1B Section 32)
☐ Fuel injection system fault (Chapter 4A or Chapter 4B)
☐ Engine management system fault (Chapter 4A or Chapter 4B)
☐ Crankcase ventilation system blocked (Chapter 4C)
☐ Tyres under-inflated (see *Weekly checks*)
☐ Brakes binding (Chapter 1A, Chapter 1B or Chapter 9)
☐ Fuel leak, causing apparent high consumption (Chapter 1A Section 7 or Chapter 1B Section 7)

Fuel leakage and/or fuel odour

☐ Damaged or corroded fuel tank, pipes or connections (Chapter 4A Section 8 or Chapter 4B Section 8)
☐ Evaporative emissions system fault – petrol models (Chapter 4C Section 2)

Excessive noise or fumes from exhaust system

☐ Leaking exhaust system or manifold joints (Chapter 1A Section 14 or Chapter 1B Section 14)
☐ Leaking, corroded or damaged silencers or pipe (Chapter 1A Section 14 or Chapter 1B Section 14)
☐ Broken mountings causing body or suspension contact (Chapter 1A Section 14 or Chapter 1B Section 14)

Clutch

Pedal travels to floor – no pressure or very little resistance

- [ ] Air in hydraulic system/faulty master or slave cylinder (Chapter 6 Section 2)
- [ ] Faulty hydraulic release system (Chapter 6)
- [ ] Clutch pedal return spring detached or broken (Chapter 6 Section 5)
- [ ] Faulty clutch release cylinder (Chapter 6 Section 4)
- [ ] Broken diaphragm spring in clutch pressure plate (Chapter 6 Section 6)

Clutch fails to disengage (unable to select gears)

- [ ] Air in hydraulic system/faulty master or slave cylinder (Chapter 6 Section 2)
- [ ] Faulty hydraulic release system (Chapter 6)
- [ ] Clutch disc sticking on transmission input shaft splines (Chapter 6 Section 6)
- [ ] Clutch disc sticking to flywheel or pressure plate (Chapter 6 Section 6)
- [ ] Faulty pressure plate assembly (Chapter 6 Section 6)
- [ ] Clutch release mechanism worn or incorrectly assembled (Chapter 6)

Clutch slips (engine speed increases, with no increase in vehicle speed)

- [ ] Faulty hydraulic release system (Chapter 6)
- [ ] Clutch disc linings excessively worn (Chapter 6 Section 6)
- [ ] Clutch disc linings contaminated with oil or grease (Chapter 6 Section 6)
- [ ] Faulty pressure plate or weak diaphragm spring (Chapter 6 Section 6)

Judder as clutch is engaged

- [ ] Clutch disc linings contaminated with oil or grease (Chapter 6 Section 6)
- [ ] Clutch disc linings excessively worn (Chapter 6 Section 6)
- [ ] Faulty or distorted pressure plate or diaphragm spring (Chapter 6 Section 6)
- [ ] Worn or loose engine or transmission mountings (Chapter 2A Section 19, Chapter 2B Section 20, Chapter 2C Section 18 or Chapter 2D Section 18)
- [ ] Clutch disc hub or transmission input shaft splines worn (Chapter 6 Section 6)

Noise when depressing or releasing clutch pedal

- [ ] Faulty clutch release cylinder (Chapter 6 Section 4)
- [ ] Worn or dry clutch pedal bushes (Chapter 6 Section 5)
- [ ] Faulty pressure plate assembly (Chapter 6 Section 6)
- [ ] Pressure plate diaphragm spring broken (Chapter 6 Section 6)
- [ ] Broken clutch disc cushioning springs (Chapter 6 Section 6)

Manual transmission

Noisy in neutral with engine running

Note: *Fault finding for the Easytronic transmission should be entrusted to a Vauxhall/Opel dealer.*

- [ ] Lack of oil (Chapter 7A Section 2)
- [ ] Input shaft bearings worn (noise apparent with clutch pedal released, but not when depressed) (Chapter 7A)*
- [ ] Clutch release cylinder faulty (noise apparent with clutch pedal depressed, possibly less when released) (Chapter 6 Section 4)

Noisy in one particular gear

- [ ] Worn, damaged or chipped gear teeth (Chapter 7A)*

Difficulty engaging gears

- [ ] Clutch fault (Chapter 6)
- [ ] Worn, damaged, or poorly-adjusted gearchange (Chapter 7A Section 3)
- [ ] Lack of oil (Chapter 7A Section 2 or Chapter 7C Section 2)
- [ ] Worn synchroniser units (Chapter 7A)*

Jumps out of gear

- [ ] Worn, damaged, or poorly-adjusted gearchange (Chapter 7A)
- [ ] Worn synchroniser units (Chapter 7A)
- [ ] *Worn selector forks (Chapter 7A)*

Vibration

- [ ] Lack of oil (Chapter 7A Section 2 or Chapter 7C Section 2)
- [ ] Worn bearings (Chapter 7A)*

Lubricant leaks

- [ ] Leaking driveshaft or selector shaft oil seal (Chapter 7A Section 5)
- [ ] Leaking housing joint (Chapter 7A)
- [ ] *Leaking input shaft oil seal (Chapter 7A)*

Although the corrective action necessary to remedy the symptoms described is beyond the scope of the home mechanic, the above information should be helpful in isolating the cause of the condition, so that the owner can communicate clearly with a professional mechanic.

Automatic transmission

Fluid leakage

Note: *Due to the complexity of the automatic transmission, it is difficult for the home mechanic to properly diagnose and service this unit. For problems other than the following, the vehicle should be taken to a dealer service department or automatic transmission specialist. Do not be too hasty in removing the transmission if a fault is suspected, as most of the testing is carried out with the unit still fitted. Remember that, besides the sensors specific to the transmission, many of the engine management system sensors described in Chapter 4A and 4B are essential to the correct operation of the transmission.*

☐ Automatic transmission fluid is usually dark red in colour. Fluid leaks should not be confused with engine oil, which can easily be blown onto the transmission by airflow. To determine the source of a leak, first remove all built-up dirt and grime from the transmission housing and surrounding areas using a degreasing agent, or by steam-cleaning. Drive the vehicle at low speed, so airflow will not blow the leak far from its source. Raise and support the vehicle, and determine where the leak is coming from. The following are common areas of leakage:
   a) *Fluid pan*
   b) *Dipstick tube (Chapter 7B)*
   c) *Transmission-to-fluid cooler unions (Chapter 7B)*

Transmission fluid brown, or has burned smell

☐ Transmission fluid level low (Chapter 7B Section 2)

General gear selection problems

☐ Chapter 7B deals with checking the selector cable on automatic transmissions. The following are common problems which may be caused by a faulty cable or sensor:

   a) *Engine starting in gears other than Park or Neutral.*
   b) *Indicator panel indicating a gear other than the one actually being used.*
   c) *Vehicle moves when in Park or Neutral.*
   d) *Poor gear shift quality or erratic gear changes.*

Transmission will not downshift (kickdown) with accelerator pedal fully depressed

☐ Low transmission fluid level (Chapter 7B Section 2)
☐ Engine management system fault (Chapter 4A or Chapter 4B)
☐ Faulty transmission sensor or wiring (Chapter 7B)
☐ Incorrect selector cable adjustment (Chapter 7B Section 3)

Engine will not start in any gear, or starts in gears other than Park or Neutral

☐ Faulty transmission sensor or wiring (Chapter 7B)
☐ Engine management system fault (Chapter 4A or Chapter 4B)
☐ Incorrect selector cable adjustment (Chapter 7B Section 3)

Transmission slips, shifts roughly, is noisy, or has no drive in forward or reverse gears

☐ Transmission fluid level low (Chapter 7B Section 2)
☐ Faulty transmission sensor or wiring (Chapter 7B)
☐ Engine management system fault (Chapter 4A or Chapter 4B)

Note: *There are many probable causes for the above problems, but diagnosing and correcting them is considered beyond the scope of this manual. Having checked the fluid level and all the wiring as far as possible, a dealer or transmission specialist should be consulted if the problem persists.*

Driveshafts

Vibration when accelerating or decelerating

☐ Worn inner constant velocity joint (Chapter 8 Section 6)
☐ Bent or distorted driveshaft (Chapter 8 Section 2)
☐ Worn intermediate bearing (Chapter 8 Section 4)

Clicking or knocking noise on turns (at slow speed on full-lock)

☐ Worn outer constant velocity joint (Chapter 8 Section 6)
☐ Lack of constant velocity joint lubricant, possibly due to damaged gaiter (Chapter 8 Section 5)

Braking system

Vehicle pulls to one side under braking

Note: *Before assuming that a brake problem exists, make sure that the tyres are in good condition and correctly inflated, that the front wheel alignment is correct, and that the vehicle is not loaded with weight in an unequal manner. Apart from checking the condition of all pipe and hose connections, any faults occurring on the anti-lock braking system should be referred to a Vauxhall/Opel dealer for diagnosis.*

☐ Worn, defective, damaged or contaminated brake pads on one side (Chapter 1A Section 10, Chapter 1B Section 10 or Chapter 9)
☐ Seized or partially-seized brake caliper piston (Chapter 9)
☐ A mixture of brake pad lining materials fitted between sides (Chapter 1A Section 10, Chapter 1B Section 10 or Chapter 9)
☐ Brake caliper mounting bolts loose (Chapter 9)
☐ Worn or damaged steering or suspension components (Chapter 1A Section 12, Chapter 1B Section 12 or Chapter 10)

Noise (grinding or high-pitched squeal) when brakes applied

☐ Brake pad friction lining material worn down to metal backing (Chapter 1A Section 10 or Chapter 1B Section 10)
☐ Excessive corrosion of brake disc (may be apparent after the vehicle has been standing for some time (Chapter 1A Section 10 or Chapter 1B Section 10)
☐ Foreign object (stone chipping, etc)
☐ trapped between brake disc and shield (Chapter 1A Section 10 or Chapter 1B Section 10)

Excessive brake pedal travel

☐ Faulty master cylinder (Chapter 9 Section 9)
☐ Air in hydraulic system (Chapter 9 Section 2)
☐ Faulty vacuum servo unit (Chapter 9 Section 11)

Brake pedal feels spongy when depressed

☐ Air in hydraulic system (Chapter 9 Section 2)
☐ Deteriorated flexible rubber brake hoses (Chapter 1A Section 11 or Chapter 1B Section 11)
☐ Master cylinder mounting nuts loose (Chapter 9 Section 9)
☐ Faulty master cylinder (Chapter 9 Section 9)

Excessive brake pedal effort required to stop vehicle

☐ Faulty vacuum servo unit (Chapter 9 Section 11)
☐ Faulty vacuum pump – diesel models (Chapter 9 Section 19)
☐ Disconnected, damaged or insecure brake servo vacuum hose (Chapter 9 Section 12)
☐ Primary or secondary hydraulic circuit failure (Chapter 9)
☐ Seized brake caliper piston (Chapter 9)
☐ Brake pads incorrectly fitted (Chapter 9)
☐ Incorrect grade of brake pads fitted (Chapter 9)
☐ Brake pad linings contaminated (Chapter 1A Section 10 or Chapter 1B Section 10)

Judder felt through brake pedal or steering wheel when braking

Note: *Under heavy braking on models equipped with ABS, vibration may be felt through the brake pedal. This is a normal feature of ABS operation, and does not constitute a fault.*

☐ Excessive run-out or distortion of discs (Chapter 9 Section 6)
☐ Brake pad linings worn (Chapter 1A Section 10 or Chapter 1B Section 10)
☐ Brake caliper mounting bolts loose (Chapter 9)
☐ Wear in suspension or steering components or mountings (Chapter 1A or Chapter 1B)
☐ Front wheels out of balance (see *Weekly checks*)

Brakes binding

☐ Seized brake caliper piston (Chapter 9)
☐ Faulty master cylinder (Chapter 9 Section 9)

Rear wheels locking under normal braking

☐ Rear brake pad linings contaminated or damaged (Chapter 1A Section 10 or Chapter 1B Section 10)
☐ Rear brake discs warped (Chapter 9 Section 6)

Suspension and steering

Vehicle pulls to one side

Note: *Before diagnosing suspension or steering faults, be sure that the trouble is not due to incorrect tyre pressures, mixtures of tyre types, or binding brakes.*

☐ Defective tyre (see *Weekly checks*)
☐ Excessive wear in suspension or steering components (Chapter 1A, Chapter 1B or Chapter 10)
☐ Incorrect front wheel alignment (Chapter 10 Section 23)
☐ Accident damage to steering or suspension components (Chapter 1A or Chapter 1B)

Wheel wobble and vibration

☐ Front wheels out of balance (vibration felt mainly through the steering wheel) (see *Weekly checks*)
☐ Rear wheels out of balance (vibration felt throughout the vehicle) (see *Weekly checks*)
☐ Roadwheels damaged or distorted (see *Weekly checks*)
☐ Faulty or damaged tyre (see *Weekly checks*)
☐ Worn steering or suspension joints, bushes or components (Chapter 1A, Chapter 1B or Chapter 10)
☐ Wheel bolts loose (Chapter 1A or Chapter 1B)

Excessive pitching and/or rolling around corners, or during braking

☐ Defective shock absorbers (Chapter 1A or Chapter 1B)
☐ Broken or weak spring and/or suspension component (Chapter 1A or Chapter 1B)
☐ Worn or damaged anti-roll bar or mountings (Chapter 10 Section 8)

Wandering or general instability

☐ Incorrect front wheel alignment (Chapter 10 Section 23)
☐ Worn steering or suspension joints, bushes or components (Chapter 1A or Chapter 1B)
☐ Roadwheels out of balance (see *Weekly checks*)
☐ Faulty or damaged tyre (see *Weekly checks*)
☐ Wheel bolts loose (Chapter 1A or Chapter 1B)
☐ Defective shock absorbers (Chapter 10 Section 4 or Chapter 10 Section 10)
☐ Power steering system fault (Chapter 10 Section 19)

Excessively-stiff steering

☐ Seized steering linkage balljoint or suspension balljoint (Chapter 1A or Chapter 1B)
☐ Incorrect front wheel alignment (Chapter 10 Section 23)
☐ Steering rack damaged (Chapter 10 Section 18)
☐ Power steering system fault (Chapter 10 Section 19)

Excessive play in steering

☐ Worn steering column/intermediate shaft joints (Chapter 10)
☐ Worn track rod balljoints (Chapter 10 Section 21)
☐ Worn steering rack (Chapter 10 Section 18)
☐ Worn steering or suspension joints, bushes or components (Chapter 1A or Chapter 1B)

Lack of power assistance

☐ Power steering system fault (Chapter 10 Section 19)
☐ Faulty steering rack (Chapter 10 Section 18)

Tyre wear excessive

Tyres worn on inside or outside edges

☐ Tyres under-inflated (wear on both edges) (see *Weekly checks*)
☐ Incorrect camber or castor angles (wear on one edge only) (Chapter 10 Section 23)
☐ Worn steering or suspension joints, bushes or components (Chapter 1A or Chapter 1B)
☐ Excessively-hard cornering or braking Accident damage

Tyre treads exhibit feathered edges

☐ Incorrect toe-setting (Chapter 10 Section 23)

Tyres worn in centre of tread

☐ Tyres over-inflated (see *Weekly checks*)

Tyres worn on inside and outside edges

☐ Tyres under-inflated (see *Weekly checks*)

Tyres worn unevenly

☐ Tyres/wheels out of balance (see *Weekly checks*)
☐ Excessive wheel or tyre run-out Worn shock absorbers (Chapter 10 Section 4 or Chapter 10 Section 10)
☐ Faulty tyre (see *Weekly checks*)

Electrical system

Battery will not hold a charge for more than a few days

Note: *For problems associated with the starting system, refer to the faults listed under 'Engine' earlier in this Section.*

☐ Battery defective internally (Chapter 5A Section 3)
☐ Battery terminal connections loose or corroded (see *Weekly checks*)
☐ Auxiliary drivebelt worn or faulty automatic adjuster (Chapter 1A Section 23 or Chapter 1B Section 24)
☐ Alternator not charging at correct output (Chapter 5A Section 5)
☐ Alternator or voltage regulator faulty (Chapter 5A Section 5)
☐ Short-circuit causing continual battery drain (Chapter 5A or Chapter 12 Section 2)

Ignition/no-charge warning light remains illuminated with engine running

☐ Auxiliary drivebelt broken, worn, or or faulty automatic adjuster (Chapter 1A Section 23, Chapter 1B Section 24 or Chapter 5A Section 7)
☐ Internal fault in alternator or voltage regulator (Chapter 5A Section 9)
☐ Broken, disconnected, or loose wiring in charging circuit (Chapter 5A or Chapter 12 Section 2)

Ignition/no-charge warning light fails to come on

☐ Broken, disconnected, or loose wiring in warning light circuit (Chapter 5A or Chapter 12 Section 2)
☐ Alternator faulty (Chapter 5A Section 8)

Electrical system (continued)

Lights inoperative

- ☐ Bulb blown (Chapter 12)
- ☐ Corrosion of bulb or bulbholder contacts (Chapter 12)
- ☐ Blown fuse (Chapter 12 Section 3)
- ☐ Faulty relay (Chapter 12 Section 3)
- ☐ Broken, loose, or disconnected wiring (Chapter 12)
- ☐ Faulty switch (Chapter 12 Section 4)

Instrument readings inaccurate or erratic

Fuel or temperature gauges give no reading

- ☐ Faulty gauge sender unit (Chapter 4A Section 6 or Chapter 4B Section 6)
- ☐ Wiring open-circuit (Chapter 12 Section 2)
- ☐ Faulty gauge (Chapter 12 Section 9)

Fuel or temperature gauges give continuous maximum reading

- ☐ Faulty gauge sender unit (Chapter 3 Section 6, Chapter 4A Section 6 or Chapter 4B Section 6)
- ☐ Wiring short-circuit (Chapter 12 Section 2)
- ☐ Faulty gauge (Chapter 12 Section 9)

Horn inoperative, or unsatisfactory in operation

Horn operates all the time

- ☐ Horn push either earthed or stuck down (Chapter 12 Section 2)
- ☐ Horn cable-to-horn push earthed (Chapter 12 Section 2)

Horn fails to operate

- ☐ Blown fuse (Chapter 12 Section 3)
- ☐ Cable or connections loose, broken or disconnected (Chapter 12 Section 2)
- ☐ Faulty horn (Chapter 12 Section 11)

Horn emits intermittent or unsatisfactory sound

- ☐ Cable connections loose (Chapter 12 Section 2)
- ☐ Horn mountings loose (Chapter 12 Section 11)
- ☐ Faulty horn (Chapter 12 Section 11)

Windscreen wipers inoperative, or unsatisfactory in operation

Wipers fail to operate, or operate very slowly

- ☐ Wiper blades stuck to screen, or linkage seized or binding (Chapter 12 Section 13)
- ☐ Blown fuse (Chapter 12 Section 3)
- ☐ Battery discharged (Chapter 5A Section 3)
- ☐ Cable or connections loose, broken or disconnected (Chapter 12 Section 2)
- ☐ Faulty relay (Chapter 12 Section 3)
- ☐ Faulty wiper motor (Chapter 12 Section 13)

Wiper blades sweep over too large or too small an area of the glass

- ☐ Wiper blades incorrectly fitted, or wrong size used (see *Weekly checks*)
- ☐ Wiper arms incorrectly positioned on spindles (Chapter 12 Section 12)
- ☐ Excessive wear of wiper linkage (Chapter 12 Section 13)
- ☐ Wiper motor or linkage mountings loose or insecure (Chapter 12 Section 13)

Wiper blades fail to clean the glass effectively

- ☐ Wiper blade rubbers dirty, worn or perished (see *Weekly checks*)
- ☐ Wiper blades incorrectly fitted, or wrong size used (see *Weekly checks*)
- ☐ Wiper arm tension springs broken, or arm pivots seized (Chapter 12 Section 12)
- ☐ Insufficient windscreen washer additive to adequately remove road film (see *Weekly checks*)

Windscreen washers inoperative, or unsatisfactory in operation

One or more washer jets inoperative

- ☐ Blocked washer jetDisconnected, kinked or restricted fluid hose (Chapter 12 Section 15)
- ☐ Insufficient fluid in washer reservoir (see *Weekly checks*)

Washer pump fails to operate

- ☐ Broken or disconnected wiring or connections (Chapter 12 Section 2)
- ☐ Blown fuse (Chapter 12 Section 3)
- ☐ Faulty washer switch (Chapter 12 Section 4)
- ☐ Faulty washer pump (Chapter 12 Section 15)

Washer pump runs for some time before fluid is emitted from jets

- ☐ Faulty one-way valve in fluid supply hose (Chapter 12 Section 15)

Electric windows inoperative, or unsatisfactory in operation

Window glass will only move in one direction

- ☐ Faulty switch (Chapter 12 Section 4)

Window glass slow to move

- ☐ Battery discharged (Chapter 5A Section 3)
- ☐ Regulator seized or damaged, or in need of lubrication (Chapter 11 Section 14)
- ☐ Door internal components or trim fouling regulator (Chapter 11)
- ☐ Faulty motor (Chapter 11 Section 14)

Window glass fails to move

- ☐ Blown fuse (Chapter 12 Section 3)
- ☐ Faulty relay (Chapter 12 Section 3)
- ☐ Broken or disconnected wiring or connections (Chapter 12 Section 2)
- ☐ Faulty motor (Chapter 11 Section 14)

Central locking system inoperative, or unsatisfactory in operation

Complete system failure

- ☐ Remote handset battery discharged, where applicable (Chapter 1A Section 26 or Chapter 1B Section 28)
- ☐ Blown fuse (Chapter 12 Section 3)
- ☐ Faulty relay (Chapter 12 Section 3)
- ☐ Broken or disconnected wiring or connections (Chapter 12 Section 2)
- ☐ Faulty motor (Chapter 11 Section 13)

Latch locks but will not unlock, or unlocks but will not lock

- ☐ Remote handset battery discharged, where applicable (Chapter 1A Section 26 or Chapter 1B Section 28)
- ☐ Faulty master switch (Chapter 12 Section 4)
- ☐ Broken or disconnected latch operating rods or levers (Chapter 11 Section 13)
- ☐ Faulty relay (Chapter 12 Section 3)
- ☐ Faulty motor (Chapter 11 Section 13)

One solenoid/motor fails to operate

- ☐ Broken or disconnected wiring or connections (Chapter 12 Section 2)
- ☐ Faulty operating assembly (Chapter 11 Section 13)
- ☐ Broken, binding or disconnected latch operating rods or levers (Chapter 11 Section 13)
- ☐ Fault in door latch (Chapter 11 Section 13)

A

ABS (Anti-lock brake system) A system, usually electronically controlled, that senses incipient wheel lockup during braking and relieves hydraulic pressure at wheels that are about to skid.

Air bag An inflatable bag hidden in the steering wheel (driver's side) or the dash or glovebox (passenger side). In a head-on collision, the bags inflate, preventing the driver and front passenger from being thrown forward into the steering wheel or windscreen.

Air cleaner A metal or plastic housing, containing a filter element, which removes dust and dirt from the air being drawn into the engine.

Air filter element The actual filter in an air cleaner system, usually manufactured from pleated paper and requiring renewal at regular intervals.

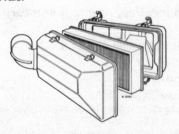

Air filter

Allen key A hexagonal wrench which fits into a recessed hexagonal hole.

Alligator clip A long-nosed spring-loaded metal clip with meshing teeth. Used to make temporary electrical connections.

Alternator A component in the electrical system which converts mechanical energy from a drivebelt into electrical energy to charge the battery and to operate the starting system, ignition system and electrical accessories.

Ampere (amp) A unit of measurement for the flow of electric current. One amp is the amount of current produced by one volt acting through a resistance of one ohm.

Anaerobic sealer A substance used to prevent bolts and screws from loosening. Anaerobic means that it does not require oxygen for activation. The Loctite brand is widely used.

Antifreeze A substance (usually ethylene glycol) mixed with water, and added to a vehicle's cooling system, to prevent freezing of the coolant in winter. Antifreeze also contains chemicals to inhibit corrosion and the formation of rust and other deposits that would tend to clog the radiator and coolant passages and reduce cooling efficiency.

Anti-seize compound A coating that reduces the risk of seizing on fasteners that are subjected to high temperatures, such as exhaust manifold bolts and nuts.

Asbestos A natural fibrous mineral with great heat resistance, commonly used in the composition of brake friction materials. Asbestos is a health hazard and the dust created by brake systems should never be inhaled or ingested.

Axle A shaft on which a wheel revolves, or which revolves with a wheel. Also, a solid beam that connects the two wheels at one end of the vehicle. An axle which also transmits power to the wheels is known as a live axle.

Axleshaft A single rotating shaft, on either side of the differential, which delivers power from the final drive assembly to the drive wheels. Also called a driveshaft or a halfshaft.

B

Ball bearing An anti-friction bearing consisting of a hardened inner and outer race with hardened steel balls between two races.

Bearing The curved surface on a shaft or in a bore, or the part assembled into either, that permits relative motion between them with minimum wear and friction.

Bearing

Big-end bearing The bearing in the end of the connecting rod that's attached to the crankshaft.

Bleed nipple A valve on a brake wheel cylinder, caliper or other hydraulic component that is opened to purge the hydraulic system of air. Also called a bleed screw.

Brake bleeding Procedure for removing air from lines of a hydraulic brake system.

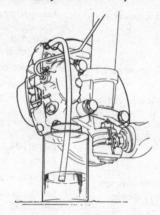

Brake bleeding

Brake disc The component of a disc brake that rotates with the wheels.

Brake drum The component of a drum brake that rotates with the wheels.

Brake linings The friction material which contacts the brake disc or drum to retard the vehicle's speed. The linings are bonded or riveted to the brake pads or shoes.

Brake pads The replaceable friction pads that pinch the brake disc when the brakes are applied. Brake pads consist of a friction material bonded or riveted to a rigid backing plate.

Brake shoe The crescent-shaped carrier to which the brake linings are mounted and which forces the lining against the rotating drum during braking.

Braking systems For more information on braking systems, consult the *Haynes Automotive Brake Manual*.

Breaker bar A long socket wrench handle providing greater leverage.

Bulkhead The insulated partition between the engine and the passenger compartment.

C

Caliper The non-rotating part of a disc-brake assembly that straddles the disc and carries the brake pads. The caliper also contains the hydraulic components that cause the pads to pinch the disc when the brakes are applied. A caliper is also a measuring tool that can be set to measure inside or outside dimensions of an object.

Camshaft A rotating shaft on which a series of cam lobes operate the valve mechanisms. The camshaft may be driven by gears, by sprockets and chain or by sprockets and a belt.

Canister A container in an evaporative emission control system; contains activated charcoal granules to trap vapours from the fuel system.

Canister

Carburettor A device which mixes fuel with air in the proper proportions to provide a desired power output from a spark ignition internal combustion engine.

Castellated Resembling the parapets along the top of a castle wall. For example, a castellated balljoint stud nut.

Castor In wheel alignment, the backward or forward tilt of the steering axis. Castor is positive when the steering axis is inclined rearward at the top.

Catalytic converter A silencer-like device in the exhaust system which converts certain pollutants in the exhaust gases into less harmful substances.

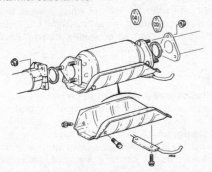

Catalytic converter

Circlip A ring-shaped clip used to prevent endwise movement of cylindrical parts and shafts. An internal circlip is installed in a groove in a housing; an external circlip fits into a groove on the outside of a cylindrical piece such as a shaft.

Clearance The amount of space between two parts. For example, between a piston and a cylinder, between a bearing and a journal, etc.

Coil spring A spiral of elastic steel found in various sizes throughout a vehicle, for example as a springing medium in the suspension and in the valve train.

Compression Reduction in volume, and increase in pressure and temperature, of a gas, caused by squeezing it into a smaller space.

Compression ratio The relationship between cylinder volume when the piston is at top dead centre and cylinder volume when the piston is at bottom dead centre.

Constant velocity (CV) joint A type of universal joint that cancels out vibrations caused by driving power being transmitted through an angle.

Core plug A disc or cup-shaped metal device inserted in a hole in a casting through which core was removed when the casting was formed. Also known as a freeze plug or expansion plug.

Crankcase The lower part of the engine block in which the crankshaft rotates.

Crankshaft The main rotating member, or shaft, running the length of the crankcase, with offset "throws" to which the connecting rods are attached.

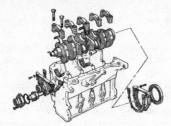

Crankshaft assembly

Crocodile clip See Alligator clip

D

Diagnostic code Code numbers obtained by accessing the diagnostic mode of an engine management computer. This code can be used to determine the area in the system where a malfunction may be located.

Disc brake A brake design incorporating a rotating disc onto which brake pads are squeezed. The resulting friction converts the energy of a moving vehicle into heat.

Double-overhead cam (DOHC) An engine that uses two overhead camshafts, usually one for the intake valves and one for the exhaust valves.

Drivebelt(s) The belt(s) used to drive accessories such as the alternator, water pump, power steering pump, air conditioning compressor, etc. off the crankshaft pulley.

Accessory drivebelts

Driveshaft Any shaft used to transmit motion. Commonly used when referring to the axleshafts on a front wheel drive vehicle.

Drum brake A type of brake using a drum-shaped metal cylinder attached to the inner surface of the wheel. When the brake pedal is pressed, curved brake shoes with friction linings press against the inside of the drum to slow or stop the vehicle.

E

EGR valve A valve used to introduce exhaust gases into the intake air stream.

Electronic control unit (ECU) A computer which controls (for instance) ignition and fuel injection systems, or an anti-lock braking system. For more information refer to the *Haynes Automotive Electrical and Electronic Systems Manual*.

Electronic Fuel Injection (EFI) A computer controlled fuel system that distributes fuel through an injector located in each intake port of the engine.

Emergency brake A braking system, independent of the main hydraulic system, that can be used to slow or stop the vehicle if the primary brakes fail, or to hold the vehicle stationary even though the brake pedal isn't depressed. It usually consists of a hand lever that actuates either front or rear brakes mechanically through a series of cables and linkages. Also known as a handbrake or parking brake.

Endfloat The amount of lengthwise movement between two parts. As applied to a crankshaft, the distance that the crankshaft can move forward and back in the cylinder block.

Engine management system (EMS) A computer controlled system which manages the fuel injection and the ignition systems in an integrated fashion.

Exhaust manifold A part with several passages through which exhaust gases leave the engine combustion chambers and enter the exhaust pipe.

F

Fan clutch A viscous (fluid) drive coupling device which permits variable engine fan speeds in relation to engine speeds.

Feeler blade A thin strip or blade of hardened steel, ground to an exact thickness, used to check or measure clearances between parts.

Feeler blade

Firing order The order in which the engine cylinders fire, or deliver their power strokes, beginning with the number one cylinder.

Flywheel A heavy spinning wheel in which energy is absorbed and stored by means of momentum. On cars, the flywheel is attached to the crankshaft to smooth out firing impulses.

Free play The amount of travel before any action takes place. The "looseness" in a linkage, or an assembly of parts, between the initial application of force and actual movement. For example, the distance the brake pedal moves before the pistons in the master cylinder are actuated.

Fuse An electrical device which protects a circuit against accidental overload. The typical fuse contains a soft piece of metal which is calibrated to melt at a predetermined current flow (expressed as amps) and break the circuit.

Fusible link A circuit protection device consisting of a conductor surrounded by heat-resistant insulation. The conductor is smaller than the wire it protects, so it acts as the weakest link in the circuit. Unlike a blown fuse, a failed fusible link must frequently be cut from the wire for replacement.

G

Gap The distance the spark must travel in jumping from the centre electrode to the side electrode in a spark plug. Also refers to the spacing between the points in a contact breaker assembly in a conventional points-type ignition, or to the distance between the reluctor or rotor and the pickup coil in an electronic ignition.

Adjusting spark plug gap

Gasket Any thin, soft material - usually cork, cardboard, asbestos or soft metal - installed between two metal surfaces to ensure a good seal. For instance, the cylinder head gasket seals the joint between the block and the cylinder head.

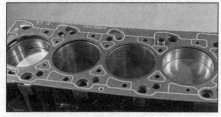

Gasket

Gauge An instrument panel display used to monitor engine conditions. A gauge with a movable pointer on a dial or a fixed scale is an analogue gauge. A gauge with a numerical readout is called a digital gauge.

H

Halfshaft A rotating shaft that transmits power from the final drive unit to a drive wheel, usually when referring to a live rear axle.

Harmonic balancer A device designed to reduce torsion or twisting vibration in the crankshaft. May be incorporated in the crankshaft pulley. Also known as a vibration damper.

Hone An abrasive tool for correcting small irregularities or differences in diameter in an engine cylinder, brake cylinder, etc.

Hydraulic tappet A tappet that utilises hydraulic pressure from the engine's lubrication system to maintain zero clearance (constant contact with both camshaft and valve stem). Automatically adjusts to variation in valve stem length. Hydraulic tappets also reduce valve noise.

I

Ignition timing The moment at which the spark plug fires, usually expressed in the number of crankshaft degrees before the piston reaches the top of its stroke.

Inlet manifold A tube or housing with passages through which flows the air-fuel mixture (carburettor vehicles and vehicles with throttle body injection) or air only (port fuel-injected vehicles) to the port openings in the cylinder head.

J

Jump start Starting the engine of a vehicle with a discharged or weak battery by attaching jump leads from the weak battery to a charged or helper battery.

L

Load Sensing Proportioning Valve (LSPV) A brake hydraulic system control valve that works like a proportioning valve, but also takes into consideration the amount of weight carried by the rear axle.

Locknut A nut used to lock an adjustment nut, or other threaded component, in place. For example, a locknut is employed to keep the adjusting nut on the rocker arm in position.

Lockwasher A form of washer designed to prevent an attaching nut from working loose.

M

MacPherson strut A type of front suspension system devised by Earle MacPherson at Ford of England. In its original form, a simple lateral link with the anti-roll bar creates the lower control arm. A long strut - an integral coil spring and shock absorber - is mounted between the body and the steering knuckle. Many modern so-called MacPherson strut systems use a conventional lower A-arm and don't rely on the anti-roll bar for location.

Multimeter An electrical test instrument with the capability to measure voltage, current and resistance.

N

NOx Oxides of Nitrogen. A common toxic pollutant emitted by petrol and diesel engines at higher temperatures.

O

Ohm The unit of electrical resistance. One volt applied to a resistance of one ohm will produce a current of one amp.

Ohmmeter An instrument for measuring electrical resistance.

O-ring A type of sealing ring made of a special rubber-like material; in use, the O-ring is compressed into a groove to provide the sealing action.

Overhead cam (ohc) engine An engine with the camshaft(s) located on top of the cylinder head(s).

Overhead valve (ohv) engine An engine with the valves located in the cylinder head, but with the camshaft located in the engine block.

Oxygen sensor A device installed in the engine exhaust manifold, which senses the oxygen content in the exhaust and converts this information into an electric current. Also called a Lambda sensor.

P

Phillips screw A type of screw head having a cross instead of a slot for a corresponding type of screwdriver.

Plastigage A thin strip of plastic thread, available in different sizes, used for measuring clearances. For example, a strip of Plastigage is laid across a bearing journal. The parts are assembled and dismantled; the width of the crushed strip indicates the clearance between journal and bearing.

Plastigage

Propeller shaft The long hollow tube with universal joints at both ends that carries power from the transmission to the differential on front-engined rear wheel drive vehicles.

Proportioning valve A hydraulic control valve which limits the amount of pressure to the rear brakes during panic stops to prevent wheel lock-up.

R

Rack-and-pinion steering A steering system with a pinion gear on the end of the steering shaft that mates with a rack (think of a geared wheel opened up and laid flat). When the steering wheel is turned, the pinion turns, moving the rack to the left or right. This movement is transmitted through the track rods to the steering arms at the wheels.

Radiator A liquid-to-air heat transfer device designed to reduce the temperature of the coolant in an internal combustion engine cooling system.

Refrigerant Any substance used as a heat transfer agent in an air-conditioning system. R-12 has been the principle refrigerant for many years; recently, however, manufacturers have begun using R-134a, a non-CFC substance that is considered less harmful to the ozone in the upper atmosphere.

Rocker arm A lever arm that rocks on a shaft or pivots on a stud. In an overhead valve engine, the rocker arm converts the upward movement of the pushrod into a downward movement to open a valve.

Rotor In a distributor, the rotating device inside the cap that connects the centre electrode and the outer terminals as it turns, distributing the high voltage from the coil secondary winding to the proper spark plug. Also, that part of an alternator which rotates inside the stator. Also, the rotating assembly of a turbocharger, including the compressor wheel, shaft and turbine wheel.

Runout The amount of wobble (in-and-out movement) of a gear or wheel as it's rotated. The amount a shaft rotates "out-of-true." The out-of-round condition of a rotating part.

S

Sealant A liquid or paste used to prevent leakage at a joint. Sometimes used in conjunction with a gasket.

Sealed beam lamp An older headlight design which integrates the reflector, lens and filaments into a hermetically-sealed one-piece unit. When a filament burns out or the lens cracks, the entire unit is simply replaced.

Serpentine drivebelt A single, long, wide accessory drivebelt that's used on some newer vehicles to drive all the accessories, instead of a series of smaller, shorter belts. Serpentine drivebelts are usually tensioned by an automatic tensioner.

Serpentine drivebelt

Shim Thin spacer, commonly used to adjust the clearance or relative positions between two parts. For example, shims inserted into or under bucket tappets control valve clearances. Clearance is adjusted by changing the thickness of the shim.

Slide hammer A special puller that screws into or hooks onto a component such as a shaft or bearing; a heavy sliding handle on the shaft bottoms against the end of the shaft to knock the component free.

Sprocket A tooth or projection on the periphery of a wheel, shaped to engage with a chain or drivebelt. Commonly used to refer to the sprocket wheel itself.

Starter inhibitor switch On vehicles with an automatic transmission, a switch that prevents starting if the vehicle is not in Neutral or Park.

Strut See MacPherson strut.

T

Tappet A cylindrical component which transmits motion from the cam to the valve stem, either directly or via a pushrod and rocker arm. Also called a cam follower.

Thermostat A heat-controlled valve that regulates the flow of coolant between the cylinder block and the radiator, so maintaining optimum engine operating temperature. A thermostat is also used in some air cleaners in which the temperature is regulated.

Thrust bearing The bearing in the clutch assembly that is moved in to the release levers by clutch pedal action to disengage the clutch. Also referred to as a release bearing.

Timing belt A toothed belt which drives the camshaft. Serious engine damage may result if it breaks in service.

Timing chain A chain which drives the camshaft.

Toe-in The amount the front wheels are closer together at the front than at the rear. On rear wheel drive vehicles, a slight amount of toe-in is usually specified to keep the front wheels running parallel on the road by offsetting other forces that tend to spread the wheels apart.

Toe-out The amount the front wheels are closer together at the rear than at the front. On front wheel drive vehicles, a slight amount of toe-out is usually specified.

Tools For full information on choosing and using tools, refer to the *Haynes Automotive Tools Manual*.

Tracer A stripe of a second colour applied to a wire insulator to distinguish that wire from another one with the same colour insulator.

Tune-up A process of accurate and careful adjustments and parts replacement to obtain the best possible engine performance.

Turbocharger A centrifugal device, driven by exhaust gases, that pressurises the intake air. Normally used to increase the power output from a given engine displacement, but can also be used primarily to reduce exhaust emissions (as on VW's "Umwelt" Diesel engine).

U

Universal joint or U-joint A double-pivoted connection for transmitting power from a driving to a driven shaft through an angle. A U-joint consists of two Y-shaped yokes and a cross-shaped member called the spider.

V

Valve A device through which the flow of liquid, gas, vacuum, or loose material in bulk may be started, stopped, or regulated by a movable part that opens, shuts, or partially obstructs one or more ports or passageways. A valve is also the movable part of such a device.

Valve clearance The clearance between the valve tip (the end of the valve stem) and the rocker arm or tappet. The valve clearance is measured when the valve is closed.

Vernier caliper A precision measuring instrument that measures inside and outside dimensions. Not quite as accurate as a micrometer, but more convenient.

Viscosity The thickness of a liquid or its resistance to flow.

Volt A unit for expressing electrical "pressure" in a circuit. One volt that will produce a current of one ampere through a resistance of one ohm.

W

Welding Various processes used to join metal items by heating the areas to be joined to a molten state and fusing them together. For more information refer to the *Haynes Automotive Welding Manual*.

Wiring diagram A drawing portraying the components and wires in a vehicle's electrical system, using standardised symbols. For more information refer to the *Haynes Automotive Electrical and Electronic Systems Manual*.

Note: *References throughout this index are in the form* **"Chapter number"** • **"Page number"**. *So, for example, 2C•15 refers to page 15 of Chapter 2C.*

A

Accelerator pedal/position sensor – 4A•3
Air cleaner – 1A•13, 1B•17
    assembly and intake ducts – 4A•2, 4B•4
Air conditioning system – 3•9
Airbag system – 12•15
Alternator – 5A•5
Anti-lock Braking and Traction Control systems – 9•16
Anti-theft alarm system – 12•15
Automatic transmission – 7B•1 *et seq*
    fault finding – REF•22
    fluid – 7B•2
Auxiliary drivebelt – 1A•11, 1B•14, 5A•5
    tensioner – 5A•5

B

Battery – 0•15, 5A•2, 5A•3, REF•9
Body electrical systems – 12•1 *et seq*
Body exterior fittings – 11•18
Bodywork and fittings – 11•1 *et seq*
Bonnet – 11•5
    lock spring – 11•6
    release cable – 11•6
Braking system – 9•1 *et seq*
    bleeding – 9•2
    caliper – 9•10, 9•11
    disc – 1B•9, 9•9
    fault finding – REF•23
    fluid – 0•14, 1A•12, 1B•16
    master cylinder – 9•11
    pads – 1A•8, 1B•9, 9•4, 9•7
    pedal – 9•12
    pipes – 1A•8, 1B•9
Bulbs (exterior) – 12•4
Bulbs (interior) – 12•8
Bumpers – 11•4

C

Camshafts – 2D•11
    cover – 2A•4, 2B•4, 2C•5
    followers and hydraulic tappets – 2A•10, 2B•12, 2C•10, 2D•13
    housing – 2B•13, 2D•9
    oil seals – 2A•9, 2B•11, 2C•9, 2D•9

Catalytic converter – 4C•8
Centre console – 11•26
Charging system – 5A•4
Clutch – 6•1 *et seq*
    assembly – 6•5
    bleeding – 6•2
    finding – REF•21
    fluid – 0•14, 1A•8, 1A•12, 1B•16
    master cylinder – 6•3
    model with MTA control unit – 7C•4
    pedal – 6•4
    release cylinder – 6•3
Compression test – 2A•4
    and leakdown test – 2B•3, 2C•3, 2D•3
Conversion factors – REF•6
Coolant – 0•14, 1B•16
    pump – 3•5
    renewal – 1A•12
    temperature sensor – 3•5
Cooling, heating and air conditioning systems – 3•1 *et seq*
    fault finding – REF•20
    hoses – 3•2
Crankshaft – 2E•12, 2E•14, 2E•16
    oil seals – 2A•15, 2B•18, 2C•15, 2D•18
    pulley – 2A•5, 2B•8
    pulley/vibration damper – 2C•6, 2D•6
Cylinder block – 2E•13
Cylinder head – 2A•12, 2B•13, 2C•11, 2D•14, 2E•9, 2E•11
    and valves – 2E•10

D

Diesel 1.7 litre engine in-car repair procedures – 2B•1 *et seq*
Diesel 1.9 litre DOHC engine in-car repair procedures – 2D•1 *et seq*
Diesel 1.9 litre SOHC engine in-car repair procedures – 2C•1 *et seq*
Diesel engine emissions control systems – 4C•3
Diesel injection system electrical components – 4B•6
Dimensions and weights – REF•1
Door – 11•6
    handles and lock components – 11•9
    inner trim panel – 11•8
    window glass and regulator – 11•13
Driveshafts – 8•1 *et seq*
    check – 1A•9, 1B•10
    fault finding – REF•22
    joint gaiters – 8•4
    oil seals – 7C•4

Note: *References throughout this index are in the form* **"Chapter number"** • **"Page number"**. *So, for example, 2C•15 refers to page 15 of Chapter 2C.*

E

Easytronic transmission – 7C•1 *et seq*
Electric cooling fan – 3•4
Electrical system check – 0•17, 1A•10, 1B•11
Electrical system fault finding – 12•2, REF•24
Electro-hydraulic power steering pump – 10•16
Electronic control unit (ECU) – 7B•5
Emissions control systems – 4C•1 *et seq*
Engine fault finding – REF•18
Engine oil and filter – 0•13, 1A•6, 1B•6
Engine removal and overhaul procedures – 2E•1 *et seq*
Engine/transmission mountings – 2A•16, 2B•18, 2C•16
Exhaust system – 1A•9, 1B•10, 4A•11
   emission check – 1A•13, 1B•17
   manifold – 4A•10
   manifold and turbocharger – 4B•19
Exterior light units – 12•10
Exterior mirrors and associated components – 11•17

F

Facia panel components – 11•27
Fault finding – REF•16 *et seq*
   automatic transmission – REF•22
   braking system – REF•23
   clutch – REF•21
   cooling system – REF•20
   driveshafts – REF•22
   electrical system – 12•2, REF•24
   engine – REF•18
   fuel and exhaust systems – REF•20
   manual transmission – REF•21
   suspension and steering – REF•24
Fluid cooler – 7B•5
Flywheel/driveplate – 2A•16, 2B•17, 2C•16
Front anti-roll bar – 10•10
Front hub bearings – 10•5
Front subframe – 10•8
Front suspension – 1A•9, 1B•9
   lower arm – 10•8
   strut – 10•5
Front swivel hub – 10•3
Fuel and exhaust systems – diesel engines – 4B•1 *et seq*
Fuel and exhaust systems – petrol engine – 4A•1 *et seq*
Fuel and exhaust systems fault finding – REF•20
Fuel economy – REF•2
Fuel filter – 1B•8, 1B•12
   crash box – 4B•5

Fuel gauge sender unit – 4A•3
Fuel injection systems – 4A•6
   depressurisation – 4A•3
   injectors – 4B•12
Fuel rail – 4B•10
Fuel supply pump – 4A•5, 4B•5
Fuel system priming and bleeding – 4B•5
Fuel tank – 4A•5, 4B•5
Fuses and relays – 12•3

G

Gearchange mechanism – 7A•3, 7A•5
Glossary of technical terms – REF•26
Glovebox – 11•27
Glow plugs – 5A•9

H

Handbrake – 1A•12, 1B•15
   cables – 9•14
   lever – 9•14
   warning light switch – 9•16
Headlight beam alignment – 1A•12, 1B•16, 12•11
Heated seats – 12•15
Heating and ventilation system – 3•6
High-pressure diesel injection system – 4B•3
High-pressure fuel pump – 4B•8
Horn – 12•11
Hydraulic fluid renewal – 1A•12, 1B•16
Hydraulic pipes and hoses – 9•3

I

Ignition system – petrol models – 5B•1 *et seq*
   module – 5B•2
   testing – 5B•2
   timing – 5B•2
Ignition switch/steering column lock – 10•14
Information display unit – 12•11
Instrument panel – 12•11
Intake manifold – 4A•9, 4B•15
   changeover flap actuator drive – 4B•17
Intercooler – 4B•18
Interior trim – 11•23
Intermediate shaft – 8•3
   bearing – 8•4
Introduction – 0•4

Note: *References throughout this index are in the form "**Chapter number**" • "**Page number**". So, for example, 2C•15 refers to page 15 of Chapter 2C.*

J

Jacking and vehicle support – REF•9
Jump starting – 0•7

K

Knock sensor – 5B•2

L

Leaks – 0•10, 1A•7, 1B•8
Lubriants and fluids – 0•17

M

Main and big-end bearings – 2E•14
Manual transmission – 7A•1 *et seq*
    fault finding – REF•21
Mode switches – 7B•5
MOT test checks – REF•12
Multec-S Injection system components – 4A•7

O

Oil filter housing – 2B•17, 2C•14, 2D•17
    (VVT engines) – 2A•15
Oil level sensor – 5A•8
Oil pressure warning light switch – 5A•8
Oil pump – 2A•13, 2B•16, 2C•13, 2D•16
    seal – 2B•17
Oil seals – 7A•6, 7B•5

P

Petrol engine in-car repair procedures – 2A•1 *et seq*
    emissions control systems – 4C•2
Piston rings – 2E•15

Pistons/connecting rods – 2E•12, 2E•14, 2E•17
Pollen filter – 1A•11, 1B•12
Power steering fluid – 1A•7, 1B•8
Power steering hydraulic system – 10•16
Pre/post-heating system – 5A•9
    control unit – 5A•10

R

Radiator – 3•2
Radio/CD player – 12•14
    aerial – 12•15
Rear hub bearings – 10•11
Rear shock absorber – 10•11
Rear suspension – 1A•9, 1B•10
    coil spring – 10•12
    torsion beam and trailing arms – 10•12
Relays and fuses – 12•3
Remote control battery renewal – 1A•12, 1B•16
Reversing light switch – 7A•6
Road test – 1A•10, 1B•11
Roadwheel bolt tightness – 1A•10, 1B•11
Routine maintenance and servicing – diesel models – 1B•1 *et seq*
Routine maintenance and servicing – petrol models – 1A•1 *et seq*

S

Safety first! – 0•5
Seats – 11•20
    belt components – 11•22
Selector cable – 7B•3
Selector lever assembly – 7B•4, 7C•2
Selector lever position switch – 7B•5
Service interval indicator reset – 1A•11, 1B•11
Simtec 75.1 injection system components – 4A•8
Spark plug – 1A•14
Speakers – 12•15
Starter motor – 5A•7
Starting and charging systems – 5A•1 *et seq*

Note: *References throughout this index are in the form* **"Chapter number"** • **"Page number"**. *So, for example, 2C•15 refers to page 15 of Chapter 2C.*

Steering – 10•1 *et seq*
    column – 10•14
    electronics module – 12•14
    intermediate shaft – 10•15
    lock/ignition switch – 10•14
    gear – 10•15
    gear rubber gaiters – 10•15
    wheel – 10•13
Stop-light switch – 9•15
Sump – 2A•13, 2B•15, 2C•12, 2D•15
Sunroof – 11•18
Suspension and steering – 10•1 *et seq*
    fault finding – REF•24
Switches – 12•3

T

Tailgate and support struts – 11•15
Tailgate lock components – 11•16
Tailgate wiper motor – 12•13
Thermostat – 3•4
Throttle housing – 4A•5
Timing belt – 2A•6, 2B•9, 2C•6, 2D•6
    covers – 2A•6, 2B•8
    sprockets – 2A•7
    sprockets, tensioner and idler pulley – 2C•7, 2D•7
    tensioner and sprockets – 2B•10
Top Dead Centre (TDC) – 2A•4, 2B•4, 2C•4, 2D•4
Towing – 0•10
Track rod – 10•17
    end – 10•16

Transmission input/output speed sensors – 7B•5
Transmission oil – 7A•2, 7A•8, 7C•2
Transmission shift module – 7C•3
Turbocharger – 4B•18
Tyres – 0•16, 0•17

U

Unleaded petrol – 4A•3

V

Vacuum pump – 9•17
Vacuum servo unit – 9•12
    check valve and hose – 9•14
Valve clearances – 2A•9, 2B•11, 2C•9
Valve timing – 2C•5, 2D•5
Vehicle identification – REF•7
VVT oil control valves – 2A•8

W

Washer fluid – 0•15
Wheel alignment and steering angles – 10•17
Wheel changing – 0•8
Windscreen and fixed window glass – 11•18
Windscreen wiper motor and linkage – 12•12
Windscreen/tailgate washer system components – 12•13
Wiper arm – 12•12
Wiper blades – 0•17
Wiring diagrams – 12•17 *et seq*

Preserving Our Motoring Heritage

< *The Model J Duesenberg Derham Tourster. Only eight of these magnificent cars were ever built – this is the only example to be found outside the United States of America*

Almost every car you've ever loved, loathed or desired is gathered under one roof at the Haynes Motor Museum. Over 300 immaculately presented cars and motorbikes represent every aspect of our motoring heritage, from elegant reminders of bygone days, such as the superb Model J Duesenberg to curiosities like the bug-eyed BMW Isetta. There are also many old friends and flames. Perhaps you remember the 1959 Ford Popular that you did your courting in? The magnificent 'Red Collection' is a spectacle of classic sports cars including AC, Alfa Romeo, Austin Healey, Ferrari, Lamborghini, Maserati, MG, Riley, Porsche and Triumph.

A Perfect Day Out

Each and every vehicle at the Haynes Motor Museum has played its part in the history and culture of Motoring. Today, they make a wonderful spectacle and a great day out for all the family. Bring the kids, bring Mum and Dad, but above all bring your camera to capture those golden memories for ever. You will also find an impressive array of motoring memorabilia, a comfortable 70 seat video cinema and one of the most extensive transport book shops in Britain. The Pit Stop Cafe serves everything from a cup of tea to wholesome, home-made meals or, if you prefer, you can enjoy the large picnic area nestled in the beautiful rural surroundings of Somerset.

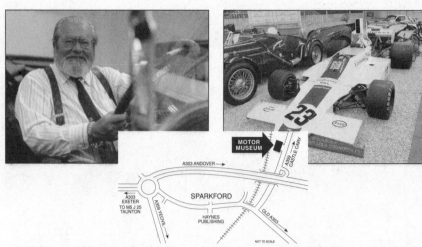

John Haynes O.B.E., Founder and Chairman of the museum at the wheel of a Haynes Light 12. >

< *Graham Hill's Lola Cosworth Formula 1 car next to a 1934 Riley Sports.*

The Museum is situated on the A359 Yeovil to Frome road at Sparkford, just off the A303 in Somerset. It is about 40 miles south of Bristol, and 25 minutes drive from the M5 intersection at Taunton.
Open 9.30am - 5.30pm (10.00am - 4.00pm Winter) 7 days a week, *except Christmas Day, Boxing Day and New Years Day*
Special rates available for schools, coach parties and outings Charitable Trust No. 292048